The Clinical and Forensic Assessment of Psychopathy

A Practitioner's Guide

The LEA Series in Personality and Clinical Psychology
Irving B. Weiner, Editor

Calhoun/Tedeschi • Facilitating Posttraumatic Growth: A Clinician's Guide

Dana (Ed.) • Handbook of Cross-Cultural and Multicultural Personality Assessment

Exner (Ed.) • Issues and Methods in Rorschach Research

Frederick/McNeal • Inner Strength: Contemporary Psychotherapy and Hypnosis for Ego-Strengthening

Gacono/Meloy • The Rorschach Assessment of Aggressive and Psychopathic Personalities

Ganellen • Integrating the Rorschach and the MMPI-2 in Personality Assessment

Goodman/Rudorfer/Maser (Eds.) • Obsessive-Compulsive Disorder: Contemporary Issues in Treatment

Handler/Hilsenroth (Eds.) • Teaching and Learning Personality Assessment

Hy/Loevinger • Measuring Ego Development, Second Edition

Kelly • The Assessment of Object Relations Phenomena in Adolescents: TAT and Rorschach Measures

Kelly • The Psychological Assessment of Abused and Traumatized Children

Kohnstamm/Halverson/Mervielde/Havill (Eds.) • Parental Descriptions of Child Personality: Developmental Antecedents of the Big Five?

Loevinger (Ed.) • Technical Foundations for Measuring Ego Development: The Washington University Sentence Completion Test

McCallum/Piper (Eds.) • Psychological Mindedness: A Contemporary Understanding

Meloy/Acklin/Gacono/Murray/Peterson (Eds.) • Contemporary Rorschach Interpretation

Needleman • Cognitive Case Conceptualization: A Guidebook for Practitioners

Nolen-Hoeksema/Larson • Coping With Loss

Rosowsky/Abrams/Zweig (Eds.) • Personality Disorders in the Elderly: Emerging Issues in Diagnosis and Treatment

Sarason/Pierce/Sarason (Eds.) • Cognitive Interference: Theories, Methods, and Findings

Silverstein • Self Psychology and Diagnostic Assessment: Identifying Selfobject Functions Through Psychological Testing

Taylor (Ed.) • Anxiety Sensitivity: Theory, Research, and Treatment of the Fear of Anxiety

Tedeschi/Park/Calhoun (Eds.) • Posttraumatic Growth: Positive Changes in the Aftermath of Crisis

Van Hasselt/Hersen (Eds.) • Handbook of Psychological Treatment Protocols for Children and Adolescents

Weiner • Principles of Rorschach Interpretation

Wong/Fry (Eds.) • The Human Quest for Meaning: A Handbook of Psychological Research and Clinical Applications

Zillmer/Harrower/Ritzler/Archer • The Quest for the Nazi Personality: A Psychological Investigation of Nazi War Criminals

The Clinical and Forensic Assessment of Psychopathy

A Practitioner's Guide

Edited by

Carl B. Gacono
Center for Therapeutic Assessment

LEA

LAWRENCE ERLBAUM ASSOCIATES, PUBLISHERS
2000   Mahwah, New Jersey   London

Lawrence Erlbaum Associates, Inc., Publishers
10 Industrial Avenue
Mahwah, NJ 07430

Cover design by Richard Rasulis, Jr., PhD.

Library of Congress Cataloging-in-Publication Data

The clinical and forensic assessment of psychpathy : a practitioner's guide /[compiled] by Carl B. Gacono
     p. cm.
Includes bibliographical references and index.
ISBN 0-8058-3038-3 (cloth : alk. paper)
1. Antisocial personality disorders. 2. Antisocial personality disorders—Diagnosis. I. Gacono, Carl B.
  RC555.C53 2000
  616.85'82075—dc21

                99-058743
                CIP

Printed in the United States of America
10 9 8 7 6 5 4 3

This book is dedicated to Lynne, whose love and support helped me weather the "slings and arrows" of its preparation. She also taught me that life offers more than studying psychopaths or writing research papers.

"*Plato is dear to me, but dearer still is the truth.*"
—Aristotle

"*Crime and politics, they're the same thing*"
—Godfather III

"*If the principle of outward adaptation is made the keystone to success in society, what sort of human qualities will be encouraged and what sort of people, one may ask, will come to the fore.*"

—Vaclav Havel (Living in Truth)

Carl B. Gacono, PhD, is a licensed psychologist who maintains a clinical and forensic private practice in Austin, Texas. Formerly the Assessment Center Director at Atascadero State Hospital and later, the Chief Psychologist at the Federal Correctional Institution, Bastrop, Texas, he has more than 20 years of correctional and institutional experience. He is co-author of *The Rorschach Assessment of Aggressive and Psychopathic Personalities* and co-editor of *Contemporary Rorschach Interpretation*. He has authored or

co-authored more than 50 scientific articles and book chapters. He is the 1994 recipient of the Samuel J. And Anne G. Beck Award for excellence in early career research, a member of the American Board of Assessment Psychology, and a Fellow of the Society for Personality Assessment. Dr. Gacono is sought as an expert in the area of criminal behavior, psychopathy and clinical, forensic, and research applications of the Rorschach and Psychopathy Checklists. Address correspondence to: Carl B. Gacono, PhD, P.O. Box 140633, Austin, Texas, 78714. E-mail: DRCARL14@aol.com

Contents

CONTENTS

List of Contributors

Arthur I. Alterman, University of Pennsylvania/Philadelphia Veterans Administration

Paul Babiak, Private Practice, Hopewell Junction, New York

Robert H. Bodholdt, U.S. Department of Justice, Bastrop, Texas

S. Doug Bodie, University of Alabama, Tuscaloosa, Alabama

Christopher T. Bodin, University of Alabama, Tuscaloosa, Alabama

Shelley L. Brown, Research Branch Correctional Service of Canada, Ottawa, Ontario

John S. Cacciola, University of Pennsylvania/ Philadelphia Veterans Administration

Keith R. Cruise, University of North Texas, Denton, Texas

Roberto Di Fazio, Millhaven Institution, Ontario, Canada

Philip S. Erdberg, Private Practice, Corte Madera, California

Adelle E. Forth, Carleton University, Ottawa

Paul J. Frick, University of New Orleans, Louisiana,

Carl B. Gacono, Center for Therapeutic Assessment, Austin, Texas

James L. Greenstone, Fort Worth Police Department, Forth Worth, Texas

Jerald V. Justice, California Department of Mental Health Psychiatric Program, Vacaville, California

David S. Kosson, Finch University of Health Science, The Chicago Medical School, Wisconsin

Martin L. Lalumière, University of Toronto, Ontario

David R. Lyon, Simon Fraser University, Burnaby, British Columbia

Donna L. Mailloux, Carelton University, Ottawa

J. Reid Meloy, University of California, San Diego

Joseph P. Newman, University of Wisconsin, Madison, Wisconsin

James R. P. Ogloff, Simon Fraser University, Burnaby, British Columbia

Henry R. Richards, Johnson, Bassin, & Shaw, Inc., Silver Spring, Maryland

Richard Rogers, University of North Texas, Denton, Texas

Megan J. Rutherford, University of Washington

William A. Schmitt, University of Wisconsin, Madison, Wisconsin

Ralph C. Serin, Frontenac Institution, Kingston, Ontario

Michael C. Seto, University of Toronto, Ontario

Barbara J. Sparrow, University of Texas, Austin, Texas

Brian L. Steuerwald, Developmental Associates, Inc., Indianapolis, Indiana

Jennifer E. Vitale, University of Wisconsin, Madison, Wisconsin

John F. Wallace, Carroll Regional Counseling Center, Carroll, Iowa

Glenn D. Walters, Federal Correctional Institution, Schuylkill, Pennsylvania

Myla H. Young, California Department of Mental Health Psychiatric Program, Vacaville, California

Preface

From November 27 to December 7, 1995, 85 participants from 15 countries met in Alvor, Portugal, under the support of a North Atlantic Treaty Organization (NATO) Advanced Study Institute (ASI) on psychopathy. This serene oceanside setting allowed participants to maintain high levels of energy and interest over 10 consecutive 9-hour days of lectures, meetings, and small-group discussions. Group discussion frequently continued into the late evening hours over plates of grilled swordfish and glasses of full-bodied port wine. Participants were provided with the state-of-the-art knowledge on current theory and research in psychopathy. Thirty-five published abstracts (Cooke, Forth, Newman, & Hare, 1996) and a text (Cooke, Forth, & Hare, 1998) attest to the importance of the information disseminated at the ASI conference.

The conference was stimulating and provocative. Difficult concepts, hard to fathom with one or two readings of the original manuscript or article, crystallized as authors articulated the process through which their research had developed. Sharing ideas and discussing research with participants who were concerned with "science, not politics" was welcomed and unexpected. The conference's apolitical atmosphere enlivened the intellectual process. Participants were informed of "what we currently know" and stimulated concerning "what we need to learn."

Despite a few "informal work groups (were) established to apply theory and research on psychopathy to practical issues" (Hare, 1998b, p. 2), the translation of theory and research into practice and intervention was less obvious. There were notable gaps between the ivory tower and the clinic. I came away from the NATO conference with a sense of urgency and a renewed conviction that 30 years of empirical findings investigating psychopathy begged for translation into applied procedures and methods for the practitioner.

This volume is a direct result of that conviction. *The Clinical and Forensic Assessment of Psychopathy: A Practitioner's Guide* is an applied text.

An earlier version of this book was withdrawn and reissued to safeguard the copyright issues described in Chapter 17.

It is a resource book that offers guidelines toward a standard of care for psychopathy assessment in general (Gacono & Hutton, 1994), and the use of the Psychopathy Checklists in particular (Forth, Kosson, & Hare, 1997; Hare, 1991; Hart, Cox, & Hare, 1995). The purpose is to make fast the link between research and practice.

SOCIOPATHY, ANTISOCIAL PERSONALITY, AND PSYCHOPATHY

Despite a wealth of published research on psychopathy (Hare, 1966, 1996, 1998a), clinicians and authors continue to confuse sociopathy, antisocial personality disorder (ASPD) and psychopathy—inappropriately viewing them as synonymous (Losel, 1998; Millon, Simonsen, Birket-Smith, & Davis, 1998). Originating from separate theoretical lines, these constructs manifest empirically measurable and clinically relevant differences (Gacono, Nieberding, Owen, Rubel, & Bodholdt, 2000; Hare, 1998a; Hare, Hart, & Harpur, 1991). Wherever terms such as ASPD or *sociopathy* arise in the text, we have endeavored to explicate the basis for their use and their nonequivalence to the construct of *psychopathy*. Throughout the text, *psychopathy* is defined in the traditional manner (Cleckley, 1942; Meloy, 1988; Hare, 1991), with any necessary qualifications duly noted. For example, some authors have chosen to further differentiate the Cleckley psychopath from the Hare psychopath.

Sociopathy (American Psychiatric Association, 1952) and ASPD (American Psychiatric Association, 1994) are terms that have been used in various editions of the American Psychiatric Associations' *Diagnostic and Statistical Manual of Mental Disorders* (DSM). An antiquated term lacking contemporary clinical meaning, *sociopathy* was used in the first *DSM* (American Psychiatric Association, 1952) to describe a variety of conditions such as sexual deviation, alcoholism, and dyssocial/antisocial reactions. The antisocial reaction criteria were closest to those of psychopathy (Jenkins, 1960). Sociopathy's dyssocial/antisocial reactions were subsumed under the rubric of ASPD in DSM–II (American Psychiatric Association, 1968). Many of the traditional characteristics of psychopathy disappeared from ASPD with the introduction of *DSM–III* (American Psychiatric Association, 1980). Subsequent versions of the *DSM* (American Psychiatric Association, 1980, 1987, 1994) have reflected the influence of a social deviancy model (Robins, 1966) through the manuals' continued reliance on behavioral criteria.[1]

Unlike ASPD, psychopathy (Cleckley, 1942; Meloy, 1988; Hare, 1996; see Table P. 1)[2] is composed of trait and behavioral criteria. As measured by the

Psychopathy Checklists (Hare, 1991; Forth et al., 1990; Hart et al., 1995), *psychopathy* contains two stable, oblique factors. The first factor, *aggressive narcissism* (Meloy, 1992; Factor 1), is characterized by egocentricity, callousness, and remorselessness; it correlates with narcissistic and histrionic personality disorders, low anxiety, low empathy, and self-report measures of Machiavellianism and narcissism (Harpur, Hare, & Hakstian, 1989; Hart & Hare, 1989). The second factor, *antisocial lifestyle* (Meloy, 1992; Factor 2), represents an irresponsible, impulsive, thrill-seeking, unconventional, and antisocial lifestyle; it correlates most strongly with criminal behaviors, lower socioeconomic background, lower IQ and less education, self-report

TABLE P.1
Psychopathic Traits and Behaviors (Hare, 1980; Hare et al., 1990)

*1. Glibness/superficial charm
*2. Grandiose sense of self-worth
 +3. Need for stimulation/proneness to boredom
*4. Pathological lying
*5. Conning/manipulative
*6. Lack of remorse or guilt
*7. Shallow affect
*8. Callous/lack or empathy
 +9. Parasitic lifestyle
 +10. Poor behavioral controls
11. Promiscuous sexual behavior
 +12. Early Behavioral problems
 +13. Lack of realistic long-term goals
 +14. Impulsivity
 +15. Irresponsibility
*16. Failure to accept responsibility for own actions
17. Many short-term marital relationships
 +18. Juvenile delinquency
 +19. Revocation of conditional release
20. Criminal versatility

---

[1]Conduct Disorder (CD) is a juvenile prerequisite for an adult ASPD diagnosis. Community base rates for CD are 3% to 5% of school-age children, with a male to female ratio of between 4:1 and 9:1. ASPD rates are 5.8% of males and 1.2% of females with 45% to 75% in forensic settings. ASPD is predominantly a male diagnosis. Low base rates in community outpatient settings make the ASPD diagnosis more clinically relevant than in forensic, correctional, or institutional treatment settings where its presence may exceed 50% (Gacono & Meloy, 1994)

[2]The Hare Psychopathy Checklist–Revised (PCL–R; Hare, 1991) is a 20-item 40-point scale (≥ 30 = psychopathy). The PCL–R score for a combined prison population is 23.37 ($SD = 7.96$); the score for forensic psychiatric population is 20.56 ($SD = 7.79$). The Psychopathy Checklist: Screening Version (PCL:SV; Hart, Cox, & Hare, 1995) is a 12-item, 24-point scale (≥ 18 suggests psychopathy). It is a screening tool, not a substitute for the PCL–R. The Psychopathy Checklist:Youth Version (PCL:YV; Forth, Kosson, & Hare, 1997) is modified for adolescent offenders.

self-report measures of antisocial behavior, and the diagnoses of CD and ASPD (Hare, 1991; Harpur et al., 1989). Although most criminal psychopaths meet criteria for ASPD, the majority of ASPD patients are not psychopaths. One might say that criminal psychopaths are to antisocial adjustment what butter is to milkfat.

Although cross-cultural investigation of psychopathy is only beginning, a shared worldview of psychopathy is acknowledged by the majority of NATO countries (Cooke, Forth, & Hare, 1998). Labels for personality and behavior patterns akin to that seen in the clinical syndrome of psychopathy exist in most cultures, including many absent the trappings of modern urban settings (Cooke, 1998; Murphy, 1976). Murphy (1976) noted that, in the Inuit (Northwest Alaska) community, the word *kunlangeta* describes

> a man who…repeatedly lies and cheats and steals things and does not go hunting and, when the other men are out of the village, takes sexual advantage of many women—someone who does not pay attention to reprimands and who is always being brought to the elders for punishment. (p. 1026)

Similarly, the rurally isolated Yorubas of Nigeria use the term *aranakan* to describe an individual who "always goes his own way regardless of others, who is uncooperative, full of malice, and bullheaded" (Murphy, 1976, p. 1026).

With slight risk of overstatement, one could argue that studies of psychopathy have revealed the existence of a distinct phenotype of human personality, seemingly as distinct and uniform as that of a primary color. For example, although there are many shades of blue, no shade of blue is likely to be mistaken for yellow; this appears to be the case in psychopathy. This growing consensus about the nature of psychopathy has been enhanced by the ability to measure psychopathy in a reliable and valid manner. This has been accomplished through the development of the Psychopathy Checklists (Hare, 1991; Hart et al., 1995; Forth et al., 1997), which have literally catalyzed research and clinical interest in assessing the construct.

High psychopathy levels predict increases in quantity and variety of offenses committed (Hare & Jutai, 1983; Hart, Kropp, & Hare, 1988), frequency of violent offenses (Hare & McPherson, 1984), reoffense rates (Hare, McPherson, & Forth, 1988), poor treatment response (Ogloff, Wong, & Greenwood, 1990; Rice, Harris, & Cormier, 1992), and institutional misbehavior (Gacono, Meloy, Sheppard, Speth, & Roske, 1995; Gacono, Meloy, Speth, & Roske, 1997).[3] These findings remain stable even when culture, gender, and the presence or absence of a major mental disorder are controlled (Cooke, Forth, & Hare, 1998).

From the clinical observations of Pinel, through Cleckley's refined criteria, the empirical design of Hare, and the object relations understanding of the psychopath's inner life (Meloy, 1988; Meloy & Gacono, 1998), and the use of empirical measurement to flesh out the inner dynamics of the psychopath and related syndromes (Gacono, 1998; Gacono & Meloy, 1994), psychopaths have enjoyed more attention and research than any other character disorder. Psychopaths are difficult to ignore. They are involved in many of today's most serious problems: war, drugs, murder, and political corruption.

Hare (1996, p. 25) noted that "Psychopathy (was): a clinical construct whose time has come." This text represents a next step in the construct's evolution. Specifically, the authors apply recent advances in relevant research to clinical and forensic issues as they are typically confronted by the practicing clinician. As a construct, psychopathy has journeyed beyond confusing origins and a mishmash of labels into an empirically measurable syndrome (Hare, 1991). We are far from the days when psychopathy was *understood* as a disorder a step beyond our comprehension (Cleckley, 1976). Yet the journey is far from finished; goals involving prevention, prediction, and effective treatment pull us forward. This book takes us another step. It is written for all those whose caring and dedication led them to risk much by working with this most difficult population and become participants in a process that Brittain (1970) described some 30 years ago: "We cannot treat, except empirically, what we do not understand and we cannot prevent, except fortuitously, what we do not comprehend" (p. 206).

Acknowledgments

First, I would like to acknowledge the individual contributors for their courage in rising to the challenge inherent in bridging the academic—clinical gap. Often forced to conceptually move beyond their traditional roles (academic or clinical), all brought their particular virtuosity and insight, which should be evident in the exceptional quality of the text. Special appreciation is extended to Drs. Bodholdt and Kosson, who helped as the editor's editor providing time and energy well beyond that required of their individual contributions. Dr. Lynne Bannatyne must be commended for her tireless focus in reviewing many of the original manuscripts. I wish to thank Susan Milmoe and Kate Graetzer of Lawrence

---

[3] Rorschach findings reveal the psychopath's inner life (Gacono & Meloy, 1994; Meloy & Gacono, 1998). They also provide convergent validity to other trait and behavioral measures finding that psychopathic ASPDs produce more indexes associated with borderline personality organization (Gacono, 1990), are more narcissistic (Gacono, Meloy, & Heaven, 1990), and show less attachment and anxiety (Gacono & Meloy, 1991) than nonpsychopathic ASPDs.

Erlbaum Associates for their patience in keeping me on track and offering encouragement throughout this project. Also, a special thanks to Lawrence (Larry) Erlbaum, always appreciated, who provided valued guidance and perspective unique among publishers.

—Carl B. Gacono

REFERENCES

American Psychiatric Association. (1952). *Diagnostic and statistical manual of mental disorders*. Washington, DC: Author.

American Psychiatric Association. (1968). *Diagnostic and statistical manual of mental disorders* (2nd ed.). Washington, DC: Author.

American Psychiatric Association. (1980). *Diagnostic and statistical manual of mental disorders* (3rd ed.). Washington, DC: Author.

American Psychiatric Association. (1987). *Diagnostic and statistical manual of mental disorders* (3rd ed. rev.). Washington, DC: Author.

American Psychiatric Association. (1994). *Diagnostic and statistical manual of mental disorders* (4rd ed.). Washington, DC: Author.

Brittain, R. (1970). The Sadistic Murderer. *Medical Science and the Law, 10*, 198–207.

Cleckley, H. (1976). *The mask of sanity* (5th ed.). St. Louis MO: Mosby. (Original work published 1941)

Cooke, D. J. (1998). Cross-cultural aspects of psychopathy. In T. Millon, E. Simonsen, M. Birket-Smith, & R. Davis (Eds.), *Psychopathy: Antisocial, criminal, and violent behavior* (pp. 260–276). New York: Guilford.

Cooke, D. J., Forth, A. E., & Hare, R. D. (1998). *Psychopathy: Theory, research and implications for society*. London: Kluwer.

Cooke, D. J., Forth, A. E., Newman, J., & Hare, R. D. (Eds.). (1996). International perspectives on psychopathy: Abstracts from the Alvor NATO ASI on psychopathy. In D. J. Cooke, A. E. Forth, J. Newman, & R. D. Hare (Eds.), *Issues in criminology and legal psychology* (No.24)., Leicester, England: British Psychological Society.

Forth A. E., Hart, S. D., & Hare, R. D. (1990). Assessment of Psychopathy in Male Young Offenders. *Psychological Assessment, 2*, 432–344.

Forth, A. E., Kosson, D. S., & Hare, R. D. (1997). *The Hare Psychopathy Checklist: Youth Version*. Toronto, Ontario: Multi-Health Systems.

Gacono, C. B. (1990). An empirical study of object relations and defensive operations in antisocial personality. *Journal of Personality Assessment, 54*, 589–600.

Gacono, C. B. (1998). The use of the Psychopathy Checklist–Revised (PCL–R) and Rorschach for treatment planning with antisocial personality disordered patients. *International Journal of Offender Therapy and Comparative Criminology, 42(1)*, 49–64.

Gacono, C. B., & Hutton, H. E. (1994). Suggestions for the clinical and forensic use of the Hare Psychopathy Checklist–Revised (PCL–R). *International Journal of Law and Psychiatry, 17(3)*, 303–317.

Gacono, C. B., & Meloy, J. R. (1991). A Rorschach investigation of attachment and anxiety in antisocial personality. *Journal of Nervous and Mental Disease, 179,* 546–552.

Gacono, C. B., & Meloy, J. R. (1994). *The Rorschach assessment of aggressive and psychopathic personalities.* Hillsdale, NJ: Lawrence Erlbaum Associates.

Gacono, C. B., Meloy, J. R., & Heaven, T. (1990). A Rorschach investigation of narcissism and hysteria in antisocial personality disorder. *Journal of Personality Assessment, 55,* 270–279.

Gacono, C. B., Meloy, J. R., Sheppard, K., Speth, E., & Roske, A. (1995). A clinical investigation of malingering and psychopathy in hospitalized insanity acquittees. *Bulletin of the American Academy of Psychiatry and the Law, 23(3),* 387–397.

Gacono, C. B., Meloy, J. R., Speth, E., & Roske, A. (1997). Above the law: Escapees from a maximum security forensic hospital. *Bulletin of the American Academy of Psychiatry and the Law, 25(4),* 547–550.

Gacono, C. B., Nieberding, R., Owen, A., Rubel, J., & Bodholdt, R. (2000). Treating juvenile and adult offenders with conduct disorder, antisocial, and psychopathic personalities. In J. Ashford, B. Sales, & W. Reid (Eds.), *Treating clients with special needs.*

Hare, R. D. (1966). Psychopathy and choices of immediate and delayed punishment. *Journal of Abnormal Psychology, 71,* 25–29.

Hare, R., (1980). A research scale for the Assessment of Psychopathy in criminal populations. *Personality and Individual Differences, 1,* 111–119.

Hare, R. D. (1991). *The Hare Psychopathy Checklist–Revised.* Toronto, Ontario: Multi-Health Systems.

Hare, R. D. (1996). Psychopathy: A clinical construct whose time has come. *Criminal Justice and Behavior, 23(1),* 25–54.

Hare, R. D. (1998a). Psychopaths and their nature: Implications for the mental health and criminal justice systems (pp. 188–212). In T. Millon, E. Simonsen, M. Birket-Smith, & R. Davis (Eds.), *Psychopathy: Antisocial, criminal, and violent behavior.* New York: Guilford.

Hare, R. D. (1998b). The Alvor Advance Study Institute. In D.J. Cooke, A.E. Forth, & R.D. Hare (Eds.), *Psychopathy: Theory, research and implications for society* (pp. 1–11). London: Kluwer Academic Publishers.

Hare, R. D., Harpur, T. J., Hakstian, A. R., Forth, A. E., Hart, S. D., & Newman, J. P. (1990). The Revised Psychopathy Checklist: Descriptive statistics, reliability, and factor structure. *Psychological Assessment, 2,* 338–341.

Hare, R. D., Hart, S. D., & Harpur, T. J. (1991). Psychopathy and the *DSM–IV* criteria for antisocial personality disorder. *Journal of Abnormal Psychology, 100,* 391–398.

Hare, R. D., & Jutai, J. (1983). Criminal history of the male psychopath: Some preliminary data. In K. Van Dusen & S. Mednick (Eds.), *Prospective studies of crime and delinquency* (pp. 225–236). Boston: Klyuner Mijhoff.

Hare, R. D., & McPherson, L. (1984). Violent and aggressive behavior by criminal psychopaths. *International Journal of Law and Psychiatry, 7,* 35–50.

Hare, R. D., McPherson, L., & Forth, A. (1988). Male psychopaths and their criminal careers. *Journal of consulting and Clinical Psychology, 56,* 710–714.

Harpur, T., Hare, R., & Hatistian, R., (1989). Two-factor conceptualization of psychopathy: Construct validity and assessment implications. Psychological Assessment: *A Journal of Consulting and Clinical Psychology, 1,* 6–17.

Hart, S., & Hare, R. (1989). Discriminant validity of the Psychopathy Checklist in a forensic psychiatric population. Psychological Assessment: *A Journal of Consulting and Clinical Psychology, 1,* 211–218.

Hart, S., Cox, D., & Hare, R. D. (1995). *The Hare Psychopathy Checklist: Screening Version.* North Tonawanda, NY. Multi-Health Systems.

Hart, S. D., Kropp, P., & Hare, R. D. (1988). Performance of male psychopaths following conditional release from prison. *Journal of Consulting and Clinical Psychology, 56,* 227–232.

Jenkins, R. (1960). The psychopathic or antisocial personality. *Journal of Nervous and Mental Disease, 131,* 318–334.

Losel, F. (1998). Treatment and management of psychopaths. In D. Cooke, A. Forth, & R. Hare (Eds.), *Psychopathy: Theory, research and implications for society* (pp. 303–354). The Netherlands: Kluwer Academic Publishers.

Meloy, J. R. (1988). *The psychopathic mind: Origins, dynamics, and treatment.* Northvale, NJ: Aronson.

Meloy, J. R. (1992). *Violent attachments.* Northvale, NJ: Aronson.

Meloy, J.R., & Gacono, C. B. (1998). The internal world of the psychopath: A Rorschach investigation. In T. Millon, E. Simonsen, & M. Birket-Smith (Eds.), *Psychopathy: antisocial, criminal, and violent behaviors* (pp. 95–109). New York: Guilford.

Millon, T., Simonsen, E., Birket-Smith, M., & Davis, R. (1998). *Psychopathy: Antisocial, criminal, and violent behavior.* New York: Guilford.

Murphy, J. (1976). Psychiatric labeling in cross-cultural perspective. *Science, 191,* pp. 1019–1028.

Ogloff, J. R., Wong, S., & Greenwood, A. (1990). Treating criminal psychopaths in a therapeutic community. *Behavioral Sciences and the Law, 8,* 181–190.

Rice, M. E., Harris, G., & Cormier, C. (1992). An evaluation of a maximum security therapeutic community for psychopaths and other mentally disordered offenders. *Law and Human Behavior, 16,* 399–412.

Robins, L. (1966). *Deviant children grown up: A sociological and psychiatric study of sociopathic personality.* Baltimore: Williams & Wilkins.

I

CONCEPTUAL CONTRIBUTIONS

Applying the Concept of Psychopathy to Children: Implications for the Assessment of Antisocial Youth

Paul J. Frick
University of New Orleans

Christopher T. Barry
S. Doug Bodin
University of Alabama

Understanding the causes of aggressive and antisocial behavior in children has long been a major focus of research efforts by clinical child psychologists. This focus is understandable given the frequency with which children with conduct disorders (CDs) are referred to mental health clinics (Frick, Lahey, Strauss, & Christ, 1993). In recent years, societal concerns over the dramatic rise in juvenile crime, especially violent crime, has reaffirmed the importance of this research (Office of Juvenile Justice and Delinquency Prevention, 1995). Through this research, it has become clear that children with CD constitute a very heterogeneous group in terms of the types of behaviors they exhibit, the causes of their behavior problems, and their developmental course. The implications of this heterogeneity for causal theory (Richters, 1997) and clinical practice (Frick, 1998) have been well documented. Unfortunately, despite the large amount of research documenting the heterogeneous nature of CD, there is little consensus as to the most appropriate way to distinguish among children with this disorder.

SUBTYPING APPROACHES FOR CHILDREN WITH CONDUCT DISORDERS

There have been two influential traditions for classifying children with CD and defining important subtypes within this diagnostic category. The multivariate approach categorizes aggressive and antisocial behaviors based on the strength of their covariance within individuals. This approach isolates patterns or factors of intercorrelated conduct problems and defines groups of children based on their scores on these factors (see Achenbach, 1995; Quay, 1986, for a review). Frick et al. (1993) conducted a meta-analysis of over 60 published factor analyses of aggressive and antisocial behavior that involved a combined sample of over 28,401 children and adolescents. The results suggest that conduct problems are generally described by two bipolar dimensions. The first dimension was a covert–overt dimension. The overt pole consisted of directly confrontational behaviors (e.g., oppositional defiant behaviors and mild aggression), whereas the covert pole consisted of nonconfrontational behaviors (e.g., stealing, lying). The second dimension was a destructive–nondestructive dimension. With this dimension, the overt behaviors were divided into those that were overt-destructive (aggression) and those that were overt-nondestructive (oppositional), whereas the covert behaviors were divided into those that were covert-destructive (property violations) and those that were covert-nondestructive (status offenses). This categorization of conduct problems is consistent with legal distinctions made within delinquent behaviors, which distinguish among violent offenses (overt-destructive), status offenses (covert-nondestructive), and property offenses (covert-destructive; e.g., Office of Juvenile Justice and Delinquency Prevention, 1995).

The second method for classifying and subtyping children with CD is the clinical method exemplified by the most recent revisions of the *Diagnostic and Statistical Manual of Mental Disorders* (*DSM*; American Psychiatric Association, 1980, 1987, 1994). In this method, distinct syndromes or patterns of aggressive and antisocial behavior are classified based on their severity, duration (e.g., over extended periods of time), and impairment they cause to a child's psychosocial adjustment (Lahey et al., 1994). A consistent distinction made across the recent versions of *DSM* is between (a) hostile, argumentative, defiant, and angry behaviors that have been considered to be indicative of oppositional disorder (OD; American Psychiatric Association, 1980) or oppositional defiant disorder (ODD; American Psychiatric Association, 1987, 1994); and (b) more serious aggressive and antisocial behaviors that involve violating the rights of others or major societal norms, labeled conduct disorder (CD; American Psychiatric Association, 1980, 1987, 1994). Although the distinction between ODD and CD has been fairly consistent, there have been numerous changes in the subtypes that are recognized within the CD diagnosis. The primary symptoms used to diagnose CD and the subtypes recognized in the recent versions of the *DSM* are provided in Table 1.1.

In *DSM–III* (American Psychiatric Association, 1980), subtypes of CD were defined based on two dimensions. The first dimension was whether a

TABLE 1.1
The Changes in Criteria for Conduct Disorder Across the Most Recent
Versions of the *Diagnostic and Statistical Manual of Mental Disorders*

DSM-III *(American Psychiatric Association, 1980)*	DSM-III-R *(American Psychiatric Association, 1987)*	DSM-IV *(American Psychiatric Association, 1994)*
	Primary Symptoms	

1. Physical violence against persons or property.
2. Thefts outside the home involving confrontation.
3. Chronic violations of rules.
4. Repeated running away overnight.
5. Persistent serious lying.
6. Stealing not involving confrontation of victim.
	1. Stealing without confrontation of victim.
	2. Running away from home overnight.
	3. Often lies.
	4. Deliberately engages in fire-setting.
	5. Often truant.
	6. Broken into someone else's house, building, or car.
	7. Deliberately destroyed others' property.
	8. Physically cruel to animals.
	9. Forced someone into sexual activity.
	10. Used a weapon in a fight.
	11. Often initiates physical fights.
	12. Has stolen with confrontation of victim.
	13. Has been physically cruel to people.
		A. Aggression to people and animals
		  1. Bullies others.
		  2. Initiates physical fights.
		  3. Has used weapon in fight.
		  4. Physically cruel to others.
		  5. Physically cruel to animals.
		  6. Stolen with confrontation.
		  7. Forced sexual activity.
		B. Destruction of property
		  8. Deliberate fire-setting.
		  9. Vandalism.
		C. Deceitfulness or theft
		  10. Broken into house, building, or car.
		  11. Lies for own gain.
		  12. Stolen without confrontation.
		D. Serious violations of rules
		  13. Often stays out at night.
		  14. Run away from home.
		  15. Often truant.

	Subtypes	
1. Undersocialized, Aggressive 2. Undersocialized, Nonaggressive 3. Socialized, Aggressive 4. Socialized, Nonaggressive	1. Group 2. Solitary Aggressive 3. Undifferentiated	1. Childhood-onset 2. Adolescent-onset

child or adolescent with CD was (a) capable of sustaining social relationships and tended to commit antisocial behavior with other deviant peers (socialized type), or (b) unable to sustain social relationships and committed antisocial acts alone (undersocialized type). The second dimension was whether a child or adolescent with CD (a) showed a pattern of aggressive behavior in which the rights of others were violated (aggressive type), or (b) showed only nonaggressive antisocial behavior (nonaggressive type). The validity of this subtyping approach was supported by studies showing that youth who were classified as undersocialized and aggressive tended to have poorer adjustment in juvenile institutions and were more likely to continue to show antisocial behavior into adulthood compared with youth who exhibited the socialized-nonaggressive pattern of CD (Frick & Loney, 1999; Quay, 1987). The undersocialized-aggressive group was also more likely to show neuropsychological correlates to their antisocial behavior, such as low serotonin levels and autonomic irregularities (Lahey, Hart, Pliszka, Applegate, & McBurnett, 1993). Furthermore, the socialized subgroup captured the phenomenon of gang delinquency in which the antisocial behavior seemed to be heavily influenced by contact with and support of an antisocial subculture (Quay, 1987).

Despite the promising findings for this method of subtyping children with CD, there was considerable confusion concerning the critical features that distinguished the undersocialized and socialized subgroups (see Hinshaw, Lahey, & Hart, 1993; Lahey, Loeber, Quay, Frick, & Grimm, 1992, for reviews). For example, some definitions focused on the child's ability to form and maintain social relationships, whereas others focused primarily on the context (alone or as a group) in which the antisocial acts were typically committed. Furthermore, some definitions even focused on specific causes for the inability to maintain social relationships. For example, the description of undersocialized CD, which was provided in *DSM–III*, focused on personality traits that impaired the formation of social relationships, such as a lack of affection and empathy toward others, egocentrism and manipulativeness, absence of remorse, and a willingness to blame others for mistakes.

In an effort to overcome this definitional confusion, *DSM–III–R* criteria for CD focused solely on whether the antisocial acts were committed alone (solitary type) or with other antisocial peers (group type) and whether the child with CD showed physical aggression (aggressive type; American Psychiatric Association, 1987). The rationale for defining subtypes in this way was twofold. First, children with undersocialized CD tended to be highly aggressive, whereas most children identified with socialized CD tended to show nonaggressive symptoms. Second, there was less ambiguity about the measurement of physical aggression and in determining who was typically present when a child engaged in antisocial behavior, in comparison to the difficulty in measuring more subjective personality traits related to children's empathic concern to others and feelings of guilt (Hinshaw et al., 1993; Lahey et al., 1992).

Within the *DSM* tradition, there was another approach to subtyping children with CD that focused on the presence of other disorders (i.e., comorbidities) to defined distinct subgroups of children with CD. For example, a significant proportion (65%–90%) of children with CD also exhibit severe problems of inattention and impulsivity and can be diagnosed with attention deficit hyperactivity disorder (ADHD; Abikoff & Klein, 1992). Children with both CD and ADHD show a number of characteristics that distinguish them from other CD children. They tend to develop their conduct problems at an earlier age, they tend to be more aggressive, and they are more likely to start using illegal drugs at an earlier age (Thompson, Riggs, Mikulich, & Crowley, 1996; Walker, Lahey, Hynd, & Frame, 1987). Children with both CD and ADHD also show a number of differences on neuropsychological measures from other children with CD, such as greater deficits in executive functioning (Moffitt & Henry, 1989), more problems in inhibiting a dominant response (Halperin et al., 1990), and lower autonomic reactivity (Pelham et al., 1991). Based on this research, Lynam (1996) proposed that this group of children with CD and ADHD shows a qualitatively distinct form of CD with different causal processes underlying their behavior. Furthermore, the severity of their behavior and the distinct pattern of neuropsychological deficits led Lynam (1996) to suggest that this group was a childhood precursor to psychopathy.

As Lynam's (1996) approach illustrates, many of the *DSM* subtyping approaches for CD, such as the personality traits included in the definition of undersocialized-aggressive CD and the comorbidity of CD and ADHD, could provide a link to research on adults with psychopathic traits. However, *DSM–IV* (American Psychiatric Association, 1994) chose a dramatically different focus for defining subtypes of CD. This version emphasized the different developmental trajectories through which children may develop CD. It distinguishes between CD children whose antisocial behavior begins in childhood and those whose onset of severe antisocial behavior coincides with the onset of adolescence (Hinshaw et al., 1993; Moffitt, 1993a). This method of subtyping children with CD has proved to have great predictive utility. That is, longitudinal studies have consistently shown that one of the best predictors of which children with CD will continue to show antisocial behavior into adulthood is the onset of severe conduct problems prior to adolescence (e.g., Frick & Loney, 1999).

In addition to the predictive utility of this distinction, children with the childhood-onset pattern of CD are characterized by having higher rates of cognitive/neuropsychological dysfunction, such as low intelligence (especially on measures of verbal intelligence and indexes of executive functioning and planning abilities) and much higher rates of ADHD than children with the adolescent-onset pattern of behavior (Moffitt, 1993a). In addition, children with childhood-onset CD tend to come from more dysfunctional family environments, characterized by high rates of parental psychopathology, high rates of family conflict, and the presence of dysfunctional parenting practices (see also Frick, 1994; Loeber & Stouthamer-Loeber, 1986). Based on these characteristics, Moffitt (1993a) proposed that childhood-onset CD develops through a transactional process of a temperamentally difficult infant being raised in a home that does not provide an optimal rearing environment. As a result, these children often develop a more characterological disturbance that can be highly stable throughout the life span. In contrast, children in the adolescent-onset group seem to show an exaggerated normative pattern of rebellion that coincides with the onset of puberty and often subsides as a child enters adulthood.

Although descriptively the use of age of onset to subtype children with CD does not provide a direct link to adult conceptualizations of psychopathy, several characteristics of children within the childhood-onset group make their disturbance seem more closely analogous to psychopathy in adults as compared with the adolescent-onset group. First, the more characterological nature of the disturbance and the severity and chronicity of the antisocial behavior in the childhood-onset group are consistent with the psychological profile of the psychopathic adult (Hare, Hart, & Harpur, 1991). Second, the higher rate of ADHD in the childhood-onset group makes them fit more closely with Lynam's (1996) conceptualization of the fledgling psychopath. Third, many children in the childhood-onset group show a personality profile characterized by impulsive and impetuous behavior and a cold, callous, alienated, and suspicious interpersonal style (Moffitt, Caspi, Dickson, Silva, & Stanton, 1996). These traits are quite consistent with the callous and unemotional traits characteristic of adults with psychopathy (Cleckley, 1976; Hare, 1993; McCord & McCord, 1964). Therefore, it is quite likely that the closest link with the concept of psychopathy in adulthood will be found within the childhood-onset CD group.

EXTENDING THE CONCEPT OF PSYCHOPATHY TO CHILDREN

From this review of the various methods for dividing children with CD into more homogenous subgroups, there are two critical issues that clearly illustrate the potential importance of extending the concept of psychopathy to children. First, this research illustrates that children with CD are a heterogeneous group; if we are to advance our understanding of the causes of such behavior patterns, we must define meaningful subgroups within this diagnostic category. Second, many of the methods for dividing children with CD into subgroups have identified a particularly severe subgroup of children with many characteristics similar to adults with psychopathy. However, none of these approaches has attempted to explicitly measure the full range of psychopathic traits in children and use this construct as the primary basis for determining subtypes of children and adolescents with CD. The closest attempt at such an extension was the *DSM–III* category of undersocialized-aggressive CD, which, as mentioned previously, was not clear in defining the core features of this subtype. This lack of clarity led to substantial variations in how this category was used. Otherwise, research has primarily focused on defining subgroups of children with CD and determining which subgroup shows features that are analogous to adults with psychopathy (e.g., Lynam, 1996; Moffitt et al., 1996), rather than using callous and unemotional traits as the explicit method for differentiating groups. In the following sections, we present a line of research that has attempted to make this explicit extension of the concept of psychopathy to children.

Before discussing this line of research, however, it is important to note that legitimate concerns have been raised about applying the construct of psychopathy to children (see Quay, 1987). The first concern is over the negative connotations that the label *psychopathy* has for treatment success and overall long-term outcome. The second concern is that psychopathy implies an intrinsic and biological basis to the dysfunction. These concerns highlight the importance of not assuming that the negative prognosis found for psychopathic adults applies to children. They also highlight the importance of a child's environmental context in the development of all personality traits, including those associated with psychopathy. Unfortunately, the common alternative to explicitly applying the concept of psychopathy to children is to implicitly consider all children with CD as showing a "childhood manifestation of psychopathy" (e.g., Richters & Cicchetti, 1993). This alternative is even more problematic because many of the malignant, impairing, and unique dispositional features associated with psychopathy may only apply to a subset of children with CD. By being more precise in categorizing which children with CD exhibit early signs of psychopathy, we can begin to address the critical questions related to the stability of these traits in children and to understanding the complex interaction between dispositional and environmental factors involved in the development of these traits.

Development of the Psychopathy Screening Device in Clinic-Referred Samples

To begin our research on psychopathy in children, we developed an assessment format that would provide an adequate coverage of the key aspects of psychopathy. We used the Psychopathy Checklist–Revised

(PCL–R; Hare, 1991) as a model for defining our content because the PCL–R has an extensive coverage of many different aspects of psychopathy and it has been widely used in adult forensic samples to identify psychopathic adults. Research suggests that the content of the PCL–R can be divided into two correlated dimensions of behavior (Hare, Hart, & Harpur, 1991; Harpur, Hare, & Hakstian, 1989). One dimension includes the interpersonal characteristics (such as superficial charm, callous use of others, absence of empathy) and emotional style (absence of guilt, shallow emotions, lack of anxiety) that have been hallmarks of the psychopathic personality in many clinical descriptions (see Cleckley, 1976; McCord & McCord, 1964). The second dimension includes the unstable and deviant lifestyle (such as multiple marriages, poor employment history, multiple arrests, aggression) that is characteristic of antisocial personality disorder (ASPD) in recent versions of the *Diagnostic and Statistical Manual of Mental Disorders* (*DSM*; American Psychiatric Association, 1994).

To capture these dimensions in children, each of the 20 items included on the PCL–R was made into an analogous item that was more applicable to children. This measure was labeled the Psychopathy Screening Device (PSD; Frick & Hare, in press; see Table 1.2). Although the PCL–R is completed through a semistructured interview coupled with a review of collateral information, such as institutional records and arrest history, the assessment format of the childhood PSD was designed differently. First, the items are in a rating scale format in which each item is rated on a 3-point scale as 0 (*not at all true*), 1 (*sometimes true*), or 2 (*definitely true*). Second, the PSD uses two separate rating formats: One is completed by a child's parent and the other by a child's teacher. The use of parent and teacher ratings was based on the questionable validity of children's self-report, especially of young children, for assessing their emotional and behavioral functioning (Kamphaus & Frick, 1996). Furthermore, research suggests that parents and teachers are the optimal informants for assessing childhood aggression and antisocial behavior (Loeber, Green, Lahey, & Stouthamer-Loeber, 1991). Because a major focus in the construct validation of the PSD was on the divergent validity of psychopathic traits from conduct problem behavior, it was important that the same assessment format be used to assess both dimensions.

In the initial test of the PSD, Frick, O'Brien, Wootton, and McBurnett (1994) obtained parent and teacher ratings on 92 clinic-referred children between the ages of 6 and 13. Children were consecutive referrals to two university-based outpatient child mental health clinics and the sample was predominantly male (84%) and White (82%). A principal components analysis was conducted on the PSD items using a combination of parent and teacher ratings for each item, and this analysis revealed two dimensions. The first dimension (eigenvalue of 5.9) included items tapping poor impulse control, irresponsibility, narcissism, and antisocial behavior. The second dimension (eigenvalue of 2.4) included items related to a callous and unemotional interpersonal style similar to the psychopathic traits isolated in adult samples. Although these two dimensions were similar in content to the dimensions that have emerged in adult samples using the PCL–R (Harpur et al., 1989), one notable difference was that items related to narcissism (e.g., "Thinks he/she is more important than others") were more highly associated with the impulsive and antisocial behavior dimension in children, whereas in adult samples the narcissistic items tend to be more associated with callous and unemotional traits (Factor 1 on the PCL–R). However, other authors have also documented developmental differences in narcissism and its relation to antisocial behavior (Gacono & Meloy, 1994).

To test the divergent validity of these two dimensions, Frick et al. (1994) formed two scales based on this principal components analysis. The items on each scale are provided in Table 1.2. The Impulsive-Conduct Problems (I/CP) scale contained 10 items and had a coefficient alpha of .82. The Callous Unemotional (CU) scale contained six items and had a coefficient alpha of .73. These two scales were significantly correlated ($r = .50, p < .001$). The first test of the divergent validity of these two scales was in their association with traditional conduct problems measures, such as symptoms of ODD and CD and conduct problem subscales from standardized behavior rating scales. The I/CP scale of the PSD was highly correlated with these traditional conduct problems measures (ranging from .53 to .71) and differentiated children with an ODD or CD diagnosis from other clinic-referred

TABLE 1.2
A Summary of the Two Factors of the Psychopathy Screening Device
in Clinic-Referred Children

Callous-Unemotional Traits	Poor Impulse Control-Conduct Problems
Unconcerned about schoolwork	Brags about accomplishments
Does not feel bad or guilty	Becomes angry when corrected
Emotions seem shallow and not genuine	Thinks he or she is more important than others
Does not show feelings or emotions	Acts without thinking of the consequences
Acts charming in ways that seem insincere	Blames others for own mistakes
Is unconcerned about the feelings of others	Teases or makes fun of others
	Engages in risky or dangerous activities
	Engages in illegal activities
	Does not keep the same friends
	Gets bored easily

Note. These dimensions were formed using a principle components analysis with an oblique rotation (Frick et al., 1994). The items were assessed for each child using a combination of parent and teacher reports.

children [$t(62)$ = 5.6, p < .05]. However, the CU scale was less strongly, yet still significantly, associated with traditional conduct problem measures (ranging from .30 to.45). This scale did not differentiate children with an ODD or CD diagnosis from other clinic-referred children [$t(62)$ = 1.4, p = ns].

Callous-Unemotional Traits as a Predictor of Severe Conduct Disorders

One important use of measures of psychopathy, such as the PCL–R, has been to designate prisoners who show an especially severe and violent pattern of behavior and who show a poor response to treatment (see Hare et al., 1991). Therefore, a key question concerning the usefulness of the PSD in children was whether it could also designate a severe subgroup of children with CD or a severe subgroup of juvenile delinquents. Christian, Frick, Hill, Tyler, and Frazer (1997) studied 120 consecutive outpatient clinic referrals between the ages of 6 and 13 (mean = 8.68, SD = 2.07) and were able to isolate two distinct clusters of children with conduct problem diagnoses. The first cluster (n = 29) had either an ODD (90%) or CD (45%) diagnosis, was high in the I/CP scale of the PSD, but was low on the CU scale. This was labeled the *impulsive conduct cluster*. The second conduct problem cluster (n = 11) also had either an ODD diagnosis (100%) or CD diagnosis (55%) and scored high on the I/CP scale of the PSD. However, this second cluster, labeled the *psychopathic conduct cluster*, also scored high in the CU scale of the PSD. Therefore, the CU scale of the PSD divided children with conduct problem diagnoses into two groups.

The psychopathic conduct cluster, which was also high on the CU scale, showed higher rates and greater variety of ODD and CD symptoms and scored higher on rating scale measures of conduct problems than the other conduct problem cluster. Also, this psychopathic conduct cluster was the only cluster to show higher rates of police contacts and higher rates of parental diagnoses of ASPD compared with other clinic-referred children. The differences in the rates of police contacts were particularly striking, with 36% of the psychopathic conduct cluster having had a police contact, compared with 14% of the children in the impulsive conduct cluster and none of the other clinic-referred children. This finding is illustrated in Fig. 1.1. These findings are important because the number and variety of conduct problems (Frick & Loney, 1999; Loeber, 1982, 1991), early police contact (Quay, 1987), and a family history of ASPD (Lahey et al., 1995) have all predicted poor outcomes for children with CD.

Given these findings in a clinic sample, we extended our work to forensic samples to determine if callous and unemotional traits predicted a severe pattern of delinquency in these samples as well. Due to the older age of these samples (ranging from 12 to 18 years), we modified the PSD

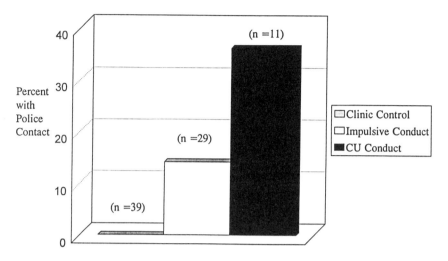

FIG. 1.1.   Figure illustrates the percentage of children with police contacts in three clinic clusters. CU refers to the cluster of children with conduct disorders and high rates of callous and unemotional rates. Data taken from Table 4 in "Psychopathy and Conduct Problems in Children: II. Subtyping Children With Conduct Problems Based on Their Interpersonal and Affective Style" by R. Christian, P. J. Frick, N. Hill, L. A. Tyler, and D. Frazier, 1997, *Journal of the American Academy of Child and Adolescent Psychiatry, 36.*

to include a self-report format. Self-report becomes more reliable and valid as a child enters adolescence, especially for assessing antisocial tendencies and attitudes that may not be observable to parents and other significant adults (Kamphaus & Frick, 1996). Also, in many of the forensic samples, parents or teachers with sufficient knowledge of the child's personality to complete rating scales were often unavailable.

This self-report version of the PSD was given to a sample of 72 adolescents (mean age = 15.17, SD = 1.32) who had been adjudicated for serious illegal behavior and placed in a secure detention facility (Silverthorn, Frick, & Reynolds, 1998). Boys in this sample could be divided into those with a childhood onset to their antisocial behavior (i.e., had first CD symptom or first police contact before age 10; n = 11) and those with an adolescent onset to their antisocial behavior (i.e., had first CD symptom and first police contact after age 11; n = 13). Those boys with a childhood onset to their antisocial behavior were more likely to show elevated CU scores on the PSD than the boys with an adolescent onset to their behavior. In a second sample of 69 adjudicated male adolescents (mean age = 16.18, SD = 1.08), scores on the CU scale of the PSD differentiated violent sex offenders (n = 23) from other violent offenders (n = 17) and nonviolent offenders (n = 29;

Caputo, Frick, & Brodsky, 1999). Specifically, although the three offender groups did not differ on I/CP scores, the violent sex offender group showed a greater percentage of juveniles elevated on the CU scale. Taken together, callous and unemotional traits were associated with patterns of offending (e.g., early onset of antisocial behavior, violent sex offending) that are frequently associated with severity and poor outcome in juvenile offenders.

Callous-Unemotional Traits and Multiple Causal Pathways to Conduct Disorder

Antisocial adults who also show callous and unemotional traits manifest a number of distinct correlates (e.g., less dysfunctional family backgrounds, less intelligence impairments, deficits in processing of emotional stimuli) compared with other antisocial adults (Hare et al., 1991). These differences in correlates could relate to different causal processes underlying the behavior of the two groups (see Lykken, 1995; Newman & Wallace, 1993). In our use of the PSD in children, we have also found differences between CD children with and without callous and unemotional traits, which could suggest differences in the etiology of CD depending on the presence of these traits. For example, we have found that children with CD who have callous and unemotional traits show a preference for thrill- and adventure-seeking activities (Frick et al., 1994) and show a greater sensitivity to rewards than punishments (O'Brien & Frick, 1996). These children are less likely than other children with CD to come from families in which the parents engage in ineffective parenting strategies (Wootton, Frick, Shelton, & Silverthorn, 1997), and they are less likely to show deficits in intellectual functioning (Christian et al., 1997; Loney, Frick, Ellis, & McCoy, 1998).

Based on these findings, combined with the fact that callous and unemotional traits seem to be primarily related to the childhood-onset pattern of CD (Moffitt et al., 1996; Silverthorn et al., 1998), we have proposed that callous and unemotional traits can be used to divide children within the childhood-onset category of CD into two distinct subgroups (Frick, 1998). In both subgroups, children have dispositional vulnerabilities that interact with their rearing context and lead to difficulties in their ability to modulate their behavior in response to authority figures, social norms, or to respect the rights of other people (Moffitt, 1993a). This commonality across the two childhood-onset pathways suggests that problems of impulse control are central to both groups. This commonality accounts for the findings that the impulsive and deviant lifestyle dimension of psychopathy (e.g., the I/CP scale of the PSD) does not differentiate subgroups within the childhood-onset group. It also provides a clear point of differentiation between these two groups and the adolescent-onset pattern of CD (see Moffitt et al., 1996; Silverthorn et al., 1998).

In contrast to other views of the childhood-onset group, however, we propose that these children may develop their problems of impulse control and antisocial behavior through several different causal pathways; a major division is between the CD children with and without callous and unemotional traits. In children without callous and unemotional traits, their poor impulse control is related to a diverse set of interacting causal factors. For example, some children may come from problematic rearing environments in which they are not taught to control their impulses and respect the rights of others (Frick, 1994). Others may have difficulty anticipating the consequences of their behavior or delaying gratification due to low intelligence (Loney et al., 1998). Furthermore, they may have developed a hostile attributional bias (i.e., a tendency to attribute hostile intent to the actions of others) resulting from factors such as being raised in an abusive home environment (Dodge, Bates, & Pettit, 1990). Still others may fail to develop appropriate behavioral controls due to a combination of an impulsive/overactive temperament combined with suboptimal parental socialization practices (Colder, Lochman, & Wells, 1997).

We propose that children with CD who also show callous and unemotional traits constitute a more homogeneous group with respect to the etiology of their lack of behavioral controls. In our model, we propose that their behavior is more related to a temperament defined by low behavioral inhibition. Low behavioral inhibition is characterized physiologically by autonomic nervous system irregularities and behaviorally by low fearfulness to novel or threatening situations and poor responsiveness to cues to punishment (Kagan & Snidman, 1991; Rothbart, 1989). As mentioned previously, children with CD and callous and unemotional traits show high levels of thrill and adventure seeking (i.e., low fearfulness) and are less sensitive to punishment cues, which is consistent with low behavioral inhibition. This temperament can be related to the development of callous and unemotional traits in several ways (see Kochanska, 1993, for seven different theories to account for this link). For example, children low in fearful inhibitions may not be as responsive to parental discipline, especially punishment-oriented discipline, because they do not experience as much anxiety associated with their misdeeds or with the possibility of disapproval from their parents. Furthermore, if they do respond to parental discipline or other socializing pressures (e.g., teacher reprimands), the lower level anxiety that they experience makes it more likely for them to attribute the motivation for appropriate behavior to external pressures and not to intrinsic motivation. As a result, they may be less likely to generalize their behavior to other situations in which the discipline does not occur. In contrast, the internal arousal experienced by children who do not lack fearful inhibitions make them more likely to perceive their arousal over misdeeds as "coming from inside" (Kochanska, 1993; p. 331). Thus, the more anxious children should show greater internalization of norms and values, rather than modulating their behavior solely as a function of the external consequences provided by parents or other significant adults (Kochanska, 1993).

Further Validation of the PSD in a Community Sample

The initial validation of the PSD and our resulting theoretical model has been based largely on clinical and forensic samples. As a result, there is limited information on how the dimensions of psychopathy are manifested in community samples of children. Research in community samples could be quite informative in defining differences between normative and non-normative levels of these traits. Such differences have important clinical applications by establishing when levels of psychopathic traits begin to predict clinically significant levels of impairment or predict risk for future violent behavior. Also, research in community samples can help determine whether psychopathy is best considered a continuous trait, with similar processes leading to variations at low and high levels of the trait, or whether it is best considered a taxon, with different causal processes underlying extreme variations in the trait (Harris, Rice, & Quinsey, 1994; Newman & Wallace, 1993). Finally, understanding how psychopathic traits are manifested in nonreferred samples could identify factors that protect persons with subclinical levels of these traits from showing more severe patterns of behavior, which could help advance the prevention and treatment of psychopathy.

As a result, we recently embarked on a 5-year study of callous and unemotional traits in a community sample of elementary school-age children funded by the National Institute of Mental Health (NIMH). In the first phase of the study, we gathered information on 1,136 children (mean age 10.7; SD = 1.6) measuring both psychopathic traits and conduct problem symptoms. The sample was 53% girls, 22% African American, and covered a broad range of socioeconomic statuses (SESs). In this sample, we conducted a factor analysis of the PSD using parent report (n = 878), teacher report (n = 1,065), and a combined parent and teacher report (n = 810) to see whether the dimensions of psychopathy in a community sample were similar to those reported in the clinic sample (Frick et al., 1994).

The results of this factor analysis are reported in Table 1.3. This analysis revealed that, in a community sample, the PSD items could be divided into three dimensions rather than the two found in the clinic sample (see Table 1.2). In this analysis, the callous and unemotional dimension that emerged in previous samples and was used to identify subgroups of children with the childhood-onset type of CD remained largely unchanged.

TABLE 1.3
Factor Structure of PSD in a Community Sample
of Third-, Fourth-, Sixth-, and Seventh-Grade Students

Traits	Narcissism Factor			Impulsivity Factor			Callous-Unemotional Factor		
	C	P	T	C	P	T	C	P	T
16. Thinks more important	.78	.59	.82						
8. Brags excessively	.67	.58	.69						
10. Uses or cons others	.52	.52	.51	.33		.40			
14. Can be charming	.51	.56	.54						
11. Teases others	.40	.35	.43			.41			
15. Becomes angry when corrected	.37	.30	.46			.36			
5. Emotions seem shallow	.36	.44	.39						
4. Acts without thinking				.70	.71	.72			
17. Does not plan ahead				.65	.67	.61			
13. Engages in risky activities				.50	.38	.53			
1. Blames others for mistakes	.31	.32		.48	.45	.55			
9. Gets bored easily					.33	.42			
18. Is concerned for feelings of others (I)			.30				.69	.67	.65
12. Feels bad or guilty (I)							.61	.69	.62
3. Is concerned about schoolwork (I)				.34			.57	.52	.71
7. Keeps promises (I)							.46	.52	.56
19. Does not show emotions							.45		.41
20. Keeps the same friends (I)							.36	.36	.35
6. Lies easily and skillfully		.35	.33	.44		.41			
Preliminary Eigenvalues	11.1	7.5	17.3	1.5	.92	.85	.78	1.14	2.24
Final Eigenvalues	12.2	8.2	18.8	1.8	1.16	1.07	1.02	1.39	2.75

Note. The results are from a principal factor analysis using maximum likelihood estimation for initial factor extraction and an oblique (Promax) rotation. Rotated factors scores of .30 or greater are reported in the table. C = combined parent and teacher report (n = 810), P = parent report only (n = 878), and T = teacher report only (n = 1,065). (I) refers to items that were inversely scored prior to the factor analysis.

However, the I/CP scale of PSD divided into two factors: one containing items assessing narcissism and another with items assessing impulsivity.

To study the relations of these three dimensions of the PSD with *DSM–IV* criteria, three subscales of the PSD were formed based on the factor loadings reported in Table 1.3. The three were intercorrelated, with the Callous and Unemotional (CU) subscale correlating .55 ($p < .001$) with the Narcissism subscale and .57 ($p < .001$) with the Impulsivity subscale. The Narcissism and the Impulsivity subscales were correlated .67 ($p < .001$). In this screening sample, measures of *DSM–IV* symptoms of CD,

ODD, and ADHD were assessed using the Child Symptom Inventory–4 (CSI–4; Gadow & Sprafkin, 1995), a parent- and teacher-completed rating scale used to assess each symptom of the *DSM–IV* disorders. Each *DSM–IV* symptom was rated on a 4-point scale, ranging from the symptom *never* being present to a symptom being present *very often*.

The correlations between the *DSM–IV* symptom scores and the three subscales of the PSD are presented in Table 1.4. In Table 1.4, the zero correlations between the *DSM–IV* symptom scores and the PSD dimensions are presented, as well as the semipartial correlations (standardized beta weights) to test the association of each PSD dimension with the *DSM–IV* symptoms scores while controlling for the other two subscales of the PSD. As evident from Table 1.4, all three subscales of the PSD were significantly correlated with *DSM–IV* composites, with correlations ranging from .50 to .74 (all $p < .001$). Also, the three dimensions accounted for 48% to 60% of the variance in the *DSM–IV* composites in multiple regression analyses. With one exception, the PSD subscales each contributed independently to the prediction of the *DSM–IV* composites. This final result suggests that the three PSD dimensions are each associated with somewhat unique aspects of the *DSM–IV* symptom lists.

There were some differences in terms of which PSD dimensions were most strongly related to the various *DSM–IV* categories. The CU subscale of the PSD generally accounted for the least amount of unique variance in the *DSM–IV* composites, suggesting that this dimension of psychopathy shows the least overlap with the *DSM–IV* definitions of disruptive behavior disorders. Also, the Narcissism subscale accounted for the largest

TABLE 1.4

Association Between the Three Dimensions from the PSD
and *DSM–IV* Symptoms of Disruptive Behavior Disorders

			PSD Subscale				
	Narcissism		Impulsivity		Callous-Unemotional		Overall
DSM–IV Symptom Scores	R	Beta	R	Beta	R	Beta	R^2
Conduct Disorder	.65***	.42***	.58***	.20***	.52***	.17***	.48***
Oppositional Defiant Disorder	.72***	.45***	.69***	.34***	.53***	.08**	.60***
Impulsivity-Hyperactivity	.64***	.27***	.72***	.52***	.50***	.05	.57***
Inattention-Disorganization	.49***	−.09**	.74***	.64***	.60***	.28***	.60***

Note. *DSM–IV* symptom scores are based on ratings from the CSI-4 (Gadow & Sprafkin, 1995). Both the PSD and CSI-4 scores are based on a combination of parent and teacher reports ($n = 810$). *$p < .05$, **$p < .01$, ***$p < .001$.

amount of independent variance in the conduct problem composites (ODD and CD), whereas the Impulsivity composite accounted for the most variance in the ADHD composites. Taken together, these findings are consistent with the findings from the clinic sample (Frick et al., 1994) — in that the Narcissism and Impulsivity dimensions of the PSD, which in the previous analyses combined to form the Impulsive-Conduct Problems scale, are the dimensions of psychopathy that were most strongly associated with traditional measures of conduct problems.

Also consistent with the early analyses in the clinic sample, the Callous-Unemotional scale was significantly correlated with measures of conduct problems, especially CD. However, the association was low to moderate especially after controlling for the other dimensions of psychopathy. This provides further support for our contention that the *DSM* criteria do not capture many of the traits that are critical to the construct of psychopathy. It remains to be seen whether CU traits predict severity and chronicity, poor treatment response, and different correlates to CD in this community sample.

SUMMARY AND CLINICAL IMPLICATIONS

We believe that the line of research developing the PSD and extending the concept of psychopathy to children with CD could have important implications for our understanding of severe antisocial behavior in youth. However, it is also important to recognize that this research is still in its early stages and, as a result, there remains substantial limitations in this research. For example, the PSD is still in the early stages of development and is not ready for clinical use. Most important, the PSD lacks adequate normative data. The large community sample within which the factor analysis was conducted was geographically limited (to one moderate size city in the southern United States) and limited in its age range (students in Grades 3, 4, 6, and 7). There are also few data on which to base empirically defined cutoff scores on the PSD, such as determining scores that predict significant impairment in functioning for a child, scores that predict response to interventions, or scores that predict risk for arrest or recidivism in adjudicated youth.

For example, PSD scores could be tested to determine a cutoff that predicts a high risk for recidivism after youth have been released from juvenile institutions. Another limitation in the use of the PSD is the lack of conclusive data as to the best informant or combination of informants to assess psychopathy in children and adolescents. For example, the ratings of parents, teachers, and children should be compared in terms of their prediction of clinically important (e.g., risk for violence) or theoretically important (e.g., low fearfulness) external criteria to determine the differential validity of the various informants. Based on research on other forms of childhood psychopathology, the optimal assessment strategy is likely to be a combination of different informants, with the optimal combination (e.g., parent and teacher; parent and child) being dependent on the age of the child (Kamphaus & Frick, 1996).

Much of the research presented in this chapter comes from one research group. Therefore, it is important that the findings be replicated by others to better determine how robust they may be. Also, other than the factor analyses reported earlier, there is still little information on psychopathy in community samples. An especially intriguing question is whether there is a significant number of children who show callous and unemotional traits but do not show severe conduct problems. If these children can be identified, do these children show correlates that make them seem similar to CD children with these traits (e.g., a reward dominant response style)? What prevents these children from showing antisocial behavior despite their cold and callous unemotional style? These issues are the focus of the later stages of the NIMH funded project described previously.

Clearly there is a significant amount of research that remains to be conducted. However, our findings to date strongly support further extensions of the concept of psychopathy to children. Consistent with the findings in adults (Hare et al., 1991), the callous and unemotional dimension of psychopathy does not seem to be captured well by traditional definitions of antisocial behavior, such as the *DSM–IV* definitions of CD. Furthermore, callous and unemotional traits seem to designate a unique subgroup of children with CD who show a more severe pattern of behavior. Also consistent with the adult literature, callous and unemotional traits may help designate a group of children with CD who have a unique constellation of causal factors underlying their behavioral difficulties.

As we summarized in this chapter, the usefulness of callous and unemotional traits for subtyping children with CD has led to some intriguing possibilities for advancing our understanding of the multiple causal pathways through which children develop severe patterns of aggressive and antisocial behavior. This enhanced understanding could be critical for designing interventions that are more individualized to the specific needs of children and adolescents with CD. For example, the current focus in designing interventions for children with CD is to use a multimodal treatment strategy that addresses the many interacting factors that can cause and maintain antisocial behavior and is tailored to the unique constellation of factors that are clinically relevant to an individual child (Frick, 1998). As argued throughout this chapter, the presence of psychopathic traits, combined with the *DSM–IV* subtypes of CD based on the age of onset, define unique subgroups of children with CD who are likely to need different approaches to intervention.

Another important clinical implication is that most of the interventions that have been systematically developed and tested for the treatment of CD have largely focused on the processes that are most important for children with CD who do not show callous and unemotional traits. For example, helping parents use more effective behavior management strategies, helping children control their anger and impulsivity, and helping children use better social problem-solving skills have all been key components to most treatment packages for children and adolescents with CD (Frick, 1998). As we learn more about children with CD who also have CU traits, hopefully additional interventions can be developed and tested to more specifically address the processes underlying the antisocial behavior in these children. For example, interventions could focus on (a) enhancing other aspects of the family environment (e.g., parent–child attachment), (b) reward-oriented approaches to socialization rather than punishment, or (c) helping these children develop skills or hobbies in which they can become invested (e.g., sports, music), which they would not want to lose due to the consequences of antisocial or delinquent behavior. These types of intervention may be more effective for CD children who show callous and unemotional traits given their reward-oriented and narcissistic interpersonal style. This contention is only speculative at this point because controlled studies of these types of intervention with children who show callous and unemotional traits have not been conducted. However, it illustrates the potential importance of differentiating children with CD based on important characteristics and designing treatments that take into account these characteristics.

Finally, our developmental model of psychopathy could provide a more explicit link to the literature on adult psychopathy and some of the rich theoretical discussions of the basic processes underlying psychopathic behavior (e.g., Newman & Wallace, 1993). As previously mentioned, this link to the adult literature can also have harmful effects if potential developmental differences are ignored. However, it provides researchers and clinicians alike with a more precise conceptualization of what are childhood manifestations of psychopathy. Such methods of discrimination have a very immediate clinical application: They alert clinicians that not all children who exhibit severe antisocial behavior, even those that can be diagnosed with CD, should be considered budding psychopaths (see also Lynam, 1996). Instead, it suggests that this may be best reserved for a distinct subgroup of children and adolescents with CD. This chapter provides a glimpse of the emerging picture that is being formed of this group of children. As this picture develops further, it may provide us with our best chance of reducing the impact of psychopathic behaviors on our society. Namely, it could provide clinicians with the necessary tools to alter the development of these traits early in life — when they may be more malleable.

ACKNOWLEDGMENTS

The authors would like to thank all of the staff of Alabama School-Aged Assessment Service who participated in the data collection for many of the studies reviewed in this chapter. Also, work on this chapter was supported by grant R29 MH55654-02 from the National Institute of Mental Health made to the first author.

REFERENCES

Abikoff, H., & Klein, R. G. (1992). Attention-deficit hyperactivity and conduct disorder: Comorbidity and implications for treatment. *Journal of Consulting and Clinical Psychology, 60,* 881–892.
Achenbach, T. M. (1995). Empirically based assessment and taxonomy: Applications to clinical research. *Psychological Assessment, 7,* 261–274.
American Psychiatric Association. (1980). *The diagnostic and statistical manual of mental disorders* (3rd ed.). Washington, DC: Author.
American Psychiatric Association. (1987). *The diagnostic and statistical manual of mental disorders* (3rd ed. rev.). Washington, DC: Author.
American Psychiatric Association. (1994). *The diagnostic and statistical manual of mental disorders* (4th ed.). Washington, DC: Author.
Caputo, A. A., Frick, P. J., & Brodsky, S. L. (1999). Family violence and juvenile sex offending: Potential mediating roles of psychopathic traits and negative attitudes toward women. *Criminal Justice and Behavior, 26,* 338–356.
Christian, R., Frick, P. J., Hill, N., Tyler, L. A., & Frazer, D. (1997). Psychopathy and conduct problems in children: II. Subtyping children with conduct problems based on their interpersonal and affective style. *Journal of the American Academy of Child and Adolescent Psychiatry, 36,* 233–241.
Cleckley, H. (1976). *The mask of sanity* (5th ed.). St. Louis, MO: Mosby.
Colder, C. R., Lochman, J. E., & Wells, K. C. (1997). The moderating effects of children's fear and activity level on relations between parenting practices and childhood symptomatology. *Journal of Abnormal Child Psychology, 25,* 251–263.
Dodge, K. A., Bates, J. E., & Pettit, G. S. (1990). Mechanisms in the cycle of violence. *Science, 250,* 1678–1683.
Frick, P. J. (1994). Family dysfunction and the disruptive behavior disorders: A review of recent empirical findings. In T. H. Ollendick & R. J. Prinz (Eds.), *Advances in clinical child psychology* (Vol. 16, pp. 203–222). New York: Plenum.
Frick, P. J. (1998). *Conduct disorders and severe antisocial behavior.* New York: Plenum.
Frick, P. J., & Hare, R. D. (in press). *The Psychopathy Screening Device.* Toronto: Multi-Health.
Frick, P. J., Lahey, B. B., Loeber, R., Tannenbaum, L. E., Van Horn, Y., Christ, M. A. G., Hart, E. A., & Hanson, K. (1993). Oppositional defiant disorder and conduct disorder: A meta-analytic review of factor analyses and cross-validation in a clinic sample. *Clinical Psychology Review, 13,* 319–340.
Frick, P. J., Lahey, B. B., Strauss, C. C., & Christ, M. A. G. (1993). Behavior disorders of children. In H. E. Adams & P. B. Sutker (Eds.), *Comprehensive handbook of psychopathology* (2nd ed., pp. 765–789). New York: Plenum.
Frick, P. J., & Loney, B. R. (1999). Outcomes of children and adolescents with conduct disorder and oppositional defiant disorder. In H. C. Quay & A. Hogan (Eds.), *Handbook of disruptive behavior disorders* (pp. 507–524). New York: Plenum.

Frick, P. J., O'Brien, B. S., Wootton, J. M., & McBurnett, K. (1994). Psychopathy and conduct problems in children. *Journal of Abnormal Psychology, 103*, 700–707.
Gadow, K. D., & Sprafkin, J. (1995). *Manual for the Child Symptom Inventory* (4th ed.). Stony Brook, NY: Checkmate Plus.
Gacono, C. B., & Meloy, J. R. (1994). *The Rorschach assessment of aggressive and psychopathic personalities.* Hillsdale, NJ: Lawrence Erlbaum Associates.
Halperin, J. M., O'Brien, J. D., Newcorn, J. H., Healey, J. M., Pascuaslvaca, D. M., Wolf, L. E., & Young, J. G. (1990). Validation of hyperactive, aggressive, and mixed disorders. *Journal of Child Psychology and Psychiatry, 31*, 455–459.
Hare, R. D. (1991). *The Hare Psychopathy Checklist–Revised.* Toronto: Multi-Health.
Hare, R. D. (1993). *Without a conscience: The disturbing world of the psychopaths among us.* New York: Pocket.
Hare, R. D., Hart, S. D., & Harpur, T. J. (1991). Psychopathy and the *DSM–IV* criteria for antisocial personality disorder. *Journal of Abnormal Psychology, 100*, 391–398.
Harpur, T. J., Hare, R. D., & Hakstian, A. R. (1989). Two-factor conceptualization of psychopathy: Construct validity and assessment implications. *Psychological Assessment, 1*, 6–17.
Harris, G. T., Rice, M. E., & Quinsey, V. L. (1994). Psychopathy as a taxon: Evidence that psychopaths are a discrete class. *Journal of Consulting and Clinical Psychology, 62*, 387–397.
Hinshaw, S. P., Lahey, B. B., & Hart, E. L. (1993). Issues of taxonomy and co-morbidity in the development of conduct disorder. *Development and Psychopathology, 5*, 31–50.
Kagan, J., & Snidman, N. (1991). Temperamental factors in human development. *American Psychologist, 46*, 856–862.
Kamphaus, R. W., & Frick, P. J. (1996). *The clinical assessment of children's emotion, behavior, and personality.* Boston: Allyn & Bacon.
Kochanska, G. (1993). Toward a synthesis of parental socialization and child temperament in early development of conscience. *Child Development, 64*, 325–347.
Lahey, B. B., Applegate, B., Barkley, R. A., Garfinkel, B., McBurnett, K., Kerdyck, L., Greenhill, L., Hynd, G. W., Frick, P. J., Newcorn, J., Biederman, J., Ollendick, T., Hart, E. L., Perez, P., Waldman, I., & Shaffer, D. (1994). *DSM–IV* field trials for oppositional defiant disorder and conduct disorder in children and adolescents. *American Journal of Psychiatry, 151*, 1163–1171.
Lahey, B. B., Hart, E. L., Pliszka, S., Applegate, B., & McBurnett, K. (1993). Neurophysiological correlates of conduct disorder: A rationale and a review of research. *Journal of Clinical Child Psychology, 22*, 141–153.
Lahey, B. B., Loeber, R., Hart, E. L., Frick, P. J., Applegate, B., Zhang, Q., Green, S. M., & Russo, M. F. (1995). Four-year longitudinal study of conduct disorder in boys: Patterns of predictors of persistence. *Journal of Abnormal Psychology, 104*, 83–93.
Lahey, B. B., Loeber, R., Quay, H. C., Frick, P. J., & Grimm, J. (1992). Oppositional defiant disorder and conduct disorder: Issues to be resolved for *DSM–IV*. *Journal of the American Academy of Child and Adolescent Psychiatry, 31*, 539–546.
Loeber, R. (1982). The stability of antisocial and delinquent child behavior: A review. *Child Development, 53*, 1431–1446.
Loeber, R. (1991). Antisocial behavior: More enduring than changeable? *Journal of the American Academy of Child and Adolescent Psychiatry, 30*, 393–397.
Loeber, R., Green, S. M., Lahey, B. B., & Stouthamer-Loeber, M. (1991). Differences and similarities between children, mothers, and teachers as informants on disruptive child behavior. *Journal of Abnormal Child Psychology, 19*, 75–95.
Loeber, R., & Stouthamer-Loeber, M. (1986). Family factors as correlates and predictors of juvenile conduct problems and delinquency. In M. Tonry & N. Morris (Eds.), *Crime and justice* (Vol. 7, pp. 29–149). Chicago: University of Chicago Press.
Loney, B. R., Frick, P. J., Ellis, M., & McCoy, M. G. (1998). Intelligence, psychopathy, and antisocial behavior. *Journal of Psychopathology and Behavioral Assessment, 20*, 231–247.

Lykken, D. T. (1995). *The antisocial personalities*. Hillsdale, NJ: Lawrence Erlbaum Associates.

Lynam, D. R. (1996). Early identification of chronic offenders: Who is the fledgling psychopath? *Psychological Bulletin, 120*, 209–234.

McCord, W., & McCord, J. (1964). *The psychopath: An essay on the criminal mind*. Princeton, NJ: Van Nostrand.

Moffitt, T. E. (1993a). Adolescence-limited and life-course persistent antisocial behavior: A developmental taxonomy. *Psychological Review, 100*, 674–701.

Moffitt, T. E. (1993b). The neuropsychology of conduct disorder. *Development and Psychopathology, 5*, 135–152.

Moffitt, T. E., Caspi, A., Dickson, N., Silva, P., & Stanton, W. (1996). Childhood-onset versus adolescent-onset antisocial conduct problems in males: Natural history from ages 3 to 18 years. *Development and Psychopathology, 8*, 399–424.

Moffitt, T. E., & Henry, B. (1989). Neuropsychological assessment of executive functions in self-reported delinquents. *Development and Psychopathology, 1*, 105–118.

Newman, J. P., & Wallace, J. F. (1993). Diverse pathways to deficient self-regulation: Implications for disinhibitory psychopathology in children. *Clinical Psychology Review, 13*, 699–720.

O'Brien, B. S., & Frick, P. J. (1996). Reward dominance: Associations with anxiety, conduct problems, and psychopathy in children. *Journal of Abnormal Child Psychology, 24*, 223–240.

Office of Juvenile Justice and Delinquency Prevention. (1995). *Juvenile offenders and victims: A focus on violence*. Pittsburgh, PA: National Center for Juvenile Justice.

Pelham, W. E., Milich, R., Cummings, M. E., Murphy, D. A., Schaughency, E. A., & Greiner, A. R. (1991). Effects of background anger, provocation, and methylphenidate on emotional arousal and aggressive-responding in attention-deficit hyperactivity disordered boys with and without concurrent aggressiveness. *Journal of Abnormal Child Psychology, 19*, 407–426.

Quay, H. C. (1986). Classification. In H. C. Quay & J. S. Werry (Eds.), *Psychopathological disorders of childhood* (3rd ed., pp. 1–42). New York: Wiley.

Quay, H. C. (1987). Patterns of delinquent behavior. In H. C. Quay (Ed.), *Handbook of juvenile delinquency* (pp. 118–138). New York: Wiley.

Richters, J. E. (1997). The Hubble hypothesis and the developmentalist's dilemma. *Development and Psychopathology, 9*, 193–230.

Richters, J. E., & Cicchetti, D. (1993). Toward a developmental perspective on conduct disorder. *Development and Psychopathology, 5*, 1–4.

Rothbart, M. K. (1989). Temperament in childhood: A framework. In G. A. Kohnstamm, J. A. Bates, & M. K. Rothbart (Eds.), *Temperament in childhood* (pp. 59–73). New York: Wiley.

Silverthorn, P., Frick, P. J., & Reynolds, R. (1998). *Timing of onset and correlates of severe conduct problems in adjudicated girls and boys*. Manuscript submitted for publication.

Thompson, L. L., Riggs, P. D., Mikulich, S. K., & Crowley, T. J. (1996). Contribution of ADHD symptoms to substance problems and delinquency in conduct-disordered adolescents. *Journal of Abnormal Child Psychology, 24*, 325–348.

Walker, J. L., Lahey, B. B., Hynd, G. W., & Frame, C. L. (1987). Comparison of specific patterns of antisocial behavior in children with conduct disorder with and without coexisting hyperactivity. *Journal of Consulting and Clinical Psychology, 55*, 910–913.

Wootton, J. M., Frick, P. J., Shelton, K. K., & Silverthorn, P. (1997). Ineffective parenting and childhood conduct problems: The moderating role of callous-unemotional traits. *Journal of Consulting and Clinical Psychology, 65*, 301–308.

Psychopathy in Youth: What Do We Know?

Adelle E. Forth and Donna L. Mailloux
Carleton University, Ottawa

Psychopathy is a personality disorder associated with a constellation of affective, interpersonal, and behavioral characteristics, central to which are a profound lack of guilt and a callous disregard for the feelings, rights, and welfare of others (Cleckley, 1976; Hare, 1991). Psychopaths are impulsive, deceitful, selfish, sensation-seeking, and irresponsible. Among adults, psychopathy has been linked to serious repetitive crime, violent behavior, and poor treatment prognosis (for reviews, see Hare, 1998a; Hart & Hare, 1997). Although a considerable amount of research has focused on psychopathy in adults, substantially less research has been conducted among children and adolescents. However, interest in the developmental aspects of this disorder has intensified (Forth & Burke, 1998; Frick, 1998; Frick, O'Brien, Wootton, & McBurnett, 1994; Lynam, 1996). Given psychopaths' resistance to treatment as adults (Ogloff, Wong, & Greenwood, 1990; Rice, Harris, & Cormier, 1992), the optimal strategy to attenuate psychopathic behavior may be to identify and intervene early in development. Early intervention strategies may modify the pathway to persistent, diverse, and serious antisocial behaviors associated with psychopathy. It is also important to differentiate psychopathic youth from other aggressive youth because not all aggressive youth will become high-rate offenders.

Most clinicians and researchers would agree that many psychopathic characteristics are first manifested at an early age. Whether these characteristics are similar to the presentation of psychopathy in adults remains to be determined. Nevertheless, researchers measuring psychopathy in children and adolescents have implicitly assumed a continuity across development. This assumption is analogous to research indicating a relation between early temperament and adult personality traits (Henry, Caspi, Moffitt, & Silva, 1996; Kruger et al., 1994). This provides the rationale for using assessment tools developed for use with adults with younger populations.

Despite the tacit assumption of continuity of psychopathy across development, the precise etiology of psychopathy is unknown. Similar to other personality traits, it is likely that a range of genetic and environmental factors influence the onset, development, and presentation of psychopathy. Knowledge of these developmental risk factors, particularly those factors that are changeable, may enhance our ability to provide more appropriate intervention programs.

The only instrument used to operationalize psychopathy in adults with demonstrated reliability and validity (Cooke, 1998; Hare, 1996, 1998a; Hart & Hare, 1997) is the Hare Psychopathy Checklist–Revised (PCL–R; Hare, 1991). The PCL–R is a clinical construct rating scale completed on the basis of a semistructured interview and a review of collateral information. A number of instruments have been adapted from the PCL–R to measure psychopathy in children and adolescents: Psychopathy Checklist: Youth Version (PCL:YV; Forth, Kosson, & Hare, in press), Psychopathy Screening Device (PSD; Frick et al., 1994), and the Childhood Psychopathy Scale (CPS; Lynam, 1997). Two strategies have been used in the development of these instruments. The first strategy extends the adult version into adolescence and, depending on its validity, extends it further into childhood. The second strategy attempts to adapt the adult version for use with children. The PCL:YV was based on the former strategy, whereas the PSD and CPS were based on the latter strategy.

This chapter reviews the empirical research relevant to understanding the manifestation of psychopathy in youth. First, a description of the instruments adapted from the PCL–R for use with children and adolescents is provided. Second, research on developmental correlates of psychopathy is reviewed. Finally, the association between psychopathy and criminal conduct in adolescence is considered.

ASSESSMENT OF PSYCHOPATHY

Although the etiology and conceptual boundaries of psychopathy have yet to be fully understood, there is consensus across mental health professionals, experimental psychologists, criminal justice personnel, and the lay public that the core features of psychopathy comprise both personality and behavioral characteristics (Albert, Brigante, & Chase, 1959;

Cleckley, 1976; Rogers, Dion, & Lynett, 1992; Tennent, Tennent, Prins, & Bedford, 1990). In an effort to assess these characteristics among children and adolescents, three instruments have been adapted from the PCL-R.

PCL:YV

Forth, Hart, and Hare (1990) were the first to examine the construct of *psychopathy* in adolescent offenders. Because the PCL-R was designed for use in the assessment of adult offenders, it was necessary to revise the scale to make it more appropriate for use with adolescents. Adolescents typically have a limited work history and few marital relationships, thus Items 9 (parasitic lifestyle) and 17 (many short-term marital relationships) were deleted. Furthermore, because adolescent offenders have had less opportunity to come into contact with the judicial system than adult offenders, it was necessary to modify two other items: Item 18 (juvenile delinquency) and Item 20 (criminal versatility). Referred to as the 18-item PCL-R, this scale has been used in several of the studies discussed in this chapter.

As researchers gained experience using the 18-item PCL-R with adolescents, three modifications were made that would further take into account the restricted life experience of adolescents. First, a scoring system was developed that reflected the greater involvement of peers, family, and school in the lives of adolescents. Second, Items 9 and 17 were reintroduced but were modified so that it was possible to assess these characteristics in youth. Third, when scoring individual items, the focus is on enduring features of the youth displayed across settings and situations. For example, when assessing poor anger control, if the adolescent displays anger toward specific people (i.e., parents, authority figures) or in limited contexts, this would not be sufficient evidence to score this item as high. This modified version of the PCL-R was named the Psychopathy Checklist: Youth Version (PCL:YV; Forth et al., in press). A draft version of the PCL:YV has been made available to researchers for use in a variety of research studies.

Two studies have investigated the factor structure of the 18-item PCL-R and the PCL:YV (Brandt, Kennedy, Patrick, & Curtin, 1997; Forth, 1995). Both studies reported a similar two-factor structure replicating that found with adult offenders (Hare et al., 1990). Factor 1 reflects the interpersonal and affective characteristics, such as grandiosity, glibness, manipulativeness, callousness, and lack of remorse. Factor 2 reflects behavioral features associated with an impulsive, irresponsible, and antisocial lifestyle.

Both the 18-item PCL-R and PCL:YV are reliable instruments. Indexes of internal consistency (alpha coefficient, mean interitem correlation) and interrater reliability are high (Brandt et al., 1997; Forth, 1995, Gretton,

1998; McBride, 1998). The PCL:YV has high interrater reliabilities with correlations between independent raters of .90 or above (see Forth & Burke, 1998). The issue of interrater reliability is of particular importance when assessment instruments developed in research settings are used for clinical assessment.

PSD

The Psychopathy Screening Device (PSD; Frick et al., 1994) is the only instrument to date that has been developed specifically to assess psychopathy in childhood. As a 20-item scale, ratings are completed based on observations made from parents or teachers (see chap. 1, this volume, for a review of the research findings). Factor analysis of the PSD in a sample of 95 clinic-referred children (ages 6–12 years) revealed a two-factor solution that the authors concluded were similar to the two-factor structure found with adults (Hare et al., 1990). The first factor, labeled *impulsivity/ conduct problems* (I/CP), consisted of 10 items (e.g., brags about accomplishments, acts without thinking). The second factor, labeled *callous/ unemotional* (C/U), consisted of 6 items (e.g., does not show emotions, lack of guilt). Various discrepancies between the factor structure found in children and adults have been noted (Frick et al., 1994; McBride, 1998). For example, items relating to grandiosity (brags about accomplishments, thinks s/he is more important than others), callousness (teases others), and failing to take responsibility for actions (blames others) were associated with the I/CP factor, whereas in adults and adolescents these are associated with Factor 1 of the PCL–R/PCL:YV. In addition, three items relating to manipulation and lying, which are also associated with PCL–R/PCL:YV Factor 1, were associated with both factors in the children. Finally, an item that should have been related to the I/CP factor (does not plan ahead) was more strongly related to the CU factor (this item was not included in the CU factor). Subsequent research by Frick and his colleagues (Christian, Frick, Hill, Tyler, & Frazer, 1997; Frick, 1998; Wootton, Frick, Shelton, & Silverthorn, 1997) have used these two scales of the PSD to investigate the differential pattern of associations with a variety of external variables. To date no study has yet attempted to replicate this factor structure in children.

Research has demonstrated a relatively low interrater agreement between parent and teacher ratings on the CU factor ($r = .29$ in the Frick et al. [1994] study and $r = .34$ in the Christian et al. [1997] study). Moreover, a recent study has found that the PSD demonstrated poor concurrent validity with the PCL:YV. McBride (1998) had 75 mothers of adolescent offenders complete the PSD and compared this to PCL:YV scores obtained from file ratings. The total PSD was correlated $r = .35$ with the

PCL:YV total scores. Both the CU (r = .28) and I/CP (r = .43) scales were correlated with Factor 2 of the PCL:YV but were not significantly correlated with Factor 1 (r = .16 and .19, respectively). In addition to the low interrater agreement, the failure of the CU scale to be strongly related to Factor 1 of the PCL:YV has raised considerable concern about how well this subscale captures the personality features it was designed to measure. These findings may in fact be due to inherent differences in the item content between the PCL:YV and the PSD. For example, each item on the PCL:YV consists of a one-page description, including examples of that characteristic and explicit criteria for coding the item. In contrast, the PSD items are simple statements derived from the PCL-R items but that are not anchored in operational definitions (e.g., thinks s/he is more important than others; his/her emotions seem shallow and not genuine).

CPS

More recently, Lynam (1997) developed the 13-item Childhood Psychopathy Scale (CPS), which is also based on the PCL-R. This scale was based on archival data of child behavior and personality that were completed by mothers as part of a large-scale study of 430 boys ages 12 to 13 years. To measure psychopathy, items were drawn from the Child Behavior Checklist (CBCL; Achenbach, 1991) and the Common Language Q-sort (Block & Block, 1980). Only 13 of the 20 PCL-R items could be operationalized using items from the two prior scales (each of the 13 items consisted of two or more items). Factor analysis of the 13-item scale also revealed a two-factor structure similar to that found using the PCL-R with adults. However, because the two factors were so highly correlated (r = .95), only the total score was used.

A variety of variables were used to assess the validity of the CPS, including self-reported antisocial behavior at ages 10 and 13. The CPS was positively correlated with serious thefts, violent acts, serious delinquency at age 10, measures of self-reported and teacher ratings of impulsivity, and negatively correlated with internalizing problems. In addition, boys who engaged in serious delinquency at both age periods (10 and 12–13) had significantly higher scores on the CPS than did the other boys. Although initial results from the CPS are promising, Lynam (1997) acknowledged that, due to the archival nature of the study, the optimal range of psychopathy traits could not be measured (only 13 of the 20 PCL-R items). Moreover, he noted that there was an overreliance on behavioral descriptors and that some of the items, such as glibness/superficial charm and shallow affect, did not adequately capture the intent of the PCL-R item.

In summary, research with the PSD and CPS provide some evidence that the construct of psychopathy can be assessed in children and young adolescents. However, both scales appear to focus primarily on behavioral descriptors without adequate coverage of the core affective and interpersonal features that most clinicians consider fundamental to psychopathy in adults. The PCL:YV is much more closely related to the PCL–R: It uses a similar methodology to assess psychopathic traits (a review of case history information and when possible clinical interviews) and provides for the assessment of the full range of relevant symptoms (affective, interpersonal, and behavioral). The remainder of this chapter focuses on research using both the modified 18-item PCL–R scale and the PCL:YV.

PREVALENCE OF PSYCHOPATHIC CHARACTERISTICS

Research conducted with the PCL–R in adult offenders has reported considerable cross-group consistency in the prevalence of psychopathy. In North America, similar PCL–R scores have been obtained across male and female offender samples (Hare, 1991; Mailloux, 1999; Neary, 1991; Strachan, 1993), Native Canadian offenders (Wong, 1985), Francophone Canadian offenders (Hodgins, Côté, & Ross, 1992), and African-American offenders in the United States (Kosson, Smith, & Newman, 1990). Although similar scores are obtained in samples of North American offenders, mean PCL–R scores do differ across samples. For example, lower scores are found in adult male European offenders (for review, see Cooke, 1998), forensic psychiatric patients, substance abusers, and noncriminals. The extent to which the prevalence of psychopathy differs across groups of adolescents is presented next.

Males

Incarcerated male adolescents display the most psychopathic characteristics, with mean scores ranging from 23 to 26 and a standard deviation from 5 to 7 (Brandt et al., 1997; Forth, 1995; Forth et al., 1990; Gretton, 1998; Hume, Kennedy, Patrick, & Partyka, 1996; Laroche, 1996; McBride, 1998; Pan, 1998). This mean is slightly higher than that found in adult male offenders whose PCL–R scores range from about 22 to 24, with a standard deviation from 6 to 8 (Hare, 1991). This relatively high score is not surprising because these youth represent a subset of adolescent offenders who have been convicted of violent offenses or who repeatedly engage in crime. For incarcerated male adolescent sex offenders, the mean score is somewhat lower at 21.40 ($SD = 7.30$; McBride, 1998). Mean scores for male adolescent psychiatric inpatients range from 14 to 17 (Myers,

Burket, & Harris, 1995; Stafford, 1997; Stanford, Ebner, Patton, & Williams, 1994). The lowest mean scores are found in samples of male high school students, ranging from 4 to 9 (Forth, 1995; Ridenour, 1996). Most of these youth had no significant problems at home, school, or in the community. Research with adult noncriminal samples has also shown a similar low score on measures of psychopathy (Forth, Brown, Hart, & Hare, 1996).

Females

Until recently there has been limited research assessing the manifestation of psychopathic traits in females. Recent research using the PCL–R suggests that female offenders have similar prevalence, factor structures, and correlates as male adult offenders. Mean PCL–R scores in incarcerated adult female offenders range from 18 to 24 (Mailloux, 1999; Neary, 1991; Strachan, 1993). In substance-abusing adult females, the scores are typically around 14 (Rutherford, Alterman, Cacciola, & McKay, 1998; Rutherford, Alterman, Cacciola, & Snyder, 1996). To date, three studies have collected data on the prevalence of psychopathy among female adolescents. In these studies, scores ranged from 21 for incarcerated female adolescents (n = 43; Gretton, 1998) to 18 for delinquent adolescents in a community-based intervention program (n = 54; Rowe, 1997), with a low of 10 for female adolescent inpatients (n = 30; Stanford et al., 1994). Due to the small number of participants in these studies, caution is required when interpreting the results. In each study, the female participants scored lower than the male participants, but this difference was only significant in the Stanford et al. (1994) study (female patients obtained scores 3 points lower than their male counterparts).

Race

Several studies have compared psychopathy scores in adolescents across racial groups. For instance, Forth et al. (1990) found significantly higher scores for White as compared with Native Canadians. In contrast, in a larger sample assessing psychopathy using only file-information, no significant differences were found between White and Native-Canadian adolescent sex offenders (McBride, 1998). Other studies comparing adolescent Whites and African Americans have reported no significant differences on psychopathy scores between these two groups (Brandt et al., 1997; Hume et al., 1996; Myers et al., 1995; Pan, 1998). In addition, the one study that compared psychopathy scores across White, African-American, and Hispanic adolescents also found no significant differences (Pan, 1998).

Age

Three studies have examined the relationship between psychopathy and age at time of assessment. None of these studies (Brandt et al., 1997; Forth et al., 1990; Forth & Burke, 1998) have found a significant association between age and psychopathy scores. These results indicate that psychopathic traits are expressed in both older and younger adolescents.

In summary, the prevalence of psychopathic characteristics across samples is different (i.e., incarcerated male adolescents obtaining the highest scores and noncriminal high school students the lowest scores). Nevertheless, the research to date provides evidence that the PCL:YV/ PCL-R is reliable across gender, race, and age groups. However, given the small sample sizes in some of these studies (e.g., Pan [1998] had fewer than 18 participants in each of his racial groups), caution should be exercised when making generalizations.

SELF-REPORT MEASURES OF PSYCHOPATHY

Self-report inventories are widely used to assess personality and psychopathology. Their appeal stems from their extensive standardization, objective nature, and relative ease of administration and scoring; the range of personality features they measure; and, for many, the inclusion of validity scales to assess invalid profiles and control for self-presentation strategies. Attempts to use self-report scales to assess psychopathy is primarily motivated by the resource-intensive nature of the PCL:YV. The PCL:YV ratings are based on an extensive semistructured interview plus a review of available collateral data. It takes upward of 2 hours to complete a PCL:YV and, in some cases, considerably longer if extensive file information is available. Unfortunately, past research has found only low to moderate correlations between self-report measures of psychopathy and the PCL-R in adult offenders. These results may be due primarily to the failure of self-report scales to capture the core personality features of psychopathy (Hare, 1996; Harpur, Hare, & Hakstian, 1989; Hart, Forth, & Hare, 1991).

Minnesota Multiphasic Personality Inventories

The Minnesota Multiphasic Personality Inventory (MMPI; Hathaway & McKinley, 1943) and the adolescent version (MMPI-A; Butcher et al., 1992) are two of the most frequently used objective self-report personality instruments with adolescents (Archer, 1992). Three studies have examined the association between the MMPI/MMPI-A and psychopathy in adolescent offenders with limited success. Brandt et al. (1997) examined the association between the 18-item PCL-R and the MMPI in a sample of 130 persistent male juvenile delinquents. The total score was significantly correlated with Scale 4 (r = .23) and Scale 4 + 9 (r = .26). Factor 2 scores were significantly associated with Scale 4 (r = .23), Scale 9 (r = .22), and Scale 4 + 9 (r = .29).

Sullivan (1996) examined the association between MMPI–A and the PCL:YV in a sample of 95 incarcerated male adolescent offenders. Significant correlations were found between PCL:YV total scores and the Psychopathic Deviate scale (r = .23), Conduct Problems content scale (r = .29), Alcohol/Drug Acknowledgment scale (r = .34), and the Anger content scale (r = .34). Consistent with findings obtained from adult offenders, these scales were more highly correlated with Factor 2 than with Factor 1 of the PCL:YV. In addition, the presence or absence of psychopathy, as assessed using the PCL:YV, could not be accurately predicted by the MMPI–A.

Hume et al. (1996) reported no significant correlations between MMPI–A scales and psychopathy. In addition, no differences between MMPI–A scores of psychopaths (score of 30 or greater on prorated 18-item PCL-R) and nonpsychopaths (scores of less than 30) were found. Using discriminant analysis, it was possible to use the 15 MMPI–A scores to correctly classify 78% of the psychopathic and nonpsychopathic group. However, there was a 60% false-positive and 40% false-negative rate.

Self-Report Psychopathy Scales

More promising results have emerged when self-report scales specially designed to measure psychopathic personality traits are used. For example, the correlations between the Psychopathy Checklist: Screening Version (PCL:SV; Hart, Cox, & Hare, 1995) and the Self-Report Psychopathy Scale (SRP; Hare, 1991) were moderate to large in magnitude in a sample of adult offenders (r = .69, total PCL:SV, r = 41, Factor 1; r = .70, Factor 2; Hart et al., 1995). More recently, in a sample of 50 young adult prisoners, Poythress, Edens, and Lilienfeld (1998) found that the Psychopathic Personality Inventory (PPI; Lilienfeld & Andrews, 1996) correlated moderately with 16-item PCL-R total (r = .54), Factor 1 (r = .54), and Factor 2 (r = .40) scores.

In summary, these results indicate that the MMPI/MMPI–A are not highly associated with the construct of psychopathy and have limited utility in screening for psychopathy. Although recent self-report inventories show more promise (e.g., SRP and PPI), the magnitude of the correlations with psychopathy continues to be moderate. Moreover, the predictive validity of these self-report scales with important outcome criteria (treatment response, recidivism, institutional maladjustment) has yet to be established. Therefore, it is recommended that clinicians not use self-report inventories, particularly the MMPI/MMPI–A, to assess psychopathic traits.

ASSOCIATION WITH CONDUCT DISORDER, ATTENTION DEFICIT DISORDER, PERSONALITY, AND SUBSTANCE ABUSE

This section reviews the studies that have looked at the association between psychopathy and the following measures: conduct disorder, attention deficit disorder, personality, and substance use.

Conduct Disorder

Conduct disorder (CD), as described in the *Diagnostic and Statistical Manual for Mental Disorders* (*DSM–IV*; American Psychiatric Association, 1994), refers to persistent serious antisocial actions that results in significant problems for the youth. *DSM–IV* diagnostic criteria require 3 of 15 symptoms to be present over the course of the last year. The criteria are separated into four main categories: aggressive conduct (seven symptoms), deceitfulness or theft (three symptoms), destruction of property (two symptoms), and serious violations of rules (three symptoms). CD is the most prevalent diagnosis found in delinquent youth (Grisso, 1998). The occurrence of CD in adolescence is a predictor of adult antisocial behavior (see review by Lahey & Loeber, 1997). However, CD constitutes a heterogeneous group; most youth with CD do not become antisocial adults (White, Moffitt, Earls, Robins, & Silva, 1990).

A moderate relation has consistently been reported between symptoms of CD and psychopathy in adolescent offenders. The correlations between psychopathy scores and CD symptoms are relatively large (.48–.64) in samples of adolescent offenders (Brandt et al., 1997; Forth, 1995; Forth et al., 1990; Gretton, 1998). However, the prevalence rates vary dramatically. According to *DSM* criteria, almost all incarcerated adolescent offenders meet the diagnostic criteria for CD. For example, 97% of the adolescent offenders in the Forth (1995) study met the criteria for *DSM–IV* CD. This high prevalence is not surprising because the CD criteria primarily focus on antisocial behaviors. An asymmetric relation has been reported between antisocial personality disorder as measured by the *DSM* criteria and psychopathy as measured by the PCL–R (Hare, 1983, 1985; Stålenheim & von Knorring, 1996). A similar asymmetric relation has also emerged when comparing the *DSM* CD and PCL:YV. In the Forth (1995) study, all adolescent offenders who met the criteria for psychopathy (cutoff of 30 or greater) also met the *DSM–IV* criteria for CD. However, only 30% of the CD adolescents met the criteria for psychopathy using the PCL:YV.

Psychopathic traits are clearly related to CD symptoms. However, a different pattern of correlations emerged when comparing the correlations between CD symptoms and the two psychopathy factors. Factor 2 (about $r = .42$ to .58) is more strongly correlated with the number of CD symptoms than Factor 1 (about $r = .32$ to .36; Brandt et al., 1997; Forth, 1995; Toupin, Mercier, Déry, Côté, & Hodgins, 1996). Interestingly, this differential pattern of correlations does not emerge when correlating PCL:YV factor scores and the number of aggressive CD symptoms. Forth (1995) correlated PCL:YV total and factor scores with the number of aggressive CD symptoms. A significant correlation was found between PCL:YV total score and number of aggressive CD symptoms ($r = .47$). However, when focusing on aggressive CD symptoms, both factors were equally correlated with Factor 1 ($r = .32$) and Factor 2 ($r = .31$).

DSM–IV has proposed two different subtypes of CD based on the age at onset, with childhood-onset type having one symptom prior to age 10 and the adolescent-onset type displaying no symptoms prior to age 10. Gretton (1998) compared the prevalence of childhood-onset CD diagnoses across 157 adolescent offenders classified as psychopaths (PCL:YV score 29 or greater), mixed group (PCL:YV score between 18 and 28), and nonpsychopaths (PCL:YV score less than 18). Across these groups, the prevalence of childhood-onset CD was 66%, 51%, and 21%, respectively. Similar results were found in a study by Smith, Gacono, and Kaufman (1997) with 48 male CD adolescent offenders. The psychopathic (scores of 29 or greater) group was more likely to be assessed with childhood onset (58%) as compared with the nonpsychopathic group (scores lower than 20; 10%).

Attention Deficit Disorder

Several studies indicate that youth who exhibit both CD and attention deficit hyperactivity disorder (ADHD) engage in higher rates of antisocial and criminal behavior and display greater persistence (Mannuzza, Klein, Bessler, Malloy, & LaPadula, 1993; Walker, Lahey, Hynd, & Frame, 1987). Lynam (1996) suggested that children who demonstrate symptoms of conduct problems and a combination of hyperactivity, impulsivity, and attention deficits are at the greatest risk for engaging in persistent antisocial behavior. He also speculated that children who manifest this combination of symptoms are the fledging psychopaths who later manifest the symptoms of psychopathy in adulthood.

To date only one study has investigated the association between psychopathy and attention deficit disorder (ADD; American Psychiatric

Association, 1980). In a sample of 233 sex offenders, McBride (1998) found that psychopathy was significantly related to the presence or absence of ADD (r = .40). Interestingly, scores on Factors 1 and 2 were equally related to ADD (r = 32 and .34, respectively). Psychopathic offenders (score of 30 or greater) were three times more likely to receive a diagnosis of ADD (57%) as compared with the nonpsychopathic group (score of 29 or below; 18%). Given the lack of research in this area, future research must study the co-occurrence of ADHD and CD in psychopathic youth.

Personality Assessment

Only one study has investigated the association between psychopathy and Axis II personality disorders. In a sample of 30 adolescent psychiatric inpatients (Myers et al., 1995), youth meeting the diagnostic criteria for CD and narcissistic personality disorder possessed significantly more psychopathic traits than those patients who did not meet the diagnostic criteria. In contrast, patients who met the criteria for avoidant or self-defeating personality disorder had lower psychopathy scores. These preliminary results replicate research with adults, which demonstrate a relation between psychopathy and antisocial, narcissistic, and borderline personality traits (Hare, 1991; Hart & Hare, 1989).

To date only one study has examined Rorschach variables in a sample of 48 CD male adolescent offenders assessed for psychopathy (Smith, Gacono, & Kaufman, 1997). Consistent with research with adult psychopaths (Gacono & Meloy, 1994), psychopathic CD youth produced elevated scores on the egocentricity indexes as compared with nonpsychopathic CD youth. There were no other significant differences on the other Rorschach measures. The authors concluded that psychopathic adolescents are more self-centered, self-absorbed, and narcissistic compared with nonpsychopathic CD youth. Although scores on the two factors of psychopathy were obtained, the Rorschach variables were not correlated with the two factors. Future research should include an analysis of the two factors with respect to Rorschach variables.

Substance Use

The comorbidity of psychopathy and substance abuse in adult offenders is high (Hemphill, Hart, & Hare, 1994; Smith & Newman, 1990). Mailloux, Forth, and Kroner (1997) examined the association between psychopathy and substance use in 40 male adolescent offenders. Psychopathy scores were correlated r = .42 with the Michigan Alcohol Screening Test (Selzer, 1971), and r = .42 with the Drug Abuse Screening Test (Skinner, 1982). Psychopathic youth started using alcohol and drugs at an earlier age and tried a greater number of drugs than did the nonpsychopathic offenders.

In summary, some clinicians might be tempted to consider CD in youth as a precursor to adult ASPD and psychopathy. However, the majority of youth with CD do not develop adult antisocial personality disorder or psychopathy. Psychopathic youth resemble youth with severe childhood-onset CD and youth with comorbid diagnosis of CD and ADHD. The primary difference between psychopathic youth and these other subtypes is that the majority of CD youth do not possess the affective and interpersonal features of the prototypical psychopath. This research suggests that CD and adolescent psychopathy, as with APD and adult psychopathy, are constructs that cannot be used interchangeably.

DEVELOPMENTAL CORRELATES OF PSYCHOPATHY

Considerable research implicates the link between adverse family background and delinquency and the perpetration of violence (Haapasalo & Tremblay, 1994; Loeber & Stouthamer-Loeber, 1986; Widom, 1997). Recent research has focused on the association between psychopathy and factors such as separation from parents, early physical and emotional abuse, parental pathology, and parenting strategies. To date, five studies have examined the relationship between psychopathy and family variables using a retrospective self-report design.

Investigating the relation between family factors and psychopathy in 106 offenders and 50 community male adolescents, Burke and Forth (1996; Forth & Burke, 1998) coded 10 variables: childhood (physical, sexual and emotional abuse, neglect), parental (marital discord, antisocial parents, alcohol history), and family background (lack of supervision, inconsistent discipline, separated from parents during childhood). From an interview and file review, the variables were coded dichotomously (present or absent) and summed to provide a composite score reflecting poor family background. The results indicate that poor family background was positively associated with PCL:YV total and both factor scores. However, among the offenders, family background was only associated with Factor 2 scores. Moreover, although family factors were not meaningful predictors of psychopathy scores among adolescent offenders, they were among the community youth. For example, PCL:YV total scores were predicted from a combination of antisocial parent, inconsistent discipline, and parental alcoholism.

On the basis of file information, Gretton (1998) coded the following four family background variables: history of adoption, age of separation from biological mother, age of separation from biological father, and history of physical, sexual, or emotional abuse in a sample of 157 adolescent offenders. Psychopathic offenders were separated at an earlier age both from their biological mothers ($M = 7.8$) and their fathers ($M = 4.2$) as compared with nonpsychopathic offenders ($M = 10.1$ from mothers; $M = 7.3$ from fathers). The groups did not differ according to the percent of adolescents adopted or in rates of childhood abuse.

Adolescent psychopathy has been found to correlate positively with biological parental criminality. Watt, Ma, Lewis, Willoughby, and O'Shaughnessy (1997) assessed 155 male juvenile offenders between the ages of 12 and 17 who were detained at an inpatient psychiatric assessment facility in British Columbia. Parental criminal behavior was determined based on a review of the youths' file and categorized according to whether the offense was violent or nonviolent. PCL:YV Total scores were found to correlate with maternal criminality ($r = .18$) and maternal nonviolent offenses ($r = .15$). Maternal ($r = .16$) and paternal ($r = .19$) criminality correlated more strongly with Factor 2 than Factor 1; however, only paternal violent behavior correlated with Factor 2 ($r = .21$).

McBride (1998) investigated the association between family background variables and psychopathy in two adolescent offender samples. In the first study, the files of 233 sex offenders were used to code psychopathy and the following nine family background variables: physical abuse, sexual abuse, emotional abuse, maternal criminality, maternal drug abuse, maternal alcohol abuse, paternal criminality, paternal drug abuse, and paternal alcohol abuse. The parental variables were collapsed to form a global maternal and paternal social deviance score. A history of physical abuse and maternal social deviance were related to PCL:YV Total and factor scores. Furthermore, a history of sexual abuse and paternal social deviance was significantly related to Total and Factor 2 scores. No significant correlations were found between psychopathy and emotional abuse.

In the second sample, the association among psychopathy, physical abuse, maternal social deviance, and parental rearing practices was assessed in 74 male adolescent offenders and their mothers. Similar to the previous study, a history of physical abuse by the father (but not the mother) and negative parental rearing practices were significantly related to PCL:YV scores. Maternal psychopathy (measured by a self-report psychopathy scale completed by the mothers) was significantly related to PCL:YV Total and Factor 2 scores.

Laroche and Toupin (1996) examined the association among parental characteristics (maternal psychopathology, paternal antisocial personality), parent–child relationships (level of supervision, physical and nonphysical punishment, communication, attachment, rules, and family activities), and psychopathy in a sample of 60 adolescent male offenders.

Level of supervision and involvement in family activities were the only variables that differentiated psychopaths from nonpsychopaths. Nonpsychopathic offenders were more likely to be adequately supervised by their parents and participated more in family activities as compared with the psychopathic offenders.

These studies provide evidence that psychopathy is associated with a range of adverse family factors: physical abuse, sexual abuse, parental criminality, parental alcoholism, childhood separation, maternal psychopathic traits, and poor parenting strategies (inadequate parental supervision, inconsistent discipline). However, for many of these variables, the relation with psychopathy has not been consistent across studies. The failure to replicate could be partly due to methodological issues (e.g., most are based on retrospective self-report from the adolescent, others on maternal self-report) or in the manner in which the variables were operationalized.

It is unlikely that one variable or cluster of variables (e.g., family background) acts in isolation in the development of psychopathy. What may be more probable is that the developmental pathways to psychopathy are multiple and varied. More than likely, this pathway is composed of an interaction between genetic, child, and parental factors and environmental stressors.

ASSOCIATION WITH CRIMINAL CONDUCT AND VIOLENCE

The characteristics that define psychopathy are compatible with an antisocial lifestyle and a lack of concern for societal rules and regulations. Traits that normally help to inhibit aggressive behavior are missing in psychopaths (consideration of the feelings of others, good impulsive control, strong emotional bonds). To examine the association between psychopathy and criminal conduct, research on the following variables is reviewed: institutional behavior, age onset, frequency and versatility of nonviolent and violent criminal behaviors, severity of violence, offender subtypes, and self-directed aggression.

Institutional Behavior

Psychopathy is associated with aggression both in institutions and in the community. Forth et al. (1990) found the 18-item PCL–R was strongly associated with the number of violent or aggressive institutional charges ($r = .46$). Brandt et al. (1997) correlated the 18-item PCL–R total and factor scores with the number of institutional infractions. PCL–R scores were significantly related to the number of verbal and physical aggressive incidents and to the number of times the adolescent was placed in the Intensive Supervision program (program where residents who are endangering themselves or others are placed for a limited time). Interestingly, only PCL–R Total and Factor 2 scores were significantly related to more negative monthly evaluations by staff. Failure of Factor 1 to correlate may be a function of an "individual high on Factor 1 were able to charm their way out of negative reviews" (Brandt et al., 1997, p. 434).

Among adolescent psychiatric patients, psychopathy has also demonstrated a strong association with overall aggression. Stafford (1997) looked at the association between psychopathy and the frequency and types of aggressive acts in 72 male and female adolescent psychiatric patients. Psychopathy was correlated with overall aggression ($r = .49$). Psychopathic youth engaged in more peer- and staff-directed aggression in addition to more covert expressions of aggression (exploiting others for personal gain). Furthermore, youth with fewer psychopathic traits exhibited reactive forms of aggression, whereas those with more psychopathic traits exhibited both instrumental (goal-directed) and reactive (evoked during emotional arousal) forms of aggression. In the prediction of institutional aggressive acts, psychopathy explained more variability than criminal or aggression history, seriousness of criminal history, or past hospitalizations.

Among adolescent offenders from a residential treatment program, psychopathy was associated with institutional adjustment. Rogers, Johansen, Chang, and Salekin (1997) correlated psychopathy scores with three measures of institutional adjustment in 81 adolescent offenders. Psychopathy was significantly correlated with treatment noncompliance ($r = .25$) and physical aggression infractions ($r = .28$) but not with verbal aggression. Pan (1998) found that in a sample of 49 violent adolescent offenders the only variables to predict institutional violence (number of violent infractions within the first 4 months incarcerated) were race and Factor 2 scores.

Although psychopathic youth have difficulty adjusting to institutions, they are also at an increased risk to escape from institutions. Gretton (1998) found that 68% of psychopathic adolescents had attempted to escape as compared with 26% of nonpsychopathic adolescents. This may be due to psychopaths' risk-taking nature, defiance of authority, and impulsivity.

Age of Onset

Psychopathic adolescent offenders start engaging in criminal behaviors at a young age. Forth (1995) assessed a sample of 106 adolescent offenders using the PCL:YV and found that age of onset for nonviolent and violent offenses was correlated $r = -.33$ and $r = -.26$ with the PCL:YV, respectively. The mean age of onset of nonviolent criminal behaviors was 11.9 for nonpsychopaths and 9.3 for psychopathic adolescent offenders. A similar age-related difference was found for violent criminal behaviors with the more psychopathic group starting at age 12.1 versus 14.5 for the less psychopathic group. Four other studies have examined the association between psychopathy and age at first arrest and found similar results. Forth et al. (1990), McBride (1998), and Brandt et al. (1997) found a correlation of $r = -.25$, $-.35$, and $-.46$, respectively, whereas Gretton (1998) found no difference between high-, mixed-, and low-psychopathy groups (14.7, 14.9, and 15.2, respectively).

Frequency of Criminal Conduct

Psychopathic adolescents engage in a greater amount of nonviolent and violent delinquent behaviors than nonpsychopathic adolescents. In their study of 52 CD youth, Toupin et al. (1996) reported a correlation of $r = .46$ between psychopathy and number of delinquent acts and $r = .30$ with the number of aggressive behaviors.

Forth (1995) found that PCL:YV scores were significantly related to the number of self-reported nonviolent behaviors ($r = .31$), violent behaviors ($r = .25$), versatility of nonviolent behaviors ($r = .35$), and versatility of violent behaviors ($r = .28$). With respect to types of antisocial behaviors committed, psychopathic youth were more likely to have threatened others with a weapon, be sexually aggressive, and commit robbery and arson. Although psychopathy was not related to the number of physically aggressive acts within dating relationships, it was related to scores on the Psychological Maltreatment of Woman Inventory (Tolman, 1989). PCL:YV Total and Factor 1 scores were significantly correlated with the Total, dominance-isolation subscale, and verbal–emotional abuse subscales. Psychopathic youth were more likely to control their partners by limiting their social network, restricting her activities, and demanding obedience from her.

Psychopathic youth commit more violent offenses than nonpsychopathic youth when in the community. In Gretton's (1998) sample of 157 offenders, PCL:YV Total, Factor 1, and Factor 2 scores were significantly correlated with violent offenses per year free ($r = .23$, .19, and .20, respectively) and unrelated to nonviolent or sex offenses. Psychopathic offenders were more likely to have a prior history of violent offending (26%) as compared with nonpsychopathic offenders (7%).

Smith et al. (1997) reported that all the psychopathic adolescent offenders in their study had a history of violence as compared with only 33% of nonpsychopathic adolescents. Myers et al. (1995) compared adolescent psychiatric inpatients who did and did not engage in specific delinquent behaviors. Psychopathy scores were higher in adolescent inpatients who fought, caused serious injury in a fight, stole, engaged in vandalism, and purposely injured or killed animals.

Across teacher-rated subscales of the Child Behavior Checklist (CBCL; Achenbach & Edelbrock, 1983), psychopathy scores were most strongly related to the aggressive subscale (r = .31; Brandt et al., 1997). This indicates that, even using nonclinician observer ratings, the link between aggression and psychopathy is evident.

The association between criminality and psychopathy has also been found in adolescent sex offenders. McBride (1998) found that the PCL:YV Total score was significantly related to the number of prior nonviolent crimes (r = .33), number of prior violent crimes (r = .26), and versatility of crimes (r = .36). Psychopathy was not related to the number of prior sexual crimes (r = .05). The failure to find an association with prior sexual crimes has also been reported by Brown and Forth (1997) in a study of 60 male adult rapists (r = −.02). However, the failure to observe a reliable relationship between sexual offenses and psychopathy may be an artifact due to the low prevalence of sexual offenses.

Severity of Crime

The association between psychopathic characteristics and the severity of crime has been investigated in two studies. Brandt et al. (1997) found a correlation between the 18-item PCL-R Total and Factor 1 scores and crime severity (r = .25 and .24, respectively). Gretton, McBride, Lewis, O'Shaughnessy, and Hare (1994) reported that adolescent sex offenders with high PCL:YV scores threatened their victims more and used more severe violence during their sexually assaultive acts than did nonpsychopathic sexual offenders.

Subtypes of Offenders

In a recent study, Dixon, Robinson, Hart, Gretton, McBride, and O'Shaughnessy (1995) examined the association between PCL:YV scores and the FBI's Crime Classification Manual (CCM; Douglas, Burgess, Burgess, & Ressler, 1992). The CCM was used to classify 50 male adolescent sexual offenders. Both the CCM and psychopathy were based on a review of case history information. Psychopathy scores were significantly higher for the three juveniles classified as Anger and Sadistic rapists (M = 28.8) as compared with those who committed nuisance offenses (M = 18.8), domestic sexual assault (M = 19.5), and entitlement rape (M = 18.8).

In another study using the CCM, Dempster and Hart (1996) classified the motive for offending in 43 male juveniles charged with attempted murder or murder. Similar to the previous study, both CCM and PCL:YV scores were derived from a review of the offenders' institutional files. Those juveniles meeting the criteria for Sexual Homicide scored significantly higher on psychopathy than those classified as Criminal Enterprise, Personal Cause, or Group Excitement.

Self-Directed Aggression

Only one study has examined the issue of self-directed aggression among psychopathic adolescents. Gretton (1998) found that psychopathic offenders were more likely to have a history of self-injury (37%) as compared with nonpsychopaths (21%). This finding is not surprising given the link between self- and other-directed aggression (see Plutchik & van Praag, 1997). Recent research has suggested that poor impulse control might mediate this association (Webster & Jackson, 1997). Interestingly, Myers et al. (1995) found that adolescent inpatients with three or more impulse behaviors had significantly higher psychopathy scores as compared with less impulsive patients. However, the impulsivity of the behaviors in this study is questionable because the presence or absence of a behavior was coded, not its intentionality. In addition, using the Conners' Parent Rating Scales (Conners, 1989), McBride (1998) found a significant and positive correlation ($r = .27$) between the impulsive-hyperactive problems subscale and Factor 2 of the PCL:YV.

In summary, the association between psychopathy and violence seen across studies suggests that violence is an integral part of the behavioral repertoire of psychopathic youth. However, to develop optimal strategies to lower this psychopathy–violence association, research is needed that explores the motivations and specific antecedents of violent behavior. This more fine-grained approach will lead to better risk management techniques with psychopathic youth.

STABILITY OF CRIMINAL BEHAVIOR

Two studies have examined age-related changes in patterns of offending from early adolescence to early adulthood in psychopathic and nonpsychopathic youth. Forth and Burke (1998) examined the age-related change in a sample of psychopathic and nonpsychopathic adolescent offenders. Using the 18-item PCL–R, offenders were divided into a high-psychopathy group ($n = 23$, score of ≥ 30) and a low-psychopathy group ($n = 40$; score ≤ 24). Official criminal records were used to code the mean number of nonviolent and violent offenses across three 2.5-year age periods from 13 to 20.5. To control for individual differences in the amount of time incarcerated, the offense rate was converted to the number of offenses committed per 6 months free. There were no significant differences between psychopathic and nonpsychopathic offenders in the rate of nonviolent offending across the age periods. However, psychopathic offenders engaged in significantly more violence in the first and last age period.

Results from a larger sample found a similar pattern of age-related change in offending (Gretton, 1998). Participants were 157 adolescent offenders who were followed-up on average for 10 years. The PCL:YV was coded retrospectively using file-information data. The participants were divided into three groups: psychopaths (n = 38; score of $\geq$ 29), a mixed group (n = 77; score between 18 and 28), and nonpsychopaths (n = 42; score of $\leq$ 17). Criminal records were used to calculate rates of nonviolent and violent offending per year free in the community across three age periods: early adolescence (13–15), mid-adolescence (16–18), and early adulthood (19–21). All three groups committed lower rates of nonviolent offenses in early adolescence as compared with the two older age periods. Psychopathic youth committed significantly more nonviolent offenses only during late adolescence. With respect to violent offenses, the psychopathic and mixed groups were significantly more violent during late adolescence and early adulthood than in early adolescence. The psychopathic group was significantly more violent than the mixed group during early and late adolescence. In early adulthood, the psychopathic group was significantly more violent than the nonpsychopathic group, but no differences were noted when compared with the mixed group.

The results of these studies confirm that the propensity for violence in psychopathic youth remains relatively persistent. Further research following these offenders as they age will determine whether this pattern is chronic. Persistence in offending has particular relevance to issues surrounding the transfer of youth to adult court and is discussed in more detail later.

RECIDIVISM

Over the past decade, there has been considerable focus on the importance of the construct of psychopathy as a risk factor for violence in adult forensic psychiatric and correctional samples (see reviews by Hemphill, Hare, & Wong, 1998; Salekin, Rogers, & Sewell, 1996). Emerging research indicates that psychopathy is also a major risk factor for violence in adolescent samples.

In the first recidivism study, Forth et al. (1990) administered the 18-item PCL–R to a sample of 75 male adolescent offenders prior to their release from a secure custody facility. This sample was followed-up for an average of 27.2 months to determine failure rates. Any charge or conviction for a new offense subsequent to release was considered a failure. The majority of the sample was released during the follow-up period (94%) in which 79% of those released recidivated. Psychopathy correlated only with the number of postrelease offenses ($r = .26$).

A retrospective 10-year review of 157 male adolescents (Gretton, 1998) referred by the courts for psychological assessment is the longest period over which recidivism has been evaluated thus far. Overall, 97% of this sample committed some offense and 68% committed a violent offense during the follow-up period. Psychopaths (84%) were more likely to reoffend violently than the mixed group (70%) followed by the nonpsychopaths (50%). The groups did not differ with respect to nonviolent or overall reoffenses. In addition, psychopaths committed their violent offense significantly sooner (on average, 43 months) as compared with the mixed group (on average 92 months) and nonpsychopath group (on average 95 months). Although prior history of violence is a major risk factor, in this study psychopathic offenders who had no prior history of violent offenses were at the same risk of violence in the follow-up periods as psychopaths with a history of violent offenses.

Lewis and O'Shaughnessy (1998) investigated a number of violent risk predictors in a sample of 209 male ($n = 172$) and female ($n = 37$) adolescent offenders who were being assessed in a juvenile forensic psychiatric unit in British Columbia. It was found that psychopathy was a better predictor of violence than other standard sociological (e.g., violent crime by mother or father, age of onset of drug/alcohol use) and criminological risk factors (e.g., age at first arrest, number of prior violent and nonviolent charges, and/or convictions). However, using the PCL:YV, only 65% of the offenders were correctly classified.

Brandt et al. (1997) investigated the association between psychopathy and the length of time before rearrest for nonviolent and violent offenses. No group differences were found in the length of time prior to arrest for nonviolent offenses, although the high psychopathy group was rearrested for a violent offense significantly sooner than the low psychopathy group.

These findings demonstrate the utility of psychopathy as a major risk factor for violence. An assessment of psychopathy has practical implications in the decision-making process within the juvenile justice system. For example, assessment of risk of harm occurs at several points within the juvenile justice system. Juveniles can be held in a secure detention facility prior to adjudication. The decision to detain a youth varies from state to state, but typically involves consideration of the following issues: the likelihood the youth will fail to show up for the adjudication proceedings, the likelihood the youth will engage in serious violence toward self or others, or the likelihood the youth may be in danger if not detained. The assessment of psychopathy is most relevant to decisions concerning the likelihood the youth will engage in future aggressive acts against others while in the community.

Another judicial decision where risk of harm is a pertinent factor is waiver to criminal/adult court. A youth who has committed a serious offense who is above a certain age (often 14 or 15) may be transferred to an adult court for adjudication. Recent changes in the juvenile laws in both Canada and the United States have resulted in the automatic transfer of youth charged with specific serious offenses (murder and other major assaultive offenses) and being of a certain age (often 14) to adult court. The issues discussed next are still likely to be relevant in many of these cases because most states and Canada provide for a hearing to determine whether the case should proceed to trial or be remanded to juvenile court. These youths who are transferred and found guilty are sentenced as an adult (although in Canada, certain restrictions relating to the length of sentence applies). In light of the potential negative consequences of a transfer to adult court, ranging from less serious (nonconfidential nature of proceedings, record of conviction on adult record) to extremely serious (lengthy incarceration periods to the death sentence), the highest standards of practice must be used. The focus of transfer hearing is on the danger the youth proposes to society and the juveniles' amenability to rehabilitation (Kruh & Brodsky, 1997).

The issue of danger includes the likelihood of harm to others across a variety of contexts. Grisso (1998) suggested that a youth's potential harm to others be addressed with respect to the likelihood of harm to other youth and staff in juvenile facilities, the likelihood of the youth engaging in violence if he escapes from a juvenile facility, and the likelihood that the youth will persist in offending as an adult. The findings summarized earlier point to the potential of harm posed by psychopathic youth both within institutions and in the community. Moreover, the studies by Forth and Burke (1998) and Gretton (1998) demonstrate the serious and stable nature of psychopathic youths' offending pattern.

RECIDIVISM FOLLOWING TREATMENT

To date there have been no controlled evaluations of intervention programs for psychopathic youth. Only two studies have assessed treatment outcome in youth assessed for psychopathy. The first study provided preliminary data from 220 adolescent sex offenders released after treatment assessed using the PCL:YV and followed up for an average of 56 months

(Gretton, McBride, O'Shaugnessy, & Hare, 1999). Offenders were divided into three groups based on their PCL:YV scores: high-psychopathy group (n = 29), mixed-psychopathy group (n = 111), and low-psychopathy group (n = 80). Offenders in the high-psychopathy group recidivated sooner than the other offenders. On average, the high-psychopathy group recidivated within 19 months versus 27 months for those in the middle group and 36 months for those in the low-psychopathy group. Furthermore, the rate of nonviolent recidivism was twice as high for the high group (66% vs. 27% for the low group), whereas the rate of violent nonsexual recidivism was almost triple for the high group (35% vs. 13%, respectively). The rates for sexual recidivism were about double the rates for the high- and low-psychopathy groups (30% vs. 16%, respectively). The treatment provided to these adolescents was focused on their sexual deviance. However, in light of the relatively high rates of nonsexual reoffending rates, targeting their more generalized antisocial tendencies is likely necessary (Hare, 1998b).

Ridenour (1996) correlated the 18-item PCL–R scores with three measures of treatment outcome in 26 adolescent offenders in a behaviorally based residential treatment unit. Psychopathy was correlated with the number of Level 1 setbacks (r = .61; Level 1 is the lowest level of the five-level system), number of offenses committed in 1-year follow-up (r = .36), and the highest level obtained in the program (r = −.34). Psychopathy identified those offenders who did poorly in treatment versus those who succeeded in the program.

The primary focus of research should be on creating, implementing, and evaluating intervention programs for youth with psychopathic characteristics. Lösel (1998) suggested that the optimal intervention program is multimodal (school, family, peers, community), long-lasting, early starting, and targets both the characteristics of the youth and parental behavior.

CONCLUSIONS

Research summarized in this chapter provides evidence that the concept of psychopathy can be extended from adults to adolescents. Although the empirical research is still in its early stages, there are a number of conclusions that can be drawn:

1. Psychopathic youth resemble youth with severe CD with childhood-onset type and youth with comorbid diagnosis of CD and ADHD and impulsivity. However, most youth with childhood-onset type CD or with comorbid CD and ADHD do not possess the affective and interper-

sonal features of the prototypical psychopath. Any assessment of psychopathy in adolescence should be based on the PCL:YV.

2. Psychopathy as measured by the PCL:YV is a dimensional measure of the degree to which the adolescent matches the prototypical psychopath. Although a categorical diagnosis of psychopathy is useful for some research and clinical applications, it is not possible to specify an optimal cutoff that would maximize diagnostic efficiency across all situations. For clinical applications (e.g., risk assessment, treatment planning), dimensional ratings of psychopathy provide the most relevant information for decision-making purposes. In addition, dimensional ratings permit clinical users to make distinctions among adolescents even in settings where the base rate of psychopathy is very high or very low.

3. Assessing psychopathic traits in adolescence provides meaningful information about the long-term risk for violence. Studies have shown that psychopathic adolescent offenders engage in more serious and frequent offenses and are more stable in their offending across time as compared with their nonpsychopathic counterparts.

4. Assessment of risk for violence should include psychopathy as a risk factor, but should also include other risk factors that have been empirically demonstrated as relating to violent behavior in youth (such as frequency and severity of past violent behaviors, substance use, association with deviant peers, antisocial attitudes, lack of social supports; see Grisso, 1998).

5. Psychopathic adolescents engage in more disruptive behavior within institutions, respond poorly to supervision, and are more likely to escape than are nonpsychopathic adolescents. To facilitate individual case management planning, clinical staff should be knowledgeable of psychopathic characteristics in the youth (e.g., level of security, amount of supervision required).

6. Youth with psychopathic features are resistant to intervention. However, this does not mean that intervention will not have an impact. Moreover, in light of the poor prognosis for these youth, the challenge facing researchers and clinicians is to develop, implement, and evaluate intervention programs.

This chapter amply demonstrated the importance of the construct of psychopathy to the juvenile criminal justice and mental health systems. There are some legitimate concerns with the potential for misuse of any scale designed to assess psychopathy in youth—in particular, with respect to accessibility to intervention (Ogloff & Lyon, 1998; Zinger & Forth, 1998). Concerns about the potential misuse of the PCL–R have recently been described by Hare (1998b). In adult court proceedings, a diagnosis of psychopathy is typically equated with a high risk of violent recidivism and an inability to benefit from treatment (Zinger & Forth, 1998). Moreover, once diagnosed as psychopathic, it is likely that this label will remain with the person and have ongoing negative repercussions. The ultimate goal for developing an assessment instrument to detect characteristics of psychopathy in younger people is to provide appropriate intervention programs proactively. Given the persistent nature of this disorder, the personal, social, and financial costs of not investing in early intervention is not an ethically acceptable alternative.

REFERENCES

Achenbach, T. M. (1991). *Manual for the Child Behavior Checklist and 1991 Profile*. Burlington, VT: University of Vermont, Department of Psychiatry.

Achenbach, T. M., & Edelbrock, C. (1983). *Manual of the Child Behavior Checklist and Revised Child Behavior Profile*. Burlington, VT: University of Vermont, Department of Psychiatry.

Albert, R. S., Brigante, T. R., & Chase, M. (1959). The psychopathic personality: A content analysis of the concept. *Journal of General Psychology, 60*, 17–28.

American Psychiatric Association. (1980). *Diagnostic and statistical manual of mental disorders* (3rd ed.). Washington, DC: Author.

American Psychiatric Association. (1994). *Diagnostic and statistical manual of mental disorders* (4th ed.). Washington, DC: Author.

Archer, R. P. (1992). *MMPI–A: Assessing adolescent psychopathology*. Hillsdale, NJ: Lawrence Erlbaum Associates.

Block, J., & Block, J. H. (1980). *The California Q-Set*. Palo Alto, CA: Consulting Psychologists Press.

Brandt, J. R., Kennedy, W. A., Patrick, C. J., & Curtin, J. J. (1997). Assessment of psychopathy in a population of incarcerated adolescent offenders. *Psychological Assessment, 9*, 429–435.

Brown, S. L., & Forth, A. E. (1997). Psychopathy and sexual assault: Static risk factors, emotional precursors, and rapist subtypes. *Journal of Consulting and Clinical Psychology, 65*, 848–857.

Burke, H. C., & Forth, A. E. (1996). *Psychopathy and familial experiences as antecedents to violence: A cross-sectional study of young offenders and nonoffending youth*. Unpublished manuscript, Carleton University, Ottawa, Ontario, Canada.

Butcher, J. N., Williams, C. L., Graham, J. R., Archer, R., Tellegen, A., Ben-Porath, Y. S., & Kaemmer, B. (1992). *MMPI–A manual for administration, scoring, and interpretation*. Minneapolis: University of Minnesota Press.

Christian, R. E., Frick, P. J., Hill, N. L., Tyler, L., & Frazer, D. R. (1997). Psychopathy and conduct problems in children: II. Implications for subtyping children with conduct problems. *Journal of the American Academy of Child and Adolescent Psychiatry, 36*, 233–241.

Cleckley, H. R. (1976). *The mask of sanity*. St. Louis, MO: Mosby.

Cooke, D. J. (1998). Psychopathy across cultures. In D. J. Cooke, A. E. Forth, & R. D. Hare (Eds.), *Psychopathy: Theory, research, and implications for society* (pp. 13–45). Dordrecht, The Netherlands: Kluwer.

Conners, C. K. (1989). *Conners' Parent Rating Scales–48*. Toronto: Multi-Health Systems.

Dempster, R. J., & Hart, S. D. (1996, March). *Utility of the FBI's Crime Classification Manual: Coverage, reliability and validity for adolescent murderers*. Paper presented at the biennial meeting of the American Psychology-Law Society (APA DIV. 41), Hilton Head, South Carolina.

Dixon, M., Robinson, L., Hart, S. D., Gretton, H., McBride, M., & O'Shaugnessy, R. (1995). Crime Classification Manual: Reliability and validity in juvenile sex offenders [Abstract]. *Canadian Psychology, 36,* 20.

Douglas, J. E., Burgess, A. W., Burgess, A. G., & Ressler, R. K. (1992). *The Crime Classification Manual: A standard system for investigating and classifying violent crimes.* New York: Lexington.

Forth, A. E. (1995). *Psychopathy and young offenders: Prevalence, family background, and violence* (Program Branch Users Report). Ottawa, Ontario, Canada: Ministry of the Solicitor General of Canada.

Forth, A. E., Brown, S. L., Hart, S. D., & Hare, R. D. (1996). The assessment of psychopathy in male and female noncriminals: Reliability and validity. *Personality and Individual Differences, 20,* 531–543.

Forth, A. E., & Burke, H. (1998). Psychopathy in adolescence: Assessment, violence, and developmental precursors. In R. D. Cooke, A. E. Forth, & R. D. Hare (Eds.), *Psychopathy: Theory, research, and implications for society* (pp. 205–229). Dordrecht, The Netherlands: Kluwer.

Forth, A. E., Hart, S. D., & Hare, R. D. (1990). Assessment of psychopathy in male young offenders. *Psychological Assessment: A Journal of Consulting and Clinical Psychology, 2,* 342–344.

Forth, A. E., Kosson, D. S., & Hare, R. D. (in press). *The Psychopathy Checklist: Youth Version.* Unpublished test manual, Multi-Health Systems.

Frick, P. J. (1998). Callous-unemotional traits and conduct problems: Applying the two-factor model of psychopathy to children. In R. D. Cooke, A. E. Forth, & R. D. Hare (Eds.), *Psychopathy: Theory, research, and implications for society* (pp. 161–187). Dordrecht, The Netherlands: Kluwer.

Frick, P. J., O'Brien, B. S., Wootton, J. M., & McBurnett, K. (1994). Psychopathy and conduct problems in children. *Journal of Abnormal Psychology, 103,* 700–707.

Gacono, C. B., & Meloy, J. R. (1994). *Rorschach assessment of aggressive and psychopathic personalities.* Hillsdale, NJ: Lawrence Erlbaum Associates.

Gretton, H. M. (1998). *Psychopathy and recidivism in adolescence: A ten-year retrospective follow-up.* Unpublished doctoral dissertation, University of British Columbia, Vancouver, British Columbia.

Gretton, H. M., McBride, M., Lewis, K., O'Shaughnessy, R., & Hare, R. D. (1994). Predicting patterns of criminal activity in adolescent sexual psychopaths [Abstract]. *Canadian Psychology, 35,* 50.

Gretton, H. M., McBride, M., O'Shaughnessey, R., & Hare, R. D. (1999). *Psychopathy and recidivism in adolescent sex offenders.* Manuscript in preparation.

Grisso, T. (1998). *Forensic evaluation of juveniles.* Sarasota, FL: Professional Resource Press.

Haapasalo, J., & Tremblay, R. E. (1994). Physically aggressive boys from ages 6 to 12: Family background, parenting behavior, and prediction of delinquency. *Journal of Consulting and Clinical Psychology, 62,* 1044–1052.

Hare, R. D. (1980). A research scale for the assessment of psychopathy in criminal populations. *Personality and Individual Differences, 1,* 111–119.

Hare, R. D. (1983). Diagnosis of antisocial personality disorder in two prison populations. *American Journal of Psychiatry, 140,* 887–890.

Hare, R. D. (1985). Comparison of procedures for the assessment of psychopathy. *Journal of Consulting and Clinical Psychology, 53,* 7–16.

Hare, R. D. (1991). *The Hare Psychopathy Checklist–Revised.* Toronto: Multi-Health Systems.

Hare, R. D. (1996). Psychopathy: A clinical construct whose time has come. *Criminal Justice and Behavior, 23,* 25–54.

Hare, R. D. (1998a). Psychopaths and their nature: Implications for the mental health and criminal justice systems. In T. M. Millon, E. Simonsen, M. Birket-Smith, & R. Davis (Eds.), *Psychopathy: Antisocial, criminal and violent behavior* (pp. 188–212). New York: Guilford.

Hare, R. D. (1998b). The Hare PCL–R: Some issues concerning its use and misuse. *Legal and Criminological Psychology, 3*, 101–122.

Hare, R. D., Harpur, T. J., Hakstian, A. R., Forth, A. E., Hart, S. D., & Newman, J. P. (1990). The Revised Psychopathy Checklist: Reliability and factor structure. *Psychological Assessment: A Journal of Consulting and Clinical Psychology, 2*, 338–341.

Harpur, T. J., Hare, R. D., & Hakstian, A. R. (1989). Two-factor conceptualization of psychopathy: Construct validity and assessment implications. *Psychological Assessment: A Journal of Consulting and Clinical Psychology, 1*, 6–17.

Hart, S. D., Cox, D. N., & Hare, R. D. (1995). *Manual for the Psychopathy Checklist: Screening Version (PCL:SV)*. Toronto: Multi-Health Systems.

Hart, S. D., Forth, A. E., & Hare, R. D. (1991). The MCMI–II as a measure of psychopathy. *Journal of Personality Disorders, 5*, 318–327.

Hart, S. D., & Hare, R. D. (1989). Discriminant validity of the Psychopathy Checklist. *Psychological Assessment: A Journal of Consulting and Clinical Psychology, 1*, 211–218.

Hart, S. D., & Hare, R. D. (1997). Psychopathy: Assessment and association with criminal conduct. In D. M. Stoff, J. Brieling, & J. Maser (Eds.), *Handbook of antisocial behavior* (pp. 22–35). New York: Wiley.

Hathaway, S. R., & McKinley, J. C. (1943). *The Minnesota Multiphasic Personality Inventory* (rev. ed.). Minneapolis: University of Minnesota Press.

Hemphill, J. F., Hare, R. D., & Wong, S. (1998). Psychopathy and recidivism: A review. *Legal and Criminological Psychology, 3*, 139–170.

Hemphill, J. F., Hart, S. D., & Hare, R. D. (1994). Psychopathy and substance use. *Journal of Personality Disorders, 8*, 169–180.

Henry, B., Caspi, A., Moffitt, T. E., & Silva, P. A. (1996). Temperamental and familial predictors of violent and nonviolent criminal convictions: From age 3 to age 18. *Developmental Psychology, 32*, 614–623.

Hodgins, S., Côté, G., & Ross, D. (1992). Predictive validity of the French version of Hare's Psychopathy Checklist [Abstract]. *Canadian Psychology, 33*, 301.

Hume, M. P., Kennedy, W. A., Patrick, C. J., & Partyka, D. J. (1996). Examination of the MMPI–A for the assessment of psychopathy in incarcerated adolescent male offenders. *International Journal of Offender Therapy and Comparative Criminology, 40*, 224–233.

Kosson, D. S., Smith, S. S., & Newman, J. P. (1990). Evaluation of the construct validity of psychopathy in Black and White male inmates: Three preliminary studies. *Journal of Abnormal Psychology, 99*, 250–259.

Kruger, R. F., Schmutte, P. S., Caspi, A., Moffitt, T. E., Campbell, K., & Silva, P. A. (1994). Personality traits are linked to crime among men and women: Evidence from a birth cohort. *Journal of Abnormal Psychology, 103*, 328–338.

Kruh, I. P., & Brodsky, S. L. (1997). Clinical evaluations for transfer of juveniles to criminal court: Current practices and future research. *Behavioral Sciences and the Law, 15*, 151–165.

Lahey, B. B., & Loeber, R. (1997). Attention-deficit/hyperactivity disorder, oppositional defiant disorder, conduct disorder, and adult antisocial behavior: A life span perspective. In D. M. Stoff, J. Brieling, & J. Maser (Eds.), *Handbook of antisocial behavior* (pp. 51–59). New York: Wiley.

Laroche, I. (1996). *Les composantes psychologiques et comportementales parentales associées à la psychopathie du contrevenant juvénile* [Psychological factors and parental behaviors associated with psychopathy in juvenile delinquents]. Unpublished doctoral thesis, University of Montreal, Montreal, Quebec.

Laroche, I., & Toupin, J. (1996, August). *Psychopathic delinquents: A family contribution?* Paper presented at the XXVI International Congress of Psychology, Montreal, Quebec.

Lewis, K., & O'Shaughnessy, R. (1998, June). *Predictors of violent recidivism in juvenile offenders*. Poster presented at the annual convention of the Canadian Psychological Association, Edmonton, Alberta.

Lilienfeld, S. O., & Andrews, B. P. (1996). Development and preliminary validation of a self-report measure of psychopathic personality traits in noncriminal populations. *Journal of Personality Assessment, 66*, 488–534.

Loeber, R., & Stouthamer-Loeber, M. (1986). Family factors as correlates and predictors of juvenile conduct problems and delinquency. In M. Tonry & N. Morris (Eds.), *Crime and justice* (Vol. 7, pp. 29–149). Chicago: University of Chicago Press.

Lösel, F. (1998). Treatment and management of psychopaths. In D. Cooke, A. E. Forth, & R. D. Hare (Eds.), *Psychopathy: Theory, research, and implications for society* (pp. 303–354). Dordrecht, The Netherlands: Kluwer.

Lynam, D. R. (1996). Early identification of chronic offenders: Who is the fledging psychopath? *Psychological Bulletin, 120*, 209–234.

Lynam, D. R. (1997). Pursuing the psychopath: Capturing the fledgling psychopath in a nomological net. *Journal of Abnormal Psychology, 10*, 425–438.

Mailloux, D. (1999). *Victimization, coping, and psychopathy: Associations with violent behaviour among female offenders.* Unpublished master's thesis, Carleton University, Ottawa, Ontario, Canada.

Mailloux, D. L., Forth, A. E., & Kroner, D. G. (1997). Psychopathy and substance use in adolescent male offenders. *Psychological Reports, 81*, 529–530.

Mannuzza, S., Klein, R. G., Bessler, A., Malloy, P., & LaPadula, M. (1993). Adult outcome of hyperactive boys: Educational achievement, occupational rank, and psychiatric status. *Archives of General Psychiatry, 50*, 565–576.

McBride, M. (1998). *Individual and familial risk factors for adolescent psychopathy.* Unpublished doctoral dissertation, University of British Columbia, Vancouver, British Columbia.

Myers, W. C., Burket, R. C., & Harris, H. E. (1995). Adolescent psychopathy in relation to delinquent behaviors, conduct disorder, and personality disorders. *Journal of Forensic Sciences, 40*, 436–440.

Neary, A. (1991). DSM-III and Psychopathy Checklist assessment of antisocial personality disorder in Black and White female felons. *Dissertation Abstracts International, 51*(7–B), 3605.

Ogloff, J. R. P., & Lyon, D. R. (1998). Legal issues associated with the concept of psychopathy. In D. Cooke, A. E. Forth, & R. D. Hare (Eds.), *Psychopathy: Theory, research, and implications for society* (pp. 401–422). Dordrecht, The Netherlands: Kluwer.

Ogloff, J. R. P., Wong, S., & Greenwood, A. (1990). Treating criminal psychopaths in a therapeutic community program. *Behavioral Sciences and the Law, 8*, 81–90.

Pan, V. (1998, March). *Institutional behavior in psychopathic juvenile offenders.* Poster presented at the biennial conference of the American Psychology-Law Society, Redondo Beach, CA.

Plutchik, R., & van Praag, H. M. (1997). Suicide, impulsivity, and antisocial behavior. In D. M. Stoff, J. Brieling, & J. Maser (Eds.), *Handbook of antisocial behavior* (pp. 101–108). New York: Wiley.

Poythress, N. G., Edens, J. F., & Lilienfeld, S. O. (1998). Criterion-based validity of the Psychopathic Personality Inventory in a prison sample. *Psychological Assessment, 10*, 426–430.

Rice, M. E., Harris, G. T., & Cormier, C. A. (1992). An evaluation of a maximum security therapeutic community for psychopaths and other mentally disordered offenders. *Law and Human Behavior, 16*, 399–412.

Ridenour, T. A. (1996). *Utility analyses of the Psychopathy Checklist, Revised and Moffitt's taxonomy for a rehabilitation program for juvenile delinquents.* Unpublished doctoral dissertation, Bell State University, Muncie, Indiana.

Rogers, R., Dion, K. L., & Lynett, E. (1992). Diagnostic validity of antisocial personality disorder: A prototypical analysis. *Law and Human Behavior, 16*, 677–689.

Rogers, R., Johansen, J., Chang, J. J., & Salekin, R. T. (1997). Predictors of adolescent psychopathy: Oppositional and conduct-disordered symptoms. *Journal of the American Academy of Psychiatry and the Law, 25*, 261–271.

Rowe, R. (1997). [Psychopathy and female adolescents]. Unpublished raw data. Carleton University, Ottawa, Ontario, Canada.

Rutherford, M. J., Alterman, A. I., Cacciola, J. S., & Snyder, E. C. (1996). Gender differences in diagnosing antisocial personality disorder in methadone patients. *American Journal of Psychiatry, 152*, 1309–1316.

Rutherford, M. J., Alterman, A. I., Cacciola, J. S., & McKay, J. R. (1998). Gender differences in the relationship of antisocial personality disorder criteria to Psychopathy Checklist–Revised scores. *Journal of Personality Disorders, 12*, 69–76.

Salekin, R. T., Rogers, R., & Sewell, K. W. (1996). A review and meta-analysis of the Psychopathy Checklist and Psychopathy Checklist–Revised: Predictive validity of dangerousness. *Clinical Psychology: Science and Practice, 3*, 203–215.

Selzer, M. L. (1971). The Michigan Alcoholism Screening Test: The quest for a new diagnostic instrument. *American Journal of Psychiatry, 127*, 89–94.

Skinner, H. (1982). The Drug Abuse Screening Test. *Addictive Behavior, 7*, 363–371.

Smith, A. M., Gacono, C. B., & Kaufman, L. (1997). A Rorschach comparison of psychopathic and nonpsychopathic conduct disordered adolescents. *Journal of Clinical Psychology, 53*, 289–300.

Smith, S. S., & Newman, J. P. (1990). Alcohol and drug abuse/dependence disorders in psychopathic and nonpsychopathic criminal offenders. *Journal of Abnormal Psychology, 99*, 430–439.

Stafford, E. (1997). *Psychopathy as a predictor of adolescents at risk for inpatient violence.* Unpublished doctoral dissertation, University of Virginia, Virginia.

Stålenheim, E. G., & von Knorring, L. (1996). Psychopathy and Axis I and Axis II psychiatric disorders in a forensic psychiatric population in Sweden. *Acta Psychiatrica Scandinavica, 94*, 217–223.

Stanford, M., Ebner, D., Patton, J., & Williams, J. (1994). Multi-impulsivity within an adolescent psychiatric population. *Personality and Individual Differences, 16*, 395–402.

Strachan, C. (1993). *Assessment of psychopathy in female offenders.* Unpublished doctoral dissertation, University of British Columbia, Vancouver.

Sullivan, L. E. (1996). *Assessment of psychopathy using the MMPI–A: Validity in male adolescent forensic patients.* Unpublished master's thesis, Simon Fraser University, Burnaby, British Columbia.

Tennent, G., Tennent, D., Prins, H., & Bedford, A. (1990). Psychopathic disorder: A useful clinical concept? *Medicine, Science, and the Law, 30*, 38–44.

Tolman, R. M. (1989). The development of a measure of psychological maltreatment of women by their partners. *Violence and Victims, 4*, 159–177.

Toupin, J., Mercier, H., Déry, M., Côté, G., & Hodgins, S. (1996). Validity of the PCL–R for adolescents. In D. J. Cooke, A. E. Forth, J. P. Newman, & R. D. Hare (Eds.), *Issues in criminological and legal psychology: No. 24. International perspectives on psychopathy* (pp. 143–145). Leicester, United Kingdom: British Psychological Society.

Walker, J. L., Lahey, B. B., Hynd, G. W., & Frame, C. L. (1987). Comparison of specific patterns of antisocial behavior in children with conduct disorder with and without coexisting hyperactivity. *Journal of Consulting and Clinical Psychology, 55*, 910–913.

Watt, K., Ma, S., Lewis, K., Willoughby, T., & O'Shaughnessy, R. (1997, June). *The relationship between parental criminal behavior and youth psychopathy.* Poster presented at the annual convention of the Canadian Psychological Association, Toronto, Ontario.

Webster, C. D., & Jackson, M. A. (1997). *Impulsivity: New directions in research and clinical practice.* New York: Guilford.

White, J. L., Moffitt, T. E., Earls, R., Robins, L., & Silva, P. A. (1990). How early can we tell? Predictors of childhood conduct disorder and adolescent delinquency. *Criminology, 28*, 507–533.

Widom, C. S. (1997). Child abuse, neglect, and witnessing violence. In D. M. Stoff, J. Brieling, & J. Maser (Eds.), *Handbook of antisocial behavior* (pp. 159–170). New York: Wiley.

Wootton, J. M., Frick, P. J., Shelton, K. K., & Silverthorn, P. (1997). Ineffective parenting and childhood conduct problems: The moderating role of callous-unemotional traits. *Journal of Consulting and Clinical Psychology, 65,* 301–308.

Wong, S. (1985). *The criminal and institutional behaviors of psychopaths.* Ottawa: Programs Branch User Report, Ministry of the Solicitor General of Canada.

Zinger, I., & Forth, A. E. (1998). Psychopathy and Canadian criminal proceedings: The potential for human rights abuses. *Canadian Journal of Criminology, 40,* 237–276.

3

Assessing Psychopathy in Adults: The Psychopathy Checklist–Revised and Screening Version

Robert H. Bodholdt
U.S. Department of Justice, Bastrop, Texas

Henry R. Richards
Johnson, Bassin, & Shaw, Inc., Silver Spring, Maryland

Carl B. Gacono
Private Practice, Austin, Texas

The purpose of this chapter is to provide a brief introduction—or a refresher—to the revised version of the Hare (1991) Psychopathy Checklist (PCL–R). Research examining the PCL–R has reached a stage where it has become a subject for analysis and review, as in the case of meta-analytic studies of the PCL–R and recidivism. Various issues associated with the introduction of a new assessment device have passed the point of mere identification and provide the basis for what we hope is an engaging review.

The clinician chooses assessment instruments and methods based on the clinical setting, referral question, and patient presentation. In forensic and correctional settings, where referral questions often involve issues of prediction, advances in psychopathy assessment have accorded the PCL–R a central role in many types of evaluations. Numerous and replicated findings indicate that psychopathy acts as a robust predictor of criminal activity and violent recidivism (Hare, 1991; Quinsey, Harris, Rice, & Cormier, 1998). Fulero (1995) wrote of the PCL–R: "state of the art . . . both clinically and in research use" (p. 454). Altogether, one could argue that clinicians working in settings where referral for evaluation of psychopathy might be indicated have some obligation to be familiar with the PCL–R and its use (Gacono, Nieberding, Owen, Rubel, & Bodholdt, 2001).

HISTORICAL ANTECEDENTS

Understanding psychopathy requires understanding of personality, personality disorder, links to other forms of pathology, and developmental psychology at large (Kernberg, 1975, 1984; Meloy, 1988; Millon, 1981). Similarly, examination of historical roots of the construct provides unique insight into some of the forces that shape current understanding of psychopathy.

Pinel (1806) presaged modern conceptualizations of psychopathy in his description of a disorder of affect and impulse that otherwise appeared to spare intellectual functioning. Such persons were described as given to social transgressions of almost any sort, including those that might otherwise be regarded as evidence of a diseased mind. Termed *manie sans delire*, or madness without confusion, the idea that any certain madness could spare central attributes of mind was revolutionary. The next 150 years — and further in the nosology of the *Diagnostic and Statistical Manual of Mental Disorder (DSM)* — were marked by a variegated striking of terms with only limited degrees of overlap with current views of psychopathy (Millon, 1981; Millon & Davis, 1996).[1]

At a time of acute interest surrounding the use of insanity as a legal defense, Kraeplin's (1907) adaptation under the term *psychopathic personality* is sometimes credited with anchoring the construct of psychopathy in a developmental framework. In other words, unlike disorders such as schizophrenia, a defining characteristic of the Kraeplin's psychopathic personality is developmental continuity with an earlier age. Still it is only Cleckley's (1941, 1976) prodigious collection of observations that unites present-day conceptualizations of psychopathy with historical attempts to characterize the disorder.

In contrast to Pinel, Cleckley's (1976) book *The Mask of Sanity* betrayed a contempt for the nature of psychopathy:

> Without restraint and without any treatment worthy of the name, the psychopath continues, woe, confusion, despair, farce and disaster, beyond any measure of these things I can convey, progressively accumulating in his social wake. (p. 539)

As outlined in Table 3.1 the Cleckley psychopath is exemplified by a combination of 16 characteristics — interpersonal, affective, cognitive, behavioral — associated with an impulsive, irresponsible, and deceitful lifestyle. With some modification, the theoretical basis of the PCL–R rests on Cleckley's initial model.

Due to the broad acceptance of the *DSM* as a diagnostic reference (American Psychiatric Association, 1952, 1968, 1980, 1987, 1994), expanded coverage is allotted in this section to highlight areas of divergence in the five *DSM* editions. The *DSM* has recapitulated many early controversies, spanning the time of Pinel to Cleckley (see Millon & Davis, 1996),

TABLE 3.1

Comparison of Cleckley's 16 Characteristics of Psychopathy and DSM-IV Criteria

Criteria	Characteristics
DSM-IV Criteria for ASPD (American Psychiatric Association, 1994)	*Cleckley's Psychopathy Criteria*
A. At least three of the following since age 15:	1. Superficial charm and good intelligence
1. Failure to conform to social norms	2. Absence of delusions and other signs of irrational thinking
2. Deceitfulness, lying	3. Absence of nervousness or psychoneurotic manifestations
3. Impulsivity	4. Unreliability
4. Irritability and aggressiveness, fights and assaults	5. Untruthfulness and insincerity
5. Reckless disregard for safety of self or others	6. Lack of remorse or shame
6. Irresponsibility	7. Inadequately motivated antisocial behavior
7. Lacks remorse	8. Poor judgment and failure to learn by experience
	9. Pathologic egocentricity and incapacity for love
B. Current age at least 18	10. General poverty in affective reactions
	11. Specific loss of insight
C. Conduct disorder, onset before 15	12. Unresponsiveness in general interpersonal relations
	13. Fantastic and uninviting behavior with or without drink
D. Occurrence of antisocial behavior not exclusively during the course of schizophrenia or manic episode.	14. Suicide rarely carried out
	15. Sex life impersonal, trivial, and poorly integrated
	16. Failure to follow any life plan

particularly as this relates to the shift away from higher order personality trait formulations and toward what some have suggested is a model
unduly focused on patently criminal behavior.

The original *DSM* (American Psychiatric Association, 1952) category
antisocial reaction describes a nexus of traits and behaviors seen as uncon-
fined to any particular disorder or patient presentation:

> . . . always in trouble, profiting neither from experience or punishment and
> maintaining no loyalties to any person, group or code. They are frequently
> callous and hedonistic, showing marked emotional immaturity with lack of
> sense of responsibility, lack of judgement, and an ability to rationalize their
> behavior so that it appears warranted, reasonable, and justified. (p. 38)

At a time when the etiologically suggestive term *reaction* came under
greater scrutiny, the *DSM–II* (American Psychiatric Association, 1968)
introduced a section comprising personality disorders, with ASPD coopt-
ing antisocial reaction. Often recognizable by adolescence, the personality disorders were characterized by deeply ingrained, inflexible, and
maladaptive traits and behaviors. Qualitatively distinct from neurotic
and psychotic disorders, the *DSM–II* sought to specify distinct and devel-
opmentally continuous personality types—hence, a greater emphasis on
characterological dimensions or personality traits.

Perhaps closest of all versions to the Cleckley or Hare psychopath, the
DSM–II ASPD is distinguished from other personality disorders by incor-
rigible antisocial traits and behaviors. Incapable of significant loyalty to
individuals, groups, or social values, the antisocially disordered individual was described as unusually selfish, callous, irresponsible, impulsive,
as well as unable to feel guilt or learn from experience or punishment.
Additional characteristics included low frustration tolerance, a tendency
to blame others, and the proffering of rationalizations for problematic
personal behavior (American Psychiatric Association, 1968).

In a time of increasing popular concern about crime in America, and
based largely on the prospective longitudinal study of Robins (1966), the
DSM–III (American Psychiatric Association, 1980) firmly embraced a
social deviance model. Absent most earlier higher order trait descriptors,
such as those involving selfishness, egocentricity, callousness, manipulativeness, and lack of empathy, there was a decided shift in the direction
of focusing on criminal behavior. As personality traits were thought by
many to be more difficult to operationalize than behavioral events, the
use of behavioral criteria also promised increased reliability of ratings in
the domain of the personality disorders, which had been a source of great
concern with previous *DSM* editions. However, as Millon and Davis
(1996) took pains to question, had the *DSM* opted to spare more fortunate
or talented psychopaths from the diagnostic roster:

(DSM formulation of ASPD) . . . fails to recognize that the same fundamental personality structure, with its characteristic pattern of ruthless and vindictive behavior, is often displayed in ways that are not socially disreputable, irresponsible or illegal. (p. 443).[2]

The *DSM-III-R* formulation of ASPD added a criterion (albeit in the last and presumably least informative position) — "lacks remorse (feels justified in having hurt, mistreated, or stolen from another)" — but drew more emphasis on violent criminal acts, including through the required linkage to Conduct Disorder (CD). *DSM-III*, *DSM-III-R*, and *DSM-IV* required evidence of CD with onset before age 15 and excluded the diagnosis of ASPD in instances were antisocial behavior occurred exclusively during the course of schizophrenia or manic episodes. Attempts at retrospective diagnosis are complicated by limits of reliability inherent to the diagnosis of any of these disorders.

The *DSM-IV* criteria for ASPD (contrasted with Cleckley's model in Table 3.1) introduced a remarkable change in format.[3] Criteria were dropped, simplified, and condensed, with at least an initial goal of bringing the *DSM-IV* more in line with the joint personality trait-behavior approach seen in other personality disorder criteria and more in line with criteria such as those used by Cleckley and Hare (Millon & Davis, 1996). Although *DSM-IV* ASPD criteria have been streamlined, interpretation requires much greater reliance on translation of the introductory narrative, which in turn preserves much of the letter of previous *DSM* editions.

THE HARE PSYCHOPATHY CHECKLISTS

The Psychopathy Checklist gained momentum as a promising research diagnostic tool in large measure due to increasingly recognized limitations of standardized testing and extant structured interviews, including those anchored in a *DSM* format, in identifying psychopathy. Although *DSM-IV* ASPD criteria may be useful in mental health settings where baserates are relatively low (community = males 3%, females 1%; clinical settings = 3%-30%; American Psychiatric Association, 1994), identification of ASPD in forensic settings is something like finding ice in your refrigerator; estimates range as high as 80% (American Psychiatric Association, 1994; Hare, 1991). Further, because child and adolescent history may be obscured (e.g., through sealing of records, patient portrayal of childhood relationships as idyllic), individuals with a pervasive adulthood pattern of violating the rights of others cannot be diagnosed as *DSM-IV* ASPD.

Initial work on a psychopathy screening instrument was begun by Robert Hare and colleagues in the form of a simple 7-point global rating scale anchored in Cleckley's model of psychopathy. Although high interrater reliability could be achieved through this method, the test existed within the clinician's head (i.e., relied too heavily on implicit knowledge of expert raters). To open this form of assessment to other researchers, criteria were operationalized in the form of the initial 22-item narrative Psychopathy Checklist. As interest and attention grew, several item descriptions were modified, scoring criteria were made more explicit, and two items were dropped—thus, the PCL-R (Table 3.2; Hare, 1991; with adaptation from Cooke & Michie, 1997).[4]

Comparison of Cleckley's criteria (see Table 3.1) with the PCL-R items (Table 3.2) reveals some interesting modifications. For example, Cleckley's first characteristic, Superficial Charm and Good Intelligence, limits reliability by combining two constructs that have no expected intercorrelation and is replaced by PCL-R Item 1, Glibness/Superficial Charm. Good Intelligence was probably eliminated on several grounds, such as failing to differentiate psychopathic from nonpsychopathic offenders. O'Kane, Fawcett, and Blackburn (1996) reported a negative correlation between PCL-R scores and IQ. Also, one can see the addition of Items 18, 19, and 20 to the PCL-R that reflect the type of criminal activity more often seen in psychopathic offenders relative to nonpsychopathic offenders. These latter items are coded given access to the criminal record.

The following summarizes the relationship between psychopathy and ASPD:

1. *Psychopathy* is defined in terms of personality traits and behaviors (Cleckley 1941, 1976; Hare, 1980), whereas ASPD (American Psychiatric Association, 1980, 1987, 1994) is based largely on a social deviance model defined predominantly in terms of antisocial and criminal behaviors.

2. *DSM-IV* (American Psychiatric Association, 1994) references *psychopathy* under Associated Features and Disorders of ASPD, but these diagnoses or sets of criteria are not interchangeable. Psychopathy can be understood as a disorder composed of selected features of all Cluster B syndromes, including Narcissistic, Histrionic, and Borderline.

3. Most psychopaths meet criteria for diagnosis of ASPD, whereas most ASPDs are not psychopaths. In forensic populations, baserates for ASPD are 50% to 80%, compared with only 15% to 25% meeting criteria for diagnosis of psychopathy.

PCL-R Factor Structure

Psychopathy, as measured by the PCL-R, at least initially appeared to be a higher order unidimensional construct composed of two moderately correlated factors (Hare, 1991). Factor analysis has fairly consistently revealed a stable, oblique two-factor structure. When subjected to item

TABLE 3.2
PCL–R Factor Structure

Item	2-Factor Solution	3-Factor Solution
1. Glibness/superficial charm	I/A	Interpersonal
2. Grandiose sense of self-worth	I/A	Interpersonal
3. Need for stimulation/proneness to boredom	IMP/DEV	Lifestyle
4. Pathological lying	I/A	Interpersonal
5. Conning/manipulative	I/A	Interpersonal
6. Lack of remorse or guilt	I/A	Affective
7. Shallow affect	I/A	Affective
8. Callous/lack of empathy	I/A	Affective
9. Parasitic lifestyle	IMP/DEV	Lifestyle
10. Poor behavioral controls	IMP/DEV	– –
11. Promiscuous sexual behavior	– –	– –
12. Early behavior problems	IMP/DEV	– –
13. Lack of realistic long-term goals	IMP/DEV	Lifestyle
14. Impulsivity	IMP/DEV	Lifestyle
15. Irresponsibility	IMP/DEV	Lifestyle
16. Failure to accept responsibility for own actions	I/A	Affective
17. Many short-term marital relationships	– –	– –
18. Juvenile delinquency	IMP/DEV	– –
19. Revocation of conditional release	IMP/DEV	– –
20. Criminal versatility	– –	– –

Note. Adapted using the original two-factor solution described by Hare (1991) and others. I/A denotes items loading on the interpersonal/affective factor, whereas IMP/DEV denotes items loading on the impulsive/deviant lifestyle factor. Adapted from the item response theory (IRT) three-factor derivation of Cooke and Michie (1997) and Hare and Hart (1999). Core psychopathic items are identified by their loadings on the interpersonal, affective, or lifestyle factor.

response theory (IRT) analysis, however (Cooke & Michie, 1997), several PCL–R items yield to a more select 13- or 14-item set particularly discriminating of psychopathy. In turn, the IRT derived set produces a three-factor solution: interpersonal, affective, and lifestyle. This is presented in Table 3.2 beside the original two-factor solution.[5] Note that three items (promiscuity, marital relationships, and criminal versatility) are eliminated from the original two-factor solution due to marginal factor loadings and are similarly eliminated by IRT due to poor discriminative strength. Items that appear to be the most discriminating of overall high scorers are Callous/Lack of Empathy, Lack of Remorse or Guilt, and Shallow Affect.

The original two-factor solution is deeply embedded in the last 15 years of research and commentary, and may yet offer practical advantages in the conceptualization of certain populations, particularly criminal populations. Factor 1 (Items 1–2, 4–8, and 16) has been described as aggressive narcissism (Meloy, 1992) or callous and remorseless disregard for the rights and feelings of others (Hare, 1991). Not surprisingly, Factor 1 correlates with narcissistic and histrionic personality diagnoses (Hare, 1991) and self-report measures of Machiavellianism and narcissism (Harpur, Hare, & Hakstian, 1989; Hart & Hare, 1989). PCL–R Factor 1 yields negative correlations with avoidant and dependent personalities, intensity of affect, and anxiety.

Factor 2 (Items 3, 9–10, 12–15, and 18–19), described in terms of chronically unstable and antisocial lifestyle (Hare, 1991), is characterized by an irresponsible, impulsive, thrill-seeking, and antisocial lifestyle. It correlates more highly than Factor 1 with the *DSM–III–R* ASPD diagnosis. Factor 2 is also more closely associated with lower socioeconomic status (SES), IQ, education, higher criminal recidivism, and higher self-report of various forms of antisocial behavior (Hare, 1991; Harpur et al., 1989; see Table 3.3). Most self-report measures, such as the MMPI (PD, MA, PD+MA, PD-So), CPI (So[-]), and MCMI–II (Antisocial) correlate more strongly with this factor.

With a few notable exceptions, many studies support the two-factor solution proposed by Hare (1991), including those of 122 English male prison inmates (Raine, 1985), 104 male inmates admitted to a therapeutic prison (Hobson & Shine, 1998), 2067 "North American participants" (Cooke & Michie, 1997), and 1,119 male offenders in a split-half cross-validation study of six samples drawn from the United States, Canada, and England (Harpur, Hakstian, & Hare, 1988). Using a modified version of the PCL–R, Brandt, Kennedy, Patrick, and Curtin (1997) replicated a similar two-factor structure in a racially mixed sample of adolescent male offenders. Difficulty replicating the initial two-factor solution has occurred in a number of select samples, including female offenders (Salekin, Rogers, & Sewell, 1997), African-American offenders (Kosson, Smith, & Newman, 1990), and a large mixed sample of community- and prison-based methadone patients (Darke, Kaye, Finley-Jones, & Hall, 1998).

Alternative conceptualizations of dimensions that might underlie the PCL–R have been advanced by various researchers in addition to those advocates of an IRT approach. Raine (1985) suggested that the items could be divided into four clusters: Emotional Detachment, Superficial Relationships, Egocentricity, and Impulsiveness. Two Finnish researchers, Haapasalo and Pulkkinen (1992), using what was described as a person-oriented cluster analysis with 92 nonviolent male offenders, identified three groupings: Cluster 1, corresponding to Factor 1; Cluster 2, corresponding to Factor 2; and Cluster 3, a group of low scorers on both factors. Darke et al. (1998) proposed a five-factor structure for the PCL–R based on a confirmatory factor analysis of ratings of methadone maintenance patients, but acknowledge a superordinate grouping along two dimensions: one primarily psychological (consisting of Glibness/Manipulative, Callousness, Irresponsibility) and one primarily behavioral (consisting of Criminal Behaviors and Promiscuity).

PCL–R Administration

Use of the PCL–R requires specialized training and is most often found in clinical and forensic psychologists with considerable experience assessing and treating individuals seen in correctional or other forensic settings (cf. chap. 7; Gacono & Hutton, 1994). We cannot duplicate that experience, but can provide a brief outline of basic administration steps:

1. Establish a basis for use of the instrument. Evaluate purpose of referral, use of findings, and whether prospective interviewee is well represented in normative studies.
2. Review collateral records, including automated criminal records (*rap sheets*), offense reports, and hospital and treatment records.
3. Note events and situations to be queried or probed during interviews.
4. Tentatively score items from record information.
5. Interview persons with significant knowledge and experience of the subject, such as family members, friends, other professionals.
6. Perform a clinical interview with rated person.
7. Integrate information through item-by-item scoring.
8. Calculate scale scores.
9. Compare the resulting scores to those of relevant normative samples.
10. Interpret scores.
11. Integrate psychopathy-related findings with other assessment data (see chap. 9).

We should emphasize that assessment findings have the potential to seriously affect the course of interviewees' lives, which should further strengthen the clinician's resolve against misuse of the PCL–R (see Hare, 1998). The assessment approach advocated is one of conservative judgment, with a recognition that data sources (such as the interviewee) may withhold or obscure information relevant to conducting an examination of this sort. Use of multiple data sources is assumed, with sound clinical judgment required to weigh issues such as source credibility in instances of conflicting information. Where uncertainty cannot be resolved, there are several options, including omitting the item and prorating the cumulative score. Clinicians may also rate their degree of confidence in the overall procedure and score based on factors such as completeness of records reviewed in the evaluation.

The PCL–R procedure consists of a synthesis of collateral information, record review, and a clinical interview. Review of collateral and historical information precedes and helps guide the clinical interview. Some examiners find it convenient to think of the procedure as bound by a series of interrelated organizing categories, such as offense history, early developmental history, social and occupational history, accounts of third-person impressions of behavior, and so on. Numerous response queries are provided for each item (Hare, 1991) and, with memorization and practice, provide for a more fluid interview (see Appendix A). Tentative positive scoring of items can begin during the record review process. Even after extensive experience is established, scoring of items should occur with the PCL–R Rating Booklet in hand, with the content of each item and its anchoring indicators being read prior to scoring.

Although the PCL–R was never designed to be used without a clinical interview, some studies suggest that record review alone might be acceptable for research purposes (Grann, Langstrom, Tengstrom, & Stalenheim, 1998). For example, Wong (1988) was able to obtain reliability with file ratings alone, but found that this method underestimated high scorers. Serin (1993) found much less than desirable correspondence between full procedure and file-only ratings of probationers, but found no clear evidence of underestimation bias in the file-only condition. Alterman, Cacciola, and Rutherford (1993) found that increasing the amount of information available to raters resulted in significantly higher PCL–R scores and more positive diagnoses. File-only rating, with due qualification of findings, may be justifiable in certain circumstances where consent is not possible, as in personality profiling during a hostage or crisis negotiation situation. Generally, the more information gathered, the greater the confidence in the overall evaluation. Interestingly, Serin (1992) found no significant score differences under conditions of guarantee of confidentiality versus a condition where subjects were advised that testing would be part of their preparole assessment.

PCL–R Norms and Scores

The PCL–R combines elements of categorical and dimensional assessment in a format (record review and interview) potentially quite sensitive to detecting and highlighting individual differences.[6] Further, a *score* may best be considered a range of true scores, expanding in both directions by one or more standard errors of measurement (SEM) depending on context and the imperative to reduce false positives or false negatives. Apart from research, where cut-off scores for psychopathy range from about 25 to the more standard 30 points, the present authors eschew a taxon approach as needlessly limiting and fraught with additional complications. In clinical settings, we argue that a person's obtained PCL–R score is but one bit of important information obtained during interview and testing. Among considerably much more information, the score does indeed inform the clinician in probabilistic form of the individual's level or degree of psychopathy as measured by the PCL–R. Although research studies may employ a threshold PCL–R Total score as low as 25 for comparing group differences (see Harris, Rice, & Quinsey, 1994), in clinical usage, where idiographic considerations are foremost, the PCL–R true score range serves as only one anchor point around which other data are integrated and linked to recommendations specific to the particular individual referred for assessment. As clinicians, we are much more concerned with the relative weight of an individual's psychopathy level (true score range) as one piece of data for making clinical decisions than whether an individual is a psychopath.

Estimates of the prevalence of psychopathy vary considerably within and across cultures. IRT analysis (see Cooke, 1998; Cooke & Michie, 1997; Cooke, Michie, Hart, & Hare, 1999) allows for examination of an individual's score on a particular item relative to the strength of the latent trait being measured. In contrast to Classical Test Theory (CTT) analysis, IRT analysis is independent of the sample used to generate item parameters and so may be particularly well suited to cross-cultural research. Somewhat akin to the contrast between phenotype (observed expression of a gene or combination of genes given interaction with environment at large) and genotype (the genetic blueprint providing certain constraints on possible phenotypic expressions), environment or culture may be said to subtly influence behavioral expression of the presumed latent trait—in this case, psychopathy. Citing one of a number of specific item examples, Cooke (1998) noted that Scottish prisoners may require higher levels of the latent trait of psychopathy before behavioral expression of Glibness and Superficial Charm becomes apparent. A combination of similar effects with additional PCL–R items has led Cooke to suggest that a lower PCL–R score drawn from their Scottish prison samples may be roughly equivalent to a higher score drawn from an otherwise similar North American sample. Nonetheless, using this lower threshold score yielded a psychopathy prevalence estimate of only 8% in the Scottish prison sample, contrasted with a prevalence estimate of 29% in a North American prison sample (Cooke, 1998; Cooke & Michie, 1997).

Drawn from North American samples, PCL–R rating forms provide descriptive statistics for adult male prison inmates of 23.6 ($SD = 7.9$, $N = 1,192$), which contrasts only slightly with that of adult male forensic psy-

chiatric patients (Mean = 20.6, SD = 7.8, N = 440; Hare, 1991). Fairly intensive validation studies of the PCL–R with females are underway (Hare &
Hart, 1999), and a revised manual is anticipated to update and expand
coverage for a number of additional populations of interest. We should
emphasize that contextual factors such as structure, level of supervision,
and staffing interact with and influence behavioral expression of psychopathic traits. Clinicians are encouraged to become aware of baserates for
psychopathy in their particular setting, as well as the implications of even
moderate to low scores in those settings. To dramatize, a patient with a
PCL–R score of 15 to 20 might function well and without incident in a
forensic psychiatric setting, and yet bring mayhem to a subsequent community-based placement geared toward treatment of more vulnerable
seriously mentally ill patients.

Examining construct validity of the PCL–R in African-American
offenders, Kosson, Smith, and Newman (1990) concluded that the construct of psychopathy "appears tentatively applicable to Blacks although
its components may be somewhat different than for Whites" (p. 250).
Specifically, they found the following commonalities between African-
American and White offenders: (a) measures of internal consistency and
reliability of the PCL–R were generally acceptable, (b) correlations of the
PCL–R with measures of socialization were similar in the two populations, and (c) African Americans identified as psychopaths by the PCL–R,
like their White counterparts, had committed more violent and nonvio-
lent crimes and displayed greater criminal versatility than African-
American offenders not identified as psychopaths. Divergence between
the two populations was noted as: (a) larger proportions of African
Americans relative to Whites were identified as psychopaths by the
PCL–R; (b) the correlations between the PCL–R and self-report measures
of impulsivity and anxiety were weaker in African Americans than in
Whites; (c) there were some differences between African Americans and
Whites in the factor loadings of individual items; and (d) deficits in passive avoidance learning were less marked among African Americans
identified as psychopaths than among Whites identified as psychopaths,
the latter recently replicated by Newman and Schmitt (1998).

The implications of these findings for the construct validity of the
PCL–R in African Americans are unclear, except to note that, in most
cases, the raters were White, raising the possibility that racially based
rater–offender interactions influenced the scoring of some items. Second,
the correlations between the PCL–R and various self-report inventories
may be as much (or more) influenced by the nature of the inventories than
by the nature of the PCL–R. Third, the passive learning deficits found in
White psychopathic offenders are not particularly strong or consistent
across studies, and the absence of these deficits in African-American psy-

chopathic offenders could be related to racial differences in motivational factors, perceptions of the task requirements, or the fact that the experimenters in these studies all have been White. An additional factor in need of investigation has to do with the variations in acculturation within groups of White and African-American offenders. For example, the PCL-R Total and item scores of Aboriginal (Native-American) offenders in Canada who have been raised in urban settings are more or less the same as those of White offenders, whereas those of Aboriginals raised in nonurban settings differ in several respects from those of White offenders (e.g., lower PCL-R scores; R. Hare, personal communication (HJR), August 17, 1999). With respect to the current issue, we do not know to what extent the urban–rural dimension might influence scoring of the PCL-R items in African Americans (or in Whites, for that matter). Clearly, research is needed on the racial, ethnic, and cultural factors associated with psychopathy and its measurement.

Meanwhile, we do not believe that the predictive validity of the PCL-R in African-American offenders is called into question seriously by the available research and its limitations, although potential differences must always be in the clinician's mind. For example, although given that the mean score of African-American offenders is, on average, as much as three points higher than that of Whites, this does not mean that African-American offenders are more likely to be psychopaths than are White offenders. Preliminary findings from IRT analyses conducted by Cooke on reasonably large North American samples suggest that the higher mean PCL-R Total score for African-American offenders may be due to measurement differences rather than differences in the underlying trait of psychopathy (D. Cooke, personal communication (HJR), August 24, 1999). Earlier, Cooke and Michie (1997) concluded:

> Analysis based on item response theory (IRT) indicate that the performance of the PCL-R in different settings and cultural groups reveals remarkable consistency . . . (and that) there is no evidence detectable in these comparatively large samples that suggests that the test is biased due to race or presence of mental disorder. (p. 10; cited in Hare, 1998)

Although the exact magnitude of these measurement differences has not been established, they are large enough for Hare to suggest that they should be taken into account in the interpretation of PCL-R scores of African Americans to avoid the harm that may come from a spuriously high rate of false positives for psychopathy in these offenders (R. Hare, personal communication (HJR), 1999).

In all cases, sensitivity to the issue of using the PCL-R score for designating an individual as a *psychopath* (a taxon) is always relevant and a process that has been assiduously argued against throughout this text. We have emphasized using PCL-R scores as one organizing point within a much larger body of data brought to bear in clinical decisions or recommendations for the particular individual referred, in all their individuality, and relative to the particular setting, circumstances, and other relevant environmental factors at hand. At some point, norms or score adjustments for specific populations will be available. Meanwhile, as it has done with White offenders (Cooke & Michie, 1997; Cooke, Michie, Hart, & Hare, 1999), IRT analyses should be able to determine which PCL-R items are most discriminating of the construct of psychopathy in African-American offenders.

Obviously, responsible clinicians should be on the alert for new research reports that are forthcoming on this topic. In the meantime, racial differences notwithstanding, higher PCL-R scores will continue to mean greater risk for recidivism. One of us (Richards, an African American) has initiated and consulted to a large alternative to incarceration program in Maryland. It relies, to a great extent, on the PCL-R to determine risk for future dangerousness and amenability for substance abuse treatment. African Americans are over 70% of offenders assessed for the program. Program evaluation data indicate that the PCL-R significantly predicts rearrest rates, ratings of progress in treatment, and adjustment on parole. Over the last 4 years, all of the adverse incidents involving violent crime or threat of violence by individuals screened by the program have been by individuals with PCL-R Total scores above 28.[7] Confidence in the assessment process has been strengthened by the experience of correspondence between assessed and observed behavior of program participants, and by the use of a well-trained, multiracial team of program administrators, clinical supervisors, and assessors.

PCL-R RELIABILITY

Although nearly all data have been collected by rigorously trained clinicians and researchers, to our knowledge, no study has credibly challenged the reliability of the PCL-R even when mental disorder, gender, and ethnicity are considered. The test holds together well, tapping into little stray area, as judged by measures of internal consistency. Test–retest data are indicative of affective, behavioral, and interpersonal stability of the disorder, although factors that may serve to mask this presentation may yet be identified. Increasingly, evidence accrues for fibers of developmental continuity throughout the life span with certain qualifications. Interrater reliability is high, with appropriate training and periodic calibration or retraining (Gacono & Hutton, 1994; see chap. 7).

Internal Consistency. Internal consistency has not been an issue, although recent IRT analysis indicates the PCL–R might well withstand even further refinement (Cooke & Michie, 1997). Cronbach's alphas are almost universally cited above .80. Hare (1991) reported an alpha of .87 for a pooled prison sample (N = 1,192) and .85 for a pooled forensic patient sample (N = 440). Of the studies providing reliability statistics in the most recent meta-analysis by Hemphill, Hare, and Wong (1998), all Cronbach's alphas were above .80. Internal consistency in a test of this sort is much less susceptible to the types of pressures inherent to self-report tests, such as impaired comprehension, concentration, effort, or dissimulation. Cronbach's alpha is now being examined in less typical populations, such as female methadone patients (alpha = .87; Rutherford, Alterman, Cacciola, & McKay, 1996).

Interrater Reliability. PCL–R intraclass correlation coefficients (ICCs) are described by Hare (1991) as ranging from .78 to .95. Of the studies reporting reliability statistics in the most recent meta-analytic study from Hemphill et al. (1998), interrater or intraclass correlation coefficients all exceeded .80. Studying psychopathy in 376 methadone maintenance patients, Darke et al. (1998) reported weighted kappas ranging from .51 to 1.00 for PCL–R Total score, with a remarkably high interrater agreement in diagnosis of psychopathy. In a high-security forensic state hospital known for orientation toward forensic assessment, research, and training, Gacono and Hutton (1994) obtained psychologist trainee results wherein 92% of psychologist trainee full score ratings (n = 135 ratings) differed by no more than two points from that of the trainer.

Test–Retest, Age, and Stability Over Time. The standard error of measurement (SEM), which can be used to estimate test–retest reliability, is estimated to be just over three points out of a total possible score of 40 (20 items × 2 points; Hare, 1991). Using the original PCL, Cacciola, Rutherford, and Alterman (1990) obtained a 1-month test–retest reliability coefficient of .94 in a sample of 10 male methadone maintenance patients. Later, studying 1-month test–retest results in another 88 male methadone maintenance patients, Alterman, Cacciola, and Rutherford (1993) obtained similar test–retest results despite that increased information about patients at retest resulted in significantly higher PCL–R scores and more positive diagnoses.

Using a cross-sectional approach, however vulnerable to possible cohort effects and other confounds, Harpur and Hare (1994) examined PCL–R scores of 889 male prison inmates between the ages of 16 and 69. Finding a decline in Factor 2 scores with age, as well as ratings of PCL–R-defined psychopathy, the authors suggested that Factor 1 traits related to egocentrism, manipulativeness, and callousness appear to remain relatively intact over the course of the life span. From a slightly different angle, researchers are increasingly identifying a remarkably high occurrence of childhood behavior problems in the histories of adults identified as psychopathic (Harris, Rice, & Quinsey, 1994; Marshall & Cooke, 1996; Vitelli, 1998).

Last, there are indications that the PCL–R is reliable in multiple assessment contexts, and reliability results have extended to populations including African-Americans (Kosson, Smith, & Newman, 1990), forensic psychiatric patients (Gacono & Hutton, 1994; Hart & Hare, 1989), substance abusers (Rutherford, Alterman, & Cacciola, 1995; Rutherford, Alterman, Cacciola, & McKay, 1996), and women (Forth, Brown, Hart, & Hare, 1996; Neary, 1991; Rutherford et al., 1996; Strachan, 1993).

PCL–R Validity

There is much overlap between types of construct and criterion-related validity. In his article "Validity on Parole: How Can We Go Straight?", Cronbach (1980) wrote, "All validation is one, and in a sense all is construct validation" (p. 99). We use this introduction to exhort the reader's acceptance of our decision to narrow the focus of this section, group studies into construct or predictive validity, and accord factor analytic data and meta-analytic studies their own sections. We are aware that others might parse these topics differently.

Construct Validity. Ten years later, Hare's (1991) introduction to the topic of construct validity stands:

> There is increasing evidence that PCL scores are related, in appropriate ways, to a variety of clinical, self-report, and demographic variables. At the same time, they are unrelated to, or only weakly related to, variables that theoretically should not be associated with psychopathy. (p. 48)[8]

Hare (1991) described several important monomethod-multitrait studies simultaneously assessing convergent and divergent validity. Using a 10-point prototypicality procedure in rating the presence of nine *DSM–III* personality disorders and Schizophrenia in a sample of 80 male forensic patients, Hart and Hare (1989) found convergent correlations with PCL–R Total scores on Antisocial, Narcissistic, and Histrionic (.71, .39, and .33, respectively) and divergent correlations on Avoidant, Dependent, and Schizophrenia (−.30, −.27, and −.15, respectively). Examining the relationship between PCL–R scores and MMPI scale elevation in 139 male inmates, Harpur et al. (1989) obtained converging correlations on Scale 4

(.26) and Scale 9 (.27), with divergent correlations on all other clinical scales except Scale 8 (.01). In a similar study examining relationships between MCMI–II scale elevations and PCL–R scores in 119 male inmates, Hart, Forth, and Hare (1991) obtained the largest converging correlations on Antisocial (.45), Aggressive-Sadistic (.36), Thought Disorder (.34), and Delusional Disorder scales (.37), with the greatest divergence noted on Dependent (–.20), Anxiety (–.16), and Dysthymic (–.13).

More recently, construct validity has been examined in a number of populations. Salekin, Rogers, and Sewell (1997) employed a multitrait-multimethod approach (Campbell & Fiske, 1959) with female offenders and obtained expected convergence and divergence with the PCL–R relative to the Antisocial Scale of Personality Assessment Inventory, Antisocial Scale of Personality Disorder Examination, as well as staff ratings of violence, verbal aggression, manipulativeness, lack of remorse, and noncompliance. Divergence with the PCL–R was noted on somatic complaints and hysteroid personality features.

Examining *DSM* Axis I and Axis II diagnoses in 251 male methadone patients, Rutherford, Alterman, and Cacciola (1997) found strong correlations between PCL–R scores and diagnosis of Cluster B personality disorders, with much lower correlations with Axis I diagnoses (less alcohol- and substance-related disorders). Examining Danish male forensic patients, Stalenheim and von Knorring (1996) found that PCL–R-defined psychopathy positively correlated with the presence of substance use disorders and diagnoses of antisocial and borderline personality disorders (*DSM–III–R*, American Psychiatric Association, 1980), but negatively correlated with depressive disorders.

The PCL–R has been found useful in discriminating inclusion in a number of group types: Rapists most likely to be classified as an opportunistic/angry subtype (Brown & Forth, 1997), as perpetrators of instrumental versus reactive violence (Cornell et al., 1996), as successfully malingered insanity acquittees versus nonmalingered acquittees (Gacono, Meloy, Sheppard, Speth, & Roske, 1995), as belonging to a group of child molesters that killed their victims versus those that did not (Firestone, Bradford, Greenberg, Larose, & Curry, 1998), as more prone to treatment failure (Hughes, Hogue, Hollin, & Champion, 1997), as demonstrating impairment in object relations and reality testing on the Bell Object Relations and Reality Testing Inventory (Rutherford, Alterman, Cacciola, McKay, 1996), and as more likely than other offender groups to have engaged in the offense of fraud (Haapasalo, 1994).

Predictive Validity. Predictive validity is particularly important to risk assessment and is discussed further in the following section on meta-analysis. Advances in prediction of dangerousness have been criticized as hampered by the idiosyncratic use of an admixture of theoretically and methodologically weak predictor variables (Monahan & Steadman, 1994). Successful prediction of relatively low-frequency events can be particularly difficult to accomplish, especially when efforts are made to screen the event—such as a violent crime—from public attention.

Early data indicate that the PCL might provide significant incremental validity, and perhaps stand solidly on its own, in the prediction violence and recidivism. Hart, Kropp, and Hare (1988) examined PCL scores of 231 male offenders participating in an early release program in Canada. Among three groups, psychopaths (PCL score 34 and above; n = 69), nonpsychopaths (PCL score 24 and below; n = 68), and a middle group (PCL score 23–33; n = 94) violated conditions of release at a rate of 65%, 24%, and 49%, respectively, and had a probability of remaining out of prison for at least 1 year of .38, .80, and .54, respectively. Moreover, members of the psychopathic group were found to be four times more likely to commit a violent offense than those identified as nonpsychopathic.

Again using the initial PCL, Harris, Rice, and Cormier (1991) conducted a postdictive file-only study that is remarkable on several counts, including the low score used to designate psychopathy (PCL = 25+), the length of follow-up (approximate average was 10 years), and the examination of approximately 50 other potential predictive variables relative to the Psychopathy Checklist. Subjects were a group of 169 male mentally disordered offenders released from a maximum security psychiatric hospital. Violent failure or reoffense was set as the (dichotomous) dependent measure. Results indicate that 40 of the 52 psychopaths violently recidivated, whereas only 24 of the 114 nonpsychopathic patients did so—an almost fourfold difference between groups. The best 16 non-PCL multiple-regression variables, including previous violent offense, predicted violent reoffense with a relative improvement over chance (RIOC, where chance for a dichotomous outcome is 50–50) of approximately 51.5%, with the PCL alone producing an RIOC of 62.4%.

Since these early studies, the PCL–R has been found useful as a predictor of behavior in a number of different settings: violent behavior in forensic hospitals (Pham, Remy, Dailliet, & Lienard, 1998); other drug (cocaine) use in methadone patients (Alterman, Rutherford, Cacciola, McKay, & Boardman, 1998); recidivism in female offenders (Salekin, Rogers, Ustad, & Sewell, 1998); general as well as violent recidivism in a random sample of 298 male prison inmates (Wong, 1995); inpatient and postdischarge aggression in 218 male forensic psychiatric patients (Heilbrun et al., 1998); violent recidivism in male offenders (Rice & Harris, 1995; Serin, 1996; Serin & Amos, 1995); and sexual/violent reoffense in released violent sexual offenders (Furr, 1993).

In some contrast, Firestone, Bradford, McCoy, Greenberg, Curry, and Larose (1998) found the PCL-R of limited use in predicting sexual, violent, or any criminal recidivism in a group of convicted male rapists. Quinsey, Lalumiere, Rice, and Harris (1995), although using the PCL-R as one variable in two actuarial prediction equations (one for violent reoffense and one for sexual reoffense) with a large group of sexual offenders (see chap. 14), noted that PCL-R scores alone accounted for only a small amount of variance in either regression analysis. However, one must note that an intuitive interpretation of analysis of variance (ANOVA) in cases where the dependent measure involves a dichotomous variable may lead the casual reader to mistakenly underestimate the predictive value of psychopathy (Hare & Hart, 1999; see also Cohen, 1988). This tends to be much more readily appreciable when data are presented in the form of group odds ratios or survival curves and preferably with the use of recommended PCL-R cutoff scores to establish groups. Indeed, again examining findings in a large group of sexual offenders, Quinsey, Rice, and Harris (1995) found that the 1-year violent recidivism rate for psychopaths was five times that of nonpsychopaths.

Meta-Analytic Studies

Meta-analysis involves a set of statistical procedures that allows for examination of effects of a particular variable, such as psychopathy, across multiple independent studies. Data are typically summarized in terms of effect size,[9] which, in studies using trait or dispositional variables to predict circumscribed behaviors, have traditionally been rather modest.

In an early meta-analysis of the PCL/PCL-R, Simourd, Bonta, Andrews, and Hoge (1990) obtained a combined recidivism (reincarceration, parole violation, violent offense) mean effect size of .28, with an effect size of .25 for violent reoffense. In a meta-analysis of four studies and 200 male prison inmates, Hemphill, Hart, and Hare (1994) found a consistent moderate association between psychopathy and drug abuse/dependence. A meta-analysis by Hemphill and Hare (1995) found that both PCL-R factors contributed to prediction of violent recidivism, whereas Factor 2 (social deviance) was stronger than Factor 1 (interpersonal/affective dimensions) in predicting general (nonviolent) recidivism.

Salekin, Rogers, and Sewell (1996) reported moderate to strong effect sizes in their examination of 18 studies investigating the relationship between the PCL/PCL-R/PCL:SV and violent and nonviolent recidivism. Using 18 studies (prediction and postdiction studies, all with at least a 1-year follow-up period to track reoffense), heterogeneity of effect size was rejected, thus providing greater assurance for the pooling of data across studies.[10] Meta-analysis produced an average psychopathy effect size of .68 across the combined 18 studies. The mean effect size of 13 studies of violence was .79, with a high of 1.92 in a study using the PCL:SV to predict institutional aggression in a psychiatric facility (Hill, Rogers, & Bickford, 1996) and a low of .42 in a postdictive study of violent offenses (Kosson et al., 1990). Three studies examining sexual sadism and deviant sexual arousal produced a mean psychopathy effect size of .61. The one study predicting sexual sadism using the PCL–R obtained an effect size of .77, with Factor 2 having a substantially larger contribution to the prediction (.73) relative to Factor 1 (.42). The 10 studies examining prediction of general recidivism produced a mean effect size of .55, with a range of .93 (examining prediction of recidivism while on community release; Serin, Peters, & Barabaree, 1990) to .24 in a study predicting recidivism in youthful offenders (Forth et al., 1990).

We close with the most recent meta-analytic study wherein Hemphill, Hare, and Wong (1998) examined seven recidivism prediction studies, each with a follow-up period of at least 1 year. The combined subject pool of this meta-analysis consisted of just over 2,800 predominantly White male offenders, including adolescent offenders, rapists, child molesters, violent offenders, mentally disordered and schizophrenic offenders, and treated and untreated offenders. The legal status categories of the offenders included accused persons found not competent to stand trial, NCR offenders, and sentenced offenders, with a full range of security levels represented. The authors examined general recidivism, violent recidivism, and sexual recidivism and compared the PCL–R to other risk assessment instruments.

The Hemphill et al. (1998) meta-analysis produced PCL–R score correlations,[11] weighted by degrees of freedom, of .27 for predicting general recidivism, .27 predicting violent recidivism, and .23 predicting sexual recidivism, which are discussed in order next. Across the six studies examining general recidivism, the average correlation of .27 had a range of .10 (in treated nonpsychotic patients from Hemphill, 1992) to .39 in a group of incarcerated inmates (Ross et al., 1992). Findings indicate that general recidivism was more highly correlated with PCL–R Factor 2 than PCL–R Factor 1. General recidivism rate within 1 year was approximately three times higher in psychopaths relative to nonpsychopaths. As anticipated, PCL–R group classification (low, medium, high) was related to general recidivism in the expected direction. Demographic and criminal history data collected in the studies did not contribute unique information for prediction of general recidivism over that offered by the PCL–R. The PCL–R was more strongly associated with general recidivism than *DSM–III* personality diagnoses, including ASPD. Of the studies examining actuarial prediction formulas (e.g., LSI, SIR, VRAG), the

PCL-R had a similar and expected predictive relationship to general recidivism and added significant incremental predictive strength to respective regression equations.

Classification by level of psychopathy was significantly related to violent recidivism, such that offenders with low, medium, or high scores demonstrated significantly different rates of violent reoffense. Unlike general recidivism, which was more strongly associated with Factor 2, violent recidivism was not particularly more associated with either of the two PCL-R factors. Also, unlike the findings for general recidivism, the relationship of the PCL-R to violent recidivism was statistically less homogeneous across studies, indicating less consistent findings of effect size across methods and samples. In the first year of track, and across all subjects with a history of violence, psychopathic offenders were three to five times more likely to violently recidivate than offenders identified as nonpsychopathic. The one prospective study of sexual recidivism (Quinsey et al., 1995) found a correlation of .23 between the PCL-R Total score and reoffending in a group of sexual offenders undergoing pretrial psychiatric assessments.

Table 3.3 is adapted with modification from a recent and particularly engaging workshop presented by Hare and Hart (1999) to provide the reader with an overview of general PCL findings before moving to the PCL:SV. There are only so many ways to report that, relative to nonpsychopaths, psychopaths recidivate, including violently, at a much higher rate, continue to do so while mere criminals may not, and appear unusually adept at withstanding most efforts made in the name of treatment or rehabilitation (Gacono et al., 2000).

PSYCHOPATHY CHECKLIST: SCREENING VERSION (PCL:SV)

The 12-item PCL:SV (Hart, Cox, & Hare, 1995) is an abridged screening version of the PCL-R. It shows great promise as a research tool and a screen for identifying persons requiring further assessment; it was not designed for diagnostic or predictive use or to replace the PCL-R (see S. Stein in Hart et al., 1995). Again, ratings are made on a scale of zero to two, with a maximum possible score of 24. Although research examining the use of the PCL:SV continues to generate results indicative of sound reliability and validity, the PCL-R remains the *sine qua non* for assessment of psychopathy. A cutoff score ≤ 12 yields near 100% specificity that psychopathy does not exist. Scores of ≥ 13 signal the need for further evaluation with the PCL-R, and scores ≥ 18 yield a sensitivity of 100% with a specificity of 82%. Preliminary results using a Receiver Operating Char-

TABLE 3.3

Modified Summary of Validity Related Findings Adapted From Hare and Hart (1999)

Variable	Findings
Criminal Behavior	* Psychopaths begin their criminal careers earlier, commit more types of offenses, and offend at a higher rate than do nonpsychopaths (Cooke, 1994; DeVita et al., 1990; Haapasalo, 1994; Forth et al., 1990; Hare, 1991; Hare & McPherson, 1984; Hare et al., 1988; Kosson et al., 1990; Serin, 1991; Smith & Newman, 1990; Wong, 1984). * There is some evidence of burnout in the antisocial behavior of psychopaths (around age 35). However, this burnout holds true only for nonviolent offenses (not for violent ones). Even after age 35, psychopaths still commit crimes at a rate equal to that of serious and persistent nonpsychcpathic offenders (Hare et al., 1988; Hare & Forth, 1992; Harris et al., 1991). * Psychopathy predicts recidivism on conditional release as well as or better than do actuarial risk instruments. In general, psychopaths recidivate at a rate three or four times higher than nonpsychopaths. (Forth et al., 1990; Harris et al., 1991, 1993; Hart et al., 1988; Hodgins et al., 1992; Serin et al., 1990). * Even whiie incarcerated or institutionalized, psychopaths engage in more disruptive behavior than do nonpsychopaths (Forth et al., 1990; Hare & McPherson, 1984; Heilbrun et al., 1993; Hill et al., 1996; Ogloff et al., 1990; Rice et al., 1992; Wong, 1984; Gacono et al., 1995, 1997; Young, Justice, Erdberg, & Gacono, chap. 13, this volume). * Malingering and psychopathy significantly correlate in hospitalized insanity acquittees. Escape behavior and psychopathy correlate in forensic psychiatric patients (Gacono, Meloy, Sheppard, Speth, & Roske, 1995; Gacono, Meloy, Speth, & Roske, 1997).
Violence and Risk	* Psychopathy is a robust predictor of violence and violent recidivism even among mentally disordered offenders, where the baserate for psychopathy is much lower (Conacher & Quinsey, 1992; Forth et al., 1990; Gacono et al., 1995; Hare & Hart, 1993; Hare & McPherson, 1984; Harris et al., 1991, 1993; Heilbrun et al., 1998; Hill et al., 1996; Rice et al., 1992; Serin, 1991, 1996; Wintrup et al., 1994; Young, Justice, Erdberg, & Gacono, chap. 13, this volume).

* Psychopaths tend to engage in instrumental (predatory) violence as opposed to expressive (affective) violence. Psychopaths tend to threaten strangers with weapons and are motivated by vengeance, retribution, sadism, or money. Nonpsychopaths tend to batter, sexually assault, or use weapons against female relatives (spouses, daughters) and are motivated by anger, jealousy, or sexual arousal (Cornell et al., 1996; Meloy, 1988, 1992; Serin, 1991; Williamson et al., 1987).

* Psychopathy is associated with sexual sadism and violent recidivism among sex offenders. Rapists may be more psychopathic than other types of sexual and nonsexual offenders. Psychopathy is associated with recidivism among rapists (Barbaree et al., 1994; Dixon et al., 1995; Prentky & Knight, 1991; Quinsey et al., 1995; Rice et al., 1990; Serin et al., 1994).

* Even while incarcerated or institutionalized, psychopaths commit more violent misconducts than do nonpsychopaths (Forth et al., 1990; Gacono et al., 1995; Hare & McPherson, 1984; Heilbrun et al., 1998; Rice et al., 1992; Wong, 1984; Young, Justice, Erdberg, & Gacono, chap. 13, this volume).

* PCL–R correlates highly with actuarial risk scales – predictive validity equal or superior to other scales (Cooke, 1994; Gacono et al., 1995; Harris et al., 1991; Serin, 1996; Serin et al., 1990).

Treatment
* In studies evaluating the effectiveness of intensive milieu therapy programs for incarcerated or institutionalized offenders, psychopaths showed less motivation, effort, and improvement in treatment than did nonpsychopaths; psychopaths were also more likely to have multiple, serious, or violent security-related problems during treatment and to terminate treatment prematurely (Harris et al., 1991; Ogloff et al., 1990; Rice et al., 1992; Young, Justice, Erdberg, & Gacono, chap. 13, this volume).

* After treatment, psychopaths have a higher rate of general and violent recidivism than do nonpsychopaths; there is some evidence that milieu therapy may even increase the recidivism rate of psychopaths (Rice et al., 1992).

acteristics paradigm found that an upper cutoff of 19 maximized predictive accuracy, providing a true positive rate of 81% and a false positive rate of 15%, whereas false negative errors were reduced to nil using a lower cutoff of 12 (Cooke et al., 1999).

Items and factor loadings from the PCL:SV (Hart, Cox, & Hare, 1995) are presented in Table 3.4. A two-factor solution similar to the PCL–R has also been identified in the PCL:SV (Hart, Cox, & Hare, 1995). However, it may not be replicable in nonclinical samples (Forth, Brown, Hart, & Hare, 1996).[12] Generally, and consistent with PCL–R findings (Cooke & Michie, 1997), interpersonal and affective items, such as Lacks Remorse and Lacks Empathy, appear to be more discriminating of overall high scorers than are lifestyle-coded items, such as Adolescent Antisocial Behavior (Cooke et al., 1999).

Reliability statistics for the screening version look good. The test manual (Hart, Cox, & Hare, 1995) reported reliability statistics for 586 subjects from 11 different samples collected as part of the MacArthur Risk Study. Subjects included correctional offenders, forensic psychiatric patients, civil psychiatric patients, and university students. Item to total correlations were all above .40. Cronbach's alpha for the total score is identified as .84, with PCL:SV Parts 1 and 2 achieving alpha coefficients of .81 and .75 — a remarkable level of internal consistency given scale length.

TABLE 3.4
PCL:SV Factor Structure and IRT-Derived Discriminative Power

Item	Two-Factor Loadings	IRT Alpha
1. Superficial	I/A (.609)	1.5
2. Grandiose	I/A (.649)	1.6
3. Deceitful	I/A (.631)	1.7
4. Lacks Remorse	I/A (.851)	3.2
5. Lacks Empathy	I/A (.812)	2.9
6. Doesn't Accept Responsibility	I/A (.774)	2.4
7. Impulsive	S/D (.740)	2.0
8. Poor Behavioral Controls	S/D (.639)	1.6
9. Lacks Goals	S/D (.661)	1.6
10. Irresponsible	S/D (.803)	2.3
11. Adolescent Antisocial Behavior	S/D (.628)	1.4
12. Adult Antisocial Behavior	S/D (.756)	2.5

Note. Adapted from the original two-factor solution described by Hart, Cox, & Hare (1995). I/A identifies items and their estimated loading on the interpersonal/affective factor, whereas S/D identifies items and their estimated loading on the socially deviant lifestyle factor. Adapted from the item response theory (IRT) derivation of Cooke, Michie, Hart, and Hare (1999), higher alphas (representing the slope of the logistic curve at point of inflection on a trait by probability of response curve) are seen in items with greater discriminating power. Note that Items 4 and 5 appear particularly solid relative to Items 1 and 11.

Interrater reliability measured by intraclass correlation coefficient (ICC) for one rater was .84, .77, and .82 for Total, Part 1, and Part 2, respectively. For two raters, the ICCs were .92, .88, and .91 for Total, Part 1, and Part 2, respectively. Raters must strive to rate items independently to overcome possible halo effects. Test–retest reliability is estimated to be .91, with temporal instability accounting for no more than 17% of variance in scores. The SEM has been estimated to range from 1.34 in noncriminal/nonpsychiatric samples to 1.92 in civil psychiatric individuals, with an intermediate SEM of 1.18 in criminal offenders.

Hill, Rogers, and Bickford (1996) found the PCL:SV useful in predicting aggression and treatment noncompliance in a sample of 55 patients in a maximum security forensic psychiatric hospital. Although failing to replicate the two-factor solution in 150 male and female college students, Forth, Brown, Hart and Hare (1996) did find significant correlations between Total PCL:SV scores and symptoms of ASPD, substance use, self-reported criminal activities, and observer ratings of interpersonal behavior.

The clinician is on the safest ethical and practice grounds when using the PCL:SV in the manner for which it was designed — that is, to screen not to assess psychopathy. In this regard, the PCL:SV is extremely useful for evaluating the appropriateness of new or potential admissions, to determine the need for further PCL–R assessment, and to enhance preliminary data concerning institutional management (see chap. 7). The PCL:SV should never be used as a substitute for the PCL–R for addressing legal-forensic questions.

CONCLUSION

The PCL–R and PCL:SV represent substantial advances in the assessment of psychopathy. These instruments also represent a solid step forward in the prediction of recidivism, including violent recidivism. Appropriate use of the Psychopathy Checklists requires a level of training and experience that allows for integration of multiple sources and types of relevant information, with a sensitivity to race and ethnicity, age, gender, contextual or environmental factors impacting expression of psychopathy, as well as an awareness of contemporary developments in the field and the limitations of our expertise. Equipped with much more solid assessment procedures, we look forward to typically much more labor-intensive life span-longitudinal and cross-cultural studies to more fully elaborate the developmental history of psychopathy, to contribute to a better understanding of etiological and mitigating factors, and to form a better understanding of more effective efforts at early intervention.

ACKNOWLEDGMENT

The material presented in this chapter may not reflect the views of any of the authors' past, present, or future affiliations.

ENDNOTES

1. Terms such as *sociopathy* and *antisocial personality* mistakenly continue to be interchanged with the term *psychopathy* (Gacono et al., 2001). To reduce confusion, the authors have adopted a nomenclature to identify typology source, as in Cleckley psychopath, Hare psychopath, and *DSM–IV* Antisocial Personality Disorder (ASPD).
2. Regardless of the merits of attempting to achieve a value-free psychiatric taxa, the authors would argue that it would be difficult to imagine a set of criteria that truly capture the essence of psychopathy that would not in practice evoke some sense of antipathy.
3. Field trials for *DSM–IV* ASPD involved examination of three different sets of criteria: ICD-10, *DSM–III–R*, and a set similar in tone and substance to that of Hare and Cleckley. None of these sets was used in the *DSM–IV*. Instead, the *DSM–IV* ASPD criteria were chosen rationally by way of committee.
4. Initial PCL items were derived from a pool of over 100 items generated from two content domains: the Cleckley criteria—and behavioral, lifestyle, and criminal conduct characteristics of offenders judged to be close matches to the Cleckley prototype. A 3-point scoring procedure was adopted: (0) *absent/no*, (1) *maybe/in some respects*, and (2) *yes*. The winnowing process of item elimination was based on redundancy, problems with reliable rating of an item, and poor discrimination between individuals identified as psychopathic and nonpsychopathic offenders. Item content was further adjusted to the most clinically meaningful level of specificity or abstraction.
5. Examination of item content and clustering by way of IRT and factor analysis provides a means for better understanding the various ways in which an individual may be psychopathic and why highly psychopathic individuals may nonetheless display significant differences in how the syndrome is expressed. As examples, high Factor 1 scorers might be better known for their cold and calculated cunning, whereas high Factor 2 scorers might be perceived in terms of social deviance or identification with criminal subculture. Dr. Hare and colleagues are currently investigating the various types of presentation that might occur given the three-factor solution derived from IRT.
6. Whether personality disorders in general, and psychopathy in particular, may best be classified using a dimensional, categorical, or prototypal approach is far from clear, yet no method is necessarily incompatible the others. For example, an analogy using visible light: A prototypal color (say, azure blue-or very severe psychopathy), falls within the category *blue* (or psychopathy) and can be defined in terms of the dimensional measure, wavelength (PCL–R score = 36–40).
7. Findings consistently indicate that PCL–R scores correlate with recidivism and particularly violent recidivism, regardless of race, gender, or presence of a concurrent Axis I psychotic disorder. "Studies have found that the PCL–R predicts recidivism in samples of adolescent offenders (Gretton, 1997; Gretton, McBride, O'Shaughnessy, & Hare, 1995; Toupin, Mercier, Dery, Cote, & Hodgins, 1996), female offenders (Loucks, 1995; Zaparniuk & Paris, 1995), male federal offenders (Hemphill et al., 1998; Zamble & Palmer, 1996), forensic psychiatric patients (Hill, Rogers, & Bickford, 1996; Wintrup, Coles, Hart, & Webster, 1994), civil psychiatric patients (Douglas, Ogloff, & Nichols, 1997), Black offenders (Hemphill, Newman, & Hare, 1997), and sex offenders (Rice & Harris, 1997)" [Hemphill et al., 1998, p. 161].

8. One might contend that the interpersonal-affective presentation of certain manic or hypomanic bipolar patients might at least temporarily masquerade as psychopathic. The reverse may more often be the case and is usually resolvable by way of more detailed review of history, including response to treatment and use of a timed series of interviews and testing, including the PCL-R. Whereas bipolar disorders (and possibly attention deficit disorders) can be understood as dysregulation syndromes, separable but potentially comorbid with psychopathy, psychopaths are generally known for trait and behavioral consistency.

9. Effect size = (M1 − M2)/SD, where M1 is the mean for the psychopathic group, M2 is the mean for the nonpsychopathic group, and SD is the (pooled) standard deviation for the two groups. Thus, effect sizes are expressed in units of standard deviation.

10. Without some heterogeneity in effect size across studies, there would be little point to meta-analysis because any single study could then be considered representative of the relationship between PCL-R scores, however attained, and the outcome measure, however defined and tracked. Interestingly, similar effect sizes were noted for postdictive and predictive studies.

11. These analyses used the PCL-R as a correlational predictor variable.

12. Forth, Brown, Hart, and Hare (1996) were unable to replicate this factor structure in a sample of 150 university students, where the range of scores fell significantly lower than expected in forensic populations.

REFERENCES

Alterman, A. I., Cacciola, J. S., & Rutherford, M. J. (1993). Reliability of the Revised Psychopathy Checklist in substance abuse patients. *Psychological Assessment, 5,* 442–448.

Alterman, A., Rutherford, M., Cacciola, J., McKay, J., & Boardman, C. (1998). Prediction of seven months methadone maintenance treatment response by four measures of antisociality. *Drug and Alcohol Dependence, 49,* 217–223.

American Psychiatric Association. (1952). *Diagnostic and statistical manual of mental disorders.* Washington, DC: Author.

American Psychiatric Association. (1968). *Diagnostic and statistical manual of mental disorders* (2nd ed.). Washington, DC: Author.

American Psychiatric Association. (1980). *Diagnostic and statistical manual of mental disorders* (3rd ed.). Washington, DC: Author.

American Psychiatric Association. (1987). *Diagnostic and statistical manual of mental disorders* (3rd ed., rev.). Washington, DC: Author.

American Psychiatric Association. (1994). *Diagnostic and statistical manual of mental disorders* (4th ed.). Washington, DC: Author.

Barbaree, H., Seto, M., Serin, R., Amos, N., & Preston, D. (1994). Comparisons between sexual and nonsexual rapist subtypes. *Criminal Justice and Behavior, 21,* 95–114.

Brandt, J. R., Kennedy, W. A., Patrick, C. J., & Curtin, J. (1997). Assessment of psychopathy in a population of incarcerated adolescent offenders. *Psychological Assessment, 9,* 429–435.

Brown, S., & Forth, A. (1997). Psychopathy and sexual assault: Static risk factors, emotional precursors, and rapist subtypes. *Journal of Consulting and Clinical Psychology, 65,* 848–857.

Cacciola, J. S., Rutherford, M. J., & Alterman, A. (1990, June). *Use of the Psychopathy Checklist with opiate addicts.* Paper presented to Committee on problems In Drug Dependence, National Drug Administration, Richmond, VA.

Campbell, D. T., & Fiske, D. W. (1959). Convergent and discriminant validation by the multitrait-multimethod matrix. *Psychological Bulletin, 56,* 81–105.

Cleckley, H. (1941). *The mask of sanity.* St. Louis, MO: Mosby.

Cleckley, H. (1976). *The mask of sanity* (5th ed.). St. Louis, MO: Mosby.

Cohen, J. (1988). *Statistical power analysis for the behavioral sciences* (2nd ed.). Hillsdale, NJ: Lawrence Erlbaum Associates.

Conacher, G. N., & Quinsey, V. L. (1992). Predictably dangerous psychopaths. *The Lancet, 340,* 794.

Cooke, D. J. (1994). *Psychological disturbance in the Scottish prison system: Prevalence, precipitants, and policy.* Edinburgh: Scottish Home and Health Department.

Cooke, D. (1998). Cross-cultural aspects of psychopathy. In T. Millon (Ed.), *Psychopathy: Antisocial, criminal, and violent behaviors* (pp. 260–276). New York: Guilford.

Cooke, D. J., & Michie, C. (1997). An item response theory analysis of the Hare Psychopathy Checklist. *Psychological Assessment, 9,* 3–14.

Cooke, D. J., Michie, C., Hart, S. D., & Hare, R. D. (1999). Evaluating the screening version of the Hare Psychopathy Checklist–Revised (PCL:SV): An item response theory analysis. *Psychological Assessment, 11,* 3–13.

Cornell, D., Warren, J., Hawk, G., Stafford, E., Oram, G., & Pine, D. (1996). Psychopathy in instrumental and reactive violent offenders. *Journal of Consulting and Clinical Psychology, 64,* 783–790.

Cronbach, L. J. (1980) Validity on parole: How can we go straight? *New Directions for Testing and Measurement, 5,* 99–108.

Darke, S., Kaye, S., Finlay-Jones, R., & Hall, W. (1998). Factor structure of psychopathy among methadone maintenance patients. *Journal of Personality Disorders, 12,* 162–171.

Devita, Enegodo, Forth, A. E., & Hare, R. D. (1990). Family background of male criminal psychopaths [Abstract]. *Canadian Psychology, 31,* 346.

Dixon, M., Robinson, L., Hart, S. D., Gretton, H., McBride, M., & O'Shaugnessy, R. (1995). Crime classification manual: Reliability and validity in juvenile sex offenders [Abstract]. *Canadian Psychology, 36,* 20.

Douglas, K., Ogloff, J., & Nichols, T. (1997, June). Personality disorders and violence in civil psychiatric patients. In C. D. Webster (Chair), Personality Disorders and Violence. Symposium conducted at the meeting of the 5th International Conference on the Disorders of Personality, Vancouver, British Columbia, Canada.

Firestone, P., Bradford, J., Greenberg, D., Larose, M., & Curry, S. (1998). Homicidal and non-homicidal child molesters: Psychological, phallometric, and criminal features. *Sexual Abuse: Journal of Research and Treatment, 10,* 305–323.

Firestone, P., Bradford, J., McCoy, M., Greenberg, D., Curry, S., & Larose, M. (1998). Recidivism in convicted rapists. *Journal of the American Academy of Psychiatry and the Law, 26,* 185–200.

Forth, A. E., Brown, S. L., Hart, S. D., & Hare, R. D. (1996). The assessment of psychopathy in male and female noncriminals: Reliability and validity. *Personality and Individual Differences, 20,* 531–543.

Forth, A. E., Hart, S. D., & Hare, R. D. (1990). Assessment of psychopathy in male young offenders. *Psychological Assessment, 2,* 342–344.

Fulero, S. M. (1995). Review of the Hare Psychopathy Checklist–Revised. In J. C. Conoley & J. C. Impara (Eds.), *Twelfth Mental Measurements Yearbook* (pp. 453–454). Lincoln, NE: Buros Institute.

Furr, K. (1993). Prediction of sexual or violent recidivism among sexual offenders: A comparison of prediction instruments. *Annals of Sex Research, 6,* 271–286.

Gacono, C. B., & Hutton, H. E. (1994). Suggestions for the clinical and forensic use of the Hare Psychopathy Checklist–Revised (PCL-R). *International Journal of Law and Psychiatry, 17,* 303–317.

Gacono, C., Meloy, R., Sheppard, K., Speth, E., & Roske, A. (1995). A clinical investigation of malingering and psychopathy in hospitalized insanity acquittees. *Bulletin of the American Academy of Psychiatry and the Law, 23,* 387–397.

Gacono, C. B., Meloy, J. R., Speth, E., & Roske, A. (1997). Above the law: Escapees from a maximum security forensic hospital and psychopathy. *Journal of the American Academy of Psychiatry and the Law, 25,* 547–550.

Gacono, C. B., Nieberding, R., Owen, A., Rubel, J., & Bodholdt, R. (2001). Treating juvenile and adult offenders with conduct disorder, antisocial, and psychopathic personalities. In J. Ashford, B. Sales, & W. Reid (Eds.), *Treating adult and juvenile offenders with special needs* (pp. 99–129). Washington, DC: American Psychological Association.

Grann, M., Langstrom, N., Tengstrom, A., & Stalenheim, E. (1998). Reliability of file-based retrospective ratings of psychopathy with the PCL–R. *Journal of Personality Assessment, 70,* 416–426.

Gretton, H. (1997). *Psychopathy and recidivism from adolescence to adulthood: A ten-year retrospective follow-up.* Unpublished doctoral dissertation, University of British Columbia, Vancouver, Canada.

Gretton, H., McBride, O'Shaughnessy, R., & Hare, R. (1995, October). *Psychopathy in adolescent sex offenders: A follow-up study.* Paper presented at the 14th annual research and treatment conference for the association for the treatment of sexual abusers, New Orleans, LA.

Haapasalo, J. (1994). Types of offense among the Cleckley psychopath. *International Journal of Offender therapy and Comparative Criminology, 38,* 59–67.

Haapasalo, J., & Pulkkinen, L. (1992). The psychopathy checklist and nonviolent offender groups. *Criminal Behavior and Mental Health, 2,* 315–328.

Hare, R. D. (1980). A research scale for the assessment of psychopathy in criminal populations. *Personality and Individual Differences, 1,* 111–119.

Hare, R. D. (1991). *The Hare Psychopathy Checklist-Revised Manual.* Toronto: Multi-Health Systems.

Hare, R. D. (1993). *Without conscience: The disturbing world of the psychopaths among us.* New York: Simon & Schuster.

Hare, R. (1998). The Hare PCL–R: Some issues concerning its use and misuse. *Legal and Criminal Psychology, 3,* 99–119.

Hare, R. D., Harpur, T. J., Hakstian, R., Forth, A. E., Hart, S. D., & Newman, J. P. (1990). The Revised Psychopathy Checklist: Reliability and factor structure. *Psychological Assessment, 2,* 338–341.

Hare, R. D., & Hart, S. D. (1999, June). *Psychopathy and the PCL–R.* Workshop presented to the Department of Justice, Federal Bureau of Prisons, Washington, DC.

Hare, R. D., & McPherson, L. M. (1984). Violent and aggressive behavior by criminal psychopaths. *International Journal of Law and Psychiatry, 7,* 35–50.

Hare, R. D., McPherson, L. E., & Forth, A. E. (1988). Male psychopaths and their criminal careers. *Journal of Consulting and Clinical Psychology, 56,* 710–714.

Harpur, T. J., & Hare, R. D. (1994). Assessment of psychopathy as a function of age. *Journal of Abnormal Psychology, 103,* 604–609.

Harpur, T. J., Hare, R. D., & Hakstian (1989). Two-factor conceptualization of psychopathy: Construct validity and assessment implications. *Psychological Assessment, 1,* 6–17.

Harris, G. T., Rice, M. E., & Cormier, C. A. (1991). Psychopathy and violent recidivism. *Law and Human Behavior, 15,* 625–637.

Harris, G. T., Rice, M. E., & Quinsey, V. L. (1993). Violent recidivism of mentally disordered offenders: The development of a statistical prediction instrument. *Criminal Justice and Behavior, 20,* 315–335.

Harris, G. T., Rice, M. E., & Quinsey, V. L. (1994). Psychopathy as a taxon: Evidence that psychopaths are a discrete class. *Journal of Consulting and Clinical Psychology, 62,* 387–397.

Hart, S. D., Cox, D. N., & Hare, R. D. (1995). *Manual for the Psychopathy Checklist: Screening Version (PCL:SV).* Toronto: Multi-Health Systems.

Hart, S. D., Forth, A. E., & Hare, R. D. (1991). The MCMI-II as a measure of psychopathy. *Journal of Personality Disorders, 5,* 318–327.

Hart, S. D., & Hare, R. D. (1989). Discriminant validity of the Psychopathy Checklist in a forensic psychiatric population. *Psychological Assessment, 1,* 211–218.

Hart, S. D., Kropp, P. R., & Hare, R. D. (1988). Performance of male psychopaths following conditional release from prison. *Journal of Consulting and Clinical Psychology, 56,* 227–232.

Heilbrun, K., Hart, S., Hare, R., Gustafson, D., Nunez, C., & White, A. (1998). Inpatient and postdischarge aggression in mentally disordered offenders: The role of psychopathy. *Journal of Interpersonal Violence, 13,* 514–527.

Hemphill, J., & Hare, R. (1995). Psychopathy checklist factor scores and recidivism. *Issues in Criminological and Legal Psychology, 24,* 68–73.

Hemphill, J., Hare, R., & Wong, S. (1998). Psychopathy and recidivism: A review. *Legal and Criminological Psychology, 3,* 139–170.

Hemphill, J., Hart, S., & Hare, R. (1994). Psychopathy and substance use. *Journal of Personality Disorders, 8,* 169–180.

Hemphill, J., Newman, J. P., & Hare, R. D. (1997). [Psychopathy and recidivism among black offenders]. Unpublished raw data.

Hemphill, J. (1992). *Psychopathy and recidivism following release from a therapeutic community treatment program.* Unpublished Master's thesis, Department of Psychology, University of Saskatchewan, Saskatoon, Saskatchewan.

Hill, C. D., Rogers, R., & Bickford, M. E. (1996). Predicting aggressive and socially disruptive behavior in a maximum security forensic psychiatric hospital. *Journal of Forensic Sciences, 41,* 56–59.

Hodgins, S., Cote, G., & Ross, D. (1992). Predictive validity of the French version of Hare's Psychopathy Checklist [Abstract]. *Canadian Psychology, 33,* 301.

Hobson, J., & Shine, J. (1998). Measurement of psychopathy in a UK prison population referred for long-term psychotherapy. *British Journal of Criminology, 38,* 504–515.

Hughes, G., Hogue, T., Hollin, C., & Champion, H. (1997). First-stage evaluation of a treatment program for personality disordered offenders. *Journal of Forensic Psychiatry, 8,* 515–527.

Kernberg, O. F. (1975). *Borderline conditions and pathological narcissism.* New York: Jason Aronson.

Kernberg, O. F. (1984). *Severe personality disorders.* New Haven, CT: Yale University Press.

Kosson, D. S., Smith, S. S., & Newman, J. P. (1990). Evaluation of the construct validity of psychopathy in Black and White male inmates: Three preliminary studies. *Journal of Abnormal Psychology, 99,* 250–259.

Kraepelin, E. (1907). *Clinical psychiatry* (A. R. Diefendorf, Trans.). New York: Macmillan.

Loucks, A. (1995). *Criminal behavior, violent behavior, and prison maladjustment in federal female offenders.* Unpublished doctoral dissertation. Queen's University, Kingston, Ontario, Canada.

Marshall, L., & Cooke, D. J. (1996). The role of childhood experiences in the aetiology of psychopathy. In D. J. Cooke, A. E. Forth, J. P. Newman, & R. D. Hare (Eds.), *Issues in Criminological and legal psychology: No. 24. International perspectives on psychopathy* (pp. 107–108). Leicester, UK: British Psychological Society.

Meloy, J. R. (1988). *The psychopathic mind: Origins, dynamics, and treatment.* Northvale, NJ: Jason Aronson.

Meloy, J. R. (1992). *Violent attachments.* Northvale, NJ: Jason Aronson.

Millon, T. (1981). *Disorders of personality: DSM–III, Axis II.* New York: Wiley.

Millon, T., & Davis, R. D. (1996). *Disorders of Personality: DSM–IV and Beyond* (2nd ed.). New York: Wiley.

Monahan, J., & Steadman, H. (1994). *Violence and mental disorder: Developments in risk assessment.* Washington, DC: American Psychological Association.

Neary, A. (1991). DSM–III and Psychopathy Checklist assessment of antisocial personality disorder in Black and White female felons. *Dissertation Abstracts International, 51*(7-B), 3605.

Newman, J. P., & Schmitt, W. A. (1998). Passive avoidance in psychopathic offenders: A replication and extension. *Journal of Abnormal Psychology, 107,* 527–532.

Ogloff, J., Wong, S., & Greenwood, A. (1990). Treating criminal psychopaths in a therapeutic community program. *Behavioral Sciences and the Law, 8,* 81–90.

O'Kane, A., Fawcett, D., & Blackburn, R. (1996). Psychopathy and moral reasoning: Comparison of two classifications. *Personality and Individual Differences, 20,* 505–514.

Pham, T., Remy, S., Dailliet, A., & Lienard, L. (1998). Psychopathy and evaluation of violent behavior in a psychiatric security milieu. *Encephale, 24,* 173–179.

Pinel, P. (1806). *A treatise on insanity* (D. Davis, Trans.). New York: Hafner.

Prentky, P., & Knight, R. (1991). Identifying critical dimensions for discriminating among rapists. *Journal of Consulting and Clinical Psychology, 59,* 643–661.

Quinsey, V. L., Harris, G. T., Rice, M. E., & Cormier, C. A. (1998). *Violent offenders: Appraising and managing risk.* Washington, DC: American Psychological Association.

Quinsey, V. L., Lalumiere, M. L., Rice, M. E., & Harris, G. T. (1995). Predicting sexual offenses. In J. C. Campbell (Ed.), *Assessing dangerousness: Violence by sexual offenders, batterers, and child abusers* (pp. 114–137). Thousand Oaks, CA: Sage.

Quinsey, V. L., Rice, M. E., & Harris, G. T. (1995). Actuarial prediction of sexual recidivism. *Journal of Interpersonal Violence, 10,* 85–105.

Raine, A. (1985). A psychometric assessment of Hare's checklist for psychopathy in an English prison population. *British Journal of Clinical Psychology, 24,* 247–258.

Rice, M. E., & Harris, G. T. (1995). Psychopathy, schizophrenia, alcohol abuse, and violent recidivism. *International Journal of Law and Psychiatry, 18,* 333–342.

Rice, M. E., Harris, G. T., & Cormier, C. A. (1992). An evaluation of a maximum security therapeutic community for psychopaths and other mentally disordered offenders. *Law and Human Behavior, 16,* 399–412.

Rice, M. E., Harris, G. T., & Quinsey, V. L. (1990). A follow up of rapists assessed in a maximum security psychiatric facility. *Journal of Interpersonal Violence, 4,* 435–448.

Rice, M. E., & Harris, G. T. (1997). Cross-validation and extension of the violence risk appraisal guide for child molesters and rapists. *Law and Human Behavior, 21,* 231–241.

Robins, L. (1966). *Deviant children grown up.* Baltimore: Williams & Wilkens.

Ross, D., Hodgins, S., & Cote, G. (1992). *The predictive validity of the French Psychopathy Checklist: Male inmates on parole.* Montreal, Quebec: Report No. 29, Department of Psychology, University of Montreal.

Rutherford, M., Alterman, A., Cacciola, J., & McKay, J. (1996). Object relations and reality testing in psychopathic and antisocial methadone patients. *Journal of Personality Disorders, 10,* 312–320.

Rutherford, M., Alterman, A., Cacciola, J., McKay, J., & Cook, T. (1997). Validity of the Psychopathy Checklist–Revised in male methadone patients. *Drug and Alcohol Dependence, 44,* 143–149.

Salekin, R., Rogers, R., & Sewell, K. (1996). A review and meta-analysis of the Psychopathy Checklist and Psychopathy Checklist–Revised: Predictive validity of dangerousness. *Clinical Psychology: Science and Practice, 3,* 203–215.

Salekin, R., Rogers, R., & Sewell, K. (1997). Construct validity of psychopathy in a female offender sample: A multitrait-multimethod evaluation. *Journal of Abnormal Psychology, 106,* 576–585.

Salekin, R., Rogers, R., Ustad, K., & Sewel, K. (1998). Psychopathy and recidivism among female inmates. *Law and Human Behavior, 22,* 109–128.

Serin, R. C. (1991). Psychopathy and violence in criminals. *Journal of Interpersonal Violence, 6,* 423–431.

Serin, R. C. (1992). The clinical application of the Psychopathy Checklist–Revised (PCL–R) in a prison population. *Journal of Clinical Psychology, 48*, 637–642.

Serin, R. C. (1993). Diagnosis of psychopathy with and without an interview. *Journal of Clinical Psychology, 49*, 367–372.

Serin, R. C. (1996). Violent recidivism in criminal psychopaths. *Law and Human Behavior, 20*, 207–217.

Serin, R. C., & Amos, N. L. (1995). The role of psychopathy in the assessment of dangerousness. *International Journal of Law and Psychiatry, 18*, 231–238.

Serin, R. C., Malcolm, P. B., Khanna, A., & Barbaree, H. E. (1994). Psychopathy and deviant sexual arousal in incarcerated sexual offenders. *Journal of Interpersonal Violence, 9*, 3–11.

Serin, R. C., Peters, R. D., & Barbaree, H. E. (1990). Predictors of psychopathy and release outcome in a criminal population. *Psychological Assessment, 2*, 419–422.

Simourd, D., Bonta, J., Andrews, D., & Hoge, R. D. (1990). Criminal behavior and psychopaths: A meta-analysis [Abstract]. *Canadian Psychology, 31*, 347.

Smith, S. S., & Newman, J. P. (1990). Alcohol and drug abuse/dependence disorders in psychopathic and nonpsychopathic criminal offenders. *Journal of Abnormal Psychology, 99*, 430–439.

Stalenheim, E. G., & von Knorring, L. (1996). Psychopathy and Axis I and Axis II psychiatric disorders in a forensic psychiatric population in Sweden. *Acta Psychiatrica Scandinavica, 94*, 217–223.

Strachan, C. E. (1993). *The assessment of psychopathy in female offenders.* Unpublished doctoral dissertation, University of British Columbia, Vancouver, British Columbia.

Templeman, R., & Wong, S. (1994). Determining the factor structure of the Psychopathy Checklist: A converging approach. *Multivariate Experimental Clinical Research, 10*, 157–166.

Toupin, J., Mercier, H., Dery, M., Cote, G., & Hodgins, S. (1996). Validity of the PCL–R for adolescents. In D. Cooke, A. Forth, J. Newman, & R. Hare (Eds.), *Issues in criminological and legal psychology: 24. International Perspectives on Psychopathy* (pp. 143–145). Leicester, England: British Psychological Society.

Vitelli, J. E., Smith, S. S., Brinkley, C. A., & Newman, J. P. (1998). *Evaluating the Psychopathy Checklist–Revised in female offenders.* Submitted for publication.

Vitelli, R. (1998). Childhood disruptive behavior disorders and adult psychopathy. *American Journal of Forensic Psychology, 16*, 29–37.

Williamson, S. E., Hare, R. D., & Wong, S. (1987). Violence: Criminal psychopaths and their victims. *Canadian Journal of Behavioral Science, 19*, 454–462.

Wintrup, A., Coles, M., Hart, S., & Webster, C. D. (1994). The predictive validity of the PCL–R in high-risk mentally disordered offenders [Abstract]. *Canadian Psychology, 35*, 47.

Wong, S. (1984). *Criminal and institutional behaviors of psychopaths.* Ottawa: Ministry of the Solicitor-General of Canada.

Wong, S. (1988). Is Hare's Psychopathy Checklist reliable without the interview? *Psychological Reports, 62*, 931–934.

Wong, S. (1995). Recidivism and criminal career profiles of psychopaths: A longitudinal study. *Issues in Criminological and Legal Psychology, 24*, 147–152.

Zamble, F., & Palmer, W. (1996). Prediction of recidivism using psychopathy and other psychologically meaningful variables. In D. Cooke, A. Forth, J. Newman, & R. Hare (Eds.), *Issues in criminological and legal psychology: 24. International perspective on psychopathy* (pp. 153–156). Leicester, England: British Psychological Society.

Zaparniuk, J., & Paris, R. (1995, April). *Female psychopaths: Violence and recidivism.* Paper presented at a conference entitled "Mental Disorder and Criminal Justice: Changes, Challenges, and Solutions," Vancouver, British Columbia, Canada.

4

Experimental Investigations of Information-Processing Deficiencies in Psychopaths: Implications for Diagnosis and Treatment

John F. Wallace
Carroll Regional Counseling Center, Carroll, Iowa

William A. Schmitt, Jennifer E. Vitale,
& Joseph P. Newman
University of Wisconsin, Madison

In recent years, psychopathy has become an increasingly prominent construct in the field of criminal justice. Its growing importance is due largely to the development and use of the Psychopathy Checklist (PCL; Hare, 1980) and the Psychopathy Checklist–Revised (PCL–R; Hare, 1991), which have afforded clinicians and researchers highly reliable and valid methods of assessing psychopathy (e.g., Hare, 1996). Although their numbers in the general population are small, psychopaths contribute disproportionately to the prison population—on the order of 15% to 25% (Hare, 1996). Moreover, psychopathic offenders (i.e., those who attain high PCL or PCL–R scores) commit more than twice as many crimes and, compared with nonpsychopaths, are two to five times more likely to reoffend (Hare, 1996; Hemphill, Templeman, Wong, & Hare, 1998; Kosson, Smith, & Newman, 1990; Serin, 1996). For example, Quinsey, Rice, and Harris (1995) followed a cohort of offenders for 6 years after their release from prison. These researchers found that over 80% of the psychopaths from this group committed violent offenses during that 6-year period, compared with only 20% of the nonpsychopaths.

Psychopaths' propensity for both violent and nonviolent offending has contributed substantially to interest in the construct. However, investigators have disagreed as to whether psychopathy is primarily a predisposition to commit antisocial acts or reflects a more general affective or cognitive deficit. The latter view is epitomized by the writings of Cleckley (e.g., 1976), which have contributed greatly to the modern conceptualization of psychopathy.

For instance, Cleckley (1976) proposed that antisocial behavior does not constitute an essential feature of psychopathy and, indeed, that psychopaths are not particularly prone to strong impulses or urges of any sort. Rather, given even a relatively modest impulse (i.e., a response set or behavioral goal), psychopaths are unlikely to exercise restraint.

It was also proposed by Cleckley (1976) that the behavioral manifestations of psychopathy result from a profound psychological (i.e., affective and/or information-processing) deficit that acts as a predisposition to behave in ways that are harmful both to the psychopath and society. He acknowledged that psychopaths present a convincing *mask of sanity* that includes superficial charm, good intelligence, and absence of irrational thinking. Nonetheless, they typically are unreliable, insincere, impulsive, egocentric, afflicted by poor judgment, and relatively incapable of shame or remorse (Cleckley, 1976).

Cleckley (1976) observed that, "in complex matters of judgment involving ethical, emotional, and other evaluational factors . . . [the psychopath] shows no evidence of a defect. So long as the test is verbal or otherwise abstract, so long as he is not a direct participant, he shows that he knows his way about." Nevertheless, "when the test of action comes to him we soon find ample evidence of his deficiency" (p. 346). That is, psychopaths have the capacity for sound judgment and genuine affect, but the information required for these activities is less accessible when they are engaged in goal-directed behavior.

Numerous examples exist in the clinical literature. For example: "I always know damn well I shouldn't do these things, that they're the same as what brought me to grief before. I haven't forgotten anything. It's just that when the time comes I don't think of anything else. I don't think of anything but what I want now" (Grant, 1977, p. 60). In summary, although antisocial or criminal behavior may be the most conspicuous feature of psychopathy, the lack of ability to regulate or adjust a response set may be the most integral.

However, notwithstanding the demonstrated utility of the construct, as well as its substantial clinical history, the *Diagnostic and Statistical Manual of Mental Disorders* (4th ed. [*DSM–IV*]; American Psychiatric Association, 1994) does not recognize psychopathy as a unique psychiatric diagnosis. Rather, individuals who meet the PCL–R criteria for psychopathy are likely to be diagnosed as suffering from antisocial personality disorder (ASPD). In addition, whereas Cleckley (1976) suggested that psychological factors, rather than criminal and antisocial behavior, are the defining features of psychopathy, the *DSM–IV* ASPD diagnosis is based primarily on behavioral criteria, such as the repeated commission of illegal acts, deceitfulness, impulsivity, irritability, aggressiveness, and disregard for the safety of self or others.

INFORMATION-PROCESSING DEFICIENCIES
IN PSYCHOPATHS

This chapter discusses why psychopaths should be considered distinct from other ASPD individuals for the purposes of diagnosis and treatment. Central to these arguments is the distinction between *cognitive deficiencies* and *cognitive distortions*. According to Kendall and Dobson (1993), a cognitive deficiency involves a lack or deficit in some specific type of information-processing activity (e.g., amnestic disorders, which entail an inability to learn new information or to recall previously learned information). Cognitive distortions, on the other hand, are the result of intact, but dysfunctional, processes (e.g., excessively negative thoughts about oneself, one's current life situation, and one's future [the negative cognitive triad]; Beck, 1967, 1976).

We hypothesize that psychopaths' diminished ability to anticipate potential adverse consequences of their actions and profit from past experience results from several related cognitive deficiencies, rather than from cognitive distortions. One of these is a deficit in *response modulation* (Patterson & Newman, 1993), which entails brief and relatively automatic shifts of attention from the organization and implementation of goal-directed behavior to the evaluation of the ongoing behavior or the current response set (see also Newman & Wallace, 1993). This type of attentional shift is an *automatic* information-processing activity in that it involves a fast, fairly effortless process, which can occur in parallel with other information-processing activities (e.g., Schneider, Dumais, & Shiffrin, 1984). Such processes are activated automatically and do not require conscious control or attention to function properly (e.g., Schneider & Shiffrin, 1977).

One important function of response modulation is the initiation of *self-regulatory processes*. Self-regulation entails three conceptually distinct phases: (a) self-monitoring, or carefully observing one's own behavior; (b) self-evaluation, or comparing one's observed performance with one's performance standards; and (c) self-reinforcement, or one's positive or negative reactions to the self-evaluation (Kanfer & Gaelick, 1986). Each of these phases entails *controlled* information processing (Kanfer & Gaelick, 1986), which is a relatively slow processing mode that requires effort and conscious attention (e.g., Schneider et al., 1984). Should attention be drawn elsewhere, a controlled process (e.g., adding a column of numbers) ceases to operate.

When self-regulatory processes are functioning properly, behavior that is judged to be appropriate is continued. If available information indicates that a relatively minor modification is necessary, then the appropriate adjustments are made in the ongoing behavior. Finally, if the behavior is judged to be inappropriate or maladaptive, then it is inhibited and replaced with another response strategy or set.

In summary, the relatively automatic attentional process involved in response modulation is the initial link in a causal chain that culminates in the initiation of higher order (i.e., controlled) cognitive processes that are fundamental to adaptive self-regulation (see Patterson & Newman, 1993). Therefore, because psychopaths manifest a response modulation deficit, they also suffer from impairment in their ability to engage in the controlled self-regulation of their behavior.

EXPERIMENTAL EVIDENCE

This section reviews research (see also Newman, 1998) that is relevant to the hypothesis that: (a) the automatic direction of attention to stimuli or information occurs less readily in psychopaths, but (b) this is only true when the information is peripheral to ongoing goal-directed behavior or a current response set. In other words, when engaged in goal-directed behavior, information that is not salient with respect to the immediate behavioral goal is less likely to attract the attention of psychopaths than of nonpsychopaths. It is this specific attentional deficiency that constitutes the psychopaths' impairment of the response modulation process (i.e., that causes psychopaths to be impaired in their ability to shift attention automatically from the organization and implementation of goal-directed behavior to the evaluation of that behavior).

As a consequence of this attentional deficiency, the controlled processing of peripheral stimuli also is impaired. That is, this attentional deficit results in a decreased ability to evaluate, and suspend if necessary, the current goal-directed behavior or response set (i.e., engage in controlled self-regulation). We believe that this—rather than a more general intellectual, motivational, or affective deficit—is the core feature of psychopathy.

Participants in the experiments described next were male prison inmates who were diagnosed using the PCL (Hare, 1980) or PCL–R (Hare, 1991; see chap. 3). Following the usual procedure (Hare, 1991), psychopaths were those having PCL–R scores of greater than or equal to 30.

In addition, we have used the Welsh Anxiety Scale (Welsh, 1956) to subdivide psychopaths and nonpsychopaths into high- and low-anxious subgroups. This procedure has allowed us to examine and control for the potentially confounding effects of anxiety (see Newman & Brinkley, 1997; Schmitt & Newman, 1999).

An initial series of experiments was designed to examine the extent to which psychopaths are able to use peripheral or nonsalient information to alter the primary focus of their ongoing goal-directed behavior or response set. It was predicted that psychopaths would be less able than nonpsychopaths to alter their goal-directed behavior. One experiment

(Newman, Patterson, & Kosson, 1987) utilized a computerized card game that afforded participants the opportunity to win money. By making the initial probability of winning quite high, a response set to play additional cards, and thus win more money, was established. However, the probability of winning decreased and that of losing increased as the game progressed. Hence, the participants had to alter their response set (i.e., stop playing additional cards).

As predicted, psychopaths played more cards and lost more money than did nonpsychopaths: Psychopaths were less likely to alter their response set based on the changing probabilities of the computer game, although it clearly was in their best interests to do so (see also Siegel, 1978). This sort of maladaptive response perseveration (i.e., difficulty in altering an established response set) is characteristic of the real-world behavior of the psychopath and has been observed in children who were assessed as having psychopathic tendencies (Fisher & Blair, 1998; O'Brien & Frick, 1996).

In a second study of the psychopath's difficulty in altering a response set (Newman & Kosson, 1986), participants were to press a button when designated target numbers appeared on a computer monitor and not press when nontarget numbers appeared. However, in one condition, participants won money for correct responses (button presses), which established a response set to press the button. In the other condition, participants lost money for incorrect responses, but did not win money for correct responses. Hence, a strong response set to press the button was not established in the second condition.

In the condition in which a strong set to press the button was established, psychopaths made more incorrect responses (i.e., they failed to inhibit the button-press response when a nontarget number was present). In the condition involving punishment only, psychopaths and nonpsychopaths did not differ in their task performance. This result suggests that psychopaths have difficulty in evaluating and appropriately altering their behavior primarily when a strong response set has been established or they have a clear behavioral goal.

We also have studied several other control conditions. In one, the task design induced participants at the outset of the task to process both reward and punishment contingencies. We expected this manipulation to prevent the opportunity for reward from becoming the dominant focus, thus eliminating the need to alter a response set while performing the task (Newman, Patterson, Howland, & Nichols, 1990). Other variations have promoted the processing of peripheral information by using relatively long intertrial intervals, thereby providing ample time to process less salient information (Arnett, Howland, Smith, & Newman, 1993; Newman et al., 1987). The task performance of psychopaths and nonpsychopaths did not differ under these conditions, which served to minimize the need to engage in response modulation to alter a response set (for a review, see Newman & Wallace, 1993).

This first set of experiments demonstrated that psychopaths apparently are motivated and able to make adaptive use of information (including cues for punishment) when there is no need to alter their response set. However, they tend to experience difficulties when it is necessary to process information or task requirements that are peripheral to an established response set or behavioral goal.

A second set of experiments was designed to examine the extent to which psychopaths actually fail to pause to process peripheral information. This was accomplished by recording response times after correct (i.e., rewarded) and incorrect (i.e., punished) responses. By subtracting response times following rewarded responses from response times following punishment, it was possible to determine how long participants suspended their goal-directed behavior to process unexpected, negative feedback.

In one experiment (Newman et al., 1990), participants performed a version of the number recognition task described earlier (i.e., Newman & Kosson, 1986). The main variation was that, following the response feedback, they were required to press a button a second time to initiate the next trial. Participants could spend as much (up to 5 seconds) or as little time as they liked processing the response feedback. As predicted, low-anxious psychopaths paused less following punished responses and made more incorrect responses than did low-anxious nonpsychopaths.

Moreover, for both psychopaths and nonpsychopaths, the longer that participants paused after punishment relative to pauses following reward, the fewer incorrect responses they made. Thus, the length of pausing following a punished response is an index of the extent to which feedback that is inconsistent with, or peripheral to, the current response set is processed.

In another study (Newman & Howland, 1987), a computerized version of the Wisconsin Card Sorting Task was used. Participants' task was to sort four-symbol stimulus displays on the basis of color, shape, or number of symbols. After 10 consecutive correct responses, the rule for sorting the displays was changed without warning (e.g., from sorting based on color to sorting based on shape). This required participants to revise their established sorting strategy or response set on the basis of feedback that was inconsistent with that set. Low-anxious nonpsychopaths paused after rule changes, whereas low-anxious psychopaths did not. Again, we conclude from these results that psychopaths tend to pause less and process less fully information that is peripheral to the current response set (see also Arnett, Smith, & Newman, 1997).

Furthermore, because the extent of processing of the peripheral information was related to the length of pausing, limited-capacity controlled processes were indicated as the processes that were not utilized as fully by psychopaths as by nonpsychopaths. This is because an automatic process would not be dependent on the suspending of goal-directed activity and information processing, but rather would proceed in parallel with other processing activities. In consequence, we suggest that psychopaths' voluntary or controlled processing of peripheral (i.e., nonsalient) information is inadequate. This conclusion is consistent with our hypothesis that, when engaged in goal-directed behavior, psychopaths are impaired in their ability to engage in controlled processing of the sort that is a requisite for adaptive self-regulation.

It is also noteworthy that, in all the results reported previously, there was no benefit to the psychopaths for failing to alter their response sets. Indeed, it was the psychopath, and no one else, who was deprived of monetary gain due to the failure to engage in adaptive self-regulation. Therefore, the failure to process peripheral information in these studies cannot plausibly be construed as arising from self-serving or antisocial motivations because it was detrimental to no one but the psychopath.

A current focus of our research is to determine the extent to which psychopaths' failure to process fully or utilize information that is peripheral to the current response set is associated with involuntary/automatic as well as with voluntary/controlled processes. Before reviewing our results, we discuss several experiments by other investigators that are also relevant to this research question.

In one study, Jutai and Hare (1983) examined event-related brain potentials (ERPs) that were evoked by brief tones. The index of the extent to which attention was directed to the tones was the amplitude of the N100 ERP component, which is considered to reflect primarily the involuntary or automatic direction of attention (e.g., Näätänen, 1988). Participants heard the tones either while not engaged in any other activity or while playing video games; they were told that the tones were not relevant to their task of scoring as many points as possible in the video games.

Psychopaths and nonpsychopaths did not differ in N100 amplitude when the tones were presented in the absence of a competing activity (i.e., playing a video game). Conversely, when the competing activity was introduced, the amplitude of psychopaths' N100 was significantly less than that of nonpsychopaths. That is, relative to nonpsychopaths, psychopaths were deficient in their involuntary or automatic direction of attention to the tones. Furthermore, this study demonstrated that psychopaths and nonpsychopaths do not differ substantially with respect to the automatic direction of attention when attention is not already allocated to the attain-

ment of a behavioral goal. Rather, the disparity is evident when the elicit-
ing stimulus is peripheral to ongoing goal-directed behavior.

Cleckley (1976) and others have proposed that an "inability to experience or appreciate the emotional significance of everyday life events"
(Williamson, Harpur, & Hare, 1991, p. 260) is a fundamental deficit associated with psychopathy. Williamson et al. (1991) examined this proposition in an experiment in which participants were asked to determine
whether a string of letters was a word or nonword. Previous studies have
shown that words having affective significance are identified more quickly than are words lacking a strong emotional valence. From the hypothesized emotional processing deficit, it was predicted that this effect would
be less apparent in psychopaths than in nonpsychopaths. Indeed, psychopaths did manifest smaller behavioral and electrocortical differences
in their responses to the words that had strong emotional significance.
This experiment demonstrated that the emotional significance or meaning
of the stimulus items—which was peripheral to participants' manifest
task of identifying the letter strings as words or nonwords—had less
influence on psychopaths' reactions.

Recently, we (Newman, Schmitt, & Voss, 1997) used a computerized
task developed by Gernsbacher and Faust (1991; Experiment 3) to examine whether the meaning of *affectively neutral* peripheral information
would affect the task-relevant information processing to a lesser degree in
psychopaths than in nonpsychopaths. Participants were to determine
whether two sequentially presented stimuli (e.g., the word *coat* followed
by the word *shirt*) were conceptually related. That is, they were to indicate
as rapidly as possible whether the first stimulus was related to the second
stimulus, and they won money based on the speed and accuracy of their
responses.

In addition, on each trial, an irrelevant stimulus, which participants
were told to ignore, was presented simultaneously with the first of the
relevant stimuli. This irrelevant stimulus could be distinguished from the
relevant stimuli by its appearance: If the relevant stimuli were words,
then the irrelevant stimulus was a picture and vice versa. The key to this
experiment was that the to-be-ignored irrelevant stimulus was either conceptually related or unrelated to the second of the relevant stimuli.
Although the relation of the irrelevant or peripheral stimulus to the relevant stimulus had no bearing on participants' manifest task, this relationship did have a marked effect on their task performance. Specifically,
when the two relevant stimuli were conceptually unrelated (e.g., the
words *coat* and *sweep*), but the irrelevant stimulus (e.g., a picture of a
broom presented simultaneously with the word *coat*) was conceptually
related to the second of the relevant stimuli (i.e., the word *sweep*), participants were slower to determine that the two relevant stimuli were unre-

lated (Gernsbacher & Faust, 1991). Because participants were explicitly instructed to ignore the stimulus that was irrelevant to performance of the manifest task, the interference caused by the irrelevant cue was presumed to be relatively involuntary and automatic.

As was the case with normal samples (Gernsbacher & Faust, 1991), low-anxious nonpsychopaths responded more slowly when the to-be-ignored stimulus was related to the second relevant stimulus. Conversely, low-anxious psychopaths showed no interference: They responded just as quickly when the irrelevant stimulus was related to the relevant stimulus as they did when irrelevant and relevant stimuli were unrelated. In other words, psychopaths were less affected than were nonpsychopaths by the affectively neutral peripheral information.

This finding has been replicated conceptually with a picture-word Stroop task (Schmitt & Newman, 1999), in which participants name pictures while attempting to ignore superimposed, incongruent words (see Fig. 4.1). The conflicting peripheral information (words) reliably slows the picture-naming of normal samples (Golinkoff & Rosinski, 1976; Rosinski, Golinkoff, & Kukish, 1975). Again, like normal controls, low-anxious nonpsychopaths displayed significant interference when attempting to ignore the incongruent words. Low-anxious psychopaths differed significantly from their nonpsychopathic counterparts in that their task performance was not impaired by the presence of the incongruent words.

Psychopaths' lack of responsiveness to the peripheral or task-irrelevant stimuli in these studies suggests that their attentional and controlled processing resources were not allocated to the processing of the peripheral information. If those limited-capacity information-processing resources had been allocated to the processing of the irrelevant stimuli, then some impairment in the performance of the manifest task would have been apparent (as was the case for nonpsychopaths, as well as for normal samples of participants). This suggestion, in turn, is consistent with the hypothesis that, for psychopaths, the automatic direction of attentional and controlled processing resources to peripheral information occurs less readily than is the case for nonpsychopaths.

Furthermore, because the stimuli in these two studies did not have a strong emotional valence, this result indicates that the psychopath's deficit is not dependent on the emotional content of the stimuli involved. Rather, psychopaths are less influenced by the meaning of affectively neutral stimuli as well as by the meaning of affectively significant stimuli, provided that this information is peripheral to their ongoing goal-directed behavior or response set.

Combined, the prior findings suggest that psychopaths are less likely to process adequately and revise their response strategies in accord with peripheral information that would be of benefit to them, especially while

FIG. 4.1. Picture-word Stroop task stimuli used by Schmitt and Newman. Adapted from "Automatic Semantic Processing in a Picture-Word Interference Task," by R. R. Rosinski, R. M. Golinkoff, & K. S. Kukish, 1975, *Child Development*, 46, pp. 247–253. Copyright © 1975 by Society for Research in Child Development. Adapted with permission.

they are engaged in goal-directed behavior. Moreover, this deficiency does not involve an impairment in the ability to process information when doing so is the focus of the psychopath's attention or the current response set. Psychopaths' task performance is comparable to that of nonpsychopaths when the task does not require the use of automatic processes to direct limited-capacity attentional and controlled processing resources to peripheral stimuli or information (Arnett et al., 1993; Newman & Kosson, 1986; Newman et al., 1987, 1990). Instead, the deficit involves the processing of peripheral information when this processing activity is dependent on relatively automatic shifts of attention (such as those that are involved in response modulation).

In summary, we suggest that psychopaths suffer from a deficiency in the automatic allocation of attentional and controlled processing resources. This deficit diminishes the awareness and processing of potentially useful peripheral information and consequently interferes with the ability to regulate dominant response inclinations and goal-directed activity. Note that we do not postulate a complete absence of the processing of peripheral information. Rather, under certain conditions, this sort of processing is less effective for psychopaths than for nonpsychopaths. This point is well illustrated by Jutai and Hare's (1983) psychophysiological findings: When engaged in an ongoing activity, psychopaths' N100 responses to peripheral information were not absent, but rather the amplitude was less than for nonpsychopaths.

SYNTHESIS

Unlike most people who have a substantial capacity for anticipating the consequences of their actions in a relatively automatic manner, psychopaths tend to be aware of those sorts of considerations only when they are (a) central to the current response set or ongoing activity, or (b) made salient prior to the initiation of goal-directed behavior or a response set. In other words, when information is central to the intentional or controlled focus of attention, it may be utilized readily by the psychopath. Conversely, when the information is peripheral to the current response set and its accessibility thus depends on the automatic allocation of limited-capacity cognitive resources (i.e., when those resources are engaged elsewhere), the ability to utilize that information is diminished substantially.

This emphasis on the interaction between automatic and controlled processes is compatible with Cleckley's (1976) observation that the impaired judgment shown by psychopaths is specific to circumstances in which they are engaged in goal-directed behavior. Psychopaths display little evidence of impairment when providing abstract answers to verbal questions. However, when the regulation of their behavior depends on automatic processes because attentional and controlled processing resources are allocated to the attainment of immediate goals, the impairment becomes much more pronounced. This does not mean that psychopaths are incapable of regulating behavior—only that for them the redirection of attention and hence self-regulation is more effortful (i.e., dependent on controlled processing capacity rather than on automatic processes). In consequence, the capability to utilize peripheral information is especially vulnerable to disruption when available attentional and controlled processing resources are reduced, such as when psychopaths are engaged in goal-directed behavior, when they are emotionally caught up in a situation, or when processing capacity is reduced due to the use of drugs or alcohol.

IMPLICATIONS FOR THE DIAGNOSIS
AND TREATMENT OF PSYCHOPATHY

Psychopathy and ASPD Should Be Considered
Distinct Diagnostic Entities

Cognitive therapy theorists (e.g., Beck, Freeman, & Associates, 1990; Young, 1994) propose that many psychiatric disorders, including personality disorders such as ASPD, reflect the influence of dysfunctional or maladaptive schemas. Schemas may be conceived as cognitive structures that (a) are based on past experience, (b) guide or bias information processing, and (c) may be thought of as beliefs about the self and one's physical and social environment. The function of schemas is to "serve as templates for the processing of later experience" (Young, 1994, p. 9). The results, products, or outcomes of schema-based information processing include judgments, inferences, and attributions, such as interpretations of one's own or others' actions (e.g., social inferences) and specific thoughts and expectations about the present and future.

Dysfunctional schemas give rise to judgments, interpretations, and inferences that are consistently biased in an erroneous manner (i.e., they cause cognitive distortions). For instance, one who believes that others are likely to be hostile is at risk of (a) interpreting an ambiguous or even innocuous interaction as reflecting an aggressive intent (e.g., Dodge & Crick, 1990; Dodge et al., 1990), and (b) acting in accord with this misperception (e.g., in an aggressive manner). A number of maladaptive schemas have been implicated in the manifestations of ASPD, including "I need to be the aggressor or I will be the victim" (Beck et al., 1990, p. 48), "People are there to be taken" (Beck et al., 1990, p. 26), "Others are exploitive, and therefore I'm entitled to exploit them back" (Beck et al., 1990, pp. 48–49), "If I don't push others around (or manipulate, exploit, or attack them), I will never get what I deserve" (Beck et al., 1990, p. 49), and "One should be able to do or have whatever one wants, regardless of what others consider reasonable or the cost to others" (Young, 1994, p. 59).

Although the concept of psychopathy historically has been associated with antisocial personality traits, in our view there is no necessary relationship between the hypothesized information-processing deficiency and any specific personality type. In this regard, psychopathy is similar to attention-deficit/hyperactivity disorder (ADHD): Although many persons bearing the ADHD diagnosis also exhibit significant conduct problems (e.g., have concurrent diagnoses of oppositional defiant disorder or conduct disorder [American Psychiatric Association, 1994]), conduct problems are by no means necessary features of ADHD (American Psychiatric Association, 1994). Likewise, antisocial behavior is not an essential feature of psychopathy (Cleckley, 1976). Rather, personality traits and the psychopath's information-processing anomalies are conceptually independent: Any type of personality structure (e.g., schemas that cause specific sorts of cognitive distortions) can overlie the psychopath's cognitive deficiencies (cf. Widiger, 1998).

Nevertheless, an individual's personality structure certainly influences the maladaptive manifestations of the psychopath's information-processing deficiencies (e.g., aggressive behavior, sexual improprieties, substance abuse, imprudent financial decisions, abrasive or otherwise inappropriate interpersonal behavior). Moreover, in a manner analogous to that in which ADHD constitutes a predisposition to conduct problems, so, too, a deficiency in the ability to evaluate the appropriateness of responses or response sets may lead to the sorts of life experiences (e.g., frequent interpersonal conflicts) that promote the development of antisocial schemas (e.g., "Others are hostile, therefore I am justified in taking advantage of them"). That is, this sort of information-processing deficiency is neither necessary nor sufficient to explain the psychopath's violent, antisocial behavior. However, such a deficit, combined with an antisocial cognitive or personality style, provides a compelling explanation for psychopaths' prolific criminal acts. For example, although hostile schemas would be expected to increase hostile thoughts and intentions in anyone, due to the hypothesized cognitive deficiencies, such reactions are less likely to be evaluated or inhibited by psychopaths (see also Serin & Kuriychuck, 1994).

However, clinical descriptions indicate that, even when no benefits result from noncompliance, psychopaths are less likely than nonpsychopaths to follow societal rules or norms (see also Blair, 1997). This may be, at least in part, a consequence of a decreased accessibility of adaptive schemas, rather than of the activity of schema-based information processing. Much of one's knowledge of social norms is based on prior experience and stored in schemalike cognitive structures (e.g., Nisbett & Ross, 1980). Examples of such schema-based expectations include the sequences of events that occur in familiar situations such as visiting a restaurant (e.g., being seated, ordering from a menu, dining, paying the bill, and leaving) or the understanding of what is expected when meeting with one's parole officer (e.g., expressing remorse, displaying an even temper, presenting a plan for prosocial adaptation, and conveying a commitment to succeed). Most people are able to benefit from this sort of schema-based information not only prior to initiating, but also during, social interactions, whereas psychopaths' ability to use such information is limited once they have established a response set. Thus, rather than simply being indicative of deliberate noncompliance with societal rules and expectations, the chronic violation of social norms displayed by psychopaths may also stem from their inability to access rule-related schemas once goal-directed behavior or a response set has been initiated (see also Gough, 1948).

We propose, then, that psychopathy is not fundamentally a reflection of schema-based information processing that results in cognitive distortions, as is the case for the nonpsychopath with ASPD. On the contrary, the current analysis suggests that many of the maladaptive manifestations of psychopathy are the result of failures of schema-based processes. This formulation highlights an important distinction in conceptualizing the antisocial behavior of nonpsychopathic individuals with ASPD on the one hand and of psychopaths on the other: The former intentionally or purposefully violate societal norms, whereas the latter often violate societal norms due to being momentarily oblivious to their existence. In other words, the antisocial behavior of the nonpsychopath with ASPD reflects primarily cognitive distortions, whereas specific cognitive deficiencies contribute substantially to the maladaptive and antisocial behavior of the psychopath.

For example, if a psychopath and nonpsychopath with ASPD each were to find a purse on a park bench, both might react in an antisocial manner by taking the purse and removing the valuables, rather than using identification to find the owner. Nevertheless, this same bit of behavior might occur for quite different reasons for the nonpsychopathic person with ASPD and the psychopath. For the ASPD nonpsychopath, the antisocial action presumably would be motivated by beliefs such as "People who can't take care of themselves deserve to be exploited," whereas the psychopath simply might act on his or her *good fortune* with little or no consideration of the distress that this course of action will cause to the purse's owner.

In summary, even if the behavioral manifestations at times appear similar, it does not seem to serve the purposes of diagnosis to group etiologically dissimilar persons within the same diagnostic category if the underlying causal processes markedly differ. In consequence, because the psychopathology of the psychopath in all likelihood results from cognitive processes that differ qualitatively from those that characterize the nonpsychopath with ASPD (i.e., specific information-processing deficiencies vs. normal schema-based information processing involving antisocial schemas), it is not sufficient to categorize the psychopath's problem as ASPD. Rather, psychopathy merits a separate diagnosis.

Diagnostic Implications of the PCL-R

As noted earlier, the PCL-R (Hare, 1991) is a reliable and valid measure of psychopathy (e.g., Hare, 1996) and is gaining considerable influence in the criminal justice system. However, there is some debate as to whether psychopathy — as assessed by the PCL-R — should be considered to reflect a dimensional trait or is better conceived as a discrete category. Continuous or dimensional traits are distributed to differing degrees, but appear throughout the population as a whole (e.g., height or weight). A discrete or categorical entity, on the other hand, is not distributed throughout the entire population: Some persons have it and some do not (e.g., Down syndrome).

Rather than viewing the PCL-R as assessing either the level of a dimensional trait or the presence of a categorical entity, we suggest that PCL-R scores reflect both a continuous variable and a discrete category. Two lines of evidence provide support for this conjecture. First, Vitale, Newman, and Serin (1999) examined the relationship between PCL-R scores and the tendency to make hostile attributions. The tendency to attribute the actions of others to hostile motivations may be conceived as reflecting the effects of hostile cognitive schemas, which give rise to expectations and interpretations that others are inherently inimicable or harbor aggressive intentions (e.g., Beck et al., 1990; Young, 1994). We found that hostile attributions, and hence the influence of hostile schemas, increase with PCL-R scores to approximately a score of 30 and then remain relatively constant as PCL-R scores continue to increase. That is, PCL-R scores below about 30, which is the usual cutoff score for diagnosing psychopathy, were associated with a continuum reflecting the influence of hostile schemas, whereas those above 30 (which are associated with the psychopathy diagnosis) were not. Indeed, the correlation between PCL-R scores and hostile attributions in White offenders was .371 ($p < .01$) when psychopaths were eliminated from the distribution. This correlation dropped to .274 ($p < .05$) when the psychopaths were reinserted in the sample. It dropped further, to a nonsignificant .159, when participants with midrange scores were removed from the sample (i.e., only psychopaths and controls were included). Although unconventional, these analyses clearly demonstrate that midrange, rather than high, PCL-R scores were most related to hostile attributional style.

Second, factor analytic studies of the PCL-R have consistently demonstrated the presence of two primary factors (i.e., categories or types of

PCL-R items). Factor 1 items appear to be related to the fundamental or core features of psychopathy that were emphasized by Cleckley (1976). Conversely, Factor 2 is related primarily to the commission of antisocial acts, such as those that are the focus of the diagnostic criteria for ASPD.

Analyses of PCL-R data performed by Cooke and Michie (1997) found that Factor 1 items are more strongly associated with the higher range of scores, whereas Factor 2 items are primarily associated with scores below 30. That is, the discriminating power of the items associated with Factor 2, which reflects mainly antisocial behavior, decreases markedly above the level at which a diagnosis of psychopathy commonly is ascribed. Moreover, these researchers concluded that Factor 2 items bear a strong association to environmental factors, such as socioeconomic status, educational attainment, and family of origin. However, at the higher range of PCL-R scores, the core features of psychopathy are relatively independent of the social context, and "the absence of any moderating effect of social context on Factor 1 tends to implicate biological processes" (Cooke & Michie, 1997, p. 12).

Based on these results, we suggest that PCL-R scores of less than 30 are likely to reflect differences in influence of acquired or environmentally based antisocial schemas of the sort associated with ASPD (e.g., schemas that produce erroneous hostile attributions), with lower scores indicating relatively little influence and higher scores indicating greater influence. Scores of 30 or more are indicative of the presence of the psychopathy diathesis (i.e., the attentional, response modulation, and self-regulatory deficits). In other words, we propose that the PCL-R measures both a continuous variable (i.e., the strength of antisocial schemas), which relate more strongly to PCL-R scores below 30, and a discrete variable (i.e., the presence of the hypothesized cognitive deficiencies), which becomes increasingly influential at levels of approximately 30 or more.

Although our proposal is, as yet, somewhat speculative, clinicians may wish to consider that scores from 1 to 29 are likely to reflect the strength of antisocial schemas (and the resulting cognitive distortions), such as those associated with ASPD. On the other hand, scores of 30 or more are likely to be indicative of the presence of the fundamental attentional, response modulation, and self-regulatory deficits that characterize psychopathy.

Nonetheless, we should emphasize that, although the PCL-R cutpoint of 30 is the most common value, both in research and applied settings, it should be used to generate diagnostic and treatment hypotheses only (as is the case for any psychometric assessment instrument). Some true psychopaths may score somewhat less than 30, and some ASPD nonpsychopaths may score somewhat above 30.

For example, an individual's culture or environment may influence the point at which the PCL-R score reflects primarily psychobiological cognitive deficiencies, rather than social influences that may give rise to anti-social cognitive distortions. Indeed, the proposal that both types of factors contribute to an individual's PCL–R score has the potential to clarify cross-cultural differences in the use of the PCL–R to assess psychopathy.

In samples of North American White males, the score at which PCL–R ratings reflect mainly cognitive deficiencies rather than social influences appears to be 30. However, for any particular individual, this point might vary somewhat depending on the environmental influences to which that person had been exposed. For example, if a person were raised in a rela-tively stable environment with numerous socially appropriate role models, the point at which his PCL–R score reflected primarily psychobiological rather than environmental factors might be expected to be lower than it would be for one whose social environment was characterized by high lev-els of aggression or hostility. This latter individual might attain a PCL–R score of 30 or more due primarily to the presence of high levels of antiso-cial behaviors and beliefs resulting from his less-than-optimal social envi-ronment, rather than to the presence of specific cognitive deficiencies.

Lorenz, Smith, Bolt, Schmitt, and Newman (1999) speculated that differ-ences that are evident in the laboratory performance of White and African-American offenders diagnosed as psychopaths on the basis of the PCL–R may reflect the differential influences of social and psychobiological fac-tors. A score of 30 on the PCL–R may indicate the point at which cogni-tive deficiencies begin to have the greatest influence on White offenders, whereas this may not be the case for African Americans. Thus, although we propose that both the effects of social factors (e.g., antisocial schemas and cognitive distortions) and psychobiological influences (specific infor-mation-processing deficiencies) contribute to PCL–R scores, the balance of the two may not be consistent across environments and cultures.

Nonetheless, it should be emphasized again that, for White males, the PCL–R cutpoint of 30 has been demonstrated repeatedly to predict accu-rately differences both in criminal offending (Hare, 1996; Kosson, Smith, & Newman, 1990; Quinsey et al., 1995; Serin, 1996) and in laboratory per-formance (e.g., Hare, 1996; Newman, 1998). Therefore, at least for White males, the suggestions presented in this chapter regarding the diagnostic and treatment implications of PCL–R scores have substantial plausibility.

Treatment Considerations for Psychopathy and ASPD

As just suggested, for clinical purposes, PCL–R scores of less than 30 might best be conceived as providing an assessment of a dimensional or continuous variable reflecting the strength of antisocial schemas of the sort associated with ASPD, whereas at levels of 30 or more, the cognitive deficiencies associated with psychopathy would be the preferred focus of the case formulation. In consequence, when using the PCL–R to guide treatment recommendations, it might be useful to consider separately scores of less than 30 and those of 30 and above. This follows from our view that differences in the etiological processes associated with nonpsychopathic ASPD and psychopathy (i.e., specific maladaptive schema contents vs. information-processing abnormalities) are likely to lead to differences in treatment outcomes for standard cognitive therapy interventions.

Specifically, we expect cognitive therapy to be less effective for psychopaths than for ASPD nonpsychopaths. This is because cognitive therapy presupposes that "the products of [schema-based information processing] are largely in the realm of awareness" (Beck et al., 1990, p. 5). Furthermore, the awareness of schema products (e.g., specific judgments, interpretations, and inferences) often entails the use of limited-capacity attentional and controlled information-processing resources for the processing of those cognitions. This direction or allocation of attention can occur in a controlled manner if, for example, the schema is intentionally accessed due to its relevance to the current behavioral goal or response set. Nevertheless, as discussed earlier, the direction of attention and controlled processing both to external and internal stimuli (such as schema products) often proceeds in an automatic manner (Wallace & Newman, 1997, 1998). Hence, the awareness and processing of schema products often depends on the automatic allocation of limited-capacity cognitive resources.

However, we have postulated that psychopaths suffer from a deficiency in the automatic direction of attentional and controlled processing resources to external and internal stimuli. Hence, for psychopaths, internal stimuli such as schema products receive substantially less processing from automatically allocated limited-capacity resources especially when those cognitions are peripheral to an ongoing response or response set. Consequently, schema-based information processing is less influential than would be the case for nonpsychopaths, especially after a response or response set has been initiated. Therefore, standard cognitive therapy focused on altering maladaptive schema contents is expected to be less effective for psychopaths than for nonpsychopathic individuals with ASPD or for nonpsychopaths in general.

We are not asserting that schemas and schema products are without influence in psychopaths. First, the ability of psychopaths to access schema contents or products in a controlled or intentional, rather than in an automatic, manner is comparable to that of nonpsychopaths. Second, prior to the initiation of goal-directed behavior or a response set, the accessing of schemas using automatic cognitive resource allocation is not compromised to the extent that it is subsequent to response or response set initiation.

This second point implies that schema-based processing that occurs prior to the initiation of a response set may influence the types of responses or response sets that subsequently are initiated. For example, psychopaths who, in addition to having the hypothesized information-processing deficiencies, have developed antisocial schemas are more prone to initiate antisocial responses than a psychopath whose schemas are relatively prosocial (e.g., that do not produce cognitive distortions, such as hostile attributions for others' actions).

More generally, we propose that maladaptive (as well as compensatory or otherwise adaptive) schemas are more influential for shaping the behavior of psychopaths prior to initiating response sets, whereas their information-processing deficiencies are the primary psychopathological influences once a response set has been initiated. Two conclusions follow. First, standard cognitive interventions aimed at modifying antisocial schemas are likely to have some efficacy in controlling the psychopath's premeditated antisocial behavior. However, because most persons, including psychopaths, at times experience fleeting inappropriate or antisocial thoughts and impulses, changing the antisocial schemas of psychopaths will not, in our view, significantly curtail their chronic antisocial behavior. Second, to control antisocial and other maladaptive response sets, psychopaths are likely to require compensatory strategies for circumventing their information-processing deficiencies. This is because (a) people are dependent on response modulation (i.e., automatic shifts of attention) to initiate self-regulation and modify ongoing, maladaptive responses or response sets, and (b) it is precisely this automatic attentional process, and the resulting impairment in self-regulation, that are deficient in psychopaths.

Because the research documenting the psychopath's information-processing deficiencies is relatively new, efforts to develop compensatory strategies have scarcely begun (Serin & Kuriychuck, 1994). Nevertheless, despite the dearth of relevant research, we are inclined to believe that behavioral interventions will prove to be the most effective strategies for ameliorating the psychopath's cognitive deficits and the expression of maladaptive response sets. Behavioral interventions might include rehearsing the act of pausing (i.e., establishing and strengthening a response set to pause and reflect before acting) to promote the processing of peripheral information prior to initiating a goal-directed response. Recall that the longer a person pauses before acting, the greater the likelihood that information peripheral to the current response set is processed and utilized to affect behavior in an adaptive manner (e.g., Newman et al., 1990). Moreover, experimental manipulations that promote pausing to process peripheral information have been shown to eliminate all evidence of the psychopath's deficit (Arnett et al., 1993; Newman et al., 1987).

In addition to teaching psychopaths to pause, it might be especially useful to teach the proactive avoidance of situations that require protracted self-control. The protracted self-control situation is substantially more difficult to negotiate successfully than is a situation that requires only decisional self-control (Kanfer & Gaelick, 1986). This is because the former requires continuous and prolonged resistance in the face of temptation to engage in a desirable but maladaptive action (e.g., choosing to abstain from alcohol while sitting in a bar), whereas the latter entails only a single decision that terminates the exposure to temptation (e.g., choosing not to visit the bar in the first place).

The conscious decision to engage in decisional, rather than protracted, self-control (i.e., to avoid problematic situations) most commonly occurs after pausing and reflecting on immediate response options. However, it also can be associated with long-term lifestyle choices, such as making a habit of returning home directly after work, rather than stopping off at a bar, or choosing law-abiding individuals as friends, thereby limiting exposure to others' antisocial schemas. In either case, the primary benefit of exercising decisional self-control is eliminating the necessity of engaging in the more effortful protracted self-control, which requires the use of automatic response modulation processes to monitor the appropriateness of ongoing behavior sequences or response sets.

Summary

We have proposed in this chapter that, unlike other persons bearing the ASPD diagnosis (whose psychopathology is due primarily to schema-based information processing involving antisocial schemas and cognitive distortions), psychopaths are not characterized primarily by the activity of specific dysfunctional schemas. Rather, the psychopath suffers from a more general information-processing deficiency involving the automatic direction of attention to stimuli or information that are peripheral to ongoing goal-directed behavior or a current response set. This deficiency is detrimental to the psychopath because it constitutes an impairment in the response modulation process. Response modulation (a) entails brief and relatively automatic shifts of attention from the implementation of goal-directed behavior to its evaluation, and (b) is crucial to initiating controlled processes associated with self-regulation. Because this deficiency differs qualitatively from the schema-based etiology for other ASPD individuals, and in fact decreases the influence of schema-based information processing, the present formulation implies that psychopaths and ASPD nonpsychopaths merit separate diagnoses.

We also have speculated that the primary instrument for diagnosing psychopathy—the PCL-R (Hare, 1991)—should be conceived as reflecting (a) a continuous variable (i.e., the strength of antisocial schemas of the sort associated with ASPD) at scores of less than 30, and (b) a discrete category indicating the presence of attentional, response modulation, and self-regulatory deficiencies at levels of 30 and above.

With respect to treatment implications, the range of PCL–R scores from 1 to 29 might be used to estimate the extent to which antisocial schemas and cognitive distortions are influential, and hence the extent to which standard cognitive therapy interventions aimed at altering those schemas might be useful. Cognitive interventions aimed at altering maladaptive schemas might also produce some benefit for psychopaths (i.e., those scoring 30 or above on the PCL–R) in decreasing premeditated antisocial behavior. Behavioral interventions, such as those described earlier, might aid psychopaths in compensating more directly for their attentional and response modulation deficits and, in turn, make them more likely to benefit from adaptive self-regulatory processes.

ACKNOWLEDGMENTS

Research described in this manuscript was supported by the National Institute of Mental Health. We are indebted to the Wisconsin Department of Corrections and staff at Oakhill Correctional Institution for making the research possible. Finally, we thank Chad Brinkley and Amanda Lorenz for their helpful suggestions during preparation of the manuscript.

REFERENCES

American Psychiatric Association. (1994). *Diagnostic and statistical manual of mental disorder* (4th ed.). Washington, DC: Author.

Arnett, P. A., Howland, E. W., Smith, S. S., & Newman, J. P. (1993). Autonomic responsivity during passive avoidance in incarcerated psychopaths. *Personality and Individual Differences, 14,* 173–185.

Arnett, P. A., Smith, S. S., & Newman, J. P. (1997). Approach and avoidance motivation in incarcerated psychopaths during passive avoidance. *Journal of Personality and Social Psychology, 72,* 1413–1428.

Beck, A. T. (1967). *Depression: Clinical, experimental, and theoretical aspects.* New York: Harper & Row.

Beck, A. T. (1976). *Cognitive therapy and the emotional disorders.* New York: International Universities Press.

Beck, A. T., Freeman, A., & Associates. (1990). *Cognitive therapy of personality disorders.* New York: Guilford.

Blair, R. J. R. (1997). Moral reasoning and the child with psychopathic tendencies. *Personality and Individual Differences, 22,* 731–739.

Cleckley, H. (1976). *The mask of sanity* (5th ed.). St. Louis, MO: Mosby.

Cooke, D. J., & Michie, C. (1997). An item response theory evaluation of Hare's Psychopathy Checklist–Revised. *Psychological Assessment, 9,* 2–13.

Dodge, K. A., & Crick, N. R. (l990). Social information-processing bases of aggressive behavior in children. *Personality and Social Psychology Bulletin, 16,* 8–22.

Dodge, K. A., Price, J. M., Bachorowski, J., Newman, J. P. (1990). Hostile attributional tendencies in severely aggressive adolescents. *Journal of Abnormal Psychology, 99,* 385–392.

Fisher, L., & Blair, R. J. R. (1998). Cognitive impairment and its relationship to psychopathic tendencies in children with emotional and behavioral difficulties. *Journal of Abnormal Child Psychology, 26,* 511–519.

Gernsbacher, M. A., & Faust, M. E. (1991). The mechanism of suppression: A component of general comprehension skill. *Journal of Experimental Psychology: Learning, Memory, and Cognition, 17,* 245–262.

Golinkoff, R. M., & Rosinski, R. R. (1976). Decoding, semantic processing, and reading comprehension skill. *Child Development, 47,* 252–258.

Gough, H. G. (1948). A sociological theory of psychopathy. *American Journal of Sociology, 53,* 359–366.

Grant, V. W. (1977). *The Menacing Stranger: A primer on the psychopath.* Oceanside, NY: Dabor Science Publications.

Hare, R. D. (1980). A research scale for the assessment of psychopathy in criminal populations. *Personality and Individual Differences, 1,* 111–119.

Hare, R. D. (1991). *The Hare Psychopathy Checklist–Revised.* Toronto: Multi-Health Systems.

Hare, R. D. (1996). Psychopathy: A clinical construct whose time has come. *Criminal Justice and Behavior, 23,* 25–54.

Hemphill, J. F., Templeman, R., Wong, S., & Hare, R. D. (1998). Psychopathy and crime: Recidivism and criminal careers. In D. J. Cooke, R. D. Hare, & A. Forth (Eds.), *Psychopathy: Theory, research and implications for society* (pp. 81–104). The Netherlands: Kluwer Academic Publishers.

Jutai, J. W., & Hare, R. D. (1983). Psychopathy and selective attention during performance of a complex perceptual-motor task. *Psychophysiology, 20,* 146–151.

Kanfer, F. H., & Gaelick, L. (1986). Self-management methods. In F. H. Kanfer & A. P. Goldstein (Eds.), *Helping people change: A textbook of methods* (3rd ed.). Elmsford, NY: Pergamon.

Kendall, P. C., & Dobson, K. S. (1993). On the nature of cognition. In P. C. Kendall & K. S. Dobson (Eds.), *Psychopathology and cognition* (pp. 3–17). New York: Academic Press.

Kosson, D. S., Smith, S. S., & Newman, J. P. (1990). Evaluating the construct validity of psychopathy in Black and White male inmates: Three preliminary studies. *Journal of Abnormal Psychology, 99,* 250–259.

Lorenz, A. R., Smith, S. S., Bolt, D. M., Schmitt, W. A., & Newman, J. P. (1999). *Reevaluating the construct of psychopathy in Caucasian and African American offenders,* submitted.

Näätänen, R. (1988). Implications of ERP data for psychological theories of attention. *Biological Psychology, 26,* 117–163.

Newman, J. P. (1998). Psychopathic behavior: An information processing perspective. In D. J. Cooke, R. D. Hare, & A. Forth (Eds.), *Psychopathy: Theory, research and implications for society* (pp. 81–104). The Netherlands: Kluwer Academic Publishers.

Newman, J. P., & Brinkley, C. A. (1997). Reconsidering the low-fear explanation for primary psychopathy. *Psychological Inquiry, 8,* 236–244.

Newman, J. P., & Howland, E. W. (1987). *The effect of incentives on Wisconsin Card Sorting Task performance in psychopaths.* Unpublished manuscript.

Newman, J. P., & Kosson, D. S. (1986). Passive avoidance learning in psychopathic and nonpsychopathic offenders. *Journal of Abnormal Psychology, 95,* 257–263.

Newman, J. P., Patterson, C. M., Howland, E. W., & Nichols, S. L. (1990). Passive avoidance in psychopaths: The effects of reward. *Personality and Individual Differences, 11,* 1101–1114.

Newman, J. P., Patterson, C. M., & Kosson, D. S. (1987). Response perseveration in psychopaths. *Journal of Abnormal Psychology, 96,* 145–148.

Newman, J. P., Schmitt, W. A., & Voss, W. (1997). The impact of motivationally neutral cues on psychopathic individuals: Assessing the generality of the response modulation hypothesis. *Journal of Abnormal Psychology, 106,* 563–575.

Newman, J. P., & Wallace, J. F. (1993). Psychopathy and cognition. In P. C. Kendall & K. S. Dobson (Eds.), *Psychopathology and cognition* (pp. 293–349). New York: Academic Press.

Nisbett, R., & Ross, L. (1980). *Human inference: Strategies and shortcomings of social judgment.* Englewood Cliffs, NJ: Prentice-Hall.

O'Brien, B. S., & Frick, P. J. (1996). Reward dominance: Associations with anxiety, conduct problems, and psychopathy in children. *Journal of Abnormal Child Psychology, 24,* 223–240.

Patterson, C. M., & Newman, J. P. (1993). Reflectivity and learning from aversive events: Toward a psychological mechanism for the syndromes of disinhibition. *Psychological Review, 100,* 716–736.

Quinsey, V. L., Rice, M. E., & Harris, G. T. (1995). Actuarial prediction of sexual recidivism. *Journal of Interpersonal Violence, 10,* 85–105.

Rosinski, R. R., Golinkoff, R. M., & Kukish, K. S. (1975). Automatic semantic processing in a picture-word interference task. *Child Development, 46,* 247–253.

Schmitt, W. A., & Newman, J. P. (1999). *Psychopathy and the response modulation hypothesis: Conceptual replications using Stroop-like tasks.* Manuscript submitted for publication.

Schmitt, W. A., & Newman, J. P. (1999). Are all psychopathic individuals low-anxious? *Journal of Abnormal Psychology, 108,* 353–358.

Schneider, W., Dumais, S. T., & Shiffrin, R. M (1984). Automatic and control processing and attention. In R. Parasuraman & D. R. Davies (Eds.), *Varieties of attention* (pp. 1–27). New York: Academic Press.

Schneider, W., & Shiffrin, R. M. (1977). Controlled and automatic human information processing: I. Detection, search, and attention. *Psychological Review, 84,* 1–66.

Serin, R. C. (1992). The clinical application of the Psychopathy Checklist–Revised (PCL-R) in a prison population. *Journal of Clinical Psychology, 48,* 637–642.

Serin, R. C. (1996). Violent recidivism in criminal psychopaths. *Law and Human Behavior, 20,* 207–217.

Serin, R. C., & Kuriychuck, M. (1994). Social and cognitive processing deficits in violent offenders: Implications for treatment. *International Journal of Law and Psychiatry, 17,* 431–441.

Shapiro, D. (1965). *Neurotic styles.* New York: Basic Books.

Siegel, R. A. (1978). Probability of punishment and suppression of behavior in psychopathic and nonpsychopathic offenders. *Journal of Abnormal Psychology, 87,* 514–522.

Vitale, J. E., Newman, J. P., & Serin, R. C. (1999). *Hostile attributions in incarcerated adult male offenders: An exploration of two associated pathways.* Manuscript submitted for publication.

Wallace, J. F., & Newman, J. P. (1997). Neuroticism and the attentional mediation of dysregulatory psychopathology. *Cognitive Therapy and Research, 21,* 135–156.

Wallace, J. F., & Newman, J. P. (1998). Neuroticism and the facilitation of the automatic orienting of attention. *Personality and Individual Differences, 24,* 253–266.

Welsh, G. (1956). Factor dimensions A and R. In G. S. Welsh & W. G. Dahlstrom (Eds.), *Basic readings on the MMPI in psychology and medicine* (pp. 264–281). Minneapolis: University of Minnesota Press.

Widiger, T. A. (1998). Psychopathy and normal personality. In D. J. Cooke, R. D. Hare, & A. Forth (Eds.), *Psychopathy: Theory, research and implications for society* (pp. 161–187). The Netherlands: Kluwer Academic Publishers.

Williamson, S., Harpur, T. J., & Hare, R. D. (1991). Abnormal processing of affective words by psychopaths. *Psychophysiology, 28,* 260–273.

Young, J. E. (1994). *Cognitive therapy for personality disorders: A schema-focused approach.* Sarasota, FL: Professional Resource Exchange.

Emotional Experiences of the Psychopath

Brian L. Steuerwald
Developmental Associates, Inc., Indianapolis, Indiana

David S. Kosson
Finch University of Health Sciences,
The Chicago Medical School, Illinois

Although accounts of the disorder vary, psychopathy is generally regarded as a chronic clinical condition associated with extreme egocentricity and interpersonal callousness, unusual emotional experiences, impulsivity, and an antisocial lifestyle. Most investigators and clinicians agree that the disorder (a) is manifested at a relatively early age (Hare, 1991; Robbins, 1972), (b) remains generally stable over the course of a lifetime (Hare, McPherson, & Forth, 1988), and (c) is typically resistant to successful treatment (Meloy, 1988; Millon, 1981). Given the chronicity of the disorder, its resistance to treatment, and the impact of psychopaths' behavior on themselves, others, and society, the condition is considered extremely serious.

The unusual emotional experiences associated with psychopathy occupy a central role in many descriptions of the disorder (Cleckley, 1976; Craft, 1966, McCord & McCord, 1964; Meloy, 1988; Millon, 1981; Yochelson & Samenow, 1976). In this chapter, we summarize the major theoretical positions regarding emotions and psychopathy, review relevant empirical studies, and provide preliminary suggestions for clinicians working with psychopaths, as well as suggestions for future directions. To provide a context for this discussion, we first clarify our use of the psychopathy construct.

Although a detailed history of the psychopathy construct is beyond the scope of this chapter (for such accounts, see Gacono & Meloy, 1994; Millon, 1981), it is fair to say that the history of this disorder has been marked by extensive controversy over the necessity and nature of specific psychological dysfunctions. Whereas some conceptualizations have highlighted the antisocial behavior or presumed moral depravity of the psychopath (e.g., American Psychiatric Association [APA], 1987; Pritchard, 1835; Rush, 1812), others have focused on underlying personality structures or psychological functions (Cleckley, 1976; Meloy, 1988; Millon, 1981). Still other conceptualizations have suggested a "catch-all" category for various disturbances that did not readily fit into other forms of psychopathology (e.g., Koch, 1889; cited in Millon, 1981).

Our conceptualization of psychopathy is most consistent with the clinical descriptions presented by Cleckley (1976) and Hare (1991). Originally published in 1941, Cleckley posited 16 characteristics of the disorder. Of particular relevance to this chapter, four of these characteristics directly addressed emotional function in the psychopath: absence of nervousness, general poverty of major affective reactions, lack of guilt and remorse, and incapacity for deep affectional bonds. Although Cleckley's account of the condition was mainly descriptive, he proposed that the psychopath suffers from a dissociation between emotion and cognition. Consequently, the psychopath is unable to use emotional reactions to modify his behavior in a socially acceptable way and fails to appreciate many life experiences.

The Psychopathy Checklist (PCL; Hare, 1985) and the Psychopathy Checklist–Revised (PCL–R; Hare, 1991) are diagnostic tools based largely on the descriptions presented by Cleckley (1976). They are designed to supply the trained clinician with reliable methods for measuring these dispositions. However, the PCL and PCL–R have also been influenced by conceptualizations of psychopathy emphasizing antisocial behavior. Thus, the 20 criteria or items of the PCL–R provide a comprehensive assessment of interpersonal, emotional, and behavioral features linked to psychopathy. Considerable support has been reported for its reliability and validity within correctional settings, making it a highly attractive measure to assess psychopathy (Harpur, Hare, & Hakstian, 1989), particularly with White males (cf. Kosson, Smith, & Newman, 1990).

Factor analyses of the PCL criteria have revealed two interrelated yet distinct factors (Harpur et al., 1989). Factor 1 describes many interpersonal and emotional characteristics associated with the disorder (e.g., callousness, egocentricity, grandiosity, poverty of affect, superficial charm), whereas Factor 2 describes many of the behavioral features (e.g., early behavior problems, impulsivity, criminal versatility). Notably, several indexes commonly used to diagnose psychopathy are strongly related only to Factor 2. These include the Psychopathic Deviate scale of the Minnesota Multiphasic Personality Inventory (MMPI; Hathaway & McKinley, 1943), Gough's (1957) Socialization Scale, and the diagnostic criteria for antisocial personality disorder (ASPD) in the *Diagnostic and*

Statistical Manual for Mental Disorders (3rd ed., rev. [*DSM–III–R*]; American Psychiatric Association, 1987).

Although *DSM*-identified ASPD and PCL-identified psychopathy are intended to identify a common construct and many clinicians use the two terms interchangeably, they are not equivalent. Typically more than 50% of an inmate population meet current criteria for *DSM* ASPD, but only 15% to 25% of an inmate population meet criteria for PCL-identified psychopathy (Harpur et al., 1989). Although many PCL-identified psychopaths also meet *DSM* criteria for ASPD, most *DSM*-identified ASPD individuals do not meet PCL–R criteria for psychopathy (Gacono & Meloy, 1994). Thus, our conceptualization of psychopathy may be viewed as a specific extreme form of ASPD.[1] Given this distinction, our review of empirical studies is limited, unless otherwise noted, to those that have used Cleckley's or Hare's criteria for identifying psychopaths.

EMOTIONAL EXPERIENCES OF PSYCHOPATHS

A perspective shared by many professionals and nonprofessionals alike is that psychopaths are relatively emotionless. However, such sweeping generalizations about the emotional experiences of psychopaths are both contradicted by the complexity and heterogeneity of the disorder and inconsistent with current research on psychopathy. Further, to the extent that assumptions regarding the absence of emotions significantly impact management or treatment strategies, such generalizations are potentially maladaptive or dangerous.

This is not to say that this popular perspective is entirely inconsistent with descriptions of the disorder. Among the first to describe the syndrome, Pinel (1801/1962) considered the psychopath to suffer from deficits in passion and affect rather than deficits in reasoning. His term *manie sans delire* translates to madness without confusion.

Similarly, Cleckley's (1976) descriptions of psychopathy have contributed substantially to the view that psychopaths are emotionless. His proposals for lack of nervousness, incapacity for love, absence of shame and remorse, and general poverty of major affective reactions all suggest the absence of emotion. Cleckley suggested that most seemingly emotional reactions by the psychopath are merely dramatic displays that lack an affective basis. Even Cleckley, however, did not see the psychopath as totally devoid of emotional experiences: He may experience "vexation, spite, quick and labile flashes of quasi-affection, peevish resentment, shallow moods of self-pity, puerile attitudes of vanity, and absurd and showy poses of indignation" (p. 380). However, Cleckley argued that deep and sustained emotional reactions are likely to be absent.

Further, Cleckley proposed that the absence of genuine, sustained emotional experience may be the fundamental deficit from which all other symptoms of the disorder follow. According to Cleckley, the lack of genuine affective experience prohibits the psychopath from modifying and directing his behavior in an appropriate way. In essence, "he cannot be taught the awareness of significance which he fails to feel" (p. 410).

The view of the psychopath as relatively and essentially emotionless is also influenced by the belief of many clinicians and theorists that the psychopath is free of shame, guilt, and remorse. In addition to the prominence of shamelessness in Cleckley's (1976) account, McCord and McCord (1964) considered the absence of guilt as one of the two hallmark characteristics of psychopathy. Attenuated shame, remorse, and guilt are also prominent in other descriptions of psychopathy (Craft, 1966; Hare, 1991; Meloy, 1988; Millon, 1981). Indeed, the psychopath's repeated interpersonal difficulties, callousness, manipulative behavior, and criminal activity all provide compelling anecdotal support for attenuated shame, guilt, and remorse.

Yet shame and guilt are complex emotional states whose development is strongly influenced by interpersonal factors and moral development. For example, *guilt* is sometimes defined as a tension state resulting from the violation of an internalized moral code and *shame* as a tension state resulting from a failure to live up to our own or others' expectations (Lazarus, 1991). Given that psychopaths' chronic interpersonal difficulties may include their earliest relationships, and given that compromised moral development may reflect factors other than emotional capacity, it may be inappropriate to conclude that the psychopath is emotionless just because he seems unable to experience these complex emotional states. In short, the psychopath's ability to experience emotions may be richer than is commonly believed. Thus, it may be a mistake to exclude all treatments that deal with the management or treatment of emotional states.

We now examine the theories and research addressing the relationship between psychopathy and four primary emotions: fear/anxiety, anger, sadness, and happiness. Not only are these four emotions widely considered to be fundamental or core emotions (e.g., Ekman, 1992; Izard, 1977; Plutchik, 1962; Tomkins, 1962); they are also commonly experienced by most individuals on a regular basis. Therefore, a review of the psychopath's experience of these emotions provides important information about similarities and differences between psychopaths and nonpsychopaths. Moreover, although this approach does not encompass all research and theory on emotion, it does provide a straightforward framework for discussing the majority of empirical studies of emotion and psychopathy.

Following a discussion of these four emotions, we also examine recent research examining the processing of emotional information in psychopathic individuals. Not included in this chapter is a discussion of the association of empathy and psychopathy. Although we consider this is an important area in understanding psychopathy, it is beyond the scope of this chapter. Similarly, it has been argued that psychopaths are characterized by unusual motivational states (Arnett, Smith, & Newman, 1997) and that motivational states associated with left hemisphere activation underlie some of psychopaths' cognitive and behavioral deficits (e.g., Kosson, 1995, 1998). However, a discussion of this perspective is also beyond the scope of this chapter.

FEAR AND ANXIETY

Fear and anxiety are emotions often used interchangeably to describe an unpleasant state of apprehensive tension. Fear and anxiety typically involve changes in the physiological state including increases in heart rate, pulse, respiration, and sweating. On a psychological level, there is a desire to avoid, escape, and reduce the perceived tension. Some prefer to use these terms as distinct, with *anxiety* defined as feelings associated with an ambiguous threat and *fear* reserved for feelings associated with a specific immediate or identified threat (Lazarus, 1991). Although this differentiation may be useful, we do not distinguish the two emotions in this discussion.

Without question, the psychopath's hypothesized deficiency in fear and anxiety has received the most theoretical and empirical attention. Millon (1981) asserted that the psychopath is fearless—undaunted by danger and punishment. Cleckley (1976) argued that the psychopath is relatively free of anxiety and worry that might be judged normal in distressing situations and may even appear calm and serene under such circumstances. Others, such as Arieti (1963), suggested that the psychopath is capable of experiencing momentary discomfort or fear of an immediate danger but not the kind of worry about future consequences that is the essence of most anxiety.

Deficient fear and anxiety have been suggested as the mechanism for the psychopath's failure to appropriately modify his behavior in situations that most people would find punishing (Lykken, 1957). These deficiencies have also been hypothesized as critical elements in underarousal and sensation-seeking theories of psychopathy (Quay, 1965; Zuckerman, 1974). Other biologically based (Fowles, 1980; Gray, 1975) theories of psychopathy also posit attenuated fear or anxiety responses as a central feature of the disorder.

Yochelson and Samenow (1976) presented one of the few positions that diverge from a view of attenuated fear and anxiety in psychopaths. They asserted that the psychopath experiences frequent fears and worries.

However, he is said to be extremely cautious about revealing his fears because it represents a weakness and vulnerability in his character. To cope with this affective state, the psychopath may use cognitive strategies to alleviate the fear or convert the fear into anger. It should be noted, however, that Samenow and Yochelson's conceptualization of psychopathy, which they termed the *criminal personality*, is largely untested, and the extent to which such individuals resemble PCL-identified psychopaths remains unclear.

Deficient fear and anxiety responses have received extensive study in psychopathy research. In a commonly used research paradigm, autonomic activity (e.g., heart rate, skin conductance) is measured before and while an aversive stimulus (e.g., loud noise, brief shock, unpleasant picture) is presented. Several studies have reported reduced physiological activity associated with fear and anxiety in psychopathic individuals (Blankenstein, 1969; Hare, 1972; Hinton & O'Neil, 1976; Mathis, 1970).

However, there are two important caveats about findings of these studies. First, reduced physiological responses in psychopaths have more consistently been reported when the onset of the aversive stimulus is forewarned than when it is not. Consequently, it appears that psychopaths are not generally underresponsive to aversive stimuli. Rather they appear to employ a coping style that buffers them from the negative effects of an aversive stimulus if they have the opportunity to prepare for the onset of the stimulus (see Hare, 1978, 1982; Ogloff & Wong, 1990). Second, the findings have been relatively consistent with respect to palmar skin conductance or electrodermal activity and relatively less consistent in heart rate and cardiovascular indexes (see Hare, 1978, for a review). Moreover, because there are multiple determinants of electrodermal activity, it is not clear whether the findings reflect differences in psychopaths' peripheral arousal response, in the attention they allocate to aversive stimuli, or in the central nervous system response to aversive stimuli.

It has also been suggested that hyporesponsiveness to aversive stimuli is part of a more general physiological underarousal in psychopaths. Although there are some reports of lower tonic heart rate or skin conductance in psychopaths, most empirical studies do not report significant differences in resting physiological activity between psychopaths and nonpsychopaths (e.g., see reviews by Hare, 1978; Raine, 1997). Psychopaths' attenuated event-related potentials (ERPs; changes in scalp electrical activity following a discrete stimulus) have also been interpreted as consistent with an underarousal hypothesis (Raine, 1989). However, this interpretation has been challenged (Howard, 1989; Jutai, 1989). In short, although the underarousal theory of psychopathy has its supporters (Ellis, 1987), it remains more convincing as a hypothesis for criminality or for a subtype of ASPD than as a basis for distinguishing between psychopathic and nonpsychopathic criminals.

Fewer studies have investigated fear with more than one response system. However, one such study was reported by Patrick, Cuthbert, and Lang (1994). Inmates with high scores on both PCL–R factors and inmates with high scores on only the social deviance dimension (Factor 2) display smaller increases than nonpsychopathic inmates in both heart rate and skin conductance when asked to imagine fear-provoking versus neutral situations. Thus, some of the reduced responsiveness to fear stimuli may be a function of ASPD, not psychopathy.

Patrick and his colleagues have also reported that psychopaths display an unusual attenuation of startle responses to intense stimuli presented during the viewing of negative affective slides. Whereas nonpsychopaths display larger eyeblinks if startled while viewing slides of negative valence, psychopaths display smaller blinks under such conditions (Patrick, 1994; Patrick, Bradley, & Lang, 1993). Although the negative slides used in these studies are not necessarily fear-inducing, Patrick (1996) recently reported that psychopaths also display smaller increases in blink magnitude while viewing slides depicting threats than do nonpsychopaths. Such group differences are interpreted as reflecting reduced activity in a defense/withdrawal system in psychopathic individuals. Of course, that psychopaths, like nonpsychopaths, display larger (not smaller) eyeblinks when startled while viewing threat stimuli demonstrates some capacity for fear, although their increases in startle response are relatively small (Patrick, 1996). It is also interesting that, in contrast to the fear imagery findings, psychopaths' reduced startle responses have been specifically linked to Factor 1 of the PCL–R (Patrick, 1994). It is possible that different aspects of psychopathy contribute to different kinds of emotional deficits. Alternatively, the links between specific deficits and dimensions of psychopathy may turn out not to be reliable.

In addition, two studies have used film clips to induce fear and anxiety in PCL-identified psychopaths and nonpsychopaths. Patterson's (1991) and Forth's (1992) studies included subjective responses, facial expressions, and, in one case, autonomic and electrocortical responses. These studies are further discussed next, because they examined not only fear but also anger, sadness, and happiness in prisoner participants. With respect to the film employed to elicit fear or anxiety, these studies indicate no significant group differences in facial expression, heart rate, skin conductance, electrocortical response, or self-reported anxiety or fear.

These studies represent advances in the study of emotional experiences in psychopaths in that they examined several types of emotions. Nevertheless, the attempt to induce and measure several emotions within the same study may have overwhelmed participants and washed out group differences for specific emotions. In addition, Forth (1992) suggested that incarcerated individuals may learn to inhibit emotional reactions (particularly fear and anger) because of the potential negative consequences associated with displaying these emotions, which could reduce the sensitivity of the emotion inductions employed in these studies.

Overall, empirical evidence seems to indicate that psychopaths show attenuated fear and anxiety responses at least in some instances. Attenuated fear and anxiety responses are most often reported in electrodermal response systems when the psychopath is forewarned about the presentation of an unpleasant event and in various systems when the psychopath is engaged in processing imagery or visual images. Nevertheless, in all these cases, findings are not entirely consistent across studies, and differences in cognitive mechanisms provide alternative explanations for observed group differences. Thus, the mechanisms responsible for attenuated fear/anxiety responsiveness under these conditions warrant further investigation.

ANGER

Anger is a commonly experienced emotion, occurring in most people one or more times a week (Averill, 1982). Anger most often develops in the context of interpersonal interactions; people are more likely to become angry at someone than at something. Frustration associated with the blocking of a goal (Berkowitz, 1962; Dollard, Doob, Miller, Mower, & Sears, 1939) and unjustified threats to self-esteem and self-image are among the most frequently cited causes of anger (Averill, 1982; Lazarus, 1991). Anger is a particularly powerful emotion because of its potential negative impact on both interpersonal relations and on the person experiencing the emotion (Lazarus, 1991).

Although many theoretical accounts suggest psychopaths display deficient or abnormal experiences of fear and anxiety, there is more disagreement as to the psychopath's experience of anger. Cleckley's (1976) view of anger in psychopaths follows from his suggestion of a general poverty of affect. Although he asserted that psychopaths may experience minor frustrations and annoyances, genuine anger is said to be absent. Thus, in psychopaths, the overt actions commonly associated with anger episodes (e.g., facial expressions, gestures, verbalizations) are no more than dramatic displays that lack an affective basis.

Although there is general agreement that psychopaths may feign anger to achieve a goal, several investigators assert that they also experience genuine anger. For example, McCord and McCord (1964) argued that psychopaths frequently experience anger as a result of ineffective strategies for coping with everyday frustrations. Millon's (1981) description of psychopathy includes frequent hostile behavior and temper outbursts. Placing the psychopath's anger in the context of interpersonal relationships, Millon argued that psychopaths are easily angered when faced with embarrassment. Similarly, Meloy (1988) proposed that most instances of anger in the psychopath arise when others' behavior provokes real or imagined threats to feelings of specialness and entitlement. Yochelson and Samenow (1976) presented the most extreme position regarding anger in psychopaths. According to these investigators, psychopaths experience intense, chronic anger that creates serious consequences for themselves and others. Anger in psychopaths tends to metastasize, such that an isolated event spreads and intensifies until all perspective is lost. Under these conditions, the psychopath's overwhelming anger is said to interfere with his ability to function. When angered, the psychopath "attempts to reassert the worth of his entire being" (p. 273) often through aggressive or criminal behavior.

Similar to the positions of Meloy (1988) and Millon (1981), Yochelson and Samenow (1976) asserted that the psychopath is overly sensitive to criticism. He interprets even slight criticisms as putdowns and responds with anger. Moreover, the psychopath responds angrily to anything perceived as preventing him from getting what he wants. Even when the psychopath is responsible for his own mistakes, his frustrations are usually directed toward others.

Despite these divergent descriptions, few empirical studies have examined anger in psychopaths. Sterling and Edelman (1988) examined reactions to provocative hypothetical scenarios. Psychopaths and nonpsychopaths were identified by offender status (incarcerated criminals vs. community noncriminals) and low versus high scores on Gough's (1957) Socialization Scale. Two anxiety and two anger scenarios were presented; participants rated the amount of anxiety, anger, fear, and threat they would feel in each situation. Compared with nonpsychopaths, psychopaths appraised both the anxiety and anger scenarios as significantly more anger provoking. Psychopaths also rated the anxiety scenarios as more threatening and the anger scenarios as less threatening. Because the Socialization Scale correlates with the antisocial lifestyle but not the emotional and interpersonal features of psychopathy (Harpur et al., 1989), it is unclear to what extent the participants in this study were characterized by psychopathy versus ASPD. However, similar findings were reported by Serin (1991) using PCL-identified psychopaths. In particular, inmates with high PCL scores self-reported experiencing greater amounts of anger than inmates with low PCL scores in response to some hypothetical vignettes describing provocation.

These studies suggest that psychopaths may differ from nonpsychopaths in the intensity of their anger experiences and the types of situations that lead to anger. However, the exclusive reliance on self-reports and focus on hypothetical situations temper generalizations to emotional reactions in real-life situations. This concern is particularly relevant given descriptions of psychopaths as pathological liars who lack insight into their behavior and who sometimes display emotional reactions lacking a true affective basis. The psychopaths in these studies could have reported what they thought they should feel instead of what they would actually feel had the scenarios been real.

Only two studies have attempted to induce anger directly in incarcerated PCL-identified psychopaths and nonpsychopaths. As noted earlier, both Patterson (1991) and Forth (1992) used film clips to induce anger. Although the chosen clips had been used in prior studies of emotion, Patterson reported no significant group differences on self-reported anger or facial expression for an anger-inducing film. Similarly, Forth reported no significant group differences on self-reported anger, heart rate, skin conductance, or facial expression for an anger-inducing film. Some possible limitations of the methods of these studies were discussed previously. In addition, it may be difficult to induce anger simply by presenting a brief film clip.

Kelly and Kosson (1998) attempted to design a more powerful set of film clips to induce anger. They did so by increasing the length of the clips and including more contextual details to enhance identification with a film protagonist and/or clarify the lack of justification for a film antagonist's behavior. Participants in this study were college students selected solely on the basis of low versus high scores on Gough's Socialization Scale. Thus, they may be more aptly characterized by ASPD traits than by psychopathic traits. However, the less socialized participants also had significantly higher scores on an interview-only measure of PCL–R Factor 1 traits than did the more socialized participants. As in Forth's (1992) and Patterson's (1991) studies, less socialized participants self-reported as much anger following the film clips as the more socialized participants. However, in contrast to earlier studies, less socialized participants displayed fewer facial expressions of anger while watching the film clips. Thus, Kelly and Kosson suggested that psychopathic traits may be associated with a disjunction between subjective experience and the expression of emotion, at least with respect to anger.[2]

These findings notwithstanding, the presentation of film clips may constitute a relatively weak technique for inducing anger because anger is usually experienced in the context of interpersonal relationships (Averill, 1982). Although a person may become angry when others are treated unjustly, anger is most often experienced when perceived injustices are directed at one's self. In addition, psychopaths are frequently characterized as lacking empathy. Therefore, film studies of psychopaths' capacity for emotion may be confounded by psychopaths' inability to empathize with film characters.

To circumvent the potential limitations in using film clips to elicit anger, Steuerwald (1996) employed the performer–evaluator paradigm as an anger-induction technique. In this paradigm, a participant performing a task adequately is unjustly criticized for a poor performance by either the experimenter or a confederate of the study. Numerous studies have demonstrated that this technique induces substantial anger in the participant (for a review of the reliability and validity of the performer–evaluator paradigm, see Zillmann, 1979).

Because there are ethical and safety concerns about inducing substantial anger in incarcerated inmates, participants in this study were college students with and without psychopathic traits. To ensure that participants had personality features consistent with both empirically validated dimensions of psychopathic traits, group selection was determined by both a measure based on Hare's (1991) PCL–R Factor 1 and Gough's (1957) Socialization Scale. Socialization scale scores have been reported to be moderately related to PCL–R Factor 2 scores but not Factor 1 scores (Harpur et al., 1989). PCL–R Factor 1 traits were assessed by trained raters during a 30- to 60-minute interview. Although Hare (1991) suggested that the PCL–R should be completed based on both interview and file information, he and his colleagues have published studies using the PCL: Screening Version (PCL:SV) on the basis of interview information alone (e.g., Forth, Brown, Hart, & Hare, 1996).

The dependent measures in the study were blood pressure, pulse, facial electromyography (EMG), subjective anger, and the amount of retaliation directed toward the confederate following provocation. Results indicate that the induction technique was successful in inducing substantial anger. Following the provocation, participants in both groups showed similar increases in blood pressure, pulse, and self-reported anger. Moreover, both groups retaliated toward the confederate at a similar level. Groups did differ on two of the three facial EMG measures (at corrugator and zygomatic facial muscle sites), indicating smaller increases in facial EMG activity following provocation in the group with psychopathic traits. The pattern of findings suggested that the more psychopathic and less psychopathic groups were characterized by comparable responsiveness to the anger induction, but the more psychopathic participants were characterized by reduced facial expression of the anger they experienced.

Although it is unclear whether a similar pattern of results would be observed in clinically diagnosed psychopaths, it is of interest that the disjunction between the experience and expression of anger in this study appears similar to that reported by Kelly and Kosson (1998). Of course, more studies are needed with different kinds of anger inductions and multiple measures of emotional response. There is also a need for studies that distinguish between the intensity of anger responses and frequency of anger episodes in the real world. However, extant research provides a relatively consistent preliminary picture of anger and psychopathy across studies. Whereas psychopaths report a greater sensitivity to anger provocation in hypothetical scenarios, they do not show greater or lesser responsiveness than nonpsychopaths to direct anger inductions. Nevertheless, psychopathic traits may be associated with a disjunction between anger responsiveness and facial expressions of anger, which may sometimes contribute to a perception that psychopaths do not experience anger or behave violently (e.g., retaliate against others) in the absence of apparent emotion.

SADNESS AND DEPRESSION

Sadness may be defined as an unpleasant emotional state resulting from real or imagined deprivation or loss. In its more extreme and enduring forms, sadness is closely related to clinical depression. It represents one of the most distressing emotions experienced by humans.

There appears to be general agreement among clinicians and theorists regarding the psychopath's attenuated sadness and depressive states. Even so, not all theorists conclude that psychopaths are exempt from states of dysphoria. Cleckley (1976) wrote that the psychopath may show "shallow moods of self-pity" (p. 380), but genuine grief and despair are absent. Even as the psychopath frequently works himself into situations of "squall and misery," he fails to feel "woe or despair or serious sorrow" (p. 381).

Similarly, Meloy (1988) argued that the psychopath may experience sudden feelings of dysphoria but is unlikely to experience sustained sadness and depression. His position is based largely on a psychodynamic conceptualization of psychopathy. Accordingly, psychopathy is considered an aggressive variant of narcissistic personality disorder (Bursten, 1989; Kernberg, 1975; Millon, 1981). Like the narcissist, the psychopath possesses primitive defense mechanisms, excessive feelings of specialness, self-righteousness, and a sense of entitlement. Unlike the pure narcissist, however, the psychopath is less able to use anxiety adaptively, has poorer moral development, and displays less impulse control. Consequently, the psychopath has greater difficulty controlling aggressive tendencies that are typically directed at others.

Based on this perspective, Meloy (1988) proposed that the psychic structure of the psychopath is incompatible with the conditions necessary for developing depression. The experience of depression is said to require a failure of denial as a defense mechanism, a discrepancy between the actual self- and ideal self-representations, and an ability to mourn actual and symbolic loss. However, these conditions are generally absent for psychopaths. First, denial is a frequently employed defense mechanism, if not a defining quality, of the psychopath. Second, the narcissistic, grandiose self-concept of the psychopath is said to prevent the formation of a discrepancy between the actual self-representation and ideal self-representation. Finally, the ability to mourn requires feelings of ambivalence and the capacity for repression as a defense mechanism, both of which are lacking within the primitive intrapsychic structure of the psychopath.

The theoretical construct that most closely resembles depression in psychopathy is Yochelson and Samenow's (1976) *zero state*. According to these investigators, the zero state in the psychopath is composed of three necessary conditions. The first condition is intense feelings of emptiness and worthlessness; hence the name *zero*. The second condition is a belief that thoughts and feelings of emptiness and worthlessness are readily apparent to others. The third is a belief in the permanence of the condition.

Yochelson and Samenow (1976) held that the zero state is frequently experienced by the psychopath, a consequence of his underlying fears of failure, although it is masked by feelings of grandiosity, specialness, and entitlement. Despite the similarities to depression, however, Yochelson and Samenow pointed out several characteristics that distinguish the zero state from a genuine depressive state. Unlike a depressive process, the zero state in the psychopath evokes fear — an intolerable state for the psychopath. Further, although depression is typically marked by decreased motor activity, the psychopath reacts to the zero state with an increase in motor activity to alleviate the condition. To reduce feelings of emptiness and worthlessness, the psychopath is also likely to respond with anger and hostility. Finally, although the zero state is said to be all-consuming for the psychopath, it is usually a transient condition and rapidly alleviated. The relatively brief duration of this state is inconsistent with characterizing it as a genuine depressive state.

Empirical studies examining sadness in psychopaths are quite rare. Only the studies by Patterson (1991) and Forth (1992) have attempted to induce sadness in PCL–identified psychopaths. As mentioned, both studies used film clips. As with anger, both studies reported no group differences for any measure of responsiveness to a sadness induction.

The findings of no group differences between psychopathic and nonpsychopathic participants in the studies of Patterson (1991) and Forth (1992) are consistent with the positions of several theorists that psychopaths have the capacity to experience at least brief periods of sadness or dysphoria. Based on only these two studies with a very similar design, it is inappropriate to make generalized statements about the experience of sadness in psychopaths. Further, there is a paucity of studies examining either more sustained periods of sadness or the hypothesized transient zero state in psychopathic individuals. The dearth of empirical studies highlights an important gap in our understanding of psychopathy. Additional studies could clearly make a critical contribution given the contradictory clinical theories regarding sadness and depressive states in the psychopath.

HAPPINESS

Happiness may be defined as a pleasant emotional state resulting from obtaining and having what we want and feeling good (Lazarus & Lazarus, 1994). Happiness is one of the emotional states most desired by people. On a continuum, happiness lies close to the middle of a range of pleasant emotional experiences ranging from milder states of contentment to more intense states of ecstasy. Here we use the terms *happiness* and *pleasure* interchangeably.

Cleckley (1976) argued that, as in the case of other emotions, the psychopath fails to experience genuine happiness/pleasure or make an affective connection with humor. However, other clinicians and theorists suggested that the psychopath experiences genuine, albeit brief periods of happiness and pleasure. Perhaps the most cited theoretical evidence is the psychopath's engagement in risk-taking and sensation-seeking behavior to experience brief periods of excitement and pleasure (Quay, 1965; Yochelson & Samenow, 1976; Zuckerman, 1974). There are also suggestions that the psychopath's overresponsiveness to immediate rewards (e.g., see chap. 4, this volume) is associated with motivational states of goal-orientation or excitement—states sometimes associated with left hemisphere activation (Kosson, 1995).

Writing within an object relations perspective, Meloy (1988) presented one of the most thorough descriptions of pleasure experiences in psychopaths. He suggested that the psychopath is unable to experience pleasure in the same ways as nonpsychopaths. In particular, the psychopath's experience of pleasure is restricted by the absence of empathy and affectional bonds, an inability to repress negative affect, and difficulty overcoming an anhedonic state. Without the capacity for empathy, the psychopath is unable to derive pleasure through observing happiness in others. Others' pleasure leads only to envy and greed in the psychopath.

Nonetheless, several theorists have argued that the psychopath achieves genuine pleasure through acts of contempt. Meloy (1988) suggested that the psychopath experiences a feeling of exhilaration through the successful manipulation and deception of others. Considered a distinctive feature of psychopathy, *contemptuous delight* serves the basic purpose of restoring the psychopath's pride. Along similar lines, Yochelson and Samenow (1976) asserted that the psychopath derives pleasure through manipulation and successful attempts to control others. Bursten (1973) added that the thrill associated with deceiving another plays an important role in maintaining a distorted sense of self-esteem and power for psychopaths, although he prefers to refer to them as manipulative personalities.

Psychopaths are also characterized as unable to form enduring affectional bonds and romantic relationships with others. Although the experience of enduring affectional bonds is more complex than the experience of brief periods of pleasure and happiness, it is not entirely separate from the realm of pleasure or happiness. Cleckley (1976) considered the psychopath's inability to love one of the 16 principal symptoms of the disorder. Several other theorists also note the inability to form genuine, enduring affectional relationships as an important feature of the disorder (Craft, 1966; McCord & McCord, 1964; Meloy, 1988; Millon, 1981).

As with the case of sadness and to a lesser extent anger, there are few empirical studies that have examined the experience of happiness and pleasure in psychopathic individuals. Patterson's (1991) and Forth's (1992) studies are the only ones of which we are aware that have attempted to induce happiness in psychopaths and nonpsychopaths. As reported earlier, both studies used film clips to induce happiness and other emotions.

Under the happiness condition, Patterson (1991) reported no significant group differences for facial expressions or self-reported happiness. Along similar lines, Forth (1992) reported no significant group differences for self-reported happiness, facial expression, heart rate, skin conductance, or ERPs under the happiness condition.

The lack of empirical studies examining the association between psychopathy and happiness represents another critical deficit in our understanding of the disorder. Our understanding of the psychopath's emotional life is not complete until empirical evidence converges with theory regarding positive affective experiences in the psychopath. For example, Meloy's (1988) concept of contemptuous delight suggests an intriguing association between psychopathy and the experience of pleasure. Not only does this concept suggest a specific kind of motivation underlying the psychopath's behavior, but it represents a unique process absent from most other psychological disorders. Moreover, the hypothesis of contemptuous delight appears relatively easy to operationalize and test using existing methods for studying emotion.

EMOTIONAL INFORMATION PROCESSING

A great deal of attention in recent years has focused on the processing of emotional information. Some of the more robust findings in this relatively new area of research include evidence for primacy of emotional over nonemotional information and evidence that emotional states facilitate retrieval and processing of emotionally relevant stimuli. Several recent studies have examined the processing of emotional information in psychopathic individuals.

The majority of these studies examined the ability to respond to emotional language (i.e., emotional information presented in the form of words). For example, when participants are asked to decide whether a presented letter string is a word, such lexical decisions are typically faster and more accurate for emotion words than for neutral words. This phenomenon is commonly referred to as *affective facilitation of lexical decision* and is sometimes attributed to a brief but automatic physiological arousal resulting from a semantic analysis of emotionally relevant information (Graves, Landis, & Goodglass, 1981; Strauss, 1983). There have been several studies of psychopathic individuals' ability to complete lexical decision with affective and nonaffective words.

Williamson, Harpur, and Hare (1991) first examined psychopaths' and nonpsychopaths' processing of emotional words, neutral words, and nonwords in a lexical decision task. Participants were asked to decide whether a presented letter string was a word, and classification accuracy, response latency, and electrocortical activity were recorded. Consistent with previous research, nonpsychopaths' reaction times were faster for emotional words than for neutral words. In contrast, psychopaths did not show this facilitation of response latency for emotional words. In addition, nonpsychopaths showed larger ERPs during the presentation of emotional words than during neutral words, but psychopaths showed no ERP differences for word type. Both groups showed the expected advantage in classification accuracy for emotional words and did not differ from each other.

Newman, Lorenz, and Schmitt (1998) replicated this absence of affective facilitation of lexical decision in a group of PCL–R-identified psychopaths. However, the absence of the response facilitation effect was only for a subgroup of psychopaths who self-reported low levels of trait anxiety and psychological distress. PCL–R-identified psychopaths who reported high trait anxiety showed the response facilitation effect as did nonpsychopathic participants.

Steuerwald (1996) reported an interesting twist on the affective facilitation effect. As reported earlier, participants in this study worked on a task and then were unjustly criticized by a confederate in an attempt to induce anger. The task they completed was a lexical decision task containing emotionally neutral words, anger-relevant words, and nonwords. Participants completed one block of trials prior to being provoked by the confederate and another block of trials immediately after being provoked.

Replicating previous empirical findings, Steuerwald (1996) reported that prior to provocation participants without psychopathic traits showed the response facilitation, whereas participants with psychopathic traits did not show the facilitation effect. After provocation, however, both groups showed the facilitation effect. Thus, after participants with psychopathic features were angered or energized, they processed the emotional information similarly to individuals without psychopathic traits. This finding provides convergent evidence for the comparability of anger responses in individuals with and without psychopathic traits. Moreover, to the extent that affective facilitation reflects an automatic access to the arousing properties of emotional stimuli, the pattern of findings raises this possibility: Psychopaths' usual lack of affective facilitation in this paradigm under nonemotional conditions may reflect a reduced access to the automatically arousing effects of emotional stimuli, rather than an inability to experience emotion-induced arousal. By contrast, when psychopaths are in an emotional state, they appear to react quickly to emotion-relevant information.

Similar evidence for a lack of responsiveness to emotionality was reported by Christiansen et al. (1996). Using a memory paradigm, they found that nonpsychopaths' retrieval was narrowed by emotional information, leading to relatively better memory for central information but reduced memory for peripheral information. By contrast, when a verbal retrieval test was administered, psychopaths' retrieval was less narrowed than that of nonpsychopaths by the introduction of affective information.

Other studies have reported emotional processing deficits for psychopaths only when classifying linguistic stimuli, not when classifying nonverbal stimuli.[3] However, a variety of factors limit the conclusions that can be drawn from these studies. For example, Williamson, Harpur, and Hare (1990) reported deficits for psychopaths when they attempted to match emotional phrases on the basis of affective meaning but not when they attempted to match emotional pictures. However, in this study, the lack of group differences with nonlinguistic stimuli may reflect a ceiling effect: The nonverbal task was relatively easy and produced little variance in participants' performance (Williamson et al., 1990).

Similarly, Patterson (1991) reported no deficits for psychopaths while classifying nonverbal emotion using the Profile of Nonverbal Sensitivity (PONS; Rosenthal, Hall, DiMatteo, Rogers, & Archer, 1979). Psychopaths were as accurate as nonpsychopaths at selecting the correct descriptor for interpersonal affective stimuli. However, supplementary analyses, including a measure of neuroticism, revealed deficits for neurotic psychopaths in classifying stimuli presented in several nonverbal channels. Even so, stimuli in this test are classified on the basis of dominance and valence rather than on the basis of the specific emotion depicted. Moreover, because the PONS presents affective stimuli in various artificial combinations (e.g., via content-filtered speech; via body but not facial cues), its correspondence with more naturalistic measures of emotional processing remains uncertain. Similarly, Forth (1992) reported no differences between psychopaths' and nonpsychopaths' ratings of affective slides on dimensions of dominance and valence.

In summary, although previous studies of nonverbal emotional processing suggest no deficits for psychopaths, there have been relatively few studies in this area. Further, interpretation of psychopaths' performance in previous studies is limited by the presentation of emotion in unnatural contexts, by ceiling effects, and by researchers' decisions to investigate participants' ability to assess the dominance and valence of nonverbal emotional stimuli rather than the ability to classify emotion into discrete categories.

One additional study merits brief discussion. Kosson and Mayer (1998) asked PCL-identified psychopathic and nonpsychopathic inmates to classify the emotion depicted on faces presented briefly. Participants completed the task either alone or paired with a demanding finger-tapping task. Under both conditions, psychopaths classified emotion relatively poorly compared with nonpsychopaths.[4] Thus, psychopaths' emotional processing deficits are not entirely limited to the processing of emotional language, but extend to the processing of nonverbal emotion at least under some conditions.

In summary, evidence from recent studies of emotional information processing suggests that psychopaths are relatively less influenced by the emotionality of stimuli than are nonpsychopaths and may also be relatively deficient at classifying emotional information. Although the evidence is more consistent from studies employing emotional language as stimuli, there is converging evidence from at least one recent study employing nonverbal emotional material. Finally, preliminary evidence from two studies suggests that psychopathic individuals' reduced sensitivity to emotion may be moderated by their own affective state and/or their general proneness to experience negative affect. Therefore, given the limited evidence that psychopaths are as responsive to emotion inductions as nonpsychopaths, it appears likely that psychopaths' impairments in processing emotional information may be specific to situations in which they are not experiencing strong emotion.

At the same time, it should be kept in mind that, although theories of emotional function in psychopaths have been stable for decades, research in this area is relatively new. Our understanding of psychopaths' emotional function is likely to change appreciably in the next decade, and all of the empirical findings reviewed in this chapter should be considered preliminary and tentative.

SUGGESTIONS FOR CLINICIANS WORKING WITH PSYCHOPATHS

Our review of theory and research on emotional function in psychopaths suggests a few implications for clinical work with psychopaths.

First, given our core operationalizations of psychopathy, clinicians should not assume that what the psychopath portrays is what he truly feels. Psychopaths may be characterized by a lack of insight into their affective state and may have difficulty accessing affective material when in nonaffective states. In fact, we do not even know the extent to which psychopaths in one affective state are able to access affective material from other affective states of similar valence.

Even to the extent that psychopaths may sometimes know their true feelings, they may often have reasons to lie about these or may be more interested in managing clinicians' impressions of them than in conveying an accurate picture. In fact, some theories (e.g., Meloy, 1988) suggest that, even in the absence of a good reason to lie, many psychopaths may lie to or manipulate clinicians just for the sheer (contemptuous) delight of it.

Clinicians should never underestimate the capacity of psychopathic clients for expressing private agendas other than those they state. On the one hand, these private agendas may be more determinative of the material presented than are the underlying true emotions. On the other hand, some of the true emotions of the psychopathic client may be largely a function of idiosyncratic interpersonal agendas than of long-standing emotional conflicts with people outside the immediate interpersonal context. (For a more extensive discussion of the psychopath's interpersonal behavior, see chap. 8, this volume.) This would be consistent not only with psychodynamic perspectives emphasizing narcissism and manipulation, but also with Arieti's (1963) emphasis on the psychopaths' relatively exclusive involvement in immediate emotional events.

Second, the limited evidence seems to suggest that psychopaths are quite capable of experiencing some emotional states. Laboratory studies suggest that psychopaths appear to be capable of experiencing as much anger as nonpsychopaths. Studies with hypothetical scenarios raise the possibility that psychopaths may be prone to experiences of heightened anger relative to nonpsychopaths. Thus, any signs that a psychopathic client is becoming increasingly angry should be taken seriously. Moreover, the clinician should be aware of the possibility that the anger (or other emotions) may not be expressed facially or interpersonally in the usual ways. Thus, clinician judgment about intense underlying affect in the absence of a clear facial display may be an important guide. Similarly, clinicians should be attentive not only to subjective reports of affect, but also to physiological signs of arousal and behavior consistent or inconsistent with specific emotions.

Although current evidence suggests that psychopaths may be less responsive than nonpsychopaths to some situations that typically elicit fear or anxiety, their hyporesponsiveness may often be limited to one specific response system (e.g., electrodermal or startle responses). Moreover, because current findings could also be explained by attentional differences, coping mechanisms, or dissociations between different emotional response systems, it seems premature to disbelieve all reports or signs of apparent fear or anxiety.

Whether psychopaths are capable of sadness and happiness has not been established empirically. However, when conventional expressions of sadness and happiness are manifested, it appears prudent for the clinician to investigate further cautiously. It remains possible that, consistent with clinical descriptions and theory, such emotional responses reflect immediate disappointments, pleasures, or idiosyncratic underlying causes, yet the possibility that such responses reflect longer range losses or joys cannot yet be eliminated. We advocate neither ignoring apparent emotions in these categories nor confronting the psychopath repeatedly for shamming such emotions unless the clinician has learned that such displays are not indicative of true underlying emotions.

Third, considerable attention to the facial displays of psychopaths and to the degree of connection between facial expression and other indexes of emotional experience appear warranted. Again, available evidence suggests some emotions (e.g., anger) that the psychopath feels inside may not be displayed in facial expressions. In the absence of collateral information, physiological information, or overt behavioral displays that would clue the clinician to the psychopath's emotional state, we may need to rely more on subjective reports than on facial expressions. In such cases, where possible, self-reports should be integrated with behavioral observations, knowledge of the individual, and clinical judgment to understand the psychopath's true emotional state.

Fourth, clinicians should try to take advantage of emotional episodes that do occur to find out more about the nature of these emotional states and about a psychopath's processing of emotion when in these states. It should be kept in mind that, at least according to some theories, psychopaths may be extremely reluctant to display certain negative affective states (e.g., fear, sadness). Hence, it may be important to explore these states carefully and to remember that they may be short-lived while remaining attentive to the possibility of being duped or manipulated.

Fifth, although not discussed in this chapter, there is clear evidence for important motivational states in psychopaths associated with an orientation toward achieving immediate goals or obtaining immediate rewards. Such states have been referred to elsewhere as states of left hemisphere activation. There is evidence that psychopaths may be particularly prone to a variety of cognitive dysfunctions only when in such states. Indeed, Kosson (1995) argued that it may be important to work with psychopaths in such states to help them become aware of their state-dependent cognitive dysfunctions.

Sixth, clinicians should be careful not to assume that the apparent absence of complex emotional states such as shame and guilt also implies an absence of other emotional states in the psychopath. We often find ourselves treating psychopathic individuals because they have engaged in repetitive, antisocial activities against others, consistent with attenuated guilt, shame, and remorse. However, the experience of these emotions relies in part on levels of socialization and morality, which may be underdeveloped in the psychopath. Thus, the seeming absence of these emotions may be related to other factors than an incapacity to experience emotions per se. It is far too common for clinicians to base evaluations of the psychopath's emotional capacity (or lack thereof) on attenuated guilt, shame, and remorse. Such sweeping generalizations of the psychopath as being emotionless are inconsistent with available empirical findings, bias our perspective on this disorder, and can limit our use of therapeutic inventions that may be effective.

Finally, it is important to keep in mind the wide range of individual differences among psychopathic individuals. Although the possibility of distinct subtypes of psychopaths remains controversial and research on the heterogeneity of psychopathy is limited, most clinicians agree that contemporary measures of the disorder identify a heterogeneous group of individuals (e.g., see Gacono, 1998). The likelihood of individual differences among psychopaths should encourage the clinician to attempt to construct an individual profile of emotional capacity/responsiveness and emotional processing aptitude to select the therapeutic techniques that maximize the chances for effective treatment. Whereas ignoring all apparent emotional displays may be appropriate for some psychopathic clients, careful attention to some apparent experiences of emotion may turn out to be quite productive for others.

ENDNOTES

1. One exception to this characterization is that, unlike the *DSM*, neither Cleckley's nor Hare's formulation requires that a history of childhood conduct disorder (CD) be present to diagnose psychopathy in an adult. Nevertheless, studies suggest that most adults diagnosed with psychopathy according to the PCL or PCL–R also have histories that meet *DSM* criteria for CD.
2. In fact, similar trends toward reduced facial expressiveness were reported for film clips designed to induce sadness and happiness. The apparent generality of reduced facial expressiveness suggests that the disjunction between experience and expression of emotion may be more general than the domain of anger.
3. To our knowledge, only one study has examined detection of emotion in psychopaths. Results for this study also suggest greater differences between groups for verbal than for nonverbal emotion. However, the results of this study are not easily integrated with the other studies reviewed in this chapter. Day and Wong (1996) reported reduced lateralization for psychopaths in detecting which of two lateralized words was emotional but

not in detecting which of two lateralized faces was emotional. However, inspection of their data shows that psychopathic participants detected emotional words more accurately than nonpsychopaths (78% vs. 69% correct) when emotional words occurred in the right visual field. Although the authors did not report the reliability of this apparent group difference, it raises the possibility that detection of emotion may reflect different processes than classification of emotion.

4. Under single-task conditions, the difference between groups fell short of but approached statistical significance ($p = .07$). Under dual-task conditions, the group difference was statistically significant.

REFERENCES

American Psychiatric Association. (1987). *Diagnostic and statistical manual of mental disorders* (3rd ed., rev.). Washington, DC: Author.

Arieti, S. (1963). Psychopathic personality: Some views on its psychopathology and psychodynamics. *Comprehensive Psychiatry, 4,* 301–302.

Arnett, P. A., Smith, S. S., & Newman, J. P. (1997). Approach and avoidance motivation in psychopathic criminal offenders during passive avoidance. *Journal of Personality and Social Psychology, 72,* 1413–1428.

Averill, J. R. (1982). *Anger and aggression: An essay on emotion.* New York: Springer-Verlag.

Berkowitz, L. (1962). *Aggression: A social psychological analysis.* New York: McGraw-Hill.

Blankenstein, K. R. (1969). *Patterns of autonomic functioning in primary and secondary psychopaths.* Unpublished master's thesis, University of Waterloo, Canada.

Bursten, B. (1973). Some narcissistic personality types. *International Journal of Psychoanalysis, 54,* 287–299.

Bursten, B. (1989). The relationship between narcissistic and antisocial personalities. *Psychiatric Clinics of North America, 12,* 571–584.

Christianson, S., Forth, A. E., Hare, R. D., Strachan, C., Lidberg, L., & Thorell, L. (1996). Remembering details of emotional events: A comparison between psychopathic and nonpsychopathic offenders. *Personality and Individual Differences, 20,* 437–443.

Cleckley, H. C. (1976). *The mask of sanity* (5th ed.). St. Louis: Mosby.

Craft, M. (1966). Conclusions. In M. Craft (Ed.), *Psychopathic disorders and their assessment* (pp. 206–225). Oxford: Pergamon.

Day, R., & Wong, S. (1996). Anomalous perceptual asymmetries for negative emotional stimuli in the psychopath. *Journal of Abnormal Psychology, 105,* 648–652.

Dollard, J., Doob, L., Miller, N., Mower, O., & Sears, R. (1939). *Frustration and aggression.* New Haven, CT: Yale University Press.

Ekman, P. (1992). Are there basic emotions? *Psychological Review, 99,* 550–553.

Ellis, L. (1987). Relationships of criminality and psychopathy with eight other apparent behavioral manifestations of sub-optimal arousal. *Personality and Individual Differences, 8,* 905–925.

Forth, A. (1992). *Emotion and psychopathy: A three-component analysis.* Unpublished doctoral dissertation, University of British Columbia, Vancouver, Canada.

Forth, A. E., Brown, S. L., Hart, S. D., & Hare, R. D. (1996). The assessment of psychopathy in male and female noncriminals: Reliability and validity. *Personality and Individual Differences, 20,* 531–543.

Fowles, D. C. (1980). The three arousal model: Implications of Gray's two-factor learning theory for heart rate, electrodermal activity, and psychopathy. *Psychophysiology, 17,* 87–104.

Gacono, C. B. (1998). The use of the PCL–R and Rorschach in treatment planning with ASPD patients. *International Journal of Offender Therapy and Counseling, 42,* 47–55.

Gacono, C. B., & Meloy, J. R. (1994). *The Rorschach assessment of aggressive and psychopathic personalities.* Hillsdale, NJ: Lawrence Erlbaum Associates.

Gough, H. (1957). *Manual for the California Psychological Inventory*. Palo Alto, CA: Consulting Psychologists Press.

Graves, R., Landis, T., & Goodglass, H. (1981). Laterality and sex differences for visual recognition of emotional and non-emotional words. *Neuropsychologia, 19*, 95–102.

Gray, J. A. (1975). *Elements of a two-process theory of learning*. New York: Academic Press.

Hare, R. D. (1972). Cardiovascular components of orienting defensive responses. *Psychophysiology, 9*, 606–614.

Hare, R. D. (1978). Electrodermal and cardiovascular correlates of psychopathy. In R. D. Hare & D. Schalling (Eds.), *Psychopathic behavior: Approaches to research* (pp. 107–144). New York: Wiley.

Hare, R. D. (1980). A research scale for the assessment of psychopathy in a prison population. *Personality and Individual Differences, 1*, 111–119.

Hare, R. D. (1982). Psychopathy and physiological activity during anticipation of an aversive stimulus in a distraction paradigm. *Psychophysiology, 19*, 266–271.

Hare, R. D. (1985). *The Psychopathy Checklist*. Unpublished manuscript, University of British Columbia, Vancouver, Canada.

Hare, R. D. (1991). *Manual for the Revised Psychopathy Checklist*. Toronto, Ontario: Multi-Health Systems.

Hare, R. D., McPherson, L., & Forth, A. (1988). Male psychopaths and their criminal careers. *Journal of Consulting and Clinical Psychology, 56*, 710–714.

Harpur, T. J., Hare, R. D., & Hakstian, A. R. (1989). Two-factor conceptualization of psychopathy: Construct validity and assessment implications. *Psychological Assessment: A Journal of Consulting and Clinical Psychology, 1*, 6–17.

Hathaway, S. R., & McKinley, J. C. (1943). *Manual for the Minnesota Multiphasic Personality Inventory*. New York: Psychological Corporation.

Hinton, J., & O'Neil, M. (1976, May). *Psychophysiological response profiles: An outline of pilot research leading to possible computer predictions of recidivism*. Paper presented at NATO Advanced Institute on Computer Prediction in Parole, Cambridge.

Howard, R. (1989). Evoked potential and psychopathy: A commentary on Raine. *International Journal of Psychophysiology, 8*, 23–27.

Izard, C. E. (1977). *Human emotions*. New York: Plenum.

Jutai, J. W. (1989). Psychopathy and P3 amplitude: A commentary on Raine. *International Journal of Psychophysiology, 8*, 17–22.

Kelly, J. C., & Kosson, D. S. (1998). *Emotional and empathetic ability in psychopaths: Verbal and nonverbal indices in an analogue group*. Unpublished manuscript.

Kernberg, O. F. (1975). *Borderline conditions and pathological narcissism*. New York: Science House.

Kosson, D. S. (1995, November). *Psychopathy and deficits in divided attention*. Paper presented at the NATO Advanced Study Institute: Psychopathy: Theory, Research, and Implications for Society, Alvor, Portugal.

Kosson, D. S. (1998). Divided visual attention in psychopathic and nonpsychopathic offenders. *Personality and Individual Differences, 24*, 373–391.

Kosson, D. S., & Mayer, A. (1998, November). *Facial affect recognition in criminal psychopaths*. Paper presented at the annual meeting of the Society for Research in Psychopathology, Cambridge, Massachusetts.

Kosson, D. S., Smith, S. S., & Newman, J. P. (1990). Evaluating the construct validity of psychopathy on black and white male inmates: Three preliminary studies. *Journal of Abnormal Psychology, 99*, 250–259.

Lazarus, R. S. (1991). *Emotion and adaptation*. New York: Oxford.

Lazarus, R. S., & Lazarus, B. N. (1994). *Passions and reason: Making sense of our emotions*. New York: Oxford University Press.

Lykken, D. T. (1957). A study of anxiety in the sociopathic personality. *Journal of Abnormal and Social Psychology, 55*, 6–10.

Mathis, H. (1970). *Emotional responsivity in the antisocial personality.* Unpublished doctoral dissertation, University of Michigan, Ann Arbor, MI.

McCord, W., & McCord, J. (1964). *The psychopath: An essay on the criminal mind.* New York: Van Nostrand.

Meloy, J. R. (1988). *The psychopathic mind: Origins, dynamics, and treatment.* Northvale, NJ: Jason Aronson.

Millon, T. (1981). *Disorders of personality: DSM–III: Axis II.* New York: Wiley.

Newman, J. P., Lorenz, A. R., & Schmitt, W. A. (1998, November). *Linking the cognitive and affective information-processing deficiences of psychopathic offenders.* Paper presented at the annual meeting of the Society for Research in Psychopathology, Cambridge, MA.

Ogloff, J., & Wong, S. (1990). Electrodermal and cadiovascular evidence of a coping response in psychopaths. *Criminal Justice and Behavior, 17,* 231–245.

Patrick, C. J. (1994). Emotion and psychopathy: Startling new insights. *Psychophysiology, 31,* 319–330.

Patrick, C. J. (1996, November). *Probing emotional processes in psychopathic criminals.* Paper presented at the meeting of the American Society of Criminology, Chicago, IL.

Patrick, C. J., Bradley, M. M., & Lang, P. J. (1993). Emotion in the criminal psychopath: Startle reflex modulation. *Journal of Abnormal Psychology, 102,* 82–92.

Patrick, C. J., Cuthbert, B. N., & Lang, P. J. (1994). Emotion in the criminal psychopath: Fear image processing. *Journal of Abnormal Psychology, 103,* 523–534.

Patterson, C. M. (1991). *Emotion and interpersonal sensitivity in psychopaths.* Unpublished dissertation, University of Wisconsin–Madison.

Pinel, P. (1962). *A treatise on insanity* (D. D. Davis, Trans.). New York: Hafner. (Original work published 1801)

Plutchik, R. (1962). *Emotion: A psychoevolutionary synthesis.* New York: Harper & Row.

Pritchard, J. (1835). *A treatise on insanity.* London: Sherwood, Gilbert, & Piper.

Quay, H. C. (1965). Psychopathic personality as pathological stimulation-seeking. *American Journal of Psychiatry, 122,* 180–183.

Raine, A. (1997). Antisocial behavior and psychophysiology: A biosocial perspective and a prefrontal dysfunction hypothesis. In D. Stoff, J. Breiling, & J. Maser (Eds.), *Handbook of antisocial behavior* (pp. 289–304). New York: Wiley.

Raine, A. (1989). Evoked potentials and psychopathy. *International Journal of Psychophysiology, 8,* 1–16.

Robbins, L. (1972). Follow-up studies of behavior disorders in children. In H. Quay & J. Werry (Eds.), *Psychopathological disorders of childhood* (pp. 414–446). New York: Wiley.

Rosenthal, R., Hall, J. A., DiMatteo, M. R., Rogers, P. L., & Archer, D. (1979). *Sensitivity to nonverbal communication: The PONS test.* Baltimore: Johns Hopkins University Press.

Rush, B. (1812). *Medical inquiries and observations upon diseases of the mind.* Philadelphia: Kimber & Richardson.

Serin, R. (1991). Psychopathy and violence in criminals. *Journal of Interpersonal Violence, 6,* 423–431.

Sterling, S., & Edelman, R. J. (1988). Reactions to anger and anxiety-provoking events: Psychopathic and nonpsychopathic groups compared. *Journal of Clinical Psychology, 44,* 96–100.

Steuerwald, B. L. (1996). *Anger following provocation in individuals with psychopathic characteristics.* Unpublished doctoral dissertation, University of North Carolina at Greensboro, Greensboro, NC.

Strauss, E. (1983). Perception of emotional words. *Neuropsychologia, 21,* 99–103.

Tomkins, S. S. (1962). *Affect, imagery, consciousness: The positive affects* (Vol. 1). New York: Springer.

Williamson, S., Harpur, T. J., & Hare, R. D. (1990, August). *Sensitivity to emotional polarity in psychopaths.* Paper presented at the meeting of the American Psychological Association, Boston.

Williamson, S., Harpur, T. J., & Hare, R. D. (1991). Abnormal processing of affective words by psychopaths. *Psychophysiology, 28,* 260–273.
Yochelson, S., & Samenow, S. E. (1976). *The criminal personality: Volume 1. A profile for change.* New York: Jason Aronson.
Zillmann, D. (1979). *Hostility and aggression.* Hillsdale, NJ: Lawrence Erlbaum Associates.
Zuckerman, M. (1974). The sensation seeking motive. In B. A. Maher (Ed.), *Progress in experimental personality research* (Vol. 7, pp. 79–148). New York: Academic Press.

II

CLINICAL ISSUES AND APPLICATIONS

6

Legal and Ethical Issues in Psychopathy Assessment

David R. Lyon and James R. P. Ogloff
Simon Fraser University, Burnaby, British Columbia

Individuals manifesting psychopathy are no strangers to the law (see Ogloff & Lyon, 1998). A search of electronic legal databases for cases involving psychopathy or its conceptual cousins (i.e., sociopathy, dissocial personality disorder, and antisocial personality disorder) identifies many legal cases where diagnosis of such was deemed relevant.[1] From review of these cases, it is readily apparent that psychopathy is a powerfully pejorative diagnostic label that can exert a profound influence over the legal decisions rendered by the courts. Indeed, the connotations associated with the word *psychopath* are so negative that it has resulted in at least one defamation suit (*Anderson v. Cramlet*, 1986).

The construct of psychopathy — and related constructs — frequently arises in legal proceedings. Given the potential impact of this diagnosis, it is puzzling to discover the absence of a cogent body of jurisprudential thought regarding psychopathy. This chapter attempts to address this gap in the literature. First, the scope of legal issues in which psychopathy has been raised is surveyed with a discussion of the appropriate limits surrounding expert testimony on the disorder. Next, the application of psychopathy to the pertinent legal issues associated with various areas of the law is critically examined. We conclude by discussing a number of professional and ethical issues that arise in connection with providing information about psychopathy to the courts.

Due to the breadth of the chapter as well as the huge diversity that exists in American jurisprudence, the discussion is fairly general in nature. Cases cited may involve psychopathy, antisocial personality disorder (ASPD), or sociopathy and are noted as such. The diagnostic differences that exist between these clinical constructs are well documented (e.g., Hare & Hart, 1995; Hart & Hare, 1997). However, little distinction among these constructs is presently made in the law.[2] Nonetheless, case opinions are useful for clarifying how an understanding of psychopathy might be applied to different legal issues. Courts may benefit from greater recognition of essential diagnostic and prognostic differences among these seemingly similar disorders. We offer recommendations and caveats in this regard.

PSYCHOPATHY AND TESTIMONY

A search of American case law reveals that expert evidence about psychopathy, ASPD, or sociopathy has been offered in court on an amazingly diverse array of legal issues within both the criminal and civil law contexts. Some of the issues that psychopathy has been raised in connection with include competency to stand trial, the insanity defense, witness credibility, capital sentencing, juvenile transfers, child custody, civil torts, and civil commitment. What makes this situation all the more interesting, or perhaps perplexing, is that many times experts have offered testimony about psychopathy when it encroached on matters usually reserved for the trier of fact, did not address the legal issue(s) in question, or lacked sufficient empirical basis to justify the conclusions reached by the expert. The following exemplifies the diversity of cases in which psychopathy has been employed while serving as a focal point for exploring where the appropriate boundaries regarding psychopathy-related evidence should lie.

In *Crowston v. Goodyear Tire and Rubber Company* (1994), the Supreme Court of North Dakota affirmed the trial judge's decision to admit opinion evidence regarding the plaintiff's ASPD. The appellant plaintiff launched a civil action for injuries suffered from an exploding tire when he attempted to place an undersized tire on a large wheel rim. To rebut the legal presumption that the plaintiff would have read and heeded a warning had one been supplied, the defendant tire manufacturer introduced psychiatric evidence that the plaintiff had an ASPD that, in the words of the court, would ". . . cause him to act on his own internal impulses, have poor judgment, act impulsively, and do the opposite of directions or warnings" (p. 410).

Although it was remanded back to the lower court on other issues, the *Crowston* case highlights the dilemma over the propriety of raising the concept of psychopathy (or related concepts) in court. Considering what little probative value psychopathy (or ASPD) bears on the issue of whether a written warning would be heeded compared to its prejudicial impact, such testimony arguably should never have been given. Furthermore, even if the psychiatrist believed that the plaintiff's ASPD would have affected his behavior concerning the reading of warning labels, the reality is that the psychiatrist had an obligation to ensure that his opinion was firmly grounded in the empirical literature (see Ogloff, 1999).

For example, there are no empirical data linking ASPD (or psychopathy) with the failure to follow warning labels. In this situation, it may be more appropriate to simply describe the relevant behaviors or characteristics of the litigant (e.g., impulsive, poor judgment, etc.) and how they relate to the material issue (reading the warning label) rather than making reference to diagnostic labels like ASPD or psychopathy. This avoids unnecessary extrapolations and gratuitous opinions that do little toward providing the court with the valid information it requires to make an informed decision.

Others might object to this stance and suggest the testimony in question is really no different than providing evidence that the plaintiff was intoxicated, blind, or illiterate. Ultimately, the (in)admissibility of evidence is a question of law, and therefore courts act as gatekeepers for regulating which evidence is presented to the trier of fact (Ogloff & Lyon, 1998). However, it is our view that merely because the court is the final arbiter on issues of admissibility does not alleviate the expert of his or her professional and ethical responsibilities for the testimony he or she may provide (Ogloff, 1999). At this point, rather than attempt to discuss all the possible circumstances where the concept of psychopathy might become extraneous or inappropriate, a better approach may be to reemphasize those areas where it is most germane.

It is worth remembering that much of the recent interest generated in the construct of psychopathy is attributable to the Psychopathy Checklist–Revised (PCL–R; Hare, 1991) and its relationship to future criminal behavior (see chap. 3). The PCL–R (Hare, 1991) is a powerful predictor of future criminal behavior, particularly violent behavior (Hart, 1998; Hemphill, Hare, & Wong, 1998; Salekin, Rogers, & Sewell, 1996; see chaps. 3, 10, & 14). Logically, then, expert evidence pertaining to psychopathy is most germane when it is closely tied to the concept's utility as a risk factor and to issues surrounding relapse and treatment amenability (see chaps. 15 and 16 & Appendix B).

The rationale for this recommendation is twofold. First, there is ample empirical evidence establishing psychopathy's relationship to risk and, to a lesser extent, treatment amenability and relapse. Second, neither assessments of risk generally, nor psychopathy specifically, are matters that might be considered within the knowledge and experience of ordinary persons, and therefore expert opinions on these subjects may be particularly helpful to the trier of fact. Conversely, once opinion evidence of psychopathy moves beyond issues related to risk, the empirical validity for such evidence is generally weaker, and therefore the concept is likely to have less probative value (or legal relevance). For some legal issues, there is so little empirical basis to the testimony that it should not be offered. Admittedly, the empirical research of psychopathy has developed along a number of different lines, and cases may arise involving material issues unrelated to risk, but for which the evidence of psychopathy is still legally relevant and firmly grounded in the empirical literature. Broadly speaking, however, the concept of psychopathy manifests the greatest probative value (relative to its prejudicial effect) in connection with risk-related issues. Accordingly, we propose that these issues should constitute the focus of most cases where the concept is introduced.

THE APPLICATION OF PSYCHOPATHY IN THE LAW

This section is divided into two main parts, each dealing with one facet of the law. The first part focuses on matters pertaining to criminal law. The second part addresses aspects of civil or private law. For each area, there is a brief introduction to the relevant legal principles followed by a discussion of how psychopathy has been applied to these principles.

PSYCHOPATHY IN CRIMINAL SETTINGS

The vast majority of reported cases involving psychopathy occur within the criminal law context. Because it is impossible to provide an exhaustive review, discussion focuses on the following areas: witness credibility, competency to stand trial, insanity, capital sentencing, as well as sexual psychopath and habitual offender laws.

Witness Credibility[3]

It is generally for the trier of fact to assess witness credibility. Consequently, the law is reluctant to usurp this function of judge or jury by admitting opinion evidence on the matter. Nevertheless, witness credibility may become the subject of expert evidence in some circumstances. Under the Federal Rules of Evidence (FRE, 608), opinion evidence is permitted for the purpose of bolstering or undermining witness credibility with the following exceptions: (a) character evidence may relate only to truthfulness or untruthfulness, and (b) character evidence relating to witness honesty may only be introduced to rebut opinion or reputational evidence designed to impeach that witness. Although the original purpose behind the rule was merely to expand the permissibility of lay testimony on witness credibility, one of the unintended side effects has been to facilitate the admissibility of evidence supplied by mental health professionals on the issue (Melton, Petrila, Poythress, & Slobogin, 1997).

Evidence of psychopathy has been raised in connection with witness credibility for obvious reasons: As a disorder characterized by deceit and manipulation, the diagnosis may cast doubt over the veracity and accuracy of a witness' testimony. The 11th Circuit Court of Appeals dealt with the issue of credibility broadly in *United States v. Lindstrom* (1983) and concluded that *psychopathic personalities* was one of several conditions that might be relevant for issues of credibility. There are also a number of reported cases bearing more directly on the admissibility of psychopathy-related evidence for this purpose. In at least two decisions, the courts have permitted the use of expert testimony to attack the credibility of a psychopathic witness (*United States v. Hiss*, 1950; *United States v. Jerkins*, 1989).

For the most part, courts have not been inclined to permit information on psychopathy for the purpose of attacking witness credibility. In *Lewis v. Velez* (1993), the U.S. Court of Appeals dismissed an appeal that psychiatric records disclosing the plaintiff's ASPD diagnosis were improperly excluded. In its judgment, the court held that a psychiatric history should only be admitted to discredit a witness if the impugned records reveal impairments in the perception or ability of the witness to testify accurately.

Elsewhere, the courts have disallowed evidence of psychopathy because witness credibility is a matter reserved for the trier of fact (*United States v. Barnard*, 1973; *United States v. Pacelli*, 1975), it is time-consuming to introduce this evidence (*United States v. Barnard*, 1973), and it is only likely to distract the fact finders from their central task (*United States v. Daileda*, 1964). The U.S. District Court eloquently summarized many of these concerns in *United States v. Daileda* (1964), when it affirmed a lower court decision to exclude evidence of psychopathy introduced to undermine the credibility of the prosecution's principal witness. In denying the defense's appeal, the District Court stated,

> . . . the reception of this type of testimony is fraught with danger and great caution must be exercised before this precarious step is taken. It may well open Pandora's box of diversion, confusion, and remoteness, and the remedy may be more dangerous than the disease it seeks to cure. (p. 154)

It is apparent from these cases that efforts to impeach witness credibility through psychopathy-related testimony have achieved mixed success over the years. Although this type of credibility testimony has been admitted on occasion, the courts appear reticent to do so for fear that juries will give undue deference to the experts, thereby usurping their own role as the fact finders in the case. Because trial judges typically wield wide discretionary powers to determine issues of admissibility, the variable results exhibited in the preceding cases may continue in the future.

Competency to Stand Trial

The Anglo-American system of law is inherently adversarial. In the civil setting, the plaintiff is pitted against the defendant; in the criminal setting, the state is pitted against the accused. As a result of the adversarial nature of the criminal justice system, it is essential—from a fairness perspective— that the accused be able to participate in his or her defense (Reich & Wells, 1985). The capacity to comprehend and participate in legal proceedings is referred to as *competency* (Ogloff, Wallace, & Otto, 1991). Issues of competency may arise at any stage of the criminal justice system including: competency to confess, competency to plead guilty, competency to stand trial, competency to waive counsel, competency to be sentenced, and, in some jurisdictions, competency to be executed (Roesch & Golding, 1987). One of the most prominent of these issues is the competency to stand trial.

Federal and state standards surrounding competency to stand trial flow primarily from the Supreme Court decision in *Dusky* v. *United States* (1960). Notwithstanding the considerable variation that exists in these legal standards, there appear to be two essential elements: (a) the accused must understand the nature of the proceedings against him or her, and (b) the defendant must have the ability to consult/communicate with his or her lawyer (Appelbaum, 1993). A smaller number of states also requires that a mental disorder or illness must be the source of the accused's inability to communicate with counsel or understand the proceedings.

In most of the cases reviewed, individuals diagnosed with psychopathy, sociopathy, or ASPD were found competent (*Boag* v. *Raines*, 1985; *Henderson* v. *Dugger*, 1988; *State* v. *Bolger*, 1983; *United States* v. *Aponte*, 1978). The Fifth Circuit Court of Appeals in *Bruce* v. *Estelle* (1976) went so far as to remark that, "a sociopath suffers from no disability which could affect competency. The medical term solely describes manipulative, egocentric persons who frequently commit antisocial acts without feelings of remorse" (p. 1060). The Fifth Circuit Court's *obiter dictum* remarks in *Bruce* should not be viewed as a binding legal principle, but their impact has been felt in other decisions (e.g., *Boag* v. *Raines*, 1985).

However, the presence of psychopathy does not eliminate the possibility of incompetency. There are at least two appellant decisions involving sociopathic defendants who were found incompetent (*Blazack* v. *Ricketts*, 1993; *Bruce* v. *Estelle*, 1976). These cases were characterized by conflicting diagnoses of sociopathy and paranoid schizophrenia, numerous documented episodes of bizarre behavior, and extensive histories of psychiatric admissions or treatment with antipsychotic medication. The only exception to this pattern appears to be *People* v. *Mouson* (1989), where the court noted that earlier in the proceedings the defendant, who had been diagnosed with ASPD, originally had been found incompetent because he was too impulsive to cooperate with his lawyer. The outcome of this case is interesting because normally an accused will only be found incompetent if he or she lacks the capacity to cooperate with counsel, and not where the accused simply fails to cooperate with counsel (Melton et al., 1997).

The lack of a relationship between psychopathy and incompetency should not be unexpected because no characteristic symptom of the disorder interferes with the basic cognitive and communicative functioning necessary for competency to stand trial. In addition, empirical investigations have failed to demonstrate any relationship between PCL total scores and standard measures of intelligence (e.g., Hart & Hare, 1989; Kosson, Smith, & Newman, 1990). The cases reviewed suggest that psychopaths are not likely to be found incompetent to stand trial unless additional psychiatric symptoms (e.g., delusions) or secondary diagnoses (e.g., schizophrenia) are present.

Although there has not been a great deal of research addressing the comorbidity of psychopathy and other psychiatric symptomatology, there is evidence to suggest that some psychopaths, albeit a very small number, also suffer from schizophrenia and other major mental disorders (e.g., Nedopil, Hollweg, Hartmann, & Jaser, 1998; Rice & Harris, 1995; see chap. 13). Where psychopathy does coexist with another serious mental disorder, it is the features of the other disorder, not psychopathy, that are likely to lead to a finding of incompetency. A far more probable scenario is that psychopaths will not cooperate with their counsel or decide to represent themselves. However (and perhaps contrary to *People* v. *Mouson*, 1989), bad legal decisions do not necessarily signal incompetency.

One area of concern that has not been addressed in the literature is that psychopaths may attempt to malinger to be incompetent to stand trial. As with all forensic evaluations, the potential for malingering must be assessed. This is particularly true for a defendant who is apparently experiencing a major mental illness while exhibiting the characteristics of psychopathy (Melton et al., 1997). One study found that psychopaths were more likely to acknowledge feigning mental illness in the past, although their efforts to malinger were no more sophisticated than other offenders (Kropp, 1992; see chap. 11). Careful assessments conducted on more than one occasion to verify consistency as well as probing for unusual and statistically rare symptomatology are two useful techniques that may be employed for detecting dissimulation.

Insanity

The law assumes that we are all rationale agents who freely decide our actions and therefore we should be held responsible for our conduct. To the extent that mental illness interferes with a person's ability to make rational and voluntary choices, it should serve to excuse an accused from responsibility (Simon & Aaronson, 1988). The insanity defense is one of the legal mechanisms through which individuals who possess a sufficient mental impairment may be relieved of criminal liability. There are three requisite elements common to most insanity standards: (a) the accused suffered from a mental disorder or defect, (b) the mental disorder was of legally sufficient nature and degree, and (c) the criminal act occurred as a result of the mental disorder (Melton et al., 1997; Ogloff, Roberts, & Roesch, 1993). If even one of these elements is absent, the defense will fail. Insanity defenses can be classified as either *cognitive* or *volitional* (or a combination of both) according to the nature and degree of the required impairment. Cognitive standards excuse persons from unlawful acts arising out of altered thoughts or perceptions that do not reflect reality, whereas volitional standards exculpate an accused whose criminal acts result from a defect of will or an inability to control one's behavior (Miller, 1992; Perlin, 1994).

It should be apparent from the preceding discussion that the first step under most insanity defenses turns on the presence of a legally sufficient mental disease or disorder. If the accused's condition does not qualify as a mental disease or defect, the insanity defense will fail; if the legal definition is satisfied, consideration will proceed to the other elements of the defense.

The view that psychopaths are bad and criminally responsible, rather than mad, together with concerns that psychopaths might use the insanity defense to escape culpability, has exerted a strong influence on how mental disease or defect has been defined. Generally speaking, the legal concept of mental disease or defect as contemplated by most insanity defense provisions does not include psychopathy. In some jurisdictions, statutory regimes define mental disease or defect according to the type and severity of impairment required. Usually the accused must exhibit substantial impairments of perception or reality testing. For instance, both Maine and Colorado require a mental condition that ". . . grossly and demonstrably impair[s] a person's perception or understanding of reality . . ." (ME. Rev. Stat. Ann. tit. 17-A, § 39(2) (West 1997); Colo. Rev. Stat. Ann. § 16-8-101.5(2)b (West 1998)). Psychopathy per se, is not associated with the gross mental impairments demanded by this type of statute. It is possible that a psychopathic individual might meet these criteria, but only where the disorder coexists with some other serious mental illness.

Other jurisdictions utilize exclusionary definitions of mental disease or defect. The emphasis in this type of approach is on specifying those conditions or diagnostic classes that do not qualify as a mental disease or defect rather than trying to define what does qualify. Here, the intent to bar psychopathy (and other personality disorders) from the insanity defense is unmistakable.[4] For example, Arizona lists ". . . character defects, psychosexual disorders or impulse control disorders . . ." among the conditions that are statutorily excluded from its insanity defense (Ariz. Rev. Stat. Ann. § 13-502(A) (West 1998)). Similarly, California law stipulates the insanity defense is not available to an accused ". . . solely on the basis of a personality or adjustment disorder . . ." (Cal. Penal Code § 25.5 (West 1998)). In other jurisdictions, judicial rulings have held that personality disorders do not constitute a mental disease or defect (*People* v. *Uppole*, 1981; *State* v. *Richey*, 1992).

Perhaps the most common exclusionary definitions are variations on the caveat paragraph originally intended to accompany the American Law Institute's (ALI) proposed test of insanity. The caveat states, ". . . the terms 'mental disease and defect' do not include an abnormality manifested only by repeated criminal or otherwise antisocial conduct" (American Law Institute, 1962, p. 4.01). This paragraph was formulated in direct response to fears that mental health professionals might diagnose a mental disorder solely on the presence of criminal or antisocial behavior, which, in turn, might be inferred as a legally sufficient basis for invoking the insanity defense (Bursten, 1982; Campbell, 1992; Uelmen, 1980).

To some extent, the ALI's fears were realized in 1980 when the American Psychiatric Association released the *Diagnostic and Statistical Manual of Mental Disorders* (3rd ed. [*DSM–III*]; American Psychiatric Association, 1980), which contained diagnostic criteria for antisocial personality disorder (ASPD) that were composed primarily of criminal behaviors (Uelmen, 1980). As Table 6.1 illustrates, the behavioral focus of ASPD has continued into *DSM–IV* (American Psychiatric Association, 1994). Furthermore, using the *DSM–IV* criteria, it is possible to receive a diagnosis of ASPD based exclusively on the existence of antisocial or criminal behavior.

Psychopathy, as operationalized by the PCL–R (Hare, 1991; see chap. 3), taps a much broader range of behavioral, affective, and interpersonal symptoms of psychopathy than ASPD (see Table 6.1). More important, and in contrast to ASPD, it is impossible to obtain a score high enough on the PCL–R to be considered a psychopath without manifesting some of the affective and interpersonal features of the disorder (see chap. 3). The presence of these other symptoms alone establishes a prima facie case for arguing that the ALI caveat does not apply to the PCL psychopath. Moreover, there is case law suggesting that any evidence of an abnormality beyond repeated antisocial and unlawful conduct may be sufficient to

TABLE 6.1
Comparison of PCL–R and ASPD Criteria by Domain

Domain	PCL–R Criteria[a]	ASPD Criteria[b]
Behavioral	Impulsivity	Impulsivity or failure to plan ahead
	Parasitic lifestyle	Disregard for the safety of others
	Irresponsibility	Irresponsibility
	Need for stimulation/ proneness to boredom	
	Lack of realistic, long-term goals	
Interpersonal	Pathological lying	Deceitfulness
	Glibness/superficial charm	
	Grandiose sense of self-worth	
	Conning/manipulative	
Affective	Lack of remorse or guilt	Lack of remorse
	Shallow affect	
	Callous/lack of empathy	
	Failure to accept responsibility for own actions	
Other	Poor behavior controls	Irritability and aggressiveness
	Criminal versatility	Repeated behaviors that are grounds for arrest
	Early behavior problems	Conduct disorder prior to age 15
	Promiscuous sexual behavior	
	Many short-term marital relationships	
	Juvenile delinquency	
	Revocation of conditional release	

Note. The organization of items by domain is based on analyses conducted by Cooke and Michie (1998) using the PCL–R.

[a]PCL–R items are scored as either 0, 1, or 2 based on the concordance between the item description and the corresponding behavioral or personality trait of the assessee. The recommended diagnostic cutoff for psychopathy is a score of 30 or more (Hare, 1991).

[b]For a diagnosis of ASPD, there must be at least three of the above listed criteria that do not occur exclusively during the course of schizophrenia or a manic episode. There also must be evidence of conduct disorder with onset prior to age 15. This diagnosis is only available to persons 18 years or older (American Psychiatric Association, 1994).

overcome the caveat (*People* v. *Fields*, 1983). Empirical evidence that psychopaths may have deficits in their ability to process emotional and affective stimuli or other cognitive abilities may bolster this argument further. Fortunately, as the Supreme Court of California noted in *People* v. *Fields* (1983), it is not sufficient to merely prove that these deficits exist in psychopaths generally. Rather, it must also be proved that they reside specifically in the accused.

Should the definition of mental disease or defect be satisfied, the next consideration is whether the accused has the necessary cognitive or volitional impairment. The classic cognitive test is the M'Naghten standard, which was formulated by the English Supreme Court of Judicature in 1843 (Perlin, 1994). To be found insane under M'Naghten, the accused must have been incapable either of appreciating the nature and quality of the act or of knowing that it was wrong (R. v. M'Naghten, 1843). It is extremely rare to find anyone who is incapable of appreciating the nature and quality of their actions (Perlin, 1994). This is the so-called *lemon squeezer* exception: It requires a cognitive impairment of such severity and degree, so the analogy runs, that an accused who is choking another person believes he or she is in fact squeezing lemons (Perlin, 1994). There is no evidence indicating that psychopaths suffer from this type of impairment. Furthermore, any legal argument along this line will likely prove exceedingly difficult to advance in the face of the motivational goals that usually lie behind the criminal behavior of most psychopaths (e.g., greed, power, or revenge) and the rational connection that usually exists between those goals and their behavior.

The second possibility under the cognitive standard is to show that an accused does not know his or her actions were wrong. The concept of wrongfulness contemplated in cognitive standards has been interpreted to connote legally wrong as well as morally wrong. If the applicable standard is legal wrong, it turns on the accused's ability to appreciate the criminal nature of his or her actions. If the accused was unable to appreciate that the act committed was illegal, the accused is not held criminally responsible. Again, there is no evidence at present indicating that psychopathy interferes with such a basic cognitive ability as understanding the difference between what is legally right and wrong. Hence, it is extremely unlikely that psychopaths will be found insane where these standards exist.

Other interpretations of *wrong* broaden the concept to incorporate the ability to appreciate what is morally wrong. Under these standards, individuals who appreciate the criminality of their acts may still be found insane if their mental disease or defect renders them unable to appreciate that their act is morally wrong.[5] Some commentators suggest that the courts do not, and should not, consider psychopaths to exhibit the necessary moral impairment to warrant exculpation (Dinwiddle, 1996; Elliot, 1992). From a legal perspective, the critical issue is whether the psychopathic condition caused the person to be unable to appreciate the wrongfulness of his or her actions. In the past, there has been no evidence of this link, but recent experimental data may lend an air of credibility to this type of legal argument. For example, Blair and colleagues (Blair, 1995; Blair, Jones, Clark, & Smith, 1995) found that higher PCL–R scores were associated with significantly poorer abilities to discriminate moral transgressions (i.e., acts that affect the rights and welfare of others) from conventions (behaviors that simply violate social norms). The evidence at this point is too limited to be legally persuasive, but it is an area of research that may hold serious implications for the issue of criminal responsibility in the future.

Cognitive approaches, such as M'Naghten, have been criticized on the ground that no consideration is given to individuals who demonstrate normal perceptual and intellectual functioning but have serious deficits in their behavioral controls.[6] The American Law Institute (1962) standard of insanity was developed to address these concerns. The ALI test is composed of both a cognitive and volitional prong. The cognitive prong concerns whether an accused can appreciate the criminality of his or her behavior. The volitional prong addresses whether the accused can conform his or her behavior to the requirements of the law. An accused needs to satisfy only one prong or the other to be relieved of criminal culpability.

With respect to psychopathy, the legal issue under volitional tests of insanity is whether the accused's incapacity to conform to the law was a result of his or her psychopathic condition. Certainly the tendency to act impulsively is one of the hallmark symptoms of psychopathy (Hart & Dempster, 1997). However, it is not clear that psychopaths are unable to conform to the law as opposed to merely disinterested in abiding by the law when it does not suit their own selfish ambitions. One suspects it is the latter description, rather than the former, which applies to most psychopaths, but this cannot be easily determined. As the American Psychiatric Association (1982) stated, "the line between an irresistible impulse and an impulse not resisted is probably no sharper than the line between twilight and dusk" (p. 11). In fact, it may well have been the fear that psychopaths would escape culpability through the volitional prong of the ALI test that prompted lawmakers to draft the caveat paragraph.

When the capacity to conform to the law must be assessed, it is likely accomplished through a thoughtful and comprehensive evaluation of the behavioral antecedents to the crime and an investigation of the crime scene characteristics. The defense is generally more tenable in cases where the accused engaged in criminal behavior that would inevitably and unavoidably result in immediate detection and arrest.

In summary, the legislatures and judiciary in most jurisdictions have attempted to exclude psychopathy from the insanity defense by keeping it outside the definitional boundaries of mental disease or defect. Because psychopathy generally fails to qualify as a mental disease or defect, little jurisprudence has developed around how psychopathy applies to the other elements of the defense. This situation may change, however, because the ALI caveat, which traditionally has barred psychopathy from the insanity defense, clearly does not apply to the construct of the disorder diagnosed by the PCL–R (Hare, 1991). The ALI caveat precludes disorders characterized only by repeated antisocial and criminal behavior, whereas the diagnosis of psychopathy based on the PCL–R encompasses interpersonal, affective, and behavioral characteristics.

If psychopathy indeed qualifies as a mental disease or disorder, the danger is that psychopaths might be found to satisfy the necessary cognitive or volitional impairments and hence escape criminal liability for their actions. This situation is unlikely to unfold in jurisdictions relying exclusively on cognitive standards unless some other relatively severe psychopathology is present in addition to psychopathy. The status of psychopathy under volitional standards is somewhat less certain due to the characteristic impulsiveness of this disorder, coupled with the difficulty in assessing the capacity to conform to the law. As a result, there appears to be a somewhat greater risk that psychopaths could be found insane in jurisdictions where volitional standards of insanity exist.

Finally, evidence that psychopathy may be associated with a higher risk for malingering has important implications for insanity evaluations (Gacono et al., 1995). As was discussed in relation to assessments of competency, the dual presence of psychopathic traits and other serious psychopathology should immediately alert the clinician to the possibility of malingering and may warrant the use of specific assessment techniques for detecting dissimulation.

Repeat or Habitual Offender Laws

In recent years, there has been a widespread increase in the number of repeat or habitual offender laws enacted in the United States (Heilbrun, Ogloff, & Picarello, 1999). These statutes usually mandate the imposition of lengthier sentences for any offender who has repeated felony convictions (Melton et al., 1997). The threshold number of convictions necessary to trigger habitual offender penalty provisions varies by jurisdiction, but typically it ranges from one to four (Heilbrun et al., in press). The invocation of many habitual offender statutes is simply a function of whether an offender has met the requisite number of convictions. Consequently, this type of statute precludes any consideration of psychopathy during the sentencing phase.

Laws that involve considerations of public safety or dangerousness openly invite the introduction of evidence on psychopathy. For example, in *Wingett* v. *State* (1994), the appellant's habitual offender status and enhanced 30-year sentence was reviewed by the Supreme Court of Indiana. The court carefully examined the various aggravating and mitigating circumstances. Among the aggravating factors listed was the accused's ASPD diagnosis, which, according to one expert at trial, prevented the accused from functioning within the parameters of the law. The Supreme Court upheld the accused's sentence, concluding that it was not manifestly unreasonable and that the trial judge had properly considered all the aggravating and mitigating factors.

The Supreme Court of North Carolina ruled in *State* v. *Todd* (1985) that mental disorders, including sociopathy, cannot serve as aggravating factors for the purpose of imposing a life sentence on a habitual offender. Nevertheless, the court went on to explain that such a finding may be justified where the accused poses a threat to other people because his or her mental disorder (a) is associated with serious criminal behavior, and (b) shows no prospects for rehabilitation. On this basis, the court dismissed the appeal and upheld the accused's life sentence. Of course, had this case occurred more recently, the construct of psychopathy would have been more relevant than ASPD to both criteria set out in the court's judgment because psychopathy demonstrates a stronger relationship to serious (i.e., violent) reoffending and it has so far proved unresponsive to therapeutic intervention.

Sexual Psychopath and Sexual Predator Laws

Various legislative measures aimed at sexual psychopaths or sexual predators have been enacted throughout the United States over the years. Sexual psychopath laws were prevalent from the late 1930s to the mid-1970s, when mounting criticism over their merits culminated in most being repealed (Grubin & Prentky, 1993). The wide-scale abandonment of sexual psychopath laws proved only to be temporary. In the early 1990s, a second wave of legislation dealing with sexually dangerous persons appeared under the rubric of *sexual predator laws*. Notwithstanding some temporal and jurisdictional differences, three requisite criteria appear common to most of these sexual offender laws: (a) the existence of some kind of mental condition, (b) the commission of a sexual offense, and (c) a high risk of future sexual violence (Group for the Advancement of Psychiatry, 1977; Janus, 1996). Once deemed a sexual psychopath or predator, these laws usually permit indeterminate confinement until the individual no longer poses a danger to society (Hammel, 1995). Perhaps the most notable difference between the two generations of laws is that sexual psychopath laws usually were created as an alternative to traditional criminal sentences, whereas sexual predator laws were designed to confine sex offenders on the expiration of their criminal sentence (Janus, 1996).

Because sexual psychopath and sexual predator laws often involve civil confinement, the law broadly pertaining to civil commitment also applies to these statutes and vice versa.[7] At this point, it should be stressed that the terms *psychopathic* or *psychopathy* contained in sexual psychopath statutes are legal constructs that are distinct from the clinical construct of psychopathy—they are common terms, but they are not terms in common. It is fitting to examine Minnesota's statute, in part, because it served as the prototype for many sexual psychopath laws, but also because it is one of only a handful that are still in use (Grubin & Prentky, 1993). Minnesota's criminal code defines a sexual psychopathic personality as:

> the existence in any person of such conditions of emotional instability, or impulsiveness of behavior, or lack of customary standards of good judgement, or failure to appreciate the consequences of personal acts, or a combination of any of these conditions, which render the person irresponsible for personal conduct with respect to sexual matters, if the person has evidenced, by habitual course of misconduct in sexual matters, an utter lack of power to control the person's sexual impulses and, as a result, is dangerous to other persons. (Minn. Stat. Ann. § 253B.02 (18b) (West 1998))

It is apparent that the legal construct referred to in the statute does not resemble the psychological construct of psychopathy conceptualized in the PCL–R (see chap. 3; Hare, 1991). Undoubtedly, the constructs exhibit some overlap (e.g., see *In the Matter of Robert Archie Kunshier*, 1994[8]), but the correspondence between the two is not perfect. Some PCL-defined psychopaths meet the legal criteria required for a sexual psychopath, but there are also some individuals found to be sexual psychopaths according to the law who do not meet the clinical criteria for psychopathy. Put succinctly, a clinical diagnosis of psychopathy is neither a necessary nor sufficient condition for legal purposes.

Simply because the legal and psychological constructs are not isomorphic does not mean that psychopathy is irrelevant or unhelpful in sexual psychopath or sexual predator proceedings. Indeed, evaluations of psychopathy conducted with the PCL–R (Hare, 1991) may be particularly well suited for this task. To begin, it is apparent from a recent U.S. Supreme Court decision that it is constitutionally permissible to incorporate personality disorders like psychopathy into the legal criteria of sexual predator laws (*Kansas* v. *Hendricks*, 1997).[9] Second, the aim of these laws is to identify the most dangerous sexual offenders. Because the PCL–R is one of the most robust predictors of future violence, it constitutes a critical component of any evaluation of risk for sexual violence (Hart, 1998; see chap. 14). In fact, some jurisdictions like California routinely administer the PCL–R as part of the risk assessment process conducted with all sexually violent predators (see Quinsey, Harris, Rice, & Cormier, 1998; see also chaps. 10 & 14).

Finally, where possible, it is also wise to evaluate sexual deviance. Not only does sexual deviance exhibit a relationship to sexual recidivism

(Hanson & Bussière, 1998; Quinsey, Lalumière, Rice, & Harris, 1995; Quinsey, Rice, & Harris, 1995), but recent empirical data indicate that it may interact with psychopathy in a manner that enhances its predictive power (Rice & Harris, 1997). In short, the PCL-R still has considerable application in sexual psychopath or sexual predator proceedings, despite the gap between legal and psychological conceptualizations of psychopathy.

Capital Sentencing

The development of contemporary death penalty jurisprudence began with the U.S. Supreme Court's ruling in *Furman* v. *Georgia* (1972), which effectively struck down the statutory schemes existing at the time. In a series of decisions shortly after *Furman*, the U.S. Supreme Court made it clear that capital sentencing schemes should provide guided discretion (Hesseltine, 1995; Liebman & Shepard, 1978). To withstand constitutional challenge now, a capital sentencing regime must set some limitations on who is eligible for the death penalty as well as permit the sentencing authority to consider the individual characteristics of the accused's case (Hesseltine, 1995). Case-specific consideration or individualization is typically achieved by examining the aggravating and mitigating factors in the case to determine whether the death penalty is warranted.[10]

Considering the general format of capital sentencing statutes described earlier, the concept of psychopathy may enter capital sentence hearings in several ways. In approximately eight states, the accused's risk for engaging in future acts of violence is among the list of possible aggravating factors (Melton et al., 1997). Psychopathy as one indication of risk for future violence could be used to establish this aggravating factor. The PCL-R is better suited in this role than a global diagnosis of sociopathy or ASPD because it carries greater predictive weight than do the latter two diagnoses. Even psychopathy, as defined by the PCL-R, is more appropriately treated as a dimensional score rather than a taxon when future risk is being considered (see chaps. 3, 10, & 14).

It is also possible for psychopathy to function in a mitigating role. Approximately half the states with death penalty provisions invite the sentencing authority to consider mental conditions as mitigating factors. This is so where it can be shown that the defendant was under the influence of an extreme mental or emotional disturbance or, at the time of the offense, the capacity of the defendant to appreciate the criminality of his conduct or to conform his conduct to the requirements of the law was impaired (Berkman, 1989; Melton et al., 1997). Under these provisions, it is conceivable that psychopathy could be considered a mitigating factor, although it is a result that does not appear to occur in practice (e.g., *Shriner*

v. *State*, 1980; *State* v. *Vickers*, 1981). The U.S. Supreme Court ruled in *Lockett* v. *Ohio* (1978) that the sentencing authority must be able to consider and give effect to any relevant mitigating circumstance. As a consequence, psychopathy could serve as a mitigating factor even when it appears unrelated to the factors enumerated in the capital sentencing scheme.

Legal tension over whether psychopathy is a mental disorder worthy of mitigation, or whether it merely identifies habitual and violent offenders who deserve harsher sanctioning by the criminal justice system (see Berkman, 1989), has created a confusing picture within the case law. Evidence of psychopathy, sociopathy, or ASPD frequently has been used, directly or indirectly, to demonstrate the existence of aggravating circumstances (e.g., *Adams* v. *State*, 1979; *Bradford* v. *State*, 1993; *Cook* v. *State*, 1991; *Earhart* v. *State*, 1991; *Satterwhite* v. *Texas*, 1988). Yet there are also cases where the disorder has been viewed as a mitigating factor (e.g., *Clisby* v. *State*, 1982; *State* v. *Caldwell*, 1990), and still others where it was considered for mitigation purposes but rejected (e.g., *Shriner* v. *State*, 1980; *State* v. *Lorraine*, 1993). In Arizona, several judicial rulings rejected the argument that character or personality disorders could constitute mitigating factors on their own, but they accepted that this evidence should be considered to see whether it warrants mitigation on other grounds (*State* v. *Gerlaugh*, 1985; *State* v. *Richmond*, 1977; *State* v. *Vickers*, 1981).

The potential contradictory role of psychopathy in capital sentencing schemes also emerges within the context of individual cases. For example, in *Richard* v. *State* (1992), a psychiatrist had testified at trial that the appellant was a sociopathic personality, antisocial type. The Court of Criminal Appeals of Texas accepted the defendant's sociopathic disorder as a mitigating factor because it could be inferred that the "appellant's conduct in this cause was 'attributable to' his sociopathic personality disorder, which in turn was brought on by the trauma emanating from his 'disadvantaged background' " (p. 283). Yet the court also relied on the accused's sociopathic personality to affirm the jury's conclusion that the defendant constituted a continuing threat to society. Again, such a conclusion is much more defensible where the accused has been carefully assessed for psychopathy and found to have a relatively high score on the PCL–R, rather than simply diagnosed as sociopathic.

At present, the U.S. Supreme Court has not definitively answered whether disorders like psychopathy should be properly considered mitigating or aggravating circumstances, but it has addressed the issue indirectly (Berkman, 1989; Sevilla, 1990; Sondheimer, 1990). In *Zant* v. *Stephens* (1983), the U.S. Supreme Court stated in obitur that it would be reversible error to use a defendant's mental illness as an aggravating factor for purposes of the death penalty. Equally as telling was the court's reference to *Miller* v. *Florida* (1979) to support its judgment (Sevilla, 1990). In *Miller*, a schizophrenic, defendant was found guilty for the sexual homicide of a cab driver. At sentencing, the judge noted the defendant would never recover from his schizophrenia, and therefore the only method of guaranteeing he would not engage in future violence was to impose the death penalty. The Florida Supreme Court overturned the sentence on appeal. In its reasoning, the court ruled that an aggravating factor cannot be the direct consequence of a defendant's mental illness. Together, the holdings in *Miller* and *Zant* hint that if the Supreme Court were to decide this issue, it would rule that mental illness cannot constitute an aggravating factor (Melton et al., 1997).

Even if the U.S. Supreme Court resolves the status of mental illness as either an aggravating factor, a mitigating factor, or both aggravating and mitigating factors, the answer only poses another question: Should psychopathy be considered a mental illness for this purpose? The Ninth Circuit Court of Appeals addressed this issue in *Harris* v. *Pulley* (1988). During the sentencing hearing in this case, the appellant expressed remorse for his crimes and recanted earlier claims that he was innocent. To rebut the accused's apparent remorse, the prosecution introduced psychiatric evidence that the defendant had ASPD. The psychiatrist opined inter alia that individuals with this disorder tend to project blame and do not feel remorse (a likely attribute of psychopathy, but a less certain trait of ASPD). On appeal, it was advanced that the charge to the jury had been in error because it allowed his mental or physical condition to be used as an aggravating factor. The defendant leaned heavily on the holding in *Zant*, claiming that his mental condition could only serve to mitigate his sentence. The court dismissed the appeal, stating,

> Zant suggested that "mental illness" might actually mitigate in favor of a penalty less than death. The "mental disorder" of such antisocial personality is not "mental illness" in the sense used by Zant. (p. 1383)

The court reasoned further that it was quite possible everyone who committed a crime carrying a capital sentence might suffer from a recognized mental disorder. Therefore, to recognize conditions such as ASPD as mitigating factors would make death penalty proceedings irrelevant.

Thus, psychopathy's legal status as a mitigating or aggravating factor is a function of both the capital sentencing scheme and applicable case law. Currently, psychopathy is likely to serve as an aggravating factor in death penalty schemes that permit the sentencing authority to examine the likelihood of future violence. However, according to the legal principle laid down in *Lockett*, the sentencing authority is always free to consider mitigating evidence. Using evidence of psychopathy to demonstrate the existence of a mental disorder in the accused for the purpose of mitigation should not be undertaken lightly. As a result of the negative connotations associated with psychopathy, this information may be of only minimal benefit. Worse, it could even backfire and have a detrimental effect. This possibility is not unfathomable because some death penalty schemes list the factors that may be considered for aggravation and mitigation, but do not specify the direction in which they are valenced (Sondheimer, 1990).

Juvenile Transfers to Adult Court

Public concern over the perceived problem of juvenile crime has led to pressure for more juveniles to stand trial in adult court and face the harsher sentences available in this system (Cintron, 1996; Strottman, 1998). The minimum age for transfer in most jurisdictions is 14, although in some jurisdictions the minimum age is lower than this and in others there is no minimum age at all (Heilbrun, Leheny, Thomas, & Huneycutt, 1997). Presently, decisions to transfer juveniles to adult court are either made by the judiciary, prosecutor, or legislative transfer schemes that mandate automatic transfer for certain specified offenses (Cintron, 1996). Where there is discretionary authority to transfer a juvenile, there are usually several factors that must be considered. Heilbrun et al. (1997) identified several factors that are common to many juvenile transfer schemes and may be relevant to forensic assessments. Psychopathy may be a relevant consideration for three of these factors, including treatment amenability, violence risk, and, possibly, presence of a mental illness.

In juvenile transfer cases, diagnoses of psychopathy, ASPD, or sociopathy are most frequently raised in reference to the juvenile's amenability to treatment. For instance, in *Matter of R.P.R.G.* (1978), the juvenile's ASPD diagnosis[11] was cited by the court as one indication that he was not amenable to treatment, and the court accordingly had the accused transferred to adult court. In several cases involving juveniles diagnosed with ASPD (inappropriately) or sociopathy, the court ordered transfers to adult court not because the juvenile was unamenable to treatment per se, but because there was no prospect for rehabilitation based on the services available within the juvenile system (*Matter of Fox*, 1981; *Matter of M.E.*, 1978; *Morgan v. State*, 1977). Other treatment considerations related to ASPD or sociopathy have included the likelihood of success (*Matter of Fox*, 1981; *Morgan v. State*, 1977) and the possibility that treatment could be achieved within the limited period of incarceration permitted under the juvenile system (*Matter of Fox*, 1981). In cases like these where treatment amenability is at issue, it is more instructive to consider the level of psychopathy rather than a global diagnosis of conduct disorder (CD) or ASPD (Gacono, Nieberding, Owen, Rubel, & Bodholdt, 2001).

The decision in the *Matter of Welfare of D.T.H.* (1997) raised the issues of both amenability for treatment and risk of violence. The court-appointed psychologist in this case opined that the juvenile defendant could be diagnosed with ASPD except that as a juvenile he did not satisfy the minimum age requirement. However, the accused did meet the diagnostic criteria for CD. The psychologist further testified that treatment would be fruitless because there was no cognitive or emotional problem to treat.[12] The psychologist also concluded that the accused should be tried as an adult because he posed a risk to public safety. In a split decision, the majority upheld the lower court decision to send D.T.H. to adult court, citing, among other things, his CD diagnosis, lack of conscience, and the expert evidence that he was dangerous. The dissent took a decidedly different approach, stating that,

> although D.T.H. was not diagnosed with any treatable disorder, his compliance with juvenile programming can certainly be measured in the future, and he should not be punished, in effect, for the fact that he has not been diagnosed as suffering from a psychosis. (p. 747)

In essence, it was the dissent's view that transferring the accused on the premise that he is not amenable to treatment simply amounts to punishing him because he has CD rather than a disorder with brighter treatment prospects.

These cases raise a number of issues that deserve further comment. Most notably, the presence of psychopathy is associated with decisions to transfer youths to adult court usually on the premise that he or she cannot be treated within the juvenile system. However, the absence of psychopathy does not necessarily mean that a juvenile will not be transferred. For example, in *State v. Nevels* (1990), psychopathy was explicitly ruled out as a possible diagnosis, yet the court still decided to transfer the juvenile into the adult system. It is also interesting to find that psychopathy's implications have been largely dominated by concerns over treatability. The relative emphasis on treatment may reflect the rehabilitative model of the 1970s. However, as the current policy trend toward protection of the public continues, it is likely that information on psychopathy will focus more on the risk of violence and less on suitability for treatment. Where the risk of violence is being considered, evidence of psychopathy should be an important factor favoring transfer to adult court.

Finally, in several cases, experts diagnosed youths with ASPD despite that this diagnosis is only available to people 18 years and older. Clearly, the onus is on mental health professionals to ensure their testimony is comprehensive, balanced, and accurate. In addition, legal representatives who familiarize themselves with mental health concepts through reading and consultation should be well prepared to ferret out any inaccuracies that might occur.

CIVIL CONTEXT

The civil context is a broad area of the law (e.g., civil suits relating to contracts or torts, marriage and family matters, mental health issues, etc.), thus the variety of cases in which evidence of psychopathy potentially could arise is equally wide. In practice, however, cases involving psychopathy in the civil setting seem to primarily concern either child custody disputes or civil commitment procedures. This section discusses both of these issues.

Child Custody Issues

Evidence of psychopathy has emerged in a number of cases involving state motions to terminate parental rights. Because a successful application leads to the permanent severance of the parent's ties with the child, the courts must consider carefully what is in the best interests of the child (Melton et al., 1997). In these cases, diagnoses of ASPD or related disorders are inevitably raised on behalf of the state to support the application for severing parental rights, although few cases detail the exact connection between the disorder and the inability to parent. In *J.C.O. v. Anderson* (1987), the father's diagnosis as a sociopath was cited along with numerous other undesirable traits and behaviors as a sign of his general unfitness or incompetence as a parent (see also *Application of L.L.*, 1995). In several other cases, ASPD diagnoses served as the foundation for testimony that the child in question would not be provided with necessary care and support (*In Interest of K.L.*, 1998; *In Interest of W.S.M.*, 1993; *Matter of Yavapai Cty. Juv. A. No. J-9365*, 1988; *State In Interest of Townzen*, 1988).

In some instances, the characteristics of the disorder have been related to specific harmful effects on the child. In *In Re Christina H.* (1992), particular reference was made to the narcissistic characteristics of ASPD as an indication that the father would attend to his own needs before considering the welfare of his child (see also *In Interest of T.T.*, 1995). In another case, evidence of the father's sociopathic disorder was linked to a risk of ongoing sexual abuse (*In Interest of T.T.*, 1983). In this case, there were allegations the father had sexually abused his daughter. One expert at trial testified that the father was a sociopath who had no sense of right or wrong and would continue sexually abusing his daughter if she was returned into his care. Additionally, expert testimony that these disorders are enduring and not amenable to treatment was used in several cases to counter arguments the parent might change (*In Interest of T.T.*, 1983; *In interest of W.S.M.*, 1993; *Matter of Yavapai Cty. Juv. A. No. J-9365*, 1988). Courts have also occasionally relied on evidence that a child was developing into a sociopath to justify terminating parental rights (*State in the Interest of T.S.*, 1996) or revoking a joint custody arrangement in favor of granting sole custody to one parent (*Mettenbrink v. Mettenbrink*, 1985).

As clinical descriptions of psychopathy remind us, it is many of the core personality characteristics' of this disorder (e.g., narcissism, shallow emotions, lack of empathy, etc.) that make psychopaths particularly unsuitable for the role of parent. These same characteristics cannot be assumed to characterize all ASPDs without careful assessment to verify their presence. Given these diagnostic differences, it is likely that psychopathy will be a stronger indicator of parental unfitness than ASPD. Not only are the characteristics of psychopathy incommensurate with supporting and caring for children, but they also suggest that psychopaths are unlikely to engage in protracted and costly legal proceedings to maintain custody of their children. When they do, psychopaths may be motivated more by factors relating to revenge, control, or money than by any bond they have with their children. In fact, the exact opposite is probably more often the case—psychopaths are likely to take little interest or responsibility in raising their children and they probably account for a substantial proportion of ex-partners who fail to pay spouse and child support.

Civil Commitment

In certain limited circumstances, the state can involuntarily confine individuals regardless of whether a criminal offense was committed. The boundary between civil commitment and criminal justice sanctions is not always distinct, and there are circumstances when civil confinement may flow from particular criminal justice system outcomes (e.g., sexual predator laws). One legal consequence of the separation between civil and criminal confinement is that civil commitment laws do not have many of the safeguards available in criminal law. As a result, major differences can exist between civil and criminal confinement, both in terms of substantive law (e.g., definition of mental illness or disorder) and procedural law (e.g., the requirements of due process).

Commitment laws vary widely from state to state, but there are two common features. Before a person may be civilly committed, every state requires the presence of a mental illness or disorder (as defined by that state) and the existence of at least one other secondary condition (Melton et al., 1997). Usually the list of secondary precommitment conditions includes such things as an inability to care for oneself, the individual poses a danger to him or herself, or the individual poses a danger to others (Melton et al., 1997). For two reasons, it is unlikely that a psychopath would satisfy the conditions of most traditional civil commitment laws (i.e., excluding sexual psychopath or sexual predator commitment laws) without the presence of another major mental illness (e.g., *Thornblad* v. *Olson*, 1992). First, psychopaths are not perceived to manifest the serious disorders of thought, mood, or perception that result in the gross impairments of cognition or functioning required by most civil commitment definitions of mental illness. Second, some jurisdictions specifically exclude personality disorders or antisocial personalities as mental conditions for the purposes of civil commitment (Melton et al., 1997).

Two cases recently handed down by the U.S. Supreme Court have important implications for who and under what conditions a person may be civilly confined. The central issue in *Foucha* v. *Louisiana* (1992) was whether a person who is no longer mentally ill can be civilly committed solely on the basis of perceived dangerousness. Foucha originally was found not guilty by reason of insanity because of a drug-induced psychosis and was civilly committed to a forensic hospital. At a judicial hearing commenced 4 years later to determine whether Foucha should be released, one expert testified that Foucha had recovered from the drug-induced psychosis he had been suffering from and that he was now mentally healthy. The court was also informed that Foucha had an antisocial personality, which the expert noted did not constitute a mental disease and was untreatable. After considering Foucha's personality disorder as well as several institutional altercations in which he had been involved, the doctor concluded he would not "feel comfortable in certifying that [Foucha] would not be a danger to himself or other people" (p. 1782). The court ruled that Foucha was dangerous and should not be released.

Foucha appealed the trial decision unsuccessfully through the state courts before the case eventually made its way to the U.S. Supreme Court. Reversing the lower court's ruling in a five to four decision, the plurality for the Supreme Court held that Foucha's continued confinement violated his due process rights. Although the judgment in *Foucha* has been described as *murky* (Janus, 1996), it is widely accepted that the main legal principle to emerge is that civil commitment based on dangerousness will be constitutionally permissible only if the person is also mentally ill (Janus, 1996; Pollock, 1998). Civil commitments based purely on dangerousness will be found unconstitutional (Janus, 1996; Pollock, 1998). Because Foucha's detainment was found unconstitutional despite his ASPD diagnosis, it also might be inferred that ASPD does not legally qualify as a mental illness for civil commitment purposes (Winick, 1995). If indeed this was the intent of the court, it could jeopardize attempts to civilly commit psychopaths through postinsanity or sexual predator commitments.

Two reasons exist for being wary of this interpretation, however. First, Louisiana did not attempt to convince the court that ASPD was a mental illness (Janus, 1996; Pollock, 1998). Second, the primary argument advanced by the state was that civil commitment could be founded exclusively on the basis of dangerousness without the presence of a mental illness (Janus, 1996; Pollock, 1998). Given the possibility that the court never truly addressed the issue of whether ASPD was a mental illness, a more decisive conclusion on this issue would have to await more definitive rulings.

The U.S. Supreme Court's ruling in *Kansas* v. *Hendricks* (1997) resolved some of the ambiguity created by *Foucha*. *Hendricks* involved the validity of a sexual predator law; however, because the scheme utilizes a civil commitment procedure, the implications of this ruling are seen as extending to civil commitment laws in general. Under Kansas law, to be civilly committed as a sexual predator, it must be shown that the person: (a) was convicted or charged with a sexual offense; (b) suffers from a mental abnormality or personality disorder; and (c) due to the abnormality or disorder, is likely to engage in sexual violence (Kansas Stat. Ann. § 59-29a02(a) (1998). The term *mental abnormality* is statutorily defined as

> a congenital condition affecting the emotional or volitional capacity which predisposes the person to commit sexually violent offenses in a degree constituting such person a menace to the health and safety of others. (Kansas Stat. Ann. § 59-29a02(b) (1998)

Shortly before the expiration of Hendricks' prison sentence for taking *indecent liberties* with two 13-year-old boys, the state of Kansas petitioned to commit him indefinitely as a sexual predator. In testimony at trial, one expert informed the court that Hendricks was a pedophile and his condition constituted a mental abnormality. Hendricks admitted being a pedophile who could not control his urges to molest children when he was stressed out. The jury in the case found Hendricks to be a sexual predator and he was committed accordingly. On appeal to the Kansas Supreme Court, Hendricks argued inter alia that the law violated his substantive due process rights because the definition of *mental abnormality* in the Act did not meet the mental illness requirement for civil commitment determined in *Foucha*. The state Supreme Court agreed with Hendricks and struck down the Act—a decision that was appealed to the U.S. Supreme Court.

In a five to four decision, the U.S. Supreme Court overturned the lower court decision and upheld the Kansas sexual predator law. The majority confirmed the decision in *Foucha* that dangerousness may serve as grounds for civil commitment so long as it is paired with some other additional factor such as the presence of a mental illness. In the words of the court,

[t]he precommitment requirement of a "mental abnormality" or "personality disorder" is consistent with . . . other statutes that we have upheld in that it narrows the class of persons eligible for confinement to those who are unable to control their dangerousness. (p. 513)

As this passage indicates, the Court linked the presence of mental illness with impaired volitional control. At this time, it is not apparent whether this link is a mandatory ingredient for a committable mental illness, whether it is merely a reference to the Kansas law, or whether it is simply a general assumption held by the majority (McAllister, 1998; Pollock, 1998).

The *Hendricks* ruling also has important implications for the utility of psychopathy within civil commitment procedures. Although the general right to statutorily define *mental illness* was deferred to state legislatures, the majority clearly endorsed personality disorders as acceptable criteria when and if a state chooses to include them. Thus, depending on the governing statutory language, psychopathy may constitute a legally sufficient mental illness.

Pollock (1998) suggested that ASPD meets substantive due process requirements because it functions to narrow the pool of civilly committable persons, and the impulsiveness associated with the disorder demonstrates a sufficient lack of control to fulfill any volitional impairment element that might be required. Although this position may be correct, there are two reasons for recommending the use of psychopathy over ASPD. First, ASPD diagnoses exist in approximately 60% to 80% of all incarcerated male offenders (Hare, 1991), whereas only 15% to 30% of comparable populations are diagnosed with psychopathy using the PCL-R (see chap. 3). As a result, any constitutional safeguard that ASPD may create by limiting the prospective pool of persons who can be civilly committed, is further strengthened using the PCL-R.

The second reason for favoring the use of the PCL-R over a diagnosis of ASPD exists in the minority judgment of *Hendricks*. Writing for the minority, Justice Breyer supported the validity of the Kansas law because "Hendricks' abnormality does not consist simply of a long course of antisocial behavior." As outlined earlier, ASPD is more vulnerable to this type of criticism because it relies predominantly on antisocial behaviors. By contrast, it is difficult to level this argument against the PCL-R because it taps a much more diverse range of symptoms (see Table 6.1).

Before leaving the topic of civil commitment, brief reference should be made to the issue of treatability because it has important implications for psychopathy. Following *Foucha*, it was theorized that treatability might be one of the key factors that legally distinguished committable from noncommittable mental conditions (Winick, 1995). This supposition was firmly rejected by both the majority and minority opinions in *Hendricks*, who clearly articulated that states may civilly confine the untreatable mentally ill. Although the amenability of psychopaths to treatment has not been the subject of rigorous scientific study, the results to date show a general absence of treatment effects; in some cases, treatment even appears to have a negative effect (Ogloff, Wong, & Greenwood, 1990; Rice, Harris, & Cormier, 1992). These results do not necessarily mean that psychopaths are untreatable, but they do indicate that the treatments studied so far fail to achieve tangible benefits. Thus, if treatability was held to be a requisite condition, it would have raised questions over the use of civil commitment procedures or sexual predator laws with individuals whose only apparent mental condition was psychopathy.

SUMMARY OF THE LAW APPLYING TO PSYCHOPATHY

During the course of reviewing how psychopathy has been applied to various legal issues in this chapter, two broad themes constantly reemerged. The first theme relates to the law's persistent concern that certain legal procedures, especially those that are punitive in nature (e.g., sexual predator laws), only be available to a limited class of individuals. The law's concern with restricting the eligibility pool should impact how psychopathy is assessed because different diagnostic strategies result in a vastly different proportion of psychopaths. Specifically, the prevalence of ASPD within prison populations is substantially higher than PCL-R-determined psychopaths. Because the courts may be more willing to utilize the concept of psychopathy if they believe it identifies a narrow pool of individuals, assessments conducted using the PCL-R may be more legally palatable than assessments conducted using the criteria for ASPD contained in the *DSM-IV*.

The second theme pertains to the relationship of psychopathy to the concept of mental illness. The law generally has not considered this disorder as it has other more conventional mental illnesses. To put it simply, the law looks on psychopaths as *bad*, but not *mad*—a viewpoint that has profoundly influenced legal conceptions of mental disorders. One result of this legal perspective has been to define mental disease and disorder differentially according to the context and purpose of the law. Where the presence of a mental disease or disorder is accorded special considerations under the law, the concept typically has been framed in a narrow manner that excludes psychopathy.

In contrast, where the existence of a mental disease or disorder permits the law to impose more punitive measures, the concept has been construed in sufficiently broad terms to encompass psychopathy. A comparison of insanity and sexually dangerous offender laws illustrate how these divergent legal concepts of mental disease or defect impact the legal treatment of psychopathy. Under most insanity laws, specific steps have been taken to reject psychopathy (e.g., the ALI caveat) as an exculpatory mental disorder or defect. By comparison, the statutory language of many sexual psychopath or sexual predator laws has been purposefully formulated to encompass psychopathy (and other personality disorders, etc.) as qualifying mental abnormalities. In light of *Hendricks* (1997), the legal validity of this approach is not in jeopardy, although it is somewhat inconsistent and illogical.

PROFESSIONAL AND ETHICAL ISSUES IN THE ASSESSMENT OF PSYCHOPATHY IN LEGAL CONTEXTS

The expert who brings the concept of psychopathy into the courtroom also carries with him or her a whole host of ethical and professional issues. It is imperative that mental health experts be cognizant and attend to these issues throughout the course of their participation in legal proceedings. Those experts who fail to do so not only risk casting themselves and possibly their profession into an unfavorable light, but they may even threaten the validity of the legal proceedings.

Mental health professionals are limited to those areas of professional practice for which they are demonstrably competent. Accordingly, mental health professionals must have obtained the proper training and supervised experience necessary to develop the skills and knowledge they purport to possess (Gacono & Hutton, 1994). Moreover, each time mental health professionals offer their services, they must exercise the requisite degree of skill and care to meet or surpass the minimum standards expected for a member of the profession.

Applying these guidelines to the assessment of psychopathy, it should be apparent that mental health professionals need to have a thorough understanding of the disorder (e.g., the prevalence, symptomatology, and implications of the disorder) as well as specialized training in the specific diagnostic tool(s) employed during the assessment process (see chap. 9). Additionally, mental health professionals must maintain their expertise in an area by keeping abreast of new findings and developments. This is particularly true of psychopathy, which has become the subject of intense empirical investigation over the past few years. Mental health professionals can keep up to date by reading the current scientific literature, attending relevant educational workshops and seminars, or conducting research on the topic.

Psychologists and psychiatrists should never conduct an assessment without first obtaining informed consent from the person being assessed. Although the necessity of obtaining informed consent does not vary with the type, purpose, or context of the assessment, the absence of consent for assessments conducted within the legal context may be especially egregious because of the serious consequences that may flow from it. Consent is informed only when the client voluntarily, knowingly, and intelligently agrees to partake in the assessment. This means that the prospective assessee must be apprised of the following minimum information: (a) his or her legal rights with respect to the anticipated forensic service, (b) the purpose of the evaluation, (c) the nature of the procedures to be employed, (d) how the assessment will be used, and (e) the party retaining the services of the assessor.

In assessments that are conducted for legal purposes, the client frequently is a third party (e.g., courts, an institution, etc.) and not the assessee. Nevertheless, the person conducting the assessment still holds an ethical and legal obligation to the examinee that is not vacated unless the assessment is court ordered. Although traditional obligations regarding confidentiality do not attach to assessments ordered by a third party, the fact that the results of the assessment and any information gathered during the assessment process are revealed to a third party must be conveyed to the assessee.

Forensic assessments must be thorough and comprehensive in nature. Although there are a variety of reasons why information about psychopathy might be of legal relevance, it should be clear that psychopathy is highly relevant whenever the risk of future violence is a material legal issue. Furthermore, the comprehensiveness of a forensic assessment is in doubt where the legal issue relates to risk but psychopathy has not been considered (Hart, 1998). In these situations, evaluators who are unable to provide a strong justification for not considering psychopathy may not be fulfilling their ethical obligations. It is doubtful that psychopathy will ever be the only piece of relevant evidence, and therefore mental health professionals must not focus on this disorder to the exclusion of other information that may also be relevant (see chaps. 7 & 9). This is true even where the issue pertains to the likelihood of future violence because other factors also play a role in raising or lowering assessments of risk (Quinsey et al., 1998).

With respect to the actual assessment of psychopathy, it should be conducted using a recognized assessment scheme that includes detailed diagnostic or scoring criteria and empirically established validity and reliability norms. When evidence of psychopathy is tendered in connection with legal issues relating to the risk of future violence, it is critical that the assessment is made using the PCL–R because virtually all the research demonstrating the predictive validity of the disorder is based on these instruments (Hart, 1998). Also, because psychopaths by definition are conning, manipulative, and dishonest, any assessment of this disorder should utilize multiple sources of information, including a personal interview, a review of pertinent file information (e.g., records from schools, employers, and criminal justice system agencies), and interviews with people familiar with the assessee (e.g., partners, friends, relatives etc.; see chaps. 3, 7, & 9).

The assessments conducted by mental health professionals and the conclusions they reach should be firmly grounded in empirical or professional knowledge. Pointing to empirical support is a relatively straightforward task when risk of violence is the issue, but it becomes more difficult, although not necessarily impossible, when other issues are addressed. For their part, opposing counsel should take full advantage of their opportunities to explore the basis for opinions offered by experts to verify that they indeed can be reasonably supported.

Mental health professionals offering opinion evidence are of greatest service to the court when their testimony is framed around the applicable legal standards. To achieve this, experts must familiarize themselves with the relevant law and legal nomenclature—they need to become "a comfortable guest, if not an insider, in the legal system" (Melton, 1987, p. 494). Relatedly, mental health professionals should avoid ultimate issue testimony whenever possible and leave it to the trier of fact to resolve the legal issues. Opinion evidence that is put in conclusionary terms often degenerates into the proverbial *battle of the experts*, and the trier of fact is left with the task of choosing which expert to accept (instead of their true task, which is to carefully examine and weigh the evidence in the case). In short, the role of the expert is best limited to providing information that assists the trier of fact with his or her final determination, and experts should avoid making the final determination for the trier of fact.

Finally, mental health professionals must openly and candidly reveal any limitations associated with their assessment or testimony. Some of the most notorious examples of inappropriate testimony include statements by Dr. Grigson, who routinely testified that an accused was a severe psychopath and would absolutely commit future acts of violence (e.g., *Satterwhite* v. *Texas*, 1988; *Smith* v. *Estelle*, 1977). Clearly, one can never be absolutely certain that someone will perpetrate further acts of violence, although there may be plenty of evidence indicating the person is high risk. The message here is simply that any informational gaps faced by mental health professionals during the assessment process, uncertainties in the final clinical conclusions, or controverted areas of the scientific field need to be explicitly expressed.

ACKNOWLEDGMENTS

The authors are grateful to Stephen D. Hart for his helpful comments and suggestions during the preparation of this chapter.

ENDNOTES

1. As has been emphasized throughout this volume (see chap. 3), many terms have been mistakenly considered synonymous with *psychopathy*. Historically, the courts have echoed clinical confusion in this regard by not expressing an appreciation for the distinction between psychopathy and these other labels.
2. It is difficult to criticize the law for its confusion over the diagnostic and clinical differences that exist between ASPD and psychopathy because the same confusion is evident among many health professionals (see chap. 3). This situation is only exacerbated by the *DSM–IV* (American Psychiatric Association, 1994), which merely states that antisocial personality disorder "has also been referred to as psychopathy, sociopathy, or dissocial personality disorder" (p. 645).
3. Witness credibility is an evidentiary issue that applies in both criminal and civil law contexts.
4. We are not suggesting that jurisdictions attempting to exclude personality disorders from the insanity defense are completely successful in this regard. For example, Reichlin, Bloom, and Williams (1990) report that statutory changes eliminating personality disorders from Oregon's insanity defense did not prevent some personality disordered individuals from being found not guilty by reason of insanity (see also Gacono, Meloy, Sheppard, Speth, & Roske, 1995).
5. *Morally wrong* has been variously interpreted to be either contrary to the moral standards of society or contrary to one's personal moral standards (Ranade, 1998). Because psychopaths are generally regarded to be amoral, a personal or subjective standard may have the unintended effect of making the insanity defense more accessible to individuals with this disorder. Of course, for a defense of insanity to be successful, there must also be a causal link between the mental disease or defect and the failure to appreciate that the act was wrong.
6. Other, less prevalent insanity standards that are not addressed in this chapter are the so-called *product rule* declared in *Durham* v. *United States* (1954) and now only in effect in New Hampshire, and the *irresistible impulse* doctrine originally set out in *Parsons* v. *State* (1886) and currently employed in some form or other in Colorado, Georgia, Kentucky, and Oklahoma.
7. Readers are directed to the discussion on civil commitment in this chapter for an examination of the permissibility of committing psychopaths under sexual psychopath/predator laws and the relevance of treatability to their confinement.
8. In describing the appellant, who was deemed a sexual psychopath, it was noted that "the Cleckley criteria presents 'virtually a word portrait of Mr. Kunshier, as he has been seen clinically over the years'" (p. 883).
9. *Kansas* v. *Hendricks* (1997) is discussed in much greater detail later in the chapter.
10. Capital sentencing schemes employ either a weighing or nonweighing method to consider the aggravating and mitigating factors in a case (see Hesseltine, 1995). Weighing statutes require the sentencing authority to *qualitatively* evaluate all the evidence to determine whether the aggravating factors outweigh the mitigating factors or vice versa. By comparison, nonweighing statutes involve a quantitative evaluation, whereby the

sentencing authority determines the number of applicable aggravating and mitigating factors (i.e., three mitigating factors against two aggravating factors).

11. This case highlights the problem of inaccurate diagnoses in court. The *DSM–IV* (American Psychiatric Association, 1994) criteria clearly limit the diagnosis of ASPD to persons 18 years of age or older.

12. Although the psychologist's statement is valid for psychopathy, it may not apply to CD given the heterogeneous nature of this diagnosis (see chaps. 1 & 2).

REFERENCES

Adams v. *State*, 577 S.W.2d 717 (1979 Tex Crim).

American Law Institute. (1962). *Model penal code: Proposed official draft*. Philadelphia: Author.

American Psychiatric Association. (1980). *Diagnostic and statistical manual of mental disorders* (3rd ed.). Washington, DC: Author.

American Psychiatric Association. (1982). *Statement on the insanity defense*. Washington, DC: Author.

American Psychiatric Association. (1994). *Diagnostic and statistical manual of mental disorders* (4th ed.). Washington, DC: Author.

Anderson v. *Cramlet*, 789 F.2d 840 (10th Cir. 1986).

Appelbaum, P. S. (1993). *Godinez v. Moran*: The U.S. Supreme Court considers competence to stand trial. *Hospital and Community Psychiatry, 44*, 929–930.

Application of L.L., 653 A.2d 873 (D.C.App. 1995).

Arizona Revised Statutes Annotated § 13–502(A) (West 1998).

Berkman, E. F. (1989). Mental illness as an aggravating circumstance in capital sentencing. *Columbia Law Review, 89*, 291–309.

Blair, R. J. R. (1995). A cognitive developmental approach to morality: Investigating the psychopath. *Cognition, 57*, 1–29.

Blair, R. J. R., Jones, L., Clark, F., & Smith, M. (1995). Is the psychopath "morally insane"? *Personality and Individual Differences, 19*(5), 741–752.

Blazak v. *Ricketts*, 1 F.3d 891 (9th Cir. 1993).

Boag v. *Raines*, 769 F.2d 1341 (1985).

Bradford v. *State*, 873 S.W.2d 15 (Tex. Cr. App. 1993).

Bruce v. *Estelle*, 536 F.2d 1051 (5th Cir. 1976), cert. denied, 429 U.S. 1053, 97 S.Ct. 767, 50 L.Ed.2d 770 (1976).

Bursten, B. (1982). What if antisocial personality disorder is an illness? *Bulletin of the American Academy of Psychiatry and Law, 10*, 97–102.

California Penal Code § 25.5 (West 1998).

Campbell, E. (1992). The psychopath and the definition of "mental disease or defect" under the Model Penal Code test of insanity: A question of psychology or a question of law? In J. R. P. Ogloff (Ed.), *Law and psychology: The broadening of the discipline* (pp. 139–170). Durham, NC: Carolina Academic Press.

Cintron, L. A. (1996). Rehabilitating the juvenile court system: Limiting juvenile transfers to adult criminal court. *Northwestern University Law Review, 90*, 1254–1282.

Clisby v. *State*, 456 So.2d 86 (Ala. Cr. App. 1982).

Colorado Revised Statutes Annotated § 16-8-101.5(2)b (West 1998).

Cook v. *State*, 821 S.W.2d 600 (Tex. Cr. App. 1991).

Cooke, D. J., & Michie, C. (1998, September). *Psychopathy: Exploring the hierarchical structure.* Paper presented at the 8th European conference on Psychology and Law, Krakow.

Crowston v. *Goodyear Tire & Rubber Co.*, 521 N.W.2d 401 (N.D. 1994).

Dinwiddle, S. H. (1996). Genetics, antisocial personality disorder, and criminal responsibili-
ty. *Bulletin of the American Academy of Psychiatry and Law, 24*(1), 95–108.
Durham v. *United States,* 214 F.2d 862 (D.C. Cir. 1954).
Dusky v. *United States,* 362 U.S. 402, 80 S.Ct. 788, 4 L.Ed.2d 824 (1960).
Earhart v. *State,* 823 S.W.2d 607 (Tex. Cr. App. 1991).
Elliot, C. (1992). Diagnosing blame: Responsibility and the psychopath. *The Journal of
Medicine and Philosophy, 17,* 199–214.
Federal Rules of Evidence, 28 U.S.C.A. Rule 608 (West, 1999).
Foucha v. *Louisiana* 112 S. Ct. 1780 (1992).
Furman v. *Georgia,* 408 U.S. 238 (1972).
Gacono, C., & Hutton, H. (1994). Suggestions for the clinical and forensic use of the
Psychopathy Checklist Revised (PCL–R). *International Journal Law and Psychiatry, 17,*
303–317.
Gacono, C., Meloy, R., Sheppard, K., Speth, E., & Roske, A. (1995). A clinical investigation of
malingering and psychopathy in hospitalized insanity acquittees. *Bulletin of the American
Academy of Psychiatry and the Law, 23*(3), 1–11.
Gacono, C., Nieberding, R., Owen, A., Rubel, J., & Bodholdt, R. (2001). Treating juvenile and
adult offenders with conduct-disorder, antisocial, and psychopathic personalities, In J. B.
Ashford, B. D. Sales, & W. Reid (Eds.), *Treating adult and juvenile offenders with special
needs* (pp. 99–129). Washington, DC: American Psychological Association.
Group for the Advancement of Psychiatry. (1977). *Psychiatry and sex psychopath legislation:
The 30s to the 80s* (Report number 98). New York: Mental Health Materials Center, Inc.
Grubin, D., & Prentky, R. (1993). Sexual psychopathy laws. *Criminal Behavior and Mental
Health, 3,* 381–392.
Hammel, A. (1995). The importance of being insane: Sexual predator civil commitment laws
and the idea of sex crimes as insane acts. *Houston Law Review, 32,* 775–813.
Hanson, R. K., & Bussière, M. T. (1998). Predicting relapse: A meta-analysis of sexual offend-
er recidivism studies. *Journal of Consulting and Clinical Psychology, 66,* 348–362.
Hare, R. D. (1991). *Manual for the Psychopathy Checklist–Revised.* Toronto: Multi-Health
Systems.
Hare, R. D., & Hart, S. D. (1995). Commentary on antisocial personality disorder: The
DSM–IV field trial. In W. J. Lively (Ed.), *The DSM–IV personality disorders* (pp. 127–134).
New York: Guilford.
Harris v. *Pulley,* 885 F.2d 1354 (9th Cir. 1988).
Hart, S. D. (1998). Psychopathy and risk for violence. In D. Cooke, A. E. Forth, & R. D. Hare
(Eds.), *Psychopathy: Theory, research, and implications for society* (pp. 355–373). Dordrecht,
The Netherlands: Kluwer.
Hart, S. D., & Dempster, R. J. (1997). Impulsivity and psychopathy. In C. D. Webster &
M. A. Jackson (Eds.), *Impulsivity: Theory, assessment, and treatment* (pp. 212–232). New
York: Guilford.
Hart, S. D., & Hare, R. D. (1989). Discriminant validity of the Psychopathy Checklist in a
forensic psychiatric population. *Psychological Assessment: A Journal of Consulting and
Clinical Psychology, 1,* 211–218.
Hart, S. D., & Hare, R. D. (1997). Psychopathy: Assessment and association with criminal
conduct. In D. M. Stroff, J. Breiling, & J. Maser (Eds.), *Handbook of antisocial behavior* (pp.
22–35). New York: Wiley.
Heilbrun, K., Leheny, C., Thomas, L., & Huneycutt, D. (1997). A national survey of U.S.
statutes on juvenile transfer: Implications for policy and practice. *Behavioral Sciences and
the Law, 15,* 125–149.
Heilbrun, K., Ogloff, J. R. P., & Picarello, K. (1999). Dangerous offender statutes in the
United States and Canada: Implications for risk assessment. *International Journal of Law
and Psychiatry, 22,* 393–415.

Hemphill, J. F., Hare, R. D., & Wong, S. (1998). Psychopathy and recidivism: A review. *Legal and Criminological Psychology, 3,* 139–170.

Henderson v. *Dugger,* 522 So.2d 835 (Fla. 1988).

Hesseltine, D. (1995). The evolution of the capital punishment jurisprudence of the United States Supreme Court and the impact of *Tuilaepa* v. *California* on that evolution. *San Diego Law Review, 32,* 593–635.

In Interest of K.L., 972 S.W.2d 456 (Mo. App. W.D. 1998).

In Interest of T.T., 427 So.2d 1382 (Miss. 1983).

In Interest of W.S.M., 845 S.W.2d 147 (Mo. App. W.D. 1993).

In Re Christina H., 618 A.2d 228 (Me. 1992).

In the Interest of T.T., 541 N.W.2d 552 (Iowa App. 1995).

In the Matter of Robert Archie Kunshier, 521 N.W.2d 880 (Minn. Ct. App. 1994).

J.C.O. v. *Anderson,* 734 P.2d 458 (Utah 1987).

Janus, E. S. (1996). Predicting sexual violence: Setting principled constitutional boundaries on sex offender commitments. *Indiana Law Journal, 72,* 157–213.

Kansas v. *Hendricks,* 138 L.Ed. 2d 501, 117 S.Ct. 2072 (1997).

Kansas Statutes Annotated § 59-29a02(a) (1998).

Kosson, D. S., Smith, S. S., & Newman, J. P. (1990). Evaluating the construct validity of psychopathy on Black and White male inmates: Three preliminary studies. *Journal of Abnormal Psychology, 99,* 250–259.

Kropp, P. R. (1992). *The relationship between psychopathy and malingering.* Unpublished doctoral dissertation, Simon Fraser University, Burnaby, British Columbia.

Lewis v. *Velez,* 149 F.R.D. 474 (S.D.N.Y. 1993).

Liebman, J. S., & Shepard, M. J. (1978). Guiding capital sentencing discretion beyond the "boilerplate": Mental disorder as a mitigating factor. *The Georgetown Law Journal, 66,* 757–836.

Lockett v. *Ohio,* 438 U.S. 586 (1978).

Maine Revised Statutes Annotated title 17-A, § 39(2) (West 1997).

Matter of Fox, 625 P.2d 163 (Or. App. 1981).

Matter of M.E., 584 P.2d 1340 (Okl. Cr. 1978).

Matter of R.P.R.G., 584 P.2d 239 (Okl. Cr. 1978).

Matter of Welfare of D.T.H., 572 N.W.2d 742 (Minn. App. 1997).

Matter of Yavapai Cty. Juv. A. No. J-9365, 759 P.2d 643 (Ariz. App. 1988).

McAllister, S. R. (1998). Sex offenders and mental illness: A lesson in federalism and the separation of powers. *Psychology, Public Policy, and Law, 4,* 268–296.

Melton, G. B. (1987). Bringing psychology into the legal system: Opportunities, obstacles, and efficacy. *American Psychologist, 42*(5), 488–495.

Melton, G. B., Petrila, J., Poythress, N. G., & Slobogin, C. (1997). *Psychological evaluations for the courts: A handbook for mental health professionals and lawyers* (2nd ed.). New York: Guilford.

Mettenbrink v. *Mettenbrink,* 371 N.W.2d 310 (Neb. 1985).

Miller, G. H. (1992). Insanity standards. *Psychiatric Annals, 22,* 626–631.

Miller v. *Florida,* 373 So.2d 882 (Fla. 1979).

Minnesota Statutes Annotated § 253B.02 (18b) (West 1998).

Morgan v. *State,* 569 P.2d 474 (Okl. Cr. 1977).

Nedopil, N., Hollweg, M., Hartmann, J., & Jaser, R. (1998). Comorbidity of psychopathy with major mental disorders. In D. Cooke, A. E. Forth, & R. D. Hare (Eds.), *Psychopathy: Theory, research, and implications for society* (pp. 257–268). Dordrecht, The Netherlands: Kluwer.

Ogloff, J. R. P. (1999). Ethical and legal contours of forensic psychology. In R. Roesch, S. D. Hart, & J. R. P. Ogloff (Eds.), *Psychology and law: The state of the discipline* (pp. 405–422). New York: Kluwer Academic/Plenum.

Ogloff, J. R. P., & Lyon, D. R. (1998). Legal issues associated with the concept of psychopathy. In D. Cooke, A. E. Forth, & R. D. Hare (Eds.), *Psychopathy: Theory, research, and implications for society* (pp. 401–422). Dordrecht, The Netherlands: Kluwer.

Ogloff, J. R. P., Roberts, C. F., & Roesch, R. (1993). The insanity defense: Legal standards and clinical assessment. *Applied and Preventive Psychology, 2*, 163–178.

Ogloff, J. R. P., Wallace, D. H., & Otto, R. K. (1991). Competencies in the criminal process. In D. K. Kagehiro & W. S. Laufer (Eds.), *Handbook of psychology and law* (pp. 343–360). New York: Springer-Verlag.

Ogloff, J. R. P., Wong, S., & Greenwood, A. (1990). Treating criminal psychopaths in a therapeutic community program. *Behavioral Sciences and the Law, 8*, 81–90.

Parsons v. State, 81 Ala. 577, 2 So. 854 (1886).

People v. Fields, 673 P.2d 680 (Cal. 1983).

People v. Mouson, 540 N.E.2d 834 (Ill. App. 3d 1989).

People v. Uppole, 97 Ill. App. 3d 72, 52 Ill. Dec 564, 422 NE2d. 245 (1981).

Perlin, M. L. (1994). *The jurisprudence of the insanity defense.* Durham, NC: Carolina Academic Press.

Pollock, B. J. (1998). *Kansas v. Hendricks*: A workable standard for "mental illness" or a push down the slippery slope toward state abuse of civil commitment? *Arizon Law Review, 40*, 319–349.

Quinsey, V. L., Harris, G. T., Rice, M. E., & Cormier, C. A. (1998). *Violent offenders: Appraising and managing risk.* Washington, DC: American Psychological Association.

Quinsey, V. L., Lalumière, M. L., Rice, M. E., & Harris, G. T. (1995). Predicting sexual offenses. In J. C. Campbell (Ed.), *Assessing dangerousness: Violence by sexual offenders, batterers, and child abusers* (pp. 114–137). Thousand Oaks, CA: Sage.

Quinsey, V. L., Rice, M. E., & Harris, G. T. (1995). Actuarial prediction of sexual recidivism. *Journal of Interpersonal Violence, 10*, 85–105.

R. v. M'Naghten, 10 Cl. and F. 200, 8 Eng. Rep. 718 (H.L. 1843).

Ranade, B. V. (1998). Conceptual ambiguities in the insanity defense: State v. Wilson and the new "wrongfulness" standard. *Connecticut Law Review, 30*, 1377–1409.

Reich, J., & Wells, J. (1985). Psychiatric diagnosis and competency to stand trial. *Comprehensive Psychiatry, 26*, 421–432.

Reichlin, S. M., Bloom, J. D., & Williams, M. H. (1990). Post-Hinckley insanity reform in Oregon. *Bulletin of the American Academy of Psychiatry and Law, 18*, 405–412.

Rice, M. E., & Harris, G. T. (1995). Psychopathy, schizophrenia, alcohol abuse, and violent recidivism. *International Journal of Law and Psychiatry, 18(3)*, 333–342.

Rice, M. E., & Harris, G. T. (1997). Cross-validation and extension of the Violence Risk Appraisal Guide for child molesters and rapists. *Law and Human Behavior, 21*, 231–241.

Rice, M., Harris, G., & Cormier, C. (1992). An evaluation of a maximum security therapeutic community for psychopaths and other mentally disordered offenders. *Law and Human Behavior, 16*, 399–412.

Richard v. State, 842 S.W.2d 279 (Tex. Cr. App. 1992).

Roesch, R., & Golding, S. L. (1987). Competency to stand trial. In I. B. Weiner & A. K. Hess (Eds.), *Handbook of forensic psychology* (pp. 378–394). New York: Wiley.

Salekin, R., Rogers, R., & Sewell, K. (1996). A review and meta-analysis of the Psychopathy Checklist and Psychopathy Checklist-Revised: Predictive validity of dangerousness. *Clinical Psychology: Science and Practice, 3*, 203–215.

Satterwhite v. Texas, 108 S.Ct. 1792 (1988).

Sevilla, C. M. (1990). *Anti-social personality disorder: Justification for the death penalty?* Unpublished manuscript.

Sondheimer, J. N. (1990). A continuing source of aggravation: The improper consideration of mitigating factors in death penalty sentencing. *The Hastings Law Journal, 41*, 409–446.

Shriner v. State, 386 So.2d 525 (Fla. 1980).

Simon, R. J., & Aaronson, D. E. (1988). *The insanity defense: A critical assessment of law and policy in the post-Hinckley era.* New York: Praeger.

Smith v. Estelle, 445 F. Supp. 647 (1977).

State In Interest of Townzen, 527 So.2d 579 (La. App. 3 Cir. 1988).

State In the Interest of T.S., 927 P.2d 1124 (Utah App. 1996).

State v. Bolger, 332 N.W.2d 718 (S.D. 1983).

State v. Caldwell, 388 S.E.2d 816 (S.C. 1990).

State v. Gerlaugh, 698 P.2d 694 (Ariz. 1985).

State v. Lorraine 613 N.E.2d 212 (Ohio 1993).

State v. Nevels, 453 N.W.2d 579 (Neb. 1990).

State v. Richey, 64 Ohio St. 3d 353, 595 N.E.2d 915 (Ohio 1992).

State v. Richmond, 114 Ariz. 186, 560 P.2d 41, cert. denied, 433 U.S. 915, 97 S.Ct. 2988, 53 L.Ed.2d 1101 (1977), reh'g denied, 434 U.S. 1323, 98 S.Ct. 8, 54 L.Ed.2d 34 (1977).

State v. Todd, 326 S.E.2d 249 (N.C. 1985).

State v. Vickers, 633 P.2d 315 (Ariz. 1981).

Strottman, K. A. (1998). Creating a downward spiral: Transfer statutes and rebuttable presumptions as answers to juvenile delinquency. *Whittier Law Review, 19,* 707–755.

Thornblad v. Olson, 952 F.2d 1037 (8th Cir. 1992).

Uelmen, G. F. (1980). The psychiatrist, the sociopath and the courts: New lines for an old battle. *Loyola of Los Angeles Law Review, 14,* 1–23.

United States v. Aponte, 591 F.2d 1247 (9th Cir. 1978).

United States v. Barnard, 490 F.2d 907 (U.S. Ct. App. 1973), cert den'd, 94 S. Ct. 1976.

United States v. Daileda, 229 F. Supp. 148 (U.S.D.C. 1964).

United States v. Hiss, 88 F. Supp. 559 (U.S.D.C. 1950), appeal den'd, 185 F.2d 822.

United States v. Jerkins, 871 F.2d 598 (6th Cir. 1989).

United States v. Lindstrom, 698 F.2d 1154 (11th Cir. 1983).

United States v. Pacelli, 521 F. 2d 135 (U.S. Ct. App. 1975).

Wingett v. State, 640 N.E.2d 372 (Ind. 1994).

Winick, B. J. (1995). Ambiguities in the legal meaning and significance of mental illness. *Psychology, Public Policy, and Law, 1*(3), 534–611.

Zant v. Stephens, 462 U.S. 862 (1983).

7

Suggestions for Implementation and Use of the Psychopathy Checklists in Forensic and Clinical Practice

Carl B. Gacono
Private Practice, Austin, Texas

> *". . . but the Emperor has nothing on at all!"*
> —The Emperor's new Clothes, Hans Christian Andersen
>
> *"Silence is the virtue of fools."*
> —Sir Francis Bacon

Psychopathy has proved to be a robust construct that transcends the cultural biases associated with other characterological diagnoses such as antisocial personality disorder (ASPD; Murphy, 1976; see Table 7.1). Research with the Psychopathy Checklists (PCL, PCL–R, Hare, 1991a) has demonstrated that psychopathic traits can be assessed in a reliable fashion within forensic populations. Strong validity findings, particularly in the area of predicting reoffense and violence, indicates that psychopathy level is an essential independent measure when studying offender populations (Gacono & Meloy, 1992, 1994; Gacono, Nieberding, Owen, Rubel, & Bodholdt, 2001). The absence of this principal measurement (e.g., in treatment outcome studies) can confound findings and bring unwanted criticism to the researcher. Demographics, diagnosis, or committing offense are no longer sufficient as inclusion measures.

The emergence of the PCL–R as the *sine que non* research scale for assessing psychopathy occurred gradually. By contrast, interest in its clinical applications has grown rapidly. In fact, clinical interest has outpaced the development of clinical guidelines (Gacono, 1998; Gacono & Hutton, 1994; Meloy & Gacono, 1995; Serin, 1992). The predictive ability of the

TABLE 7.1
Psychopathy Characteristics

1. Glibness/superficial charm
2. Grandiose sense of self-worth
3. Need for stimulation/proneness to boredom
4. Pathological lying
5. Conning/manipulative
6. Lack of remorse or guilt
7. Shallow affect
8. Callous/lack of empathy
9. Parasitic lifestyle
10. Poor behavioral controls
11. Promiscuous sexual behavior
12. Early behavior problems
13. Lack of realistic, long-term goals
14. Impulsivity
15. Irresponsibility
16. Failure to accept responsibility for own actions
17. Many short-term marital relationships
18. Juvenile delinquency
19. Revocation of conditional release
20. Criminal versatility

Note. From Hare (1980) and Hare et al. (1990).

scale — particularly in the areas of institutional violence, and both violent and generic recidivism (Harris, Rice, & Cormier, 1991; Hart, Kropp, & Hare, 1988; Rice, 1997; Rice, Harris, & Quinsey, 1990; Serin, 1991, 1992; Serin, Peters, & Barbaree, 1990; Wong, 1984) — has attracted the attention of correctional researchers, forensic psychologists, mental health workers, and administrative and policy personnel. Many institutions have already begun to use the PCL–R for making decisions concerning treatment, out-placement, and conditional release (Correctional Services of Canada, 1990; Cotton, 1989; Gacono, 1998; Gacono & Hutton, 1994; Hare, 1998; Serin, 1992; Meloy, Haroun, & Schiller, 1991).

Increased interest from clinical and forensic practitioners has resulted in a growing demand for training and guidance in utilizing the PCL–R. This chapter offers guidelines for implementing the Psychopathy Checklist–Revised (PCL–R) within a correctional or forensic mental health setting. Suggestions stem from the author's use of the PCL–R in research and clinical settings, as well as training of other psychologists and psychology interns to do so.[1]

WHY USE THE PCL–R?

What institutional benefits are gained from routine assessment of psychopathy? Does the early identification of patients or inmates[2] prone to violent behavior (Hare & McPherson, 1984; Williamson, Hare, & Wong, 1987) and treatment failure (Ogloff, Wong, & Greenwood, 1990; Rice, 1997; Rice, Harris, & Cormier, 1992) offer any tangible rewards? The most likely answer to these questions is "yes," and a sampling of advantages is outlined next:

1. Prescreening prevents inappropriate admissions. When inmates with high PCL–R scores are transferred to less secure prison or hospital settings, they participate in routine psychiatric, psychological, and medical evaluations. These procedures are costly especially in light of likely recommendations involving return to higher level security. Since psychopaths are more violent than nonpsychopaths (Hare & McPherson, 1984), controlling and monitoring the disruptive behaviors of these patients involves the use of disproportionate amounts of staff time, predominantly in the form of attending to disruptive behavior, which of course detracts from patient and staff morale and available resources allotted for legitimate treatment purposes. Staff and patient injuries from violent acting out are not uncommon and result in increased financial liability (medical/hospital care; injuries). Use of an abbreviated version of the PCL–R, the PCL:SV (Hart, Cox, & Hare, 1995), in screening can aid in making clinical decisions, which decrease inappropriate referrals.[3] Elevated PCL:SV scores indicate a need for more thorough assessment.

2. Identifying high-risk offenders can guide staff in developing specialized treatment plans for monitoring, controlling, and treating behavior. At a large maximum security forensic psychiatric hospital, patients scoring ≥ 28 on the PCL–R with a history of violence toward others were required to undergo a special administrative review and a clinical assessment of dangerousness before being granted increased privileges, specifically related to less supervision. At a low security level Federal Medical Center Substance Abuse Treatment Program, elevated PCL–R scores, while not excluding inmates from substance abuse treatment, allowed high scorers to be carefully monitored with immediate consequences for rule infractions or nontherapeutic attitudes. Given their inflexible personality, these psychopaths often were expelled or withdrew voluntarily from treatment. Empirical-based PCL–R data can also help staff anchor and understand countertransference reactions (Gacono et al., 2001; Meloy et al., 1991).

3. Administrative support for assessing psychopathy protects staff while increasing their morale. Early identification of potentially violent offenders may decrease incidents involving serious injury within the institution.[4] Standardized assessment procedures allow clinicians to take a leadership role in confronting workplace violence (Davis, 1997)—an issue that should never be ignored or accepted as *part of the job*. Burnout

may be a natural correlate of working with difficult inmates; however, burnout can be reduced with the assistance of an enlightened and supportive administration.

4. Assessing psychopathy makes standardized testing a professional contribution to security. Assessment provides a collaborate bridge between mental health staff and custody. Within forensic settings, relegating professional staff to correctional duties in nonemergency situations can have a negative impact on morale while creating ethical dilemmas (Gacono et al., 2001). Psychopathy assessment elevates the professional's role by allowing their specialized education to become a valued and integral part of the institution's security procedures. Useful recommendations for managing inmates come from evaluations of psychopathy and violence risk.

5. Unmonitored high PCL–R scorers are apt to victimize other patients. Particularly within a hospital setting, low functioning patients are at risk for all manner of exploitation: monetarily, sexually, emotionally, and so on. (Gacono & Meloy, 1994). Patients are also indirectly victimized by the absence of staff attention and bed space allocated to an unresponsive psychopathic *patient* (Gacono et al., 2001).

6. PCL–R data are useful in assessing community risk. When an identifiable psychopath is released from custody prematurely and subsequently commits a heinous crime, the result is all the more tragic when validated test procedures exist to limit such instances.[5] Cases where staff have been duped by psychopaths are not atypical. Many inmates who have committed heinous offenses in the community could have been identified as high-risk offenders through PCL–R evaluation (Quinsey & Walker, 1992). Use of PCL–R scores for partialing out risk related to psychopathy can increase the precision of risk assessment schemes by allowing more careful inspection of other risk factors and risk-reduction factors among offenders with similar levels of psychopathy (H. Richards, personal communication, August 1998). Failure to incorporate such assessments has a snowballing effect in terms of mistaken public perception and policy development. It is as costly monetarily as it is to those felons who in fact are amenable to rehabilitation. In the future, mental professionals who conduct risk assessments without the PCL–R may find themselves to be at ethical or even civil risk.

These are only several of many issues that support the routine assessment of psychopathy within the institution. Unfortunately, the impetus for incorporating psychopathy assessment into institutional policy often occurs as a reaction to a serious assault or heinous community offense.[6] Serious incidents result in unwanted media attention and public scrutiny. Political and social pressures force a careful reexamination of institutional policy regarding patient evaluation. Proactive planning rather than reactive intervention is administratively desirable, ensuring the smooth assimilation of patient evaluation into institutional policy and routine (Serin, 1992). Why, one might ask, do some institutions appear to operate reactively rather than proactively only to, like the inmate residents, suddenly find *religion* after a tragic event? Policy evaluation and change is recommended over continued denial. Psychologists must accept responsibility for educating administrators regarding any specialized assessment needs within their respective treatment populations. The following procedural and ethical guidelines might reduce liability in the face of patient or inmate litigation.

FORGING AN ALLIANCE: STAFFING AND STAFF ROLES

Key administrators such as executive and medical directors (hospitals), wardens and associate wardens (corrections), and department heads need to understand the value of assessing psychopathy within their institution. An outside expert or resident staff with extensive hospital or correctional experience, well-versed in psychopathy research literature, and knowledgeable concerning clinical usage of the Psychopathy Checklists can familiarize administrators with the concept of psychopathy, review the predictive validity of the Psychopathy Scales, and present areas of potential, including financial benefits.

Typically an action plan outlining the necessary steps for implementing psychopathy assessment within the institution is developed by the chief psychologist or an equivalent position. Appointing an advisory committee to oversee the implementation process is the next logical step following introduction of the instrument to administration. Psychologists' knowledge of test construction, psychometrics, and associated ethical issues make them logical members for the core of such a committee. Ideally an advisory committee has at least one delegate from each major personnel subdivision. Examples include administration, front-line staff, social work, chemical dependency, psychology, psychiatry, and custody. Research on staff morale and motivation has fairly consistently demonstrated that cooperation and commitment are enhanced wherever workers have the perception of participation and voice (Schultz & Schultz, 1998).

The advisory committee's initial tasks include developing a proposal for staff training and formulating guidelines for the Psychopathy Checklist's (PCL, PCL-R, PCL:SV, and PCL:YV) use. Training should include all institutional staff; everyone plays a role in assessing or managing high-risk offenders. Educating staff as to their respective roles can prevent the negative effects of role ambiguity and role conflict (Keenan & Newton, 1987; Schultz & Schultz, 1998). Standards for training/certifying staff in PCL–R and PCL:SV administration and interpretation are needed. It is essential that professional staff performing evaluations have a documented history of performing proficient and reliable assessments. Raters should establish acceptable interrater agreement. Ultimately, the advisory committee is directly or indirectly involved in evaluating the scale's use (i.e., developing norms and cutoff scores, and assessing cultural effects). Hasty implementation can diminish the value of psychopathy assessment, whereas a thoughtful introduction that addresses institutional systems (Schultz & Schultz, 1998) can lead to its becoming an integral part of institutional procedures.[7]

That everyone plays a critical role in assessing or managing high-risk offenders cannot be overstated. Line staff such as correctional officers, psychiatric technicians, and nurses must be able to identify psychopathic attitudes and behaviors. Their high frequency of contact with inmates/ patients makes their observations (when recorded in an objective manner) invaluable to the evaluator. Line staff are often the front line of intervention and hence require specialized training in managing psychopaths.[8] Social workers are trained to obtain psychosocial data. They have access to independent sources of information such as family interviews and records from parole, probation, and other institutions that are essential for reliable and valid assessment. Understanding psychopathy criteria allows social workers to incorporate additional areas of inquiry into their routine interviewing and data gathering. Psychiatrists are part of the treatment team in forensic settings (hospitals/prisons). They usually appreciate how PCL–R data can be used to refine diagnosis, identify high-risk offenders, and provide empirical grounding for forensic testimony. The psychologist's assessment can be used independently from or conjointly with a psychiatric interview (Gacono & Hutton, 1994). Although any team (hospital) or unit team (corrections) member can raise issues suggesting the need for a PCL–R assessment, psychiatrists' questions concerning diagnosis, malingering, or treatment amenability often stimulate a referral. Because both psychiatrists and social workers routinely interview and refer patients for further evaluation, they should be proficient in administering the PCL:SV (Hart, Cox, & Hare, 1995).[9] Last, training in psychometrics and test theory make psychologists the best candidates for administrating, scoring, and interpreting the PCL and PCL–R (Meloy & Gacono, 1995). Other professionals who meet requirements for PCL–R usage in clinical settings (Hare, 1991) might also be considered. However, the standards for clinical administration and use exceed those required for research use. The remainder of this chapter discusses the evaluator's role and provides guidelines for the clinical and forensic use of the checklists.[10]

TRAINING FOR PSYCHOPATHY CHECKLIST USERS

The Psychopathy Checklists should only be used in client populations such as prisons and forensic psychiatric facilities, where it has been fully validated (Hare, 1991a). Clinicians should possess an advanced degree in the social or behavioral sciences; be licensed with the local, state, or provincial registration body that regulates the assessment and diagnosis of mental disorders; and have demonstrated experience with forensic populations. Training and supervision are necessary prerequisites for PCL-R usage (Hare, 1991a). Like other standardized psychological instruments, the role of thorough training needs to be underscored (Gacono & Hutton, 1994; Serin, 1992). Access to a PCL-R manual is not sufficient for administering, scoring, and interpreting the Psychopathy Checklists (Gacono & Hutton, 1994; Hare, 1991a). Like other psychological tests, ethical use of the PCL-R requires specialized training and supervision.

One acceptable training method involves trainees watching video-taped mock assessment interviews (provided by Dr. Hare), rating the subjects interviewed, and then submitting scores to Hare's lab to assess interrater reliability (Hare, 1991a). As an alternative, small clinician groups can practice rating subjects and develop their own interrater agreement (Hare, 1991a) after participating in specialized training workshops. Consultation with a skilled rater is necessary to ensure accurate administration and scoring, and to resolve scoring differences. Although adequate reliabilities over a minimum of 10 ratings are recommended before using the checklists for research purposes (Hare, 1991a), clinical standards are higher. Frequent PCL-R use after the training period and the use of two raters whenever possible is preferred (Gacono & Hutton, 1994). A two-rater protocol is encouraged in those forensic cases that are most likely to be carefully scrutinized or those that involve patients whose history suggests risk to the public; these are often one in the same.

Workshops can familiarize large numbers of institutional staff with the Psychopathy Checklist's reliability and validity and can provide potential raters with practice in administration and scoring. Small interview groups of two or three raters and individual supervision, however, are best suited for practicing the record review and live clinical interviews. Prolonged training within an institutional setting is preferred over a single workshop because conducting many PCL-R ratings with a variety of patients differing in ethnicity, diagnosis, gender, age, and psychopathy level better prepares the examiner for using the instrument.

A Training Model for Psychologists

Successful training results in reliable and valid Psychopathy Checklist administration, scoring, and interpretation. Training often begins with an introductory workshop for all staff. During this introduction, staff are introduced to the concept of psychopathy and how it differs from other diagnoses such as ASPD. Staff become familiar with psychopathy criteria and the PCL–R's reliability and validity.

Subsequent to this introduction, potential raters continue to meet and discuss administration and scoring procedures. Scoring strategies are discussed for each PCL–R item, and participants score several cases—some from record data only (Wong, 1988) and others based on record data combined with videotaped interviews. At the end of 2 to 3 days of workshops, participants typically demonstrate a rudimentary proficiency in administration and scoring.

After completing the workshops, psychologists participate in 5 to 10 PCL–R interviews with an experienced rater. These interviews generally include one to two trainees. Trainees review the medical and legal records, documented information relevant to scoring, and then observe an experienced rater complete the PCL–R interview and Information Schedule (or, in the case of the skilled interviewer, the Clinical and Forensic Interview Schedule; see Appendix A, this volume; Gacono, 1994). Prior to completing the interview, trainees pose additional questions needed for independent scoring. After raters have scored the PCL–R, the rationale for scoring individual items and differences are discussed. By the final practice session, each trainee should conduct one or two supervised interviews.

PCL–R advisory committee standards for certification at Atascadero State Hospital (ASH) required psychologists to complete a minimum of five PCL–R ratings with an experienced rater, an averaged score no greater than 2 points from the trainer's rating, no directional biases across scoring, and conducting one supervised interview. Remediation was offered to raters who failed these requirements.[11]

As depicted in Figs. 7.1 and 7.2, the ASH training resulted in reliable psychopathy ratings. Seventy-five percent ($n = 110$) of the ratings were $\leq$ 1 point from the trainers rating, 17% ($n = 25$) differed by 2 points, and 7.6% ($n = 11$) by > 2 points. Figure 7.2 addresses the issue of scorer bias. When compared with the trainer, trainees as a group did not systematically over or underscore subjects. Thirty-eight percent ($n = 55$) of the scores exceeded the trainer's rating, 39% ($n = 57$) of the scores were less than the trainer's rating, and 23% ($n = 34$) of the scores were equivalent to the trainer's rating. There were also no instances of directional bias within individual trainees. Figure 7.1 reveals the high levels of reliability possible when advanced graduate level psychology students and forensic psychologists participate in adequate training.

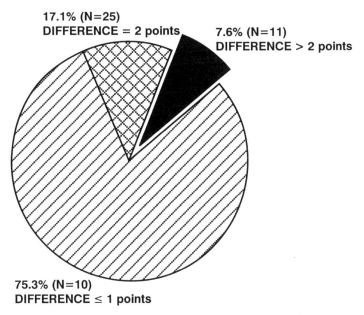

17.1% (N=25)
DIFFERENCE = 2 points

7.6% (N=11)
DIFFERENCE > 2 points

75.3% (N=10)
DIFFERENCE ≤ 1 points

FIG. 7.1. PCL-R interrater reliability (N = 146, ratings).

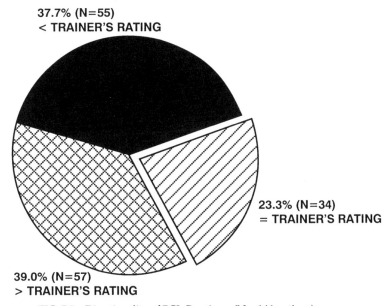

37.7% (N=55)
< TRAINER'S RATING

23.3% (N=34)
= TRAINER'S RATING

39.0% (N=57)
> TRAINER'S RATING

FIG. 7.2. Directionality of PCL-R ratings (N = 146, ratings).

HOW IS PSYCHOPATHY LEVEL ASSESSED?

The PCL–R is a 20-item, 40-point scale (see Table 7.1). For each item, raters assign a score of 0 (*trait does not apply*), 1 (*some elements of the trait exist*), 2 (*a reasonably good match in most essential aspects*), or omit (*item cannot be scored based on available information*). Data are obtained from record review and semistructured interview as recommended (Hart, Hare, & Harpur, 1992; Serin, 1992). Whenever possible, and especially in high-profile cases, two raters should evaluate the patient and average their independent ratings for the final PCL–R score (Hare, 1991a). In typical clinical practice, routine use of two raters is usually unfeasible. Alternatively, an evaluator should seek consultation and periodically participate in interviews with other experienced raters (Gacono & Hutton, 1994).

Record Review

While reviewing records for psychopathy ratings, no other competing purpose should be pursued. Clinicians should make note of other areas that might require additional evaluation or testing, but reserve this inquiry for a separate session. For example, a thorough sexual history is warranted when assessing sexual deviance; however, only a portion of such information is needed for PCL–R scoring. Although essential to assessing dangerousness, PCL–R data is only one component (Rice, 1997).

Since sufficient collateral information (records) are necessary for a valid PCL–R rating, interviews should always await the availability of record information. In hospital settings, several sources of collateral information—such as psychiatric and social histories, police reports, staff behavioral observations, and previous psychological evaluations—are frequently available. Developing a systematic method for recording historical data, such as the *Clinical and Forensic Interview Schedule* included in Appendix A, facilitates an efficient interview. The *Clinical and Forensic Interview Schedule* allow the examiner to link the data they are recording directly to specific items. This approach is useful in research settings as well.

A thorough record review with systematic note taking allows the examiner to assess certain content-based items, such as Items 18 (Juvenile Delinquency) and 20 (Criminal Versatility, the variety of offenses in the adult criminal record), prior to the interview. The record review also aids in developing hypotheses about characterological trait-based items (Gacono, 1998) and provides comparative data for information obtained during interviewing. All record information should be reviewed prior to interviewing.

Clinical Interview

The PCL–R assessment should be introduced to staff and patients as part of a psychological evaluation. Staff should not inform patients that they are going for a Hare interview or are to be assessed for psychopathy level. The reason for evaluation should be explained in the context of a referral question. Introducing a PCL–R evaluation otherwise may set a negative tone for the interview or even, given the complexity of policy that will regulate PCL–R usage, may provide the patient with inaccurate information.

After all records are reviewed and pertinent information is recorded, the examiner precedes to the interview. Hare has provided a 16-page *Interview and Information Schedule* (Hare, 1991b) to guide the PCL–R interview. This information schedule is organized into 10 sections: School Adjustment, Work History, Career Goals, Finances, Health, Family Life, Sex/Relationships, Drug Use, Childhood/Adolescent Antisocial Behavior, and Adult Antisocial Behavior. Since concomitant questions are not explicitly linked to specific ratings, psychologists utilize responses plus collateral information to address PCL–R ratings after the interview is completed (Rogers, 1995). This burdensome process is unlike most semi-structured interviews, where questioning is linked to specific ratings and scoring is completed during the interview. The *Interview and Information Schedule* format is foreign to experienced interviewers, who, as suggested by Rogers (1995), ". . . develop their own system for recording patient responses" (p. 230).

The PCL–R *Clinical and Forensic Interview Schedule* (*CIS*; see Appendix A; Gacono, 1994) typically takes less time to administer than the *Interview and Information Schedule*. Many of the same questions contained in the *Interview and Information Schedule* are used during the *CIS*; however, the sequence of questioning is linked to specific PCL–R items and item clusters. First, a chronological life history is obtained and recorded. This information provides a template for then assessing, in order, Items 20, 19, 18, 12, 17, 11, 3/14/15, 6/7/8/16, 10, 4/5, 9, 13, and 1/2 (Gacono, 1994). This sequence was developed over the course of administering hundreds of PCL–Rs (Gacono & Hutton, 1994). Rapport develops while interviewing, as the *CIS* begins with less threatening, behaviorally anchored items and progresses to less structured, personality, trait-based items. Information from early items contributes to scoring later items. For example, Glibness (1) and Grandiosity (2) can often be scored by the end of the *CIS* with few additional questions. Record data, subject presentation, and information from items such as Lack of Remorse (6) and Failure to Accept Responsibility for Own Actions (16) are frequently sufficient for scoring Items 1 and 2.

Interview efficiency increases when information is organized around item clusters (see *CIS* in Appendix A). For example, Proneness to Boredom

(3), Impulsivity (14), and Irresponsibility (15) are related and, in part, can be inferred from frequent change of address, job, or relationship, coupled with a lack of planning, substance abuse on the job, being terminated from employment, or quitting jobs without giving notice. Frequent speeding tickets and enjoyment in reckless driving are elements of both Proneness to Boredom and Irresponsibility. Efficient interviewing skills allow an item to be assessed and scored prior to proceeding with the interview. When the examiner is uncertain about scoring several items (e.g., whether an individual item should be scored as 0 versus 1 or 1 versus 2, the *Manual* suggests that half the items in question should be scored higher and half lower (Hare, 1991a). Although this procedure applies equally to clinical and forensic usage, obtaining the true score for each item prevents unwanted scrutiny of the examiner's scoring decisions. Since recorded information is linked to specific items, the examiner can quickly refer to the *CIS* to identify the data used for scoring specific items.

Examiners must question sufficiently to obtain valid ratings. Practice with the *Interview and Information Schedule* can help the beginning or inexperienced rater develop a repertoire of relevant questions. In addition, collateral records, questions from the *CIS*, and any other relevant queries (to scoring the PCL–R) should be utilized. Although with experience the examiner's efficiency will increase, initially it is better to over question than conduct a incomplete inquiry. Individual items or item clusters should be fully assessed prior to proceeding to subsequent ones.

The *CIS* format is generally nonthreatening and can be used in a manner that builds rapport. Ratings do not differ significantly when completed under the expressed promise of confidentiality (research) or as part of a preparole psychological assessment (Serin, 1992). In my clinical experience, the few subjects who did become indignant, not surprisingly, proved to be psychopathic on subsequent PCL–R assessment.

Scorer Variance

A rater needs to develop a prototype or ideal image for each item based on Hare's (1991a) criteria. This is contrasted with the tendency to base ratings on preconceived or popular definitions of the scale terms. Once a prototype is developed, a rater assesses the degree to which the subject matches this image. Beginning raters have a tendency to seek a perfect match to score an item as a 2. Rather, a 2 is scored if the

> item applies to the individual (and is) a reasonably good match in most essential respects; behavior is generally consistent with the flavor and intent of the item, even if only a few of the characteristics are displayed, providing

that, in the rater's opinion, they are sufficiently extreme in intensity, frequency, or duration. (Hare, 1991a, p. 6)

Ratings are based on life-long patterns and typical functioning.

Introspection concerning etiology may bias scoring and hence should be avoided. Psychopaths are notorious at being able to structure a naive listener's understanding of events, whereby all manner of antisocial behavior makes sense or even appears inevitable. Less naive raters learn to discern a small handful of bottom line themes to a tangled, endless array of short stories and long stories, which, framed as they are, appear briefly to capture the etiology of behavior.

Item 9, Parasitic Lifestyle, is an exception to this rule, in that *able-bodied* is included as a discriminator. For example, some psychotic patients may clearly meet the criteria for a score of 2 on a given item. Raters believing that the patient is not psychopathic may unwittingly lower an item from 2 to 1 to tailor the PCL-R score to fit their diagnostic formulation. Any subject can obtain a 2 on a few items and still obtain a low total PCL-R score. The validity data indicate that the total score will discriminate among levels of psychopathy in both correctional and forensic mental health settings (Hare, 1991a; Hart & Hare, 1989).

Confidence in the instrument can be obtained by comparison to base rates and means for like populations. Most patients in a forensic psychiatric facility are expected to score around 20 (Hart & Hare, 1989), whereas the mean for a prison population is 23 (Hare, 1991a). Repeat offenders who meet the criteria for ASPD seldom score below 18. When a patient carrying an Axis I psychotic disorder scores a standard deviation above the mean, this reflects comorbid elements of character pathology (Axis II; Gacono & Hutton, 1994). Confidence in the meaning of the final score is grounded in numerous validity studies, whereas confidence in the validity of an individual rating should be described in the Assessment Findings or similar section of the formal report.

WHEN ARE THE PSYCHOPATHY CHECKLISTS USED?

The PCL:SV is an excellent screen for admissions. Following admission, the PCL-R should be used in the following circumstances: suspected malingering; presence of a lengthy criminal history; diagnosis of ASPD (American Psychiatric Association, 1987); presence of predatory violence; referral questions involve treatment amenability or violence potential: or aid in institutional classification and management. With the exception of extent of criminal history and severity of antisocial personality, these other referral questions require additional specialized tests or procedures (see chap. 9). The PCL-R provides access to one variable, psychopathy level, whereas most clinical questions require a battery or multiple methods to provide valid recommendations (Gacono, 1998; Meloy & Gacono, 1995). Often a combination of structured and unstructured assessment tools (Gacono, 1990, 1998), such as the PCL-R, record review, Rorschach Test, the MMPI-2, and tests of cognitive functions, can address most forensic referral questions (Gacono & Hutton, 1994; Meloy & Gacono, 1995).

Assessing violence risk is important within forensic settings (see chaps. 10 & 14). The PCL-R can aid in identifying high-risk offenders (Quinsey & Walker, 1992). Used alone, the PCL-R does not discriminate among all forms of dangerousness. An assessment of dangerousness always considers both situational and personality factors (Meloy, 1987; Monahan, 1981) and addresses both affective and predatory patterns (Meloy, 1988). Among violent offenders, elevated PCL-R scores (≥ 30) signal the likelihood of planned/purposeful (predatory) violence (Hare & McPherson, 1984) and correlate with weapons use, male stranger victims, and violence related to monetary and secondary gain (Hare & McPherson, 1984). In contrast, moderate or even low scores are more frequent in psychotic or other patients prone to affective (driven by emotion) violence. Within the institution, individuals prone to predatory violence (planned/purposeful) require different management strategies than those whose violence is primarily affective (Gacono & Hutton, 1994).

Nonpsychopathic sexual sadists are part of a second violence-prone group that may not score in the high PCL-R range. In our sample of 38 sexual homicide perpetrators approximately two thirds were psychopathic (PCL-R ≥ 30; Gacono, Meloy, & Bridges, 2000). One sexual sadist (PCL-R = 20), whose offense patterns were organized (Ressler, Burgess, & Douglas, 1988) and progressing toward a sexual homicide had a history of alcoholism, sexual sadism, childhood abuse, and depression. When questioned about the impact of his behavior on victims and fairness of sentences (Items 6 & 16 — i.e., What should have happened to you? Effects of your behavior on victims? Have your sentences generally been lenient, fair, or harsh?), the patient, with intense affect, stated, "I'm a no good SOB and should have been put to death." This is in marked contrast to a second patient (PCL-R = 37.5) with similar sexually deviant behaviors who stated, in response to the same questions, "Doc, if I had buried their bodies in the desert I might have got away with it." During his hospital stay, the first patient expressed a desire to be castrated rather than be released and face the possibility of reoffending. Sexual sadists may or may not commit a variety of offenses (Item 20) or share the same juvenile precursors (Items 12 & 18) as psychopaths. Thus, despite their heinous crimes, a subgroup of sadists can score in the moderate ranges of the PCL-R (e.g.,

20–25). When sexual sadism coexists with psychopathy, however, the potential for violence becomes more ominous and likely.

HOW IS THE PCL–R DATA INTEGRATED INTO REPORTS?

Within the body of the report, PCL–R scores can be used to describe the severity of existing psychopathic characteristics (see chap. 9). Ranges can be integrated as a qualifier on Axis II within a multiaxial diagnosis. Individual items can help structure and organize clinical descriptions of the patient or inmate (Gacono, 1998; see Appendix C). For high PCL–R scorers, dangerousness can be described by referring to extant validity findings. Last, modified PCL–R scoring procedures can be used to assess offenders with lengthy institutional histories.

Describing ranges as severe, moderate, or low has been suggested (Hare, 1991a; Meloy, 1988), but does not substitute for relating findings to the specific individual within the body of the report (Gacono & Hutton, 1994). The moderate range (20–29) identifies a heterogeneous mix of psychopaths and nonpsychopaths (Hare, 1991a). For example, although many of their behaviors (Factor 2) are similar to patients scoring 28 or 29 on the PCL–R, forensic patients with a score of 21 generally have fewer Factor 1 elements (i.e., they are less aggressively narcissistic). To make finer discriminations between such offenders, PCL–R scores can be described in ranges in the report narrative (see Table 7.2). Although these ranges are not empirically derived as actuarial markers related to risk, they do allow the examiner to more accurately anchor the findings within the body of the report.

A psychopathy designation (PCL–R; Hare, 1991a) is not the same as an ASPD (American Psychiatric Association, 1994; see Gacono et al., 2000). Describing psychopathic traits helps refine and specify the much less specific diagnosis of ASPD. Ranges suggested by Hare (1991a) and

TABLE 7.2
Suggested Ranges for Reporting PCL–R scores

Value	Description
≥ 33	Severe range
30–32	Low end of severe range (low severe)
27–29	High end of moderate range (high moderate)
23–26	Moderate range
20–22	Low end of moderate range (low moderate)
≤ 19	Low range

Meloy (1988) can be included on Axis II and used to qualify an ASPD as severe (≥ 30), moderate (20–29), or mild (> 20). The following two case excerpts illustrate psychopathy descriptions for two ASPD patients with differing PCL-R scores. Items that correlate with report statements are referenced in parentheses; in clinical practice, such referents would not be included.

> Mr. P's Axis II 301.70 ASPD can be classified at the low end of the moder-
> ate range. Mr. P.'s history lacks juvenile arrests (18) or severe childhood
> behavioral problems (12). As an adult, he has worked at several jobs, the
> longest lasting 4 years (9). Although at times he exhibits attitudes of entitle-
> ment (2), this is primarily related to "felt" inadequacy. His sensitivity to
> both real and perceived criticism (2) relates to difficulty accepting responsi-
> bility for negative behaviors (16) and impairment in empathy (8). Past
> behaviors have not included cruel behavior toward animals, stealing from
> family, or other callous behaviors (8). Mr. P tends to blame others for his
> actions and does not demonstrate true remorse (6 & 16). Although at times
> he verbalizes remorse, he has done little to change his behavior. Albeit lim-
> ited, Mr. P. does experience a range of affect. At times dramatic (7), his affect
> is generally empty or depressed. He is quick to anger when he feels mis-
> treated (7). Mr. P's problems include substance abuse (primarily alcohol),
> anger and impulse management, and depressed mood.

In contrast to Mr. P (PCL-R = 22), Mr. J.'s ASPD can be classified as severe (PCL-R = 34).

> Mr. J. meets the criteria for 301.83 Borderline Personality Disorder and
> 301.70 severe ASPD. Mr. J. has little concern for others, and uses them as
> objects for immediate gratification (8). He demonstrates a chronically irre-
> sponsible lifestyle, motivated by thrill seeking and chronic boredom (3, 15).
> He readily lies to present himself in a favorable light or to get what he
> wants: "I'm a chronic liar, the best liar you've ever seen. I can talk my way
> out of anything" (4). Mr. J. is a very manipulative individual who has no
> remorse for past behaviors. He demonstrates a callous lack of empathy
> toward others. Mr. J. is also very impulsive and is unable or unwilling to
> control aggressive outbursts (10).

The PCL-R item clusters can be used to structure the content of report findings. These characteristics should be illustrated with the patient's real-world behavior. The following is a report excerpt from a mentally disordered offender (PCL-R = 34.5) whose referral questions included diagnosis and treatment amenability.

> Mr. B. clearly meets the criteria for 301.70 severe ASPD. His criminal histo-
> ry began at age 8 with stealing a purse (12). Mr. B. was in Juvenile Hall at
> age 12, the California Youth Authority during his adolescence (18), and has

been incarcerated most of his adult life (20). Between ages 18 and 37, Mr. B. has only been in the community 3 and a half years (20).

Mr. B. is a verbally facile and glib individual (1) with a very lofty opinion of himself (2). Although he talks at length about himself, he actually reveals little substantive information (1). His embellished stories demonstrate an inflated self-image and are intended to leave the examiner with a favorable impression (1, 2). Mr. B. has a great deal of difficulty empathizing with others (8). An absence of remorse is indicated, in part, through his tendency to minimize the impact of behavior on his victims (6, 16). For example, despite having committed many offenses, including robberies and assaults, he states, "I only hurt two people" during my life.

Mr. B.'s lifestyle is impulsive (14) and thrill-seeking. He consistently demonstrates a proneness to boredom and a need to be involved in exciting activities (3), many of which have been illegal (3). He describes himself as preferring to "live on the edge," "where the action is" (3). He also evidences a pattern of irresponsibility in which he does not consider the impact of his behavior on others (15). He has stolen from family members to support his drug abuse and has exploited others financially despite his ability to work (9).

Notwithstanding the limitations of predicting dangerousness (e.g., Monahan, 1981, 1984, 1992; Monahan & Steadman, 1994), psychopathy level has repeatedly been found to correlate with violent reoffense (Rice, 1997; see chaps. 3, 10, & 14). Forensic reports can cite findings demonstrating the significant relationship between high PCL–R scores and the likelihood of future violence. The following excerpt (PCL–R = 37.5) is part of a dangerousness assessment that describes psychopathy in the context of group data.[12]

> Mr. S.'s 301.70 ASPD can be classified as severe. Individuals like Mr. S. display a combination of aggressive narcissism and antisocial behavior. This results in greater criminality and violence relative to those with a milder disturbance. Research indicates that such individuals are more likely to commit violent offenses, commit more offenses, engage in predatory violence, be more verbally threatening and physically violent while in institutions, continue their offending pattern much later into life, show less investment in and poorer response to treatment, violate parole more often, and finally reoffend sooner than nonpsychopathic offenders. The research also indicates that, although some antisocial behaviors may decrease later in adult life, the pathological narcissism that often fuels violent behavior may not. Mr. S.'s severe ASPD places him in a group at higher risk for these behaviors.

Mr. S.'s sexual sadism and the lack of any appreciable personality change were identified as contributing factors to his ongoing dangerousness during testimony.

Young adult offenders whose current incarceration began prior to age 18 present special scoring problems (Forth, Kosson, & Hare, 1997). Since they have never been in the community as adults, items such as Short-Term Marital Relationships (17) and Revocation of Conditional Release (19) may have to be omitted and the final score prorated. As the following case (PCL-R = 28) indicates, adjustments should reflect the examiner's confidence in the PCL-R ratings' validity.

> Mr. D.'s 301.70 ASPD is estimated to be within the high end of the moderate range. Because Mr. D. has been incarcerated since age 17, he has not had the opportunity to engage in many of the behaviors associated with criminal psychopathy. . . . Although he does lack remorse (6) and is deficient in empathy (8), it is difficult to fully assess with a high degree of confidence his level of psychopathy.

Reporting PCL-R findings to staff and patients should follow the same guidelines as other psychological evaluations. They should be integrated with other assessment data, anchored in a specific referral question, and presented as findings. A subject's introduction to test feedback should occur in the context of a referral question, as is often the case when referred for treatment recommendations (Gacono, 1998). To prevent misuse, PCL-R scores should be treated with the same precautions as other raw test data (American Psychological Association, 1985, 1991). I am reminded of one psychopathic patient who, on inadvertently being informed of his PCL-R score of 32, proceeded to boast to other patients concerning how well he did on the *test*. Sometimes more is not better.

ETHICAL CONSIDERATIONS

The PCL-R's development has been consonant with the reliability and validation procedures outlined by *Standards for Educational and Psychological Testing* (American Psychological Association, 1985) and others (Anastasi, 1988). For clinical usage, there are several additional ethical considerations to be addressed (see chap. 6). Testing standards recommend that diagnostic classifications made from performance scores be determined empirically. Appropriate diagnostic cutoffs are currently being developed using a variety of external validation and cluster analytic studies (Hare, 1991a; Rogers, 1995). At present, recommended ranges are based on statistical ranges and clinical judgment (Hare, 1985b, 1991; Meloy, 1988; Gacono & Hutton, 1994). Clinicians using the PCL-R are advised to examine the suggested ranges and then determine the most effective diagnostic cutoffs in their settings (see chap. 11). In an outpatient day treatment program for seriously mentally ill patients, a PCL-R score of 15 to 25, although not indicating a psychopathic syndrome, could be cause for serious concern on any number of fronts.

When reporting PCL-R results, range of performance and qualitative descriptions are preferred over specific numerical scores (Anastasi, 1988;

Gacono & Hutton, 1994; Meloy & Gacono, 1995). Each score should be considered in the context of the standard error of measurement (SEM). The PCL-R has an SEM of 3.25 (Hare, 1985), which indicates that, for a score of 30 (low severe range), the odds would be roughly 2 to 1 that the *true score* (a statistical construct) would not exceed 33.25 (severe range) or fall below 26.75 (moderate range). The interval of the numerical score spans two ranges (6.5 points) and should be so noted (American Psychological Association, 1985). The use of ranges rather than numerical scores also allows for comparison to a category that provides a meaningful context. The cutoffs described in Table 7.2 provide categorical labels.[13] Interpretations are strengthened when several independently obtained sources of data are used (American Psychological Association, 1985; Heilbrun, 1992). The choice of testing battery varies related to the referral question. PCL-R cutoff scores should only be used in conjunction with other data (e.g., Gacono, 1998; Meloy & Gacono, 1995).

Cautionary statements are particularly relevant when testing minority clients (Meloy, 1992; Rogers, 1995). African-American males show similar interjudge reliability and validity findings on the PCL-R relative to White males, but do score slightly higher and show a less differentiated two-factor structure (Kosson, Smith, & Newman, 1990). There are encouraging findings from a growing body of research on the use of the PCL-R with women (Neary, 1990; Piotrowski, Tusel, Sees, Banys, & Hall, 1996; Rutherford, Cacciola, Alterman, & McKay, 1996; Salekin, Rogers, & Sewell, 1997; Strachan & Hare, 1998). Additional studies have found that the PCL-R predicts recidivism in samples of adolescent offenders (Gretton, 1997; Gretton, McBride, O'Shaughnesy, & Hare, 1995; Toupin, Mercier, Dery, Cote, & Hodgins, 1996), female offenders (Loucks, 1995; Zaparniuk & Paris, 1995), male federal offenders (Hemphill et al., 1998; Zamble & Palmer, 1996), forensic psychiatric patients (Hill, Rogers, & Bickford, 1996; Wintrup, Coles, Hart, & Webster, 1994), civil psychiatric patients (Douglas, Ogloff, & Nicholls, 1997), African-American offenders (Hemphill, Newman, & Hare, 1997), and sex offenders (Rice & Harris, 1997).

Forensic Testimony

Although the *Standards* do not specifically mention the use of psychological tests in a judicial setting, general guidelines apply. Psychologists should be prepared to describe their qualifications for using the scale (American Psychological Association, 1991). Qualifications must follow the *PCL-R Manual* (Hare, 1991a) guidelines for use in clinical settings and include adequate training (Gacono & Hutton, 1994). Adequate training always involves supervision and establishing a history of adequate interrater scoring agreement. Psychologists are responsible for following standardized administration and scoring procedures outlined in the manual (Hare, 1991a; Heilbrun, 1992). During direct or cross-examination, scale users should be prepared to present their qualifications including specific PCL–R training experiences to describe the PCL–R's development and relevant research, justify the cutting scores used to form diagnoses, and discuss the comparability of the examinee to normative groups (Butcher & Pope, 1990).

The use of PCL–R findings in the courtroom involves establishing the instrument's reliability and validity, demonstrating relevance to specific legal issues, as well as describing the instrument's acceptance into the scientific community (Heilbrun, 1992). In the past, the *Frye* rule provided a standard of general acceptance to guide the admissibility of scientific evidence. The so-called *Frye test* is no longer relevant in many jurisdictions because guidance about admissibility of the PCL–R in U.S. federal courts is now provided by *Daubert v. Merrell Dow* (U.S. Supreme Court, 1993). The judge's discretionary choice to allow introduction of the PCL–R is based largely on the PCL–R's relevance to the case and the PCL–R's *reliability* (a legal term that actually means scientific validity). In general, when the instrument is specifically constructed for the issue or question to which the psychologist is testifying, there is less challenge to the measure's appropriateness (Blau, 1984).

CONCLUSION

Paradoxically, we have witnessed a general deemphasis in the use of assessment during a period in mental health history where assessment advances have made the process invaluable (Meyer et al., 1998). Some lay professionals wrongly equate assessment with psychological testing. Assessment has been characterized as a process that,

> . . . integrat(es) the results of several carefully selected tests with relevant history information and observation . . . enabl(ing) the sophisticated clinician to form an accurate, in-depth understanding of the patient; formulate the most appropriate and cost-effective treatment plan; and later, monitor the course of intervention. (Meyer et al., 1998)

Assessment is a process of deduction, selective inquiry, and inference. Assessment is rooted in a knowledge of developmental psychology, personality and individual differences, statistics and measurement, with knowledge of limits (e.g., in predication) in cognitive science, ethics, and abnormal psychology, including dynamics and defense, with a keen awareness of various substantive issues such as acculturation, minority issues, malingering and deception, transference, countertransference, and so on (R. Bodholdt, personal communication, October 1998). Assessment forms the cornerstone of the forensic mind set—one that is data based, utilizing test data, observation, interviewing, and multisources of substantiated historical information in forming, testing, and modifying hypothesis. Ultimately, true assessment allows the clinician to articulate the steps that lead to their clinical and forensic opinions. It is not surprising that psychologists resent being supported in a testing role under the guise that testing offers the benefit of true assessment. Assessment is a multifaceted, ongoing, interactive process; as such, it often blends imperceivably with treatment, staff education, and program evaluation and development. One cannot advocate for testing and expect to achieve assessment.

This chapter extends the notion of assessment to an organizational context (see chap. 13) and must be regarded as such. By no means could the chapter attend to all layers of context beneath it, nor is it likely to anticipate the unique attendant context or proclivities/constraints within an organization or the relationship of a specific organization (prison) to the greater whole (department of corrections). The psychologist holds a special responsibility to see that this context not be lost and that a well-rounded, unbiased education (protocol) be provided about benefits and costs of introducing an instrument such as the PCL–R (R. Bodholdt). When an administration institutes a program on the scale of testing and proclaim or expect the benefit of assessment, we are obligated to identify the limits of such window dressing. In this regard, when political convenience supersedes ethical and professional considerations, it is often the psychologist's unique grounding in empirically based assessment that forces them into the, at times, awkward position of proclaiming, "the emperor has no clothes." So be it.

At a time when assessment is being devalued at large, it may be difficult to introduce this type of instrument or any instrument to an organization. At the same time, when the clinician has a professional skill of considerable use to an organization, but fails to educate about it, whose responsibility is it if a false conclusion—nobody is interested—results.

The PCL–R has reached a point where in certain situations it probably should be regarded as an essential clinical tool. Research continues into possible roles in other organizations. For example, many institutions that manage violent offenders prolong the induction of the PCL–R as part of their assessment protocol. Some of these same institutions require clinicians to make recommendations concerning early parole or community release. They offer that the PCL–R is too time-intensive. Yet the same institution promotes the routine use of window dressing protocols—specifically, empty assessment protocols filled with paper-and-pencil tests that have little relationship to risk assessment (window dressing). Information such as that offered in this chapter is needed to counter detractors. First, the collateral information necessary for scoring the PCL–R is routinely reviewed for every offender during any screening or assessment process. When the record reviewer and PCL–R administerer are one in the same, use of the *Clinical and Forensic Interview Schedule* (*CIS;* see Appendix A) allows for an expedient completion of the PCL–R. Second, not every offender needs a full PCL–R assessment. Triaging procedures help determine and guide when the PCL–R should be administered. Finally, from a cost-benefit perspective, professionals must wrestle with the potential ethical and civil liabilities involved in releasing a violent offender prematurely who has not been assessed for psychopathy level, only to have him or her violently reoffend. Since the extant research demonstrates that psychopathy assessment constitutes an essential aspect of the accepted standard of care for risk assessment, how can this practice be defended ethically or legally?

Within institutions that manage violent patients or inmates, it is essential to develop policy and procedures that guide violence management and ensure the safety of staff and patients. In this area, psychologists can embrace an assessment role that distinguishes them from other mental health professionals, allows them to walk hand in hand in clinical respectability with other staff, and provides, in certain cases, essential information that cannot be obtained with similar efficacy by other methods. Assessment should not be an afterthought; rather, the process should begin at admissions with standardized triage procedures. Unfortunately, in far too many settings, clinicians have failed to heed Brittain's (1970) warning, "We cannot treat, except empirically, what we do not understand and we cannot prevent, except fortuitously, what we don not comprehend" (p. 206), with sometimes tragic and fatal outcomes.

Psychopathy assessment plays an integral role in the management of institutional violence—as a guide to treatment planning (see Appendix C), as an aid in release decisions, and as part of a assessment battery designed to answer specific forensic questions. Implications of the Psychopathy Checklist's robust validity findings in these areas should be easily understood by clinicians and nonclinicians alike. With appropriate training, implementation of standardized procedures, and continued study of the instrument's clinical validity, the PCL–R is becoming an invaluable clinical instrument for assessing psychopathy within criminal populations (Heilbrun, 1992; Rice et al., 1992).

ENDNOTES

1. Over the past 15 years, I have used the Psychopathy Checklists in both research and clinical/forensic practice. In the fall of 1988, I introduced the PCL–R to Atascadero State Hospital (ASH; the largest maximum security forensic psychiatric facility in North America) staff. Subsequent to the PCL–R's introduction, psychopathy assessment was assimilated into policy and practice, and PCL–R training was offered to staff and students from other hospitals and correctional settings. Appreciation is extended to Dr. Robert Bodholdt for his comments and suggestions on this chapter.

2. Throughout this chapter, *patient* and *inmate* are used interchangeably depending on the setting—hospital or correctional.
3. Ethical practice dictates that treatment not be denied solely on a subject's PCL-R score. A high score on the PCL:SV, however, can alert the evaluator to the need for a thorough evaluation of treatment amenability before approving transfer. Multiple data sources are used when making clinical decisions with the PCL-R (Gacono & Hutton, 1994; Meloy & Gacono, 1995; Quinsey & Walker, 1992). PCL-R data should only be one source of information used by clinicians in considering institutional privileges.
4. At a large maximum security forensic hospital, increased emphasis was placed on assessing psychopathy level and violence potential after the unfortunate and tragic murder of a staff member by a psychopathic patient.
5. TJ was approved for early parole partially on the recommendation of his treating psychologist, who indicated treatment improvement. As part of PCL-R staff training, another psychologist interviewed TJ. Much to the dismay of TJ's treating psychologist, who observed the interview, TJ demonstrated glibness and grandiosity while boasting about his manipulation of the clinical staff. Most dramatic was TJ's revelation that, should he be detained by an officer after release, he would "just blow them away." Subsequent to the interview, TJ's treating psychologist changed his recommendation. Fortunately, TJ was not released.
6. In one state, an undiagnosed sexual psychopath (PCL-R > 30) was released from a treatment setting, as cured, only to commit several sexual murders. Several state legislatures have altered violent sex offender treatment laws after similar incidents.
7. Inappropriate use of the PCL-R, such as using a single cutoff score to deny patients treatment or access to lower security levels, can discredit the instrument and impede its acceptance. Using the PCL-R in an ethical manner, such as designating a patient with a high PCL-R score ($\geq$ 28) and a history of violence toward others for a special administrative and clinical review including a clinical assessment of violence potential prior to assignment of security status, will aid its implementation.
8. Managing psychopaths and other severe character disorders requires involvement from all staff, including administration. In forensic hospitals, treatment teams formulate specialized treatment plans that require administrative approval. Treatment teams also require administrative support for developing policies that prevent institutional violence and allow prosecution of patients who assault staff.
9. The PCL-R should be used for research, establishing norms, or answering clinical and forensic questions. The PCL:SV is an excellent tool for screening. It is not a substitute for the PCL-R. Screening is critical prior to Department of Corrections transfers to lower level security institutions, such as forensic hospitals.
10. With the permission of Pergamon Press, the remainder of this chapter is an adapted version of "Suggestions for the Clinical and Forensic Use of the Psychopathy Checklist-Revised," *International Journal of Law and Psychiatry, 17*(3), 1994.
11. One interesting scoring pattern emerged in several raters. They routinely underscored several Factor 1 items. Factor 1 of the PCL-R correlates with narcissistic and histrionic personality disorders (Harpur, Hare, & Hakstian, 1989). Whether this pattern could be attributed to personality traits of the examiner (Gacono et al., 2000; Richards, 1993) remains unexplained and merits further study.
12. Application of group data to individual cases should be done with caution because other factors influence this theoretical premise (Monahan, 1981). These factors include, but are not limited to, individual differences, score distributions within a group, sensitivity and specificity of the predictor (psychopathy), and so on (see chap. 11).
13. Serin (1992) raised the following issues in selecting an appropriate cutoff score: "(A) researcher may adopt fairly stringent criteria to identify a relatively more homogeneous group (Wong, 1988), but this increases the false negative errors (incorrectly identified

failures). Decision-makers, however, may attempt to establish a cut-off that minimizes false positives (incorrectly identified successes). Lastly, clinicians may attempt to balance between false positives and false negatives, thereby selecting the cut-off that yields the fewest errors overall. The dilemma becomes less ambiguous in the case of violent recidivism, where no subject with a PCL–R score less than 23 was recommitted for a violent offense" (p. 640).

REFERENCES

American Psychiatric Association. (1987). *Diagnostic and statistical manual of mental disorders* (3rd ed., rev.). Washington, DC: Author.
American Psychiatric Association. (1994). *Diagnostic and statistical manual of mental disorders* (4th ed.). Washington, DC: Author.
American Psychological Association. (1991). *Ethical principles of psychologists*. Washington, DC: Author.
American Psychological Association. (1985). *Standards for educational and psychological testing*. Washington, DC: Author.
Anastasi, A. (1988). *Psychological testing* (6th ed.). New York: Macmillan.
Blau, T. H. (1984). Psychological tests in the courtroom. *Professional Psychology: Research and Practice, 15,* 176–186.
Brittian, R. (1970). The sadistic murderer. *Medical Science and the Law, 10,* 198–207.
Butcher, J. N., & Pope, K. S. (1990). MMPI-2: A practical guide to clinical, psychometric, and ethical issues. *Independent Practitioner, 10,* 20–25.
Cooke, D. (1998). Psychopathy across cultures. In D. Cooke, A. Forth, & R. Hare (Eds.), *Psychopathy: Theory, research and implications for society* (pp. 13–45). The Netherlands: Kluwer Academic Publishers.
Correctional Services of Canada. (1990). *Task force on mental health care*. Ottawa, Canada: Author.
Cotton, D. J. (1989). *Forensic assessment survey results and model forensic assessment protocol recommendations*. Pinole, CA: California Department of Mental Health, Forensic Services Branch, Conditional Release Program.
Daubert v. Merrell Dow Pharmaceuticals, Inc., 113 S. Ct. 2786 (1993)
Davis, D. (1997). *Threats pending, fuses burning: Managing workplace violence*. Palo Alto, CA: Davies-Black.
Douglas, K. S., Ogloff, J. R., & Nicholls, T. L. (1997, June). Personality disorders and violence in civil psychiatric patients. In C. D. Webster (Chair), *Personality disorders and violence*. Symposium conducted at the meeting of the fifth International Congress on the Disorders of Personality, Vancouver, British Columbia, Canada.
Forth, A., Kosson, D., & Hare, R. (1997). *Psychopathy Checklist: Youth Version* (Draft Version). North Tonawanda, NY: Multi-Health Systems.
Gacono, C. B. (1990). An empirical study of object relations and defensive operations in antisocial personality disorder. *Journal of Personality Assessment, 54,* 589–600.
Gacono, C. B. (1994). *The Hare PCL–R: Clinical Interview Schedule* (Adult Form). Unpublished.
Gacono, C. B. (1998). The use of the Psychopathy Checklist–Revised (PCL–R) and Rorschach in treatment planning with antisocial personality disordered patients. *International Journal of Offender Therapy and Comparative Criminology, 42*(1), 49–64.
Gacono, C. B., & Hutton, H. E. (1994). Suggestions for the clinical and forensic use of the Hare Psychopathy Checklist–Revised (PCL–R). *International Journal of Law and Psychiatry, 17*(3), 303–317.
Gacono, C. B., & Meloy, J. N. (1992). The Rorschach and the *DSM–III–R* antisocial personality: A tribute to Robert Lindner. *Journal of Clinical Psychology, 48*(3), 393–405.

Gacono, C. B., & Meloy, J. N. (1994). *The Rorschach assessment of aggressive and psychopathic personalities*. Hillsdale, NJ: Lawrence Erlbaum Associates.

Gacono, C. B., Meloy, J. N., & Bridges, M. (2000). A Rorschach comparison of psychopaths, sexual homicide perpetrators, and nonviolent pedophiles: Where angels fear to tread. *Journal of Clinical Psychology.*

Gacono, C. B., Nieberding, R., Owen, A., Rubel, J., & Bodholdt, R. (2001). Treating juvenile and adult offenders with conduct-disorder, antisocial, and psychopathic personalities. In J. B. Ashford, B. D. Sales, & W. Reid (Eds.), *Treating adult and juvenile offenders with special needs* (pp. 99–129). Washington, DC: American Psychological Association.

Gretton, H. M. (1997). *Psychopathy and recidivism from adolescence to adulthood: A ten year retrospective follow-up*. Unpublished doctoral dissertation, University of British Columbia, Vancouver, Canada.

Gretton, H. M., McBride, M., O'Shaughnessy, R., & Hare, R. D. (1995, October). *Psychopathy in adolescent sex offenders: A follow-up study*. Paper presented at the 14th annual Research and Treatment Conference for the Association for the Treatment of Sexual Abusers, New Orleans, LA.

Hare, R. D. (1980). A research scale for the assessment of psychopathy in criminal populations. *Personality and Individual Differences, 1,* 111–119.

Hare, R. D. (1985a). *The Psychopathy Checklist*. Unpublished manuscript, University of British Columbia, Department of Psychology, Vancouver, Canada.

Hare, R. D. (1985b). Comparison of procedures for the assessment of psychopathy. *Journal of Consulting and Clinical Psychology, 53,* 7–16.

Hare, R. D. (1991a). *The Hare Psychopathy Checklist–Revised (PCL–R)*. Toronto, Ontario: Multi-Health Systems.

Hare, R. D. (1991b). *The Hare PCL–R: Interview and information schedule*. Toronto, Ontario: Multi-Health Systems.

Hare, R. D. (1998). The Hare PCL–R: Some issues concerning its use and misuse. *Legal and Criminological Psychology, 3,* 99–119.

Hare, R., & McPherson, L. (1984). Violent and aggressive behavior by criminal psychopaths. *International Journal of Law and Psychiatry, 7,* 35–50.

Hare, R. D., Harpur, T. J., Hakstian, A. R., Forth, A. E., Hart, S. D., & Newman, J. P. (1990). The Revised Psychopathy Checklist: Descriptive statistics, reliability, and factor structure. *Psychological Assessment, 2,* 338–341.

Harpur, T., Hare, R., & Hakstian, R. (1989). Two factor conceptualization of psychopathy: Construct validity and assessment implications. *Psychological Assessment: A Journal of Consulting and Clinical Psychology, 1*(1), 6–17.

Harris, G. T., Rice, M. E., & Cormier, C. A. (1991). Psychopathy and violent recidivism. *Law and Human Behavior, 15,* 625–637.

Hart, S. D., Cox, D. N., & Hare, R. D. (1995). *Psychopathy Checklist: Screen Version*. Toronto, Ontario: Multi-Health Systems.

Hart, S. D., & Hare, R. D. (1989). Discriminant validity of the Psychopathy Checklist in a forensic psychiatric population. *Psychological Assessment: A Journal of Consulting and ClinicalPsychology, 1,* 211–218.

Hart, S. D., Hare, R. D., & Harpur, T. J. (1992). The Psychopathy Checklist–Revised (PCL–R): An overview for researchers and clinicians. In J. Rosen & P. McReynolds (Eds.), *Advances in psychological assessment (Vol. 8)*. New York: Plenum.

Hart, S. D., Kropp, P. R., & Hare, R. D. (1988). Performance of male psychopaths following conditional release from prison. *Journal of Consulting and Clinical Psychology, 56,* 227–232.

Heilbrun, K. (1992). The role of psychological testing in forensic assessment. *Law and Human Behavior, 16*(3), 257–272.

Hemphill, J. F., Newman, J. P., & Hare, R. D. (1997). *Psychopathy and recidivism among Black offenders*. Unpublished raw data.

Hemphill, J. R., Templeman, R., Wong, S., & Hare, R. D. (1998). Psychopathy and crime: Recidivism and criminal careers. In D. J. Cooke, A. F. Forth, & R. D. Hare (Eds.), *Psychopathy: Theory, research, and implications for society* (pp. 375–399). Dordrecht, The Netherlands: Kluwer.

Hill, C. D., Rogers, R., & Bickford, M. E. (1996). Predicting aggressive and socially disruptive behavior in a maximum security forensic psychiatric hospital. *Journal of Forensic Sciences, 41*, 56–59.

Keenan, A., & Newton, T. J. (1987). Work difficulties and stress in young professional engineers. *Journal of Occupational Psychology, 60*, 133–145.

Kosson, D., Smith, S., & Newman, J. (1990). Evaluating the construct validity of psychopathy in Black and White male inmates: Three preliminary studies. *Journal of Abnormal Psychology, 99*(3), 250–259.

Loucks, A. D. (1995). *Criminal behavior, violent behavior, and prison maladjustment in federal female offenders.* Unpublished doctoral dissertation, Queen's University, Kingston, Ontario, Canada.

Meloy, J. R. (1987). The prediction of violence in outpatient psychotherapy. *American Journal of Psychotherapy, 41*, 38–45.

Meloy, J. R. (1988). *The psychopathic mind: Origins, dynamics, and treatment.* Northvale, NJ: Jason Aronson.

Meloy, J. R. (1992). *Violent attachments.* Northvale, NJ: Jason Aronson.

Meloy, J. R., & Gacono, C. B. (1995). Assessing the psychopathic personality. In J. Butcher (Ed.), *Clinical personality assessment: Practical approaches* (pp. 410–422). New York: Oxford University Press.

Meloy, J. R., Haroun, A., & Schiller, E. (1991). *Clinical guidelines for involuntary outpatient treatment.* Sarasota, FL: Professional Resource Exchange.

Meyer, G., Finn, S., Eyde, L., Kay, G., Kubiszyn, T., Moreland, K., Eisman, E., & Dies, R. (1998). *Benefits and costs of psychological assessment in healthcare delivery: Report of the Board of Professional Affairs Psychological Assessment Work Group, Part I.* Washington, DC: American Psychological Association Practice Directorate.

Monahan, J. (1981). *Predicting violent behavior.* Beverly Hills, CA: Sage.

Monahan, J. (1984). The prediction of violent behavior: Toward a second generation of theory and policy. *American Journal of Psychiatry, 141*(1), 10–15.

Monahan, J. (1992). Mental disorder and violent behavior: Perceptions and evidence. *American Psychologist, 47*, 511–521.

Monahan, J., & Steadman, H. J. (1994). *Violence and mental disorder: Developments in risk assessment.* Chicago, IL: University of Chicago Press.

Murphy, J. (1976). Psychiatric labeling in cross-cultural perspective. *Science, 191*, 1019–1028.

Neary, A. (1990). DSM–III *and Psychopathy Checklist assessment of antisocial personality disorder in Black and White female felons.* Unpublished doctoral dissertation, University of Missouri, St. Louis, MO.

Ogloff, J., Wong, S., & Greenwood, A. (1990). Treating criminal psychopaths in a therapeutic community program. *Behavioral Sciences and the Law, 8*, 81–90.

Piotrowski, H., Tusel, D. J., Sees, K. L., Banys, P., & Hall, S. M. (1996). Psychopathy and antisocial personality disorder in men and women with primary opioid dependence. In D. J. Cooke, A. E. Forth, J. P. Newman, & R. D. Hare (Eds.), *Issues in criminological and legal psychology: No. 24. International perspectives on psychopathy* (pp. 123–126). Leicester, United Kingdom: British Psychological Society.

Quinsey, V. L., & Walker, W. D. (1992). Dealing with dangerousness: community risk management strategies with violent offenders. In R. Peters, R. McMahon, & V. Quinsey (Eds.), *Aggression and violence through the lifespan* (pp. 244–260). Newbury Park, CA: Sage.

Ressler, R., Burgess, A., & Douglas, J. (1988). *Sexual homicide: Patterns and motives.* Lexington, MA: D.C. Heath.

Rice, M. E. (1997). Violent offender research and implications for the criminal justice system. *American Psychologist, 52*(4), 414–423.

Rice, M. E., & Harris, G. T. (1997). Cross-validation and extension of the Violence Risk Appraisal Guide for child molesters and rapists. *Law and Human Behavior, 21*, 231–241.

Rice, M. E., Harris, G. T., & Cormier, C. A. (1992). An evaluation of maximum security therapeutic community for psychopaths and other mentally disordered offenders. *Law and Human Behavior, 16*, 399–412.

Rice, M. E., Harris, G. T., & Quinsey, V. L. (1990). A follow-up of rapists assessed in a maximum-security psychiatric facility. *Journal of Interpersonal Violence, 5*, 435–448.

Richards, H. (1993). *Therapy of substance abuse syndromes.* Northvale, NJ: Aronson.

Rogers, R. (1995). *Diagnostic and structured interviewing: A handbook for psychologists.* USA: Psychological Assessment Resources, Inc.

Rutherford, M. J., Cacciola, J. S., Alterman, A. I., & McKay, J. N. (1996). Reliability and validity of the Revised Psychopathy Checklist in women methadone patients. *Assessment, 3,* 43–54.

Salekin, R., Rogers, R., & Sewell, K. (1997). Construct validity of psychopathy in a female offender sample: A multitrait-multimethod evaluation. *Journal of Abnormal Psychology, 106,* 576–585.

Schultz, D. P., & Schultz, S. E. (1998). *Psychology and work today: An introduction to industrial and organizational psychology* (7th ed.). New Jersey: Prentice-Hall.

Serin, R. C. (1991). Psychopathy and violence in criminals. *Journal of Interpersonal Violence, 6,* 423–431.

Serin, R. C. (1992). The clinical application of the Psychopathy Checklist–Revised (PCL–R) in a prison population. *Journal of Clinical Psychology, 48*(5), 637–642.

Serin, R. C., Peters, R. DeV., & Barbaree, H. E. (1990). Predictors of psychopathy and release outcome in a criminal population. *Psychological Assessment: A Journal of Consulting and Clinical Psychology, 2,* 419–422.

Strachan, C., & Hare, R. D. (1998). *Assessment of psychopathy in female offenders.* Manuscript submitted for publication.

Toupin, T., Mercier, H., Déry, M., Cote, G., & Hodgins, S. (1996). Validity of the PCL–R for adolescents. In D. J. Cooke, A. E. Forth, J. P. Newman, & R. D. Hare (Eds.), *Issues in criminological and legal psychology: 24. International perspectives on psychopathy* (pp. 143–145). Leicester, United Kingdom: British Psychological Society.

Williamson, S. E., Hare, R. D., & Wong, S. (1987). Violence: Criminal psychopaths and their victims. *Canadian Journal of Behavioral Science, 19,* 454–462.

Wintrup, A., Coles, M., Hart, S., & Webster, C. D. (1994). The predictive validity of the PCL–R in high risk mentally disordered offenders [Abstract]. *Canadian Psychology, 35*(2a), 47.

Wong, S. (1984). The criminal and institutional behaviors of psychopaths. *Ministry of the Solicitor General, Programs User Report.* Ottawa, Ontario, Canada: Ministry of the Solicitor General of Canada.

Wong, S. (1988). Is Hare's Psychopathy Checklist reliable without the interview? *Psychological Reports, 62,* 931–934.

Zamble, E., & Palmer, W. (1996). Prediction of recidivism using psychopathy and other psychologically meaningful variables. In D. J. Cooke, A. E. Forth, J. P. Newman, & R. D. Hare (Eds.), *Issues criminology and legal psychology, 24. International perspectives on psychopathy* (pp. 153–156). Leicester, United Kingdom: British Psychological Society.

Zaparniuk, T., & Paris, F. (1995). *Female psychopaths, Violence and recidivism.* Paper presented at conference on "Mental Disorder and Criminal Justice: Changes, Challenges, and Solutions," Vancouver, British Columbia, Canada.

8

Assessing Psychopathy: Interpersonal Aspects and Clinical Interviewing

David S. Kosson
Finch University of Health Sciences/
The Chicago Medical School, Illinois

Carl B. Gacono
Private Practice, Austin, Texas

Robert H. Bodholdt[1]
U.S. Department of Justice, Bastrop, Texas

Widger and Frances (1985) noted that, "each personality disorder [has] a characteristic and dysfunctional interpersonal style that is often the central feature of the disorder" (p. 620). Others have suggested that the essence of personality disorders lies in their distinctive interpersonal patterns (Millon, 1981; Vaillant, 1975). To the extent that such patterns can be specified and measured, various authors have stressed the importance of assessing interpersonal cues during the evaluation process (Lerner, 1975, 1991; Schachtel, 1966; Schafer, 1954; Sugarman, 1981). This assessment becomes particularly important when working with patients characterized as antisocial or psychopathic.

Working with psychopaths can precipitate a wide variety of emotional and defensive reactions in the clinician (Gacono, Nieberding, Owen, Rubel, & Bodholdt, 2001). Even among experienced clinicians, the psychopath may evoke a special regard—from denial of pathology to a singular intellectualized distance. As Cleckley (1976) adapted from *Macbeth*, "This disease is beyond my practice." Work with psychopathic individuals may challenge our core beliefs, including assumptions central to our identity as health care providers and, at times, our global assumptions about the nature of personality and humanity. Clinicians must have emotional maturity and psychological awareness to identify and manage these reactions constructively. The psychopath's psychodynamics and cognitive style (cf. Gacono & Meloy, 1988, 1994) provide a map from which interview strategies can be formulated. These strategies in turn can aid in managing interactions and avoiding some of the pitfalls inherent in evaluating or attempting to treat psychopathic patients.

The main purpose of this chapter is to provide an overview of interpersonal dynamics commonly observed in psychopathy. The conspicuous nature of these dynamics allowed one of us (DSK) to develop the Interpersonal Measure of Psychopathy (IM-P; Kosson, Steuerwald, Forth, & Kirkhart, 1997), which is discussed later in this chapter. Our intent is to provide the clinician with a framework for identifying and understanding common reactions to interpersonal interactions with psychopathic individuals, which is crucial for adequate assessment, treatment, and clinician equilibrium.[2] Most of our framework is conceptually driven—rooted in clinical theory and accounts of work with individuals identified as psychopathic or particularly antisocial. Where relevant research is available, it is noted. Additional research on the interpersonal behavior of psychopaths is reviewed later in the chapter.

DEFENSES THAT PSYCHOPATHS EXPRESS IN INTERACTIONS

From a psychodynamic perspective, the psychopath's internalized defensive operations and object relations invigorate transactions manifest during the interview (see Gacono & Meloy, 1988, 1994). In one form or the other, the clinician viscerally experiences being incorporated into the psychopath's web. Many of these internally felt experiences originate not within the interviewer per se, but as the interviewer experiences subtle and not so subtle pushes and pulls comprising defensive operations characteristic of psychopathic syndromes. As discussed here, defenses constitute systematic patterns of automatic, largely unconscious mechanisms for coping with intense relational impulses. It should be noted that unconscious defenses also have conscious cognitive correlates (Gacono & Meloy, 1988, 1994). A cursory review of several primitive defenses provides a context for understanding interpersonal interactions commonly observed in working with the psychopath (Gacono, 1988, 1990; Gacono & Meloy, 1994; see chap. 5, this volume, for a discussion of the psychopath's emotional life).

Splitting Defenses

Repression is seen as regulating attentional processes and the intensity of emotional experience in neurotic and normal personality, whereas *splitting* is the fundamental preoedipal defense believed to regulate the internal world of most individuals with severe personality disorders (Kernberg, 1984). Although it was once proposed that psychopaths are essentially neurotic characters (Alexander, 1935), most contemporary psychodynamic theorists agree that, although some criminals are neurotic, the personalities of psychopathic patients function at the less advanced, borderline level of organization (Grotstein, 1980; Kernberg, 1970; Meloy & Gacono, 1992, 1993).[3]

Although a borderline personality organization is considered distinct from both the more primitive kinds of functioning seen in psychosis and the more mature functioning seen in neurosis and normal personality, it does not contravene the possibility of comorbid thought disorder (Gacono & Meloy, 1994; Meloy & Gacono, 1992). A borderline level of personality organization is believed to result from a fixation at or near the second or third year of life. It is associated with a preponderance of aggressive impulses and partial representations of others (i.e., introjects linked to frustration) that the besieged ego is unable to integrate with affiliative motives (and introjects associated with gratification) to forge more comprehensive, consistent views of self and others. Theorists vary in their consideration of the relative importance of stress and diathesis: unfavorable environmental versus constitutional/temperamental contributions. Nonetheless, what we eventually observe in patients with borderline personality organization involves ego fragmentation, cognitive immaturity, and a limited capacity for integrating disparate attitudes and emotional responses. Necessary organizational and regulatory processes are subject to failure as intense relational impulses and strivings are activated.

Widespread use of splitting maintains an active separation of opposite valence introjects and identifications (Kernberg, 1966). For example, instead of an integrated and cohesive self-image comprised of elements (thoughts, images, apperceptions) with various positive and negative aspects, the individual is aware of only positive or only negative attributes at any one time. Instead of a mosaic with a unifying image or figure, there is a collage with various elements fragmented from the rest and separate to themselves. Splitting also prevents the synthesis of discrepant ideational and affective perceptions of others. Rather than appreciating important others as individuals with both good and bad characteristics, others are experienced, at different times, as all good or all bad.[4] Because psychopaths are characterized by a preponderance of introjects linked to hostility or deprivation (relative to more fully integrated, positive, or benign introjects), perceptions of others as well intentioned are likely to be transitory and susceptible to displacement by perceptions of hostility or threat. Moreover, because these perceptions are based on partial representations linked to powerful affects of pleasure and displeasure, attitudes toward others tend to be unstable, extreme, and dependent on immediate mood and circumstance.

Projective Defenses

Splitting mechanisms underlie primitive forms of projection. Through projection, the patient at the borderline level of personality organization places his or her own unwanted feelings or attributes onto the clinician. In such cases, parts of the self are externalized, placed on others, and result in misperceptions. Distorted lenses transform others into wholly positive (nurturant) or wholly negative (hostile, aggressive) entities. When the psychopath relates to the clinician in this manner, he or she may experience a peculiar sense of having been miscast or, in other words, selected to play a role in the interaction that is uncomfortably foreign. In contrast to the projections of dependent personalities, for example, who often idealize or err favorably in their characterization of staff motives, the projections of psychopaths are most often experienced as disparaging and provocative. It is not uncommon for clinicians to feel somewhat blind-sided by the interpersonal posture of the psychopath, back-peddling to regain some bearing or reacting defensively to avoid impromptu conflict in the interaction. Interviewers should be alert to statements about their motives or feelings beyond what they have disclosed. Rather than reflecting either unusual insight by the patient or a plausible but mistaken inference, these opinions usually provide more information about the underlying dynamics of the interviewee.

An overabundance of aggressive drives and impulses is prototypic of psychopathy. However, many psychopaths have a capacity for self-presentation that allows them to conceal their disorder, especially given circumstances where the prize (e.g., a favorable evaluation; see Chapter 9) is particularly salient and where a sense of private victory can be maintained (discussed further later). In such cases, projected hostility remains high but is accompanied by a facade ranging from apparent anxiety to superficial agreeableness. In such instances, the clinician may unwittingly feel a pull toward reassuring the interviewee and misjudge the dynamic origin of apparent anxiety or friendliness. In cases where projected hostility becomes unbearable, restraint may give way to preemptive attack. Such cases often involve projective identification, which is discussed in greater detail later.

Although less prominent in most psychopaths, the same splitting defenses can also operate on positive traits. In this context, psychopaths who momentarily view themselves as tough or hostile may project powerful attractions onto others, leading them to perceive an interviewer as more interested in him or her than is the case. Such a projection may encourage an unusual expression of informality and may even precipitate a shift in the psychopathic patient to more positive feelings. However, as discussed next, the projection of positive qualities onto others is typically a precursor to devaluation.

To the extent that projections of opposite valence are undetected, they can lead treatment team members to exhibit highly discrepant, polarized views of the same patient. During the interview, structure and confrontation can help contain the projection and the underlying splitting processes. However, this can be fraught with complications, even under circumstances where the projection is unduly positive. The use of assessment methods outside the interview can also help staff achieve a more balanced view of a patient's strengths and weaknesses (see chaps. 7 & 9). Managing splitting is frequently a central task when treating patients with both antisocial personality disorder (ASPD) and psychopathy (Gacono et al., 2001).

Projective Identification

Projective identification is a specific form of projection common to interactions with psychopaths. Although the term has been used in a number of different ways and remains somewhat controversial (cf. Lubbe, 1998), projective identification is an unconscious defensive process that, like projection, is usually regarded as a normal and adaptive process early in development and generally (but not always) regarded as pathological if observed frequently in adults. For our purposes, projective identification differs from projection in that it involves not only attribution of disowned aspects of the self to another but also a sense of control over the other by placing him or her in the position of enacting the projected parts of the self (Grotstein, 1980; Lubbe, 1998; Ogden, 1992). Further, there is often a reintrojection of these aspects or identification associated with taking on the role of the other person or denying differences between the self and the other. For example, the psychopathic patient projects hostility, envy, or aggressiveness onto an examiner, experiences an illusory sense of connection to the examiner, and, finally, interprets his or her own reaction as actually caused or brought on by the examiner's negative behavior. As a result, the subjective experience of projective identification involves both a continued (although altered) experience of the projected impulse and, often, a conscious fear of the recipient of the projection, which is nevertheless more tolerable than the original hostile impulse/representation.

For example, the following response to Card IV of the Rorschach demonstrates projective identification: "It's an *angry* monster that is *coming after me.*" Obviously it is just an inkblot with no inherent qualities related to movement or emotion. Yet in the prior response, aggressive impulses projected onto the blot return to persecute the patient. By contrast, in simple projection, the patient might attribute movement or emotion to the percept: "It looks like a monster with an angry face." However, the percept would not be described as showing specific interest in the patient.

When included in a projective identification cycle, the clinician is likely to internally experience the presence of foreign feelings, thoughts, or images that actually originate in the patient. This experience can be particularly distressing to the naive interviewer. Projective identification can also be seen in the following remark by Travis — a psychopath with comorbid paranoid and narcissistic features who said, with a smile, as he was being placed in room seclusion: "You (CBG) enjoy this, don't you?" Through projective identification, the psychologist had become not only the container for Travis' projected sadism, but also the vehicle through which these projections returned to persecute him (Gacono & Meloy, 1994). Theoretically, placing the aggressive impulses in the therapist makes the patient's sadistic impulses less threatening. At the same time, the patient obtains partial gratification of these impulses by identifying with the therapist's aggressiveness.

Although the sense that such feelings are foreign can help a clinician to resist them, repeated exposure to such projections may nonetheless produce some degree of control over the clinician in the form of an interpersonal pull to act in accord with the projection.[5] That is, in addition to feeling cheapened or debased, the clinician may experience an impulse to reciprocate or act out the previously foreign thoughts or feelings. For example, in situations like the earlier example, the interviewer may experience a pull to behave sadistically. A better strategy is to remain affectively neutral while confronting the projective process: "It is not that I enjoy putting you in room seclusion, but given your propensity for aggression and violence one of the few things I may have to offer you, as a professional, is to instruct you in methods for controlling your anger." When the clinician responds to the affective pull of the interaction, he or she has, in a sense, accepted the psychopath's unconscious invitation.

Alternatively, a positive projective identification cycle may be initiated in which positive traits or motives are attributed to the clinician. For example, the psychopath may perceive the clinician as powerful or unusually competent and, on this basis, experience a sense of kinship. Alternatively, the patient may project affiliative motives and experience the clinician as unusually interested in him or her (the patient). In either case, the patient may interpret the clinician's actions as driven by these qualities and may even attempt to control the clinician overtly on the basis of this interpretation. The patient's identification with the clinician affords at least partial gratification of narcissistic or affiliative impulses without the responsibility of recognizing these as his own. For the clinician, the seductiveness of being flattered or appreciated by the interviewee may be a potential trap that can undercut attention to the subtle way in which the clinician is being manipulated. In fact, as discussed below, idealization of the clinician may sometimes trigger a manipulative cycle through which the clinician is desired and then devalued (Meloy, 1988).

In summary, projective identification provides the psychopath with greater interpersonal predictability and control at the expense of a higher level of relatedness. Just as a dependent personality often finds (creates) nurturers, the psychopath often finds (creates) adversaries. Observing emotional reactions in a patient that appear more consistent with an interviewer's alleged perspective (in the prior example, sadism) than with what is allegedly being done to the individual himself points to the presence of projective identification. Consultation examining one's actual versus implied motives may also help disentangle "whose stuff is whose," which can be invaluable to those working with this population. Splitting and projective identification can trounce and befuddle and are routinely encountered in forensic settings.

Devaluation

Both theory and research suggest that devaluation is a common defense among narcissistic, antisocial, and psychopathic disorders (Gacono, 1988, 1990; Gacono, Meloy, & Berg, 1992; Helfgott, 1991, 1992). Devaluation of others reduces any potential real or perceived threat while allowing the psychopath some comfort within his or her own grandiosity. Others must be degraded — their importance diminished — for the psychopath to maintain the experience of self as special, unique, and entitled. By devaluing the goodness in others, the psychopath prevents the experience of envy or a conscious awareness of what he or she lacks. Devaluation of the interviewer or assessment instruments ("It's just an inkblot") may occur frequently during any interview and can be experienced in interactions in which the interviewer feels put down or even discarded.

According to Meloy (1988) and Bursten (1973), devaluation begins when psychopaths project ideal attributes onto others. At times psychopaths experience partial representations of others as ideal objects, which may in turn activate intense affiliative desires to control or possess those others. Although they may briefly form an identification with those others, the prevalence of frustration and aggression usually leads to experiencing these same others as withholding or unattainable and a source of envy. Consequently, to avoid the rage associated with frustration, deprivation, and envy, the psychopath defensively distorts the situation into one in which he possesses the ideal attributes (by re-introjecting the ideal) while, via use of splitting, the other person does not. In short, envy and the portent of shame underlie the psychopath's frequent devaluation of others. As noted by McKay (1986), the psychopaths' devaluation of others is often accompanied by the establishment of a new object who is briefly idealized.

Both devaluation and projective identification are involved in unilateral attempts to define the nature or rules of relationships to reduce the power of the clinician or increase the power of the psychopath. However, because these attempts are not grounded in true empathy, the suggested role definition often seems stilted or fails to provide a satisfactory mutual contract for a relationship. For example, as a sexual psychopath commented to one of us (CBG) after a brief formal introduction, "Carl, you can call me Don." In this case, reducing the status of the examiner appears to ward off unconscious, imaginary, yet threatening aspects of the examiner created via projective identification. At the same time, an assumption of premature intimacy or crossing of usual examiner–examinee boundaries links the participants symbolically and may appear to impose certain requirements on the clinician (e.g., complementarity; Keisler, 1996).

The vicissitudes of devaluation and its role in maintaining the psychopath's grandiosity are seen in this excerpt from Milton's (1968) *Paradise Lost*: "Better to reign in hell, than serve in heaven" (p. 54). There is room for only one superior being in the psychopath's world, and maintaining grandiosity supersedes all else.

The Manipulative Cycle

Bursten (1972, 1973) used the term *manipulative cycle* to characterize the unfolding of primitive defenses during psychopathic deception. The manipulative cycle involves an experienced or potential conflict, followed by an intent to deceive, a deceptive act, and a devaluation of the deceived person, which results in feelings of contemptuous delight. This cycle is commonly activated when the psychopath is confronted with behaviors inconsistent with his previous statements (or collateral information) that contradict him. However, this cycle may also underlie interactions in which the psychopath's lying seems to have no observable motive. The deception is highly affectively rewarding, as the interviewer is devalued by the psychopath for being ignorant of the truth (Meloy, 1988). Control is reestablished, and any sense of vulnerability or weakness is projected onto the interviewer.

Whereas conscious correlates of the manipulative cycle can be observed unfolding during the interview, the unconscious process is usually thought to involve protecting and regulating the underlying grandiose self-structure (Kernberg, 1975). First, unwanted introjects are purged and evacuated by projecting these onto the clinician. Then the recipient of these projections is devalued, resulting in feelings of contemptuous triumph. The manipulative cycle maintains the psychopath's internal integrity and leaves the examiner with residual feelings — perhaps embarrassment, sadness, or rage at having been violated. By putting one over on you, the psychopath remains psychologically on top. Remaining one up, however, often requires drastic intrapsychic maneuvers especially during periods of limited accomplishment or acclaim.

Both unconscious and conscious motivations for the psychopath's statements and inquiries should generally be assumed, identified, and managed. Assessed through the psychopath's verbalizations and cognitive patterns, these defenses never occur in isolation from underlying personality organization (Gacono & Meloy, 1988; Helfgott, 1991, 1992). We recommend self-monitoring: "What am I feeling, and how does this relate to what the patient is doing to me?" and asking frequently: "Why is the patient saying this now?" to help maintain an interviewer's focus.

The clinician should be cognizant that his or her own unconscious, unwanted, or unowned attributes are prime targets for the psychopath's manipulative cycling. Rest assured, psychopaths are masters at ferreting out our "weaknesses," and the cycles of devaluation and projective identification can leave the clinician affectively reeling. In fact, anticipating the inevitable uncovering of our vulnerabilities can guide the clinician to introduce information — while maintaining professional boundaries — that can diffuse the manipulative cycling at its onset. What is consciously acknowledged is less susceptible to manipulation because it no longer holds the same utility for achieving the affective reward of contemptuous delight.

Direct Expression of Impulses

At least one other class of psychopaths' interpersonal behavior deserves brief mention. Like other individuals with severe personality disorders (Kernberg, 1984), psychopaths sometimes express their impulses relatively directly, unmodulated by defenses. To the extent that few inhibitions exist, or where defenses falter under stress, psychopaths sometimes express hostility or affiliative impulses directly to the clinician. Given the unavailability of repression at the borderline level of organization, psychopaths are often assumed to be conscious of these hostile or affiliative impulses. Moreover, psychopaths' lack of ambivalence leads them to express such impulses in a more intense form than will most other interviewees. Intense expressions of contempt (e.g., "You don't know much about what goes on here"), sexualized overtures, or other bids for coalition (e.g., "Do you need a coauthor for your papers?") provide important clues to affective processes operating in psychopathic patients. As for the other defensive processes discussed here, caution is warranted in responding to such overtures.

The proposition that psychopaths function at a borderline level of personality organization implies that they are characterized by a lack of integration of negative and positive representations of others, a lack of ambivalence, and an inability to repress intense relational impulses. Thus, psychopaths may also experience powerful attractions; just as they are prone to express intense hostility directly, they may also be prone to express intense affiliative impulses directly. Because such attractions are not based on empathy or a mature appreciation of another person, these positive affectional links are often likely to be fleeting, tenuous, and based on illusory perceptions of others (Gacono, 1988, 1990; Gacono & Meloy, 1992; Gacono et al., 1992; Meloy, 1988). Although expressions of intense sexual or affiliative impulses may be somewhat less common during extremely structured interactions (e.g., court-ordered examinations), they may nevertheless exert powerful effects on clinicians who encounter them and may contribute to descriptions of some psychopaths as charming or charismatic.

A specific form of these affiliative expressions has been termed *simulation* or *pseudoidentification* by Meloy (1988). According to Meloy, simulations reflect unconscious expressions of the attitudes, feelings, and behaviors of others. These expressions resemble identifications with others, and both are assumed to be based on internalizations of others through which individuals experience a sense of connection to others. In fact, simulations are sometimes considered precursors to identifications (e.g., Gaddini, 1969). However, most theorists suggest that in true identifications the self-representations of an individual are modified temporarily to resemble the person with whom he or she identifies. By contrast, in pseudoidentifications, self-representations are not altered. Instead, the internalizations are part of the introjection–projection cycle described earlier (as underlying projective identification), in which positive qualities of another are introjected as part of an attempt to control the other person.

Whether the interaction is characterized by sexuality, friendship, alliance, or simulative behavior, clinicians should be careful to evaluate the basis and stability of those impulses. In general, clinician perceptions of stable positive alliances with psychopathic clients should signal the possibility of wishful projections on the part of the clinician rather than an attribute of the real relationship.

It must also be acknowledged that the place of idealization and affiliation in psychopaths' interpersonal interactions is controversial. Several prominent descriptions characterize psychopaths as unable to bond with others (Cleckley, 1976; Meloy, 1988) or as persistently mistrustful of and detached from others (e.g., Leary, 1957; Millon, 1981). From this perspective, apparent idealizations reflect narcissistic reactions to positive feedback, in which the psychopath's true focus is on maintaining his or her grandiose self-image or an attempt to ingratiate him or herself as part of a manipulative cycle (Gacono & Meloy, 1994). However, we suggest that all of these possibilities plausibly occur. Only careful observation, clinician judgment, and sometimes collateral input can help to differentiate unmodulated expressions of idealization from self-centered and manipulative expressions of good will.

THE CLINICIAN'S REACTIONS TO THE PATIENT

Clinician reactions ranging from retaliation and rage to fear, indifference, submission, and sexual seduction have been associated with interviewing antisocial and psychopathic patients (Bursten, 1972, 1973; Meloy, 1988). Rather than affectional relatedness and attachment, relationships with psychopaths are often based on power and control. Thus, a clinician may feel as if he or she is "under a microscope." Whether searching for weaknesses to exploit or scanning for sources of potential threat, the psychopath's scrutiny is disconcerting and can leave the examiner feeling disorganized, puzzled, confused, or inept. The examiner may even feel as if he or she is engaged in a competition with the patient—an unusual experience for someone in the role of conducting an evaluation.

Interviewers' reactions can be visceral—as, for example, a sudden chill that Meloy (1988) described as *atavistic* to highlight the similarity between a person's reaction to the psychopath's stark detachment and the prey's sense of a predator's profound detachment and lack of empathy. The clinician's sense of alarm should be explored if consultation is sought. Indeed, a failure to explore the bases for such reactions, based on a fear of appearing overly timid or paranoid, can lead to a loss of important diagnostic information and inadequate case conceptualization.

At other times, the examiner is likely to feel miscast in a reciprocal role relationship that is alien to him or her, which provides additional clues to the possibility of a significant defect in empathy or perspective-taking. At the risk of appearing disagreeable, considerable diagnostic information can be gained as the clinician attempts to renegotiate typically unspoken relationship rules on a more bilateral basis.

Countertransference

We use the term *countertransference* broadly to include both indirect forms (e.g., those stimulated by the clinician's unfinished business) and direct forms (e.g., those reflecting common reactions to specific kinds of patient dynamics and behaviors; Racker, 1968). Indirect countertransference occurs when the clinician unconsciously associates patient characteristics with other important people in his or her life, and thus experiences emotions that do not originate within the relationship to the patient. In contrast, direct countertransference consists of a clinician's own emotional reactions to the patient's personality organization (e.g., the felt emptiness empathically experienced when interviewing the patient with borderline personality disorder). Diagnostically, we are most concerned with these latter reactions, as stimulated when the clinician is placed in the position of a particular projected self- or object-representation. Direct countertransferential reactions are the silver of the photographic plate and can provide the clinician with an accurate picture of the patient's inner dynamics. These represent the chief focus of our discussion.

Difficult countertransference reactions are common fare when working with psychopaths and emerge in various forms. Awareness and management of common countertransferential thoughts, feelings, and the interpersonal role(s) associated with them frees the clinician to approach the examination process in a more fluid, flexible, hypothesis-testing manner. It is important to keep in mind that it is not the countertransference reaction per se that is necessarily limiting, but rather the attendant restriction of freedom to openly test or explore alternative hypotheses, including alternative conceptualizations of the interviewee's personality and behavior. To the extent that this freedom to explore is lacking, the clinician is no longer functioning, so to speak, as a direct photographic plate: Unexamined countertransference impressions are imbued with conclusions rather than questions. There are several common countertransferential themes of diagnostic and therapeutic significance (Gacono et al., 2001; Lion, 1978; Meloy, 1988, 1995; Strasburger, 1986). We turn to these now.

Denial and Self-Deception Reactions to the Interviewee

Blindness to dangerousness, illusory treatment alliance, and misattribution of psychological health are countertransference reactions often exhibited by mental health professionals who interact with psychopathic patients. These reactions are linked by their role in downplaying or denying the psychopath's deficits while amplifying the psychopath's real or projected favorable characteristics. They may reflect direct reactions to the behavior of the psychopath or may be associated with a variety of clinician personality characteristics, ranging from an optimistic view of human nature, to hysterical mechanisms that are adaptive in other settings for managing anxiety, to more pathological and primitive forms of denial (see Meloy, 1992, for a discussion of hysterical mechanisms in those who form attachments to psychopaths).

Blindness to Dangerousness. Some clinicians may unconsciously deny the potential dangerousness of violent patients in the service of managing anxiety (Lion & Leaff, 1973). Meloy (1988) linked this counterphobic reaction to the unwillingness of clinicians to participate in the prosecution of psychopathic patients who have seriously injured others (Hoge & Gutheil, 1987), to the underdiagnosis of ASPD, to clinicians' disbelief that a given patient has an antisocial or violent history—or even that psychopathy in all its ugliness exists (cf. Vailiant, 1975). Denial may operate at several levels. At the level of the organization, it surfaces in policies that omit procedural and structural safeguards for staff and patients alike (security systems, informed assessment triage). At the level of the individual clinician, denial shows up in decisions that ignore empirically based assessments of potential risk, to the extent that these referrals are actually made.

When interviewing antisocial patients, the clinician must always ensure his or her own safety as well as that of other staff and patients (Kernberg, 1998). Early in CBG's forensic career, a psychopathic patient with a history of violence and a tumultuous tie to his vacationing female therapist told a therapist at the clinic's entrance, "I'm so angry today I could kill Carl (CBG)." Filling in for the regular therapist, CBG was scheduled to see this patient within the hour. Never informed of the patient's threat, CBG was unprepared for the patient's anger, which escalated to the point of threatening the substitute and brandishing a knife. Just how common these apparent lapses in communication are we cannot say. Another of us (RHB), working in a similar forensic setting, learned from an antisocial patient's therapist, in passing, of the patient's thoughts about killing a staff member, only after these had been discussed in individual therapy for 2 months and after the patient had been removed from the treatment unit for setting another patient's shirt on fire "as a joke." The rationale cited for the delay in alerting staff was the need to protect confidentiality. Staff failures to explicitly consider and enforce the limits of confidentiality help promote a form of denial in which assessment of violence potential is deferred and staff and patients are exposed to unnecessary risk.

For some potentially violent patients, direct questions can circumvent an incident of violence. For example, asking "Am I safe talking with you today?" may help consciously inform the patient (and interviewer) of escalating anger or volatile instability while anchoring the interaction in the "here and now." By contrast, when interviewing psychopaths prone to predatory violence (Meloy, 1988), the use of external information such as knowledge of contingency plans (e.g., access to an escape route) and control strategies, including ensuring adequate staff back-up and frequent updates on a patient's current mental status, may provide greater safeguard than direct questions. Regardless, the clinician should always reserve the right to terminate the interview.

More conscious or preconscious self-deceptions regarding dangerousness can also contribute to catalyzing volatile situations into actual violence. For example, self-deception occurs when the clinician is frightened and, fearing the patient's rage, avoids setting limits or providing appropriate confrontation (Meloy, 1995). Such self-deception, linked to "superego problems in the clinician, the avoidance of anxiety, passive-aggressive rejection of the patient, or an identification with the deceptive skills of the patient" (Meloy, 1995, p. 2283), can also prevent a clinician from dealing with important interpersonal or relationship-anchored therapeutic issues, particularly those that require immediate attention.

Illusory Treatment Alliance.   An illusory treatment alliance occurs when the clinician assumes that a therapeutic alliance exists where there is none. This form of self-deception may result from the clinician's own wishful projections (Meloy, 1988) or may be encouraged by idealizations of the therapist, which originate from splitting. In either case, this countertransference reaction makes the clinician susceptible to the manipulative cycle discussed earlier and increases the risk that he or she will be exploited by the psychopathic patient.

Without supervision and correction, susceptibility to an illusory alliance can lead to self-devaluation, burn out, the rise of therapeutic nihilism, and the loss of professional identity. Never allow unexplored positive affective reactions to guide management considerations when they fly in the face of real-world historical and assessment data (such as an elevated PCL–R score).

Misattribution of Psychological Health.   Similar to an illusory treatment alliance is this subtle form of countertransference: rash declarations of a therapeutic miracle can be an especially tempting retreat from more realistic appraisals in settings where small, hard-won treatment gains are the norm. Commonly attributed to the therapist's wishful projections, the clinician believes that the patient's psychological maturity and complexity mirrors his or her own. Particularly common when there is no Axis I diagnosis and the patient's intelligence is above average, this interviewer reaction is facilitated by a superficial charm and verbal fluency that mask more enduring attributes and underlying personality organization in the psychopath (Meloy, 1988). Clinicians operating under this form of self-deception are unable to match appropriate intervention and management strategies to the patient. Moreover, clinicians may unwittingly mount treatment plans to increase self-esteem or bolster such attitudes as putting oneself first, or may even retrace a presumed legitimate history of personal victimization so as to justify the psychopath's ongoing transgressions against others.

Elements of misattribution of psychological health and/or illusory treatment alliance are exhibited in the following evaluative conclusions formed by interviews of serial killer Edmund Kemper:

> (After killing a victim he often engaged in sex with the corpse, even after it had been decapitated.) On one occasion Kemper visited at length with psychiatrists who stated at the conclusion of the interview that Ed was now safe and would not harm another person. They agreed at the meeting to have

Kemper's juvenile record sealed to allow him to lead a normal life. Only Ed knew that at that very moment, the head of one of his victims was in the trunk of his car. (Hickey, 1991, p. 142)

Negative Affective Reactions to the Interviewee

Negative reactions to the psychopathic patient are perhaps even more common and expectable in instances of egregious conduct. These can also originate along a direct countertransferential path or be stimulated by vulnerabilities within the clinician. If positive countertransference may introduce or reinforce eventually destructive dynamics within an assessment or treatment relationship, negative transference may bear all the more watching. In fact, professionals susceptible to overly positive reactions may also be at heightened risk for developing unduly negative reactions to the patient.

Helplessness and Guilt.   Interactions with antisocial and psychopathic patients may be governed by interpersonal rules antithetical to the clinician's belief system. For example, kindness may be viewed as weakness by antisocially oriented individuals. When interventions fail to produce any notable change, or when the clinician is repeatedly manipulated and devalued, a sense of helplessness and guilt can result. If unacknowledged, these feelings may stimulate unconscious rage expressed passively through therapist withdrawal or actively through reaction formation in the form of intensified efforts to treat (Strasburger, 1986). Clinicians whose narcissism makes it difficult to accept the limits of their ability to heal are especially susceptible to this outcome. As in the illusory treatment alliance, these feelings place a therapist at risk for subsequent self-devaluation and the loss of professional identity.

Fear of Assault or Harm.   Histories of real-world violence and the use of primitive defenses increase the likelihood that the behavior of antisocial and psychopathic patients will stimulate fears in the clinician (Strasburger, 1986). Described earlier, the atavistic response to the psychopathic predator may signal real danger even in the absence of an overt threat (Meloy, 1995). In the absence of a formal risk assessment, all of a clinician's fears should be considered realistic, and appropriate precautions should be taken to ensure his or her safety. If the situation is safe, as noted earlier, it can sometimes be valuable to explore the psychopaths' feelings, thoughts, and behaviors contributing to the alarm reaction.

Therapeutic Nihilism.   Lion (1978) used this term to describe the belief that all patients with an antisocial history are untreatable. Instead of assessing treatment prognosis through a formal evaluation of psychopathy and other relevant patient variables (see chaps. 14 & 15, Appendix C), the conclusion of untreatability rests solely on the presence of antisocial behavior in the patient's history. Aside from its potential inaccuracy, therapeutic nihilism devalues the patient, thus mirroring what the psychopath frequently does to others (Meloy, 1988). Further, a therapist's sense of futility may subtly undermine treatment efforts. Therapeutic nihilism reduces the vigor of a therapist's free exploration of issues. Further, if such a countertransference reaction is allowed to progress, it can provide the basis for heightening patients' sense that their mental health contacts are pointless. A related consequence involves the potential for the clinician to foreclose available assessment or treatment options. In turn, the clinician may be left to find his or her professional identity and work satisfaction elsewhere in a role without direct clinical responsibilities.

Hatred and the Wish to Destroy.   Prolonged work with antisocial and psychopathic patients may compel the clinician to face his or her own aggressive and destructive impulses (Meloy, 1988). These patients are often characterized by devaluation of goodness and by hateful wishes to destroy any goodness in the therapist (Redl & Wineman, 1951). Clinicians may ultimately begin to "[identify] with the patient's hatred and wish to destroy" (Meloy, 1988, p. 2284). In such cases, the clinician is at risk for developing a variety of additional problems, including destructive acting out.

RESEARCH ADDRESSING THE INTERPERSONAL BEHAVIOR OF PSYCHOPATHS

Despite its poignancy, there have been relatively few controlled studies of the interpersonal behavior of psychopaths. Many studies have documented the association between psychopathy and external behaviors such as probation violations and violent crimes, whereas few have directly studied psychopaths' behavior in interactions with other individuals (for two exceptions, see Gillstrom & Hare, 1988; Rime, Bouvy, Leborgne, & Rouillon, 1978). Several researchers have attempted to study aggressiveness in psychopaths. However, even in this domain, the majority of studies have involved hypothetical vignettes rather than overt interpersonal behavior (e.g., Blackburn & Lee-Evans, 1985; Serin, 1996).

Those studies that have directly assessed interpersonal behavior in artificial situations, such as administering shock to another (Hare & Craigen, 1974; Sutker, 1970) or participation in the Prisoner's Dilemma paradigm (Whitehill, 1986; Widom, 1976), have generally failed to reveal differences between psychopathic and nonpsychopathic participants. By

219

contrast, those that have examined behavior in less structured situations have generally reported greater aggressiveness in psychopaths. For example, psychopathic inmates are rated by prison guards as displaying more hostile and dominant interpersonal behavior (Foreman, 1988), and adolescents and students with psychopathic features are described by raters as more hostile and dominant (Forth, Brown, Hart, & Hare, 1996; see also Rime et al., 1978). Indeed, that differences have been reported across interview studies and observed interpersonal interactions suggests the possibility that such interpersonal situations may be relatively more sensitive than controlled laboratory studies in detecting psychopaths' distinctive interpersonal patterns. With this in mind, Kosson et al. (1997) developed the Interpersonal Measure of Psychopathy.

The Interpersonal Measure of Psychopathy (IM-P)

As discussed in chapter 3, the PCL–R is the best validated measure of psychopathy currently available. Although the PCL–R manual (Hare, 1991) specifically encourages raters to attend to the interpersonal maneuvers of interviewees, often the conspicuous and unique interpersonal style of the psychopath is lost. Only quotes and examples included in the formal report (see chap. 9) provide a flavor for the nature and quality of verbal and nonverbal behaviors that transpired during the interview. Moreover, although the PCL–R is one of the only contemporary measures to assess the core personality features of psychopathy (Factor 1), Factor 1 ratings often depend substantially on a clinician's ability to make inferences about the accuracy of and motives underlying an interviewee's self-reports and to integrate behavior across multiple domains.

The Interpersonal Measure of Psychopathy (IM-P) was developed to assess the core personality of the psychopath by identifying and coding some of the distinctive interpersonal features described in this chapter. At the same time, it was intended to provide a more objective record of unusual interpersonal behavior by requiring few inferences or subjective judgments. It must be emphasized that the IM-P was designed to augment, not replace, PCL–R scores.

Item Selection. IM-P items were designed to identify and quantify specific aspects of verbal interaction of interviewees, as well as some of the more distinctive nonverbal behaviors often observed in interactions with more antisocial individuals. There were three sources for items: a review of the research literature addressing interpersonal behavior of psychopaths, a survey of current experts on psychopathy, and our own clinical intuition and judgments about our interpersonal experiences with psychopaths.

Items were written to permit reliable ratings based on direct observation of behavioral events. Because interviewers often have multiple goals during assessment, we also sought items that would reflect relatively unmistakable types of interactions, freeing the clinician to attend to other aspects of the interview process. Once thoroughly trained, ratings are believed to minimally tax attentional resources of the interviewer. Because concepts like transference and countertransference have sometimes been difficult to measure reliably, we sought simple event labels that could be rated as *did* or *did not* apply. Item labels or behavioral identifiers were written to achieve an intermediate level of specificity: to describe individual features that do not occur in most interviews but that occur often enough that, averaging across many items, different interviewees may be discriminated. For example, "Unusual calmness or ease" may be indicated by reclining in a chair to an unusual degree, by putting one's feet up, by moving the furniture in the office, or by getting up and walking around the room during the interview. Similarly, "Incorporation of interviewer into personal stories" refers to the interviewee's use of examples or stories in which the interviewer is given a hypothetical role without regard to the content of the story. For example: "Let's say you wanted to buy some drugs from me. Well, I don't give you my real name. . . . " It is our experience that, in such examples, the clinician is typically placed in a role involving either antisocial behavior or a one-down position relative to the interviewee. Of the 29 items initially written, 21 were sufficiently reliable that they were retained. The items in the final instrument are depicted in Table 8.1.

Administration. Because the IM-P is usually completed in conjunction with a PCL-R, raters are encouraged to complete the file review and the PCL-R rating prior to looking at the IM-P. This separation of operations reduces the probability that a clinician's expectations regarding interpersonal behaviors captured in the IM-P can contaminate PCL-R assessment. After completing the PCL-R, raters simply estimate the extent to which each feature or interaction in the IM-P seemed characteristic of the individual, based on the frequency with which relevant behaviors or signs of the construct occurred. In comparison with the PCL-R, the IM-P requires relatively little formal training specific to the instrument, although general clinical training in assessment strategies and behavioral observation is certainly valuable. The rater is instructed simply to attend to interpersonal processes and note distinctive behaviors and interactions, as well as any personal reactions to the interviewee.

IM-P Validity. Research using the IM-P suggests that it provides a valuable contribution to our assessments of psychopathy. To date, several different kinds of evidence have been generated. Kosson et al. (1997)

TABLE 8.1
Interpersonal Measure of Psychopathy (IM-P) Items

1. Interrupts
2. Refuses to tolerate interruption
3. Ignores professional boundaries
4. Ignores personal boundaries
5. Tests interviewer
6. Makes personal comments
7. Makes requests of interviewer
8. Tends to be tangential
9. Fills in dead space
10. Unusual calmness or ease
11. Frustration with argument avoidance
12. Perseveration
13. Ethical superiority
14. Expressed narcissism
15. Incorporation of interviewer into personal stories
16. Seeking of alliance
17. Showmanship
18. Angry
19. Impulsive answers
20. Expressed toughness
21. Intense eye contact

examined interviewers' subjective emotional responses during interviews, ranging from amusement and skepticism to fear and guilt.
Consistent with the earlier discussion regarding interviewers' reactions to
psychopaths, both PCL–R factors displayed significant correlations with
several indexes of interviewer emotional response. That is, interviewers
reported more of a variety of different emotions (and less of a sense of
warmth) when interviewing men with psychopathic traits relative to
interviewees rated low on psychopathy (see Table 8.2). Interestingly, IM-P
scores also correlated significantly with interviewer emotional reactions
in six out of eight categories assessed—a number similar to that obtained
for PCL–R Factor 1, but larger than that for PCL–R Factor 2 (see chap. 3
for factor structure of the PCL–R). After controlling for participants' age
and intelligence, IM-P scores continued to predict the interviewers' reactions in six categories and, in combination with Factor 1, predicted reactions in a seventh category. That is, interviewees who demonstrated the
interpersonal behaviors measured by the IM-P elicited more confusion,
more amusement, more skepticism, less warmth, more trepidation, and a
greater desire to avoid confrontation.

IM-P ratings correlate highly with ratings of Factor 1 of the PCL–R.
Interestingly, in several different samples, IM-P ratings appear more
strongly correlated with PCL–R Factor 1 than with PCL–R Factor 2 scores

TABLE 8.2
Correlations Between Predictor and Criterion Variables for Study 1

Criterion	IM-P (n = 93–97)	F1 (n = 94–98)	F2 (n = 94–98)
Interviewer Emotional Responses			
Confusion	.34***	.35***	.27**
Attentiveness	−.06	.06	−.01
Warmth	−.26**	−.33***	−.21*
Trepidation	.36***	.23*	.07
Amusement	.36***	.46***	.26**
Disbelief/skepticism	.29**	.44***	.29**
Guilt	.03	−.07	−.18
Avoid confrontation	.37***	.23*	.18
Antisocial Behavior Criteria			
Adult fights	.35***	.28**	.23*
Violent charges	.10	.24*	.30**
Violent IDRs	−.13	−.05	.07
Nonviolent charges	.14	.30**	.26**
Nonviolent IDRs	−.10	.14	.11
Criminal versatility	.19	.45***	.52***
Drug versatility	−.01	.14	.27**

Note. Sample size varied. IM-P = Interpersonal Measure of Psychopathy; F1 = Psychopathy Checklist–Revised (PCL–R) Factor 1; F2 = PCL–R Factor 2; Avoid confrontation = desire to avoid a confrontation with a participant. IDRs = Institution discipline reports. Copyright © 1997 by the American Psychological Association. Adapted with permission.
***$p \le .001$. **$p \le .01$. *$p \le .05$.

(see Table 8.3). These correlations suggest that the interpersonal behaviors associated with psychopathy are more closely associated with the personality core of the disorder than with the various irresponsible and acting-out behaviors captured by Factor 2.

IM-P ratings have also been linked to violent interpersonal behavior. However, as noted by Kosson et al. (1997), different indexes of violent behavior correlate differently with various measures of psychopathy, and results of analyses designed to predict violent behavior do not always replicate across different studies and samples. For example, although some have argued that F2 is most predictive of violence, others suggest F1 is most predictive; still others highlight the interaction between the two (for a more detailed discussion, see chaps. 3 & 10). Nevertheless, it is noteworthy that, in Kosson et al. (1997), IM-P scores were the best predictor of one of three indexes of violence examined: inmates' self-reported involvement in physical fights. That is, whereas Factor 2 uniquely predicted the number of violent charges, only the IM-P score predicted the number of fights after taking into account PCL–R Factors 1 and 2. Again, given the conflicting findings relating different indexes of violence to specific com-

TABLE 8.3
Correlations Between IM-P Scores and Factors of the PCL–R or PCL:YV

Setting	Sample	Correlation With Factor 1	Correlation With Factor 2
Adult forensic	Male federal prison inmates[1]	.62	.31
	Male adult county jail inmates[2]	.54	.23
Adolescent forensic	Male adolescent probationers[3]	.47	.41
	Female adolescent inmates[4]	.51	.38
University	Canadian college students[1]	.33	.15
	North American college students[5]	.62	.36

[1]Kosson, Forth, Steuerwald, and Kirkhart (1997)
[2]Kosson (1999a)
[3]Kosson (1999b)
[4]Bauer (1999)
[5]Colwell (1998)

ponents of psychopathy, this finding should be interpreted cautiously until it has been replicated.[6]

More recently, Vassileva (1999), using cluster analytic techniques, found a cluster of inmates characterized by high IM-P scores and high Factor 1 scores to have more charges for violent offenses, on average, than clusters of inmates formed by other combinations of PCL–R factors. This study suggested that the combination of both high IM-P scores and high PCL–R Factor 1 ratings may describe a subset of psychopaths with more of the features classically associated with the construct, including lower scores on measures of anxiety, less consistent involvement in nonviolent criminality on average, and less comorbidity with alcohol abuse, compared with subtypes selected primarily on the basis of high Factor 1 and high Factor 2 scores.

IM-P scores also predict objective observers' ratings of dominant behavior at least as well as PCL Factors 1 and 2. In fact, even after controlling for age, education, gender, and PCL factor scores, IM-P scores uniquely predict observer-rated dominance (Kosson et al., 1997). However, whereas PCL–R factors correlate nonsignificantly more highly with ratings of hostility than with ratings of dominance, IM-P ratings correlate more highly with ratings of dominance. Moreover, whereas PCL–R factors correlate similarly with observer ratings and self-reports of dominance, IM-P ratings were not significantly correlated with self-reports. Thus, the IM-P appears to be relatively more specific than the PCL–R in predicting dominant behavior, not just negative interpersonal behavior, and in predicting behaviors that individuals do not necessarily see in themselves.

Finally, Colwell (1998) reported that IM-P scores also predict responses to TAT cards that are typically assumed to reflect preconscious projections of aggressive behavior onto characters in TAT stories. In this study, college student participants were assessed for features associated with both PCL dimensions of psychopathy. However, because file material was not available, these dimensions were assessed with measures other than the PCL–R. In particular, PCL–R Factor 1 traits were assessed based on a brief interview adapted from the longer interview used (in conjunction with files) to assess Factor 1; Gough's (1960) Socialization scale was used to measure PCL–R Factor 2 traits.[7] Like participants with both kinds of psychopathic characteristics, participants with high IM-P scores tended to generate TAT stories with heroes displaying arrogant, calculating (i.e., aggressive) personality traits. In fact, IM-P scores contributed to predicting the personalities of participants' TAT story protagonists (or central figures) even after partialing out participants' scores on the Socialization scale (Colwell, 1998).

It must be emphasized that current findings with the IM-P are tentative and based on a small number of studies. Moreover, because the instrument was not designed to be used in the absence of the PCL–R, any use of the IM-P in such contexts must be considered exploratory. In particular, there are currently no data examining the sensitivity or specificity of the IM-P. For example, it is possible that high IM-P scores reflect interpersonal manifestations of personality disorder, especially of an erratic-dramatic nature, rather than specific manifestations of psychopathy. Nevertheless, it is striking that many of the interactional measures that appear related to psychopathy also appear related to the interpersonal manifestations of the disorder as assessed by the IM-P.

CONCLUSION

Understanding the psychopath's psychodynamics and conscious cognitive style is not only helpful in developing interview strategies to manage likely interpersonal patterns; it is invaluable. Of course, the context, depth, and length of the interpersonal interaction may largely determine the kinds of interpersonal interactions that transpire. Nevertheless, both the interpersonal behavior of psychopathic individuals and clinicians' reactions to this behavior are often comprehensible. Knowing some of the common interpersonal processes and underlying dynamics can be useful not only to novitiates in forensic practice but also to seasoned forensic practitioners. However, without a rough map of the territory, attempts to chart an assessment or treatment/management course with psychopathic patients can be bewildering at best.

The current chapter attempted to provide a partial map of the area—in no sense exhaustive or exclusive, but a map nonetheless that we encourage readers to evaluate. Because several common patterns may be identified, we end by summarizing suggestions for avoiding some of the common pitfalls in interviewing psychopaths. An important caveat is that no set of strategies is likely to be effective in all cases or contexts, and that when working with psychopaths over time and in nonsecure settings, consultation is often the better part of valor.

First, safety considerations and dangerousness management must always precede treatment considerations. When psychopathy is considered, always assess before treating and prepare before interviewing. Some of the most important questions to address include: Is the setting secure? What emotional reactions are likely given the available historical data?

Second, a thorough assessment of the dynamics of the interaction should be conducted. Interactions differ not only in the frequency and rhythm with which particular defenses and therapist reactions arise, but also in their affective coloring and intensity. For example, whereas some interactions may present frequent power and control struggles, others may be characterized by the appearance of intimacy (often a pseudointimacy) and interviewer idealization. Still others may reflect overt threats and intimidation. Careful evaluation of the clinician's own reactions may provide important clues to the dynamics unfolding in the interaction.

Wherever splitting and projective identification are common, clinicians should pay special attention to their emotional reactions that seem uncharacteristic and to patients' inferences about interviewers' motives. Clinicians should also avoid reinforcing or supporting a distorted view of the therapist or treatment team. Promoting integration of conflicting motives or views of others in an individual at the borderline level of personality organization is likely to be both difficult and labor-intensive. If a therapeutic alliance is complicated by a forensic context, substantial acting out, or threats of aggression, the prognosis may be poorer still.

Nevertheless, therapists may sometimes find it useful to respond to projections in ways that violate projective expectancies. Rather than fostering a negative transference, such responses may be effective for returning projections to their source. For example, Travis, the same psychopathic patient mentioned earlier, once suggested to one of us (CBG) with a sadistic grin: "You would probably like to be there when I get the gas chamber." The psychologist replied, "Possibly, but I wouldn't be celebrating. Rather, I would be sad that you chose to waste your life in such a worthless and irresponsible manner" (Gacono & Meloy, 1994). Although the patient's initial response may be perplexity and confusion, this kind of response can interrupt the cycle of projection and projective identification. Further, the containment of projections can, over time, foster growth and integration by helping the patient face the internal struggle instead of projecting it onto the environment.

Where devaluation and antagonism are common, simply protecting the therapist's ability to work freely and constructively with a client often becomes a primary objective. In such cases, a therapist is at risk for incapacitation on a number of fronts, including the development of various countertransference reactions described earlier (e.g., therapeutic nihilism). Monitoring for countertransference reactions regularly may help mitigate their impact.

Similarly, where mirroring and apparent identification are expressed, the interviewer should be alert to a variety of traps. There is the risk of an overidentification with the patient, which may be associated with an illusory treatment alliance or misattribution of psychological health. Even in the absence of such distortions, the clinician may be at risk for feelings of helplessness or guilt. Both kinds of reactions increase the likelihood that a therapist will soon bear witness to an unhappy turn of events associated with manipulation and deceit.

Because interpersonal interaction is so much of the nuts and bolts of what we do as clinicians, we have largely focused on specific dynamic formulations of commonly observed interaction patterns and common clinician reactions. In addition, in discussing a new experimental measure, the IM-P, we attempted to draw attention to a list of so-called *event labels* or types of interactions that may be useful to consider in arriving at a case conceptualization. Although the PCL–R remains the sine qua non of psychopathy assessment and case formulation, we are heartened that additional approaches to assessing psychopaths' interpersonal behavior continue to be developed.

ENDNOTES

1. The ideas in this chapter reflect relatively equal contributions by the first and second authors, with substantial contributions by the third author.
2. There is a variety of roles in which clinicians may have reason to interact with psychopaths: therapist, interviewer, examiner, researcher. We have chosen the general term *clinician* to refer to these various roles.
3. The use of the term *borderline level of organization* is not intended to suggest similarities to the specific syndrome described elsewhere as Borderline Personality Disorder. Rather, Kernberg's use of this term denotes a broad category relevant to many personality disorders, including many but not all individuals who would meet *DSM–IV* criteria for erratic-dramatic personality disorders (Kernberg, 1970).
4. Splitting mechanisms should be suspected when patient attitudes toward the clinician vacillate between extremes of idealization and devaluation, when gross inconsistencies between affect and behavior are apparent, or when events or people are described in extreme and opposite polarities. The psychopath's conscious indifference to this fragmented experience of self and others may be almost inconceivable to the unseasoned clinician and hence may not be fully appreciated.

5. The actual interpersonal control often associated with projective identification may contribute to the view that this process is interpersonal, not just intrapsychic (Lubbe, 1998).
6. By contrast, IM-P scores predicted reduced involvement in nonviolent criminal offenses (Kosson et al., 1997). As noted later, a similar finding was also reported by Vassileva (1999).
7. For a further discussion of the validity of the interview measure of Factor 1, see Colwell (1998), Steuerwald (1996), and Forth et al. (1996). For a review of the evidence relating the Socialization scale to Factor 2, see Kosson, Steuerwald, Newman, and Widom (1994) and Harpur et al. (1989).

REFERENCES

Alexander, F. (1935). *Roots of crime.* New York: Knopf Publishers.
Bauer, D. (1999). *Psychopathy in incarcerated adolescent females: Prevalence rates and individual differences in cognition, personality and behavior.* Unpublished doctoral dissertation, Finch University of Health Sciences/The Chicago Medical School, North Chicago, Illinois.
Blackburn, R., & Lee-Evans, J. M. (1985). Reactions of primary and secondary psychopaths to anger-evoking situations. *British Journal of Clinical Psychology, 24,* 93–100.
Bursten, B. (1972). The manipulative personality. *Archives of General Psychiatry, 26,* 318–321.
Bursten, B. (1973). Some narcissistic personality types. *International Journal of Psychoanalysis, 54,* 287–299.
Cleckley, H. (1976). *The mask of sanity* (5th ed.). St. Louis: Mosby.
Colwell, J. T. (1998). *An interpersonal method for scoring the TAT: Implications for distinguishing individuals with psychopathic symptomatology using Leary's circumplex model.* Unpublished doctoral dissertation, University of North Carolina at Greensboro, Greensboro, North Carolina.
Foreman, M. (1988). *Psychopathy and interpersonal behavior.* Unpublished doctoral dissertation, University of British Columbia, Vancouver, Canada.
Forth, A. E., Brown, S. L., Hart, S. D., & Hare, R. D. (1996). The assessment of psychopathy in male and female noncriminals: Reliability and validity. *Personality & Individual Differences, 20,* 531–543.
Gacono, C. (1988). *A Rorschach analysis of object relations and defensive structure and their relationship to narcissism and psychopathy in a group of antisocial offenders.* Unpublished doctoral dissertation, United States International University, San Diego.
Gacono, C. (1990). An empirical study of object relations and defensive operations in antisocial personality. *Journal of Personality Assessment, 54,* 589–600.
Gacono, C., & Meloy, R. (1988). The relationship between cognitive style and defensive process in the psychopath. *Criminal Justice and Behavior, 15*(4), 472–483.
Gacono, C., & Meloy, R. (1992). The Rorschach and the *DSM–III–R* antisocial personality: A tribute to Robert Lindner. *Journal of Clinical Psychology, 48*(3), 393–405.
Gacono, C., & Meloy, R. (1994). *The Rorschach assessment of aggressive and psychopathic personalities.* Hillsdale: NJ: Lawrence Erlbaum Associates.
Gacono, C., Meloy, R., & Berg, J. (1992). Object relations, defensive operations, and affective states in narcissistic, borderline, and antisocial personality. *Journal of Personality Assessment, 59,* 32–49.
Gacono, C., Meloy, R., Sheppard, K., Speth, E., & Roske, A. (1995). A clinical investigation of malingering and psychopathy in hospitalized insanity acquittees. *Bulletin of the American Academy of Psychiatry and the Law, 23*(3), 1–11.
Gacono, C., Nieberding, R., Owen, A., Rubel, J., & Bodholdt, R. (2001). Treating juvenile and adult offenders with Conduct-Disorder, Antisocial, and Psychopathic Personalities. In J. B. Ashford, B. D. Sales, & W. Reid (Eds.), *Treating adult and juvenile offenders with special needs* (pp. 99–129). Washington, DC: American Psychological Association.

Gaddini, E. (1969). On imitation. *International Journal of Psycho-Analysis, 50*, 475–484.

Gillstrom, B. J., & Hare, R. D. (1988). Language-related hand gestures in psychopaths. *Journal of Personality Disorders, 2*, 21–27.

Gough, M. G. (1960). Theory and measurement of socialization. *Journal of Consulting Psychology, 24*, 23–30.

Grotstein, J. S. (1980). *Splitting and projective identification.* New York: Aronson.

Hare, R. D., & Craigen, D. (1974). Psychopathy and physiological activity in a mixed-motive game situation. *Psychophysiology, 11*, 197–206.

Harpur, T. J., Hare, R. D., & Hakstian, A. R. (1989). Two-factor conceptualization of psychopathy: Construct validity and assessment implications. *Psychological Assessment: A Journal of Consulting and Clinical Psychology, 1*, 6–17.

Helfgott, J. (1991). *A comparison of cognitive, behavioral, and psychodynamic assessments of psychopathy: Integrative measures of understanding the psychopathic personality in criminal and noncriminal populations.* Unpublished master's thesis, Pennsylvania State University, University Park.

Helfgott, J. (1992). *The unconscious defensive process/conscious cognitive style relationship: An empirical study of psychopathic dynamics in criminal and noncriminal groups.* Unpublished doctoral dissertation, Pennsylvania State University, University Park.

Hickey, E. (1991). *Serial murderers and their victims.* Pacific Grove, CA: Brooks/Cole.

Hoge, S. K., & Gutheil, T. G. (1987). The prosecution of psychiatric patients for assaults on staff: A preliminary empirical study. *Hospital and Community Psychiatry, 38*, 44–49.

Keisler, D. J. (1996). *Contemporary interpersonal theory and research.* New York: Wiley.

Kernberg, O. (1966). Structural derivatives of object relationships. *International Journal of Psychoanalysis, 47*, 236–253.

Kernberg, O. (1970). A psychoanalytic classification of character pathology. *Journal of the American Psychoanalytic Association, 19*, 595–635.

Kernberg, O. (1975). *Borderline conditions and pathological narcissism.* New York: Aronson.

Kernberg, O. (1977). The structural diagnosis of borderline personality organization. In P. Hartocollis (Ed.), *Borderline personality disorders* (pp. 87–121). New York: International Universities Press.

Kernberg, O. (1984). *Severe personality disorders: Psychotherapeutic strategies.* London: Yale University Press.

Kosson, D. S. (1999a). Psychopathy indices in male county jail inmates. Unpublished raw data.

Kosson, D. S. (1999b). Psychopathy indices in male adolescent probationers. Unpublished raw data.

Kosson, D., Steuerwald, B. L., Forth, A. E., & Kirkhart, K. (1997). A new method for assessing the interpersonal behavior of psychopathic individuals: Preliminary validation studies. *Psychological Assessment, 9*(2), 89–101.

Kosson, D. S., Steuerwald, B. L., Newman, J. P., & Widom, C. S. (1994). The relation between socialization and antisocial behavior, substance use, and family conflict in college students. *Journal of Personality Assessment, 63*, 473–488.

Leary, T. (1957). *Interpersonal diagnosis of personality.* New York: Ronald.

Lerner, P. (1975). Interpersonal relations. In P. Lerner (Ed.), *Handbook of Rorschach scales* (pp. 324–357). New York: International Universities Press.

Lerner, P. (1991). *Psychoanalytic theory and the Rorschach.* Hillsdale, NJ: Analytic Press.

Lion, J. (1978). Outpatient treatment of psychopaths. In W. Reid (Ed.), *The psychopath: A comprehensive study of antisocial disorders and behaviors* (pp. 286–300). New York: Brunner/Mazel.

Lion, J., & Leaff, L. (1973). On the hazards of assessing character pathology in an outpatient setting. *Psychiatric Quarterly, 47*, 104–109.

Lubbe, T. (1998). Projective identification fifty years on: A personal view. *Journal of Child Psychotherapy, 24*, 367–391.

McKay, J. R. (1986). Psychopathy and pathological narcissism: A descriptive and psychody-namic formulation on the antisocial personality disorder. *Journal of Offender Counseling, Services, & Rehabilitation, 11,* 77–93.

Meloy, R. (1988). *The psychopathic mind: Origins, dynamics and treatment.* Northvale, NJ: Aronson.

Meloy, R. (1992). *Violent attachments.* Northvale, NJ: Aronson.

Meloy, R. (1995). Antisocial personality disorder. In G. Gabbard (Ed.). *Treatments of psychiatric disorders* (2nd ed., pp. 2274–2290). Washington, DC: American Psychiatric Press.

Meloy, R., & Gacono, C. (1992). A psychotic sexual psychopath: "I just had a violent thought." *Journal of Personality Assessment, 58*(3), 480–493.

Meloy, R., & Gacono, C. (1993). A borderline psychopath: "I was basically maladjusted." *Journal of Personality Assessment, 61*(2), 358–373.

Meloy, R., & Gacono, C. (1994). A neurotic criminal: "I learned my lesson." *Journal of Personality Assessment, 62*(1), 27–38.

Millon, T. (1981). *Disorders of personality: DSM–III: Axis II.* New York: Wiley.

Milton. J. (1968). *Paradise lost and paradise regained.* New York: American New Library.

Ogden, T. H. (1992). The dialectically constituted/decentred subject of psychoanalysis: II. The contributions of Klein and Winnicott. *International Journal of Psycho-Analysis, 73,* 613–626.

Racker, H. (1968). *Transference and counter-transference.* New York: International Universities Press.

Redl, R., & Wineman, D. (1951). *Children who hate: The disorganization and breakdown of behavior controls.* New York: The Free Press.

Rime, B., Bouvy, H., Leborgne, B., & Rouillon, F. (1978). Psychopathy and nonverbal behavior in an interpersonal situation. *Journal of Abnormal Psychology, 87,* 636–643.

Schachtel, E. (1966). *Experiential foundations of Rorschach's test.* New York: Basic Books.

Schafer, R. (1954). *Psychoanalytic interpretation in Rorschach testing.* New York: Grune & Stratton.

Serin, R. (1996). Violent recidivism in criminal psychopaths. *Law and Human Behavior, 20,* 207–217.

Steuerwald (1996). *Anger following provocation in individuals with psychopathic characteristics.* Unpublished doctoral dissertation, University of North Carolina at Greensboro, Greensboro, NC.

Strasburger, L. (1986). Treatment of antisocial syndromes: the therapist's feelings. In W. Reid, D. Dorr, J. Walker, & J. Bonner (Eds.), *Unmasking the psychopath* (pp. 191–207). New York: Norton.

Sugarman, A. (1981). The diagnostic use of countertransference reactions in psychological testing. *Bulletin of the Menninger Clinic, 45*(6), 473–490.

Sutker, P. B. (1970). Vicarious conditioning and sociopathy. *Journal of Abnormal Psychology, 76,* 380–386.

Valliant, G. E. (1975). Sociopathy as a human process. *Archives of General Psychiatry, 32,* 178–183.

Vassileva, J. (1999). *Classification of criminal offenders based on psychopathy and theoretically-related constructs.* Unpublished master's thesis, Finch University of Health Sciences/The Chicago Medical School, North Chicago, Illinois.

Whitehill, M. B. (1986). *Psychopathy and interpersonal relationships.* Unpublished doctoral dissertation, University of Pittsburgh, Pittsburgh, Pennsylvania.

Widiger, T. A., & Frances, A. (1985). The DSM–III personality disorders. *Archives of General Psychiatry, 42,* 615–623.

Widom, C. S. (1976). Interpersonal conflict and cooperation in psychopaths. *Journal of Abnormal Psychology, 85,* 330–334.

9

Assessing Psychopathy: Psychological Testing and Report Writing

J. Reid Meloy
University of California, San Diego

Carl B. Gacono
Private Practice, Austin, Texas

Hugo Munsterberg, one of the first forensic psychologists, wrote in his 1908 book *On the Witness Stand*, "we do not grasp for the poisonous fruit, because the danger holds us back" (p. 237). We assume he was thinking about the nonpsychopathic individual who is, at times, inhibited and fearful, like many of the patients we see in our clinical practices.

On occasion, however, we are faced with the assessment of the psychopathic personality. If our work takes us into criminal forensic settings, psychopathy is a "specific constellation of deviant traits and behaviors" (Hare, 1991, p. 2) that cannot be ignored. The preceding chapter focused on the interpersonal aspects of psychopathy—specifically, the clinical interview. This chapter is devoted to the practical assessment of psychopathy, focusing on psychological testing and report writing.

FORENSIC ASSESSMENT

The purpose of assessing psychopathy varies with the nature of the setting and the functional outcome of the evaluation. Prior to sentencing, the psychologist is usually called on to aid the trier of fact—the judge or jury—in answering a psycholegal question such as dangerousness or sanity. Subsequent to institutional commitment, referral questions stem from institutional concerns and may involve severity of antisocial personality disorder (ASPD), malingering, treatment amenability or planning (Gacono, 1998;

see chap. 8), sanity, violence risk, threat management, sadism, sexual sadism, outpatient treatment, classification (Gacono & Hutton, 1994), and others related to diagnosis, treatment, and risk management. In all cases, the forensic psychologist—as evaluator rather than therapist—is performing an investigation to gather data. He or she is not an agent of change. Confusion between these two fundamentally different roles, evaluator or therapist, may lead to misuse of information and unethical behavior (Meloy, 1989). The psychologist must have a clear conception of his or her role before the assessment begins.

There is an additional problem in assessing psychopathy. Most psychopathic individuals are chronically deceptive and lie to and mislead the assessor at every turn. The deceptive behaviors often involve projection of blame and malingering or exaggeration of psychiatric symptoms, all important behaviors to be noted as part of the assessment process. The goal of the psychopathic patient is usually to gain a more dominant or pleasurable position in relation to his objects, whether it be a person, an institution, or a legal proceeding (Meloy, 1988).

This second concern is addressed by recognizing the need to gather data from three different sources: a clinical interview, independent historical information, and testing. The clinical interview involves face-to-face contact with the individual long enough to complete a mental status exam and gather self-reported problems and historical data that can be used to develop clinical hypotheses. It also allows for the emergence of transference and countertransference reactions, which can be a potent source of psychodiagnostic information (Kernberg, 1984; see chap. 9). Independent historical (or contemporaneous) information refers to any data that are not self-reported by the examinee; it includes such things as other psychiatric and psychological records, medical records, school and military records, employment records, criminal records, and interviews with historical and contemporary observers of the examinee (parents, siblings, legal and health care professionals). *Testing* refers to psychological, neuropsychological, and medical tests—historical or contemporary—that provide objective reference points to further understand the psychology or psychobiology of the examinee. The elimination of any one of these three sources of knowledge will leave the psychologist vulnerable to gross manipulation in a treatment setting and may lead to impeachment as an expert witness in a forensic setting.

Although this chapter focuses on the use of testing, we cannot overstate the importance of the other two components of the psychopathy assessment triangle: the clinical interview and the examination of independent historical data. Our subsequent discussion of tests and instruments assumes the competent and thorough completion of these other two clinical tasks. Our discussion of report writing integrates data from all three.

PSYCHOPATHY AND ANTISOCIAL PERSONALITY DISORDER

The diagnosis of antisocial personality disorder (ASPD) in the *Diagnostic and Statistical Manual of Mental Disorders* (4th ed. [*DSM–IV*]; American Psychiatric Association, 1994) is almost exclusively devoted to criminal and antisocial behaviors (see chap. 3). Although most psychopathic subjects also meet criteria for ASPD, as defined by psychiatric nomenclature, only one third of ASPD samples in maximum security prisons meet the criteria for psychopathic personality as defined by a reliable and valid measure (Cleckley, 1941/1976; Hare, 1991). The clinical importance of this fact can be stated differently. Most ASPD adults, both male and female, should not be considered severely psychopathic and do not meet the factor analytic definition of this construct: an individual whose behavior is characterized by a callous and remorseless disregard for the rights and feelings of others and a chronic antisocial lifestyle (Hare, 1991).

When reporting the results of a Psychopathy Checklist–Revised (PCL–R) evaluation, several options for clarifying the relationship between ASPD and psychopathy emerge. First, one could use the PCL–R total score to determine psychopathy level. These ranges could then be used to designate the Axis II ASPD diagnosis as mild, moderate, or severe. This would be a more refined, yet similar method of subtyping as has been applied to the juvenile conduct disorder (CD) diagnoses in *DSM–IV* (American Psychiatric Association, 1994). A mild, moderate, or severe referent could be included with the ASPD diagnosis, 301.70 Antisocial Personality Disorder (severe). Subsequently, the patient's clinical picture is clarified in the report's finding section by using factor scores and item analysis as a basis for describing existent traits and behaviors (see chap. 8; Gacono & Hutton, 1994). All protocol data, including total PCL–R score, should be maintained in the psychologist's confidential files under the same ethical guidelines as other instruments such as the Rorschach or MMPI–2.

A second approach is that the construct *psychopathy* can be integrated into Axis II by placing in parentheses the terms *mild, moderate,* or *severe psychopathy* after the *DSM–IV* recognized personality disorder if one or several exist. The subsequent paragraph should then explain how psychopathy is defined and psychologically measured. For example:

Axis I: Sexual sadism

Axis II: Antisocial Personality Disorder (severe psychopathy)

Psychopathy is a measurable construct that refers to an individual who is both aggressively narcissistic and chronically antisocial. In this case, Mr. A scored 38 on the PCL–R, the most reliable and valid measure of psychopathy. This finding has important implications for treatment amenability and future violence risk, particularly when placed in the context of his history of 12 sexually sadistic murders.

The psychologist should recognize that the term *psychopathy* does not currently appear as a psychodiagnosis or as a personality disorder in *DSM–IV*, but does extensively appear in the companion volume, *Treatments of Psychiatric Disorders*, published in 1995 by the American Psychiatric Press (Meloy, 1995). We remain hopeful that there will be further integration of psychopathy as a useful construct into mainstream American psychiatry by the time of *DSM–V*.

THE PSYCHOPATHY CHECKLIST–REVISED

The first and most important instrument for measuring psychopathy is the PCL–R (Hare, 1991; see chap. 3). This 20-item, 40-point scale is completed following a semistructured interview and a review of independent historical and contemporaneous data. Further psychological testing is not necessary to complete this behavioral trait instrument.

A growing body of research has demonstrated the reliability and validity of the PCL–R for prison and forensic psychiatric populations (Hare, 1991; Hare et al., 1990; Hart & Hare, 1989; Kosson, Smith, & Newman, 1990; Schroeder, Schroeder, & Hare, 1983; Siegel, 1998; Strachan, 1993; Taylor, 1997; see chaps. 3 & 8). The literature has demonstrated that psychopathic prisoners, compared with nonpsychopathic prisoners:

- Commit a greater quantity and variety of offenses (Hare & Jutai, 1983),
- Commit a greater frequency of violent offenses in which predatory violence (Meloy, 1988) is used against male strangers (Hare & McPherson, 1984; Williamson, Hare, & Wong, 1987),
- Have lengthier criminal careers (Hare, McPherson, & Forth, 1988),
- Have a poorer response to therapeutic intervention (Ogloff, Wong, & Greenwood, 1990), which, in some cases, may be followed by an increase in their subsequent arrest rates for violent crimes (Rice, Harris & Cormier, 1992), and
- Have a pattern of chronic cortical underarousal (Meloy, 1992; Raine, 1993) as in "habitual criminals"—a term that describes a group empirically related to psychopathy.

When the forensic evaluator uses the PCL–R in report writing and in preparation for court, particular attention should be paid to knowing (or at least knowing where to look for) (a) the most current validation studies concerning the instrument; (b) which groups the instrument has been validated on; (c) normative scores for the instrument when it has been used with young adult males; (d) distribution of scores in male, female, and delinquent incarcerated samples; (e) criticism of the test and its psychometric properties; and (f) clear and simple explanations of the test to the trier of fact, whether a judge or jury. It is important to remember that the lay person, whether educated or not, likely considers the terms *antisocial, psychopathic,* and *sociopathic* to be synonymous, essentially describing a bad person for whom they have little empathy and less compassion. The forensic psychologist is both a clinician and a teacher, especially in court.

The forensic psychologist should always be aware of several key issues related to PCL–R or PCL:SV administration and scoring. When testifying, the evaluator should be prepared to provide evidence concerning his or her qualifications and training, the appropriateness of the instruments used with this particular patient (normative samples), and that adequate collateral information was available for scoring. Prior to administering the Psychopathy Checklists, the following should be ensured:

- The evaluator is a licensed mental health professional with forensic experience,
- The evaluator has participated in adequate training that has included his or her demonstrated ability to reliably rate the instrument (see chaps. 3 & 8),
- The evaluator is familiar with the current PCL research ,
- The patient is similar to a population where the instrument has been validated (for the PCL–R; incarcerated males and females, and male juvenile delinquents),
- There is available independent historical information, and
- Collateral information is always reviewed before the interview.

The following caveats form a mind set for conducting the interview, decrease the possibility of scoring bias and halo effects, and should be foremost in the evaluator's awareness during the PCL–R administration:

- Conduct the PCL–R interview as a separate part of the overall psychological evaluation,
- Ensure that ratings are based on life-long patterns and typical functioning,
- Focus on scoring each item separately; avoid letting speculation about the total score influence individual item scoring,
- Avoid introspection about etiology or preconceived notions of psychopathy,

- Frequently refer to the PCL–R Rating Booklet to maintain the scoring prototype, and
- Remember that the PCL–R Clinical Interview Schedule (see Appendix A) is generally nonthreatening and can build rapport with and a sense of empathy for the patient.

Although a score of ≥ 30 has been used as the research convention for separating psychopathic from nonpsychopathic research subjects, we do not recommend using this cutoff for forensic purposes due to the heightened sensitivity and impact of the score on the individual being evaluated. Psychologists should consider the mean standard error of measurement (SEM; 3.14) and the mean standard error of prediction (4.26; Hare, 1991) when integrating test scores. We recommend that the term *severe psychopathy* be reserved for individuals who score at least 33 points on the PCL–R or one SEM unit above the research cutoff. Individuals scoring below this level should be considered to have psychopathic traits, and discussion should avoid labeling them as psychopathic personalities. In some cases, the evaluator may forego the use of the term *psychopathy* altogether. The majority of criminal psychopaths meet the accepted diagnostic label of ASPD and should be labeled as such, with the severity of the ASPD providing the clinician with information concerning the actual psychopathy level.

Assessment is strengthened when several independent measures are used. We recommend that several other tests be employed to further delineate the behavioral and intrapsychic characteristics of the psychopathic subject within whom many individual differences reside.

THE RORSCHACH

The Rorschach is ideally suited for contributing to the assessment of psychopathy. It avoids the face validity of self-report measures, yet provides reliable and valid information about the individual's personality structure and function (Exner, 1986). Although we hesitate to state that the Rorschach cannot be malingered, we have found that it is usually only beaten by the psychopathic patient who sufficiently constricts his or her response frequency (Perry & Kinder, 1990). Such a psychometrically invalid protocol (Exner, 1988), however, may still yield worthwhile psychodiagnostic information (Weiner, 1998). We have found that ASPD males in general produce normative response frequencies (Gacono & Meloy, 1992, 1994), at least in research settings. Rorschachs taken for forensic purposes in pretrial criminal cases may be constricted, but the examiner should aggressively pursue a valid protocol (R ≥ 14) according to Exner's guidelines.

Although the clinician should administer and interpret the Rorschach according to the Comprehensive System (Exner, 1991), other psychoanalytically informed empirical measures of the Rorschach are also quite valuable. Two methods that we ordinarily use to complement the Comprehensive System include a measure of defenses (Cooper & Arnow, 1986) and an object relations measure (Kwawer, 1980). We have found both of these measures to have acceptable interjudge reliability (Gacono & Meloy, 1992). Kwawer (1979) found that his 10 categories of primitive interpersonal modes were able to significantly differentiate between a borderline and an age- and gender-matched control sample of Rorschachs. Cooper, Perry, and Arnow (1988) reported interrater reliabilities for each of 15 defenses ranging from .45 to .80, with a median of .62 (intraclass correlation coefficients). Interrater reliability for the borderline defenses as a group, most commonly seen in psychopathic protocols, was .81. However, they did not find any particular defense mechanism related to the presence of ASPD (*DSM–III–R*) and speculated that the diagnosis of ASPD may be too psychodynamically heterogeneous. We agree.

Through a series of studies (Gacono, 1990; Gacono et al., 1990; Gacono & Meloy, 1991, 1992, 1994; Meloy & Gacono, 1992; Meloy, Gacono, & Kenney, 1994), we have validated the use of the Rorschach as a sensitive instrument to discriminate between psychopathic and nonpsychopathic ASPD subjects. Psychodynamic differences include more pathological narcissism and sadism (Gacono, Meloy, & Heaven, 1990), less anxiety, and less capacity for attachment (Gacono & Meloy, 1991). Personality organization (Kernberg, 1984) predominates at a borderline level (Gacono, 1990). Commonly used defenses include devaluation, massive denial, projective identification, omnipotence, and splitting. Idealization and higher level neurotic defenses are virtually absent. Psychopathic criminals produce significantly more narcissistic mirroring, boundary disturbance, and total primitive object relations than nonpsychopathic criminals (Gacono & Meloy, 1992).

The prototypical Rorschach protocol of the psychopathic subject evidences certain abnormal structural characteristics (Exner, 1991; see Table 9.1). The numbers represent mean scores or frequencies of the majority of the subjects in a sample of 33 male ASPD psychopaths in prison (Gacono & Meloy, 1994).

Deviations from these typical findings do not necessarily rule out a psychopathic disturbance and should deepen understanding of the individual differences within any one patient. For example, a psychopathic patient might also show histrionic features structurally evident in some idealizing defenses, a color projection (CP) response, a low lambda (L), and an elevated affective ratio (Afr). In contrast, a paranoid psychopath might produce a constricted protocol, elevated Dd responses, a low

TABLE 9.1
Select Comprehensive System Variables From a Prototypical Rorschach of a Psychopath

Variable	Value
Responses	21
Core characteristics	
Lambda	>.99
D	0
Adj D	0
Affects	
FC:CF+C	1:4
Afr	<.50
Pure C	>0
T	0
Y	0
Space	>2
Interpersonal relations	
Pure H	2
(H)+Hd+(Hd)	2.5
COP	0
Ag	0
Sx	1
Self-perception	
Rf	1
PER	>2
W:M	>3:1
Cognitions	
X+%	54
F+%	56
X–%	22
M–	1
WSum6SpecSc	17

H+A:Hd+Ad ratio, and a positive hypervigilance index (HVI). A psycho-pathic subject scoring 36 on the PCL–R might also have the biochemical disorder of schizophrenia, evident on the Rorschach in a positive schizo-phrenia index (SCZI). What begins as a gross categorization of chronic antisocial behavior (*DSM–IV*) moves to a determination of the degree of psychopathic disturbance using the PCL–R. It is further refined through the Rorschach to measure the internal structure and dynamics of the par-ticular patient.

Recent research has described the manner in which Rorschach data can be presented in court (Meloy, 1991), the admissibility of Rorschach data in court (Weiner, Exner, & Sciara, 1996), and the weight of Rorschach data in court (Meloy, Hansen, & Weiner, 1997). Forensic evaluators should be thoroughly familiar with recent validation studies of the Rorschach (Weiner, 1996) and its relationship to legal standards for admissibility of scientific evidence (McCann, 1998). If there are scoring questions, consultations should be sought, informing the colleague that his or her name may be referenced in pending litigation as a consultant *before* the talk begins. Evaluators should pay particular attention to the growing database for forensic Rorschach samples (Gacono & Meloy, 1994), keeping in mind that differences have emerged in these indexes when compared to Exner's nonpatient and clinical norms.

THE MMPI/MMPI-2

Our assessment of psychopathy turns next to the psychometric workhorse of the profession and forensic psychology in particular. Although self-report measures in criminal populations are inherently unreliable (Hare, 1985), either the Minnesota Multiphasic Personality Inventory (MMPI) or the MMPI-2 should be used with other instruments in the assessment of psychopathy for the following reasons: to provide convergent validity for other sources of data; to measure self-report of psychopathology with a method that is sensitive to distortion; to measure domains of behavior that are not empirically abnormal; and to meet evidentiary standards for admissibility as a scientific method or procedure (*Daubert v. Merrell Dow Pharmaceuticals*, 113 Sup. Ct. 2786). The latter standard, applicable in all federal jurisdictions in the United States, is met through the court's determination that the measure is relevant to the case and scientifically valid.

The clinical scale most sensitive to "a variation in the direction of psychopathy" (McKinley & Hathaway, 1944, p. 172) is, of course, Scale 4 (Pd). Most criminal populations show remarkable homogeneity by elevating on this scale. However, Scale 4 does not significantly correlate with total PCL-R scores and is more related to Factor II (chronic antisocial behavior) than Factor I (aggressive narcissism).

McKinley and Hathaway (1944) developed this scale by contrasting two normative groups—married adults and college applicants—with a sample of female and male delinquents (ages 17–22) referred by the Minnesota courts to a psychiatric setting. These young adults had a long history of minor criminal behavior: stealing, lying, truancy, sexual promiscuity, alcohol abuse, and forgery. There were no homicide offenses in the histories of these subjects of whom the majority were girls. Cross-validation indicated that a T-score of ≥ 70 was achieved by 59% of a sample of 100 male federal prisoners (McKinley & Hathaway, 1944). We note that the original criterion group was already incarcerated and had been selected for psychiatric study. Temporal reliability of this scale ranges from .49 to .61 for intervals up to a year (Dahlstrom et al., 1975) and was .71 in normals according to McKinley and Hathaway (1944).

The MMPI Scale 4 is composed of 50 items, of which half are answered true (24) and half answered false (26). Factor analysis has generally yielded five factors: Shyness, Hypersensitivity, Delinquency, Impulse control, and Neuroticism (Greene, 1980). Several texts are relevant for validation and interpretation of Scale 4 (Dahlstrom et al., 1972, 1975; Graham, 1978; Greene, 1980). Clinical interpretation should always address both elevation and configuration.

The Harris and Lingoes (1955) Pd subscales help to further understand Scale 4 nuances. Originally derived from the MMPI through a rational analysis and not separately validated, they are composed of 67 items, 12 of which are off scale and do not appear among the other Scale 4 items. Five subscale items (64, 67, 94, 146, 368) appear in more than one of the subscales. Caldwell (1988) provided a useful interpretation of these subscales for the MMPI.

The Scale 4 items have undergone virtually no changes in MMPI-2. The 50 items remain and 4 have been reworded. However, Pd T-scores are approximately 10 T points lower for males and 5 T points lower for females across the range of the scale due to the new norms. Moreover, the Pd scale is not affected by educational level in either the MMPI-2 male or female normative samples (Butcher, 1990).

The Harris and Lingoes subscales have been substantially changed on the MMPI-2. D. Nichols (personal communication, April 1993) determined that each subscale lost a certain number of items (see Table 9.2).

The MMPI-2 committee's justification for these deletions is that they were off scale items and did not contribute to clarification of elevation on the parent (Pd) scale. The Pd3 subscale, Social Imperturbability, was most heavily hit, losing half its items. This measure of what D. Nichols (personal communication, April 1993) called *insouciance* has gotten consistently high negative loadings on anxiety and may best capture the social aggression of the psychopathic personality. The MMPI-2 deletions have decreased the subscales' reliability due to increased T-score jumps for

TABLE 9.2
Harris and Lingoes Pd Subscale Items and Changes Between MMPI and MMPI-2

Subscale		MMPI	Deleted	MMPI-2
Pd1	Family Discord	11	2	9
Pd2	Authority Problems	11	3	8
Pd3	Social Imperturbability	12	6	6
Pd4a (Pd4)	Social Alienation	18	5	13
Pd4b (Pd5)	Self-Alienation	15	3	12
Total		67	19	48

Note.   Courtesy of David Nichols, Ph.D.

each remaining item and may have affected the subscales' meanings and internal consistency. Although these subscales have been compromised and may be less adequate than they were, we still think they deserve clinical attention.

The major problems with the new antisocial practices (ASP) content scale (Butcher et al., 1989) are its face validity and the fact that it is suppressed with elevations on K. It can be viewed as an attitude scale until further researched with psychopathic subjects. Lilienfeld (1991) found that it had relatively high loadings on two factors—Negative Emotionality and Fearlessness—in a sample of college undergraduates, which is consistent with expected trait characteristics of adult male psychopathic personalities.

The most useful MMPI typology for classifying criminals was developed by Megargee and Bohn (1979). Of their sample of 1,214 federal inmates, 96% of the MMPI profiles could be assigned to 1 of their 10 subtypes. Subsequent research has supported its concurrent validity (Booth & Howell, 1983; DiFrancesca & Meloy, 1989; Hutton, Miner, & Langfeldt, 1993) and questioned its predictive validity (Louscher, Hosford, & Moss, 1983). Their typology can be used to generate behavioral hypotheses concerning a particular subject's MMPI elevations and configuration, which can then be tested against other data.

The application of the Megargee–Bohn typology to the MMPI–2 necessitated revision of their classification rules and procedures. Identical classifications were then achieved with 80% to 84% of subjects in samples of youthful male offenders and male prisoners. Validation of these typology revisions for MMPI–2 needs to be done (Megargee, 1993).

How does Scale 4 and its subscales contribute to a clinical understanding of psychopathy? We compared the PCL–R, MMPI, and MMPI–2 Pd scores for two samples of male subjects who had been found not guilty by reason of insanity and were committed to an involuntary outpatient treatment program (Meloy, Haroun, & Schiller, 1990). Most of these subjects were White males diagnosed with paranoid schizophrenia who had committed a violent crime. The data are presented in Table 9.3.

The data suggest that, although there is a positive relationship between elevations on MMPI and MMPI–2 Pd and the PCL–R, the product–moment correlations are modest and nonsignificant. Our findings are consistent with Hare (1991), who found that correlations between the MMPI Pd scale and the PCL–R ranged from .19 to .25. We think this is primarily due to the Pd scale's measurement of Factor II of the PCL–R (Chronic Antisocial Behavior) rather than Factor I (Aggressive Narcissism). If the PCL–R factors are separately correlated with Pd, Factor I ranges between .05 and .11 and Factor II ranges between .28 and .31 (Hare, 1991).

The Harris and Lingoes (1955) subscales' correlations with the PCL–R indicate that Pd2, Authority Problems, are highest, and Pd1, Family Dis-

TABLE 9.3
Pearson Product–Moment Correlations Between PCL–R Scores
and MMPI and MMPI-2 Pd Scores in Samples of NGI Acquittees

Subscale	(N = 40) MMPI	(N = 34) MMPI-2
Pd	.21	.20
Pd1 Family Discord	.00	.10
Pd2 Authority Problems	.34*	.31*
Pd3 Social Imperturbability	.20	.23
Pd4 Social Alienation	−.17	−.10
Pd5 Self-Alienation	−.05	−.22

*$p < .05$ (one-directional test).

cord, are virtually nonexistent. Pd3, Social Imperturbability, is not significantly correlated but increases slightly between MMPI and MMPI-2.
Most compelling is the negative correlation between the PCL–R and the
MMPI-2 Pd5, Self-Alienation. This is consistent with our findings concerning the psychopath that he does not feel guilt, self-blame, or regret-
fulness concerning his antisocial acts (Caldwell, 1988; Gacono & Meloy,
1992, 1994). In fact, his lack of superego constraint or sense of personal
responsibility for his actions is a benchmark for his behavior (Hare, 1991;
Meloy, 1988). These findings also suggest that correlations between the
PCL–R and Pd, although modest, do not change when a forensic psychiatric sample is studied, rather than just a criminal sample. The clinician
should not hesitate to measure psychopathy despite the presence of a
major mental disorder (Hart & Hare, 1989).

Because response style should be considered (Bannatyne, Gacono, &
Greene, 1999) and distortion should be assumed in all forensic evaluations (Meloy, 1989), the MMPI/MMPI-2 validity scales take on special
importance when determining psychopathy. It appears that scales L and
F remain the most useful in classifying fake-bad and fake-good profiles
(Timbrook, Graham, Keiller, & Watts, 1993). The clinician is referred to
the extensive work of both Butcher et al. (1989) and Caldwell (1988, 1997)
for their interpretive refinements concerning deviant responding to the
MMPI-2.

MEASURES OF COGNITION AND INTELLIGENCE

Although not central to the assessment of personality, a standardized
measure of intelligence, such as the Wechsler Adult Intelligence Scale–III
(WAIS–III) or the Kaufman Adolescent and Adult Intelligence Test, should
be incorporated into the battery when assessing psychopathy level. In the

absence of time to do a complete intelligence battery, the Quick Test (Ammons & Ammons, 1977) gives a reliable estimate of intelligence and has been validated in forensic settings (Husband & DeCato, 1982; Randolph, Randolph, Ciula, Padget, & Cuneo, 1980; Sweeney & Richards, 1988). An estimate of general intelligence provides a baseline for interpretive performance on other instruments, although IQ does not correlate with psychopathy: a thoroughly replicated finding (Hare, 1991).

Neuropsychological measures may provide useful information to the clinician, but gross differences between psychopathic and nonpsychopathic subjects have yet to be consistently demonstrated (Hare, 1991). Some neuropsychological tests are also useful for suggesting malingering because of their face validity. Psychopathic malingerers often perform worse than the expected norms for neurologic or psychiatric patients. They also evidence more impairment than observed behavioral functioning would suggest (T. Wylie, personal communication, May 1993). We find two points most salient to the use of neuropsychological instruments in the assessment of psychopathy. First, any measures of performance are subject to motivational factors, and psychopathic patients may quickly realize that decrements in their performance on neuropsychological tests will contribute to their disability and perhaps avoidance of personal responsibility. Second, the genuine presence of neuropsychological impairment does not rule out psychopathy and may in fact be consistent with cognitive and emotional deficits already established in research with psychopaths (Hare, 1991; Young, Justice, & Erdberg, 1999).

Moreover, neuropsychological impairments that appear genuine may warrant further neurological workup with methods that eliminate motivational factors and measure brain structure or function. These procedures could include fMRI, CT, PET, EEG, or BEAM studies.

One sexual murderer (PCL–R = 37) produced generally invalid psychological test results due to malingering, and was diagnosed with both ASPD and NPD on Axis II. He was found, moreover, to have an abnormal visual evoked potential test using BEAM technology and an abnormal PET scan indicating decreased metabolic uptake in certain areas of his pre-frontal cortex and midbrain. Based on these findings, and corollary behaviors, he received an additional Axis I diagnosis of organic personality syndrome, explosive type. (DSM–III–R)

Raine and his colleagues (Raine & Buchsbaum, 1996; Raine, Buchsbaum, & LaCasse, 1997; Raine et al., 1994, 1998) have conducted a series of studies investigating differences in prefrontal cortical function among murderers referred for neural imaging to various comparison groups and between affective and predatory murderers. Although Raine and his colleagues did not measure psychopathy in any of these studies, their work suggests that functional impairments among psychopaths may be found in the orbital-frontal portion of the prefrontal cortex. Bold studies such as these—the first of their kind—postulating a relationship between biology and criminal behavior at a metabolic level, are not probative of criminal responsibility in any one case, but point directions for future research and the possible use of neural imaging in forensic cases. Raine (1993) also reviewed and contributed to a substantial body of work that strongly suggests biological loadings for what he referred to as *habitual criminality*, including physiological measures that create a state of chronic cortical underarousal in the habitual criminal.

Research findings such as these extend the original work of Hare (1970), which found peripheral autonomic hyporeactivity to aversive stimuli among psychopaths, and suggest that biological measures, broadly or discretely defined, may eventually play a role in the psychodiagnosis of psychopathy. Until that time, the evaluator should treat the disparate biological findings concerning psychopaths as a large, patchwork quilt that is just beginning to be woven, but will eventually help us fully understand the brain–behavior relationships within psychopathy.

INTEGRATION OF FINDINGS
AND REPORT WRITING

Perhaps the most difficult and elegant task of the psychologist is to integrate the findings from various assessment procedures into an empirically accurate and theoretically consistent clinical picture of the patient. In the case of the psychopath in a forensic setting, findings also need to withstand the rigors of cross-examination (Gacono & Hutton, 1994; Meloy, 1991; Meloy, Hansen, & Weiner, 1997; Pope, Butcher, & Seelen, 1993). Again, we cannot overstate the importance of the history and clinical interview and their usefulness to validate or invalidate test findings. Moreover, test results provide contemporaneous and objective reference points for the support or refutation of developing clinical hypotheses, as well as data relevant to the management of psychopathic patients in an institution (see chap. 8; Gacono, Nieberding, Owen, Rubel, & Bodholdt, 2001; Meloy, 1995).

In forensic evaluations, the specific psycholegal question(s) to be addressed should be clear to the examiner before work begins on the case. For example, a diagnosis may be only the first step in determining whether there is a mental disease or defect. Questions of responsibility or culpability are the next step on the causal chain, perhaps refocusing the examiner on the facts of the crime and any temporally reliable test findings that might support or refute certain states of mind in the perpetrator at the time of the criminal act. Then again, test results that address unstable emotional conditions, such as depression, may be irrelevant to prospective or retrospective hypothesis formulation. In most cases, however, psychopathy as a character or personality disorder has the temporal stability (Rutherford et al., 1999) to cast an illuminating light on the propensities and history of the individual.

The tests we have emphasized—the PCL–R, the Rorschach, and the MMPI–2—provide main avenues to understanding the psychopathic patient. The PCL–R is based on observation of the individual and his or her history, the Rorschach accesses generally unconscious personality structure and psychodynamics, and the MMPI–2 measures deliberate self-report of psychopathology and its distortion. Taken together, these instruments provide both discriminant and convergent data.

For example, a patient is scored 2 on PCL–R Item 13, Lack of Realistic or Long-Term Goals, which is partially arrived at on the basis of a series of frequent job changes in the subject's employment record. The MMPI–2 indicates a Pd2 (Authority Problems) T-score of 75, providing insight into one of the reasons for frequent job changes, which is further confirmed through the subpoena of employer records. The Rorschach is scrutinized and yields S > 2 (H: chronic anger), Lambda >.99 (H: a simple, item-by-item approach to problem solving), and FC:CF+C of 1:4, with 2 Pure C responses (H: unmodulated affect with a marked propensity to emotional explosiveness). Further study of the employment records indicates several incidents of angry outbursts toward employers. A look at the long sought after military record also indicates a less than honorable discharge. The evaluator then compares these findings with his clinical interview with the patient and recalls his countertransferential feelings of anxiety as the patient aggressively questioned his credentials before the interview began. Taken together, these approaches to understanding this hypothetical patient provide clinical understanding that is at once broader and more meaningful than the yield from any one test. It is the culmination of inference building (both convergent and divergent findings) across the three primary sources of data: the clinical interview, independent historical and contemporaneous data, and test results.

Appendix B is a report written by JRM; it focuses on a particular psycholegal question in a California case: Should a forensic inpatient be released from the hospital to a supervised outpatient treatment setting? Implicit within this question is a determination of dangerousness to self or others. This is the first step in the restoration to sanity of all forensic patients originally found not guilty by reason of insanity. This young man murdered both his parents while in a psychotic state. The evaluation was conducted pursuant to court order and was referred out of the county of commitment due to the controversial nature of the case and the relatively high stakes if the forensic evaluator committed a false negative. Forensic clinicians working with the patient were divided as to whether he was an imposturing, high-velocity psychopath or whether he had actually benefited from treatment and could go home. As indicated, the report findings suggest the latter.

The clinical assessment of psychopathic personality is a complex task that involves both nomothetic comparison and idiographic delineation. It is most frequently needed in forensic settings, but psychopathy may appear in any health care practice. The clinical psychologist, with his or her training in the appropriate use of tests, is most suited to the task.

ACKNOWLEDGMENT

This chapter is a revised and expanded version of work by the authors which originally appeared in J. Butcher, ed., *Clinical Personality Assessment*, Oxford University Press, 1995. It is reprinted with permission of the publisher.

REFERENCES

American Psychiatric Association. (1994). *Diagnostic and statistical manual of mental disorders* (4th ed.). Washington, DC: Author.

Ammons, R., & Ammons, C. (1977). The Quick Test: Provisional manual. *Psychological Reports Monograph Supplement I-VII*, 11, 111–161. (Original work published 1962)

Bannatyne, L., Gacono, C., & Greene, R. (1999). Differential patterns of responding among three groups of chronic psychotic forensic patients. *Journal of Clinical Psychology, 55*(12), 1553–1565.

Booth, R., & Howell, R. (1983). Classification of prison inmates with the MMPI: An extension and validation of the typology. *Criminal Justice and Behavior, 7*, 407–422.

Butcher, J. (1990). Education level and MMPI-2 measured psychopathology: A case of negligible influence. *MMPI-2 News and Profiles, 1*, 3.

Butcher, J., Dahlstrom, G., Graham, J., Tellegen, A., & Kaemmer, B. (1989). *MMPI-2 manual for administration and scoring*. Minneapolis, MN: University of Minnesota Press.

Caldwell, A. (1988). *MMPI supplemental scale manual*. Los Angeles: Caldwell Report.

Caldwell, A. (1997). *Forensic questions and answers on the MMPI-2*. Los Angeles: Caldwell Report.

Cleckley, H. (1941/1976). *The mask of sanity*. St Louis: C.V. Mosby.

Cooper, S., & Arnow, D. (1986). An object relations view of the borderline defenses: A Rorschach analysis. In M. Kissen (Ed.), *Assessing object relations phenomena* (pp. 143–171). Madison, CT: International Universities Press.

Cooper, S., Perry, J., & Arnow, D. (1988). An empirical approach to the study of defense mechanisms: I. Reliability and preliminary validity of the Rorschach defense scales. *Journal of Personality Assessment, 52*, 187–203.

Dahlstrom, G., Welsh, G., & Dahlstrom, L. (1972). *An MMPI handbook: Volume I. Clinical interpretation* (rev. ed.). Minneapolis, MN: University of Minnesota Press.

Dahlstrom, G., Welsh, G., & Dahlstrom, L. (1975). *An MMPI handbook: Volume II. Research applications* (rev. ed.). Minneapolis, MN: University of Minnesota Press.

DiFrancesca, K., & Meloy, J. R. (1989). A comparative clinical investigation of the "how" and "charlie" MMPI subtypes. *Journal of Personality Assessment, 53,* 396–403.

Daubert v. Merrell Dow Pharmaceuticals, 113 Sup. Ct. 2786.

Exner, J. (1986). *The Rorschach: A comprehensive system: Volume 1. Basic foundations* (2nd ed.). New York: Wiley.

Exner, J. (1988). Problems with brief Rorschach protocols. *Journal of Personality Assessment, 52,* 640–647.

Exner, J. (1991). *The Rorschach: A comprehensive system: Volume 2. Interpretation* (2nd ed.). New York: Wiley.

Gacono, C. B. (1990). An empirical study of object relations and defensive operations in antisocial personality disorder. *Journal of Personality Assessment, 54,* 589–600.

Gacono, C. B. (1998). The use of the psychopathy checklist-revised (PCL–R) and Rorschach in treatment planning with antisocial personality disordered patients. *International Journal of Offender Therapy and Comparative Criminology, 42,* 49–64.

Gacono, C. B., & Hutton, H. (1994). Suggestions for the clinical and forensic use of the Hare Psychopathy Checklist–Revised (PCL–R). *International Journal of Law and Psychiatry, 17*(3), 303–317.

Gacono, C. B., & Meloy, J. R. (1991). A Rorschach investigation of attachment and anxiety in antisocial personality disorder. *Journal of Nervous and Mental Disease, 179,* 546–552.

Gacono, C. B., & Meloy, J. R. (1992). The Rorschach and the *DSM–III–R* antisocial personality: A tribute to Robert Lindner. *Journal of Clinical Psychology, 48,* 393–405.

Gacono, C. B., & Meloy, J. R. (1994). *Rorschach assessment of aggressive and psychopathic personalities.* Hillsdale, NJ: Lawrence Erlbaum Associates.

Gacono, C. B., Meloy, J. R., & Bridges, M. R. (in press). A Rorschach comparison of psychopaths, sexual homicide perpetrators, and nonviolent pedophiles. *Journal of Clinical Psychology.*

Gacono, C. B., Meloy, J. R., & Heaven, T. (1990). A Rorschach investigation of narcissism and hysteria in antisocial personality disorder. *Journal of Personality Assessment, 55,* 270–279.

Gacono, C. B., Nieberding, R., Owen, A., Rubel, J., & Bodholdt, R. (2001). Treating juvenile and adult offenders with conduct disorder, antisocial, and psychopathic personalities. In J. Ashford, B. Sales, & W. Reid (Eds.), *Treating adult and juvenile offenders with special needs* (pp. 99–129). Washington, DC: American Psychological Association.

Graham, J. (1978). *The MMPI: A practical guide.* New York: Oxford University Press.

Greene, R. (1980). *The MMPI: An interpretive manual.* New York: Grune & Stratton.

Hare, R. D. (1970). *Psychopathy: Theory and research.* New York: Wiley.

Hare, R. D. (1985). Comparison of the procedures for the assessment of psychopathy. *Journal of Consulting and Clinical Psychology, 53,* 7–16.

Hare, R. D. (1991). *Manual for the Psychopathy Checklist–Revised.* Toronto: Multi-Health Systems.

Hare, R. D., Harpur, T., Hakstian, A., Forth, A., Hart, S., & Newman, J. (1990). The Psychopathy Checklist–Revised: Reliability and factor structure. *Psychological Assessment, 2,* 338–341.

Hare, R. D., & Jutai, J. (1983). Criminal history of the male psychopath: Some preliminary data. In K. Van Dusen & S. Mednick (Eds.), *Prospective studies of crime and delinquency.* (pp. 23–32). Boston: Kluner Mijhoff.

Hare, R. D., & McPherson, L. (1984). Violent and aggressive behavior by criminal psychopaths. *International Journal of Law and Psychiatry, 7,* 35–50.

Hare, R. D., McPherson, L., & Forth, A. (1988). Male psychopaths and their criminal careers. *Journal of Consulting and Clinical Psychology, 56,* 710–714.

Harris, R., & Lingoes, J. (1955). *Subscales for the MMPI: An aid to profile interpretation.* Unpublished manuscript.

Hart, S., & Hare, R. D. (1989). Discriminant validity of the Psychopathy Checklist in a forensic psychiatric population. *Psychological Assessment, 1,* 211–218.

Husband, S., & DeCato, C. (1982). The Quick Test compared with Wechsler Adult Intelligence Scale as measures of intellectual functioning in a prison clinical setting. *Psychological Reports, 50,* 167–170.

Hutton, H., Miner, M., & Langfeldt, V. (1993). The utility of the Megargee–Bohn typology in a forensic psychiatric hospital. *Journal of Personality Assessment, 60,* 572–587.

Kernberg, O. (1984). *Severe personality disorders.* New Haven, CT: Yale University Press.

Kosson, D., Smith, S., & Newman, J. (1990). Evaluating the construct validity of psychopathy on black and white male inmates: Three preliminary studies. *Journal of Abnormal Psychology, 99,* 250–259.

Kwawer, J. (1979). Borderline phenomena, interpersonal relations, and the Rorschach test. *Bulletin of the Menninger Clinic, 43,* 515–524.

Kwawer, J. (1980). Primitive interpersonal modes, borderline phenomena and Rorschach content. In J. Kwawer, P. Lerner, H. Lerner, & A. Sugarman (Eds.), *Borderline phenomena and the Rorschach test* (pp. 89–109). New York: International University Press.

Lilienfeld, S. (1991). Assessment of psychopathy with the MMPI and MMPI-2. *MMPI-2 News and Profiles, 2,* 2.

Louscher, P., Hosford, R., & Moss, C. (1983). Predicting dangerous behavior in a penitentiary using the Megargee typology. *Criminal Justice and Behavior, 10,* 269–284.

McCann, J. T. (1998). Defending the Rorschach in court: An analysis of admissibility using legal and professional standards. *Journal of Personality Assessment, 70*(1), 125–144.

McKinley, C., & Hathaway, S. (1944). The Minnesota Multiphasic Personality Inventory V. Hysteria, hypomania, and psychopathic deviate. *Journal of Applied Psychology, 28,* 153–174.

Megargee, E. (1993, March 28). *Using the Megargee offender classification system with the MMPI-2: An update.* Paper presented at the MMPI-2/MMPI-A Symposium, St. Petersburg, FL.

Megargee, E., & Bohn, M. (1979). *Classifying criminal offenders.* Beverly Hills, CA: Sage.

Meloy, J. R. (1988). *The psychopathic mind: Origins, dynamics, and treatment.* Northvale, NJ: Jason Aronson.

Meloy, J. R. (1989). The forensic interview. In R. Craig (Ed.), *Clinical and diagnostic interviewing* (pp. 323–344). Northvale, NJ: Jason Aronson.

Meloy, J. R. (1991). Rorschach testimony. *Journal of Psychiatry and Law, 19,* 221–235.

Meloy, J. R. (1992). *Violent attachments.* Northvale, NJ: Jason Aronson.

Meloy, J. R. (1995). Antisocial personality disorder. In G. Gabbard (Ed.), *Treatments of psychiatric disorders, second edition* (Vol. II, pp. 2273–2290). Washington, DC: American Psychiatric Press.

Meloy, J. R., & Gacono, C. B. (1992). The aggression response and the Rorschach. *Clinical Psychology, 48,* 104–114.

Meloy, J. R., Gacono, C. B., & Kenney, L. (1994). A Rorschach investigation of sexual homicide. *Journal of Personality Assessment, 62,* 58–67.

Meloy, J. R., Hansen, T., & Weiner, I. (1997). Authority of the Rorschach: Legal citations during the past fifty years. *Journal of Personality Assessment, 69,* 53–62.

Meloy, J. R., Haroun, A., & Schiller, E. (1990). *Clinical guidelines for involuntary outpatient treatment.* Sarasota, FL: Professional Resource Exchange.

Munsterberg, H. (1933). *On the witness stand.* New York: Clark Boardman Co. (Original work published 1908)

Ogloff, J., Wong, S., & Greenwood, A. (1990). Treating criminal psychopaths in a therapeutic community program. *Behavioral Sciences and the Law, 8,* 81–90.

Perry, G., & Kinder, B. (1990). The susceptibility of the Rorschach to malingering: A critical review. *Journal of Personality Assessment, 54,* 47–57.

Pope, K., Butcher, J., & Seelen, J. (1993). *The MMPI, MMPI-2, and MMPI-A in court.* Washington, DC: American Psychological Association.

Raine, A. (1993). *The psychopathology of crime.* San Diego: Academic Press.

Raine, A., & Buchsbaum, M. (1996). Violence and brain imaging. In D. M. Stoff, & R. B. Cairns (Eds.), *Neurobiological approaches to clinical aggression research* (pp. 195–218). Mahwah, NJ: Lawrence Erlbaum Associates.

Raine, A., Buchsbaum, M., & LaCasse, L. (1997). Brain abnormalities in murderers indicated by positron emission tomography. *Biological Psychiatry, 42,* 495–508.

Raine, A., Buchsbaum, M., Stanley, J., Lottenberg, S., Abel, L., & Stoddard, S. (1994). Selective reductions in prefrontal glucose metabolism in murderers. *Biological Psychiatry, 36,* 365–373.

Raine, A., Meloy, J. R., Bihrle, S., Stoddard, J., LaCasse, L., & Buchsbaum, M. (1998). Reduced prefrontal and increased subcortical brain functioning assessed using positron emission tomography in predatory and affective murderers. *Behavioral Sciences and the Law, 16,* 319–332.

Randolph, G., Randolph, J., Ciula, B., Padget, J., & Cuneo, D. (1980). Retrospective comparison of Quick Test IQs of new admissions and a random sample of patients in a maximum security mental hospital. *Psychological Reports, 46,* 1175–1178.

Rice, M., Harris, T., & Cormier, C. (1992). An evaluation of a maximum security therapeutic community for psychopaths and other mentally disordered offenders. *Law and Human Behavior, 16,* 399–412.

Rutherford, M., Cacciola, J., Alterman, A., McKay, J., & Cook, T. (1999). The 2-year test-retest reliability of the PCL-R in methadone patients. *Assessment, 6,* 285–292.

Schroeder, M., Schroeder, K., & Hare, R. D. (1983). Generalizability of a checklist for the assessment of psychopathy. *Journal of Consulting and Clinical Psychology, 51,* 511–516.

Siegel, L. (1998). *Executive functioning characteristics associated with psychopathy in incarcerated females.* Unpublished doctoral dissertation, California School of Professional Psychology, San Diego.

Strachan, C. (1993). *The assessment of psychopathy in female offenders.* Unpublished doctoral dissertation, University of British Columbia, Vancouver.

Sweeney, D., & Richards, H. (1988, March). *The Quick Test, the WAIS and the WAIS-R: Normative data, cultural bias, and psychometric properties in a forensic psychiatric population.* Paper presented at the midwinter meeting of the Society for Personality Assessment, New Orleans, LA.

Taylor, C. (1997). *Psychopathy and attachment in a group of incarcerated females.* Unpublished doctoral dissertation, California School of Professional Psychology, San Diego.

Timbrook, R., Graham, J., Keiller, S., & Watts, D. (1993). Comparison of the Wiener–Harmon subtle–obvious scales and the standard validity scales in detecting valid and invalid MMPI-2 profiles. *Psychological Assessment, 5,* 53–61.

Weiner, I. (1996). Some observations on the validity of the Rorschach Inkblot Method. *Psychological Assessment, 8*(2), 206–213.

Weiner, I. (1998). *Principles of Rorschach interpretation.* Mahwah, NJ: Lawrence Erlbaum Associates.

Weiner, I., Exner, J., & Sciara, A. (1996). Is the Rorschach welcome in the courtroom? *Journal of Personality Assessment, 67*(2), 422–424.

Williamson, S., Hare, R. D., & Wong, S. (1987). Violence: Criminal psychopaths and their victims. *Canadian Journal of Behavioral Science, 19,* 454–462.

Young, M., Justice, J., & Erdberg, P. (1999). Risk factors for violent behavior among incarcerated male psychiatric patients: A multimethod approach. *Assessment, 6,* 243–258.

The Clinical Use of the Hare Psychopathy Checklist–Revised in Contemporary Risk Assessment[1]

Ralph C. Serin
Shelley L. Brown
Research Branch, Correctional Service of Canada

As researchers, clinicians, and policymakers continue to struggle with balancing civil liberties and community safety, this past decade has witnessed a virtual explosion in the development of second- and third-generation risk assessment instruments (Monahan, 1992). Central to this work on risk appraisals has been the introduction, for clinical purposes, of the Psychopathy Checklist–Revised (PCL–R) to applied settings. For a number of reasons, the PCL–R appears to have captured the interests of clinicians, and the diagnosis is increasingly being employed in risk assessment strategies of prisoners and forensic patients at various stages within the criminal justice process—from pretrial assessments to postrelease risk management (see chap. 3). Although the PCL–R is a measure of criminal psychopathy, for reasons to be discussed shortly, it has become increasingly popular within the risk assessment paradigm.

In 1991, following over a decade of research, the PCL–R was copyrighted and marketing was initiated to make it readily available to researchers and clinicians. For those interested in using the PCL–R for risk assessment, the accompanying manual provided adequate research with large samples regarding its predictive validity across different sites and jurisdictions. During that time and more recently, other risk assessment instruments were also being made available. Nonetheless, the relationship between psychopathy and violence appeared robust (Hemphill, Hare, & Wong, 1998; Salekin, Rogers, & Sewell, 1996), likely increasing its valence to clinicians. Concurrently, there were efforts to link psychopathy

251

to theoretical models of criminality, violence, and self-regulation deficits (Cooke, Forth, & Hare, 1998), which also appealed to researchers and clinicians. Additionally, for psychologists, the focus of the PCL-R on personality (Factor 1 items) and behavioral indexes (Factor 2 items), rather than solely focusing on criminal history variables, was also of interest. Perhaps what is most striking about this evolution was that the PCL-R was not initially developed as a risk appraisal instrument, although this has become a preoccupation within applied settings. Rather, the serendipitous findings of its predictive validity (Hemphill et al., 1998; Salekin et al., 1996) have led to its expanded clinical use, both alone and within other risk appraisal strategies (*Violence Risk Assessment Guide* [VRAG]; Harris, Rice, & Quinsey, 1993; Historical Clinical Risk Scheme [HCR-20]; Webster, Douglas, Eaves, & Hart, 1997).

This chapter focuses on how clinicians might best utilize the PCL-R in completing risk appraisals. First, the predictive literature as it pertains to the PCL-R is reviewed, followed by some of the ethical, legal, and practical challenges that have emerged as a result of the PCL-R's increased popularity. Next, the need to consider baserates, type of recidivism, standard error of measurement (SEM), time to failure, overlapping confidence intervals, and the impact of differential PCL-R cutoffs on estimated failure rates and decision errors is empirically demonstrated. Last, these issues are further emphasized when we provide 10 general guidelines for using the PCL-R, which are then illustrated in the context of a case study.

PREDICTION AND THE PCL-R

Since its release, the PCL-R has consistently been shown to have high predictive validity for both correctional settings (Hart, 1998; Hemphill et al., 1998; Salekin et al., 1996) and forensic hospitals (Harris et al., 1993; Monahan, 1996). The comprehensive yet conservative meta-analytic review of the PCL-R (Hemphill et al., 1998) considered all derivations, including the original 22-item PCL (Hare, 1980), the 20-item PCL-R (Hare, 1991), the 18-item youth version (PCL:YV; Forth, Kosson, & Hare, in press), the PCL-R French version (Hare, 1996), and the 12-item screening version (PCL-SV; Hart, Cox, & Hare, 1995). Seven predictive studies ($N = 1,275$) generated an average weighted correlation of .27 between the PCL-R and general recidivism (Hemphill et al., 1998). In terms of violent recidivism, six predictive studies ($N = 1,374$) yielded an averaged weighted correlation of .27. Similarly, a more liberal meta-analytic review that included both postdictive (6) and predictive (9) studies produced an average Cohen's d of .79 (equivalent $r = .37$) between the PCL-R and violent recidivism and/or institutional violence (Salekin et al., 1996). Thus, taken together, these meta-analytic reviews demonstrate that the PCL-R predicts both general and violent recidivism moderately well.

Hemphill et al. (1998) also concluded that the PCL-R was no more accurate at predicting general recidivism when compared with actuarial tools such as the Base Expectancy Score (BES; Gottfredson & Bonds, 1961), the Level of Supervision Inventory (LSI; Andrews, 1982), the Salient Factor Score (SFS-81; Hoffman, 1983), or the Statistical Information on Recidivism Scale (SIR; Nuffield, 1982). In terms of violence prediction, Hemphill et al. (1998) reported that PCL-R scores were correlated more strongly with violent recidivism compared with their actuarial counterparts. However, a recent meta-analytic comparision of the Level of Service Inventory–Revised (LSI-R; Andrews & Bonta, 1995) and the PCL-R demonstrated that the former outperformed the latter for both general (Common Language [CL] Effect Size Indicator = 78%; McGraw & Wong, 1992) and violent recidivism (CL = 75%; Gendreau, Goggin, & Smith, 1999). Further, the VRAG has also demonstrated superior predictive validity to the PCL-R in terms of violence prediction. However, it should be noted that the VRAG includes weighted PCL-R scores in its derivation. Additionally, detailed analysis has revealed that most of the explained variance accounted for by the VRAG is attributable to the PCL-R (Harris et al., 1993).

Although more than 20 different countries use the PCL-R (Hare, 1998), its predictive validity appears strongest for North American samples of predominantly White male offenders. The evidence is less clear for using the PCL-R with adolescents, women, and non-Whites for prediction purposes (Salekin et al., 1996) and that it may not be the best index of sexual recidivism (Hanson & Bussière, 1998). Also, there is emerging evidence that there may be a multiplicative interaction between psychopathy and phallometrically determined deviant sexual preference (Rice & Harris, 1997; Serin, Mailloux, & Malcolm, 1998). Nonetheless, proponents of the PCL-R suggest that the data are encouraging for all applications (Hemphill et al., 1998).

In summary, a review of the published literature, the endorsement of the PCL-R by certain jurisdictions (e.g., state of California in sexual predator assessments), and a review of clinical reports all attest to its popularity. Prominent researchers have also endorsed its use in the completion of risk appraisals (Harris et al., 1993; Monahan, 1996; Webster et al., 1997), thereby encouraging others to utilize the PCL-R in clinical practice.

THE DOWNSIDE OF THE PCL-R'S INCREASED USE

The popularity and strong research support for the PCL-R has resulted in some disturbing trends. It appears that as some consumer groups (i.e., parole boards, case management staff, prison managers) have been exposed to some of the research, they are now demanding the inclusion of PCL-R scores in assessment reports. We consider this a precarious evolution for the discipline. First, the selection of psychological tests should be the purview of the psychologist. Second, that consumers expect to see PCL-R scores within the body of the assessment report raises concerns about standards of practice. Notably, offenders are also becoming more informed and, on reading their assessment reports (based on Canadian privacy provisions), are beginning to raise questions about informed consent and the credentials and training of the clinicians.

There is also some indication that clinicians are beginning to use the PCL-R to guide decisions about treatment placement apparently based on two relatively recent studies (Ogloff, Wong, & Greenwood, 1990; Rice, Harris, & Cormier, 1992). It may be that, in reviewing the pessimistic literature regarding the treatment of psychopaths, they have prematurely concluded that treatment is ineffective and increases risk. High PCL-R scores are then used to exclude offenders from treatment. Not only is this a questionable extrapolation of the existing data, it likely would fail to meet Charter challenges regarding the withholding of treatment. It is also inconsistent with the principle of treatment responsiveness (Andrews & Bonta, 1994), which states that higher risk offenders warrant treatment of greatest intensity. Recent efforts to provide advanced training in the clinical use of the PCL-R should assist in providing necessary guidelines to psychologists to overcome these recent developments (see chaps. 3 & 7).

Notwithstanding its popularity or perhaps because of this, several other issues regarding the clinical use of the PCL-R must be reviewed. As a psychological test and because of its diagnostic label, offenders/patients must provide informed consent for the assessment. This is a standard of practice for psychologists regarding ethical guidelines, yet the potential impact of labeling someone a *psychopath* is considerable. Similarly, raw test results are not typically provided in a psychological assessment report due to concerns about misinterpretation of such numbers. The same standard must be applied to the reporting of the PCL-R. The manual recommends a clinical cutoff of 30, yet different settings have utilized different cutoffs, creating some confusion. Presenting percentiles has also been used, but authors of reports are chastened to ensure that the reader does not confuse this figure with an estimate of likelihood of recidivism. Percentiles reflect the degree to which an individual approximates the protypical psychopath in comparison with the normative sample. Further, the cutoff for what represents a high-risk offender has not been specified in probabilistic terms, although it is likely that high PCL-R scorers would be considered high risk. More important, low and moderate scorers on the PCL-R also fail, although at lower rates in absolute and survival terms. Nonetheless, this means other assessment instruments should be incorporated into a risk appraisal strategy.

The PCL-R is also highly correlated with other risk scales such as the LSI-R, the VRAG, and the SIR. Therefore, the use of these multiple measures will not markedly increase validity because of shared method variance. However, multimethod assessment is recommended given that not every tool is applicable in every situation for every offender (Hart, 1998). Further, the consideration of additional static and true dynamic risk factors is recommended. Notably, the instructions for scoring the PCL-R over the client's lifetime and the restricted range of scoring of the items (0–3) suggest that the PCL-R is a static risk instrument and that post-treatment reassessment should not be expected to change significantly.

MAXIMIZING THE CLINICAL UTILITY
OF THE PCL-R THROUGH STATISTICS

With few exceptions, most notably the VRAG, the importance of SEM, type of recidivism, time to failure, baserate, and impact of differential cut-off scores on estimated failure rates, confidence intervals, and decision errors have not received much attention in the risk-prediction literature. Further, a consistent strategy for incorporating such information into the daily practice of offender risk assessment has yet to emerge. Consequently, this section demonstrates the impact that these factors can have on the accurate appraisal of risk using the PCL-R as an illustrative example. Reanalyzed data originally presented in Serin and Amos (1995) are used to accomplish this task.[2] Briefly, the Serin and Amos (1995) data were composed of 263 Canadian male federal offenders who were released on parole or statutory release (legislated release after two thirds of sentence is served) from either medium or minimum security institutions in the province of Ontario. All offenders were serving sentences of 2 years or more for index offenses ranging from minor crimes such as possession of stolen property to violent crimes such as murder, assault, or sexual assault. Overall, the follow-up period ranged from 1 month to 7.66 years (M = 4.32, SD = 2.11).

For illustration, assume that a clinician must complete a risk assessment for an upcoming parole hearing. As part of the assessment process, the clinician determines the offender has a PCL-R score of 28. At this stage, the clinician must reflect this information in the final risk assessment of future likelihood of recidivism. According to classical test theory, an individual's obtained score on any given test does not represent the individual's true score due to the existence of random error. Guessing, distractions in the test situation, administration errors, content sampling, scoring errors, and fluctuations in the examinee's state are potential sources of random error (Crocker & Algina, 1986). The SEM is a statistical index that quantifies the amount of random error associated with any given test. The PCL-R has an SEM of 3.25 (Hare, 1991). In practical terms, this means that the clinician can be 68% confident that an obtained score of 28 actually lies somewhere between 25 and 31. Similarly, adopting a more stringent criterion, the clinician can be 95% sure that a test score of 28 actually lies somewhere between 22 and 35. Thus, for the given example, the clinician could neither confirm nor deny that the individual meets the recommended clinical cutoff as specified in the Hare PCL-R manual.

We argue that the existing dilemma that the clinician can neither confirm nor deny that the individual meets the recommended diagnostic cutoff is not critical in the context of a risk appraisal. More relevant is information pertaining to the likelihood of recidivism associated with a PCL-R score of 28. Given that actuarial guidelines were not used to develop the PCL-R, probable failure rates associated with various PCL-R cutoff scores are currently not available for a large, normative sample. Consequently, the Serin and Amos (1995) data were used to generate both general and violent recidivism rates associated with various PCL-R cutoff scores. The reanalyzed data indicate that 81% of offenders scoring over 28 would recidivate generally within an average 4-year risk period. Alternatively, using a 95% confidence interval, 71% to 91% of offenders scoring above 28 would recidivate within this time frame.

At this stage, the clinician can at least provide the parole board with concrete information pertaining to the offender's likelihood of general recidivism within an average 4-year time span. However, an additional issue that the clinician should be aware of is the possibility and significance of overlapping confidence intervals associated with various PCL-R cutoff scores. For example, we know that 71% to 91% of offenders with a score of 28 or above will recidivate within 4 years of release. However, the Serin and Amos (1995) data also reveal that 71% to 86% of offenders with a score of 24 or above would recidivate within the same time frame. Similarly, 67% to 81% scoring over 20 would recidivate. Thus, there is substantial overlap in the probable failure rates associated with a wide range of PCL-R scores (see Table 10.1). The only group of individuals that did not share overlapping estimated failure rates (25% 50%) were those scoring below 15. Notably, however, the lack of discriminate predictive validity among a wide range of PCL-R scores was most likely exacerbated by the relatively high base rate in the current sample (65%) and the relatively small sample size (N = 263).[3] Nonetheless, it remains important for decision makers not to overestimate the importance of the recommended diagnostic cutoff of 30 when providing probability estimates of future recidivism.

An additional issue to consider is the type of recidivism that the offender is likely to perpetrate. Thus far, we have restricted our discus-

TABLE 10.1
Failure Rates and Corresponding Confidence Intervals
Associated With Various PCL-R Cutoff Scores

		Failure Rates		Confidence Interval	
PCL-R Decision Criterion	N	%	(n)	LCL[a]	UCL[b]
General recidivism					
15≤[c]	59	37.30	(22)	24.96	49.64
16≥	204	72.54	(148)	66.37	78.63
20≥	161	73.90	(119)	67.12	80.68
24≥	108	78.70	(34)	70.98	86.42
28≥	63	81.00	(51)	71.31	90.69
32≥	15	80.00	(12)	59.77	100.00
Violent recidivism					
15≤	59	6.80	(4)	3.62	13.22
16≥	202	25.20	(51)	19.21	31.19
20≥	159	29.60	(47)	22.50	36.70
24≥	106	36.80	(39)	27.62	45.98
28≥	62	37.10	(23)	25.08	49.13
32≥	15	46.70	(7)	21.45	71.95[d]

Note.   [a]LCL = lower confidence limit. [b]UCL = upper confidence limit. [c]To use the entire range of PCL-R scores, it was decided to include an inclusive bin consisting of PCL-R scores ranging from 0 to 15. The remaining cutoffs are exclusive. [d]Confidence intervals increase as sample size decreases.

sion to general recidivism. However, equally if not more important is the probability of violent or sexual recidivism. In the current example, 81% of offenders scoring 28 or more committed some form of general recidivism within 4 years of release. However, only 37%, or 25% to 49%, committed a violent crime within the same time frame. It is crucial that decision makers clearly articulate the probability of failure associated with different forms of recidivism. However, with few exceptions (i.e., the VRAG), this task is somewhat difficult given that most actuarial tools were developed to maximize their relationship with general rather than violent or sexual recidivism. However, as the field continues to evolve, this problem will most likely correct itself.

The importance of decision errors cannot be overlooked in the context of any risk appraisal. As Fig. 10.1 illustrates, a prediction of any future event can result in one of four possibilities: a true positive, a true negative, a false positive, or a false negative. True positives and true negatives refer to correct decisions, whereas false positives and false negatives refer to incorrect decisions. In the context of offender risk assessment, a true positive refers to a situation whereby a prediction is made that a given offender will recidivate and the offender actually does recidivate. Conversely, a true negative occurs when a prediction states that a given offender will not reoffend

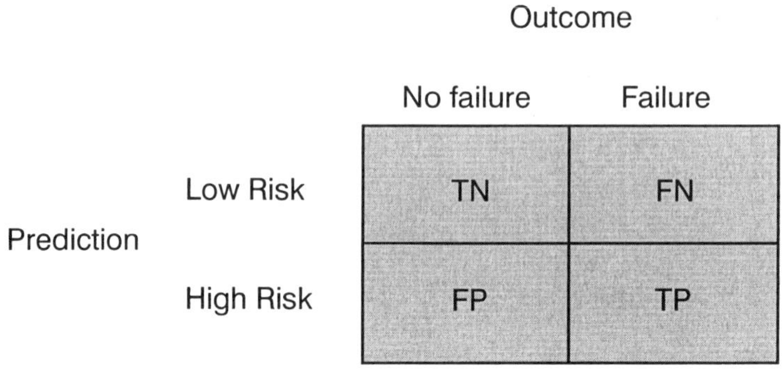

Outcome

No failure   Failure

FIG. 10.1.   Possible outcomes in the prediction of recidivism.

and the offender does not reoffend. False positives and false negatives refer to situations where the predicted outcome does not correspond with the true outcome. In the case of a false positive, an offender is predicted to recidivate; however, in actuality, he or she does not. Conversely, a false negative results when a prediction states that the offenders will not recidivate and he or she actually does recidivate. Thus, false positives and false negatives are commonly known as *decision errors*.

Extrapolating from Serin and Amos (1995), we ascertained that a score of 28 yields a false positive and a false negative rate of 18.9% and 58.20%, respectively (for violent recidivism). Furthermore, a cutoff score of 24 minimizes the total error rate producing a 32.5% false positive rate and a 29.10% false negative rate for the prediction of violent recidivism. It is important for clinicians to be aware of the trade-off that exists between false positives and false negatives along the continuum of PCL–R scores. Using violent recidivism as an example, a score of 32 yields a relatively low false positive rate (4%), which may appeal to civil liberty advocates. However, the public may not tolerate the corresponding false negative rate of 87%. Conversely, a more liberal cutoff of 16, which generates a 7% and 73% false negative and false positive rate, respectively, may be defended by the public but rebuked by offender advocates. See Table 10.2 for a complete presentation of decision errors associated with various PCL–R cutoff scores. Currently, this type of information is not readily available to clinicians or other decision makers. However, clearly this type of knowledge is warranted if risk appraisals involving the PCL–R are to meet current standards of practice.

Another crucial piece of information that is often not available to the decision maker is at what point during the 4-year risk period is the offender likely to fail. For example, in regard to violent recidivism, the clinician knows that, if released, an offender with a score of 28 or more has a 37% chance of committing a violent crime sometime within the next 4

TABLE 10.2
Decision Errors Associated With Various PCL-R Cutoff Scores

PCL-R Decision Criterion	N	False Positive Rate (%)	False Negative Rate (%)
General recidivism			
15≤[a]	59	39.80	87.10
16≥	204	60.20	12.90
20≥	161	45.20	30.00
24≥	108	24.70	50.00
28≥	63	12.90	70.00
32≥	15	3.20	92.90
Violent recidivism			
15≤	59	26.70	92.70
16≥	202	73.30	7.30
20≥	159	54.40	14.50
24≥	106	32.50	29.10
28≥	62	18.90	58.20
32≥	15	3.90	87.30

Note. [a]To use the entire range of PCL-R scores, it was decided to include an inclusive bin consisting of PCL-R scores ranging from 0 to 15. The remaining cutoffs are exclusive.

years. However, a more precise estimate of when that violent failure is likely to occur can be extrapolated from information obtained through survival analysis. Briefly, survival analysis is a statistical technique that estimates the time taken to reach an event and the rate of occurrence of that event (Chung, Schmidt, & Witte, 1991). Using the Serin and Amos (1995) data, it can be determined that offenders with a score of 28 or more on the PCL-R have a 22% chance of failing violently during the first 12 months of release. This projected failure rate is 15% lower than the original 37% estimate. Clearly such extrapolations can increase the level of precision associated with predictions of violence.

The probability that a given individual will fail is inextricably linked to the base rate. Thus, under ideal circumstances, the decision maker would be aware of the exact baserate associated with a given outcome for the population in question. For example, if the baserate is somewhat high in a given sample (i.e., 60%), then regardless of the PCL-R score 6 out of every 10 offenders will recidivate. Conversely, in situations where the baserate is substantially lower (i.e., 10%), only 1 out of every 10 offenders will recidivate. Using the Serin and Amos (1995) example, if the offender scoring 28 is being released from a medium security institution that has a known violent return rate of 40%, then clearly the projected 22%, 1-year failure rate may be an underestimation. Conversely, if the offender is being released from a lower security institution that has a known baserate of 10%, the 22% probability rate may be an overestimation. Currently we are unaware of an empirical strategy that incorporates baserates into the risk estimate. However, we are exploring various strategies to this end (see Serin & Brown, 1999). Further, if an acceptable empirical strategy is devised, future advancements must utilize an approach that automatically incorporates baserate information into the risk appraisal. The necessity for this automation is based on empirical findings demonstrating that decision makers do not systematically consider baserate information when assessing risk (Cannon & Quinsey, 1995).

Clearly this exercise demonstrates that, even when using a highly regarded risk assessment instrument with demonstrated predictive validity such as the PCL–R, there are clear limitations to the reliance on a single measure. More important, this type of research provides clinicians and decision makers with relevant information to assist them in choosing cutoffs, estimating types of failures, and managing risk by knowing when the failure is likely to occur. However, this research is clearly in its infancy and is subject to several formidable obstacles that can only be overcome using larger construction and cross-validation samples. Last, for optimal efficiency, a decision-making model that incorporates all of the aforementioned factors in a systematic and accurate fashion undoubtedly requires expert systems that utilize complex computerized algorithms.

RISK ASSESSMENT AND TREATMENT

Although the primary focus of this chapter is on risk appraisal, it seems a brief comment on treatment issues within the context of a risk management paradigm is warranted. The debate regarding the efficacy of intervention for psychopaths continues (Cooke et al., 1998). Yet it is inevitable that some offenders who are diagnosed as psychopathic will be referred and potentially admitted to treatment programs at various stages of the criminal justice process—from pretrial to postrelease. It is equally inevitable, based on conventional wisdom, that many such offenders are viewed as high risk and resistant toward treatment. Excluding them from treatment because a flawed literature has failed to demonstrate effectiveness seems at odds with what is known about offender risk management and correctional intervention (Andrews & Bonta, 1994; Gendreau, 1996). The area of treatment responsivity is gaining momentum (Bonta, 1995; Kennedy & Serin, 1997) and alternative views of treatment success such as harm reduction are emerging for high-risk or repetitive offenders (Laws, 1996). Similarly, it is unknown whether relapse prevention is a more viable conceptual model for the treatment and risk management of psychopaths. It would appear that the specific model for successful intervention remains unclear and that the gains in the area of risk assessment have yet to be applied to intervention of high-risk offenders.

SUMMARY

It is clear from the aforementioned discussion that any risk scale has limitations, including a robust tool such as the PCL-R. Equally important is the need for clinicians to attend to these issues within the context of their clinical practice. Most notable among these are: (a) the need to be aware of baserates, (b) the awareness of the SEM and its potential impact on group membership and cutoffs, (c) the probability and types of decision errors yielded by different cutoffs, (d) the importance of overlapping confidence intervals associated with different failure rates generated by different cutoffs, and (e) the benefits of knowing when a failure is most likely to occur. It is also likely that, as the PCL-R achieves greater profile and more consistent use in clinical decision making, there will be legal challenges regarding its use (Hare, 1998). An understanding of the aforementioned issues should assist clinicians facing such challenges.

To highlight these issues raised by the clinical use of the PCL-R in completing risk appraisals, we have developed Ten Commandments to Offender Risk Assessment. Each commandment is presented with a brief explanation. Following this description, a case study is presented to highlight the issues addressed in the previous discussion and the Ten Commandments. It is hoped that this exercise will both alert clinicians to potential pitfalls as well as provide direction for the completion of risk appraisals. The guidelines are not restricted to the use of the PCL-R, but were developed specifically for use in this chapter.

Ten Commandments to Offender Risk Assessment

1. Thou shalt know thy baserate.

The importance of the baserate on predictive accuracy is well known (Quinsey, 1980). Remarkably, however, few clinicians are aware of the failure rates for their population, which makes it impossible for them to anchor their appraisals in probabilistic terms. Relative to lower risk settings (e.g., minimum security settings), higher risk settings (e.g., maximum security facilities) should have higher baserates if the security and placement of offenders utilize risk factors.

2. Thou shalt use multimethod assessment strategies.

As Hart (1998) noted no single risk appraisal instrument will apply equally for all offenders or for all situations. The use of multiple measures should permit the clinician to determine convergence among risk factors and the potential for independent contributions across domains sampled.

3. Thou shalt not confuse shared method variance with increased validity.

More information does not necessarily imply increased precision (Quinsey, Harris, Rice, & Cormier, 1998). The intercorrelation among risk scales is high (Serin & Amos, 1995), meaning that clinicians must be wary of believing that the use of multiple risk scales such as the LSI–R, PCL–R, and VRAG significantly increases their predictive accuracy.

4. Thou shalt be wary of clinical overrides.

The utility and efficacy of actuarial risk scales is undisputed (Grove & Meehl, 1996), but as Hart (1998) appropriately illustrated, clinical information is not irrelevant to the risk assessment enterprise. Clinical estimates are not sufficient for accurate prediction, but they can enhance the risk appraisal process. However, there exists the need to develop decision rules to incorporate such factors as treatment response into the risk appraisal and risk management paradigm (Serin, 1998). Such rules must heed the literature on offender treatment efficacy, consider assessments by therapists and independent assessors, and guard against unchecked enthusiasm for self-reports of treatment gain.

5. Thou shalt heed statistical estimates.

In the same manner that baserates provide essential anchors, so too do statistical estimates more generally. In cases where the application of actuarial scales appear limited, an argument must be provided by the clinician in the body of the assessment report. Otherwise the statistical estimate must provide a starting point for the risk appraisal, with revisions being judiciously considered and supported. For instance, a functional analysis of an offender's offense pattern over time and across victims would be justifiable (McDougall, Clark, & Fischer, 1994), but obtuse clinical opinion should not effect a revision in the estimate. Once again, the degree to which the original actuarial estimate should be adjusted in accordance with, for example, a functional analysis remains an empirical question.

6. Thou shalt not covet thy neighbours' data.

Published data are essential to the validation of a particular instrument such as the PCL–R, but clinicians must be very sure that the population with which they work are comparable to those described. Offender populations differ and norms and validity data for one sample may not be applicable to another—or between forensic and correctional and institutional and community samples. Age, ethnicity, and risk profiles can all impact on risk management strategies, as can organizational priorities and resources. The nature of the follow-up data (i.e., length of follow-up, type of release, type of outcome, source of recidivism data, retrospective or prospective, sample size) also varies across studies, making it tenuous to conclude that results from one setting apply to another. Although not all clinicians can conduct prospective research for their respective populations, they must attend to these issues as they attempt to use published results to support clinical practice.

7. Thou shalt know the limits of thy prediction.

Consistent with Commandments 5 and 6, clinicians should be wary of extending predictions to different outcomes or for unspecified time periods. Similarly, stronger statements can be made about extreme groups (nonpsychopaths and psychopaths), but the majority of offenders will score in the middle of the mixed group. Failing to attend to this group will greatly limit the applicability of the PCL-R in risk appraisals. As well, clinicians must be aware of the reliability of the instrument (SEM) and their demonstrated competence through supervised training.

8. Thou shalt know thy false positive and false negative rates for specific cutoffs.

This chapter has illustrated that different PCL-R cutoffs yield markedly different types of decision errors. Clinicians would be well advised to consider this in their application of the PCL-R to risk prediction for violent and sexually violent outcomes. It is likely that the policies for different jurisdictions may mostly be concerned with high false negative rates.

9. Thou shalt provide conditional predictions.

Risk appraisals that provide conditional predictions (Serin, 1995) assist consumers to develop risk management strategies by articulating higher risk situations and factors. Further, this recognizes that risk is not a static entity, but rather there are dynamic features that must be considered (Hart, 1998).

10. Thou shalt follow an aide-memoire.

The development and use of aide-memoire is increasingly popular (Hart, 1998; Serin, 1995; Webster et al., 1997). In many respects, this is a backdrop against which to place the important MacArthur Foundation research. It is hardly surprising, then, that we strongly encourage clinicians to consider the use of an aide-memoire as a standard of care in offenders' risk appraisals. This should help ensure that clinicians have relevant and adequate (complete) information to complete the appraisal such that errors are reduced and information is collected using a systematic strategy. Consultation with colleagues in difficult cases is also encouraged. It is important to note that similar suggestions exist in the suicide prediction literature (Silverman, Berman, Bongar, Litman, & Maris, 1998). Such strategies should also insulate clinicians from liability in the case of false negatives, although this is an ancillary benefit and not the primary reason for employing an aide-memoire.

Case Study

(Where applicable, the relevant commandments are placed in parentheses as a aide to the reader.)

By age 34, John had amassed a remarkable criminal history. He is currently serving an 8-year sentence for armed robbery, assault, and weapons charges and is being reviewed for discretionary release or parole. His first recorded conflict with the police occurred at age 8, when he was caught stealing. Before that, however, his teachers had noticed his bullying behavior in the playground. His family life was characterized as chaotic with little structure. Soon he was involved in various petty crimes and, following several unsuccessful foster home placements, he was finally sent to a juvenile youth center at age 14. His crime continued unabated, with escalation to drug dealing, pimping, robbery, assaults, and finally armed robbery. As a youth, he frequently absconded from foster homes and training school. Although drugs and alcohol were major lifestyle factors, his impulsive and risk-taking behavior was not restricted to being under the influence. Surprisingly, in some areas of his life, John was a careful planner. For instance, he would carefully plan out certain crimes or methodically mete out revenge.

The current charges involved his robbing two banks while heavily armed. He had just been released from a federal prison after completing a 6-year sentence for robbery. During that sentence, he had often been segregated for fighting and possession of contraband drugs. He failed in his bid for a parole release and refused treatment opportunities. Prior to that incarceration, he had been in and out of jail for sentences ranging from 1 month to 12 months.

Despite this persistent pattern of antisocial behavior, John could be engaging and a charmer when he wished. This was especially noticeable around members of the opposite sex. Often, however, this allure was fleeting, lasting only until he had attained his goal. For instance, he considered sex to be a conquest and bragged to others regarding his prowess. Also he had been convicted for living off the avails in his early twenties. There are also reports of spousal assault, but there are no convictions for these offenses.

To the careful eye, however, his behavior had a grandiose quality and was typically exhibited at times when he wanted something. Equally notable was that, once he was pursuing a particular goal, his ability to consider other options was poor, such that at times he continued to act even when it was clearly not in his best interests. For example, in the past, he committed new crimes after having convinced the judge to grant him bail because of his newfound religion and intentions by a friend to offer him employment. He never showed up for work the next day.

At times he made outrageous claims, such as playing professional sports. When asked what occupation he might wish to pursue, he would propose owner of his own business, despite never having kept a job for more than 4 months. He recounted such goals with a panache that was at clear odds with his obvious situation. Further, it seemed foreign to him that this story might easily be proved false. Certainly, his interactions with others appeared shallow and egocentric from a distance, but this was disguised by guile and superficiality to those he chose to permit into his inner circle. John couldn't trust others. His self-destructive relationships precipitated moving around a great deal. He described it as wanderlust, yet partly it may be that he needed to meet new people who would accept him at his word. Those who knew him for any period of time couldn't penetrate the veneer. It was as if there were two Johns. The outward John was often outgoing and devil-may-care. The other was a loner, appearing not to require the company of others. His contact with others could be mercurial and unpredictable. For instance, he could be filled with remorse during therapy sessions (4), but then commit crimes on the way home. It was as if his words and deeds were disconnected. If guile didn't get him what he wanted, he might easily become aggressive and violent. It was as if it were all an act, with his performance delivered as part of a script. He always seemed to know the right words to say (2, 4).

Recent assessments completed during the present sentence phase identified several risk factors that, if not addressed, would likely contribute to his recidivism (2, 10). These include: (a) insight and motivation were considered marginal, although he could say the right words if it appeared as this might derive him some immediate benefits; (b) substance abuse, (c) poor employment skills, (d) egocentricity and callousness, and (e) criminal associations, criminal values, and disregard for rules.

Notwithstanding his recent interest in religion and a letter of support from chaplaincy and community volunteers, other staff are more pessimistic about his response to treatment (4). He attends Alcoholics Anonymous and says this meets his substance abuse needs. He has a new girlfriend who has offered him a place to stay if released, and she has suggested he could work in her retail business. The psychologist who completed the assessment observed that John had monopolized the interview and attempted to obscure some aspects of his history (2, 10).

His PCL–R score is 28, placing him in the moderate to high-risk category for general and violent recidivism (1, 6, 8). He had similar rankings on the LSI–R, the VRAG, and another acutarial risk scale for general recidivism (2, 3). Because of the robbery convictions, the main question is whether John will reoffend violently (5, 7, 8) and, if so, within what time frames (5, 7). Also of interest are viable risk management strategies to utilize if and when he is released (9, 10).

The purpose of this case example is not to provide a cookbook or perfunctory set of guidelines for clinicians to follow. Rather, it is an attempt to concisely illustrate a typical case and highlight where the Ten Commandments of Offender Risk Assessment could apply to facilitate good clinical decision making. It is important to note that much of the information, although necessary to provide a context for the case, is not crucial to the risk appraisal per se. In particular, much of the interpersonal descriptions are important contextually in terms of treatment response and risk management, but other information would receive greater weight in a risk appraisal.

CONCLUSION

With the exception of the LSI-R (i.e., Gendreau et al., 1999), the research to date suggests that the PCL-R has a slight competitive edge at predicting violent recidivism in comparison with less costly and less time-consuming actuarial measures such as the SIR. However, in all likelihood, existing actuarial tools (e.g., the SIR), alongside newly evolving instruments, will soon equal if not surpass the PCL-R and perhaps the LSI-R if and when they are recalibrated specifically to predict violence. Additionally, once and if the enterprise of treatment delivery and measurement is perfected, accurate measures of treatment gain, alongside careful monitoring of environmental triggers and eroded treatment effects, could, in theory, render static risk estimates (such as those provided by the PCL-R) somewhat limited in the broader context of contemporary risk appraisal.

However, this does not undermine the important role that the PCL-R—specifically, Factor 1—should play in the effective management and treatment of offenders. In summary, we recommend the continued use of instruments such as the PCL-R particularly when predictions of violence are at stake. More important, however, is that risk decision makers heed the complex issues raised throughout this chapter when using the PCL-R and other measures.

ENDNOTES

1. The points of view expressed in this chapter are those of the authors and do not necessarily reflect those of the Correctional Service of Canada.
2. It should be noted that we have developed an empirically based decision-making model using the Serin and Amos (1995) data that systematically incorporates all of the aforementioned statistical factors. However, a detailed review of this model is beyond the scope of the current discussion. Interested readers should see Serin and Brown (1999).
3. The normative sample used in the Hare PCL-R manual is composed of substantially more subjects (> 1,000).

REFERENCES

Andrews, D. A. (1982). *The level of supervision inventory*. Toronto: Ontario Ministry of Correctional Services.
Andrews, D. A., & Bonta, J. (1998). *The psychology of criminal conduct* (2nd ed.). Cincinnati, OH: Anderson.

Andrews, D. A., & Bonta, J. (1995). *The Level of Service Inventory–Revised*. Toronto, ON: Multi-Health Systems.

Bonta, J. (1995). The responsivity principle and offender rehabilitation. *Forum on Corrections Research, 7*(3), 34–37.

Cannon, C. K., & Quinsey, V. L. (1995). The likelihood of violent behavior: Predictions, postdictions and hindsight bias. *Canadian Journal of Behavioural Sciences, 27*, 92–106.

Chung, C. F., Schmidt, P., & Witte, A. D. (1991). Survival analysis: A survey. *Journal of Quantitative Criminology, 7*, 59–98.

Cooke, D. J., Forth, A. E., & Hare, R. D. (1998). *Psychopathy: Theory, research, and implications for society*. Dordrecht, The Netherlands: Kluwer.

Crocker, L., & Algina, J. (1986). *Introduction to classical and modern test theory*. New York: Harcourt Brace.

Forth, A. E., Kosson, D., & Hare, R. D. (in press). *The Hare Psychopathy Checklist: Youth Version*. Toronto, ON: Multi-Health Systems.

Gendreau, P. (1996). The principles of effective intervention with offenders. In A. T. Harland (Ed.), *Choosing correctional options that work: Defining the demand and evaluating the supply* (pp. 117–130). Thousand Oaks, CA: Sage.

Gendreau, P., Goggin, C., & Smith, (1999, May). *Is there an actuarial measure that is demonstrably superior to all others?* Symposium conducted at the meeting of the 60th annual Canadian Psychological Association Convention, Halifax, Canada.

Gottfredson, D. M., & Bonds, J. A. (1961). *A manual for intake base expectancy scoring*. San Franciso: California Department of Corrections, Research Division.

Grove, W. M., & Meehl, P. E. (1996). Comparative efficiency of informal (subjective, impressionistic) and formal (mechanical, algorithmic) prediction procedures: The clinical-statistical controversy. *Psychology, Public Policy, and Law, 2*, 293–323.

Hanson, R. K., & Bussière, M. T. (1998). Predicting relapse: A meta-analysis of sexual offender recidivism studies. *Journal of Consulting and Clinical Psychology, 66*, 348–362.

Hare, R. D. (1980). A research scale for the assessment of psychopathy in criminal populations. *Personality and Individual Differences, 1*, 111–117.

Hare, R. D. (1991). *The Hare Psychopathy Checklist–Revised*. Toronto, ON: Multi-Health Systems.

Hare, R. D. (1996). *The Hare Psychopathy Checklist–Revised*. Toronto, ON: Multi-Health Systems.

Hare, R. D. (1998). The Hare PCL–R: Some issues concerning its use and misuse. *Legal and Criminological Psychology, 3*, 99–119.

Harris, G. T., Rice, M. E., & Quinsey, V.L. (1993). Violent recidivism of mentally disordered offenders: The development of a statistical prediction instrument. *Criminal Justice and Behaviour, 20*, 315–335.

Hart, S. D. (1998). The role of psychopathy in assessing risk for violence: Conceptual and methodological issues. *Legal and Criminological Psychology, 3*, 121–137.

Hart, S. D., Cox, D. E., & Hare, R. D. (1995). *The Hare Psychopathy Checklist: Screening Version*. Toronto, ON: Multi-Health Systems.

Hemphill, J. F., Hare, R. D., & Wong, S. (1998). Psychopathy and recidivism: A review. *Legal and Criminological Psychology, 3*, 139–170.

Hoffman, P. B. (1983). Screening for risk: A revised Salient Factor Score (SFS 81). *Journal of Criminal Justice, 11*, 539–547.

Kennedy, S., & Serin, R. (1997). Treatment responsivity: Contributing to effective correctional programming. *International Community Corrections Association (ICCA) Journal, 7*(4), 46–52.

Laws, D. R. (1996). Relapse prevention or harm reduction? *Sexual Abuse, 8*, 243–247.

McDougall, C., Clark, D., & Fisher, M. (1994). The assessment of violent behaviour. In M. McMurran & J. Hodge (Eds.), *The assessment of criminal behaviour of clients in secure settings* (pp. 68–93). London: Jessica Kingsley Publishers.

McGraw, K. O., & Wong, S. P. (1992). A common language effect size statistic. *Psychological Bulletin, 111,* 361–365.

Monahan, J. (1992). Risk assessment: Commentary on Poythress and Otto. *Special Issue: Psychopathology and Crime. Forensic Reports, 5,* 151–154.

Monahan, J. (1996). Violence prediction: The past twenty and the next twenty years. *Criminal Justice and Behavior, 23,* 107–120.

Nuffield, J. (1982). *Parole decision-making in Canada: Research towards decision guidelines.* Ottawa: Supply and Services Canada.

Ogloff, J. R., Wong, S., & Greenwood, A. (1990). Treating criminal psychopaths in a therapeutic community program. *Behavioural Sciences and the Law, 8,* 181–190.

Quinsey, V. L. (1980). The baserate problem and the prediction of dangerousness: A reappraisal. *Journal of Psychiatry and Law, 8,* 329–340.

Quinsey, V. L., Harris, G. T., Rice, M. E., & Cormier, C. A. (1998). *Violent offenders: Appraising and managing risk.* Washington, DC: American Psychological Association.

Rice, M. E., & Harris, G. T. (1997). Cross-validation and extension of the Violence Risk Appraisal Guide for child molesters and rapists. *Law and Human Behaviour, 21,* 231–241.

Rice, M. E., Harris, G. T., & Cormier, C. (1992). Evaluation of a maximum security therapeutic community for psychopaths and other mentally disordered offenders. *Law and Human Behaviour, 16,* 399–412.

Salekin, R. T., Rogers, R., & Sewell, K. W. (1996). A review and meta-analysis of the Psychopathy Checklist and Psychopathy Checklist-Revised: Predictive validity of dangerousness. *Clinical Psychology: Science and Practice, 3,* 203–215.

Serin, R. C. (1995). Psychological intervention in corrections. In T. A. Leis, L. L. Motiuk, & J. R. P. Ogloff (Eds.), *Forensic psychology: Policy and practice in corrections* (pp. 36–40). Ottawa, ON: Correctional Service of Canada.

Serin, R. C. (1998). Treatment responsivity, intervention and reintegration: A conceptual model. *Forum on Corrections Research, 10,* 29–32.

Serin, R. C., & Amos, N. L. (1995). The role of psychopathy in the assessment of dangerousness. *International Journal of Law and Psychiatry, 18,* 231–238.

Serin, R. C., & Brown, S. L. (1999). *Empirical guidelines for clinicians: Enhancing the practice of offender risk assessment.* Unpublished manuscript.

Serin, R. C., Mailloux, D. L., & Malcolm, P. B. (1998). *Psychopathy, deviant sexual arousal and recidivism in sexual offenders.* Manuscript submitted for publication.

Silverman, M. M., Berman, A. L., Bongar, B., Litman, R. E., & Maris, R. W. (1998). Inpatient standards of care and the suicidal patient: Part II. An integration with clinical risk management. In B. Bongar, A. L. Berman, R. W. Maris, M. M. Silverman, E. A. Harris, & W. L. Packman (Eds.), *Risk management with suicidal patients* (pp. 83–109). New York: Guilford.

Webster, C. D., Douglas, K. S., Eaves, D., & Hart, S. D. (1997). *HCR:20 Assessing risk for violence, Version 2.* Burnaby, British Columbia: Simon Fraser University Press.

11

Malingering and Deception Among Psychopaths

Richard Rogers and Keith R. Cruise
University of North Texas

The putative link of psychopathy to various forms of dissimulation and deception has considerable intuitive appeal. In Hare's reformulation of Clecklian psychopathy, Factor 1 is characterized as "selfish, callous, and remorseless use of others" (Hare, 1991, p. 38). Clearly the exploitation of others is often based on conning and deception. Placed in a broader context, Rogers and his colleagues (Rogers, Dion, & Lynett, 1992; Rogers, Salekin, Sewell, & Cruise, in press) found that dishonest relationships were a core dimension in prototypical ratings by community and offender samples. Interestingly, forensic psychiatrists emphasized manipulativeness and lack of empathy rather than dishonest relationships per se (Rogers, Duncan, & Sewell, 1994). Within the interpersonal domain, deception and manipulation appear to be integral elements of psychopathic functioning.

Mental health professionals are justifiably concerned about the role of psychopathy in the production of different response styles. In criminal settings, a primary concern is malingering (i.e., the deliberate fabrication or gross exaggeration of psychological or physical symptoms). The external goals for malingering within the criminal justice system may include exculpation or delay of pending criminal charges, mitigation of sentencing, or serving *easy* time in a psychiatric facility (Resnick, 1997). With respect to clinical interventions with offender samples, conning and deception may impede progress or provide therapists with an overly optimistic view of treatment gains. In light of these considerations, this chapter focuses on two facets of dissimulation. The first section is devoted to the relationship between psychopathy and malingering. The second section addresses more generally the role of deception for our understanding of psychopathy.

THE RELATIONSHIP OF PSYCHOPATHY TO MALINGERING

Classificatory Models

Spanning the last two decades, the American Psychiatric Association (1980, 1987, 1994) has conceptualized antisocial personality disorder (ASPD) as one of four elements to be considered in the evaluation of malingering.[1] A second element, medicolegal context, indirectly buttresses the presumed relationship between psychopathy and malingering. The critical question remains: Does the co-occurrence of these two elements (ASPD and medicolegal context) indicate any increased risk of malingering?

Rogers (1990a, 1990b) has argued that this preoccupation with a psychopathy–malingering link may be the result of a methodological artifact. Nearly all malingering research on nonstudent populations has occurred in *criminal* forensic settings. Obviously the two common elements in such settings are (a) persons with ASPD, and (b) defendants involved in medicolegal evaluations. Although these are *common features* of forensic settings, the more germane issue is whether they constitute *distinguishing features* (i.e., reliable differentiation of malingerers from nonmalingerers). As an instructive example, the male gender is also a common feature of clinical-forensic settings and presumably of malingerers. To confuse this common feature (e.g., male gender) with a distinguishing feature would result in grave misclassifications. We suspect that a similar process occurs in evaluations of malingering with ASPD and medicolegal evaluations as common but not distinguishing features.

In our forensic experience, we have noted that different professionals are likely to be susceptible to this putative psychopathy–malingering link. In forensic hospitals, professional and paraprofessional staff are sometimes disturbed by both the heinous crimes and concomitant callousness of a psychopath. Some staff vocalize their genuine repugnance at the idea that such a person might not be found culpable for their crimes. In personal injury cases, defense counsel are often hyperalert to the possibility that a psychopath is bilking their client. Such biases, based on the psychopathy–malingering link, may impede the impartiality of malingering classifications.

The original question of whether the two elements (ASPD and medicolegal context) increase the likelihood of malingering has not been addressed directly. However, Rogers (1990a) examined a closely related question: Does the presence of ASPD in medicolegal evaluations increase the likelihood of malingering? In an inpatient forensic sample of 24 malingerers and 114 bona fide patients, each of the four *Diagnostic and Statistical Manual of Mental Disorders* (*DSM*) indices of malingering was examined. Relevant to the current discussion, ASPD was found in similar proportions for malingerers (20.8%) and bona fide patients (17.7%). More generally, the use of the *DSM* benchmark (i.e., two or more indices resulting in a strong suspicion of malingering) was not substantiated. This benchmark resulted in an unacceptably high false positive rate of 79.9%. If these findings hold true in other settings, then any blind application of the *DSM* indices is likely to result in misclassifications of malingering in four out of five cases.

Gacono, Meloy, Sheppard, Speth, and Roske (1995) provided interesting data on psychopathy and malingering. An archival review of 18 malingerers found *not guilty by reason of insanity* revealed generally high scores on the Psychopathy Checklist–Revised (PCL–R; $M = 34.9$; $SD = 1.8$). However, clinicians are cautioned that this study was not intended to address the front-end assessment of malingering and whether psychopathy would be useful in this endeavor. Beyond the methodological limitations inherent in this type of research,[2] the sample was highly restricted to persons with violent criminal offenses and antisocial histories, increasing the likelihood of high PCL–R scores. In addition, it systematically excluded persons with psychotic disorders or symptoms and addressed only persons who had been found insane and committed to a maximum security hospital.

A different issue is whether psychopaths are more skilled at malingering than other populations. Kropp (1992) addressed this issue directly in his dissertation research. His simulation study examined the ability of psychopathic and nonpsychopathic inmates[3] to feign a severe mental disorder. He found that the presence of psychopathy did not improve inmates' ability to feign on the Structured Interview of Reported Symptoms (SIRS; Rogers, Bagby, & Dickens, 1992). Kropp did not find group differences between psychopaths and nonpsychopaths, but he did proceed to examine the protocols of the more successful feigners. He found a nonsignificant trend that the most able feigners were more likely to be from the psychopathic group.

Results of the Kropp (1992) study deserve a brief commentary. The lack of group differences for psychopathy (and in supplementary analyses, the ASPD) suggests that the capacity to malinger is unlikely to be linked to the clinical classification of psychopathy. Given the polythetic nature of psychopathy with more than 15,000 variations (Salekin, Rogers, & Sewell, 1996), it is quite possible that the capacity to deceive is well represented in certain variants of this classification. The clinical issue then becomes more refined to establishing the critical features of psychopathy that are associated with a greater likelihood of successful feigning.

Other research provides indirect support for the notion that antisocial persons are no more effective than others at successful malingering. With respect to the SIRS, studies (Connell, 1991; Gothard, Viglione, Meloy, & Sherman, 1995; Kurtz & Meyer, 1994; Linblad, 1994; Rogers, Gillis, & Bagby, 1990; Rogers, Kropp, & Bagby, 1992) have consistently demonstrated that inmates from correctional settings are detectable on the SIRS primary scales. Although less clear, inspection of Minnesota Multiphasic Personality Inventory–2 (MMPI–2) studies and malingering (e.g., see individual studies cited in Rogers, Sewell, & Salekin, 1994) do not suggest any consistent pattern between offender and nonoffender samples and their elevations on MMPI–2 validity indicators. In summary, both direct and indirect research is highly consistent in providing evidence for the conclusion that antisocial persons are generally no more effective than others at feigning mental disorders.

Despite the empirical evidence to the contrary, many forensic practitioners are likely to find the intuitive appeal of the psychopathy–malingering association to be irresistible. What makes this association so compelling? We hypothesize the following logic:

- An implicit assumption is that malingering and Axis I symptoms are mutually exclusive. In many forensic reports, the consideration of any genuine symptoms is abandoned once the classification of malingering is invoked.
- The disregard of any genuine symptoms results in a polarization of clinical data with genuine disorders versus ASPD/malingering. In instances of malingering, ASPD frequently becomes the default diagnosis because criminal behavior cannot be attributed to a mental disorder.
- By extension, ASPD becomes a diagnostic simplism for malingering potential.

Clinicians in forensic practice are likely to be troubled by the implications of these conclusions. The central question remains: Should clinicians entirely disregard evidence of psychopathy in determinations of malingering? In this regard, we believe that two positions are defensible:

1. The *corrosive influence* approach would argue that previously described pitfalls far outweigh any advantage from considering psychopathy in the assessment of malingering. From this perspective, the answer is unambiguously affirmative: psychopathy should be disregarded categorically in malingering evaluations.

2. The *screen for adept malingering* approach is premised on Kropp's (1992) finding that small numbers of psychopaths eluded detection. From this perspective, all evaluatees would be screened for potential malinger-

ing. Moreover, additional care would be taken in the evaluation of individuals with high PCL scores beyond the usual screening measures. For this approach, the answer is a circumscribed "no"; the presence of psychopathy would signal *increased scrutiny* but not *increased likelihood* of malingering.

Explanatory Models

A crucial distinction must be discerned between classificatory and explanatory models. Classificatory models, analogous to diagnosis, provide critical data for establishing the presence of malingering. In contrast, explanatory models attempt to understand the primary motivation of individuals to malinger. Although the previous discussion questioned the utility of ASPD and psychopathy for classificatory purposes, their value within explanatory models merits our consideration.

Rogers and his colleagues (Rogers, Sewell, & Goldstein, 1994; Rogers, Salekin, Sewell, Goldstein, & Leonard, 1998) have conducted several prototypical analyses of malingering with highly experienced forensic psychologists. They found that a criminological model, composed of *DSM* indices of malingering and core attributes of psychopathy, was useful in explaining malingerers' motivation. Rogers et al. (1998) examined differences in motivation based on setting (forensic or nonforensic) and feigned presentation (mental disorder, cognitive deficits, or medical illness[4]). Understandably, the criminological model was more prototypical of forensic than nonforensic cases. No differences were found across feigned conditions. However, gender played an important role for the criminological model; males were judged as significantly more prototypical than females in both forensic (4.81 vs. 4.24) and nonforensic (4.35 vs. 3.44) cases. With a rating of 4 designating moderate prototypicality, nonforensic female cases were rated comparatively low on the criminological model.

Clark (1997) cautioned against the injudicious use of ASPD/psychopathy for the classification of malingering. This caution is best heeded. Available data do not support the use of psychopathy as either a screening criterion or risk factor for malingering. A crucial discrimination must be appreciated between common and distinguishing features. Although obviously common in criminal forensic settings, ASPD/psychopathy is not a distinguishing feature of malingering.

As a clinical example, the first author evaluated a 26-year-old male insurance claimant whose malingering was obviously motivated by his criminal desire for unwarranted compensation. A comprehensive evaluation revealed multiple plans to defraud others. For example, as a stockbroker, he manipulated larger accounts to skim funds from equity transactions. In addition, he misrepresented the viability of his business as he systematically liquidated its assets. With respect to feigning, he unwisely acknowledged his contempt for health care providers and blatantly misrepresented his current involvement in treatment. In summary, his efforts at malingering were simply another effort to secure undeserved financial gain. Although the claimant does not have an arrest history for criminal offenses, he warranted the ASPD diagnosis.

In summary, several conclusions are offered regarding classificatory and explanatory models of malingering:

1. Offenders in general, and psychopaths in particular, do not appear to be especially skilled at malingering. On the contrary, data summarized by Clark (1997) suggest that some offenders try too hard and are readily identifiable by the extremeness of their presentations.

2. However, data from Kropp (1992) suggest that a small proportion of psychopaths may have particular traits and skills that allow them to feign more successfully than most other psychopaths and offenders.

3. As an explanatory model, a criminological explanation of undeserved rewards and unwarranted treatment does appear relevant in clarifying the primary motivation of some malingerers. Especially among males in forensic settings, this model is moderately high in prototypicality.

4. Care must be taken not to confuse explanatory (i.e., the understanding of motivation) with classificatory (i.e., the determination of malingering) models.

DECEPTION AND PSYCHOPATHY

Some form of deception and subterfuge appears to be an essential prerequisite of most crimes. Deceptive practices may include the crime itself (e.g., scams and confidence games), the identity of the perpetrator (e.g., aliases and use of disguises), and attempts to avoid prosecution (e.g., concealment of evidence, denial of involvement, and improper use of alibis). Because of the manifest link between deception and crime, the question of whether psychopaths are deceptive is largely resolved. The more interesting question is whether psychopaths differ from other antisocial persons in their types of deception.

Current Literature

The available literature focuses on lying and deception among delinquent populations. In her classic review of seven studies, Stouthamer-Loeber (1986) found that approximately one half of conduct-disordered youth displayed chronic problems with lying. Loeber and his colleagues (Lahey & Loeber, 1994; Loeber & Schmaling, 1985) have attempted to conceptualize conduct disorders (CDs) along two dimensions (overt vs. covert and destructive vs. nondestructive). Within this framework, persistent lying is viewed as a covert act of slight destructiveness. Interestingly, lying was only associated with aggressive conduct symptoms in approximately one half of the studies. As part of the *DSM–IV* trials, Frick et al. (1994) examined the diagnostic utility of lying for the diagnosis of CD. Unlike aggressive symptoms, persistent lying was relatively ineffective at identifying youths with CDs (PPP = .56). More important, many youth without CDs also engaged in persistent lying (NPP = .49). In summary, persistent lying does not appear to be specific to CDs and delinquency.

Several studies have attempted to link deception to the early emergence of psychopathy. For example, Frick, O'Brien, Wooton, and McBurnett (1994) examined dimensions of childhood psychopathy. Several forms of deception (e.g., cons others and lies easily and skillfully) were viewed as general components of psychopathy, although they appeared to be less salient than other characteristics when considered in a two-factor model. In addition, Rogers, Johansen, Chang, and Salekin (1997) examined predictors of adolescent psychopathy. In general, the mere presence of deceit/theft constellation of *DSM–IV* conduct symptoms was not predictive of psychopathy. However, use of the total rate of deceit/theft symptoms, which considered estimated frequency of each symptom, resulted in a moderately high correlation with psychopathy (r = .65). When entered into a hierarchical multiple regression, the total rate of deceit/theft symptoms accounted for a substantial percentage of the variance (ΔR^2 = .32) in predicting adolescent psychopaths. Both studies underscore the need for further studies to explore the relationship between deception and early psychopathy.

Cogburn (1993) directly addressed the skillfulness of psychopaths to deceive others in an experimental study. When measured by ratings on the PCL–R (Hare, 1991), psychopaths were no more successful than nonpsychopaths at deception. On the contrary, participants with high ratings on psychopathy were rated as less credible—regardless of whether they were attempting to deceive or be forthright. As noted by Clark (1997), this study raises a tempting hypothesis that psychopaths simply appear more dishonest in their interactions with others, irrespective of their motivation or intent to deceive.

Millon and Davis (1998) declared that psychopathy is best understood within the framework of 10 personality subtypes. Within this typology, two subtypes emphasize deception. The *unprincipled* psychopath is indifferent to honesty and skilled at charismatically deceiving others. The *disingenuous* psychopath is characterized by his or her pervasive deceitfulness that extends from the instrumental use of others to dishonesty and scheming in close relationships. Although this model obviously requires empirical testing, it postulates that deception may be a prototypical characteristic in only a minority of psychopaths.

In summary, the empirical literature provides an incomplete picture of the deception–psychopathy relationship. Lying appears to be a common feature of both delinquent and nondelinquent populations. Although common to psychopathy, deception is unlikely to be a distinguishing feature for its classification. Results of several studies require further consideration. For example, Rogers et al. (1997) found that the simple presence of deceit/theft symptoms is unlikely to be related to psychopathy among adolescent offenders. Instead, the breadth (number of symptoms) and frequency of these symptoms appear predictive of early psychopathy. In addition, Cogburn (1993) concluded that psychopaths look dishonest irrespective of their intentions. Finally, the theoretical work of Millon and Davis (1998) proposed that our examination of deception be refocused on specific subtypes of psychopathy.

Because of this incomplete picture, we conducted a reanalysis of an extensive data set (Rogers, Salekin, Hill, Sewell, & Murdock, in press) to examine specific characteristics of deception that are associated with psychopathy. The next section summarizes this reanalysis and discusses its implications for the deception–psychopathy relationship.

Reanalysis of Rogers et al. (1998)

Rogers and his colleagues (1998) combined data from three separate studies of psychopathy with all participants administered the Psychopathy Checklist–Screening Version (PCL–SV; Hart, Cox, & Hare, 1996). The data set combined the following: (a) Murdock and Rogers' (1997) sample of 120 adolescent male offenders in a residential correctional facility; (b) Salekin, Rogers, and Sewell's (1997) sample of 103 female offenders detained in a large metropolitan jail; and (c) Hill's (1996; see also Hill, Rogers, & Bickford, 1996) sample of 150 male forensic patients in a maximum security hospital.

The three studies employed an extended PCL–SV answer sheet that was modeled after the original (Hare, Cox, & Hart, 1989). The only addition was that clinicians were asked to rate the 58 subcriteria as well as the 12 criteria. By treating the subcriteria as individual items, the psychometric properties of the 12 criteria could be examined systematically. In general, the findings provide strong empirical support for the PCL–SV's construct validity.

Components of Deception.   Of the 58 subcriteria, we found 17 (29.3%) that addressed deception, either directly or indirectly. Intuitively, the domains of deception included denial of the crime, fraud/manipulation of others, false portrayal of emotions, and general dishonesty. The empirical question remained to be addressed: Is deception a unitary construct among offender populations?

We performed a principal axis factoring (PAF) analysis on the 17 subcriteria associated with deception using an oblique rotation with Kaiser normalization. Inspection of eigenvalues and scree plots strongly suggested a three-factor model (e.g., other eigenvalues < 1.00). The three-factor solution resulted in substantial loadings (≥ .40) for each of the 17 subcriteria with no cross-loadings. As summarized in Table 11.1, three well-defined factors were established:

- *Implausible presentation* (34.84% of the variance) is characterized by an unbelievable display with respect to statements and emotional expressions.
- *Denial of criminality* (13.92% of the variance) is typified as a disavowal of criminal involvement and an externalization of responsibility.
- *Conning and manipulation* (7.44% of the variance) is represented by use of deception for furthering of the psychopath's ends at the expense of others.

These factors are not highly intercorrelated (M r = .37), suggesting that some individuals with psychopathic traits are likely to be limited to only one or two forms of deception. We recommend that clinicians examine these three forms of deception separately in their evaluations of offenders.

As a clinical example, several graduate students evaluated a 55-year-old probationer convicted of child molestation. Because the evaluation was conducted solely for research purposes, the assessment was started, although legal and clinical records were not immediately available. The results are all too familiar: The probationer told an engaging account of how this first offense was precipitated by tragic losses, and he elaborated on his postarrest efforts to rectify his wrongs. With subsequent access to his records, an entirely different picture emerged about his repetitive history, lack of known precipitators, and lackluster involvement in treatment. His deceptions clearly involved both (a) a denial and minimization of his offenses, and (b) an attempt to con and manipulate his evaluators.

An important question is whether these forms of deception are found disproportionately in psychopaths. We classified the sample by the established cut score of ≥ 18 (Hart et al., 1996) into 115 psychopaths and 137 nonpsychopaths. As an exploratory analysis, we divided each dimension into quartiles with high (≥ 75th percentile) and low (≤ 25th percentile) deception. The overlap between subcriteria for each dimension and the overall PCL–SV rating is a confound. Therefore, we also computed pro-

TABLE 11.1
Dimensions of PCL–SV Subcriteria Associated With Deception

PCL–SV Subcriteria	Factor 1	Factor 2	Factor 3
Tells unlikely stories; has convincing explanations for behavior	.84	−.04	−.10
Has shallow presentation; is difficult to believe	.80	.04	.09
Alters statements when challenged	.74	−.10	.08
Display of emotions do not appear genuine	.69	−.04	.09
Exaggerates status and reputation	.63	.03	.08
Portrays self in a good light	.49	.23	.03
Verbalizes remorse insincerely	.41	.17	.06
Rationalizes; downplays significance of acts	.02	.84	−.04
Maintains innocence or minimizes involvement in crime	−.08	.73	.03
Minimizes the effects of behavior on others	.11	.72	−.05
Projects blame onto others	.14	.68	−.08
Claims being framed or victimized; claims amnesia or blackouts	−.07	.60	.10
Manipulates without concern for others	.04	.02	.87
Deceives with self-assurance and no anxiety	.04	.06	.86
Is fraud artist or con man	−.11	−.04	.82
Enjoys deceiving others	.13	-.10	.75
Distorts the truth	.12	.10	.68
Eigenvalues	6.34	2.77	1.68
Percentage of the variance	34.84	13.92	7.44

Note. Substantial loadings (≥ .40) are italicized.

rated scores by eliminating the criterion from each analysis that contributed the most subcriteria. Both analyses are presented in Table 11.2. Focusing on the prorated classifications, several key findings emerged:

- Implausible presentation was found almost invariably among psychopaths (97.6%). In contrast, approximately one fourth (27.0%) of nonpsychopaths shared this dimension.
- Almost six out of seven psychopaths (83.0%) engaged in a denial of criminality; in comparison, slightly more than one out of three nonpsychopaths (34.9%) were high on this dimension.
- Conning and manipulation were less common than dimensions for both psychopaths and nonpsychopaths. Still more than three out of four (77.8%) psychopaths engaged in a high level of conning and manipulation as compared with approximately one fourth (22.4%) of nonpsychopaths.

Although differences in deception were expected, we were surprised by their magnitude. In general, psychopaths were three times more like-

TABLE 11.2
Types of Deception Among Psychopaths and Nonpsychopaths

Type of Deception	Original Classification		Prorated Classification	
	Psychopaths	Nonpsychopaths	Psychopaths	Nonpsychopaths
Implausible				
presentation	$\chi^2 = 137.74$	$(p < .001)$	$\chi^2 = 56.98$	$(p < .001)$
Low	4.3%	78.1%	2.4%	73.0%
High	95.7%	21.9%	97.6%	27.0%
Denial of				
criminality	$\chi^2 = 26.20$	$(p < .001)$	$\chi^2 = 28.16$	$(p < .001)$
Low	30.4%	62.8%	17.0%	65.1%
High	69.6%	37.2%	83.0%	34.9%
Conning and				
manipulation	$\chi^2 = 30.43$	$(p < .001)$	$\chi^2 = 42.61$	$(p < .001)$
Low	25.2%	59.9%	22.2%	77.6%
High	74.8%	40.1%	77.8%	22.4%

Note. Low = lowest quartile; high = highest quartile. With the *original* classification, psychopathy is not completely independent of the dimensions of deception. In each analysis, a small number of subcriteria (i.e., implausible presentation = 7 or 12.1%; denial of criminality = 5 or 8.6%; conning and manipulation = 5 or 8.6%) are shared between the type of deception and psychopathy. In the *prorated* classification, we eliminated the criterion of each analysis from which most subcriteria were derived and prorated the cut scores (i.e., ≥ 17 vs. ≥ 18).

ly to have high levels of these dimensions of deception than their nonpsychopathic counterparts. The most profound difference was found for implausible presentation.

Psychopaths primarily characterized by implausible presentations (see also Cogburn, 1993) are likely to have long-standing interpersonal difficulties. We surmise that their efforts at impression management are unsuccessful and continue to impair their attempts to form any meaningful relationships. We wonder whether underlying feelings of inadequacy, as hypothesized by Millon and Davis (1998) for disingenuous psychopaths, play an important role in producing these transparent pretenses. The extreme prevalence of implausible presentations argues against it being linked to one or two subtypes of psychopathy.

Psychopaths, typified by denial of criminality, may be responding to situational demands. Admission of criminal behavior is likely to have significant consequences at both the pretrial (e.g., admission of guilt) and posttrial (e.g., likelihood of parole) phases. Admission of criminal behavior that was previously denied may also be viewed as evidence of dishonesty or an insincere attempt to appear contrite. Beyond situational demands, however, denial of criminality appears to be associated with an antisocial perspective and characterized by an externalization of responsibility (Lilienfeld, 1996). Based on our data, substantial numbers of psychopaths and nonpsychopaths are likely to manifest this dimension.[5]

Psychopaths with conning and manipulation represent a systematic effort to deceive others to achieve personal objectives. This duplicitous misuse of others, akin to the Millon and Davis (1998) unprincipled psychopath, appears prototypical of Hare's (1991) Factor 1—namely, the "selfish, callous, and remorseless use of others" (p. 38). We surmise that psychopaths with conning and manipulation are more likely than other deceptive psychopaths to thwart treatment efforts and be disruptive to correctional units.

CONCLUSIONS

Caveats on the Assessment of Malingering

An enduring challenge to forensic evaluations is reducing the effects of confirmatory bias. As discussed by Borum, Otto, and Golding (1993), confirmatory bias influences clinicians' ability to seek information consistent with their hypotheses and accord supportive evidence with disproportionate importance. Given the intuitive appeal of considering psychopaths as deceptive individuals predisposed to malinger, confirmatory bias may lead clinicians to overvalue any supportive evidence of malingering and, conversely, devalue any countervailing evidence of nonmalingering.

The current *DSM–IV* model inadvertently reinforces this confirmatory bias because most psychopaths meet its threshold with at least two indices (i.e., ASPD and medicolegal evaluations) for being strongly suspected of malingering. If malingering is to be strongly suspected in most psychopaths, then confirmatory bias is likely to result in many misclassifications. As an egregious example, the first author was involved in a capital murder case in which a highly experienced expert reported a high likelihood of malingering because the male defendant met three of four *DSM* indices: He was an uncooperative psychopath involved in a forensic evaluation. A careful review of the defendant's inpatient record revealed a much more complex picture, with (a) his severe schizophrenia unresponsive to most treatments, (b) his gross impairment clearly compromising his cooperativeness, and (c) all standardized indices of malingering being in the expected range for genuine patients.

Forensic experts must take an active role in debiasing their evaluations of malingering among psychopaths. One method of combating confirmatory bias is to explicitly reject the *DSM–IV* indices of malingering. The best available data suggest that these indices, if treated as inclusion criteria, are likely to lead to false positives four out of five times. We have not found a scintilla of published data that would support the use of these indices, even in the seemingly innocuous role of screening. Also for debiasing, experts must evaluate all characteristics of malingering with a simple litmus test:

- Is this characteristic simply a *common* feature of malingering? If so, disregard in making determinations of malingering.
- Is this characteristic specifically a *distinguishing* feature of malingering? If so, apply judiciously in light of its validation and incremental validity.

Guidelines for the Assessment of Deception

Lying and other forms of deception are an integral component of our modern social fabric (Miller & Stiff, 1993). Moreover, lying is a common feature of many mental disorders (Ford, King, & Hollender, 1988). In studies of delinquency, lying had only marginal usefulness in distinguishing between youth with and without CDs. In summary, the mere presence of lying does not appear to be either an antecedent condition (see Rogers et al., 1997) or a primary characteristic of psychopathy. In understanding the deception–psychopathy relationship, the types of deception and their effects on assessment/intervention become the focal points.

In advancing our understanding of the deception–psychopathy relationship, the reanalysis of the Rogers et al. (in press) data provides important, albeit preliminary insights. As an initial framework, we recommend that deceptions among psychopaths be categorized according to dimensions extracted from PCL–SV subcriteria. In this regard, the following clinical issues should be addressed:

1. Are deceptions circumscribed to his or her involvement in the index crime and his or her acknowledgement of previous criminal behavior (i.e., denial of criminality)?
2. Do deceptions focus on fostering a false self-image (i.e., implausible presentation)?
3. Do deceptions generally attempt to mislead others to achieve nonlegitimate objectives (i.e., conning and manipulation)?

As summarized in Table 11.2, psychopaths are likely to engage in a broad range of deceptions. Clinicians may wish to use high PCL–R and PCL–SV scores as useful screens for when different forms of deception warrant systematic evaluation. On a practical level, adoption of a modified scoring for the PCL–SV (i.e., ratings of subcriteria) would provide psychologists and other mental health professionals with standardized ratings to address important components of lying and deceit.

ENDNOTES

1. As an important distinction, these elements are not intended as formal inclusion criteria. Rather, they serve a screening function, with any combination signaling that "malingering should be strongly suspected" (American Psychiatric Association, 1994, p. 683).
2. To be included in the study, malingering participants must have a "self-reported exaggerating or malingering to gain access to the hospital" (Gacono et al., 1995, p. 388). Insanity acquittees may have various motivations for making this type of admission. In our experience, the most common and plausible motivation for such an admission is an attempt to secure an early release from a maximum security hospital. This motivation may lead to false confessions of malingering.
3. Psychopathy scores (i.e., PCL–SV) were moderately correlated (.66) with SCID-based diagnoses of ASPD.
4. Individuals feigning more than one condition were excluded from this analysis.
5. When controlling for the baserates of psychopathy in forensic populations (i.e., 15%–25%; see Hare, 1998), denial of criminality is more likely to be observed in nonpsychopaths than psychopaths.

REFERENCES

American Psychiatric Association. (1980). *Diagnostic and statistical manual of mental disorders* (3rd ed.). Washington, DC: Author.
American Psychiatric Association. (1987). *Diagnostic and statistical manual of mental disorders* (3rd ed., rev.). Washington, DC: Author.
American Psychiatric Association. (1994). *Diagnostic and statistical manual of mental disorders* (4th ed.). Washington, DC: Author.
Borum, R., Otto, R., & Golding, S. (1993). Improving clinical judgment and decision making in forensic evaluation. *Journal of Psychiatry and Law, 21*, 35–76.
Clark, C. R. (1997). Sociopathy, malingering, and defensiveness. In R. Rogers (Ed.), *Clinical assessment of malingering and deception* (2nd ed., pp. 68–84). New York: Guilford.
Cogburn, R. A. K. (1993). A study of psychopathy and its relation to success in interpersonal deception. *Dissertation Abstracts International, 54*, 2191B.
Connell, D. K. (1991). *The SIRS and the M test: The differential validity and utility of two instruments designed to detect malingered psychosis in a correctional sample.* Unpublished dissertation, University of Louisville.
Ford, C. V., King, B. H., & Hollender, M. H. (1988). Lies and liars: Psychiatric aspects of prevarication. *American Journal of Psychiatry, 145*, 554–562.
Frick, P. J., Lahey, B. B., Applegate, B., Kerdyck, L., Ollendick, T., Hynd, G. W., Garfinkel, B., Greenhill, L., Biederman, J., Barkley, R. A., McBurnett, K., Newcorn, J., & Waldman, I. (1994). *DSM–IV* field trials for the disruptive behavior disorders: Symptom utility estimates. *Journal of the American Academy of Child and Adolescent Psychiatry, 33*, 529–539.
Frick, P. J., O'Brien, B. S., Wooton, J. M., & McBurnett, K. (1994). Psychopathy and conduct problems in children. *Journal of Abnormal Psychology, 103*, 700–707.

Gacono, G. B., Meloy, J. R., Sheppard, K., Speth, E., & Roske, A. (1995). A clinical investigation of malingering and psychopathy in hospitalized NGRI patients. *Bulletin of the American Academy of Psychiatry and Law, 23,* 387–397.

Gothard, S., Viglione, D. J., Meloy, J. R., & Sherman, M. (1995). Detection of malingering in competency to stand trial evaluations. *Law and Human Behavior, 19,* 493–505.

Hare, R. D. (1991). *Manual for the Hare Psychopathy Checklist–Revised.* Toronto, ON: Multi-Health Systems.

Hare, R. D. (1998). Psychopaths and their nature: Implications for the mental health and criminal justice systems. In T. Millon, E. Simonsen, M. Birket-Smith, & R. D. Davis (Eds.), *Psychopathy: Antisocial, criminal and violent behaviors* (pp. 188–212). New York: Guilford.

Hare, R. D., Cox, D. N., & Hart, S. D. (1989). *PCL–CV scoresheet.* Unpublished measure, University of British Columbia, Vancouver.

Hart, S. D., Cox, D. N., & Hare, R. D. (1996). *Manual for the Screening Version of Psychopathy Checklist Revised (PCL:SV).* Toronto, ON: Multi-Health Systems.

Hill, C. (1996). *Predictive validity of the PCL:SV with maximum security patients.* Unpublished doctoral dissertation, University of North Texas.

Hill, C., Rogers, R., & Bickford, M. (1996). Predicting aggressive and socially disruptive behavior in a maximum security hospital. *Journal of Forensic Sciences, 41,* 56–59.

Kropp P. R. (1992). *Antisocial personality disorder and malingering.* Unpublished doctoral dissertation, Simon Fraser University, Burnaby, British Columbia, Canada.

Kurtz, R., & Meyer, R. G. (1994, March). *Vulnerability of the MMPI-2, M Test, and SIRS to different strategies of malingering psychosis.* Paper presented at the American Psychology-Law Society, Santa Fe, NM.

Lahey, B. B., & Loeber, R. (1994). Framework for a developmental model of oppositional defiant and conduct disorder. In R. K. Routh (Ed.), *Disruptive behavior disorders in childhood* (pp. 139–180). New York: Plenum.

Lilienfeld, S. O. (1996). The MMPI-2 antisocial practices scale: Construct validity and comparison with the psychopathic deviate scale. *Psychological Assessment, 8,* 281–293.

Lindblad, A. D. (1994). Detection of malingered mental illness within a forensic population: An analogue study. *Dissertation Abstracts International, 54-B,* 4395.

Loeber, R., & Schmaling, K. B. (1985). Empirical evidence for overt and covert patterns of antisocial conduct problems: A meta-analysis. *Journal of Abnormal Child Psychology, 13,* 337–352.

Miller, G. R., & Stiff, J. B. (1993). *Deceptive communication.* Newbury Park, CA: Sage.

Millon, T., & Davis, R. D. (1998). Ten subtypes of psychopathy. In T. Millon, E. Simonsen, M. Birket-Smith, & R. D. Davis (Eds.), *Psychopathy: Antisocial, criminal and violent behaviors* (pp. 161–170). New York: Guilford.

Murdock, M. E., & Rogers, R. (1997, August). *Validity of the Psychopathy Checklist–Screening Version with adolescent offenders.* Paper presented at the American Psychological Association Convention, Chicago.

Resnick, P. J. (1997). Malingered psychosis. In R. Rogers (Ed.), *Clinical assessment of malingering and deception* (2nd ed., pp. 47–67). New York: Guilford.

Rogers, R. (1990a). Development of a new classificatory model of malingering. *Bulletin of the American Academy of Psychiatry and Law, 18,* 323–333.

Rogers, R. (1990b). Models of feigned mental illness. *Professional Psychology: Research and Practice, 21,* 182–188.

Rogers, R., Bagby, R. M., & Dickens, S. E. (1992). *Structured Interview of Reported Symptoms (SIRS) and professional manual.* Odessa, FL: Psychological Assessment Resources.

Rogers, R., Dion, K. L., & Lynett, E. (1992). Diagnostic validity of antisocial personality disorder: A prototypical analysis. *Law and Human Behavior, 16,* 677–689.

Rogers, R., Duncan, J. C., & Sewell, K. W. (1994). Prototypical analysis of antisocial personality disorder: *DSM-IV* and beyond. *Law and Human Behavior, 18,* 471–484.

Rogers, R., Gillis, J. R., & Bagby, R. M. (1990). The SIRS as a measure of malingering: A validational study with a correctional sample. *Behavioral Sciences and the Law, 8,* 85–92.

Rogers, R., Gillis, J. R., Dickens, S. E., & Bagby, R. M. (1991). Standardized assessment of malingering: Validation of the Structured Interview of Reported Symptoms. *Psychological Assessment, 4,* 89–96.

Rogers, R., Johansen, J., Chang, J. J., & Salekin, R. T. (1997). Predictors of adolescent psychopathy: Oppositional and conduct-disordered symptoms. *Journal of the American Academy of Psychiatry and Law, 25,* 261–271.

Rogers, R., Kropp, P. R., & Bagby, R. M. (1992). Faking specific disorders: A study of Structured Interview of Reported Symptoms (SIRS). *Journal of Clinical Psychology, 48,* 643–647.

Rogers, R., Salekin, R. T., Hill, C., Sewell, K. W., & Murdock, M. E. (in press). The Psychopathy Checklist–Screening Version: An examination of criteria and subcriteria. *Assessment.*

Rogers, R., Salekin, R. T., Sewell, K. W., & Cruise, K. R. (in press). Prototypical analysis of antisocial personality disorder: An insider's perspective. *Criminal Justice and Behavior.*

Rogers, R., Salekin, R. T., Sewell, K. W., Goldstein, A., & Leonard, K. (1998). A comparison of forensic and nonforensic malingerers: A prototypical analysis of explanatory models. *Law and Human Behavior, 22,* 353–367.

Rogers, R., Sewell, K. W., & Goldstein, A. (1994). Explanatory models of malingering: A prototypical analysis. *Law and Human Behavior, 18,* 543–552.

Rogers, R., Sewell, K. W., & Salekin, R. T. (1994). A meta-analysis of malingering on the MMPI-2. *Assessment, 1,* 227–237.

Salekin, R. T., Rogers, R., & Sewell, K. W. (1996). A review and meta-analysis of the Psychopathy Checklist and the Psychopathy Checklist–Revised: Predictive validity of dangerousness. *Clinical Psychology: Science and Practice, 3,* 203–215.

Salekin, R. T., Rogers, R., & Sewell, K. W. (1997). Construct validity of psychopathy in a female offender sample: Multitrait-multimethod evaluation. *Journal of Abnormal Psychology, 106,* 576–585.

Stouthamer-Loeber, M. (1986). Lying as a problem in children. A review. *Clinical Psychology Review, 6,* 267–289.

III

SPECIAL APPLICATIONS

Psychopathic Manipulation at Work

Paul Babiak
Private Practice, Hopewell Junction, New York

> *Look in the mirror and one thing's certain: what we see is not who we are.*
> — Richard Bach

The behavior of psychopaths has stimulated the interest of psychological researchers in a variety of disciplines. Psychiatrists, as well as clinical, experimental, and forensic psychologists, are frequent contributors to the literature. In recent years, interest in the psychopath as a research subject has expanded even further to include industrial and organizational psychologists (Babiak, 1995a, 1995b, 1996a; Gustafson & Ritzer, 1995).

Industrial and organizational (I-O) psychology is the study of the behavior of people at work; it includes the behaviors associated with performing a job, as well as the context in which the job is performed. While performing work, people act as individuals with unique needs, values, and motivations. They often act as members of work groups, where these same needs, values, and motivations interrelate with those of others in the context of working toward common (and sometimes conflicting) goals and objectives.

Because humans spend a considerable amount of their waking lives at work, there is quite a lot of opportunity for I-O psychologists to conduct pure and applied research and use that research to solve real-life problems. I-O psychologists make observations, collect data, build models of human behavior, and then design and implement interventions with an overriding objective toward improving the effectiveness of the individual, the team, and ultimately the organization as a whole. I–O psychologists work in academia, as independent consultants, or as full-time employees in organizations often as part of the human resources or related department.

The field has broadened since its inception during the early 1900s and now encompasses two interrelated areas of study. Industrial psychology, the oldest subdiscipline, has as its focus the individual and his or her ability to perform well in the organization. Human competence in the forms of knowledge, skill, and ability are frequent areas of research, as are the interrelationships of performance, job satisfaction, attitudes, motivation, and personality, among many other variables. For example, selection test development, which is the creation and validation of test instruments to predict performance on the job, is an important area where application of research fulfills real business needs.

In the newest subdiscipline, organizational psychology, the focus is on interactions among individuals as they perform work together. Group dynamics, organizational culture, interpersonal conflict, and leadership are frequently studied with an eye toward using the knowledge gained to improve organizational effectiveness.

WHO IS THE CLIENT: THE PSYCHOPATH, THE VICTIM, OR THE ORGANIZATION?

Although the role of the I–O psychologist is to use knowledge of human behavior to improve the effectiveness of the individual as well as the organization, it does not involve the forming of therapeutic relationships with individuals. Clearly many psychiatrists and psychologists see the psychopath in a relatively clear role — as a client in a clinical setting, there to receive some assistance in dealing with clinical issues. This is not the case for the I–O psychologist. I–O psychologists do not conduct therapy with employees, but take necessary steps to refer individuals to appropriately qualified resources should the need come to their attention. In the case of the psychopath, it is not the amelioration of his or her mental state that intrigues the I–O psychologist; rather, it is their ability to unduly influence organization members as well as business processes.

Although prisons, hospitals, and clinics are ideal settings for clinical study and survey research of psychopaths, the behavior observed is limited to interactions with other criminals, seriously ill people, or staff members (Doren, 1987). A considerable number of studies have come out of the research of psychiatrists and psychologists who work in these settings, and much is now known about the criminal psychopath. But what of the subcriminal or noninstitutionalized psychopath (Cleckley, 1976;

Hare, 1986; Levenson, Kiehl, & Fitzpatrick, 1995; Person, 1986; Widom, 1977)? Known for their ability to elude detection and their tendency to move on to other victims once their utility has been exhausted, they are a much more difficult population to study. In a traditional work setting, I–O psychologists can potentially observe the behaviors of a psychopath in real time, within normal populations, as well as their impact on coworkers who have been victimized (Babiak, 1996b); that is, if psychopaths really do hold down jobs in traditional business organizations — a position that this writer will explore in this chapter.

It is important that attention is focused on maintaining confidences, especially in the data-collection phase of organizational analysis, while avoiding participation in the interpersonal dynamics, which might be part of the organization's dysfunction. It is common for organization members to attempt to establish special relationships with the consultant — a situation that must be tactfully avoided by clarifying the nature of the relationship with the organization and individuals up front. This situation becomes much more difficult when the organization member is a psychopath or one of his or her victims, both of whom seek the consultant's help albeit for different reasons.

On the most practical of levels, the client in organizational consulting is usually the member of management who engages the I–O psychologist's services and, through that person, the organization as a whole. Rarely is the assignment (in this writer's experience) built around a client's interest in research. The I–O psychologist's ability to solve real problems often drives the relationship, with research being a means to an end or sometimes just an added outcome.

This chapter describes some research conducted over the past several years on psychopathic individuals who have successfully entered the mainstream workforce and continue to enjoy profitable careers in business. Observations and data are presented, along with models that capture the dynamics of psychopathic behavior in organizations, the impact on coworkers, and the impact on the organization. It is hoped that the reader finds value in this somewhat unique perspective and that this chapter can shed some light on the behavior of psychopaths in organizational settings.

A CASE STUDY

It would be instructive to start with a brief case history: It is the story of Frank and Dave (Babiak, 1995a). Frank hired Dave on the basis of Dave's charm, intelligence, and technical expertise as an entry-level manager in a successful, rapidly growing high-tech firm in the midwestern United

States. Dave interviewed well, impressing everyone who met him. He was hired with the unanimous approval of several interviewers and was welcomed readily into this dynamic, fast-paced organization.

Within 2 weeks of joining the staff, problems developed. Dave was late for meetings; he was disruptive when he would finally arrive, and began to display an attitude that seemed, at least to Frank, his boss, to grow more and more serious as the weeks went by. Dave would leave in the middle of meetings, citing important phone calls he needed to make, and blow up when questioned or challenged. He also began verbally abusing the support staff.

It eventually became clear to Frank that, despite Dave's impressive resumé and positive first impressions, his actual work output—both in terms of quantity and quality—was far less than that of people with less experience and education. Dave ignored assignments he found uninteresting, claiming that he was overworked. He also claimed that much of the work he was asked to do was beneath him. Dave was frequently insubordinate to his boss and openly criticized Frank to others in the organization.

Among other things of concern, Dave had a tendency to lie—even about insignificant things—and he ignored any rule that inconvenienced him. For example, Dave began to purchase supplies for personal use using company funds; when questioned by the purchasing department, he began placing orders directly with vendors. It was later discovered that he was siphoning off materials from the company to sell to clients on the side.

Frank spoke with his own superior, the director, who was initially skeptical of Frank's report on Dave's performance. Frank then began building a case against Dave by collecting evidence documenting Dave's increasingly outrageous behavior. Frank's boss was still hesitant to take any disciplinary steps against Dave despite the evidence, so they decided on a test of Dave's integrity. Frank was to meet with Dave and share some specific confidential information and ask him to maintain the confidence for a couple of days. As expected, Dave immediately went to Frank's boss to share this confidential information. Not only did he flagrantly break the confidence, but he also grossly distorted the facts in an effort to disparage Frank and enhance his own position.

With this validation of Dave's insincerity, Frank and the director went to see the president, only to find out (to their great surprise) that Dave had already been there and had forewarned him about the impending visit. The president clearly did not believe their story and told them to leave Dave alone. He subsequently informed the director that Dave was considered a high-potential employee by the other executives and was on the fast track for promotion. Within a couple of weeks, Dave was promoted and Frank was given a new job working on special projects. Soon thereafter Frank left the company. How did this happen?

Research Questions

This chapter addresses five questions typical of the I–O psychologist's perspective:

1. How can a psychopath enter and work in an organization?
2. Why would psychopaths want to work in industry anyway, where, in many respects the environment is more controlling and less controllable than self-employment or other more transient jobs in open society?
3. Can psychopathic individuals actually have successful careers in industrial organizations and what does this success entail?
4. How do psychopaths manipulate large, relatively constant groups of people over a long period of time into believing their lies and tolerating their abusive behaviors?
5. What are the opportunities for joint research between I–O psychologists and clinical colleagues?

METHOD

Longitudinal Studies in Industry

This writer's first exposure to a psychopath in industry occurred during a routine consulting assignment involving improvements to the operations of a technical department. The assignment took the form of a traditional organization development (a subdiscipline of I–O psychology) intervention: meetings with the client organization to understand the nature of the issues affecting team performance, interviews of all department members and allied colleagues, a written survey of team effectiveness to pinpoint issues, and a series of feedback and improvement sessions referred to collectively as *team-building sessions*.

Early in this process, which extended over 2 years, a request for assistance in dealing with a problem employee surfaced. This did not come as a surprise because there had been conflicting reports (both positive and negative) about an individual (Dave; not his real name) in the department forthcoming during the data-gathering phase of the intervention. This writer's personal impressions from several interactions and interviews were also mixed at this time. (Subsequent assignments in different companies have revealed other employees displaying similar behavior; data on a selection of these are reported in this chapter.)

When presented with problem employee issues, it is important for the consultant to first clarify the perceptions of the supervisor as to whether the problems are reflected in the employee's performance, work habits, willingness to work, abilities, or perceived attitude. Each suggests an approach to take to get to the root cause. Frank had concerns about Dave in all of these areas; based on what was ultimately observed, his perception was accurate. Attempts to improve the situation, including clarifying goals and expectations, more frequent performance feedback discussions, and greater involvement in decision making — normal approaches to take — all failed. The root cause of Dave's behavior was based in his psychopathic personality — a fact unknown at the time of the assignment that ended when upper management reorganized Frank out of his department.

Using The Psychopathy Checklist in Organizational Settings

As discussed in chapter 3 of this book, the cutting edge thinking on the measurement of psychopathy has been forthcoming from Robert Hare, whose measure of psychopathy, the PCL (Hare, 1985, 1991a), is the state-of-the-art instrument (Fulero, 1995) used by virtually all researchers of psychopaths.

The PCL procedure as developed by Hare and his associates involves an in-depth structured interview following a detailed protocol (Hare, 1991b) and a review of the subject's history of antisocial acts, which usually takes the form of a criminal record. The evaluator completes the instrument — either the PCL–R or the shorter screening version (PCL–SV; Hare, Hart, & Cox, 1995) — and then calculates the results. In addition to a total psychopathy score, Factor 1 and Factor 2 scales are scored.

The data-collection protocol used by I–O psychologists who consult to industrial leaders parallels the PCL–R procedure in many respects. It is particularly conducive to the completion of the PCL because of the richness of the information collected and the longitudinal nature of the overall process. This process typically includes frequent direct observation of behaviors among coworkers; face-to-face personal interviews in formal and informal settings; team-building meetings (which have as their purpose enhancing interpersonal relationships); staff meetings; review of reports by coworkers, superiors, peers, and subordinates; and analysis of organizational survey data. Written records are also reviewed. These include performance evaluations, business correspondence, supervisory files, and employment records. Critical incidents are only included in the analysis if they surface independently from two or more sources, from the subjects, or from direct observation.

For its use in the studies reported in this chapter, the PCL procedure was significantly augmented (as described earlier) to include direct observation of and interactions with the subjects over periods ranging from 2 to 4 years. Subjects were subsequently assessed using both the PCL-R (criminal population version; Hare, 1991a) and the PCL-SV (Hare, Hart, & Cox, 1995).

RESULTS

The present research is the summary of six longitudinal studies conducted over several years at six organizations undergoing dramatic organizational change. These changes included organizational restructuring, downsizing, *right sizing,* mergers, acquisitions, and a joint venture. In each setting, the presenting problem was of an organizational nature, such as improving morale and organizational effectiveness, managing change, and dealing with other issues normally in the realm of I-O psychology. In each case, however, a problem employee surfaced as a key player in the dysfunctional dynamics plaguing the client. It was only after the PCL-R evaluation was conducted that the possibility that a psychopath could be at work in each of these organizations presented itself as a reality.

Table 12.1 summarizes the total and factor scores for the PCL-R and the PCL-SV for each of the subjects. The last column describes the type of change or transition issue that characterized each organization. Each subject's total score met or exceeded the cutoff for psychopathy on the PCL-SV and some also on the PCL-R.

TABLE 12.1
PCL-R and PCL-SV Factor and Total Scores for Six Cases

	PCL-R			PCL-SV			Type of Change
Case	F1	F2	Total	F1	F2	Total	
Dave	15	11.6	29.4	11	8	19	Rapid growth
Bob	16	11.6	31.3	12	7	19	Severe downsizing
Ron	15	11.6	30.6	11	8	19	Joint venture
Jim	15	11.6	29.4	11	8	19	Downsizing
Ev	15	10.1	27.8	11	6	17	Corporate reorganization
Carol	14	10.3	25.6	12	7	19	Downsizing
Maximum score →	16	18	40	12	12	24	

Psychopathic Profiles

In many studies, it has been shown that nonpsychopathic normals score very low on the total PCL–R score as well as Factors 1 and 2 (Hare et al., 1990), whereas criminal psychopaths score high on the total and both factors (Hare, 1985, 1991a; Hare, Hart, & Cox, 1995; Harpur, Hakstian, & Hare, 1988; Harpur & Hare, 1991; Harpur, Hare, & Hakstian, 1989). Nonpsychopathic criminals, who typically score high on clinical evaluations of antisocial personality disorder (ASPD) using *Diagnostic and Statistical Manual of Mental Disorders* (*DSM*) guidelines (American Psychiatric Association, 1994), actually score low to moderate on Factor 1, the personality component, but high on Factor 2, the deviant lifestyle component (Hare, 1991a).

The industrial psychopaths found in the companies studied displayed the reverse profile (i.e., they were extremely high on Factor 1, the psychopathic personality component, and moderate on Factor 2, the deviant lifestyle component; see Fig. 12.1). They displayed the personality traits ascribed to psychopaths without exhibiting antisocial acts or a lifestyle typical of criminal psychopaths, which would have attracted the formal attention of society.

DISCUSSION

Discrepant Views of Subjects Observed

The most striking similarity across the organizations studied was the discrepancy in perception between those individuals who described their

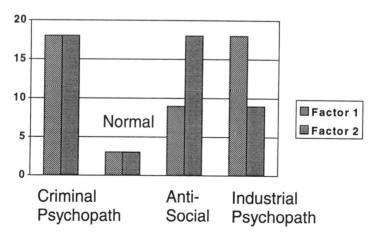

FIG. 12.1.   PCL–R profiles.

psychopathic coworkers in a favorable light and those that saw them in a negative light. This discrepancy was unlike any division that one might find based on simple political separation or, for that matter, in the case of problem employees (who tend to exhibit a different pattern).

The discrepancy also changed over time. In every case, all coworkers reported initially liking the subject. However, with continued exposure, some organization members grew to dislike the subject, whereas others interestingly grew even more attached. Eventually some in this latter group would come to actively defend the subject against the others; many even identified him or her as a close and trusted friend. At first, evidence might suggest that the psychopath was ingratiating himself with those at the top of the organization and abusing peers and the lower levels. However, the memberships of the groups did not divide neatly along organizational lines.

To illustrate how the discrepant views evolved, let us take a closer look at the case of Dave (Babiak, 1995a). If observations are limited to overall perceptions, then two groups emerged within the organization regarding Dave: supporters and detractors. In Table 12.2, supporters are listed on the right side and detractors on the left. There is a mix of levels and functions represented and no obvious distinction between the groups. If we now consider how often coworkers interacted with Dave, *often* versus *infrequently*, then these two groups can be divided further into four as illustrated in Table 12.3. This results in two groups of supporters and two groups of detractors.

There is one group of supporters (the lower right quadrant in Table 12.3) who tended to be high in organizational status and power, primarily (but not exclusively) at the executive level. Because of their position in the hierarchy and the nature of their jobs, they had only infrequent interactions with Dave. Despite admitting that they knew little about him, they quite openly stated that they liked him very much. They advocated for him against the other organization members, identified him as a key player in the future of

TABLE 12.2
Detractors and Supporters in the Case of Dave

Perceptions of Dave	
Detractors	*Supporters*
Frank [boss]	President
Coworkers	Vice presidents
Department Secretary	Department director
Some peers/managers	"Soul mate"
Purchasing manager	Staff assistant
Security guards	Some peers/managers
HR manager	

TABLE 12.3
Over Time, Discrepant Views of Dave Emerged

	Perceptions of Dave	
	Detractors	Supporters
	Utility	
Interaction	Low	High
Frequent	Department director ←	← Department director
	Frank [boss]	"Soul mate"
	Coworkers	Staff assistant
	Department secretary	Some peers/managers
	Some peers/managers	
Infrequent	Purchasing manager	President
	Security guards	Vice presidents
	HR manager	Some managers

the organization, and attributed much success to his efforts. These individuals acted as Dave's patrons, as evidenced by their willingness and ability to protect, defend, and mentor him in the organization. This pattern was also observed in other organizations reported in Table 12.1.

Like the first group, the second group (upper right quadrant) was composed of individuals who felt positively about Dave. Unlike the others, these are the people who worked with him on a daily basis, including peers, subordinates, and some superiors. It appears that some of these people held low-level positions in the hierarchy, making one wonder why a possible psychopath would find them of interest. In actuality, they possessed informal power within the organizational system, making them useful to the psychopath. Informal power holders influence the attitudes and behaviors of other employees, the work flow, adherence to rules, and communications networks. To have the support of an informal leader makes influencing the rest of the organization infinitely easier to accomplish.

For example, the staff assistant was an older woman working in a completely different department from Dave who turned out to be a major conduit of the office grapevine. She was totally charmed by Dave and enjoyed gossiping with him when he passed by her desk. Enthralled with the amount of attention she was receiving from someone much higher up in the organization (Dave was a manager), she kept him informed of behind the scenes information while also spreading positive, glowing stories about him throughout the organization.

Another example is the individual referred to in Table 12.2 as the *soul mate*—someone who had a special relationship with Dave. This special relationship was filled with infatuation and dependence, almost cultlike worship. Eventually it was revealed that the soul mate, a recognized technical expert, was doing Dave's work for him. The soul mate role was subsequently uncovered in a majority of other cases. On the whole, coworkers in this group were manipulated without their knowledge by the psychopath, essentially being used as pawns to influence the attitudes and behaviors of other employees to support the psychopath's endeavors.

The first group of detractors (upper left quadrant) was made up of individuals who despised the subject and described him as evil; *snake* was the most common epithet used in Dave's case. Most of these individuals had previously been pawns or supporters and, for reasons discussed later, now realized that they had been used; in effect, they felt like patsies.

In the case study, Frank, Dave's boss, was originally his patron, bringing him into the company and showing him the ropes. When things started getting out of hand, he tried to work with Dave to change some of his abusive behavior. However, once he discovered discrepancies in Dave's expense account and the misuse of other company resources, he changed his perception and tried to have him removed. This proved to be his own downfall because Dave turned the power holders against him.

Certainly Frank was a patsy in this case, but so was the director (Frank's boss), who really believed that he had a close relationship with Dave; he was devastated by Dave's betrayal.

The second group of detractors (lower left quadrant) was made up of individuals who held critical control functions in the organization, such as security officers, auditors, and some members of the Human Resources department. These individuals are often referred to (in a humorous vein in management literature) as the *organizational police*. Perhaps being naturally suspicious or at least trained to be skeptical, the individuals in this case quickly saw through Dave's manipulation, despite having limited interaction. Unfortunately, beyond collecting and presenting information about delinquent, abusive, and potentially criminal behavior to management, in *every* case in which they were involved, the organizational police could not influence upper management's decisions regarding the psychopath.

It is interesting to an I-O psychologist to explore how this state has developed in the organization. It is particular useful to understand the human interactions—the group dynamics—at play. It seems clear from closer study of the evolution of discrepant views that the effort exerted by the psychopath to charm each victim is directly related to the perceived utility of that individual to the psychopath. This effort goes beyond ingratiating oneself with obviously powerful people in the organization; it includes lesser players whose utility is understood by the psychopath and used by him or her. Yet in all cases when an individual's utility dissipates, so does the psychopath's interest and charming veneer, resulting in feelings of confusion, humiliation, anger, and betrayal among his or her victims.

The Psychopathic Process Model

Based on the similarities observed in many cases like Dave's, it seems reasonable to suggest that the evolving discrepancies in the perceptions of the psychopaths by their coworkers are not random. Rather, they are actually the outcome of a predictable process of organizational manipulation on the part of the psychopath (Babiak, 1996a). The acting out of this process seems to satisfy some of their power and manipulation needs and ultimately results in career success.

It is characteristic of the psychopath to leave people with positive first impressions. However, over time, with continued daily interaction, some people come to figure out what the psychopath is really like. It might be expected that, given enough time, everyone would figure out the psychopath's game. According to the discrepant view model described earlier, all of the psychopath's supporters would become detractors. However, in the constantly changing organizations from which these cases were taken, this did not happen. When the organizational manipulation of the subjects was compared, five distinct career phases become apparent. These phases have been observed in virtually all subjects studied to date and are presented as a process model.

Phase 1: Organizational Entry

Psychopaths are able to join organizations more easily than one might expect because the barriers to organizational entry are no match for the psychopath's charm. There are several reasons for this inherent in the selection and hiring practices often used by even the most sophisticated of companies.

At best, the hiring process is an imperfect art. Many hiring decisions are still based on resumés, which can be easily faked, and unstructured interviews conducted by untrained or unprepared interviewers. Technical credentials are evaluated on the basis of education and experience listed on a resumé, which, as noted, may not be accurate. For example, Dave did not have a degree in the technical specialty listed on his resumé. In fact, this writer found three different degrees listed on different documents in his file, but no one at the company had noticed the inconsistencies.

All too often an accurate evaluation of a candidate's competence is confounded by the individual's ability to convince the interviewer that he or she knows what he or she is talking about — a skill easily demonstrated by psychopaths. Personal references listed on psychopaths' resumés would no doubt be selected from among their previous patrons and provide credible testimonials to the candidates' strengths and talents. Reference checks with prior employers are sometimes made to verify experience, but many major corporations, fearing litigation from past employees, will only verify salary and employment dates when contacted. Actual performance data are rarely made available. Security checks are not all that common for most jobs in industry. However, if done, the noninstitutionalized psychopath would not be expected to have much of a record.

Personality is an extremely important factor to consider when assessing job performance in work situations (Hogan, 1991), and the ability of the typical manager to assess personality based on an interview — despite personal beliefs of the hiring manager to the contrary — is limited. Integrity and personality tests are sometimes used by municipalities and large corporations where issues of public safety are relevant (Lowman, 1989), but the ability of a paper-and-pencil instrument to measure psychopathy has not been firmly demonstrated to date (Babiak, Hemphill, & Hare, 1999). More often, simply how well the candidate behaves interpersonally during the interview contributes heavily to the decision to hire — that is, the chemistry between interviewers and the candidate are taken as an indication of personality fit.

The selection dilemma is compounded by the changing role of the hiring process in organization development. Instead of replacing employees in kind, it is becoming increasingly more common for rapidly growing companies to hire people based on perceptions of their leadership potential. That is, individuals are hired for the next job or two up the corporate ladder, not necessarily the one for which they originally applied. Given a dynamic, charming veneer, a carefully constructed resumé, and a convincing communications style, it is easy to believe that a psychopathic candidate may have leadership potential, and it is a short generalization to include knowledge, skills, and abilities necessary to do the current job. For the psychopath, the *mask of sanity* (Cleckley, 1976) used to navigate through society is easily modified to a mask of *conscientiousness, intelligence, and interpersonal skill* — the three characteristics most often sought by organizations in new employees (Hogan & Hogan, 1989; Hogan, Hogan, & Busch, 1984).

Phase 2: Assessment

Once inside the organization, psychopaths begin a rapid process of identifying the key players, the interaction patterns among employees, and the culture of the organization. They quickly assess the utility of different organization members, identifying some as pawns and others as potential patrons. Utility is based both on organizational power (gauged by access to information and control of resources) and technical ability.

While conducting the utility assessment, the psychopath is establishing a network of personal, intense, and sometimes intimate relationships (as reported by some victims). This is almost always done through private one-on-one interactions. In the case of high-level power holders, they take advantage of their newness to the organization during the *honeymoon* period to gain access to executives by being naïve about the organization's culture, bypassing chain of command boundaries that others will not normally cross. Because of their ability to form positive, lasting first impressions, these brief encounters later form the basis for more extensive manipulation.

Phase 3: Manipulation

During this phase, psychopaths manipulate the established communication networks to collect and use information to their advantage while spreading disinformation to further their own career. In each case reviewed, without exception, the psychopath's association with the disinformation was effectively cloaked from coworkers.

Communication networks are manipulated to enhance the psychopath's own reputation with supporters, disparage others, and create conflicts and rivalries between organization members, thereby keeping them from sharing information that might uncover the deceit. During this phase, they consistently spend more time socializing face to face or on the phone with their targets, avoiding virtually all group meetings where this writer believes maintaining multiple facades may be too difficult. All of the subjects reported here stated that their work was too important to be interrupted by participation in meetings.

This manipulation, or game-playing, phase is where the psychopath enjoys playing the *puppet master* (R. D. Hare, personal communication, 1998), pulling strings from behind the scenes to create a work of organizational fiction. This fiction—the psychopath as ideal employee—includes the psychopath's own persona of loyalty and competence on which he or she can solicit and receive favors and rewards from power holders and support and adulation from useful followers. Pawns are used to reinforce perceptions of the psychopath's loyalty, and soul mates, who are secretly doing the psychopath's work, are used to demonstrate competence. People with power and influence become patrons, protecting the psychopath from detractors and ensuring a fruitful career.

Meanwhile, detractors and potential rivals are painted with quite negative attributes by the psychopath. These negative attributions are almost always done surreptitiously through spontaneous and opportunistic references to otherwise innocuous behaviors and personal characteristics. In and of themselves, each is harmless; over time, they paint a disparaging mental picture that can be invoked by the psychopath at any time to dispose of the rival or sway others against him or her when necessary. A typical interchange might run as follows: Al: "Here's the report you requested; sorry, it's a bit late. You know Ed, he is quite the detail-guy! It's good that we have people like Ed to make sure things are 'perfect,' as long as they don't get in the way of our ideas and slow things down. He had no changes by the way; he said everything was perfect." In this interchange, the psychopath, Al, has deflected any criticism for being late with the report, has invoked Ed's expertise in assessing it as perfect, and has laid the groundwork for bypassing Ed in the future.

The psychopath assures that others do not share information by creating distrust among coworkers where none in reality should exist. The most common ploy is to hint to one person that another person has said something uncomplimentary about them: "Bill, you wouldn't believe what Jack said about you. . . . I really don't want to say anything more; but he isn't your friend." Then the psychopath approaches Jack, saying, "You wouldn't believe what Bill said about you. . . . I really don't want to. . . ." Techniques such as this work best in environments where trust level is low anyway, as in organizations undergoing chaotic change.

Phase 4: Confrontation

It is during this phase that interpersonal violence and abuse comes to the surface and victims begin to realize that they have been victimized. The confrontation stems from two possible dynamics. First, some pawns begin to realize that the psychopath is deceitful, manipulative, and not pulling his or her own weight on the job; they begin to feel that they have been used or conned. Angered by this realization, they begin to challenge and sometimes confront the psychopath, only to realize that they have no recourse. Whatever special relationship these individuals thought they had dissolves, and they come to find that any complaints they might make to management or coworkers fall on deaf ears. They have been neutralized by the psychopath, who has already systematically poisoned the water with doubts about their competence, loyalty, and motives through the previously established influence networks.

When questioned about these realizations, organization members reported feeling humiliated, vulnerable, and completely surprised by the change in the psychopath's behavior. This is understandable because systematic neutralization is accomplished surreptitiously, often without the victims ever suspecting that they have had a rival in the psychopath.

A second form of confrontation occurs when the psychopath, who is constantly reassessing utility of individuals in his or her network, dispenses with a pawn. Pawns who were once useful to the psychopath are no longer so and therefore abandoned—in the social sense (the psychopath stops calling) and the psychological sense (the intimacy generated early on turns cold).

Because the psychopath creates a sense of a special relationship with those they find potentially useful, they engage their victim at a deeper emotional level than is common in business relationships. In a business world that is becoming increasingly more cold and dispassionate, these close, rare, and seemingly genuine relationships are valued greatly by coworkers. Therefore, when they end, the emotion felt is greater than normally expected. It follows that the more intense, humiliating, and complex their feelings of rejection, the less likely victims are to reveal their experiences to others.

It might be expected that the psychopath's game could be uncovered as the number of employees who observe and understand the lies, deceit, and manipulation increases, but this has not been observed in the cases to date. The manipulation skills of the psychopath are challenged, perhaps adding excitement to the psychopath's game, as he or she is constantly (and successfully) called on to manage the discrepant views of fellow employees. In some cases, chaotic change has acted like an ally to the psychopath as new organization members, unfamiliar with the psychopath, join the department or, as has happened in some of these cases, the psychopath was rotated out of the department into a new position as part of a management development plan.

Phase 5: Ascension

During the first four phases of the process, the psychopath has been creating and managing a network of powerful and useful individuals. During the ascension phase, the psychopath manipulates the whole power structure of the organization in his or her favor. The fifth phase is really the most insidious part of the psychopath's entire game. All along, high-power and high-status individuals—the patrons—have protected the psychopath from doubts and accusations from other organization members until they are betrayed. At this point, the patron falls from grace and either leaves the organization or is moved aside as the psychopath moves up the organization. The patron has now become the patsy.

The Victims (Individual and the Organization) and the Victor

It is usual during an organizational analysis to gather information about employees' frustrations with work, difficulties in interpersonal relationships, and lack of career success. These feelings are taken by the consultant as input about the culture and climate of the organization and often lead to the implementation of programs to improve the work environment. However, the employees in the companies in which psychopaths were identified reported a significantly greater number of negative emotional feelings than is normally encountered. The most frequently reported feelings were confusion mixed with disbelief and self-doubt over the changing relationship with the psychopath. Many individuals reported feeling shame for being conned ("He was such a liar; I knew he was a liar, but still I believed what he said. How could I have been such a fool?"). Several who had their careers derailed by the psychopath reported feelings of betrayal and humiliation; they expressed anger at the psychopath as well as frustration toward management for not seeing what was going on.

The most perplexing feeling expressed was one of abandonment mixed with relief. That is, some victims, after describing how they were betrayed, lied to, and used by the psychopath, described how, after the psychopath broke off relationships with them, they felt abandoned and wanted the psychopath back in their life. This inconsistency was perceived and readily identified by the individuals interviewed, yet discounted in their own descriptions by recounting the good times had with the psychopath. In particular, they had felt that they were an important part of the psychopath's life and missed playing that role. (Note: the term *psychopath* was never used — *liar, cheat, deceitful, unscrupulous person* were terms used by those interviewed.) The need for mental health intervention was evident in many individuals, and referrals to the company Employee Assistance Programs (EAPs) were made as appropriate.

The organization can also be viewed as a victim of psychopathic manipulation. From the I–O psychologists' perspective, manipulation, betrayal, conflict, and insecurity generated by the psychopath lead to a breakdown in teamwork, a decline in department morale, and a general disintegration of the work unit — the true course of which is usually out of the view of executives at the top of the organization. The cost of lowered productivity, decreased quality, lessened customer service, and loss of talented staff, for example, is difficult to track under ideal circumstances and extremely difficult to link to the activities of an individual who happens to be a psychopath. The lack of a clear link makes taking corrective action by management very difficult.

Yet in every case to date, the psychopath has enjoyed career success. Promotions, salary increases, and inclusion on the corporate succession plan have almost guaranteed that the psychopath will continue his or her game, draining the organization of resources and displacing rivals as needed. As new members join the organization or as the psychopath moves from one department to another, the psychopathic process is repeated. As of this writing, only one of those reported in Table 12.1 has left his or her job, leaving with an exceptionally large severance package — including a car — only to move to a competitor at a higher level position and at greater salary. By the time this writer lost track, he or she had lost over $1 million in business investments for the new employer, but was still successfully employed.

Chaos and Transitional Organizations

Why would a psychopath want to work in industry? This writer believes that jobs in management are extremely attractive to the psychopath for several reasons. On the surface, they involve the exertion of power and control over people and resources, often do not require involvement in detail work, and command greater salary than nonmanagement jobs. A leader's ability to get people to do things (e.g., to manipulate people through charisma) is often more important than his or her technical capabilities to perform work tasks. This makes it seem like leadership is an easy job, requiring little schooling and more reliance on innate people skills, which the psychopath believes he or she possesses.

In reality, there are a limited number of leadership jobs in traditional pyramid-shaped organizations, and it truly takes hard work to get them. In a traditional bureaucracy career, movement is slow and one has to perform one's job well before getting a promotion to the next level. There can be a large number of levels to pass through on the way to a higher paying management job. There are also a lot of organizational rules to be followed—far more than the prototypical psychopath cares to deal with. This process requires a greater ability to delay gratification than psychopaths are known to possess.

Then why is Dave still at his company and why was he promoted over Frank? This writer believes the answer lies in the changing nature of work and organizational life. Since the 1980s, in the United States and throughout the world, the pace of technological change has accelerated to such a degree that slow predictable organizational growth is no longer a viable option for business survival. To remain competitive, organizations need to become more fast paced, and the organization and its members need to adapt quickly and respond to changing environments. Old rules must be broken, management controls must loosen up, traditional organizational business designs must become more flexible, and leaders must take greater risk to stay ahead of the competition and stay in business.

One major problem inherent in this growing need to change is that most managers are resistant and even a little afraid of change. Due to the tendency to continue acting in comfortable ways, few managers have the experience necessary to effectively manage rapid change. Therefore, much of this change remains uncontrolled and ends up being chaotic. In a chaotically changing organization, rules seem to be broken indiscriminately and decisions are taken with little or no time for meaningful evaluation. The psychopath has no difficulty dealing with the consequences of rapid change; in fact, he or she thrives on it.

In addition to changing business and technological environments, the increasing frequency of mergers, acquisitions, and joint ventures, which often result in downsizing, uncontrolled rapid growth, and frequent reorganizations, has increased the potential exposure to psychopathic manipulation. These alternative, less rigid, less bureaucratic organizations, although poised to meet the challenges of an accelerated business world, are (unfortunately) much more attractive to psychopaths, more conducive to their lifestyle, and open up for them career opportunities not previously available in large businesses. In contrast to old-style bureaucratic organizations, these transitional organizations are characterized by unclear, unenforceable, or nonexistent work rules and policies, inadequate measurement systems, greater tolerance for controversial and perhaps even abusive behaviors, and highly vulnerable communication networks. When these are combined with the normal levels of job insecurity, personality clashes, and political battling (inherent in virtually every organization), this chaotic milieu provides an environment that is extremely inviting to the psychopath. Organizational chaos provides both the necessary stimulation for psychopathic thrill-seeking (Quay, 1965) and sufficient cover for psychopathic manipulation and abusive behavior.

The role of the organizational consultant is to "shine light on the dark side" of human behavior—through education, assessment, and guidance about psychopaths—so that senior executives can navigate their organizations through chaotic transitions without becoming vulnerable to psychopathic manipulation and its aftermath.

THE FUTURE

Recommendations

It is of the utmost importance that those consulting to organizations consider the possibility of psychopathy when traditional explanations of individual and group behavior do not explain observed dysfunction in the organization. Organizational symptoms to look for include (a) the evolution of discrepant views of an individual along the lines of demarcation noted earlier; (b) coworkers reporting feelings of abandonment, anger, betrayal, persecution, humiliation, and shame—intense emotions more often associated with intimate relationships with people in their personal life rather than with coworkers; (c) a severe drop in morale, productivity, and communication in the department where the individual works; (d) a chaotic internal business environment characterized by unclear or unenforced rules and regulations, rapid organizational change, and job insecurity; and (e) an overall culture lacking in trust and openness. Although none of these factors alone ensures that one is dealing with an industrial psychopath, together they raise the possibility based on observations to date. Individual symptoms would include the psychopathic characteristics as evaluated using Hare's Psychopathy Checklist (PCL) of the individual who seems to be at the center of the dysfunction. A careful assessment by trained evaluator(s) should be made before drawing conclusions.

Reading this chapter—not to mention this entire book—may leave executives and HR staff wondering whether their organizations would be helpless at the hands of an industrial psychopath. Some suggestions to the practitioner are in order: The first and best line of defense is the selection procedure used by the organization to screen job candidates. All critical items on the resumé should be independently validated, including education and other credentials. Interviewers should be well trained, use a structured interview format, and make the hiring decision jointly so that inconsistencies can be more readily identified. Ideally, interviews by non-departmental and human resources staff should be used to assess non-technical factors. When properly validated, personality testing would add strength to the selection effort. Candidates described as *too good to be true* are probably not, and follow-up interviews, scheduled after the interview team has met to do a preliminary evaluation, should be considered to validate initial impressions.

The second line of defense is a culture of openness and trust, especially when the company is undergoing intense, chaotic change. Often the perception of change is different at different levels within the company due to the amount of information possessed by individuals. Executives should consider sharing more information about the future, even with the caveat that it may not be the final word in the interest of maintaining the loyalty of employees. Secrecy and chaos are the ally of the psychopath because deceitful, manipulative behavior cannot be hidden for long in an environment of openly shared information. Changing a corporation's culture from closed and distrustful to open and honest is perhaps the most difficult challenge facing the executive. Because of the benefits associated with positive organizational cultures, there has been much research in this area, yet none published to date has considering the psychopath's role in fostering negative cultures.

Opportunities for Joint Research

The number of I–O psychologists studying psychopaths in industry is relatively small (e.g., Babiak, 1995a, 1995b; Gustafson & Ritzer, 1995). In the I–O field, the inclusion of personality variables as part of the research on human resources selection processes has grown since the early 1970s (see Hogan, 1991). The focus has been on critical public safety professions such as police, firefighter, and nuclear power plant operator (Lowman, 1989), where the link between personality (and personality disorders) and performance is more clear. In recent years, it has become more acceptable to suggest that personality has an effect on how people in other professions perform on the job. Much of the research has focused on the effects of integrity (Sackett & Harris, 1984) and conscientiousness (Hogan & Hogan, 1989; Hogan, Hogan, & Busch, 1984) on performance.

There have also been some discussions of the effect of personality disorders, primarily narcissism, on executive performance (Hogan, Raskin, & Fazzini, 1990; Kernberg, 1979; Kets de Vries & Miller, 1984, 1985). Those high on narcissism are often seen as possessing leadership capabilities and are more often chosen for those roles than others. Because narcissism is an easily accepted trait of successful business leaders, and acute narcissism is an easy explanation for tough, aggressive behavior, this writer believes that individuals who are really psychopaths are often mistaken by their peers for narcissists and chosen by the organizations for promotion into leadership positions (Babiak, 1996b, 1998). Unfortunately, to the degree that psychopathic manipulation looks like narcissistic ambition, it is welcomed in the organization.

Clearly in this emerging field, there are many opportunities for the I–O psychologist and the psychiatrist or clinical psychologist to team up in research endeavors. Unfortunately, many business people have little interest in researching the psychological issues of their employees, especially when they include clinical concepts. The benefits of the research to the organization, plus adequate assurance of confidentiality and anonymity for the company and its employees, need to be clearly communicated to garner support for any research effort. The ability of the I–O psychologist to speak the language of the business executive can be a valuable asset.

Some topics of interest to I–O psychologists would include:

1. Research on the personality–performance relationship, specifically regarding the personality disorders. Are psychopaths really poor performers? Can (and should) organizations avoid hiring them?
2. Research on the effectiveness of different selection procedures designed to screen out psychopathic job candidates. Should structured interviews or testing be part of the hiring process? How effective are they in identifying psychopathic tendencies?
3. Research on the long-term impact on coworkers—the victims of psychopathic manipulation. Several people lost their jobs in the cases reviewed, and many were personally distraught by their han-

dling by the psychopath. How is their future performance affected by their experience? How does it impact their personal life?

4. Research on the effectiveness of EAPs to address issues arising from psychopathic victimization. Despite referring employees to company EAPs, this writer is somewhat doubtful that the programs were equipped to handle such issues. What protocols could be developed to assist them?

There are certainly many other research questions that would interest psychologists and psychiatrists of all types. By teaming up the strengths of several psychological disciplines, a cohesive research program can potentially add considerable knowledge to the field and have applications useful to business and society. Because of our understanding of the true nature of the psychopath, it behooves all of us to make this a reality by inviting colleagues to join our efforts.

SUMMARY

It is commonly accepted that psychopaths are neither interested in nor capable of successfully working in a large corporation. Their low tolerance for frustration and excessive need for stimulation would dissuade them from seeking employment in traditional bureaucratic organizations, defined by policies and control systems and characterized by boring, routine task requirements. Furthermore, much of the success of psychopaths in society is attributed to their ability to change venue often to evade apprehension — a characteristic not conducive with a long-term career in a corporation.

It is becoming more clear that some industrial organizations — those in the midst of rapid growth or chaotic change — not only attract psychopaths but provide an environment in which they can experience career success, all without the need to correct or change their psychopathic behavioral tendencies. Corporate downsizing, rapid growth, frequent reorganizations, mergers, acquisitions, and joint ventures offer increased opportunities for employment for individuals with psychopathic personalities.

Having now followed this phenomena in a large number of organizations over the course of several years, it seems prudent to suggest that (a) the discrepancy in the perception of psychopaths in organizations is actually the outcome of a predictable process of organizational manipulation on the part of the psychopath; (b) the effort exerted by the psychopath to charm his victim is directly related to the perceived utility of that individual to the psychopath; (c) this effort goes beyond ingratiating oneself with obviously powerful people in the organization (it includes lesser players who have utility not so obvious to the casual observer); (d) psychopathic characteristics such as interpersonal charm, cool/detached decision making, and need for stimulation are easily mistaken for leadership traits such as charisma, decisiveness, and extroversion; and (e) career success is made easier for the psychopath by the chaotic state of the organization in which he or she operates. This chaos allows psychopaths in industry, as well as in some governments, to use their manipulation skill to build relationships with powerful and useful individuals in their organization, to effectively manage the discrepant views of their supporters and detractors, and to systematically betray their way into increasingly more powerful positions of leadership.

An awareness of the possibility of the existence of a psychopath in organizations is necessary for the organizational consultant, HR manager, and executive, but it is not sufficient to protect oneself and the organization. It is commonly known that experts in the field of psychopathy can also be caught off guard by psychopaths. When plagued by doubts, it is recommended that the individual distance him or herself as much as possible from the possible psychopath and seek guidance and support from someone outside of the work environment—preferably a mental health professional, but also, if potential criminal behavior is involved, the appropriate authorities.

Finally, it is important for researchers and practitioners in the field of psychopathy to help increase the awareness of business leaders of the potential harm to their organizations from psychopaths and win their support for joint research, which can benefit not only their own company, but society's understanding of these invisible human predators (Hare, 1993).

REFERENCES

American Psychiatric Association. (1994). *Diagnostic and statistical manual of mental disorders* (4th ed.). Washington, DC: Author.

Babiak, P. (1995a). When psychopaths go to work: A case study of an industrial psychopath. *Applied Psychology: An International Review, 44*, 171–188.

Babiak, P. (1995b, December). *Psychopathic manipulation in organizations: Pawns, patrons, and patsies.* Paper presented at the NATO Advanced Study Institute, Psychopathy: Theory, Research, and Implications for Society, Alvor, Portugal.

Babiak, P. (1996a, April). Industrial psychopaths: Organizational manipulation and career success. In P. Babiak (Chair), *Shining light on the dark side: Psychopaths in organizations.* Symposium conducted at the 11th annual conference of the Society for Industrial and Organizational Psychology, San Diego, CA.

Babiak, P. (1996b, September). *Psychopathic personalities in organizations.* Paper presented at the Metropolitan New York Association for Applied Psychology, New York, NY.

Babiak, P. (1998, July). *Psychopaths in the organization: Some thoughts for the HR professional.* Paper presented at the Society for Human Resource Management, Western Connecticut Chapter, Danbury, CT.

Babiak, P., Hemphill, J., & Hare, R. D. (1999, May). Help Wanted: Psychopaths Please Apply. In P. Babiak (Chair) *Liars of the dark side: Can personality interfere with personality measurement?* Symposium conducted at the fourteenth annual conference of the Society for Industrial and Organizational Psychology, Atlanta, GA.

Cleckley, H. M. (1976). *The mask of sanity* (5th ed.). St. Louis, MO: Mosby.

Doren, D. (1987). *Understanding and treating the psychopath.* New York: Wiley.

Fulero, S. M. (1995). Review of the Hare Psychopathy Checklist–Revised. In J. C. Conoley & J. C. Impara (Eds.), *Twelfth mental measurements yearbook* (pp. 453–454). Lincoln, NE: Buros Institute.

Gustafson, S. B., & Ritzer, D. R. (1995). The dark side of normal: A psychopathy-linked pattern called aberrant self-promotion. *European Journal of Personality, 9*, 147–183.

Hare, R. D. (1985). *The Psychopathy Checklist.* Unpublished manuscript, University of British Columbia, Vancouver, Canada.

Hare, R. D. (1986). Twenty years of experience with the Cleckley psychopath. In W. H. Reid, D. Dorr, J. I. Walker, & J. W. Bonner III (Eds.), *Unmasking the psychopath* (pp. 3–27). New York: Norton.

Hare, R. D. (1991a). *The Hare Psychopathy Checklist–Revised manual.* Toronto, Canada: Multi-Health Systems.

Hare, R. D. (1991b). *The Hare PCL–R: Rating book.* Toronto, Canada: Multi-Health Systems.

Hare, R. D. (1993). *Without conscience: The disturbing world of the psychopaths among us.* New York: Simon & Schuster.

Hare, R. D., Harpur, T. J., Hakstian, A. R., Forth, A. E., Hart, S. D., & Newman, J. P. (1990). The revised psychopathy checklist: Reliability, and factor structure. *Psychological Assessment: A Journal of Consulting and Clinical Psychology, 2*, 338–341.

Hare, R. D., Hart, S. D., & Cox, D. N. (1995). *Manual for the screening version of the Hare Psychopathy Checklist–Revised (PCL: SV).* Toronto, Canada: Multi-Health Systems.

Harpur, T. J., Hakstian, A. R., & Hare, R. D. (1988). Factor structure of the psychopathy checklist. *Journal of Consulting and Clinical Psychology, 56*, 741–747.

Harpur, T. J., & Hare, R. D. (1991, August). *Psychopathy and violent behavior: Two factors are better than one.* Paper presented at the meeting of the American Psychological Association, San Francisco, CA.

Harpur, T. J., Hare, R. D., & Hakstian, A. R. (1989). Two-factor conceptualization of psychopathy: Construct validity and assessment implications. *Psychological Assessment: A Journal of Consulting and Clinical Psychology, 1*, 6–17.

Hogan, J., & Hogan, R. (1989). How to measure employee reliability. *Journal of Applied Psychology, 74*, 273–279.

Hogan, R. (1991). Personality and personality measurement. In M. D. Dunnette & L. M. Hough (Eds.), *Handbook of industrial and organizational psychology* (pp. 873–919). Palo Alto, CA: Consulting Psychologists Press.

Hogan, R., Hogan, J., & Busch, C. (1984). How to measure service orientation. *Journal of Applied Psychology, 69*, 157–163.

Hogan, R., Raskin, R., & Fazzini, D. (1990). The dark side of charisma. In K. E. Clark & M. B. Clark (Eds.), *Measures of leadership* (pp. 343–354). West Orange, NJ: Leadership Library of America.

Kernberg, O. (1979). Regression in organizational leadership. *Psychiatry, 42*, 29–39.

Kets de Vries, M. F. R., & Miller, D. (1984). *The neurotic organization: Diagnosing and changing counterproductive styles of management.* San Francisco: Jossey-Bass.

Kets de Vries, M. F. R., & Miller, D. (1985). Narcissism and leadership: An object relations perspective. *Human Relations, 38*(6), 583–601.

Levenson, M. R., Kiehl, K. A., & Fitzpatrick, C. M. (1995). Assessing psychopathic attributes in a noninstitutionalized population. *Journal of Personality and Social Psychology, 68,* 151–158.

Lowman, R. (1989). *Pre-employment screen for psychopathology: A guide to professional practice.* Sarasota: Professional Resource Exchange.

Person, E. S. (1986). Manipulativeness in entrepreneurs and psychopaths. In W. H. Reid, D. Dorr, J. I. Walker, & J. W. Bonner (Eds.), *Unmasking the psychopath: Antisocial personality and related syndromes* (pp. 256–274). New York: Norton.

Quay, H. C. (1965). Psychopathic personality as pathological stimulation seeking. *American Journal of Psychiatry, 122,* 180–183.

Sackett, P. R., & Harris, M. M. (1984). Honesty testing for personnel selection: A review and critique. *Personnel Psychology, 37,* 221–245.

Widom, C. S. (1977). A methodology for studying non-institutionalized psychopaths. *Journal of Counseling and Clinical Psychology, 45,* 674–683.

13

The Incarcerated Psychopath in Psychiatric Treatment: Management or Treatment?

Myla H. Young
Jerald V. Justice
*California Department of Mental Health Psychiatric Program,
Vacaville*

Philip S. Erdberg
Private Practice, Corte Madera, California

Carl B. Gacono
Private Practice, Austin, Texas

Like many states, California's prison population has grown. Over the past decade (1988–1998), the number of California inmates has increased from approximately 70,000 to over 150,000 (Department of Corrections, 1998). Although causal factors such as a rise in young males, increasing social stratification, the breakdown of the traditional family, inadequate societal constraints, and ineffective consequences for criminal behavior have been linked to this expansion (Toch & Adams, 1994), the decline in societal tolerance for criminal behavior has resulted in more offenders being sentenced to prison for longer periods of time.

The number of mentally ill inmates has also increased. Obtaining a true estimate of mental illness among offenders has been confounded by the lack of agreement as to what constitutes *mental illness* (Monahan, 1992). Some studies have expanded inclusion criteria beyond functional psychosis or organic impairment to include substance abuse and personality disorders. For studies that excluded substance abuse disorders and personality disorders, estimates of mental illness have ranged from 10% to 50% (Guy, Platt, Zwerling, & Bullock, 1985; Steadman, Holohean, & Dvoskin, 1991; Teplin, 1994).[1] Although actual estimates for their numbers vary (Monahan, 1992), the disproportional number of incarcerated individuals who suffer from some form of major mental illness has been a source of concern for correctional and forensic health workers (Guy et al., 1985; Steadman et al., 1991; Teplin, 1994).

Complex diagnostic issues become further confused within the forensic psychiatric setting (Marques, Haynes, & Nelson, 1993). More often than not, forensic patients have carried multiple diagnoses. The typical forensic patient may meet the criteria for schizophrenia, substance abuse, and antisocial personality disorder (ASPD; Gacono, Meloy, Sheppard, Speth, & Roske, 1995; Nedopil, Hollweg, Hartmann, & Jaser, 1995; Stalenheim & Von Knorring, 1996). These multiple and dually diagnosed patients, and particularly psychopathic schizophrenics, have continued to present correctional and psychiatric staff with unique management and treatment considerations (Gacono & Meloy, 1994). The purpose of the present chapter is to psychometrically map with assessment methods the characteristics of these patients and to provide the reader with management and treatment recommendations based on these data.

THE ANTISOCIAL SCHIZOPHRENIC

Clinical and empirical differences (Gacono & Meloy, 1994) have been noted among psychotic patients with and without concurrent personality disorders, such as ASPD (*Diagnostic and Statistical Manual of Mental Disorders, 4th ed.* [*DSM–IV*]; American Psychiatric Association, 1994). In general, the nonpersonality-disordered schizophrenic patient has responded to medical and psychosocial interventions such as psychosocial rehabilitation models. The clinician's associated countertransference has usually been positive (Gacono, Nieberding, Owen, Rubel, & Bodholdt, 2001). Violent incidents in these patients were likely to be affective in nature—that is, not planned but motivated by emotions such as fear (Meloy, 1988). However, the dually diagnosed (ASPD–schizophrenic) patient has offered a different clinical presentation. As a disorganized ASPD schizophrenic, the patient experiences increased personality organization through psychopharmacological intervention; patterns of conning and manipulation may also become apparent. The guarded character pathology of the APSD paranoid schizophrenic may regulate a superficial adjustment that masks the severity of the underlying psychosis. A certain malevolence may remain in the stabilized ASPD bipolar patient. Whereas affective violence has been noted in the nonpersonality-disordered psychotic patient, planned and organized violence (Meloy, 1988) has been initiated by these latter patients.

These dually diagnosed patients have perplexed clinicians and confounded treatment interventions. Historically, clinical confusion was compounded by diagnostic nomenclature. The *DSM–III* (American Psychiatric Association, 1980) disallowed a concurrent diagnosis of schizophrenia and ASPD. Although this demarcation attempted to increase diagnostic clarity, it further confused clinical understanding and led to interventions that focused on Axis I psychopathology while ignoring the concurrent characterological issues. Fortunately, this attempt to bring clarity to the interface between a biochemical disorder of the brain and severe character pathology was abandoned seven years later in *DSM–III–R* (American Psychiatric Association, 1987), which allowed for the dual diagnosis of schizophrenia and ASPD. This trend was continued in *DSM–IV* (American Psychiatric Association, 1994) for those patients where "the occurrence of antisocial behavior is [was] not exclusively during the course of Schizophrenia or a Manic Episode" (American Psychiatric Association, 1994, p. 650).[2]

PSYCHOPATHY AND MENTAL DISORDER

The mentally ill patient with concurrent psychopathy has presented an even more difficult management or arduous treatment challenge than the nonpsychopathic ASPD mentally ill patient. Attempts at either management or treatment with all ASPD patients should: (a) occur only after careful assessment (Gacono, 1998), (b) utilize approaches with proven efficacy, and (c) be conducted in settings that ensure the safety of the clinician and other patients. With the psychotic, psychopathic patient, stabilizing the psychosis while managing (therapeutic containment) the severe character pathology may be the preferred clinical model (Gacono & Meloy, 1994; Gacono et al., 2001).

As suggested (Hare, 1991) by the mean Psychopathy Checklist–Revised (PCL–R) scores for forensic psychiatric patients ($N = 440$; $M = 20.6$, $SD = 7.8$), base rates for psychopathy in forensic psychiatric settings (10%–15%; Hare, 1991) are lower than in nonpsychiatric prison populations ($N = 1,192$, $M = 23.6$, $SD = 7.9$; 50%–80%; Hare, 1991). However, this does not minimize the importance of assessing and understanding psychopathy in those settings (see chap. 7). In fact, in some cases, the negative impact of the psychotic psychopath within less secure hospital settings has been even more disruptive than in prison settings (Gacono et al., 1995), where staff are constantly attuned to criminality and the potential for violence. Staff from hospital settings may also have experienced positive identifications with nonpsychopathic schizophrenic patients. Hospital settings often do not prepare staff for managing dually diagnosed patients. Rather, training in these settings encourages a care-taking role— a sure template for potential victimization. One must always keep empirical findings at the forefront of intervention. One 10-year outcome study from a forensic psychiatric facility found higher rates of violent reoffense in treated psychopaths when compared with untreated psychopaths (Rice, Harris, & Cormier, 1992). Both groups included schizophrenics.

Fortunately, the use of the Psychopathy Checklists (PCL–R, Hare, 1991; PCL:SV, Hart, Cox, & Hare, 1995) has been extended to forensic psychiatric populations (Hart & Hare, 1989). Psychiatric staff have correctly used the checklists in screening out inappropriate admissions, making placement decisions, and assessing treatability and risk. Within forensic psychiatric settings, psychopathy level has been associated with the presence of concurrent substance abuse and personality disorder diagnosis (Nedopil, Hollweg, Hartmann, & Jaser, 1995; Stalenheim & Von Knorring, 1996), various forms of aggression (Heilbrun, Hart, Hare, Gustafson, Nunez, & White, 1998; Hill, Rogers, & Bickford, 1996), a wide range of institutional misbehaviors (Gacono et al., 1995; Gacono, Meloy, Speth, & Roske, 1997; Heilbrun et al., 1998; Pham, Remy, Dailliet, & Lienard, 1998), treatment noncompliance and failure (Hill et al., 1996; Quinsey et al., 1998; Rice, Harris, & Cormier, 1992), malingering (Gacono et al., 1995), escape behavior (Gacono et al., 1997), and violence (Heilbrun et al., 1998; Quinsey et al., 1998; Young, Justice, & Erdberg, 1999).

MANAGEMENT OR TREATMENT?

Although managing the mentally ill psychopath has presented a clinical challenge, treating the mentally ill psychopath has been even more challenging. Psychopaths have placed a significant burden on any treatment setting (Gacono et al., 1995, 1997; Heilbrun et al., 1998; Pham et al., 1998). In their study of 218 male mentally disordered offenders, Heilbrun et al. (1998) found significant correlations between PCL–R scores and nonphysical and physical aggression, seclusion, and restraint time during the first 2 months of hospitalization. Gacono et al. (1995) found that insanity malingerers, who were all psychopaths (PCL–R $\geq$ 30, M = 34.9, SD = 1.8), were significantly more likely to be involved in institutional violence (18:3), to sell drugs (8:0), and to be sexually involved with female staff (7:0) than a comparison group of insanity acquittees who had not malingered (PCL–R = 19.4, SD = 9.9).

Even when provided, the effectiveness of treatment in reducing violent recidivism among psychopaths has remained, at best, questionable. For example, Harris, Rice, and Quinsey (1993) studied the impact of treatment on mentally disordered patients remanded to Oak Ridge (a forensic psychiatric facility). They found that 10 years after institutional release, violent recidivism rates were high for all patients (40%), regardless of whether they received psychiatric treatment. Treated psychopaths had significantly greater rates of violent recidivism than their untreated counterparts, whereas the reverse was true for the nonpsychopaths. Harris et al. (1993) suggested that the therapeutic community had raised psychopaths' self-esteem, raised their aggression levels, and provided them with more information about ways to commit crimes without being caught. The nonpsychopaths in the program likely learned to be more empathic, whereas the psychopathic patients learned how to be better psychopaths.

THE VACAVILLE PSYCHIATRIC PROGRAM

Despite the difficulties in treating the mentally ill offender, institutional and postrelease treatment have historically been legally mandated (Meloy, Haroun, & Schiller, 1990). One program that provides treatment to mentally ill male inmates is the California Department of Mental Health Program at Vacaville, California (the Vacaville Psychiatric Program [VPP]). The VPP is a psychiatric treatment program located within a large state prison. Implemented in 1988, the VPP consists of 150 acute and 60 subacute treatment beds (N = 210 treatment beds). The VPP provides mental health services to acutely mentally ill inmates in the California Department of Corrections.

Program referrals originate from 25 prisons throughout California. The VPP is designed to treat inmates who experience a major mental disorder. Admission criteria include: (a) presence of a major Axis I mental illness in an acute phase, (b) at risk for self-harm, or (c) in need of evaluation to determine the presence of a mental disorder. Although all of the inmates meet admission criteria, 18% are discharged without a diagnosis of a major mental disorder. Assessment and treatment services utilize an interdisciplinary treatment team model, maintaining a full-time staff of psychiatrists, psychologists, psychiatric social workers, and rehabilitation therapists, in addition to a comprehensive nursing staff of registered nurses, licensed vocational nurses, and medical technical assistants.

The VPP's primary goals are to (a) provide a comprehensive mental health assessment, (b) provide treatment interventions sufficient to alleviate the acuity of the disorder, and (c) prepare the inmate patient for postrelease mental health treatment services. Given the chronicity of the population, more than a third require longer term hospitalization than is available (VPP's mean length of stay is 85 days). These refractory patients are referred to a forensic psychiatric hospital for longer term hospitalization (see Marques et al., 1993).

The VPP also maintains an Office of Program Review that conducts research designed to evaluate its treatment programs. Sociodemographic, psychiatric, neuropsychological, and emotional/personality dimensions (including psychopathy level) are routinely assessed. The findings from one study (N = 131) are summarized in the following section of this chapter, with a particular emphasis on psychopathy as a factor in understanding the psychopathology of VPP patients ($N = 118$).

Demographics

Age and Ethnicity. All inmates were male. They were relatively young, mostly unmarried, and undereducated. Their mean age was 33 (range = 19–65 years). Sixty percent were single, 22% divorced, and 18% married. Educational level ranged from third grade to college completion ($M = 10$ years). The racial distribution reflected that of the larger prison population, being weighted toward the minorities. White (36%) and African-American (36%) inmates comprised the largest racial categories, followed by Latino (23%) and *others* (5%; Asian, Native American). Socioeconomic status (SES) was assessed with a two-factor scale (education and employment; Meyers & Bean, 1968) consisting of five levels. One hundred percent of the population ranked in the lower two levels, with 61% clustered in the lowest level.

Previous Psychiatric Treatment. Sixty-two percent of the inmates received previous psychiatric treatment. Twenty-four percent of the inmates reported more than one type of neurological injury. Twenty-seven percent had experienced a head trauma resulting in loss of consciousness; 8% reported having experienced at least one seizure. Ninety-one percent acknowledged illicit drug use, and 83% reported severe polysubstance abuse. Slightly more than 40% reported a loss of consciousness for at least 30 minutes as a result of some type of illicit drug use.

Diagnosis. Most patients had a *DSM* Axis I major mental disorder or were dually diagnosed. Personality disorders, in the absence of a major mental illness, do not qualify for admission.[3] Admitting diagnoses were psychotic (47%), mood disorders (21%), organic diagnoses (14%), or other (18%). Most diagnoses in this latter category were adjustment disorders or malingering. As expected, most of the patients were prescribed psychotropic medications (primarily antipsychotics and antidepressants). Personality disorder diagnoses were divided among Cluster B (69%; antisocial, borderline, narcissistic), Cluster C (19%; dependent, personality disorder NOS), and Cluster A (6%; paranoid, schizoid, schizotypal).

Violence. Violence was prevalent in the VPP population. Seventy-one percent of these patients had committed at least one act of violence that involved a physical attack producing injury or death to a victim(s). When violence histories were categorized as either *high* (two or more offenses involving physical injury or one offense that included murder) or *low* (one or less instances of physical harm to others), 63% met the criteria for high violence. Even after incarceration, violence continued as 85% received a disciplinary action for violent behavior in prison. Psychopathic patients (PCL–R ≥ 30) were 6.6 times more likely to have histories of high violence than those who were not psychopathic (PCL–R < 30).

COMPARING VPP PSYCHOPATHS AND NONPSYCHOPATHS

To better understand the relationship between psychopathy level and the functioning of the VPP patients, we examined a random sample of 118 patients. All patients signed an informed consent and participated in a comprehensive psychometric evaluation, including a psychological/neuropsychological evaluation, record reviews, semistructured clinical interview, and neuropsychological and emotional/personality testing. Record reviews included review of correctional, medical, and psychiatric records. Semistructured clinical interviews recorded developmental, psychiatric, social, educational, work, relationship, drug, and forensic histories. Neuropsychological testing included these tests: Finger Tapping, Seashore Rhythm, Speech Sounds Perception, Trail Making A and B, Tactual Performance Test, Aphasia Test, Category Test, the WAIS–R Vocabulary and Block Design subscales, and Ravens Colored Progressive Matrices. Emotional/personality testing included the Rorschach Test, Minnesota Multiphasic Personality Inventory–II (MMPI-2), and PCL–R.

The following section compares the cognitive and personality functioning of psychopathic (PCL–R ≥ 30) and nonpsychopathic patients (PCL–R < 30) and uses these findings to suggest management and treatment strategies.

Demographic and Diagnostic Characteristics

All patients were young, poorly educated, from lower SES groups (SES = IV and V = 100%), and predominantly single (see Table 13.1). Consistent with their greater prevalence in the larger prison population, non-White patients (African American, Latino, Other) were significantly more likely to score within the high range of psychopathy.

ASPD and Psychopathy. Table 13.2 presented the PCL–R score distributions for this sample. Thirty-six percent scored in a low range (PCL–R = 0–19), 35% in a moderate range (PCL–R = 20–29), and 29% in the psychopathic range (PCL–R ≥ 30). Although consistent with the elevated histories of violence and the high security level of the institution,

TABLE 13.1
Demographic Data for Psychopathic and Nonpsychopathic VPP Inmate/Patients

Demographic	PCL–R ≥ 30 (N = 32)				PCL–R < 30 (N = 86)			
	N	M	SD	%	N	M	SD	%
Educational level	–	9.3	2.0	–	–	10.6	2.2	–
Ethnicity*								
White	10	–	–	31	39	–	–	46
African American	12	–	–	38	24	–	–	28
Latino	7	–	–	22	16	–	–	19
Other	3	–	–	9	6	–	–	7
Martial status								
Single	19	–	–	61	57	–	–	67
Married/widowed	6	–	–	19	8	–	–	9
Separated/divorced	7	–	–	20	21	–	–	24

Note. High PCL–R scores were more likely to be non-White.
*p < .01.

TABLE 13.2
PCL–R Total Scores for VPP Inmate/Patients

Classification	n	Range	%
PCL–R 0–19	43	5–19	36
PCL–R 20–29	41	20–29	35
PCL–R ≥ 30	34	30–39	29
Total	118	5–39	100

the high frequency of psychopathy is atypical for a forensic psychiatric population. Twenty-nine percent of this sample was psychopathic, whereas a frequency of 12% to 15% has been previously reported in forensic psychiatric samples (Hare, 1991).

Additionally, 69% of the sample met criteria for ASPD. The majority of VPP ASPD patients produced PCL–R scores ≥ 30 (74%) and would be classified as psychopaths. When compared with nonpsychopathic ASPDs (NP-ASPDs), psychopathic ASPDs (P-ASPDs) tended to:

1. Have higher IQs (P-ASPDs: Mean IQ = 82; NP-ASPDs: Mean IQ = 78)
2. Evidence better, although impaired, performance across all neuropsychological tests
3. Have been more violent in the community
4. Have more prison disciplinary actions (both serious and administrative)

5. Not have a consistent problem solving style (Rorschach Ambitent Style)
6. Be less likely to produce evidence of cognitive slippage on the Rorschach
7. Be more likely to provide Rorschach responses suggesting unmodulated emotionality (CF > FC + C)
8. Be more interpersonally maladjusted (Rorschach- Less T; more PER and Fr).

Although these measures all showed significant trends, only community violence and frequency of disciplinary offenses statistically differentiated the psychopathic ASPDs from the nonpsychopathic ASPDs (see Table 13.4).

Drug abuse was quite prevalent. Ninety-one percent of the patients had diagnosable substance abuse disorders and 83% reported polysubstance abuse. Although most patients preferred alcohol and/or marijuana, psychopaths preferred other drugs. They were significantly more likely to prefer opiates, cocaine, amphetamines, hallucinogens, or inhalants than alcohol and/or marijuana ($p < .05$). Psychopaths were also significantly more likely ($p < .01$) to start their drug use at a younger age ($M = 11.2$ years).

Eighty-three percent of nonpsychopathic patients were discharged with an Axis I major mental disorder. For the group of psychopathic patients, however, 56% were diagnosed with an Axis I major mental disorder and 44% were discharged without a major mental disorder. Although this finding may provide some concurrent support for the association between psychopathy and malingering in forensic psychiatric facilities (Gacono et al., 1995), it assuredly encourages careful screening for psychopathy. The use of the PCL:SV (Hart et al., 1995) when evaluating potential program candidates could reduce inappropriate admissions, thereby saving time and money (see chap. 7).

TABLE 13.3
Axis I Diagnosis for Psychopathic and Nonpsychopathic VPP Inmate/Patients

	PCL–R ≥ 30 (N = 32)		PCL–R < 30 (N = 86)	
Diagnosis	n	%	n	%
Axis I Diagnosis				
Psychotic	9	28	36	43
Mood	6	19	23	27
Organic	3	9	11	13
No diagnosis*	14	44	16	19

*No Diagnosis, Diagnosis Deferred, Diagnosis Unknown, Malingering, and Adjustment Disorder. Psychopaths were less likely to receive an Axis I diagnosis, $p < .001$.

Sixty-three percent of all patients' histories were classified within a high range of violence. Although violence histories were high for all patients, it was significantly greater for the psychopaths ($p < .001$; as noted in Table 13.4). Eighty-one percent were classified as highly violent. Psychopaths began their criminal histories at a young age, committed increasingly violent crimes, were incarcerated for highly violent offenses, and continued a pattern of violence after incarceration. Also of interest, psychopathic inmates were significantly more likely to have been placed in a juvenile state prison (61%; $p < .05$) than were nonpsychopathic patients.

A summary of the differences between psychopathic and nonpsychopathic patients indicated that psychopaths were:

1. Ten times more likely to have used drugs at a younger age,
2. Ten times more likely not to have an Axis I major mental disorder, despite being treated in an acute psychiatric facility,
3. Seven times more likely to have histories of severe violence in the community,
4. Eight times more likely to continue to be assaultive in prison,
5. Four times more likely to use drugs other than alcohol or marijuana most and five times more likely to have preferred drugs other than alcohol or marijuana,
6. Four times more likely to be non-White,
7. Three times more likely to have been placed in a state juvenile prison.

TABLE 13.4
Violence Level for Psychopathic and Nonpsychopathic VPP Inmate/Patients

	PCL–R ≥ 30 (N = 32)		PCL–R < 30 (N = 86)	
Violence	N	%	N	%
Greatest violent offense				
1–Nonviolent	1	3	1	1
2–Ambiguous violence	0	0	1	1
3–Property crimes	1	3	10	12
4–Threats to person	1	3	20	24
5–Physical attack	18	56	32	38
6–Loss of life	7	22	8	9
7–Loss of life with extreme violence	4	13	13	15
Unknown	4	13	1	1
Lifetime violence rating*				
High	26	81	43	50
Low	6	19	42	49
Not available	0	0	1	1

*$p < .001$; High PCL–R scorers produced the highest levels of violence.

TABLE 13.5
Incident Reports for Psychopathic and Nonpsychopathic VPP Inmate/Patients

	PCL–R ≥ 30 (N = 32)			PCL–R < 30 (N = 86)			
Type of Prison Offense	n	M	SD	n	M	SD	p
Administrative offenses (nonassault)	29	13.8	15.4	74	4.5	14.0	.30
Serious offenses	29	7.9	9.9	76	2.2	4.2	.001
Total offenses*	31	20.4	22.2	75	6.6	12.4	.15

*Psychopaths (97%) were more likely than nonpsychopaths (70%) to have received CDC 115 incident reports ($p < .002$).

Neuropsychological Characteristics of VPP Patients

On average, the VPP patients had low to average intellectual abilities and mild to moderate neuropsychological impairment. Using demographically corrected normative standards and considering impairment as one standard deviation below the mean, the performance for all patients was remarkably low, but psychopaths were significantly more impaired on tasks of attention ($p < .05$) and reading ($p < .001$) than nonpsychopathic patients. The average reading grade equivalent for nonpsychopaths and psychopaths was 11th grade and 8th grade, respectively.

Selected Rorschach Measures

Table 13.6 presents Rorschach variables and ratios associated with personality style (EB, Lambda), control and stress (D, Adj D), ideation (X+%, F+%, Xu%, X-%, Sum Special Scores, Level 2 Special Scores, Populars, DV), interpersonal relationships (Sum T, Cooperative, Aggressive, Morbid, Space, Personal, Egocentricity, Reflection), and Affect (FC, CF, C). Not surprisingly, the Rorschach data from these patients were significantly different from those expected in nonpatients (Exner, 1995). Consistent with other clinical samples, our patients were predominately ambient (i.e., they lack a definitive problem-solving style). Predominately high-Lambda subjects, these patients could be characterized as concrete and simplistic thinkers. Surprisingly, only a fourth of each group evidenced poor controls (AdjD < 0). However, this finding can only be accurately interpreted within the context of their psychological resources (EA; Gacono & Meloy, 1994). Unconventional thinking (Xu% > 20) and poor reality testing abounds (X-% > 15). Interpersonal deficits included a lack of bonding capacity (Sum-T); consistent with their histories of real-world aggression, there was an egosyntonic relationship to aggression (elevated Ag = 0; Gacono & Meloy, 1994).

Variable	PCL–R ≥ 30 (N = 32) %	PCL–R < 30 (N = 86) %
Personality		
Introversion	29	33
Ambitent	52	49
Extratensive	19	18
Lambda > .99	49	61
Control and stress		
D Score > 0	23	13
D Score = 0	45	57
D Score < 0	32	30
Adj D Score > 0	25	18
Adj D Score = 0	52	63
Adj D Score < 0	23	19
Ideation		
Dd > 3*	17	41
X+% > 89	0	0
< 50*	61	74
F+% > 70	7	8
Xu% > 20*	55	73
X-% > 15	79	87
WSum6 > 6*	8	15
Level2 SpecScores > 0*	15	53
Populars < 4	23	53
Dv > 0*	59	64
Interpersonal		
Sum T = 0	87	75
COP = 0*	55	33
AG = 0	58	72
MOR > 2	17	10
Space > 2	22	16
PER > 1**	42	6
EGO < 33*	39	50
> 44	39	36
Fr+rF = 0	77	89
Fr+rF > 1	23	11
Affect		
FC > 0*	46	62
CF > 0	68	50
C > 0	26	23
Constellations		
SCZI ≥ 4	35	45
DEPI ≥ 5	19	22
CDI ≥ 4	70	60

*p < .05; **p < .01.

Psychopathic patients also differed from nonpsychopathic patients in thought processes. Despite similar deficits, including pervasive perceptual accuracy problems, psychopathic patients produced less unconventional thinking (Xu%; $p < .05$) and cognitive slippage (Level 2 Special Scores > 0; $p < .05$) than their nonpsychopathic counterparts. They were also more narcissistic (Fr+rF > 0, $p = .07$), despite high levels of major mental illness in this sample (similar findings are found in Gacono & Meloy, 1994). They were less likely to compare themselves unfavorably to others (Ego < .33; $p < .01$), produced more personals ($p < .001$), and gave less evidence of expectations of cooperative human interaction (COP, $p < .05$). Given the high levels of major mental illness in this sample, the finding of relatively few reflections was not unexpected. Gacono and Meloy (1994) also found less reflections in the ASPD schizophrenic sample compared with the ASPD psychopaths. Less poorly modulated affect was also noted. However, this latter finding can only be accurately interpreted within the context of total SumC.

From the perspective of Odds Ratios, when compared with nonpsychopathic patients, psychopaths were:

1. Thirteen times more likely to have provided > 2 Personal responses,
2. Seven times more likely to have provided < 2 Special Scores,
3. Four times more likely to have provided < 1 Deviant Verbalization,
4. Three times more likely to have produced Reflection responses,
5. Three times more likely to have provided < 4 Form Color (FC) responses,
6. Three times more likely to have provided < 2 Cooperative responses,
7. Two times more likely to have Egocentricity Index Ratios < .33 or > .44.

These Rorschach differences were quite similar to those reported by Gacono and Meloy (1994; Gacono, Meloy, & Heaven, 1990) in their comparisons of ASPD inmates with and without schizophrenia. VPP's schizophrenic psychopaths are discussed next.

The VPP Psychopathic Schizophrenic

Although their numbers were small, psychopathic schizophrenics comprised 17% of the sample. When psychopathic schizophrenics were compared with their nonpsychopathic schizophrenic counterparts, they:

1. Evidenced greater impairment in perceptual accuracy and reality testing (X+% lower and X-% higher),
2. Produced more cognitive slippage (Wsum6 higher),

3. Showed less expectations of cooperative human interaction (fewer Cops),
4. Evidenced greater impairment in thinking, reasoning, and problem solving (Category Test, Wisconsin Card Sorting, Trail Making B).

DISCUSSION

VPP patients form an atypical forensic psychiatric sample. They differ from other general psychiatric patient populations across several dimensions, including their elevated levels of violence and psychopathy. Although the data analyzed do not provide definitive answers, the interaction between major mental disorders and cognitive deficits, character pathology (69% ASPD, 29% psychopathic), and a demanding, high-stress prison environment must play a major role. Therefore, generalizability of these findings is limited to similar low functioning, violent, incarcerated populations.

The psychometric data from these psychiatrically hospitalized psychopathic patients have implications for intervention. The following is a summary of significant findings that suggest approaches helpful for clinical, correctional, and administrative staff when dealing with similar populations.

Interaction With Referring Mental Health Systems. Although every psychopath in our program filtered through three levels of assessment prior to admission, almost half did not carry an Axis I disorder. Many of these inmates were skilled at convincing even experienced mental health professionals of a need for inpatient services. Every clinician who evaluates a patient within a forensic context must remember that pathological lying and conning and manipulation (Hare, 1991) are the psychopath's calling cards (see chap. 7). Although it is clinically prudent to err on the side of caution whenever suicidal or homicidal threats or bizarre behavior are presented, screening for psychopathy prior to referral is a necessity. Brief stays with close clinical observation prior to admission and a system for the rapid discharge of malingerers could improve the program's effectiveness.

Violence Potential. This is a population whose violence histories began early, typically resulting in a first conviction in their mid-teens. Escalating violence is a consistent pattern; these men continue to use physical assaultiveness even within the institution. As psychopathy level increases, inmates are more likely to have used violent episodes selectively, even if on the surface these episodes appeared volatile, unmodulated, and out of control.

Faced with the endlessly frustrating prison environment, it is likely that this habitual aggression will recur; psychopathic patients had markedly more assaultive incidents than nonpsychopathic patients. A program philosophy of enlightened self-interest, which focuses on behavior change as desirable not because of benefit to others or to society but because of benefit to the individual (Thorne, 1971), is suggested. Consistent with other cognitive-behavioral approaches (Gacono et al., 2001) and reality therapy (Glasser, 1965), this approach makes the consequences to assaultive behavior immediate and substantial. Substantial skepticism is warranted in response to explanations for violent behavior (e.g., "I don't know what happened, I just lost it"). Our data suggest that seemingly out-of-control episodes may have a planned and purposeful component (Meloy, 1988). Additionally, aggressive and proactive psychopharmacology should augment psychological interventions geared toward reducing impulsivity and violence.

Substance Abuse.   For most of these men, drugs and alcohol have been a significant part of their lives since their early teens. As psychopathy increases, so does the likelihood that the more addictive opiates, cocaine, amphetamines, and hallucinogens play a part in a largely sensation-seeking abuse picture. As psychopathy increases, so does the likelihood that the hidden agenda for interactions with the mental health system may include attempts to obtain drugs. Many of these patients are extremely sophisticated in reporting symptom patterns aimed at obtaining drug prescriptions.

It is suggested that a reality-oriented substance abuse education program during incarceration may be of value. Again, a program whose focus is enlightened self-interest, even if its impact is difficult to ascertain, may be of greatest value. A matter-of-fact, hard-hitting description of drug interactions, dangers to themselves, and brain damage consequences is a good starting point. Staff should make random and frequent substance abuse screening (urine analysis) part of the treatment package.

Cognitive and Educational Issues.   These inmates are characterized by fragmented educational histories, early school withdrawal, and mild neuropsychological impairment. It is a history that results in a confusing mosaic of psychopathy compromised by poor judgment. Although they vehemently think they understand the potential consequences of their behavior, our data suggest that their cause-and-effect reasoning may be so idiosyncratic that they typically act without accurate awareness of future implications (see chap. 4). Their approach is more likely to be on an item-by-item basis, with little ability to accomplish the sort of syntheses that would allow accurate cause-and-effect conclusions.

We see these deficits in anticipating consequences and, perhaps even more important, the unawareness of these deficits as a significant intervention target. Inservice training for staff should emphasize the necessity of ongoing description of if–then, cause-and-effect sequences.

Interpersonal and Self-Concept Issues. Our findings suggest that these men read the interpersonal world inaccurately and with a particular skew that represents others as untrustworthy potential targets whose only value may lie in their potential for being exploited. This stance occurs in the context of an intensely self-focused style, vulnerable to angry narcissistic injury when confronted. It is a particularly complex problem in correctional settings, in which the roles of mental health professionals often have administrative and clinical components. New, inexperienced staff members are particularly vulnerable. We suggest that ongoing staff support, inservice training, and case conferences can provide a truing function against over- or underresponsiveness to the interpersonal intensity that so frequently characterizes work with psychopathic inmates. Psychopharmacological intervention may be particularly useful especially in cases where reality distortions include typical psychotic symptoms such as delusions, hallucinations, and so on.

General Guidelines. Given our description of this population and our presentation of specific intervention implications, we suggest some general guidelines useful for all staff members:

1. Staff must be well trained and the environment must be secure enough to contain the multifaceted psychopathology,

2. Proactive and aggressive psychopharmacology should augment other more psychologically based interventions; treating Axis I disorders and mediating Axis II disorders (impulsivity/anger),

3. Communication should be clear, culturally informed, culturally competent, and unambiguous,

4. Emphasis throughout should be on cause-and-effect relationships and the likely consequences of behaviors,

5. An enlightened self-interest approach should accompany descriptions of cause-and-effect sequences,

6. Program routines should be structured, predictable, and consistent,

7. Communications should be reality based, factual, and presented in a calm, matter-of-fact style,

8. Programs that allow extensive staff interaction, mentoring for less experienced staff members, and frequent conferencing are more likely to achieve the levels of consistency crucial in working with this population.

VPP findings described a relatively young, undereducated, low-SES group with significant problems in multiple domains, including substance abuse, violence potential, cognitive and neuropsychological deficits, and poor interpersonal, organizational, and vocational skills. Our findings also emphasized the need for careful, comprehensive evaluation of inmates who are admitted to a psychiatric treatment program within a prison setting. The level of psychopathy that characterizes these men intensified these problems, and we share the cautious stance expressed by Quinsey, Harris, Rice, and Cormier (1998) about the possible gains that any intervention program can accomplish. However, we do hope that our findings can inform the approach they suggested when they wrote, "It is our view that the clinical leaders of an institution are obliged to use the systematic application of consequences to influence the behavior of the institutions' inhabitants . . ." (p. 213).

ACKNOWLEDGMENTS

The views expressed in this chapter are solely the authors' and may not reflect the views of any past, present, or future professional affiliation. The authors extend appreciation to Sylvia Blount, MPA, Executive Director, A. C. Lamb, MD, Medical Director, and E. Bachman and D. Pangburn, Program Directors, for their support in completing this work.

ENDNOTES

1. Guy, Platt, Zwerling, and Bullock (1985) interviewed 486 inmates in a Philadelphia jail and identified 67% as being in need of psychiatric treatment. Steadman, Holohean, and Dvoskin (1991) concluded that 16% of prisoners in New York State prisons required psychiatric treatment and 8% were severely psychotic. More recently, Teplin (1994) reported prevalence rates approaching 30% among males serving jail time.
2. Forty-two percent of our Vacaville Psychiatric Program inmates who were psychotic also had a concurrent Axis II diagnosis of ASPD. ASPD schizophrenics differed from ASPDs only on those measures that would, theoretically, be predicted. ASPD schizophrenics had more severe illogical thinking (Rorschach Level 2 Special Scores), greater indication of unmodulated affect (CF+C>FC), and more impairment on neuropsychological tests, which predominately evaluate the ability to think, reason, and problem solve. Our Rorschach findings are consistent with those of Gacono and Meloy (1994), who additionally found that ASPD schizophrenics were more narcissistic and less anxious than non-ASPD inpatient schizophrenics.
3. Some severe personality disorders with acute borderline decompensation or, as previously stated, posing a significant self-harm risk are admitted for treatment.

REFERENCES

American Psychiatric Association. (1980). *Diagnostic and statistical manual of mental disorders* (3rd ed.). Washington, DC: Author.
American Psychiatric Association. (1987). *Diagnostic and statistical manual of mental disorders* (3rd ed., rev.). Washington, DC: Author.

American Psychiatric Association. (1994). *Diagnostic and statistical manual of mental disorders* (4th ed.). Washington, DC: Author.

Department of Corrections, Offender Information Services Branch, Data Analysis Unit. (1998). *California prisoners and parolees*. Sacramento, CA: Author.

Exner, J. (1995). *A Rorschach workbook for the comprehensive system* (4th ed.). Ashville, NC: Rorschach Workshops.

Gacono, C. (1998). The use of the Psychopathy Checklist–Revised (PCL–R) and Rorschach in treatment planning with ASPD patients. *Journal of Offender Therapy and Comparative Criminology, 42*(1), 49–64.

Gacono, C., & Meloy, R. (1994). *The Rorschach assessment of aggressive and psychopathic personalities:* Hillsdale, NJ: Lawrence Erlbaum Associates.

Gacono, C., Meloy, R., & Heaven, T. (1990). A Rorschach investigation of narcissism and hysteria in antisocial personality disorder. *Journal of Personality Assessment, 55*, 270–290.

Gacono, C., Meloy, R., Sheppard, K., Speth, E., & Roske, A. (1995). A clinical investigation of malingering and psychopathy in hospitalized insanity acquittees. *Bulletin of the American Academy of Psychiatry and the Law, 23*(3), 1–11.

Gacono, C., Meloy, R., Speth, E., & Roske, A. (1997). Above the law: Escapes from a maximum security forensic hospital and psychopathy. *American Academy of Psychiatry and the Law, 25*(4), 1–4.

Gacono, C., Nieberding, R., Owen, A., Rubel, J., & Bodholdt, R. (2001). Treating juvenile and adult offenders with conduct-disorder, antisocial, and psychopathic personalities. In J. B. Ashford, B. D. Sales, & W. Reid (Eds.), *Treating adult and juvenile offenders with special needs* (pp. 99–129). Washington, DC: American Psychological Association.

Glasser, W. (1965). *Reality therapy: A new approach to psychiatry*. New York: Harper & Row.

Guy, E., Platt, J., Zwerling, I., & Bullock, S. (1985). Mental health status of prisoners in an urban jail. *Criminal Justice and Behavior, 2*, 29–53.

Hare, R. D. (1991). *The Hare Psychopathy Checklist–Revised*. Toronto, Ontario: Multi-Health Systems.

Harris, G., Rice, M., & Quinsey, V. (1993). Violent recidivism of mentally disordered offenders. *Criminal Justice and Behavior, 20*, 315–335.

Hart, S., Cox, D., & Hare, R. (1995). *The Hare PCL:SV: Psychopathy Checklist Screening Version.* Toronto, Ontario: Multi-Health Systems.

Hart, S., & Hare, R. (1989). Discriminant validity of the Psychopathy Checklist in a forensic psychiatric population. *Psychological Assessment: A Journal of Consulting and Clinical Psychology, 1*, 6–17.

Heilbrun, K., Hart, S., Hare, R., Gustafson, D., Nunez, C., & White, A. (1998). Inpatient and postdischarge aggression in mentally disordered offenders: The role of psychopathy. *Journal of Interpersonal Violence, 13*(4), 514–527.

Hill, C., Rogers, R., & Bickford, M. (1996). Predicting aggressive and socially disruptive behavior in a maximum security forensic psychiatric hospital. *Journal of Forensic Sciences, 41*, 56–59.

Marques, J., Haynes, R., & Nelson, C. (1993). Forensic treatment in the US: A survey of selected forensic hospitals. *International Journal of Law and Psychiatry, 16*, 57–70.

Meloy, J. R. (1988). *The psychopathic mind: Origins, dynamics, and treatment*. Northvale, NJ: Jason Aronson.

Meloy, R. (1995). Treatment of antisocial personality disorder. In G. Gabbard (Ed.), *DSM–IV treatments of psychiatric disorders*. Washington, DC: American Psychiatric Press.

Meloy, R., Haroun, A., & Schiller, E. (1990). *Clinical guidelines for involuntary outpatient treatment*. Sarasota, FL: Professional Resource Exchange Monahan & Steadman.

Meyers, J. K., & Bean, L. L. (1968). *A decade later: A follow-up of social class and mental illness*. New York: Wiley.

Monahan, J. (1992). Mental disorder and violent behavior. *American Psychologist, 47*(4), 511–521.

Nedopil, N., Hollweg, M., Hartmann, J., & Jaser, R. (1995). Comorbidity of psychopathy with major mental disorders. *Issues in Criminological & Legal Psychology, 24,* 115–118.

Pham, T., Remy, S., Dailliet, A., & Lienard, L. (1998). Psychopathy and evaluation of violent behavior in a psychiatric security milieu. *United Observation et de Treatment, Prison de Mons, Belgique, 24*(3), 173–179.

Quinsey, V., Harris, G., Rice, M., & Cormier, C. (1998). *Violent offenders: Appraising and managing risk.* Washington, DC: American Psychological Association.

Rice, M., & Harris, G. (1992). A comparison of criminal recidivism among schizophrenic and nonschizophrenic offenders. *Journal of Law and Psychiatry, 15,* 397–408.

Rice, M., Harris, G., & Cormier, C. (1992). An evaluation of a maximum security therapeutic community for psychopaths and other mentally disordered offenders. *Law and Human Behavior, 16,* 399–412.

Stalenheim, E., & Von Knorring, L. (1996). Psychopathy and Axis I and Axis II psychiatric disorders in a forensic psychiatric population in Sweden. *Acta Psychiatrica Scandinavica, 94*(4), 217–223.

Steadman, H., Holohean, E., & Dvoskin, J. (1991). Estimating mental health needs and service utilization among prison inmates. *Bulletin of American Academy of Psychiatry and Law, 19,* 297–307.

Teplin, L. (1994). Psychiatric and substance abuse disorders among male urban jail detainees. *American Journal of Public Health, 84,* 290–293.

Thorne, F. T. (1971). *Tutorial counseling.* Brandon, VT: Clinical Psychology Publishing Company.

Toch, H., & Adams, K. (1994). *The disturbed violent offender.* Hyattsville, MD: American Psychological Association.

Young, M., Justice, J., & Erdberg, P. (1999). Risk factors to violence among psychiatrically hospitalized forensic patients: A multimethod approach. *Assessment, 6,* 243–258.

14

Psychopathy and Sexual Aggression

Michael C. Seto
Martin L. Lalumière
University of Toronto, Ontario

Sexual aggression is a serious social problem. Over 260,000 attempted or completed rapes were reported in the United States in 1995, for an annual incidence rate of 160 per 100,000 American females over the age of 12 (Greenfeld, 1997). Estimates of the prevalence of sexual coercion experienced by females range from 14% to 25% in the majority of surveys (see Koss, 1993, for a review). A recent large-scale survey in the United States suggested that approximately 24% of females and 14% of males, retrospectively, reported being sexually abused (involving sexual touching or intercourse) as children (Finkelhor, Hotaling, Lewis, & Smith, 1990). Moreover, the psychological correlates of sexual victimization can be serious, including anxiety, depression, substance abuse, and other symptoms of posttraumatic stress disorder (PTSD; reviewed by Beitchman et al., 1992; Hanson, 1990; but see Rind, Tromovitch, & Bauserman, 1998).

Paralleling public concern, the number of Canadian sex offenders in federal custody has increased more than other types of offenders, currently accounting for approximately 20% of the federal inmate population (Motiuk & Belcourt, 1996). Five percent of the total American correctional population is identified as sex offenders, with an annual growth rate almost twice the average rate (Greenfeld, 1997). The assessment, treatment, and management of sex offenders have consequently become an important responsibility for mental health and correctional professionals. The enactment of sexual predator laws permitting the long-term incapacitation of high-risk sex offenders after serving their sentences[1] has increased the involvement of these professionals and has highlighted many issues regarding risk assessment and treatment planning.

Recent research on the correlates of sexual aggression, development of assessment tools, and effectiveness of treatment and management efforts, although far from definitive, can identify the most productive approaches to deal with sexual aggression. This research shows that psychopathy is one of the most crucial factors to consider. This chapter reviews relevant findings on sexual aggression and the central role played by psychopathy. We show how psychopathy, measured using the Psychopathy Checklist-Revised (PCL-R; Hare, 1991; see chap. 3), is an important static variable in a recently developed actuarial instrument—the Sex Offender Risk Appraisal Guide—that accurately assesses sex offenders' risk to commit future sexual (and other violent) crimes (Quinsey, Harris, Rice, & Cormier, 1998). It also discusses how individuals scoring high in psychopathy pose special challenges in treatment, particularly in the interpretation of positive treatment behavior. The role of the PCL-R in the risk assessment and management of sex offenders is illustrated using two case vignettes.

INDIVIDUAL DIFFERENCES AND SEXUAL AGGRESSION

Research has identified a number of individual differences that are empirically related to sexual aggression. Most of these individual differences can be sorted into three domains: sexual deviance, mating effort, and antisociality (see Lalumière & Quinsey, 1996; Seto & Barbaree, 1997).

Sexual Deviance

Sexual preferences are usually considered deviant when they are both statistically unusual and, when acted on, likely to inflict unwanted harm on oneself or others (Lalumière & Quinsey, 1999). Pedophilia (a sexual preference for prepubescent children) and preferential rape (a sexual preference for violent, nonconsenting sex, similar to sexual sadism) are particularly relevant here. Sexual deviance in males is currently best measured using phallometry—an objective measure of sexual arousal that is less susceptible to faking than self-report (see Lalumière & Harris, 1998; Quinsey & Lalumière, 1996). In phallometry, changes in penile erection (circumference or volume) are recorded while a man sits alone in a room and is presented with sets of sexual stimuli varying on the dimension of interest, such as pictures depicting children or adults or audiotaped vignettes describing consenting or nonconsenting sex. Circumferential devices, typically a mercury-in-rubber strain gauge placed over the midshaft of the penis, are the most common. Changes in the conductance of the mercury column reflect changes in penile circumference and can be calibrated to give a precise measure of erection. Sexual deviance is usually scored in terms of responses to inappropriate stimuli (e.g., pictures of children, description of nonconsenting sex) relative to responses to appropriate stimuli (e.g., pictures of adults, descriptions of consenting sex).

Phallometric studies consistently find that child molesters differ from nonsex offenders or nonoffenders, with child molesters as a group responding relatively more to stimuli depicting children (reviewed by Seto, Lalumière, & Kuban, 1999). Among child molesters, more deviant responding is associated with having a male victim, having more than one victim, and having younger victims. Phallometric studies also consistently find that rapists differ from nonrapists in their relative responses to scenarios describing the rape of a female by a male (quantitatively reviewed by Lalumière & Quinsey, 1993, 1994). Finally, follow-up studies of child molesters and rapists show that more deviant responding in phallometric assessments and higher scores on other indicators of sexual deviance are associated with a greater likelihood of committing a new violent or sexual offense (Hanson & Bussière, 1998; Rice, Harris, & Quinsey, 1990; Rice, Quinsey, & Harris, 1991).

Although sexual deviance has received less empirical attention among adolescent sex offenders, available phallometric data from older adolescent sex offenders are generally consistent with adult findings. In a sample of 79 juvenile sex offenders with female victims, Becker, Kaplan, and Tenke (1992) identified 29 who responded more to young children or did not discriminate between children and adults. Hunter, Goodwin, and Becker (1994) found that subjects with male victims responded more to child stimuli than those with female victims. However, no published study has compared the phallometric responses of juvenile sex offenders to an age-matched comparison group of nonsex offenders or nonoffenders. This comparison is necessary to interpret individual responding: Does the offender's pattern of responses differ from that of adolescents who have not committed sexual offenses? For example, we do not know whether it is unusual for a young adolescent boy to sexually respond to girls who are two or three years younger.

Little is known about sexual deviance in sexually coercive men recruited from college campuses or from the larger community. Malamuth (1986) showed that the degree of penile tumescence to a stimulus depicting rape was related to self-reported history of sexual coercion, but Lalumière and Quinsey (1996) did not find any difference in penile responding between sexually coercive and noncoercive men. It has been suggested that sexual deviance may be more relevant for rapists who have committed more violent or sadistic acts of sexual aggression; perhaps these men are more likely to be found in adjudicated adult samples (see Blader & Marshall, 1989).

The question of whether some subgroups of rapists show especially deviant penile responding has been addressed in two studies. Barbaree, Seto, Serin, Amos, and Preston (1994) used the Massachusetts Treatment Center rapist typology (Knight & Prentky, 1990) to classify adjudicated rapists as "nonsexually" motivated (opportunistic or vindictive types, $n = 35$) or "sexually" motivated (sadistic or nonsadistic, $n = 23$). As expected, the latter group showed more deviant phallometric responding than the former group; the sadistic rapists ($n = 8$) showed the largest relative responses to rape. PCL–R scores did not distinguish between the nonsexually and sexually motivated rapists. Langevin et al. (1985) classified 9 adjudicated rapists into a sadistic group (those judged to prefer or be particularly aroused by having control over their victims and by the victims' fear and suffering) and 11 other rapists into a nonsadistic group. Contrary to their expectations, the sadistic group showed less deviant preferences than the nonsadistic group. Despite its popularity, the idea that sexual deviance is more relevant in some subgroups of rapists has received little scientific attention.

Are psychopaths more likely to be sexually deviant? One might expect that men who exhibit little behavioral and physiological inhibition, who lack concern for the welfare of others, and who have histories of impersonal sex with multiple partners would show higher sexual responses to scenarios depicting nonconsenting sex. However, there is no published research specifically comparing the phallometric responses of psychopaths and nonpsychopaths, independent of sex offender status. One study found that PCL–R scores correlated .28 with phallometrically measured responses to children or nonconsenting sex in a sample of 65 sex offenders (Serin, Malcolm, Khanna, & Barbaree, 1994). A significant relationship was observed among extrafamilial child molesters and rapists, but not among incest offenders (who typically score lower on the PCL–R). More research is needed on this important theoretical and practical question.

Mating Effort

Mating effort is defined as energy directed to locating, courting, guarding, and sexually interacting with members of the preferred sex and age. It can be contrasted with parenting effort, in which energy is allocated to protecting and investing in one's mate and offspring (Lalumière & Quinsey, 1999). Higher scores on measures of mating effort reflect a more varied sexual history (e.g., earlier age at first intercourse, more sexual partners, more casual sexual encounters) and a greater interest in partner variety and casual sex. As predicted by Trivers's (1972) theory of parental investment, men score higher than women on measures of mating effort (reviewed by Buss, 1994, 1999), although there are also large intrasex variations on mating effort (Lalumière, Chalmers, Quinsey, & Seto, 1996; Lalumière & Quinsey, 1996).

Nonadjudicated men who report having been sexually coercive have more extensive sexual histories, a greater history of uncommitted relationships, and a greater interest in partner variety and casual sex than noncoercive men (Kanin, 1985; Lalumière et al., 1996; Lalumière & Quinsey, 1996). For example, Lalumière et al. (1996) found that a preference for partner novelty and casual sex was associated with self-reported sexual coercion in a sample of 156 young males. Malamuth and his colleagues found that male college students who scored higher on a measure of mating effort (age at first intercourse and number of sexual partners since the age of 14) were more likely than men who scored lower on this measure to report engaging in both sexual and nonsexual coercion, especially in conjunction with negative attitudes and beliefs about women and heterosocial relationships (Malamuth, Linz, Heavey, Barnes, & Acker, 1995; Malamuth, Sockloskie, Koss, & Tanaka, 1991). Recent results from our laboratory suggest that adjudicated rapists also score higher on measures of mating effort and are similar to nonadjudicated sexually coercive men on these measures. Child molesters have not yet been studied in this way. Nonetheless, the existing research suggests that some acts of sexual coercion reflect high mating effort—a mating strategy that may have been adaptive, in the Darwinian sense, in ancestral environments (see Quinsey & Lalumière, 1995).

Is psychopathy related to mating effort? Cleckley (1976) described psychopaths as having short and unstable sexual relationships, and two PCL–R items—Promiscuous Sexual Behavior and Many Short-Term Marital Relationships—refer explicitly to sexual behavior. Among men recruited from the community, Seto, Khattar, Lalumière, and Quinsey (1997) found a positive relationship between scores on a 16-item measure of psychopathy and scores on indicators of mating effort. Similarly, Seto, Lalumière, and Quinsey (1995) reported positive relationships between scores on a measure of sensation-seeking, a personality trait that is related to psychopathy, and scores on indicators of mating effort. Finally, Lalumière and Quinsey (1996) reported positive relationships between two self-report measures of psychopathy (the Psychopathy Scale described by Levenson, Kiehl, & Fitzpatrick, 1995, and the Childhood and Adolescence Taxon Scale[2]), a measure of sensation-seeking, and indicators of mating effort. All three studies recruited college and community participants. These findings are consistent with recent theoretical models of psychopathy suggesting that mating effort is an important component of a psychopathic life-history strategy (see Quinsey et al., 1998).

Antisociality

Antisociality is a broad construct representing early, varied, and chronic antisocial conduct; crime-supportive attitudes and peer associations; and personality features such as manipulativeness, impulsivity, and callousness. Psychopathy, as measured with the PCL–R, is an extreme manifestation of antisociality (see chaps. 3 and 8). Earlier clinical descriptions correctly suggested that some individuals committed sexual offenses as part of a stable pattern of delinquency or criminality (e.g., Amir, 1971; Cohen, Seghorn, & Calamus, 1969; Gebhard, Gagnon, Pomeroy, & Christenson, 1965). Rapists often have a history of antisocial behavior, juvenile delinquency, and nonsexual crimes (e.g., Bard et al., 1987; Weinrott & Saylor, 1991). Criminal history, an antisocial personality disorder (ASPD) diagnosis, and elevated scores on the Psychopathic-Deviate subscale of the Minnesota Multiphasic Personality Inventory (MMPI; see Hathaway & McKinley, 1943) are consistently associated with sexual and nonsexual recidivism among adult sex offenders (Hanson & Bussière, 1998). Rice et al. (1990) found that PCL–R scores predicted both sexual and nonsexual recidivism among adjudicated rapists, over and above variables such as age, offense history, and psychiatric history. Quinsey, Rice, and Harris (1995) also found that scores on the PCL–R predicted sexual recidivism in a sample of 178 rapists and child molesters.

There is also evidence that antisociality and sexual aggression are related among nonadjudicated adults. Studies have shown that male college students who endorse antisocial attitudes and beliefs are more likely to have engaged in sexual and nonsexual coercion (Malamuth et al., 1995); those who score higher on measures of psychopathic traits (Kosson, Kelly, & White, 1997; Lalumière & Quinsey, 1996) are more likely to have engaged in sexual coercion than college-age men who score lower.

Antisociality also has discriminative and predictive validity among juvenile sex offenders (Fagan & Wexler, 1988; Hanson & Bussière, 1998). Elliott (1994) analyzed self-report data from a longitudinal study of 1,725 juveniles and found that sexual aggression typically occurred after an increasingly serious history of nonviolent and then violent offending. In their review of primarily descriptive studies, France and Hudson (1993) suggested that approximately 50% of juvenile sex offenders have a history of nonsexual arrests and that a majority can be described as conduct disordered. Youths with more serious sexual offenses have more extensive histories of nonsexual offending; these offenders seem to be similar to other antisocial adolescents in their personality profiles, history of conduct problems, and substance abuse (e.g., Jacobs, Kennedy, & Meyer, 1997).

Although antisociality and psychopathy are important variables to consider for all types of sex offenders, there is evidence that rapists score higher than child molesters on the PCL–R (Quinsey et al., 1995; Rice & Harris, 1997a; Serin et al., 1994; Seto & Barbaree, 1999). For example, Seto and Barbaree reported that rapists (M = 19.0, SD = 7.3) scored higher, on average, than extrafamilial (M = 14.6, SD = 6.2) or intrafamilial (M = 14.4, SD = 6.2) child molesters. Brown and Forth (1997) found that rapists classified as opportunistic under the Massachusetts Treatment Center topology scored higher on the PCL–R than rapists classified as nonsadistic-sexual or vindictive.

Interrelationships Among Sexual Deviance, Mating Effort, and Antisociality

One would predict that individuals scoring high on all three factors would have the most serious and varied history of sexual offenses and would show the highest rate of sexual recidivism. In a series of studies, Malamuth described the confluence of antisociality (what he has called *hostile masculinity*) and mating effort (what he has called *impersonal sex*) in explaining variation in self-reported sexual coercion. He was able to predict, from these two factors, sexual and nonsexual conflict with female partners 10 years later (Malamuth et al., 1995; see Malamuth, 1998, for the most recent version of the confluence model). Malamuth (1986) also showed that sexual deviance (penile responses to rape scenarios), antisociality (antisocial attitudes and beliefs, particularly hostility toward women and acceptance of interpersonal violence), and mating effort (sexual experience) interacted in the prediction of self-reported sexual coercion. Finally, Rice and Harris (1997a) showed that phallometrically measured sexual deviance interacted with scores on the PCL–R in the prediction of sexual recidivism among rapists and child molesters followed for an average of 10 years. Sexually deviant men scoring high on the PCL–R ($\geq$ 25) had a much lower survival rate (26%) than men who were only sexually deviant, high on the PCL–R, or neither. We are currently investigating how the three factors individually and collectively contribute to sexual aggression. We are also investigating the role of a fourth factor — neurodevelopmental instability. It is related to lifetime violence among adjudicated offenders, but is not related to psychopathy (Harris, Rice, & Lalumière, 1998).

RISK ASSESSMENT AND MANAGEMENT

The importance of antisociality in explaining sexual aggression underscores the necessity of carefully evaluating psychopathy when dealing with sex offenders. Psychopathic sex offenders pose the greatest risk for sexual recidivism, and psychopaths seem to respond poorly to treatment when compared with other offenders (e.g., Rice, Harris, & Cormier, 1992). The following describes how the PCL–R is useful in the risk assessment and management of sex offenders and discusses some of the challenges posed by treatment participants who score high on psychopathy.

Sex Offender Risk Assessment

Assessment measures are used to appraise risk for reoffense and identify treatment and clinical needs. These purposes overlap because many risk factors (e.g., procriminal attitudes and associations, substance abuse, sexual deviance) can and should be targeted in treatment. Of note, sexual attitudes and beliefs, interpersonal difficulties, and subjective distress are commonly assessed, although there is little or no evidence that these variables are associated with risk for recidivism among adjudicated sex offenders (Hanson & Bussière, 1998), adjudicated offenders in general (Gendreau, Little, & Goggin, 1996), or mentally disordered offenders (Bonta, Law, & Hanson, 1998).

There is good evidence that the Sex Offender Risk Appraisal Guide (SORAG), a 14-item actuarial instrument, predicts violent recidivism[3] among sex offenders (reviewed in Quinsey et al., 1998). The items and the range of scores (weight) associated with each item are shown in Table 14.1. The item weights are based on the empirical relationship between the predictor and violent recidivism in the large development sample; each point

TABLE 14.1
Items on the Sex Offender Risk Appraisal Guide (SORAG)

Items	Range of Scores
1. Did not live with both biological parents until age 16	−2 . . . +3
2. Elementary school maladjustment	−1 . . . +5
3. History of alcohol problems	−1 . . . +2
4. Never married	−2 . . . +1
5. Criminal history score for nonviolent offenses	−2 . . . +3
6. Criminal history score for violent offenses	−2 . . . +6
7. Number of previous convictions for sexual offenses	−1 . . . +5
8. History of sex offenses against male children or adults	0 . . . +4
9. Failure on prior conditional release	0 . . . +3
10. Age at index offense (negatively keyed)	−5 . . . +2
11. Meets *DSM–III* criteria for any personality disorder	−2 . . . +3
12. Does not meet *DSM–III* criteria for schizophrenia	−3 . . . +1
13. Any deviant phallometric test result	−1 . . . +1
14. Psychopathy Checklist–Revised score	−5 . . . +12
Possible total range	−27 . . . +51
Range for 98% of offenders	−16 . . . +40

*The third edition of the *Diagnostic and Statistical Manual of Mental Disorders* (American Psychiatric Association, 1980).

represents an increment or decrement of 5% from the overall baserate of violent recidivism in that sample. The derivation of item weights is described in detail by Quinsey et al. As shown in Table 14.1, PCL–R scores (Item 14) contribute substantially to the final score.

After summing the item scores, the SORAG produces a percentile ranking that indicates the offender's risk of future violence relative to the development sample and a probability of violent recidivism over a specific period of time. To illustrate the actuarial nature of the SORAG: A score less than –10 is associated with an estimated probability of 9% for violently reoffending within 10 years of opportunity, a score between 8 and 13 is associated with an estimated probability of 59%, and a score over 31 is associated with an estimated probability of 100%. Rice and Harris (1997a) reported a correlation of .47 (Receiver Operator Characteristic area = .77, where an area of .50 indicates prediction at the level of chance) between SORAG scores and violent recidivism in a cross-validation study of 159 sex offenders that were at risk for an average of 10 years.

The SORAG is an actuarial instrument and was not constructed according to an explicit theory of sexual offending. It is clear, however, that most of the items shown in Table 14.1 can be viewed as indicators of antisociality, and three items (7, 8, and 13) can be viewed as indicators of sexual deviance. Notably, most of the SORAG items are the same as items from the Violence Risk Appraisal Guide (VRAG)—an actuarial instrument for the prediction of violent recidivism among offenders in general (see Quinsey et al., 1998).

Case Vignettes

To illustrate the scoring of the SORAG, we describe two men who participated in a prison-based treatment program for sex offenders in a Canadian medium security penitentiary. The PCL–R and SORAG were scored using information obtained during their clinical assessment. Information about risk is used in subsequent decision making, including recommendations for further treatment, transfers in security level, and suitability for parole. Both men were assessed by the first author (MCS). Some details have been changed or omitted to protect the confidentiality of these men and their victims.

Low PCL–R Score. Mr. Jones was 54 years old at the time he committed the index sexual offenses (SORAG Item 10 = –5), which were multiple convictions involving seven male victims (Item 8 = +4) all between the ages of 9 and 12, and possession of child pornography (videotapes of sexual acts he engaged in with teenage males). He had two prior convictions, an indecent assault against a 15-year-old male committed more than a decade ago (Item 7 = +1), and public mischief after he vandalized

SETO AND LALUMIÈRE

an acquaintance's car following a dispute (Item 5 = 0, Item 6 = +6). He ful-filled his probation requirements without incident (Item 9 = 0).

Mr. Jones described a quiet, socially isolated upbringing, although he was involved in some extracurricular activities such as team sports. This history was confirmed in interviews with his parents. He obtained good grades and exhibited no discipline or behavior problems at school (Item 2 = –1). There was no history of juvenile arrests or contact with police. Mr. Jones graduat-ed from high school and obtained full-time employment as a public sector employee. He lived with both his biological parents until moving into his own residence in his mid-20s (Item 1 = –2). Mr. Jones acknowledged that he had a series of minor problems and technical violations that eventually resulted in his dismissal after 20 years of service. He received social assis-tance and eventually filed for bankruptcy. He had been unemployed for almost 2 years at the time of his arrest. Mr. Jones denied any problems or concerns with his alcohol or drug use, there was no history of substance abuse in his family of origin, and neither alcohol nor drugs were involved in his offenses (Item 3 = –1). He did not meet the DSM–III criteria for a diag-nosis of personality disorder or schizophrenia (Item 11 = –2, Item 12 = +1).

Mr. Jones acknowledged that he was sexually attracted to adolescent males and young-looking adult males. Phallometric testing indicated that he had a sexual preference for young boys (Item 13 = +1). Mr. Jones said that he became sexually active at the age of 15 with a similar-aged male friend. He reported having approximately 300 to 400 male partners in his lifetime, most of them casual and most of them hired as prostitutes. He was never married or involved in a common-law relationship (Item 4 = +1). Mr. Jones claimed that he restricted his sexual behavior to adult males until after he was dismissed from his public sector job and became distressed by his financial and employment prospects.

Mr. Jones scored 9 out of 40 on the PCL–R (Item 14 = –3). His total SORAG score was 0, placing him at the 24th percentile in the SORAG development sample of sex offenders. Offenders with this score have an estimated probability of 39% for committing a new violent offense within an average of 10 years of opportunity. Based on this result, Mr. Jones was deemed by the treatment program providers to be at moderate risk of a new violent offense (which would include a new sexual offense involving physical contact, but not an offense involving possession of illegal pornography). After satisfactorily completing the treatment program, in accordance with case management plans, he was recommended for a graduated release to the community with ongoing supervision and involve-ment in community-based treatment.

High PCL–R Score. Mr. Smith was 32 years old at the time of his index offense (SORAG Item 10 = –1), which was a sexual assault committed against a 22-year-old female stranger (Item 8 = +4). He had consumed alcohol and smoked marijuana following an argument with his common-law spouse and had then gone driving around town. He picked up a hitch-hiker and drove to a secluded area, where he forced the woman into the back seat and ordered her to perform fellatio on him. He choked and threatened to kill the victim when she refused. She complied and was released after performing the sexual act. The victim suffered cuts and bruises as a result of the sexual assault. Mr. Smith was concurrently charged with a similar sexual offense, but was acquitted. He had no prior convictions for sexual offenses (Item 7 = –1), but admitted during the interview that he had committed two sexual assaults as a juvenile for which he was not charged.

Mr. Smith had an extensive criminal history beginning in his early adolescence, consistent with a conduct disorder (CD) diagnosis. He was convicted of breaking and entering, theft, auto theft, and possession of stolen property as a juvenile, resulting in a number of custodial placements. He committed a number of similar property offenses, as well as credit card fraud and aggravated assault, as an adult (Item 5 = +3, Item 6 = +6). Mr. Smith committed several of his offenses while on probation, resulting in charges of failure to comply (Item 9 = +3). Mr. Smith met the *DSM–III* criteria for a diagnosis of ASPD (Item 11 = +3); he received no other psychiatric diagnosis (Item 12 = +1).

Mr. Smith's parents were quite young when he was born and he was subsequently taken into custody by a child protection service at the age of 4 (Item 1 = +3). Mr. Smith described a violent and unstable upbringing in which he was moved from home to home, sometimes as a result of abuse or neglect. His longest stay in one home lasted 4 years, between the ages of 5 and 9. His attendance and grades in school were okay, but he frequently changed schools because of his moves and sometimes was not formally in school for months at a time. He was suspended several times for fighting and was eventually placed in a class for children with behavior problems in Grade 4 (Item 2 = +5). He quit school at the age of 16 and began working in a series of short-term labor or service jobs, broken up by periods of incarceration. His longest term of employment, in a restaurant, lasted 6 months.

Mr. Smith acknowledged that he had persistent problems with his alcohol and drug use. He began smoking marijuana at the age of 12 and began drinking regularly at the age of 14. He had also used cocaine, heroin, and prescription drugs. Mr. Smith was drinking and using drugs almost daily in the year preceding his current offenses and they were often involved in his offenses (Item 3 = +2).

Mr. Smith said that his first sexual experience was the first sexual assault he committed as a juvenile, at the age of 14. His first consensual experience occurred a year later. He reported 22 partners in his lifetime, all of them casual except for his common-law relationship (Item 4 = –2). The majority of these sexual contacts were with prostitutes. Phallometric testing did not indicate that he had a sexual preference for nonconsenting sex or violence (Item 13 = –1).

Mr. Smith obtained a score of 30 out of 40 on the PCL–R (Item 14 = +4). His total SORAG score was +29, placing him at the 97th percentile in the SORAG development sample of sex offenders. Offenders with the same score have an expected probability of 89% for committing a new violent offense within an average of 10 years of opportunity. Based on this result, Mr. Smith was deemed to be at very high risk of committing a new violent offense by the program providers. After completing the treatment program, he was recommended for further institutional treatment, with no change in his security status.

Treatment and Management

The research reviewed in this chapter and the research leading to the development of the SORAG and VRAG show that antisociality, exemplified by psychopathy, is a central construct to consider for sex offenders, as it also is for juvenile delinquents (Lipsey & Derzon, 1998), adult offenders in general (Gendreau et al., 1996), and mentally disordered offenders (Bonta et al., 1998). The relevance of antisociality is thus generalizable across offender groups.[4] The implications for treatment are clear: The best candidates for interventions designed to reduce recidivism among sex offenders are interventions that have been demonstrated to be effective for juvenile delinquents (Lipsey, 1998) and adult offenders (Andrews et al., 1990). These interventions are characterized by being specific, cognitive-behavioral in orientation, allocated to those at higher risk for reoffending, and focused on criminogenic needs such as procriminal attitudes and peer associations, substance use, and lifestyle stability in areas such as employment and relationships (Quinsey et al., 1998). However, few sex offender treatment programs specifically emphasize and target criminogenic needs. Instead, many programs target acceptance of responsibility, victim empathy, social skills, and other constructs that are not directly related to risk for recidivism, although they may be relevant for clinical management.

With regard to risk management, levels of intervention and supervision, ranging from long-term incapacitation to minimal supervision in the community, should (and can) be directly related to an offender's level of static risk.[5] A recent study of dynamic risk factors suggests that contemporaneous expressions of antisociality (e.g., more antisocial attitudes and values, unrealistic discharge plans) can be tracked over time and are empirically related to violent reoffending (Quinsey, Coleman, Jones, & Altrows, 1997). This means that antisociality is not only related to whether an individual will reoffend (static risk), but when he will do so (dynamic risk). Tracking temporally varying risk of violent reoffending means that levels of intervention and supervision can vary and be tailored to respond sensitively to offenders' current needs.

Psychopathy and Treatment Response

Sex offenders scoring high in psychopathy pose special challenges in treatment, as demonstrated by a recent study conducted by Seto and Barbaree (1999). How should good treatment behavior (e.g., accepting responsibility for one's sexual offenses, expressing empathy for victims, understanding treatment concepts, and being compliant with program requirements) exhibited by men scoring high in psychopathy be interpreted? Seto and Barbaree examined the relationship between treatment behavior and recidivism in a sample of 224 adult sex offenders followed for approximately 3 years after their release from prison. The measure of treatment behavior tapped appropriate interactions in group sessions and quality of homework assignments, rated by research assistants reviewing the clinical files, and positive ratings of motivation and overall change made by treating clinicians. Contrary to expectations, a positive score on the measure of treatment behavior was associated with a higher, rather than a lower, rate of serious recidivism (new sexual or nonsexually violent offense). Further analysis revealed that psychopathy was largely responsible for this finding: Sex offenders who scored higher on the PCL-R (> 15) and who also behaved well in treatment were more likely to commit a new offense of some kind and were much more likely to commit a new serious offense than men who scored lower on one or both measures. Seto and Barbaree suggested two possible explanations: First, the measure of treatment behavior may have identified a subset of men scoring higher on psychopathy who were particularly skillful at manipulating others and who could therefore learn what to say and do to receive positive treatment ratings. Second, individuals scoring higher on the PCL-R may have actually learned something in treatment that increased their risk to reoffend, such as impression management skills that would increase access to victims once they are released. Further research is needed to elucidate the nature of the relationship between good treatment behavior and recidivism among individuals scoring higher on the PCL-R.

The results of Seto and Barbaree (1999) and other investigators add to concerns about the involvement of psychopaths in treatment, especially the possibility that participation in treatment could exacerbate their already high levels of risk (see Rice & Harris, 1997b; Rice et al., 1992; Yalom, 1995). Hart and Hare (1997) recently reviewed the treatment literature on psychopaths and suggested it is possible that "group therapy and insight-oriented programs help psychopaths to develop better ways of manipulating, deceiving, and using people but do little to help them to understand themselves" (p. 31). Nonetheless, they suggested that psychopaths might respond well to treatment if there was tight supervision and the focus was on accepting responsibility and learning prosocial strategies to achieve personal goals. Others have also claimed, with caveats, that psychopaths may respond positively to treatment (e.g., Doren, 1987; Templeman & Wollersheim, 1979). Rice and Harris (1997b) cogently argued that interventions with psychopaths should focus on increasing the detection and perceived costs of their antisocial behavior; targeting psychopathic characteristics that are empirically related to recidivism, such as impulsivity; and targeting other characteristics that are related to recidivism, such as deviant sexual arousal in sex offenders. Psychopaths do respond to contingent positive reinforcement, at least under certain conditions (Newman, Kosson, & Patterson, 1992; Scerbo et al., 1990), so it is possible that carefully constructed behavioral interventions could have a positive effect on specific targets (e.g., deviant sexual arousal). However, it is also possible that psychopaths can learn treatment concepts and respond appropriately while under direct control and supervision, but do not maintain these responses when they are no longer under control or supervision. Considering the lack of empirical support for current sex offender treatment programs (Rice & Harris, 1997b) and the potential danger in providing treatment to psychopaths, we believe that at present it is ill advised to provide treatment to psychopathic sex offenders without also carefully evaluating the efficacy of the treatment using a methodologically sound research design.

ACKNOWLEDGMENTS

We would like to thank Aileen Brunet, Alberto Choy, Catherine Cormier, Grant Harris, Vern Quinsey, and Marnie Rice for their helpful comments on an earlier version of this chapter.

ENDNOTES

1. As of September 1998, 12 states in the United States have enacted statutes permitting the commitment of dangerous sex offenders following a criminal sentence (Lieb & Matson, 1998).
2. The Childhood and Adolescence Taxon Scale is an eight-item measure that is highly correlated with the PCL–R and identifies the same individuals as psychopaths in taxometric analyses (Harris, Rice, & Quinsey, 1994). The items pertain to historical indicators: arrested before age 16, did not live with both biological parents until age 16, early school problems, suspended or expelled from school, childhood aggression, conduct disorder (CD) diagnosis, alcohol abuse as a teen, and parental alcohol abuse.

3. Sexual offenses involving any physical contact with the victim are included in the definition of violent recidivism, whereas sexual offenses that do not involve physical contact (e.g., indecent exposure, pornography-related offenses) are not included.
4. As explained earlier, sexual deviance is a unique construct to consider for sex offenders because it is the only individual difference variable identified so far that clearly distinguishes sex offenders from other kinds of criminals.
5. Static risk refers to information about risk that cannot change (e.g., historical information such as number of prior offenses) or is very stable (e.g., personality traits). Dynamic risk refers to information about risk that can vary over time (e.g., substance use, compliance with supervision).

REFERENCES

American Psychiatric Association. (1980). *Diagnostic and statistical manual of mental disorders* (3rd ed.). Washington, DC: Author.

Amir, M. (1971). *Patterns of forcible rape*. Chicago: University of Chicago Press.

Andrews, D. A., Zinger, I., Hoge, R. D., Bonta, J., Gendreau, P., & Cullen, F. T. (1990). Does correctional treatment work? A clinically relevant and psychologically informed meta-analysis. *Criminology, 28,* 369–404.

Barbaree, H. E., Seto, M. C., Serin, R. C., Amos, N. L., & Preston, D. L. (1994). Comparisons between sexual and non-sexual rapist subtypes: Sexual arousal to rape, offense precursors and offense characteristics. *Criminal Justice and Behavior, 21,* 95–114.

Bard, L. A., Carter, D. L., Cerce, D. D., Knight, R. A., Rosenberg, R., & Schneider, B. (1987). A descriptive study of rapists and child molesters: Developmental, clinical, and criminal characteristics. *Behavioral Sciences and the Law, 5,* 203–220.

Becker, J. V., Kaplan, M. S., & Tenke, C. E. (1992). The relationship of abuse history, denial and erectile response profiles of adolescent sexual perpetrators. *Behavior Therapy, 23,* 87–97.

Beitchman, J. H., Zucker, K. J., Hood, J. E., DaCosta, G. A., Akman, D., & Cassavia, E. (1992). A review of the long-term effects of child sexual abuse. *Child Abuse and Neglect, 16,* 101–118.

Blader, J. C., & Marshall, W. L. (1989). Is assessment of sexual arousal in rapists worthwhile? A critique of current methods and the development of a response compatibility approach. *Clinical Psychology Review, 9,* 569–587.

Bonta, J., Law, M., & Hanson, K. (1998). The prediction of criminal and violent recidivism among mentally disordered offenders: A meta-analysis. *Psychological Bulletin, 123,* 123–142.

Brown, S. L., & Forth, A. E. (1997). Psychopathy and sexual assault: Static risk factors, emotional precursors, and rapist subtypes. *Journal of Consulting and Clinical Psychology, 65,* 848–857.

Buss, D. M. (1994). *The evolution of desire: Strategies of human mating*. New York: Basic Books.

Buss, D. M. (1999). *Evolutionary psychology: The new science of the mind*. Toronto: Allyn & Bacon.

Cleckley, H. (1976). *The mask of sanity*. St. Louis: Mosby.

Cohen, M. L., Seghorn, T., & Calamus, W. (1969). Sociometric study of sex offenders. *Journal of Abnormal Psychology, 74,* 249–255.

Doren, D. (1987). *Understanding and treating the psychopath*. New York: Wiley.

Elliott, D. S. (1994). Serious violent offenders: Onset, developmental course, and termination. *Criminology, 32,* 1–21.

Fagan, J., & Wexler, S. (1988). Explanations of sexual assault among violent delinquents. *Journal of Adolescent Research, 3,* 363–385.

Finkelhor, D., Hotaling, G., Lewis, I. A., & Smith, C. (1990). Sexual abuse in a national sample of adult men and women: Prevalence, characteristics, and risk factors. *Child Abuse and Neglect, 14*, 19–28.

France, K. G., & Hudson, S. M. (1993). The conduct disorders and the juvenile sex offender. In H. E. Barbaree, W. L. Marshall, & S. M. Hudson (Eds.), *The juvenile sex offender* (pp. 225–234). New York: Guilford.

Gebhard, P., Gagnon, J., Pomeroy, W., & Christenson, C. (1965). *Sex offenders.* New York: Harper & Row.

Gendreau, P., Little, T., & Goggin, C. (1996). A meta-analysis of the predictors of adult offender recidivism: What works! *Criminology, 34*, 575–607.

Greenfeld, L. (1997). *Sex offenses and offenders: An analysis of data on rape and sexual assault* (Report No. NCJ-163392). Annapolis Junction, MD: Bureau of Justice Statistics Clearinghouse.

Hanson, R. K. (1990). The psychological impact of sexual assault on women and children: A review. *Annals of Sex Research, 3*, 187–232.

Hanson, R. K., & Bussière, M. T. (1998). Predicting relapse: A meta-analysis of sexual offender recidivism studies. *Journal of Consulting and Clinical Psychology, 66*, 348–362.

Hare, R. D. (1991). *Manual for the revised Psychopathy Checklist.* Toronto: Multi-Health Systems.

Harris, G. T., Rice, M. E., & Lalumière, M. L. (1998). *Criminal violence: The roles of psychopathy, neurodevelopmental insults, and antisocial parenting.* Manuscript submitted for publication.

Harris, G. T., Rice, M. E., & Quinsey, V. L. (1994). Psychopathy as a taxon: Evidence and psychopaths are a discrete class. *Journal of Consulting and Clinical Psychology, 62*, 387–397.

Hart, S. D., & Hare, R. D. (1997). Psychopathy: Assessment and association with criminal conduct. In D. M. Stoff, J. Breiling, & J. D. Maser (Eds.), *Handbook of antisocial behavior* (pp. 22–35). New York: Wiley.

Hathaway, S. R., & McKinley, J. C. (1943). *The Minnesota Multiphasic Personality Inventory* (rev. ed.). Minneapolis: University of Minnesota Press.

Hunter, J. A., Jr., Goodwin, D. A., & Becker, J. V. (1994). The relationship between phallometrically measured deviant sexual arousal and clinical characteristics in juvenile sexual offenders. *Behaviour Research and Therapy, 32*, 533–538.

Jacobs, W. L., Kennedy, W. A., & Meyer, J. B. (1997). Juvenile delinquents: A between-group comparison study of sexual and nonsexual offenders. *Sexual Abuse, 9*, 201–217.

Kanin, E. J. (1985). Date rapists: Differential sexual socialization and relative deprivation. *Archives of Sexual Behavior, 14*, 219–231.

Knight, R. A., & Prentky, R. A. (1990). Classifying sexual offenders: The development and corroboration of taxonomic models. In W. L. Marshall, D. R. Laws, & H. E. Barbaree (Eds.), *Handbook of sexual assault: Issues, theories, and treatment of the offender* (pp. 23–52). New York: Plenum.

Koss, M. P. (1993). Detecting the scope of rape: A review of prevalence research methods. *Journal of Interpersonal Violence, 8*, 198–222.

Kosson, D. S., Kelly, J. C., & White, J. W. (1997). Psychopathy-related traits predict self-reported sexual aggression among college men. *Journal of Interpersonal Violence, 12*, 241–254.

Lalumière, M. L., Chalmers, L., Quinsey, V. L., & Seto, M. C. (1996). A test of the mate deprivation hypothesis of sexual coercion. *Ethology and Sociobiology, 17*, 299–318.

Lalumière, M. L., & Harris, G. T. (1998). Common questions regarding the use of phallometric testing with sexual offenders. *Sexual Abuse, 10*, 227–237.

Lalumière, M. L., & Quinsey, V. L. (1993). The sensitivity of phallometric measures with rapists. *Annals of Sex Research, 6*, 123–138.

Lalumière, M. L., & Quinsey, V. L. (1994). The discriminability of rapists from non-sex offenders using phallometric measures: A meta-analysis. *Criminal Justice and Behavior, 21*, 150–175.

Lalumière, M. L., & Quinsey, V. L. (1996). Sexual deviance, antisociality, mating effort, and the use of sexually coercive behaviors. *Personality and Individual Differences, 21,* 33–48.

Lalumière, M. L., & Quinsey, V. L. (1999). A Darwinian interpretation of individual differences in male propensity for sexual aggression. *Jurimetrics, 39,* 201–216.

Langevin, R., Bain, J., Ben-Aron, M. H., Coulthard, R., Day, D., Roper, V., Russon, A. E., Webster, C. D., & Wortzman, G. (1985). Sexual aggression: Constructing a predictive equation: A controlled pilot study. In R. Langevin (Ed.), *Erotic preference, gender identity, and aggression in men: New research studies* (pp. 39–76). Hillsdale, NJ: Lawrence Erlbaum Associates.

Levenson, M. R., Kiehl, K. A., & Fitzpatrick, C. M. (1995). Assessing psychopathic attributes in a noninstitutionalized population. *Journal of Personality and Social Psychology, 68,* 151–158.

Lieb, R., & Matson, S. (1998). *Sexual predator commitment laws in the United States: 1998 update.* Washington State Institute for Public Policy.

Lipsey, M. W. (1998). What do we learn from 400 research studies on the effectiveness of treatment with juvenile delinquents? In J. McGuire (Ed.), *What works: Reducing reoffending – guidelines from research and practice* (pp. 63–77). London: Wiley.

Lipsey, M. W., & Derzon, J. H. (1998). Predictors of violent or serious delinquency in adolescence and early adulthood: A synthesis of longitudinal research. In R. Loeber & D. P. Farrington (Eds.), *Serious and violent juvenile offenders: Risk factors and successful interventions* (pp. 86–105). London: Sage.

Malamuth, N. M. (1986). Predictors of naturalistic sexual aggression. *Journal of Personality and Social Psychology, 50,* 953–962.

Malamuth, N. M. (1998). An evolutionary-based model integrating research on the characteristics of sexually coercive men. In J. D. Adair, D. Bélanger, & K. L. Dion (Eds.), *Advances in psychological science* (Vol. 1, pp. 151–184). Hove, England: Psychology Press.

Malamuth, N. M., Linz, D., Heavey, C. L., Barnes, G., & Acker, M. (1995). Using the confluence model of sexual aggression to predict men's conflict with women: A ten year follow-up study. *Journal of Personality and Social Psychology, 69,* 353–369.

Malamuth, N. M., Sockloskie, R. J., Koss, M. P., & Tanaka, J. S. (1991). Characteristics of aggressors against women: Testing a model using a national sample of college students. *Journal of Consulting and Clinical Psychology, 59,* 670–681.

Motiuk, L., & Belcourt, R. (1996). Profiling the Canadian federal sex offender population. *Forum on Corrections Research, 8,* 3–7.

Newman, J. P., Kosson, D. S., & Patterson, C. M. (1992). Delay of gratification in psychopathic and nonpsychopathic offenders. *Journal of Abnormal Psychology, 101,* 630–636.

Quinsey, V. L., Coleman, G., Jones, B., & Altrows, I. F. (1997). Proximal antecedents of eloping and reoffending among supervised mentally disordered offenders. *Journal of Interpersonal Violence, 12,* 794–813.

Quinsey, V. L., Harris, G. T., Rice, M. E., & Cormier, C. A. (1998). *Violent offenders: Appraising and managing risk.* Washington, DC: American Psychological Association.

Quinsey, V. L., & Lalumière, M. L. (1995). Evolutionary perspectives on sexual offending. *Sexual Abuse, 7,* 301–315.

Quinsey, V. L., & Lalumière, M.L. (1996). *Assessment of sexual offenders against children.* Newbury Park, CA: Sage.

Quinsey, V. L., Rice, M. E., & Harris, G. T. (1995). Actuarial prediction of sexual recidivism. *Journal of Interpersonal Violence, 10,* 85–105.

Rice, M. E., & Harris, G. T. (1997a). Cross-validation and extension of the Violence Risk Appraisal Guide for child molesters and rapists. *Law and Human Behavior, 21,* 231–241.

Rice, M. E., & Harris, G. T. (1997b). The treatment of adult offenders. In D. M. Stoff, J. Breiling, & J. D. Maser (Eds.), *Handbook of antisocial behavior* (pp. 425–435). New York: Wiley.

Rice, M. E., Harris, G. T., & Cormier, C. A. (1992). An evaluation of a maximum security therapeutic community for psychopaths and other mentally disordered offenders. *Law and Human Behavior, 16,* 399–412.

Rice, M. E., Harris, G. T., & Quinsey, V. L. (1990). A follow-up of rapists assessed in a maximum-security psychiatric facility. *Journal of Interpersonal Violence, 5*, 435–448.

Rice, M. E., Quinsey, V. L., & Harris, G. T. (1991). Sexual recidivism among child molesters released from a maximum security psychiatric institution. *Journal of Consulting and Clinical Psychology, 59*, 381–386.

Rind, B., Tromovitch, P., & Bauserman, R. (1998). A meta-analytic examination of assumed properties of child sexual abuse using college samples. *Psychological Bulletin, 124*, 22–53.

Scerbo, A., Raine, A., O'Brien, M., Chan, C. J., Rhee, C., & Smiley, N. (1990). Reward dominance and passive avoidance learning in adolescent psychopaths. *Journal of Abnormal Child Psychology, 18*, 451–463.

Serin, R. C., Malcolm, P. B., Khanna, A., & Barbaree, H. E. (1994). Psychopathy and deviant sexual arousal in incarcerated sex offenders. *Journal of Interpersonal Violence, 9*, 3–11.

Seto, M. C., & Barbaree, H. E. (1997). Sexual aggression as antisocial behavior: A developmental model. In D. Stoff, J. Breiling, & J. D. Maser (Eds.), *Handbook of antisocial behavior* (pp. 524–533). New York: Wiley.

Seto, M. C., & Barbaree, H. E. (1999). Psychopathy, treatment behavior and sex offender recidivism. *Journal of Interpersonal Violence, 14*, 1235–1248.

Seto, M. C., Khattar, N. A., Lalumière, M. L., & Quinsey, V. L. (1997). Deception and sexual strategy in psychopathy. *Personality and Individual Differences, 22*, 301–307.

Seto, M. C., Lalumière, M. L., & Kuban, M. (1999). The sexual preference of incest offenders. *Journal of Abnormal Psychology, 108*, 267–272.

Seto, M. C., Lalumière, M. L., & Quinsey, V. L. (1995). Sensation seeking and males' sexual strategy. *Personality and Individual Differences, 19*, 669–675.

Templeman, T. L., & Wollersheim, J. P. (1979). A cognitive-behavioral approach to the treatment of psychopathy. *Psychotherapy: Theory, Research, & Practice, 16*, 132–139.

Trivers, R. L. (1972). Parental investment and sexual selection. In B. Campbell (Ed.), *Sexual selection and the descent of man* (pp. 136–179). Chicago: Aldine.

Weinrott, M. R., & Saylor, M. (1991). Self-report of crimes committed by sex offenders. *Journal of Interpersonal Violence, 6*, 286–300.

Yalom, I. D. (1995). *The theory and practice of group psychotherapy* (4th ed.). New York: Basic.

Psychopathy and Substance Abuse: A Bad Mix

Megan J. Rutherford
Alcohol and Drug Abuse Institute, University of Washington

Arthur I. Alterman
John S. Cacciola
Treatment Research Center, University of Pennsylvania/
Philadelphia Veterans Administration

Until recently, the majority of studies on antisociality in substance abusers have focused not on psychopathy as conceptualized by Cleckley and operationalized by Hare, but on the *Diagnostic and Statistical Manual of Mental Disorders* (*DSM*) measures of antisocial personality disorder (ASPD; Alterman, Rutherford, Cacciola, McKay, & Woody, 1996; Alterman, Rutherford, Cacciola, McKay, & Boardman, 1997; Brooner, Schmidt, Felch, & Bigelow, 1992; Cottler, Price, Comptom, & Mager, 1995). Studies on the relationship of psychopathy and substance abuse have mainly been conducted with male offenders and are limited in number. Some of these studies measured psychopathy with the Minnesota Multiphasic Personality Inventory (MMPI; Dush & Keen, 1995; Rogers & Bagby, 1994) or other measures of psychopathy (Fishbein & Reuland, 1994). These studies do not necessarily include truly psychopathic individuals, however, because measures of psychopathy such as the MMPI typically have strong correlations with antisocial behaviors but weak correlations with the personality traits associated with psychopathy (see chap. 3).

The Psychopathy Checklist–Revised (PCL–R) yields a global rating of psychopathy, the total score, and two factor scores. Factor 1 assesses psychopathic personality traits with items such as glibness/superficial charm, grandiose sense of self-worth, pathological lying, lack of remorse or guilt, shallow affect, and failure to accept responsibility for own actions. Factor 2, Chronically Unstable and Antisocial Lifestyle, includes items such as need for stimulation, parasitic lifestyle, poor behavioral controls, early behavioral problems, and revocation of conditional release. Behaviors that are considered related to drug use are included in the assessment of all PCL-R items. For brevity, throughout this chapter, we refer to Factor 1 as Psychopathic Personality Traits and Factor 2 as Antisocial Lifestyle. The following focuses only on published studies that utilized the PCL-R to assess psychopathy. In the first section, findings from studies of psychopathy and substance abuse in prison or forensic settings are reviewed. In the second section, results from studies of psychopathy in individuals who are receiving treatment for substance abuse problems are discussed.

PSYCHOPATHY AND SUBSTANCE ABUSE AMONG PRISON POPULATIONS

Generally research demonstrates that there is a differential relationship between substance use and the PCL-R factor scores. An early study evaluated the relationship between the presence or absence of alcohol use and drug use disorders with the PCL-R Factor 1, Factor 2, and Total scores in 80 primarily White (average age 32) forensic psychiatric patients (Hart & Hare, 1989). The mean PCL-R score in this sample was 21.9 (SD = 6.8). Only 12.5% (N = 10) of the sample were classified as *psychopathic* according to the PCL-R. Results of this study indicate that there was a significant correlation between drug dependence and abuse diagnoses and the PCL-R Total (r = .31) and Factor 2 scores (r = .40), but not with Factor 1 scores (r = .15). The same pattern of results was seen with alcohol use, but the correlations were not significant (Total, r = .24; Factor 1, r = .07; Factor 2, r = .26). This pattern of a moderate relationship between the PCL-R Total and Factor 2 scores with substance use and a weak relationship between substance use and Factor 1 scores has been found in several other studies.

Correlations between Factor 2 and the number of drug or alcohol use symptoms (r = .40 for drug and alcohol) were also found to be stronger than the correlations between Factor 1 and the number of drug or alcohol use symptoms (rs = .13 and .14, respectively) in a study of 360 White Wisconsin inmates between 18 and 40 years old (Smith-Stevens & Newman, 1990). This study included 113 (31.3%) individuals who were classified as *psychopaths*. Psychopaths in this study were found to be more likely than nonpsychopaths to have a lifetime diagnosis of alcohol abuse or dependence (92.9% vs. 65.3%) and a lifetime drug abuse or dependence diagnosis (73.5% vs. 43.5%). PCL-R Total and Antisocial Lifestyle scores were significantly associated with the age of first intoxication and first arrest. Psychopathic Personality Traits were significantly related to the age of first arrest, but not age of first intoxication. It appears that early substance use is more related to a general pattern of deviance rather than to specific personality traits associated with psychopathy.

Antisocial Lifestyle was also found to be more strongly related to substance use than Psychopathic Personality Traits when PCL–R scores were examined in relation to the drug and alcohol use scales of the Millon Clinical Multiaxial Inventory–II (MCMI–II) in 119 predominately White inmates (Hart, Forth, & Hare, 1991). The mean PCL–R score of the sample was 24.07 (*SD* = 6.98). There were 24 subjects (20.2%) who had PCL–R scores of 30 or more. Results reveal moderate correlations between the Total PCL–R score and the MCMI–II drug and alcohol use scales (.31 and .24, respectively). The correlations between Factor 2 and the drug (.40) and alcohol (.26) scales were significantly stronger than the correlations between Factor 1 and the MCMI–II drug (.15) and alcohol (.07) use scales.

Unlike the earlier study by Smith-Stevens and Newman (1990), psychopaths were not found to be significantly more likely than nonpsychopaths to be diagnosed with drug or alcohol abuse or dependence (95.7% vs. 87.6% and 57.4% vs. 58.2%, respectively) in a study of 200 primarily White inmates (average age 30; Hemphill, Hart, & Hare, 1994). The mean PCL–R Total score for this sample was 24.04 (*SD* = 6.9) and 23.5% (*n* = 47) of subjects were classified as *psychopathic*. Correlations between Antisocial Lifestyle and drug abuse or dependence diagnoses (*r* = .35) were again found to be significantly stronger than the correlations between Psychopathic Personality Traits (*r* = .09) and drug abuse or dependence diagnoses. The correlations for Factor 1 and Factor 2 with alcohol abuse or dependence diagnoses were not found to be significantly different. The overall psychopathy rating was significantly correlated with the number of substances used, the age of first alcohol intoxication, and the number of charges/convictions for drug-related offenses. Antisocial Lifestyle had a significantly stronger correlation than did Psychopathic Personality Traits with the number of substances used (*r* = .34 vs. .20). Surprisingly, Psychopathic Personality Traits was significantly correlated with the number of charges/convictions, but Antisocial Lifestyle was not (*r* = .17 vs. .05). Because number of arrests was previously found to be related to both Psychopathic Personality Traits and Antisocial Lifestyle (Smith-Stevens & Newman, 1990), it appears that individuals who present themselves as glib, grandiose, and lacking empathy or remorse are not more likely to be arrested, but are more likely to be convicted of a crime than an individual who presents with fewer such traits.

A meta-analysis of the four studies described earlier indicates that generally there is a moderate association between drug abuse/dependence and the PCL–R Total score among male inmates (Hemphill, Hart, & Hare, 1994). The association appears to be highly significant and replicable across studies. The association between alcohol abuse/dependence and the PCL-R is less consistent across studies and low to moderate in magnitude. Antisocial Lifestyle consistently had a stronger relationship than Psychopathic Personality Traits to alcohol and drug abuse/dependence among male offenders. The correlations between substance use and Factor 2 were significantly stronger than those found for Factor 1 and substance use disorders, but the correlations for Factors 1 and 2 were not significantly different for alcohol use disorders.

It is interesting that these studies did not find a significant difference between the correlations for Factors 1 and 2 with alcohol use disorders. In part, this may be explained by the fact that alcohol is a legal and relatively inexpensive drug compared with most other drugs of abuse (e.g., heroin, cocaine, amphetamines), which are costly and illegal. Most individuals who are addicted to heroin or cocaine are involved in illegal activities to one degree or another, but it is not as common for alcoholics to be involved in illegal activities other than driving under the influence. In general, individuals who are illegal drug users may be (a) more likely to take risks, (b) more impulsive, and (c) perhaps more psychopathic compared with individuals who choose to primarily use alcohol. There is more antisocial behavior associated with the acquisition and the result of illegal drugs use than with alcohol use. Neither alcohol or drug use, however, has been found to be strongly associated with the personality traits of psychopathy. Therefore, it is not unexpected that there is a significant difference in the Factor 1 and 2 correlations with drug use disorders, but not with alcohol use disorders.

Taken together, the results of these studies indicate that substance use among inmates tends to be more associated with social deviance and an antisocial lifestyle (Factor 2) than to the core personality traits associated with psychopathy (Factor 1). These findings are consistent with Cleckley's (1941) notion that, in the psychopath, alcohol or substance use serves as a catalyst that facilitates the expression of preexisting antisocial tendencies. Substance use alone, however, would not cause an individual to express an impulse that was not already present. Therefore, in psychopaths, substance use can be viewed as one of many symptoms in a general pattern of deviance. In contrast, many individuals who are dependent or abusing alcohol or drugs may have begun using drugs for a variety of reasons (e.g., escape emotional distress, be part of a peer group) and continue using, in part, because they are physically addicted. Antisocial acts by these individuals are most likely driven by the need to acquire money for drugs or the result of impairment in their lives caused by substance use (e.g., unemployment) rather than by an underlying constellation of psychopathy.

When assessing psychopathy in male offenders with either the PCL-R or the PCL-SV, if a strong Factor 2 behavioral style such as impulsivity, irresponsibility, and poor behavioral controls is present, the individual should also be assessed for substance use problems. Furthermore, it is important that clinicians ascertain the age of onset of regular substance use as well as whether, and to what degree, antisocial behaviors were present prior to the onset of substance use. If antisocial behaviors were present prior to the onset of drug use, it indicates an increased likelihood of psychopathy. These more psychopathic inmates with substance use problems are less likely to be compliant with or complete substance abuse treatment. These individuals will most likely require more structured and specialized interventions involving greater incentives (e.g., earn more hours of recreation, reduction in number of community service hours) for them to be successful in ceasing substance use. If antisocial behaviors were not present prior to the onset of substance use, it suggests that substance use may be the driving force behind much of the antisocial activity. These individuals will probably benefit from substance abuse treatment and cease the majority of their antisocial activities once substance use has abated.

CORRELATES OF PSYCHOPATHY IN SUBSTANCE ABUSERS

Over the last 8 years, our group has investigated the reliability (Alterman, Cacciola, & Rutherford, 1993; McKay, Ford, Alterman, Cacciola, & Rutherford, 1994; Rutherford, Cacciola, Alterman, McKay, & Cook, 1999) and predictive validity of alternative conceptualizations of ASPD, including psychopathy as measured by the PCL–R, in samples of methadone patients, alcoholics, and, more recently, cocaine-dependent women. To date, 397 men have been studied. The majority of men (n = 205) were opiate-dependent individuals recruited from the Philadelphia Veterans Administration (VA) methadone maintenance (MM) program. An additional 45 opiate-dependent men were recruited from an urban methadone maintenance program. The remaining 146 men were alcohol-dependent patients recruited from a community treatment program in a nearby urban center.

Demographic and historical variables for the three samples of men are presented in Table 15.1. There were many statistically significant (p < .05) differences between the three samples of men. The alcohol-dependent men were significantly younger than the men from the VA methadone program and the men from the community MM program. Men from the VA MM program had significantly more years of education and were more likely to be currently employed than either the alcohol-dependent men or community MM men. Not surprisingly, the alcohol-dependent

TABLE 15.1
Sample Characteristics

| | Men | | | | | |
| | Opiate-VA (N = 205) | | Opiate-CMM (N = 45) | | Alcohol (N = 145) | |
Variable	Mean	SD	Mean	SD	Mean	SD
% African American	58.5	—	54.5	—	52.8	—
% White	37.7	—	40.9	—	45.8	—
Age	40.9	4.7	39.7	6.1	32	7.2
Years of education	12.5	1.5	11.5	1.6	11.8	1.6
% Currently employed	41.1	—	20.5	—	22.9	—
Years of heavy alcohol use	6.5	8.9	3.8	6.1	12.1	7.8
Years of heroin use	16.4	7.6	14.1	7.6	0.1	0.6
Years of cocaine use	3.8	5.1	2.0	3.1	3.5	4.2
# Prior alcohol treatments	0.7	2.1	1.1	3.7	2.3	3.5
# Prior drug treatments	4.7	4.3	5.1	4.3	1.3	2.5
# Prior inpatient psychiatric treatments	0.5	1.1	0.1	0.3	0.3	0.9
# of arrests	7.2	11.8	13.8	20.5	4.3	8.5
Months of incarceration	19.5	29.8	39.3	39.1	9.9	20.1

men reported significantly more years of heavy drinking, but significantly fewer years of heroin use than either the VA MM men or community MM men. Community MM men reported significantly more arrests and months of incarceration than both VA MM men and alcohol-dependent men. Despite these difference, no statistical difference in PCL–R scores was found between the groups (Table 15.2). Therefore, in most of the studies discussed later, the groups of men were combined for purposes of analyses.

Because there is a relatively high degree of illegal activity among substance abuse patients and many individuals are required to enter treatment by the courts, probation officers, or their employers, one might think that there would be a high proportion of individuals in substance abuse treatment who would be diagnosed as psychopathic. However, this was not the case in our studies. PCL R scores for substance-dependent men in our studies were significantly lower than those found in prisoners. Although the prevalence of psychopathy in prison samples tends to be between 15% and 25%, it is less than 12% in our samples. Only 13 of the VA MM men, 3 of the community MM, and 17 of the alcoholic men had a PCL–R score above 30. The average Factor 1 (7.5) and Factor 2 (8.5) scores of the substance-abusing men are also significantly below those of inmates (Factor 1 = 8.6, Factor 2 = 11.4). It appears that, although substance-dependent individuals participate in many antisocial activities and

TABLE 15.2
Comparisons of PCL-R Scores for Samples of Addicted Men

	Sample		
	VA MM[1] (N = 205)	CM MM[2] (N = 45)	ADM[3] (N = 145)
Variable	PCL–R Score (SD)	PCL–R Score (SD)	PCL–R Score (SD)
Factor 1	7.3 (3.4)	8.1 (3.1)	7.7 (3.9)
Factor 2	8.2 (3.3)	9.5 (3.0)	8.7 (3.9)
Total	18.3 (7.0)	20.6 (6.3)	18.7 (8.1)
% Scoring ≥ 30	6.3	6.7	11.6

1 = Veterans Administration methadone maintained men
2 = Community methadone maintained men
3 = Alcohol-dependent men

demonstrate some of the behavioral styles associated with psychopathy such as conning and manipulation and failure to accept responsibility for their actions, the frequency of a full diagnosis of psychopathy is considerably lower in substance-dependent patients than in inmates. In our studies, only a small subset of substance abuse patients have been found to be primarily psychopathic. With so few individuals scoring above 30, it is difficult to make meaningful statistical comparisons between psychopathic and nonpsychopathic groups. Investigations of the correlations between the level of psychopathy and other measures is, however, possible. The reader should remain cognizant that, in all of the studies summarized herein, less than 10% of the samples were *psychopathic*, as defined by having a PCL-R score of 30 or more.

It is believed that psychopaths do not experience subjective distress to the same degree as normal individuals (Cleckley, 1941; Gacono & Meloy, 1991, 1994). If this is the case, higher PCL-R scores should be associated with lower rates of affective and anxiety disorders. To evaluate whether this was true for substance abusers, the relationship between the PCL-R and *DSM-III-R* affective disorders was studied in 250 male methadone patients from the VA and community clinic (Rutherford, Alterman, Cacciola, & McKay, 1997). Twenty-eight percent (27.9%) of these participants met criteria for current major depression. As expected, the correlations between major depression and the PCL-R were low for Factor 1 (.02), Factor 2 (.08), and the Total (.04) score. Only 23.9% of the sample met criteria for a current anxiety disorder (a diagnosis of either panic, agoraphobia, social or simple phobia, obsessive–compulsive, generalized anxiety, or posttraumatic stress disorder [PTSD]). Correlations between the PCL-R and anxiety disorders were also low for Factor 1 (.08), Factor 2 (.16), and the Total (.06) score.

These results indicate that methadone patients with elevated psychopathy scores are less likely than those with low psychopathy scores to experience sustained subjective distress such as major depression. Compared with prisoners, however, methadone patients demonstrated a stronger relationship between the PCL-R scores and anxiety disorders. This finding may be explained, in part, by the fact that most of our sample is composed of veterans, many who suffer from PTSD (~18% of the sample), therefore, increasing the likelihood of anxiety disorders in this sample. Moreover, the men were all assessed shortly after entering treatment and may generally have been experiencing increased levels of anxiety.

The presence of depression or anxiety often acts as an incentive for an individual to enter treatment. The ability to feel subjective distress indicates that there is some acknowledgment of a problem and usually a desire to alleviate problems causing the distress. Anxiety or depression is a relatively healthy response to difficulties compared with denying the presence of problems or taking out one's anger or frustration on others (turning anger outward). Psychopathic individuals are far more likely to take out frustrations they experience on those around them than realize that they have a problem or that their behavior is causing them difficulties.

Among prisoners, it has consistently been found that drug use disorders are more strongly related to Antisocial Lifestyle than to Psychopathic Personality Traits. Although the correlations for alcohol use disorders were also stronger for Factor 2 than for Factor 1, results are less consistent than those for drug use disorders. To determine if this was also the case in substance abusers, correlations of PCL-R scores with the total number of substance use disorders diagnosed were examined. All three PCL-R scores were found to be significantly correlated with the total number of substance use disorders (e.g., opiate dependence, cocaine dependence), but correlations were significantly stronger ($p < .01$) for Factor 2 (.44) than for Factor 1 (.23) or the Total (.35) score. The correlations between a diagnosis of alcohol dependence and the PCL-R scores were all nonsignificant (Factor 1, $r = .06$; Factor 2, $r = .12$; Total, $r = .10$). The correlation with alcohol dependence was stronger for Factor 2 than for Factor 1, but not significantly. Thus, among prisoners and substance abusers, use of drugs (and, to a lesser extent, alcohol) appears to be associated with a general pattern of antisocial behavior (Factor 2), which may contribute to and/or result from substance use. However, substance abuse appears to be largely independent of the underlying psychopathic personality structure.

Based on findings with prisoners (Hare, 1991), the association between psychopathy and *DSM-III-R* Axis II symptomatology was generally expected to be weak, with the exception of the Cluster B diagnoses, especially ASPD. The personality disorders (PDs) such as antisocial, histrionic, narcissistic, borderline, and sadistic personality disorder, which share similar features to the construct of psychopathy (e.g., callousness, lack of empathy), were expected to have at least moderate correlations with psychopathy scores. The correlations between Axis II disorders and psychopathy scores were also examined in the sample of 250 male methadone patients from the VA and community clinic. Because the majority of PDs were diagnosed in less than 10% of participants in our study, PCL–R scores were examined in relation to the number of positive PD symptoms rather than actual PD diagnoses (Rutherford et al., 1997). As anticipated, strong and significant correlations between the Total score and the symptoms of ASPD (.46), borderline (.35), narcissistic (.32), and histrionic (.26) PDs were found. All of these PDs have cold, labile, or shallow interpersonal relationships as a hallmark, a feature shared with psychopathy. There was also a strong and significant correlation between the PCL–R Total score and symptoms of sadistic PD (.31).

Factors 1 and 2 generally appeared to have similar correlations with the symptoms of Cluster B and sadistic PDs, but this was not true for ASPD. As found in prisoners, the correlation with ASPD was significantly stronger with Factor 2 (.49) compared with Factor 1 (.28). This should not be surprising because the behaviorally based ASPD criteria are more similar to Factor 2 items in content than Factor 1 items.

The correlations between the PCL–R scores and other Cluster A and C personality disorders were very low, with the exception of Factor 2 and paranoid personality disorder ($r = .22$). At first, this unexpected finding did not seem to make sense. Paranoid individuals tend to exhibit more anxiety and have more tumultuous relationships compared with psychopathic individuals. Paranoid individuals, however, are often hostile, cruel, and vigilant for opportunities to take advantage of situations. These are all traits that can also characterize psychopathic individuals. It is also possible that those with the most antisocial lifestyles are more wary and concerned about being arrested, watched, or hurt by others in their environment (e.g., drug dealer who cheated someone is concerned about retaliation). These paranoid behaviors may be enhanced by drug use, especially use of cocaine, thus becoming excessive and inappropriate. It is also possible that some paranoid behaviors may have been appropriate given the individual's circumstances, but were wrongfully included when diagnosing paranoid PD.

Psychopathic individuals are described by Cleckley (1941) as egocentric, manipulative, unable to form long-lasting bonds to people, and unlikely to express psychotic symptoms or reality-testing difficulties. Therefore, it could be hypothesized that there would be significant differences in the level of impairment in object relations, but not reality testing, between psychopathic and nonpsychopathic individuals.

To evaluate this hypothesis, two studies were conducted (using the Bell Object Relations and Reality Testing Inventory [BORRTI]; Bell, 1991) to assess object relations and reality testing. The BORRTI is a self-report questionnaire consisting of four scales that assess object relations: alienation, egocentricity, insecure attachment, and social incompetence. There are three reality subscales: reality distortion, uncertainty of perception, and hallucinations and delusions. Negative scores on all the scales are considered better, whereas higher or positive scores are more unhealthy. It was hypothesized specifically that psychopathic individuals would show pronounced deficits on the alienation scale, indicating a basic lack of trust and superficial social relationships, as well as on the egocentricity scale, indicating that an individual sees others as people to be exploited for their own means and has little regard for their feelings (Bell, 1991). Deficits on the insecure attachment scale, indicating fear of rejection and abandonment, or on the social incompetence scale, which suggests a shy and nervous individual, were not anticipated, nor were any deficits on the three reality subscales expected.

In the first study of 215 methadone patients, significant differences between subjects with high ($\geq$ 25) and low PCL–R scores were revealed (Rutherford, Alterman, Cacciola, McKay, & Cook, 1996). Individuals with high psychopathy scores demonstrated more impairments on the alienation, insecure attachment, and egocentricity object relations scales than individuals with low psychopathy scores. Bell (1991) stated that deficits on the alienation and egocentricity scale suggest a "bitter turning against the other with a profound mistrust of other's motivations and a belief that interpersonal gratification's can only occur through manipulation, coercion, and demandingness at the expense of the other" (p. 16). It is also stated that elevations on these two scales and a very low social incompetence score may indicate that an individual feels able to con others and views himself as a *smooth operator* who can manipulate others at will. The social incompetence score of the high psychopathy group in our sample was significantly lower than Bell's mean, suggesting that this was the case.

Surprisingly, individuals with high psychopathy scores were also found to have significant impairments on the reality distortion and hallucinations and delusions reality testing scales, whereas those with low psychopathy scores demonstrated no impairments on these scales. As Cleckley (1941) cogently noted long ago, despite the facade of normal human emotion and reasoning, the lack of empathy, shallow affect, manipulativeness, and grandiosity of psychopaths implies that their reality is different than that of most people. Psychopaths are unaware of this difference, but confident that their own view of reality is correct (Cleckley, 1941). These results suggest that methadone patients with high psychopathy scores have little confusion regarding perceptions of their internal and external realities (Bell, 1991), although their view of reality is distorted compared with other individuals. The descriptions of the object relations and reality testing based on BORRTI scores for the psychopathic individuals are certainly consistent with those purported by Cleckley (1941).

These findings point to the difficulties one can expect to encounter when treating an individual with high psychopathy scores. It is difficult to establish a therapeutic alliance with individuals with high psychopathy scores because they have such a high degree of mistrust of others and believe that the only way to get what they desire is by manipulating others. These individuals often feel that there are strings attached to everything. Additionally, they also tend to think that they are much smarter than you, the clinician, and may take great pleasure in trying to confuse, educate, or impress you with their knowledge of counseling, drug use, or the legal system. One result of psychopaths having different views of reality, which they feel is the correct view compared with the rest of the world, is that it is hard for them to truly appreciate, other than on a superficial basis, how their actions affect others. For example, when asked whether his actions (drug use, stealing) affected his family, one client (with a PCL–R score of 31) stated, "Yeah, I really hurt them." When asked how he hurt them, he said only, "What I did was wrong. Things would still be fine if I'd never got caught." (He stole jewelry that his father, now deceased, had given his mother to obtain drug money.) When really pushed to say more about the effect of his actions, this client got mad and stated, "I'm the one who spent time in jail not my mother, so why is she pissed off? I never got much money for anything I stole, anyway insurance covers all that crap." This client could not even see his mother as being affected by things he did, and he certainly exhibited no remorse for having stolen items of sentimental value from her.

In contrast to the findings with methadone patients, the next study of 147 alcoholic men revealed no significant differences on any BORRTI object relations or reality testing scale between those with high PCL–R scores (≥ 25) and low PCL–R scores (Snyder, 1998). It is unclear why the results in the sample of alcoholic men were so different from those of the methadone patients. One possible explanation is that the alcoholic participants either consciously or unconsciously denied their pathology in an attempt to portray themselves in a more positive light than the methadone patients. The group of alcoholics studied was of a significantly lower socioeconomic group compared with the VA and community MM patients and had much poorer employment histories. Despite a higher rate of psychopathy (~12% vs. 6% with PCL–R scores ≥ 30) in the alcoholics, there were significantly fewer arrests and less incarceration time reported by the alcoholics compared with the methadone patients. The antisocial activity of the alcoholics was less varied and appeared more related to obtaining general economic support. Therefore, it is also possible, and perhaps more likely, that alcoholics as a group tend to be less psychopathic than opiate addicts, and therefore did not demonstrate the deficits seen in the MM. Sampling error may also be responsible for the higher rate of individuals with PCL–R scores of 30 or more found in the alcoholic sample.

PSYCHOPATHY AND HIV INFECTION

AIDS and HIV infection are of great concern to society. Reducing the spread of HIV is a primary goal of health care systems. Previous research on risk for HIV infection in methadone patients demonstrated that ASPD was associated with risky behaviors such as needle sharing, which increased the risk for HIV infection (Brooner et al., 1990, 1993). The relationship between psychopathy and HIV infection has received little research attention to date. The degree to which psychopathy predicts sex and drug-related behaviors associated with HIV infection risk was compared in a sample of 257 methadone patients (Tourian et al., 1997). Individuals with high PCL–R scores (≥ 25) were found to be twice as likely as those with low scores to have multiple sexual partners and three times more likely to share needles. These findings indicate that methadone patients with high psychopathy scores are far more likely to engage in risky behaviors related to the spread of HIV. Such behaviors not only place the individual at increased risk, but increase the risk of HIV infection for the individual's sexual partners and/or those with whom they share needles. These results should not be surprising given that psychopathic individuals tend to be impulsive, have poor behavior controls, and care little for the rights and feeling of others.

PSYCHOPATHY AND SUBSTANCE ABUSE
TREATMENT OUTCOME

The question of whether high PCL–R scores predict poor substance abuse treatment outcomes was evaluated in a sample of 193 VA methadone patients (Alterman, Rutherford, Cacciola, McKay, & Boardman, 1997). This study evaluated the 7-month MM outcome for those with high (≥ 25) and low PCL–R scores. Outcome variables included treatment retention for the 7-month study period; the number of positive opiate, cocaine, and benzodiazepine urine drug screens taken while the individual was in treatment; as well as changes in the Addiction Severity Index (ASI; McLellan, Luborsky, O'Brien, & Woody, 1980) composite scores. The findings of this study indicate that the level of psychopathy at the time the individual entered treatment was a powerful predictor of 7-month treatment noncompletion. Individuals with high psychopathy scores were more likely to leave treatment prematurely than those with low scores. Positive opiate urines were not significantly predicted by Total psychopathy scores. By contrast, positive cocaine and benzodiazepine urines were predicted by Total psychopathy scores. Psychopathy was not predictive of ASI composite score improvements in any of the areas assessed (i.e., medical, employment, legal, drug, alcohol, family/social, and psychological functioning). Thus, this study provides limited support for the predictive validity of psychopathy in substance abuse treatment outcomes of substance abuse patients.

These findings suggest that individuals with high psychopathy scores are harder to keep engaged in substance abuse treatment. However, if the individual remains in treatment, he will demonstrate improvements in general areas of life functioning to the same degree as other methadone patients. It appears that, during the course of methadone treatment, the individual with high psychopathy scores will be just as successful in decreasing his heroin use as other clients, but may experience more trouble ceasing use of cocaine and benzodiazapines compared with other clients. Although methadone does alleviate the withdrawal and cravings for opiates, it does nothing to reduce the desire for cocaine. Heavy cocaine users frequently use alcohol and/or benzodiazapines to counteract the stimulating effects of the cocaine, thus enabling them to sleep. The stimulation associated with cocaine may be much harder for the impulsive, sensation-seeking individual with high PCL–R scores to resist compared with a less impulsive, stimulation-seeking individual.

TREATMENT PLANNING

Although the utility of psychopathy is somewhat more limited in a substance abuse treatment setting than in a prison, it is clearly a useful concept that imparts important information regarding an individual's behavior and psychological make-up. These data can be useful in developing appropriate treatment plans. When developing a treatment plan with substance abusers, it is important to determine whether antisocial activities are initiated and maintained primarily by substance use or whether antisocial activities occur independently of substance use. This can be accomplished easily with the PCL–R interview by evaluating the age that various behaviors (e.g., truancy, illegal activities, physical fights) began in relation to the age of onset of alcohol and drug use.

There are several PCL–R Factor 2 items that can be particularly informative in determining whether substance use is a symptom in a pattern of general deviance (psychopathy) versus initiating and maintaining the majority of antisocial behaviors. Specifically, the need for stimulation/proneness to boredom (Item 3), poor behavioral controls (Item 10), irresponsibility (Item 15), and early behavioral problems (Item 12) can be very informative. If behaviors assessed by these items occurred prior to and at times other than when the individual was intoxicated or in a state of withdrawal, the likelihood of psychopathy is much higher than if such behaviors occur only while the individual was attempting to acquire money for drugs, intoxicated, or withdrawing from drugs. Individuals with this pattern of behavior are more likely to benefit from substance abuse treatment than those whose antisocial activities are not tied solely to substance use.

Assessment of Factor 1 items provides additional information relevant to the individual's amenability to treatment. Factor 1 items, which the clinician should pay special attention to, are failure to accept responsibility (Item 16), lack of remorse (Item 6), lack of empathy (Item 8), and shallow affect (Item 7). The ability to feel true remorse regarding the effects of one's substance use and the ability to understand the negative impact that the substance use has had on others (empathy), as well as being able to experience the full range of emotions, will bode well for one's ability to benefit from treatment. Moreover, individuals who demonstrate a shallow affect, lack of empathy, and remorse are often difficult to form a therapeutic alliance with and engage in therapy. These are commonly the individuals who terminate treatment prematurely. The clinician should also consider the outcome of any prior treatment attempts and whether the individuals have taken responsibility for their use or do they blame their use on external circumstances. Numerous past treatment attempts and ongoing use are negative prognostic indicators.

Substance abuse treatment for an individual with a high PCL–R score requires added patience, structure, incentives, and monitoring. The psychopathic individual is likely to be more demanding and manipulative than the nonpsychopathic individual. For example, one psychopathic client (PCL–R = 33), Caleb, seen by the senior author, repeatedly missed scheduled counseling appointments, only to appear at unscheduled times. At those times, Caleb would demand to be seen in counseling. When told that he had no appointment and could not be seen, Caleb lied, informing me that someone, whose name he could not remember, called and told him to come to the clinic. When this strategy failed to get him an appointment, Caleb informed me that he had taken off work and had borrowed money to get to the clinic.

According to Caleb, he was only doing what he was told to do—someone had called him. Now he demanded money to get home. Someone was going to have to pay for his trip to the clinic. In a last ditch effort to obtain sympathy, Caleb said, "If I'm not seen today my probation officer will violate me for noncompliance with treatment." Caleb repeatedly stated that I did not care about him and he feels that I was trying to ruin his attempts to do better. When confronted with the reality that he had missed numerous appointments and was forewarned that his probation was in jeopardy, Caleb became louder, more belligerent, and pounded the wall in an attempt to intimidate me into seeing him. In response to firm limit setting, he stated that I was forcing him to leave treatment and get locked up again. If I let him walk out that door without seeing him, I would be responsible for his rearrest. When I still would not see Caleb, he devalued me, stating, "You know you're not a very good therapist. How long have you been doing this? Did you ever have a drug problem? Maybe you're in recovery now?" Not responding to Caleb's attempt to draw me into an argument, I again told Caleb that he could not be seen today, but could come in the following day. He stated again that I was messing up his attempts to stop using; I was forcing him to go out and use drugs. Caleb then left. This entire interaction was in a loud and quite dramatic manner and was very disruptive to others in the clinic. Caleb returned the next day at the scheduled time, behaving as if none of this had occurred. When asked about the events of the previous day, he replied, "Yeah I was just having a bad day. I am sure someone called to tell me to come to the clinic though. You're gonna tell my probation officer I'm here today though, right?" Caleb had nothing else to say about what had occurred. This client repeatedly played out similar scenarios and ultimately violated his probation and was returned to prison.

Caleb's case illustrates that external pressures are frequently the only motivation for psychopathic clients to be in treatment. Establishment of firm rules with clear consequences for violation of those rules, as well as confrontation of maladjustive and irresponsible behaviors, are essential when working with clients with high psychopathy scores (Gacono, Nieberding, Owen, Rubel, & Bodholdt, 2001). Working in cooperation with the probation officer or employer is a way to enhance treatment compliance. If a client is providing clean urine samples and is compliant with treatment, a reduction in the required number of community service hours or the required number of visits with his probation officer may be used as incentives for meeting clinical goals. Teaching the client alternative ways to remain stimulated and challenged with life (see chap. 18) may also be beneficial in helping them reduce substance use. Clients with high psychopathy scores are at increased risk for HIV infection. They should be encouraged to reduce their HIV risk behaviors, such as engaging in unprotected sexual activity and sharing needles. Cognitive behavioral intervention programs focusing on changing the specific behavioral patterns associated with HIV infection risk should be used to accomplish this in conjunction with general AIDS education.

Clinicians need to be persistent and creative in dealing with clients with high psychopathy scores. Clinicians who are especially good with difficult and manipulative clients should be the primary therapist for these patients. Experienced clinicians typically have a better understanding of the relationship issues of transference, countertransference, and resistance, which impact the therapeutic alliance (Gacono et al., 2001). If there is to be a positive treatment outcome, it is essential that the clinician successfully manage those processes that can disrupt the course of therapy. Clients with high psychopathy scores are likely to arouse intense countertransference reactions, and clinicians must have enough psychological awareness and maturity not to let these reactions damage the therapeutic alliance. The potential for burnout when dealing with a psychopathic client is tremendously high. Clinicians must have adequate support and supervision available in the clinic. Clinicians should not take the frequent failure of these clients and the clients' devaluation of them as a clinician as a reflection of their own clinical abilities. Clinicians must keep in mind that, although patients with high psychopathy scores can be helped to reduce their substance use, there is currently no effective treatment for the psychopathic personality. Clients with high psychopathy scores are one of the most difficult, trying, and perhaps least rewarding group of individuals to treat.

ACKNOWLEDGMENTS

This work was supported by the Medical Research Service of the Department of Veterans Affairs, National Institute on Drug Abuse Research Grant No. RO1 DA-05858, Center Grant DA05186, and the National Institute on Alcohol Abuse and Alcoholism Grant No. 5-R01-AA08480. We would also like to express our thanks to Ellen M. Mulholland for her tireless efforts in all of our studies.

REFERENCES

Alterman, A. I., Cacciola, J. S., & Rutherford, M. J. (1993). Reliability of the revised Psychopathy Checklist in substance abuse patients. *Psychological Assessment, 5*, 442–448.
Alterman, A. I., Rutherford, M. J., Cacciola, J. S., McKay, J. R., & Woody, G. E. (1996). Response to methadone maintenance and counseling among antisocial patients with and without major depression. *Journal of Nervous and Mental Disease, 184*, 695–702.
Alterman, A. I., Rutherford, M. J., Cacciola, J. S., McKay, J. R., & Boardman, C. R. (1997). Prediction of seven month methadone maintenance treatment response by four measures of antisociality. *Drug and Alcohol Dependence, 49*, 217–223.
Bell, M. D. (1991). *An introduction to the Bell Object Relations Reality Testing Inventory.* Available from MD Bell, Ph.D., 116B, D.V.A. Medical Center, West Haven, CT 06516, 1991

Brooner, R. K., Bigelow, G. E., Strain, E., & Schmidt, C. W. (1990). Intravenous drug abusers with antisocial personality disorder: Increased HIV risk behavior. *Drug and Alcohol Dependence, 26*, 39–44.

Brooner, R. K., Greenfield, L., Schmidt, C. W., & Bigelow, G. E. (1993). Antisocial personality disorder and HIV infection among intravenous drug abusers. *American Journal of Psychiatry, 150*, 53–58.

Brooner, R. K., Schmidt, C. W., Felch, L. J., & Bigelow, G. E. (1992). Antisocial behavior of intravenous drug abusers: Implications for diagnosis of antisocial personality disorder. *American Journal of Psychiatry, 149*, 182–187.

Cleckley, H. (1941). *The mask of sanity* (1st ed.). St. Louis, MO: Mosby.

Cottler, L. B., Price, R. K., Comptom, W. M., & Mager, D. E. (1995). Subtypes of adult antisocial behavior among drug abusers. *Journal of Nervous and Mental Disease, 183*, 154–161.

Dush, D. M., & Keen, J. (1995). Changes in cluster analysis subtypes among alcoholic personalities after treatment. *Evaluation and the Health Professions, 18*, 152–165.

Fishbein, D. H., & Reuland, M. (1994). Psychological correlates of frequency and type of drug use among jail inmates. *Addictive Behaviors, 19*, 583–598.

Gacono, C., & Meloy, J. R. (1991). A Rorschach investigation of attachment and anxiety in antisocial personality disorder. *Journal of Nervous and Mental Disease, 179*, 546–552.

Gacono, C., & Meloy, J. R. (1994). *The Rorschach assessment of aggressive and psychopathic personalities.* Hillsdale, NJ: Lawrence Erlbaum Associates.

Gacono, C., Nieberding, R. J., Own, A., Rubel, J., & Bodholdt, R. (2001). Treating juvenile and adult offenders with conduct disorder, antisocial, and psychopathic personalities. In J. Ashford, B. Sales, & W. Reid (Eds.), *Treating adult and juvenile offenders with special needs* (pp. 99–129). Washington, DC: American Psychological Association.

Hare, R. D. (1991). *The Revised Psychopathy Checklist.* Toronto, Ontario, Canada: Multi-Health Systems.

Hart, S. D., Forth, A. E., & Hare, R. D. (1991). The MCMI–II as a measure of psychopathy. *Journal of Personality Disorders, 5*, 318–327.

Hart, S. D., & Hare, R. D. (1989). Discriminate validity of the Psychopathy Checklist in a forensic psychiatric population. *Psychological Assessment, 1*, 211–218.

Hemphill, J. F., Hart, S. D., & Hare, R. D. (1994). Psychopathy and substance use. *Journal of Personality Disorders, 8*, 169–180.

McLellan, A. T., Luborsky, L., O'Brien, C. P., & Woody, G. E. (1980). An improved evaluation instrument for substance abuse patients: The Addiction Severity Index. *Journal of Nervous and Mental Disease, 173*, 412–423.

McKay, J. R., Ford, S., Alterman, A. I., Cacciola, J. S., & Rutherford, M. J. (1994, June). *Reliability of the Revised Psychopathy Checklist in alcoholics.* Paper presented at the Research Society on Alcoholism, Maui, Hawaii.

Rogers, R., & Bagby, R. M. (1994). Dimensions of psychopathy: A factor analytic study of the MMPI antisocial personality disorder scale. *International Journal of Offender Therapy and Comparative Criminology, 38*, 297–308.

Rutherford, M. J., Alterman, A. I., Cacciola, J. S., & McKay, J. R. (1997). Validity of the Psychopathy Checklist–Revised in male methadone patients. *Drug and Alcohol Dependence, 44*, 143–149.

Rutherford, M. J., Alterman, A. I., Cacciola, J. S., McKay, J. R., & Cook, T. G. (1996). Object relations and reality testing in psychopathic and antisocial methadone patients. *Journal of Personality Disorders, 10*, 312–320.

Rutherford, M. J., Cacciola, J. S., Alterman, A. I., McKay, J. R., & Cook, T. G. (1999). The two-year test-retest reliability of the PCL–R in methadone patients. *Assessment, 6*, 285–291.

Smith-Stevens, S., & Newman, J. P. (1990). Alcohol and drug abuse-dependence disorders in psychopathic and nonpsychopathic criminal offenders. *Journal of Abnormal Psychology, 99*, 430–439.

Snyder, J. B. (1998). *Relationship of psychopathy and antisocial personality disorder to the object relations and reality testing of alcoholic men.* Unpublished doctoral dissertation, Temple University.

Tourian, K., Alterman, A. I., Metzger, D. S., Rutherford, M., Cacciola, J. S., & McKay, J. R. (1997). Validity of three measures of antisociality in predicting HIV risk behaviors in methadone maintenance patients. *Drug and Alcohol Dependence, 47,* 99–107.

16

Psychopathy and the Criminal Lifestyle: Similarities and Differences

Glenn D. Walters
Federal Correctional Institution, Schuylkill, Pennsylvania

Roberto Di Fazio
Millhaven Institution, Ontario, Canada

The term *psychopathy* has its roots in late 19th-century Germany, where it was used to describe all disorders of personality (Dolan, 1994). Since that time, it has evolved into a personality syndrome marked by manipulative interpersonal relationships, lack of empathy and remorse, and antisocial behavior (Hart, Hare, & Forth, 1994). Psychopaths commit crimes, but most incarcerated criminal offenders do not meet the criteria for psychopathy (Hart & Hare, 1989). By contrast, the criminal lifestyle model was explicitly designed to clarify and explain criminal behavior (Walters, 1990). Consequently, most offenders display at least some of the elements of a criminal lifestyle and can be ordered along a continuum of increasing lifestyle involvement. In short, lifestyle theory views human behavior as a reflection of specific environmental and interpersonal influences and the manner in which the person interacts with these influences, rather than a direct manifestation of the dispositional characteristics of the individual.

Psychopathy and crime are not identical. Cleckley (1976) and others identified psychopathic individuals who avoided incarceration and functioned, although not very well, in the community. In contrast, the lifestyle approach is principally concerned with individuals who behave criminally. Persons who satisfy diagnostic criteria for psychopathy come from all walks of life, whereas those who exhibit the defining features of a criminal lifestyle can be found primarily in jails and prisons. Hence, there would appear to be substantial and seemingly irreconcilable differences in how psychopathy and the criminal lifestyle are conceptualized and only minimal overlap between the concepts in terms of the types of individuals encompassed by each. In this chapter, the relationship between psychopathy and criminal lifestyle is explored in an effort to determine whether combining the two concepts can be useful in constructing a framework for intervening with antisocial individuals.

THEORY

The literature suggests two personality-based versions of psychopathy theory. The most popular theory is the one espoused by Cleckley (1976), in which 16 individual characteristics are listed, but where the cardinal feature is a deficit in the ability to respond affectively to others. Hare's (1980) Psychopathy Checklist (PCL) is a 22-item (20 items in the revision known as the PCL–R; Hare, 1991) rating scale designed to assess the Cleckley criteria for psychopathy. The second theoretical perspective, Blackburn's (1975), establishes poor impulse control as the core feature of psychopathy and is assessed using the Special Hospitals Assessment of Personality and Socialization (SHAPS). Blackburn's concept of psychopathy has gained support in Great Britain, whereas the Cleckley conceptualization is the standard used in most NATO countries, including the United States (Cootee, Forth, & Hare, 1998). Accordingly, it is the definition utilized in this chapter.

The criminal lifestyle model utilizes a social learning perspective on antisocial behavior. Within this model, behavioral patterns, rather than personality, define lifestyle. Antisocial behavior is measured not by the degree of personality disturbance, but by the level of involvement in, commitment to, and identification with a prototypic criminal lifestyle. This lifestyle is characterized by four behavioral patterns: irresponsibility (e.g., nonsupport of child), self-indulgence (e.g., history of drug or alcohol abuse), interpersonal intrusiveness (e.g., use of a weapon during the confining offense), and social rule breaking (e.g., number of prior arrests; Walters, 1990). Irresponsibility is believed to permeate many aspects of the individual's behavior, so that social, moral, and legal obligations are ignored or forgotten. Self-indulgence reveals a lack of restraint in the pursuit of immediate gratification, with little apparent concern for the negative long-term consequences of these actions. Interpersonal intrusiveness entails callously encroaching on the rights, feelings, and private lives of others, whereas social rule breaking communicates a blatant disregard for the laws and norms of society.

Each of the four behavioral styles is postulated to fall along a continuum. The extent to which irresponsibility, self-indulgence, interpersonal intrusiveness, and social rule breaking become frequent and habitual demarcates the severity of the criminal lifestyle. However, a distinction is drawn between the individual and his or her lifestyle. The person is never the lifestyle because it is impossible for any one person to be irresponsible, self-indulgent, interpersonally intrusive, and social rule breaking 24 hours a day. The lifestyle model hypothesizes that everyone has the potential to embrace a criminal lifestyle with its promises of unlimited wealth, power, and immediate gratification. However, some people are at greater risk for initial involvement in the lifestyle because of the presence of certain dispositional and situational factors. The reason for labeling the lifestyle rather than the individual is to avoid the self-fulfilling prophecy that the labeling process promotes.

Once initiated, there is little change in the patterns that mark a criminal lifestyle. The decisions the individual makes are accordingly influenced almost exclusively by the standards and protocol of the lifestyle. Although this reduces the person's adaptive abilities and limits opportunities for internal change, it can also be highly reinforcing because it relieves the individual of personal responsibility for important life decisions. The person simply follows the rules and dictates of the lifestyle (e.g., take what you want, society owes you), which, in turn, serves to maintain the lifestyle. Maintenance and patterns, it should be noted, are hallmark signs of a lifestyle.

The criminal lifestyle is further maintained by cognitive errors and thinking styles. Based in part on the ideas of Yochelson and Samenow (1976) and influenced by Beck, Wright, Newman, and Liese's (1993) work on cognitive errors, Walters (1990) developed a system of eight thinking styles believed to be instrumental in maintaining the four behavioral patterns of a criminal lifestyle. These eight thinking styles—mollification, cutoff, entitlement, power orientation, sentimentality, superoptimism, cognitive indolence, and discontinuity—are believed to correspond with all four behavioral styles, although some of the relationships are viewed to be stronger than others (see Fig. 16.1).

Cognitive indolence and discontinuity are closely related to the behavioral style of irresponsibility. Cognitive indolence involves the inclination to engage in short-cut problem solving and uncritically accept lifestyle-promoting plans and ideas. The individual who anticipates achieving happiness, once he or she accumulates a certain degree of material wealth, is operating under the false impressions that cognitive indolence can breed. Discontinuity presumes less premeditation and greater disruption of thought processes than cognitive indolence, the consequence of which is an individual who has trouble following through on initially good intentions.

Although sentimentality and superoptimism correlate with all four behavioral patterns, they are most strongly identified with self-indulgence. *Sentimentality* is characterized by the performance of good deeds designed to justify one's actions and make one feel like a *good guy*. Over-

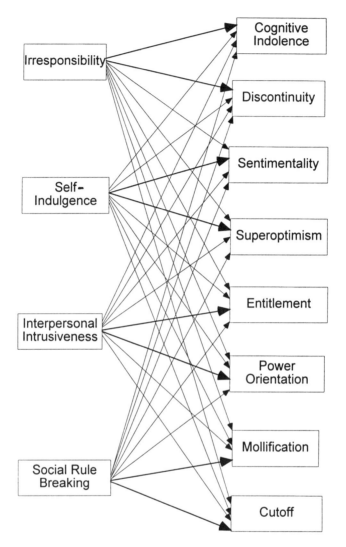

FIG. 16.1. Relationships presumed to exist between the four behavioral patterns and eight thinking styles.

estimating the chances of avoiding the negative consequences of criminal behavior comes under the classification of *superoptimism*. Hence, the fact that friends and associates are being arrested and imprisoned has little impact on the individual because he or she believes that he or she can somehow avoid a similar fate at least for the time being.

Interpersonal intrusiveness is reflected in the thinking patterns of entitlement and power orientation. Entitlement presumes a sense of privilege or ownership, in which the individual's wishes and desires take precedence over the rights of others. Entitlement is often expressed on release from prison, whereby the individual leaves the facility with the attitude that *society owes me*. Putting others down and violating their personal space to feel in control of a situation are indicative of a power-oriented individual, who when not in control feels weak and powerless.

The behavioral style of social rule breaking is perhaps most clearly captured by the thinking styles of mollification and cutoff. Mollification occurs when people justify and rationalize their rule-breaking behavior by placing blame for their actions onto other people and external events. The cutoff thinking style is employed by offenders who want to eliminate deterrents that stand in the way of them committing a particular criminal act. Offenders who entertain such thoughts as *fuck it* whenever they are frustrated are using the cutoff to deal with their problems in life.

ASSESSMENT AND INTERVENTION

Assessment Procedures

Two instruments are routinely employed in assessing the criminal lifestyle. One, the Lifestyle Criminality Screening Form (LCSF; Walters, White, & Denney, 1991), is a 14-item chart audit procedure scored from information found in a client's central file or presentence investigation (PSI) report. Total scores on the LCSF range from 0 to 22. Scores of 10 or higher on this measure indicate that the individual strongly identifies with the criminal lifestyle and correlate reasonably well with recidivism (Walters & Chlumsky, 1993; Walters & McDonough, 1998; Walters, Revella, & Baltrusaitis, 1990). Scores between 7 and 9 suggest moderate identification with the criminal lifestyle and moderate risk of recidivism, whereas scores below 7 imply low identification with the criminal lifestyle and low risk of recidivism. Mean agreement between raters independently scoring the LCSF is .92 with respect to the total score (Walters, 1998b). Although the LCSF items are broken down into theoretically meaningful clusters—irresponsibility, self-indulgence, interpersonal intrusiveness, and social rule breaking—these definitional subscales appear to have limited empirical value (Walters et al., 1991). Potentially more useful are four factor scales that have been identified and confirmed through several factor analyses of the LCSF: Antisocial Identity, Intrusiveness of the Confining Offense, Family and Interpersonal Conflict, and Poor School and Work Adjustment (Walters, 1995a, 1997a).

The Psychological Inventory of Criminal Thinking Styles (PICTS; Walters, 1995b) is a second instrument that can be used to assess the criminal lifestyle. Unlike the LCSF, the PICTS is completed by the client. The PICTS consists of 80 items organized into 10 scales: two validity scales (Confusion and Defensiveness) and eight thinking style scales (Mollification, Cutoff, Entitlement, Power Orientation, Sentimentality, Superoptimism, Cognitive Indolence, and Discontinuity). Each item is rated on a 4-point scale, with points labeled *strongly agree* (4), *agree* (3), *uncertain* (2), and *disagree* (1). This scoring system is employed with each of the eight items that comprise the eight thinking style scales and four of the validity scale items. The remaining four items on each validity scale are scored in a reverse order (i.e., *strongly agree* = 1, *agree* = 2, *uncertain* = 3, *disagree* = 4). Two-week test–retest reliability for the eight thinking style scales has been found to range between .73 and .93 (Walters, 1995b; Walters, Elliott, & Miscoll, 1998). The PICTS Cutoff and Discontinuity scales successfully predict recidivism in male felons (Walters, 1997b), while the PICTS Sentimentality scale effectively predicts recidivism in female offenders (Walters & Elliott, 1999). Exploratory and confirmatory factor analyses of the PICTS have identified four primary factors that have since been labeled Problem Avoidance, Interpersonal Hostility, Self-Deception, and Denial of Harm (Walters, 1995b; Walters et al., 1998).

The Psychopathy Checklist–Revised (PCL–R: Hare, 1991) is designed to assess psychopathy as delineated by Cleckley (1976). As noted elsewhere in this text, the PCL–R is a reliable and reasonably valid measure capable of predicting future criminality and violent recidivism (Hart, Kropp, & Hare, 1988; Rice & Harris, 1995; Serin, 1996). In factor analyses of the PCL–R, two primary factors have been identified (Hare et al., 1990). Factor 1 reflects interpersonal and affect characteristics such as egocentricity, manipulativeness, callous interpersonal relations, and lack of remorse. Factor 2 is associated with an impulsive, unstable, and antisocial lifestyle. Evidence suggests that Factor 2 is more highly correlated with a *Diagnostic and Statistical Manual of Mental Disorders* (*DSM–IV*) diagnosis of antisocial personality disorder (ASPD; American Psychiatric Association, 1994) and release outcome than is Factor 1 (Harpur, Hare, & Hakstian, 1989). In addition, cross-sectional studies indicate that, although Factor 2 correlates negatively with age, Factor 1 remains reasonably stable over the life span (Harpur & Hare, 1994). These findings imply that criminal lifestyle measures should correlate more convincingly with Factor 2 of the PCL–R than with Factor 1. We decided to empirically test this hypothesis utilizing 108 Canadian federal prisoners rated on both the PCL–R and LCSF.

Relationship Between the PCL–R and LCSF

The mean age of the 108 participants in this study was 31.23 years, and the racial breakdown was 67.6% White, 19.4% African American, 8.3% Native Canadian, and 4.6% other. Participants were serving an average sentence of 43.69 months in a federal Canadian prison, most typically for a violent offense (42.6%), with 20.4% being confined for robbery, 18.5% for property crimes, 6.5% for drugs, and 12.0% for miscellaneous felonies. The overall correlation between the LCSF and PCL–R in this sample was moderately strong ($r = .61$), although, as predicted, the LCSF correlated much higher with Factor 2 ($r = .67$) than with Factor 1 ($r = .27$).

Correlations involving the four LCSF subscales (Irresponsibility, Self-Indulgence, Interpersonal Intrusiveness, Social Rule Breaking) were also two to three times higher for Factor 2 than Factor 1. Of the four LCSF factor scales, the Antisocial Identity scale demonstrated the strongest relationship with the PCL–R Total score ($r = .59$). The correlation between Antisocial Identity and Factor 2 of the PCL–R ($r = .69$) was nearly three times that of the correlation between Antisocial Identity and Factor 1 ($r = .24$). The LCSF and PCL–R would appear to share a significant portion of variance in common, although the overlap is nonuniform in that the LCSF correlates more highly with Factor 2 than with Factor 1.

The degree of association between the PCL–R and LCSF is displayed in Table 16.1, in which standard cutting scores were employed. As the table suggests, there was minimal correspondence between a cutting score of 30 on the PCL–R and a cutting score of 10 on the LCSF. This is attributable to the fact that two thirds of the sample achieved a score of 10 or higher on the LCSF, in contrast to a mere 5% of the sample with PCL–R scores ≥ 30. In assessing the relationship between the two PCL–R factors and the LCSF, a cutting score of 10 was implemented with all three measures. Concordance between the LCSF and Factor 2 (63.9%) was higher than concordance between the LCSF and Factor 1 (52.8%). A chi-square comparison against chance revealed that only the LCSF–Factor 2 relationship achieved statistical significance [$\chi^2(1) = 4.25, p < .05$]. These findings suggest that LCSF elevation was more common than PCL–R elevation in this

TABLE 16.1
Relationship Between the PCL–R and LCSF Using Standard Cutoff Scores

PCL–R Score	LCSF Total Score	
	≥ 10	< 10
Total		
≥ 30	4.6%	0.0%
< 30	62.0%	33.3%
Factor 1		
≥ 10	24.1%	4.6%
< 10	42.6%	28.7%
Factor 2		
≥ 10	35.2%	4.6%
< 10	31.5%	28.7%

group of incarcerated Canadian offenders; as indicated in the correlational results previously reported, the LCSF is more similar to Factor 2 of the PCL-R than Factor 1.

A Three-Phase Model of Assessment

The LCSF, PICTS, and PCL-R can be combined with various behavioral skill measures to provide a comprehensive clinical assessment for use in intervening with nonpsychopathic antisocial clients. PCL-R Total scores greater than 25 (depending on the setting) may require special evaluation to determine their suitability for intervention. People preoccupied with a criminal lifestyle spend a significant portion of their day engaged in criminal activities, pursuing short-term goals, and forging identities shaped by antisocial accomplishments. Accordingly, once the client's amenability to intervention has been gauged using the PCL-R Total score, the next step is to ascertain the client's current level of criminal lifestyle involvement, commitment, and identification. This can be accomplished in several different ways, although the LCSF and Factor 2 of the PCL-R appear to provide the most reliable estimates of lifestyle involvement. A Total score of 10 or higher on the LCSF, a factor score of 7 or higher on the Antisocial Identity subscale of the LCSF, or a score of 10 or higher on Factor 2 of the PCL-R all denote significant involvement in, commitment to, and identification with the prototypic criminal lifestyle. Elevated scores on all three measures may be particularly diagnostic of a criminal lifestyle.

Once it has been established that a client satisfies the basic criteria of a criminal lifestyle, the next step is to evaluate the client's readiness for change. Prochaska and DiClemente (1992) propose a stages of change model in which the client's motivation for change is said to vary across time and situation. Borrowing from Prochaska and DiClemente, the lifestyle model postulates that change normally begins with a crisis — a *crisis* being a person's perception that the lifestyle is no longer achieving its stated aims, whether that be power, pleasure, or unlimited wealth. A crisis can just as easily arise from positive events (e.g., marriage, birth of child) as negative ones (e.g., incarceration, loss of a spouse). Furthermore, a series of minor hassles may be just as effective as a major catastrophe in temporarily arresting lifestyle activities. An early goal in working with clients, therefore, is helping them define and develop crises as a means of fostering rudimentary motivation for change. The therapist also needs to identify barriers to change, two of the more prominent being thinking patterns and fear. To the extent that the belief systems of many criminal offenders protect their lifestyles, the PICTS can be used to identify major thinking errors and patterns that may be inhibiting change. These thinking errors and patterns can be sensitively challenged during the initial interview to lay the groundwork for future interventions with the client.

The third and final phase of the lifestyle assessment process is identifying personal strengths that may support the client's efforts to exit the criminal lifestyle. Fundamental social, coping, and life skills can all be assessed using measures outlined in Walters (1996). Factor 1 of the PCL–R appears to represent a disposition to be callous and manipulative in one's ongoing interpersonal relationships, considered by many to be a classic sign of psychopathy. Low scores on this measure may symbolize a person's ability to bond with and relate to others (Gacono, 1998). Accordingly, the lower a client's score on Factor 1 of the PCL–R, the greater the likelihood that he or she possesses the personal and interpersonal resources required to enter into meaningful relationships with others. Research suggests that one of the better predictors of future outcome in criminal and drug treatment populations is social support (Booth, Russell, Soucek, & Laughlin, 1992; Hammersley, Forsyth, & Lavelle, 1990). Genuineness in one's interactions with others, as measured by a low score on Factor 1 of the PCL–R, may consequently be an important initial step in soliciting this support.

A Three-Phase Model of Intervention

Lifestyle intervention also occurs in three phases. The goal of the first phase of lifestyle intervention is to arrest the lifestyle. This phase typically begins with a crisis. As previously stated, an event need not be negative nor traumatic to qualify as a crisis. A crisis causes people to question the viability of their continued involvement in a lifestyle. The ebb and flow of crises in the natural course of an offender's daily routine presents certain opportunities for change. The key to intervention, as far as the lifestyle therapist is concerned, is developing these naturally occurring crises by holding a mirror up to clients so they can see that it is they who are responsible for the majority of negative consequences in their lives. This is most effective if there is a strong therapeutic bond between the therapist and client. The goal of the therapeutic alliance is to encourage client responsibility, hope, and self-confidence. To this end, the lifestyle therapist can assist the client in modifying his or her belief system with the help of procedures like the rational challenge (Maultsby, 1975). Three beliefs play a particularly important role in this initial phase of intervention: a belief in the necessity of change designed to promote responsibility, a belief in the possibility of change capable of instilling hope, and a belief in the ability to effect change strong enough to inspire self-confidence.

The lifestyle is viewed to be arrested when the individual shows signs of decreased involvement in routine lifestyle activities. Once this is accomplished, the next step is to assist the client in developing certain social, coping, and thinking skills. This phase of lifestyle intervention borrows extensively from the behavioral tradition. Whether the emphasis is on learning to deal with high-risk situations through stress management and resistance skills training (Ross & Fabiano, 1985), making better life decisions with the aid of values clarification and goal setting techniques (Walters, 1998a), or thinking more effectively by means of rational restructuring or cognitive relabeling (Ellis, 1970), a behavioral format is followed.

First, the global skill is separated into its component parts. Take, for instance, the case of a client learning to carry on a conversation with a stranger. Such an intervention would begin with the identification of important component skills such as learning how to select a topic for conversation, position one's body during the conversation, phrase one's ideas, and listen for feedback. Once this is accomplished, global and component skills are modeled for the client, after which the client is given the opportunity to practice the skills in simulated role-play situations. Generalization is achieved by having the client try out the skills in real-life situations and then reviewing the results in follow-up sessions with the therapist.

The third phase of lifestyle intervention centers around the construction of a substitute lifestyle designed to fill the vacuum created by the client's decision to abandon a criminal lifestyle. The criminal lifestyle accomplishes many things, including the structuring of a person's time and the avoidance of negative affect. People enmeshed in a criminal lifestyle accordingly grow accustomed to organizing their activities around lifestyle goals and objectives. Without the lifestyle to structure their time, these individuals may become lonely and bored. To maintain changes realized during the first two phases of intervention, clients must become involved in, committed to, and identified with activities incompatible with continuation of the criminal lifestyle. The authors sometimes ask clients to list what they believe they will miss once they discontinue a criminal lifestyle. This information can then be used to identify the events and experiences that draw the client to the lifestyle so that alternative avenues of achieving these experiences, objectives, and outcomes can be entertained.

CASE STUDY

Stanley is a 28-year-old White male federal Canadian prisoner serving a 39-month sentence for aggravated assault. The official version of the instant offense states that Stanley entered the home of an individual he believed owed him money and shot him in the leg and hip when he refused to pay him. On the day of the instant offense, Stanley had been drinking and became increasingly angry and agitated as he thought about how this individual had borrowed money from his girlfriend and then used it to buy drugs rather than paying her back. Stanley went to the home of this individual intent on intimidating him, but ended up shooting him after a heated argument. In discussing the instant offense, Stanley seemed genuinely remorseful for his actions and expressed relief that he did not receive a longer sentence.

Stanley had quit school in the 10th grade to work at a local bowling alley. He states that he always had trouble applying himself in academic situations and found it hard to concentrate unless he was truly interested in a topic. He reports being suspended on at least three occasions for drug use, assaulting another student, and committing vandalism — all consistent with a *DSM–IV* diagnosis of conduct disorder (CD). At the time of the instant offense, Stanley had been unemployed for 2 months because of the seasonal nature of construction work. He states that the lack of a salary made it difficult for him to support his family. Prior to being incarcerated, Stanley had been living with his common-law wife of 5 years and their 20-month-old daughter.

Stanley denied any mental health involvement, but did acknowledge a history of heavy drinking. He advised that he began drinking around age 10 and that, by age 16, he was drinking heavily, but had never participated in alcohol abuse treatment. Stanley alleges that his drinking is not a problem despite the fact nearly every one of his crimes, leading to nine arrests and three incarcerations, has occurred while under the influence of alcohol. First introduced to illegal drugs at the age of 12, Stanley has used a wide variety of psychoactive substances. Although he prefers softer drugs like marijuana, Stanley states that his drinking stimulates a craving in him for harder drugs such as cocaine and heroin and that once he starts drinking it is not long before he is using cocaine and heroin. Stanley's adult behavior is consistent with a *DSM–IV* diagnosis of ASPD.

Stanley was administered the PCL-R, LCSF, and PICTS, the results of which are reproduced in Table 16.2. Stanley's Total PCL-R score of 16 indicates a nonpsychopathic individual who scores almost one standard deviation below the mean for prison populations (seven samples, $N = 1,192$, $M = 23.6$, $SD = 7.9$; Hare, 1991). Once the individual has been triaged using the Total PCL-R score, the next order of business is to determine the level of involvement in, commitment to, and identification with the criminal lifestyle. Stanley's scores on the LCSF (15), Antisocial Identity Factor Scale (12), and PCL-R Factor 2 (10) reflect a preoccupation with and participation in criminal behavior.

The second phase of the assessment process requires that the client's readiness for change be evaluated. An initial review of Stanley's PICTS scores suggests an absence of significant criminal thinking. However, when examined in conjunction with results from the Balanced Inventory of Desirable Responding (Paulhus, 1984), Stanley's relatively high scores

TABLE 16.2
Stanley's PCL–R, LCSF, and PICTS Scores

Scale	Score	Percentile	T-Score
PCL–R			
Total Scale	16	19.1	–
Factor 1	4	13.7	–
Factor 2	10	33.6	–
LCSF			
Total score	15	–	–
Subscales			
Irresponsibility	3	–	–
Self-Indulgence	3	–	–
Interpersonal Intrusiveness	4	–	–
Social Rule Breaking	5	–	–
Factor scales			
Antisocial Identity	12	–	–
Intrusiveness of the Confining Offense	2	–	–
Family/Interpersonal Conflict	0	–	–
Poor School/Work Adjustment	2	–	–
PICTS			
Cf (Confusion)	8	–	32
Df (Defensiveness)	14	–	46
Mo (Mollification)	8	–	38
Co (Cutoff)	10	–	44
En (Entitlement)	8	–	38
Po (Power Orientation)	8	–	39
Sn (Sentimentality)	11	–	34
So (Superoptimism)	11	–	42
Ci (Cognitive Indolence)	8	–	36
Ds (Discontinuity)	11	–	44

on the LCSF, and the absence of any clearly documentable change in behavior (Stanley recently received disciplinary reports in prison for fighting and using intoxicants), it would seem that he has attempted to present himself in the best possible light on the self-report measures. This also suggests poor insight and a general lack of readiness for change. The final stage of the assessment process involves pointing out personal strengths, the most obvious in Stanley's case being the absence of a psychopathic personality (PCL–R = 16 vs. ≥ 30) despite the presence of a *DSM–IV* diagnosis of ASPD.

Intervention is marked by efforts to temporarily arrest the criminal lifestyle during the early stages. Because Stanley demonstrates low readiness for change, probably falling into Prochaska and DiClemente's (1992) precontemplation stage, intervention should focus on identifying and developing crises by confronting Stanley with the negative consequences of his behavior. Incarceration is a crisis for some, but not all, of those who enter jails and prisons. For Stanley, his first two incarcerations were little more than an inconvenience. The current incarceration, however, appears to have created more of a crisis for Stanley. Prior to the birth of his daughter, Stanley had lived from day to day. After her birth, he began to plan for the future. Separation from his daughter has become a source of distress for Stanley. The client also reported that his relationship with his common-law wife had improved and that he had made several noncriminal friends through his construction job and part-time work in a band prior to his most recent arrest and incarceration. The loss of these relationships has created a crisis for Stanley that can serve as motivation for change, provided the therapist helps Stanley see the connection between his criminal lifestyle and current distress.

Arresting the lifestyle through development of crises and extension of the arresting process with the instillation of a sense of responsibility, hope, and empowerment need to be focal points of early intervention. With the arresting of the lifestyle, the intervention moves into a second, skill-building, phase. Stanley's problem-solving, stress management, and goal setting skills are prime targets for intervention. Through a program of cognitive skills training, Stanley could improve his decision-making skills with instruction in the problem-solving method, learn to manage stress with relaxation and exercise, and augment his goal attainment by considering both the short- and long-term consequences of his actions. In the final phase of the intervention process, Stanley would be assisted in the development of a noncriminal lifestyle, in which his strengths like his lack of psychopathy and his concern for his daughter are emphasized so that he can achieve his wants and desires in ways that will not bring him back into contact with the law. During this phase of the intervention process, Stanley is asked to list all of the things he believes will be missed once he is no longer involved in a criminal lifestyle. Next, he is assisted in identifying conventional ways of achieving these goals (e.g., taking his family to the park to relax rather than drinking; playing a sport for excitement rather than committing a crime).

CONCLUSION

As suggested in this chapter, the concepts of *psychopathy* and *lifestyle* converge on some points and diverge on others. The point of convergence, as represented psychometrically by the overlap between Factor 2 of the PCL–R and the Antisocial Identity score on the LCSF, is an unstable lifestyle characterized by antisocial pursuits, goals, and images. Although this is not the sole issue addressed by lifestyle theory, it is of primary concern to those who conduct lifestyle interventions with antisocial clients.

Low guilt, reduced arousal to punishment, and other traditional psychopathic traits are viewed to be less amenable to change (Ogloff, Wong, & Greenwood, 1990). As such, the focus of lifestyle intervention is on the criminal lifestyle, which is believed to be a product of the interaction that takes place between dispositional-based trends in behavior and various environmental opportunities and learning experiences. Change is viewed by proponents of the lifestyle model as an ongoing process—a process that can be facilitated by integrating work on psychopathy with a lifestyle approach to understanding and changing antisocial and criminal behavior.

ACKNOWLEDGMENTS

Copies of the LCSF and PICTS are available from the first author. The opinions expressed in this chapter are solely the authors' and should not be construed as official or as reflecting the views of the U.S. Department of Justice, Federal Bureau of Prisons, or the Correctional Service of Canada.

REFERENCES

American Psychiatric Association. (1994). *DSM–IV: The diagnostic and statistical manual of mental disorders* (4th ed.). Washington, DC: Author.

Beck, A. T., Wright, F. D., Newman, C. F., & Liese, B. S. (1993). *Cognitive therapy of substance abuse.* New York: Guilford.

Blackburn, R. (1975). An empirical classification of psychopathic personality. *British Journal of Psychiatry, 127,* 456–460.

Booth, B. M., Russell, D. W., Soucek, S., & Laughlin, P. R. (1992). Social support and outcome of alcoholism treatment: An exploratory analysis. *American Journal of Drug and Alcohol Abuse, 18,* 87–101.

Cleckley, H. (1976). *The mask of sanity* (5th ed.). St. Louis: Mosby.

Cootee, D. J., Forth, H. E., & Hare, R. D. (1998). *Psychopathy: Theory, research and implications for society.* London: Kluwer.

Dolan, M. (1994). Psychopathy—A neurobiological perspective. *British Journal of Psychiatry, 165,* 151–159.

Ellis, A. (1970). *The essence of rational psychotherapy: A comprehensive approach to treatment.* New York: Institute of Rational Living.

Gacono, C. B. (1998). The use of the Psychopathy Checklist–Revised (PCL–R) and Rorschach in treatment planning with antisocial personality disordered patients. *International Journal of Offender Therapy and Comparative Criminology, 42,* 49–64.

Hammersley, R., Forsyth, A., & Lavelle, T. (1990). The criminality of new drug users in Glasgow. *British Journal of Addiction, 85,* 1583–1594.

Hare, R. D. (1980). A research scale for the assessment of psychopathy in criminal populations. *Personality and Individual Differences, 1,* 111–119.

Hare, R. D. (1991). *The Psychopathy Checklist.* Toronto, Ontario: Multi-Health Systems.

Hare, R. D., Harpur, T. J., Hakstian, A. R., Forth, A. E., Hart, S. D., & Newman, J. P. (1990). The revised Psychopathy Checklist: Reliability and factor structure. *Psychological Assessment, 2,* 338–341.

Harpur, T. J., & Hare, R. D. (1994). Assessment of psychopathy as a function of age. *Journal of Abnormal Psychology, 193,* 604–609.

Harpur, T. J., Hare, R. D., & Hakstian, A. R. (1989). Two-factor conceptualization of psychopathy: Construct validity and assessment implications. *Psychological Assessment, 1,* 6–17.

Hart, S. D., & Hare, R. D. (1989). Discriminant validity of the Psychopathy Checklist in a forensic psychiatric population. *Psychological Assessment, 1,* 211–218.

Hart, S. D., Hare, R. D., & Forth, A. E. (1994). Psychopathy as a risk marker for violence: Development and validation of a screening version of the Revised Psychopathy Checklist. In J. Monahan & H. J. Steadman (Eds.), *Violence and mental disorder: Developments in risk assessment* (pp. 81–98). Chicago, IL: University of Chicago Press.

Hart, S. D., Kropp, P. R., & Hare, R. D. (1988). Performance of male psychopaths following conditional release from prison. *Journal of Consulting and Clinical Psychology, 56,* 227–232.

Maultsby, M. C. (1975). *Help yourself to happiness through rational self-counseling.* New York: Institute of Rational Living.

Ogloff, J. R., Wong, S., & Greenwood, A. (1990). Treating criminal psychopaths in a therapeutic community. *Behavioral Sciences and the Law, 8,* 181–190.

Paulhus, D. L. (1984). Two-component models of socially desirable responding. *Journal of Personality and Social Psychology, 60,* 307–317.

Prochaska, J. O., & DiClemente, C. C. (1992). Stages of change in the modification of problem behavior. In M. Hersen, R. M. Eisler, & P. M. Miller (Eds.), *Progress in behavior modification* (pp. 184–214). Sycamore, IL: Sycamore.

Rice, M. E., & Harris, G. T. (1995). Psychopathy, schizophrenia, alcohol abuse, and violent recidivism. *International Journal of Law and Psychiatry, 18,* 333–342.

Ross, R. R., & Fabiano, E. A. (1985). *Time to think: A cognitive model of delinquency prevention and offender rehabilitation.* Johnson City, TN: Institute of Social Science and Art.

Serin, R. C. (1996). Violent recidivism in criminal psychopaths. *Law and Human Behavior, 20,* 207–217.

Walters, G. D. (1990). *The criminal lifestyle: Patterns of serious criminal conduct.* Newbury Park, CA: Sage.

Walters, G. D. (1995a). Factor structure of the Lifestyle Criminality Screening Form. *International Journal of Offender Therapy and Comparative Criminology, 39,* 99–108.

Walters, G. D. (1995b). The Psychological Inventory of Criminal Thinking Styles: Part I. Reliability and preliminary validity. *Criminal Justice and Behavior, 22,* 307–325.

Walters, G. D. (1996). *Substance abuse and the new road to recovery: A practitioner's guide.* Washington, DC: Taylor & Francis.

Walters, G. D. (1997a). A confirmatory factor analysis of the Lifestyle Criminality Screening Form. *Criminal Justice and Behavior, 24,* 294–308.

Walters, G. D. (1997b). Combined use of the Lifestyle Criminality Screening Form and Psychological Inventory of Criminal Thinking Styles to predict short-term release outcome. *Journal of the Mental Health in Corrections Consortium, 43,* 18–25.

Walters, G. D. (1998a). *Changing lives of crime and drugs: Intervening with substance-abusing offenders.* Chichester, England: Wiley.

Walters, G. D. (1998b). The Lifestyle Criminality Screening Form: Psychometric properties and practical utility. *Journal of Offender Rehabilitation, 27,* 9–23.

Walters, G. D., & Chlumsky, M. L. (1993). The Lifestyle Criminality Screening Form and antisocial personality disorder: Predicting release outcome in a state prison sample. *Behavioral Sciences & the Law, 11,* 111–115.

Walters, G. D., & Elliott, W. N. (1999). Predicting release and disciplinary outcome with the Psychological Inventory of Criminal Thinking Styles: Female data. *Legal and Criminological Psychology, 4,* 15–21.

Walters, G. D., Elliott, W. N., & Miscoll, D. (1998). Use of the Psychological Inventory of Criminal Thinking Styles in a group of female offenders. *Criminal Justice and Behavior, 25,* 125–134.

Walters, G. D., & McDonough, J. R. (1998). The Lifestyle Criminality Screening Form as a predictor of federal parole/probation/supervised release outcome: A 3-year follow-up. *Legal and Criminological Psychology, 3,* 173–181.

Walters, G. D., Revella, L., & Baltrusaitis, W. J. (1990). Predicting parole/probation outcome with the aid of the Lifestyle Criminality Screening Form. *Psychological Assessment, 2,* 313–316.

Walters, G. D., White, T. W., & Denney, D. (1991). The Lifestyle Criminality Screening Form: Preliminary data. *Criminal Justice and Behavior, 18,* 406–418.

Yochelson, S., & Samenow, S. E. (1976). *The criminal personality: Vol. 1. A profile for change.* New York: Jason Aronson.

17

Psychopathy and Hostage Negotiations: Some Preliminary thoughts and findings[1,2]

James L. Greenstone
Fort Worth Police Department

David S. Kosson
Finch University of Health Science, The Chicago Medical School, Wisconsin

Carl B. Gacono
Private Practice, Austin, Texas

Since the development of modern police hostage negotiations techniques in the 1970's, several typologies have been offered for categorizing hostage takers (Fowler & Greenstone, 1996; Greenstone, 1989; Greenstone, 1998; Lanceley, 1981; McMains & Mullins, 1996; Strentz, 1983; Arieti, 1963). Some typologies are based on whether the perpetrator has a mental disorder or is a criminal (in some cases, including an additional category for terrorists). Others emphasize whether the

---

[1]In this chapter we provide a brief overview of hostage negotiations. For a more detailed discussion see Greenstone (1998) and McMains (1996). The authors wish to thank Dr. Robert Hare for his helpful comments and suggestions.

[2]Material included in Appendix 1, which appeared in the first printing of this book, was written by Dr. Robert Hare, Dr. Stephen Hart, and Dr. David Cox. Although their authorship was noted in the title of the appendix, this material was inadvertently published without permission. Drs. Greenstone, Kosson, and Gacono apologize for the inadvertent unauthorized publication of this material. The authors caution readers and others that this material is copyrighted by Dr. Hare and may not be reproduced or distributed without the written permission of Dr. Hare and his publisher, Multi-Health Systems, Inc.

victim is a stranger versus a family member. Negotiation strategies utilized by hostage negotiators are based on these typologies. Newer conceptualizations also include subjects in domestic crises (Fowler, 1997; Fowler & Greenstone, 1989; Greenstone, 1993; Greenstone & Leviton, 1996; Greenstone & Leviton, 1993; McMains & Lanceley, 1995). Regardless of typology, an initial assessment and subsequent diagnostic profile is essential for defining the resolution strategies.

One accepted typology for discriminating among hostage takers involves two major categories and four subcategories (Bolz, 1979; Cooper, 1997; Fuselier, 1981; Greenstone, 1998; Strentz, 1979). As shown in Table 17.1, psychotic disorders are distinguished from personality or character disorders, and then further divided into Paranoid Schizophrenia and Bipolar Disorder. Despite its absence from the *Diagnostic and Statistical Manual of Mental Disorders* (4th ed. [DSM–IV]; American Psychiatric Association, 1994), the term *manic-depression* has been retained as a useful working diagnosis for hostage negotiators (Greenstone, 1998; Strentz, 1979). Character disorders are subdivided into the inadequate personality and the *antisocial personality*. Even though *inadequate personality* is not an accepted DSM–IV diagnosis (APA, 1994), it has demonstrated usefulness in discriminating among hostage takers.

Field diagnoses inform negotiation strategies (see Table 17.1). Approaches effective with highly depressed and suicidal individuals may prove less useful with psychotic or antisocial subjects. Although there are still some negotiators who utilize a shotgun approach, an increasing number rely on diagnosis and an in depth understanding of the subject to guide their intervention strategies. For instance, although problems sustaining effective work relationships are common to inadequate and antisocial personalities, understanding their underlying difficulties can be very useful. While the inadequate personality may be overwhelmed with their work environment, the antisocial personality may *create* a tumultuous employment setting. Subsequently, the former frequently quits their job; the latter often gets fired. Understanding such nuances guides the selection of negotiations strategies. The inadequate personality may respond to reassurance that he is doing the best that he can despite his sense of repeated failures. The antisocial individual may need to be approached with ego-enhancing statements that mirror his grandiosity and foster an alliance. For an antisocial person, it might be suggested that it is the employer's fault, not theirs, that they were fired.

TABLE 17.1

Hostage Takers and Victim Classifications

Classification	Characteristics Taught to Police Negotiators	Negotiations Guidelines
Schizophrenia, Paranoid Type	Delusions Hallucinations Chemical imbalance Not Multiple Personality Unrealistic concerns about autonomy Unrealistic concerns about sexual identity Feels controlled by external forces Disturbance of affect Ambivalence Autistic thinking Association difficulties	Do not crowd or stare at the subject Do not offer unrequested intimacy Do not argue with their delusions Do not argue with their hallucinations Mental health interventions Do not use family members Consider use of opposite sex negotiator Let them talk and establish rapport Ally yourself with the individual Negotiator may be rejected with time Large body space requirement Expect *weird* demands from this subject
Manic-Depression-Depressed State (Bipolar)	Extreme depression Unrealistic sadness and hopelessness Slowed thinking and responding Difficulty with thought processes Possibly acutely suicidal	Avoid projecting life into the future Deal in the here-and-now Beware of sudden improvements in mood May need to wait longer for responses Relatives may escalate feelings of guilt Go slow; develop rapport With rapport, may be more directive Offer reassurance as often as needed Expect honesty from this subject Small body space requirement Demands: *Leave me alone or Go Away*

continued on next page

TABLE 17.1 *(continued)*
Hostage Takers and Victim Classifications

Classification	Characteristics Taught to Police Negotiators	Negotiations Guidelines
Inadequate Personality (DSM II)	History of problems, often petty in nature History of repeated failures in life Ineffectual responses to life's demands Inadaptability in most areas of life Ineptness and poor judgment Social instability Very manipulative Unable to keep a job and poor planning Sexual irregularities Suicide potential Overuse of fantasy Uses others to get what they want Presents as calm, cool, quiet and polite Strong bonding under traumatic situations	Do not use non-police negotiators Show understanding Build self-esteem Provide uncritical acceptance Consider opposite sex negotiator With rapport, may be more directive Subject may not want incident to end May have a problem with loyalty Demands may be exorbitant

Antisocial Personality	Asocial	Do not get into a contest of wills
	Amoral	Do not use non-police negotiators
	Short-run hedonist	Non-police may worsen situation
	Inability to sustain work relationships	Do not expect interpersonal bonding
	Knows the rules; they do not apply to him	Ego stimulation and ego threat motivate
	Lacks ability to be responsible parent	Remember subjects' egocentricity
	Fails to accept social norms	Release of hostages to subjects' gain
	Unable to keep lasting personal relations	Keep subject in problem solving mode
	Self centered	Negotiations should be reality oriented
	Out for self to point of hurting others	Tactical intervention may be needed
	Makes a model prisoner	Demands will be realistic and precise
	Very manipulative	
	May end up interviewing the negotiator	
	High verbal skills	
	Blames others for his problems	
	May be very cool and calculating	

Additions and exceptions to Table 17.1 classifications are also seen in the field and are considered when training negotiators. Many who suffer from depression are not bipolar, but are reacting to a specific loss (*reactive depression*) or experiencing a unipolar major depression. Not all persons who commit crimes are antisocial. Some petty criminals spontaneously take hostages to use as leverage against the police. For example, a perpetrator who was surprised in the act of robbery took a hostage to use as a shield. The primary motive was robbery, not hostage taking. Additionally, diagnostic characteristics may overlap in profiling actual subjects (Biggs, 1987; Davis, 1987; Dolan & Fuselier, 1989; Fuselier, 1986; Soskis & Van Zandt, 1986; Wesselius, 1983).

HOSTAGE NEGOTIATION FIELD ASSESSMENT

Developing instruments to aid in psychological profiling is one of the primary goals of field assessment. This chapter addresses the possibility of differentiating among hostage takers based on their psychopathy level; it also discusses our preliminary efforts to adapt existing psychopathy measures to the requirements of a hostage crisis. In adapting assessment instruments to fieldwork, it is necessary to understand that police negotiators have many and varied responsibilities; the development of perpetrator profiles is only one of several responsibilities of the hostage negotiations team members. As differentiated from most other situations in which psychopathy is assessed, police negotiators operate as members of specially trained teams with both discrete and overlapping responsibilities (see Table 17.2). Successful operations require knowledge and abilities both unique to police and common to other negotiation situations. Moreover, an officer's specific role on the negotiations team may vary from one incident to another, depending on characteristics of the situation, availability of other personnel, and preferences of the team leader.

The organization of a police negotiations team can take various forms. The model depicted in Table 17.2 is widely used. Its basic structure can be modified under special conditions. Some negotiations teams will define themselves differently, designating roles with alternative labels. Regardless of titles or structure, however, the goals remain the same—to get everyone out safely.[3]

---

[3]The FBI is currently studying the organization of negotiations teams in order to improve the structure and function of hostage negotiations teams.

TABLE 17.2

Hostage Negotiations Team Responsibilities

Job Number	Assignment	Duties
1	Primary Negotiator	Negotiates with subject
2	Secondary Negotiator	Assists #1; Listens to negotiations; gathers intelligence
3	Coach/Police Psychologist	Monitors negotiations; Provides input to Negotiator
4	Intelligence Coordinator	Gathers, evaluates and disseminates intelligence; provides plans and strategies
5	Negotiations Team Leader	Runs Team; Coordinates with S.W.A.T.
	Technicians	Maintain, install and repair negotiations equipment

A negotiations team may be comprised of as few as one or two members (particularly in small police departments). Although, a smaller team can be effective, in some instances as a larger one, a five-member team is optimal for addressing the essential responsibilities of a hostage negotiation team. The nature and duration of the incident can require a need for additional negotiators. Specifically, incidents that extend over long periods of time may require added negotiators or even separate negotiations. Nevertheless, the five-person structure provides a useful model for summarizing the chief roles and responsibilities of the hostage negotiations team.

Within the five-person team, the *primary negotiator* is responsible for interacting with the hostage taker or crisis victim. All other team members and functions support the primary negotiator. The *secondary negotiator* ensures that all intelligence information is conveyed in a timely and efficient manner to the primary negotiator, monitors all negotiations, and substitutes for the primary as needed. The *coach* provides a third set of ears in the negotiations process. The coach may be utilized in various additional capacities at the request of the primary negotiator (e.g., maintaining the negotiations log or conveying information to the intelligence coordinator or team leader) and is often the police department psychologist. He/she monitors the stress level of the primary and the hostage-taker, usually referred to as the *subject*, and is available to provide perspective and input. The *intelligence coordinator* gathers, organizes, and updates information utilized in completing field diagnostic assessments and developing negotiations strategies. Data accumulation is an ongoing process throughout the hostage situation. Logs and records organize incoming data (see Table 17.3). Finally, the *negotiations team leader* coordinates and monitors the hostage negotiations process. She/he ensures the efficient functioning of the team while being available to liaise with other teams and ancillary personnel, such as the special weapons and tactics team and the incident command staff. The effectiveness of the negotiations team depends on the team leader.

As with most crises, hostage situations seldom are expected. Team members are required to respond to sensitive and potentially deadly situations at any time, day or night. Table 17.3 describes the typical police hostage or crisis situation process. The procedures listed in Table 17.3, however, may be modified depending on the specific situation. As can be seen from the table, developing the data for diagnostic assessments is only one of many negotiations teams' responsibilities. Successful resolution of any incident requires knowledge of the steps that are typically experienced in hostage negotiations. The potential for imminent violence (immediate risk), the lack of face to face contact with the subject, and the absence of a structured formal interview setting differentiate the hostage negotiations situation from most other clinical contexts in which psychopathy might be assessed. These factors make the psychopathic hostage taker difficult to manage during negotiations and increase the importance of "rapid" profiling.

PSYCHOPATHY

Although hostage negotiations team members are often not instructed on how to differentiate antisocial personality from psychopathy, this difference may be of considerable value, because psychopathy has been associated with specific forms of violence, including both higher rates of planned and purposeful violence (Hare

TABLE 17.3

Steps in Hostage Negotiation Resolution

Sequence	Specific Time-Related Segments
First	The initial call-out at anytime, day or night
Second	Response of S.W.A.T. and Negotiators
Third	Arrival of S.W.A.T. and securing scene
Fourth	Arrival and set-up of Negotiations Team
Fifth	Initial gathering of intelligence information
Sixth	Preparations by Negotiations Team
Seventh	Ongoing intelligence gathering
Eighth	Coordination with S.W.A.T. commander
Ninth	Initial contact between negotiator and subject
Tenth	Attempts to establish rapport with subject
Eleventh	Initial profiling of hostage taker or victim
Twelfth	In-depth intelligence gathering
Thirteenth	Evaluation of intelligence material
Fourteenth	Goal setting by Negotiations Team
Fifteenth	Continuing negotiations based on strategies
Sixteenth	Continued profiling/check of mental status
Seventeenth	Confirmation of initial observations
Eighteenth	Threat assessment
Nineteenth	Assessment of needs and interests
Twentieth	Information sharing with S.W.A.T.
Twenty-first	Bargaining or Crisis Intervention
Twenty-second	Problem solving and rapport building
Twenty-third	Development of surrender plan
Twenty-fourth	Orchestration of surrender with the subject
Twenty-fifth	Execution of surrender plan with S.W.A.T.
Twenty-sixth	Subject taken into custody
Twenty-seventh	Decision making regarding disposition
Twenty-eighth	Post-incident interviews with subject
Twenty-ninth	Post-incident interviews with hostages
Thirtieth	Negotiations Team debriefing
Thirty-first	Full tactical debriefing
Thirty-second	Training for future incidents

& McPherson, 1984; Hare, 1991; Porter, Birt, & Boer, in press). Psychopathy level also contributes to the assessment of violence risk
(Dolan & Doyle, 2001; Hemphill, Hare, & Wong, 1998; Quinsey, Harris, Rice & Cormier, 1998; Gacono & Bodholdt, 2002, in press; see
chaps. 3, 10 & 14). As discussed in chapter 3 [this text], the DSM–IV
diagnosis of antisocial personality disorder (ASPD; APA, 1994) reflects mainly overt antisocial and criminal behavior, and therefore
characterizes not only most prison inmates but also many offenders
with mental disorders. It is less useful than psychopathy in distinguishing those who are likely to commit further crimes (Hare, 1995).
One reason may be that the presence of traits such as egocentricity,
shallow affect, manipulativeness, and lack of empathy or remorse
may differentiate the psychopathic ASPD from the nonpsychopathic
ASPD subjects (Hare, 1995). These traits are components of Factor 1
on the Psychopathy Checklist—Revised (PCL–R) but not well represented in the DSM–IV ASPD criteria. Thus, to the extent that these
traits predict behavior during a hostage crisis, this differentiation
may hold utility for the negotiator.

PSYCHOPATHY ASSESSMENT
AND HOSTAGE NEGOTIATION

In order to explore the usefulness of psychopathy assessments made
by police negotiators during actual hostage or crisis situations, we
used 1) the Interpersonal Measure of Psychopathy (IM–P; Kosson,
Steuerwald, Forth, & Kirkhart, 1997; see chap. 8) and 2) a draft version of guidelines for scoring the 12 items in the Hare Psychopathy
Checklist: Screening Version (PCL:SV; Hart, Cox & Hare, 1995). Qualified users (see chaps. 3 & 7) can obtain the current published version
of the Scoring Guidelines for the Hare PCL:SV (Hare, 1998) from
Multi-Health Systems (MHS). We used the draft scoring guidelines
for all 12 PCL:SV items in order to obtain measures of Factors 1 and 2,
solely for the purpose of conducting the research project discussed in
this chapter.[4, 5, 6]

---

[4]It is emphasized that the information in this chapter is not intended to encourage use of
the PCL–R or the PCL:SV by hostage negotiators without proper qualifications and training.
Individuals who wish to use PCL-related material should pursue specialized training and
supervision.   (continued on next page)

There are several limitations of using assessment instruments during actual crisis situations. First, during a hostage situation, assessment instruments must be completed in coordination with other team responsibilities such as gathering intelligence information, coordinating with the special weapons and tactics team, setting up equipment, establishing contact with the hostage-taker, maintaining rapport, dealing with hostages, continuing the bargaining process, dealing with the subject surrender, and finally conducting post-incident interviews and team debriefings (Greenstone, 1998, 1999; Hillmann, 1988). Whatever the techniques, tests, procedures or equipment are used must be modified to fit within the parameters of these rather unusual circumstances. Simplicity is the key.

Second, because information about the subject and hostages or other victims is generally not immediately available, the amount of intelligence and profiling information varies greatly from subject to subject. Historical information is needed to complete the PCL:SV. Background data is gathered continuously from family members, police records, medical reports, friends, public records, bystanders, the subject in question, and so forth. Even so, less extensive background data is available than commonly found in forensic settings. The paucity of data was an important consideration in our field use of the Draft Guidelines for the PCL:SV and the IM–P. Attempts were made to revise the procedures typically used with these instruments only enough to reduce the workload, ease the completion of items, and allow for the integration of accumulating data.

Third, the nature of the situation may change rapidly, and negotiators cannot always wait until complete information is available.

(continued from previous page)

[5] As discussed in chapter 3, Factor 1 of the PCL:SV is often considered the personality core of psychopathy, while Factor 2 is more behaviorally oriented and correlates with the DSM–IV ASPD diagnosis.

[6] The authors apologize to Dr. Hare for an error in endnote 3 in the first printing of this chapter. The draft version of the PCL:SV Scoring guidelines used here dates to 1992 (R. D. Hare, S. D. Hart, & D. N. Cox). Published versions were made available to qualified users, as Scoring Guidelines for the Hare PCL:SV in 1995 and 1998 (see Hare, 1998). These works are also the original predecessors of the Hare P–Scan. Hostage negotiators without specialized training in the PCL–R or PCL:SV who wish to screen individuals for psychopathy should use the Hare P–Scan.

The intelligence coordinator decides when information is relayed to the primary negotiator. Field instruments must be used interactively or while the information is being collected. Because most situations are negotiated on the telephone, it was important that the instruments be modified so that they *could* be completed without a face-to-face interview. Some negotiations are conducted face-to-face; hence, the modified instruments were designed to utilize this information as well. Finally, the scoring of the instruments was also altered to indicate only a "presence" or "absence" (0 or 1) rating rather than the more differentiated scoring schemes (0, 1, 2) used in the original instruments.

In summary, our use of the PCL:SV Draft Guidelines (PCL:SV–DG) and the IM–P differed from typical scoring of the parent instruments in several ways: a) extensive background information on the hostage-taker and crisis victim was usually not available; b) items were modified to permit scoring based on information gathered by telephone; c) field intelligence formed the basis for determining item scores; d) individual items were completed in an incremental fashion; e) police negotiators received only basic, rudimentary training on scoring; f) the PCL:SV–DG and the IM–P were only one part of the intelligence gathering function of the hostage negotiations team; and, g) each item or trait disposition was scored as either present or absent.

In this preliminary research, we sought to determine whether: a) the instruments could be completed during hostage situations; b) the modified procedures could be used by paraprofessionals in a reliable manner; and, c) psychopathy scores could differentiate among hostage takers in relationship to their real-world behavior.

FIELD TRIALS

Each instrument was duplicated and placed in the negotiations command post. Multiple revisions and updates were made with the IM–P. New modifications were routinely incorporated into data gathering. For this reason, a 21-item version of the IM–P was used for the first 6 incidents, and a 30-item version was used for the remaining incidents. Subsequent to each of the 14 incidents, the PCL:SV–DG and the IM–P were given to negotiators. The primary negotiator, secondary negotiator and the intelligence coordinator were responsible for completing the instruments within 24-hours after each incident. In a typical field situation, the intelligence coordinator or his/her designee would complete the instruments.

As noted earlier, the primary negotiator is the officer with the responsibility for talking with the subject and for negotiating a resolution. The secondary negotiator assists the primary and monitors the verbal interactions between hostage taker and primary negotiator. The secondary does not speak directly to the subject except in the absence of the primary. The intelligence coordinator is the prime repository for all information relevant to the hostage or crisis scene. Although the intelligence coordinator can hear the negotiations, she/he does not speak directly to the subject. Information from the intelligence coordinator is passed to the secondary negotiator during negotiations.

Each negotiator independently completed the modified IM–P and scored the PCL:SV–DG, and forwarded the data immediately to the senior author. In a small number of cases, there were fewer than three negotiators involved in the incident. Basic instruction was given to each non-negotiator prior to completing each instrument. Where the 21-item version of the modified IM–P was completed, scores were prorated to 30 for the purposes of this study.

PRELIMINARY FINDINGS

Between October, 1996 and June, 1998, 14 cases were processed. With regard to post incident status of the subjects in these scenarios, 71.4% were taken to the county hospital for involuntary psychiatric evaluation. Two subjects (14.28%) were arrested and jailed post incident. Two subjects died during their incidents. During the crisis situation, 86% of the subjects were suicidal and 14% were homicidal. Seven percent were involved in domestic situations. Only one incident was considered a domestic incident, in which the subject was both suicidal and homicidal (see Table 17.4).

Despite their limitations, a few of the findings bear mentioning. Interrater agreement for the IM–P total scores ranged from .56 to .76 for the various combinations of raters. Interrater agreement for the PCL:SV–DG total scores ranged from .45 to .62. Because this level of

TABLE 17.4

Mean PCL:SV-DG Factor 1 Scores and IM-P Scores
as a Function of Axis I Diagnoses.

Axis I Diagnosis	PCL:SV	IMP:HN	Cases
	Factor 1		
None	5.7	18.1	1
Bipolar—Depressed	4.7	16.2	2
Major Depression	1.5	6.7	9
Anxiety	1.0	6.7	1
Full Sample	2.3	9.1	13

Note. Each of the 6 items in Factor 1 of the PCL:SV was scored as 0 or 1. Scores on Factor 1 can range from 0 to 6. The IM-P scores may range from 0-30.

agreement was lower than expected, interrater agreement was also computed for the individual factors measured by the PCL:SV–DG. Agreement for the Factor 1 score was adequate, ranging from .64 to .69. However, interrater agreement for Factor 2 was only .41 at best and, in one case, as low as −.31. Although these correlations are lower than those typically obtained with clinical/research use of these instruments, they indicate that both the PCL:SV Factor 1 and the IM–P may be reliably rated in hostage situations. By contrast, PCL:SV Factor 2, which requires more historical data to accurately assess, may be difficult to reliably score.

Next, correlations between the measures were examined. The correlations between the IM–P and both the PCL:SV–DG total score and Factor 1 score were similar to those previously reported ($rs = .59$ and .72, respectively, both $ps < .05$). However, neither the IM–P nor the PCL:SV Factor 1 was significantly correlated with the PCL:SV Factor 2 rating (both $rs < .10$). Consequently, further analyses were restricted to the Factor 1 score obtained from the PCL:SV–DG and to the IM–P score.

When field diagnoses were examined, only the Factor 1 score was highly (although not significantly) correlated with a field diagnosis of antisocial personality, $r = -.52, p = .10$. By contrast, the IM–P score was not ($r = -.11$). Similarly, only the Factor 1 score reliably predicted the negotiation team's rating of the subject as homicidal. However, the correlations for both the Factor 1 and the IM–P ratings were in the expected direction ($r = -.64, p < .05$ for Factor 1; $r = -.36$, ns for IM–P). These analyses demonstrate that, even with a sample as small as 14, the PCL:SV–DG scoring critera for Factor 1, adapted for use in hostage situations, was highly correlated with some of the field diagnoses of the negotiations team.

Axis I field diagnoses also appeared related to PCL:SV Factor 1 and IM–P scores. Although no statistical tests were conducted for these data, as shown in Table 17.5, the one subject with no Axis I diagnoses received higher psychopathy scores than those subjects with Axis I diagnoses. Further, those with field diagnoses of bipolar disorder received relatively higher scores than those with diagnoses of major depression. Finally, even among those subjects with major depression, those with an Axis II diagnosis of antisocial personality had higher scores than those with an Axis II diagnosis of inadequate or borderline personality.

One additional finding appears interesting. In this small sample, only one crisis was determined to have sufficient lethality potential to warrant actual entry by the special weapons and tactics team. The PCL:SV Factor 1 and IM–P scores for this subject (5.7 and 10.3 respectively) were also relatively high.

CONCLUSION

Several interesting relationships emerged that tentatively suggest that the the concept of psychopathy, as reflected in Draft Guidelines for the PCL:SV and the IM–P (Kosson et al., 1997), may prove useful to police negotiators. In particular, elevated PCL:SV Factor 1 scores and IM–P scores in a hostage taker suggest added caution for hos-

400

TABLE 17.5.
PCL:SV-DG Factor 1 and IM-P Scores with Major Depression as a function of Axis II Diagnoses.

Axis I	Axis II	PCL:SV		IMP:HN		Cases
Field Diagnosis	Field Diagnosis	Factor 1				
		Mean	SD	Mean	SD	
Major Depression	Antisocial	2.5	1.6	7.6	2.3	4
Major Depression	Inadequate or Borderline	0.3	0.7	6.5	7.7	4
Major Depression	Antisocial and Inadequate	2.3	–	4.0	–	1
Major Depression	(all)				1.5	1.5

tage negotiators. Moreover, among those subjects with depression, even lower cutoffs may be useful in predicting Antisocial Personality Disorder and violence proneness.

Nevertheless, substantial additional work in this area is needed, including evaluation of the reliability and validity of instruments used to assess psychopathy in the context of hostage and crisis negotiations. The IM–P and the PCL:SV–DG (Hare, 1998) may prove useful, although use of the latter is restricted to qualified users. The Hare P–Scan (Hare & Hervé, 1999), was developed as a nonclinical tool to estimate the presence of psychopathic features, and may be helpful to hostage negotiators. Also needed are additional training for negotiators who utilize these instruments, development of other measures to rule out psychopathy and to detect other mental disorders more precisely, and the use of larger and more diverse samples on which to gather data with these instruments. Only further examination and refinement of these instruments can tell us whether they will help negotiators to protect citizens and each other from those who threaten society with sudden violence.

REFERENCES

American Psychiatric Association (1994). *Diagnostic and statistical manual of mental disorders* (4th. ed.). Washington, DC: Author.

Arieti, S. (1963). Psychopathic personality: Some views on its psychopathology and psychodynamics. *Comprehensive Psychiatry, 4*, 301–312.

Biggs, J. (1987). Defusing hostage situations. *The Police Chief, 54*, 17–25.

Bolz, F. (1979). *Hostage cop.* New York: Rawson, Wade Publishers.

Cooper, H. (1997). Negotiating with terrorists. *The International Journal of Police Negotiations and Crisis Management, 1*, 47–54.

Davis, R. (1987). Three prudent considerations for hostage negotiators. *Law and Order, 10*, 54–57.

Dolan, M., & Doyle, M. (2000). Violence risk prediction: Clinical and actuarial measures and the role of the Psychopathy Checklist. *British Journal of Psychiatry, 177*, 303–311

Dolan, J., & Fuselier, G. (1989). A guide for first responders to hostage situations. *FBI Law Enforcement Bulletin, 59*, 6–11.

Fowler, W. (1997). Dealing with defenestrators: Immediate intervention. *The International Journal of Police Negotiations and Crisis Management, 1*, 5–11.

Fowler, W., & Greenstone, J. (1989). *Crisis intervention compendium.* Littleton, MA: Copley Publishing Group.

Fowler, W., & Greenstone, J. (1996). Hostage negotiations for police. In R. Corsini (Ed.), *Concise encyclopedia of psychology 2nd ed.*, (pp. 530–531). New York: John Wiley & Sons.

Fuselier, G. (1986). What every negotiator would like his chief to know. *FBI Law Enforcement Bulletin, 56*, 12–15.

Fuselier, G. (1981). A practical overview of hostage negotiations. *FBI Law Enforcement Bulletin, 50*, 10–15.

Gacono, C., & Bodholdt, R. (2002). The role of the Psychopathy Checklist-Revised (PCL–R) in risk assessment. *Journal of Threat Assessment.*

Gacono, C., & Bodholdt, R. (in press). Assessing dangerous and violent individuals. In R. F. Ballesteros (Ed.), *Encyclopedia of Psychological Assessment.* Sage Publications.

Greenstone, J. L. (1989) *A hostage negotiations team training manual for police departments.* Dallas: Lancaster Police Department.

Greenstone, J. (1993) Crisis Intervention: Skills Training for Police Negotiators in the 21st Century. *Command, 1*, 7–10.

Greenstone, J. (1998). *Basic course for hostage and crisis negotiators*, Arlington, Texas: Regional Police Academy, North Central Texas Council of Governments.

Greenstone, J., & Leviton, S. (1993). *Elements of crisis intervention.* Pacific Grove: Brooks/Cole.

Greenstone, J., & Leviton, S. (1996). Crisis intervention. In R. Corsini (Ed.), *Concise encyclopedia of psychology* 2nd edition, (pp. 269–270). New York: John Wiley & Sons.

Hare, R. (1991). *The Hare Psychopathy Checklist-Revised Manual.* Toronto: Multi-Health Systems.Hare, R. (1995) Psychopaths: New trends and research. *The Harvard Mental Health Newsletter, 5*, 1–3.

Hare, R. D. (1998). *Scoring Guidelines for the Hare PCL:SV.* Toronto: Multi-Health Systems.

Hare, R. D., & Hervé, H. S. (1999). *The Hare P–Scan: Research Version.* Toronto: Multi-Health Systems.

Hare, R., & McPherson, L. (1984). Violent and aggressive behavior by criminal psychopaths. *International Journal of Law and Psychiatry, 7*, 35–50.

Hart, S., Cox, D., & Hare, R. (1995). Manual for the Psychopathy Checklist: Screening Version (PCL:SV). Toronto: Multi-Health Systems.

Hemphill, J. F., Hare, R. D., & Wong, S. (1998). Psychopathy and recidivism: A review. *Legal and Criminological Psychology, 3*, 141–172.

Hillmann, M. (1988). Tactical intelligence operations and support during a major barricade/hostage event. Alexandria, VA: International Association of Chiefs of Police.

Kosson, D. (1997) *Notes for using the interpersonal measures of psychopathy.* Unpublished manuscript.

Kosson, D., Steuerwald, B., Forth, A., & Kirkhart, K. (1997). A new method for assessing the interpersonal behavior of psychopaths: Preliminary validation studies. *Psychological Assessment, 9*, 89–101.

Lanceley, F. (1981) The antisocial personality as a hostage taker. *Journal of Police Science and Administration, 8*, 12–25.

McMains, M., & Lanceley, F. (1995) The use of crisis intervention principles by police negotiators. *The Journal of Crisis Negotiations.*

McMains, M., & Mullins, W. (1996). *Crisis negotiations: Managing critical incidents and hostage situations in law enforcement and corrections.* Cincinnati: Anderson Publishing Company.

Quinsey, V., Harris, G., Rice, M., & Cormier, C. (1998). Violent offenders: Appraising and managing risk. Washington, DC: American Psychological Association.

Porter, S., Birt, A. R., & Boer, D. P. (in press). Report on the criminal and conditional release profiles of Canadian federal offenders as a function of psychopathy and age. *Law and Human Behavior.*

Soskis, D., & Van Zandt, C. (1986). Hostage negotiations: Law enforcements most effective non-lethal weapon. DOJ, *FBI Management Quarterly, 6,* 1–9.

Strentz, T. (1979). Law enforcement policy and ego defenses of the hostage. *FBI Law Enforcement Bulletin, 48,* 20–30.

Strentz, T. (1983). The inadequate personality as a hostage taker. *Journal of Police Science and Administration, 10,* 1–5.

Wesselius, C. (1983) The anatomy of a hostage situation. *Behavioral Sciences and the Law,* 1(2), 53–61.

Epilogue

Carl B. Gacono
Private Practice, Austin, Texas

Over the past 30 years, psychopathy has evolved into a reliably measurable construct essential to assessing the clinical needs of offenders and addressing certain forensic-legal questions (chapter 6). The Psychopathy Checklists (PCL, PCL–R, PCL:SV, PCL:YV, PSD) represent substantial advances in the assessment of psychopathy (chapters 1–3). These instruments not only provide data which informs and guides our clinical thinking, they also represent a solid step forward in addressing the clinical-forensic issues of prediction and risk, including violent recidivism, treatability, and offender management. Psychopathy assessment is required when examining, intervening, or researching all offender populations (chapters 7, 10, 13–15).

With the advent of a reliable and valid means of assessing psychopathy, clinicians are faced with considering the relevance of psychopathy evaluations to their clinical practice (see chapter 7). One should ask, Is psychopathy assessment relevant to my private practice? To the institutional setting where I work? Do I work with violent individuals or offenders? Knowledge of the implications of psychopathy assessment in any particular setting, including failure to appropriately refer for assessment of psychopathy, may suffice for administrators and the majority of clinicians (chapters 1–7). If nothing else, a working knowledge of psychopathy forces CEOs to consider integrating psychopathy assessment into their institutions' evaluation procedures and should guide clinicians in making appropriate referrals (chapters 7 & 12). Learning the actual nuts and bolts of using the Psychopathy Checklists is the task of those thoroughly trained in assessment in general, and the PCL–R in particular, as well as those organizing implementation within institutional settings, or training others in any of the former tasks (chapters 7–9, 12). While an appreciation of the importance of psychopathy assessment is essential for administrators and practitioners, proficiency in assessing psychopathy is not.

One of several challenges (see chapter 7 for others) for clinicians is applying robust nomothetic findings idiographically. The research-practitioner must determine optimal PCL–R dimensional scores for various risk paradigms within respective settings, including amenability to available treatment, potential for disrupting or seriously undermining the treatment of others, supervision or custody requirements, potential to recidivate, including violently, and so on. A low to moderate level of psychopathy in a day treatment program for more vulnerable or seriously mentally ill patients could easily be anticipated to produce unwelcome results, whereas a low to moderate level of psychopathy in higher security prison-based treatment programs might well be fairly typical; as such, treatment and supervision must be adapted to suit the population.

Ethical use of the Psychopathy Checklists also requires the use of multiple methods for answering referral and predictive questions with a sensitivity to age, gender, and ethnicity (see chapters 3 & 9). While comparative data from like-settings and similar subject populations is essential, the work of Quinsey et al. (1998; VRAG & SORAG; see chapters 10 & 14) provides a useful conceptual model for integrating psychopathy data into clinical practice. Programmatic research continues examining psychopathy as one weighted factor in a battery of other data geared toward prediction of violence. This actuarial approach provides a template for developing models to inform other clinical decisions. Psychopathy becomes important as a dimensional construct, as one aspect of any assessment. In this regard, psychopathy assessment requires researchers and clinicians to walk hand in hand. Nomothetic research findings inform and guide individual clinical decisions while clinical observations point toward the need for research related to individual differences. Assessment necessitates rejuvenation of the scientist-practitioner model, as nomothetic and idiographic data combine to inform clinical judgment.

The forensic clinician is always cognizant that any behavior occurs in a "context" that must also be assessed. Social, psychological, and biological factors must be considered as they contribute to the clinical picture. Clinical opinions are improved when subjected to the same rigors as forensic ones. Forensic evidence must conform to legal tests for admissibility, such as the *Daubert* standard,[1] which requires careful articulation of the thinking which forms forensic-clinical opinions (McCann, 1998). Similar standards might be advanced by any "treater" or "evaluator" whose relationship to offenders is a professional one.

Other issues pull us on as well. Beyond serving as a guide to the presence or absence of psychopathy (taxon) or as one point in an actuarial risk assessment, PCL–R data, specifically clinical item and item cluster analysis, provides valuable information concerning treatment planning and characterological diagnosis in "nonpsychopathic offenders" (Gacono, 1998). Specific item configurations may ultimately identify "behaviorally" different subtypes among high PCL–R scorers. Determining the relevance of individual PCL–R item scores to such clinical issues has only begun (Gacono, 1998; see Appendix C).

Much remains to be done; the journey is far from complete. This text is offered as another logical step in the evolutionary process of the construct of psychopathy, that is as a bridge among theory, research, and practice. Now equipped with much more solid assessment procedures, we are hopeful that new inroads may be found examining etiology and more effective early intervention. To Hare's (1996, p. 25), "Psychopathy (was): a clinical construct whose time has come," I now add, "Psychopathy is a construct that is likely here to stay." For those dedicated clinicians who work with these complex, sometimes dangerous, and enigmatic patients, I end with my own experience which is one of perpetual transition, engagement, and evaluation: "Once more unto the breach, dear friends, once more" (Shakespeare; *Henry V*, Act 3, Scene 1).

ENDNOTES

1. *Daubert v. Merrell Dow Pharmaceuticals, Inc.*, 113 S.Ct. 2786 (1993). Also see, McCann, J. (1998), "Defending the Rorschach in Court: An Analysis of Admissibility Using Legal and Professional Standards," 70:1, 125–144.

REFERENCES

Gacono, C. B. (1998). The use of the Psychopathy Checklist–Revised (PCL–R) and Rorschach for treatment planning with antisocial personality disordered patients. *International Journal of Offender Therapy and Comparative Criminology, 42:1,* 49–64.
Hare, R. D. (1996). Psychopathy: a clinical construct whose time has come. *Criminal Justice and Behavior, 23:1,* 25–54.
McCann, J. T. (1998). Defending the Rorschach in Court: an analysis of admissibility using legal and professional standards. *Journal of Personality Assessment, 70:1,* 125–144.
Quinsey, V., Harris, G., Rice, M., & Cormier, C. (1998). Violent offenders: appraising and managing risk. Washington, DC: American Psychological Association.

Appendix A: PCL–R Clinical and Forensic Interview Schedule

Carl B. Gacono
Private Practice, Austin, Texas

Examinee: _____ DOB: _____ Age: _____
Gender: _____ Ethnicity: _____ Education Level:_____
Examiner(s): _____
_____
Evaluation Date(s): _____ Place: _____
Psychiatric History: _____
Reason for Referral: _____
_____
_____
_____
_____
_____

Collateral Data and Records Reviewed: _____
_____
_____
_____
_____
_____
_____
_____
_____
_____

CLINICAL INTERVIEW PROCEDURES

The role of interviewing in PCL-R assessments is described in the Manual and the Rating Booklet. The *CIS* is designed for completing the PCL-R as part of a clinical or forensic evaluation (Gacono, 1998; Gacono & Hutton, 1994). The *CIS* has three parts: (a) collateral information and record review, (b) chronological life history, and (c) item interviewing. A final PCL-R score is obtained by the completion of item interviewing.

I. Record Review

Adequate collateral information (e.g., records) is essential to PCL-R administration. Interview alone is never sufficient. Prior to interviewing, the examiner reviews all collateral information and records relevant data in Section III under the appropriate item or items. Scoring impressions should be noted in the margins next to items on the *Scoring Sheet* (i.e., *collateral information suggests at least a 1 on Poor Behavioral Controls [Item 10] prior to the interview*). Scores are then modified during subsequent phases of the evaluation.

II. Chronological Adult Life History

Questions asked during the Chronological Adult Life History elicit information specific to PCL-R scoring. Record the history chronologically in the following section. It adds to record review data and provides an anchor for subsequent information obtained during Section 3, Individual Item Scoring.

Begin the adult history at age 18 or when the examinee left their parents' or designated guardian's home. Life events such as onset of incarceration, marriage, divorce, relocation, and so on suggest natural breaks. For example, an examinee leaves home at 17 and is subsequently incarcerated at 22. The 5-year period (17–22) is thoroughly assessed with questions such as: (*During that time* . . .) Where did you live? Live in an apartment? Own home? Lived with whom? How many marriages, live-ins, etc.? With parents? Who paid the bills? Ever late on rent? Bills? Utilities turned off? Evicted from an apartment? How often did you move? Default on loans? Have loans? Did you work? For how long? For who? Support self? Longest period without employment? Percentage of income obtained by illegal means? Was your main job crime? Fired from jobs? Quit jobs without giving notice? Drugs and/or alcohol on the job? Contacts with law enforcement? Arrests? Speeding tickets? DUIs? Drove while intoxicated? Drugs? Alcohol? Assess the frequency of specific behaviors; repeat "So during that period" often and summarize each section; "Just to clarify, you said that during those 5 years you. . . ." Then proceed with "and than what happened?", "After the divorce you. . . ?" Similar questions are repeated for subsequent periods leading to the examinee's current age.

The experienced PCL–R administrator will have little trouble in correlating this historical information with specific PCL–R items. Record related data under corresponding items in Section 3, Item Interviewing.

CHRONOLOGICAL LIFE HISTORY

CHRONOLOGICAL LIFE HISTORY (CONT.)

_____

_____

_____

_____

_____

_____

_____

_____

_____

_____

_____

_____

_____

_____

_____

_____

_____

_____

_____

_____

_____

_____

_____

_____

_____

_____

III. Item Interviewing[1]

PCL-R items are assessed in the following sequence: 20, 19, 18, 12, 17, 11, 3/14/15, 6/7/8/16, 10, 4/5, 9, 13, 1/2. This sequence transitions from behavioral to more trait-influenced items and item clusters. It aids in establishing rapport while creating a natural, time-efficient method for gathering PCL-R data. When the examinee spontaneously offers information out of sequence, the examiner should be flexible. Items and item clusters, however, should always be fully assessed and scored prior to proceeding. _Frequent deviations from the interviewing sequence can result in a prolonged PCL-R administration._

ITEM INTERVIEWING (CONT.)

When co-interviewing, the primary examiner should, after several items or a single item cluster (e.g., item clusters 6, 7, & 8; 4 & 5; or 2, 14, & 15), inquire of the co-interviewers, "Do you have any other questions for that section?" Periodic inquiry elicits additional information, increases inter-rater agreement (research), and ensures the completion of all scoring by interview's end. Although some items such as 20 (Criminal Versatility) can be scored reliably from the record review prior to interviewing, they should also be reviewed in this phase of the evaluation (note examinee attitudes and discrepancies). Items like Glibness/Superficial Charm and Grandiose Sense of Self-Worth are frequently scored reliably based on the examinee's presentation during the interview. They may require few additional questions. Keep in mind that the PCL–R Manual requires that *discrepancies between record and interview data be scored in the direction of psychopathology* (Hare, 1991a).

ITEM 20 CRIMINAL VERSATILITY: *Review with the examinee* their documented charges and/or convictions ≥ 18 (adult rap sheet). Code them by offense categories (see *Rating Booklet*). Refer to the *Rating Booklet* during the interview (Hare, 1991b). Review other possible offense categories.

List offense, category, and age: _____

_____

_____

_____

_____

_____

_____

_____

_____

_____

_____

_____

_____

_____

_____

_____

_____

_____

_____

ITEM 19 REVOCATION OF CONDITIONAL RELEASE: Escape, parole & probation violations, failure to appear, etc.

_____
_____
_____
_____
_____
_____
_____
_____
_____

ITEM 18 JUVENILE DELINQUENCY: Review charges and/or convictions between ages 13 and ≤ 17. Code by seriousness [see *Rating Booklet*]. Comment on behavior between 13 and 17.

List offense and age: _____

_____
_____
_____
_____
_____
_____
_____
_____

ITEM 12 EARLY BEHAVIORAL PROBLEMS: Assess the presence and frequency of behaviors in the *Rating Booklet* [≤ 12]. *Repeat "before age 13" after every second or third inquiry.* Ever see a psychiatrist or psychologist before 13? Truant from school? How often? Expelled or suspended from school before 13?

Attend an alternative school? Why? Get into fights? etc.

_____
_____
_____
_____
_____
_____
_____
_____
_____

ITEM 17 SHORT-TERM MARITAL RELATIONSHIPS: Record number; include common law. How many sexual partners did you live with for more than 4 weeks? Did you have any sexual partners that you lived with for several days at a time over a period of 6 or more months? Kept clothes at their house? Had keys to their apartment or house? If sexually unfaithful, did you keep it secret? How?

_____

_____

_____

_____

_____

_____

ITEM 11 PROMISCUOUS SEXUAL BEHAVIOR: Number of sexual partners. How many sexual partners have you had? How many were one-night stands? Did you maintain several liaisons at the same time? How many? Sexual offenses? Types of behavior: sado-masochism, bisexuality, use of prostitutes, worked as prostitute, etc.?

_____

_____

_____

_____

_____

_____

ITEM 3 NEED FOR STIMULATION/PRONENESS TO BOREDOM: Are you easily bored? Why do you say that? Have you done illegal things when you're bored (e.g., broke into houses as a juvenile)? Have you ever done dangerous things just for the thrill of it? Wasn't part of the drug usage, promiscuity, quitting jobs, etc., related to your boredom?

_____

_____

_____

_____

_____

_____

_____

_____

_____

_____

ITEM 14 IMPULSIVITY: Are you an impulsive person? Why do you say that? Itchy feet? Quit jobs without notice? Moved from place to place? Pick up and go? Value spontaneity? Tend to act without thinking? Examples? Give me examples of when you haven't been impulsive? Assess specific offenses and determine the degree of planning versus impulsivity. *A few planned offenses, however, do not negate a lifetime of impulsivity* (score of 2).

ITEM 15 IRRESPONSIBILITY: Used drugs and alcohol at work? Drove under the influence with others in car? Fired from jobs? Left without giving notice? Behaviors that put others at risk? How are your children supported? Failed to pay child support? Bought drugs rather than providing for family? (see Rating Booklet)

ITEM 6 LACK OF REMORSE OR GUILT: Have you ever felt remorse? What does it feel like? If so, why didn't you change your behaviors? *Don't provide a definition of remorse for the examinee; carefully assess for remorse/guilt (feels bad due to harm caused to others) versus shame (self-pity). Minimize verbalized "remorse" toward one idealized parental figure:* "I feel bad for what I put my mother through." (Are behaviors consistent with verbalizations?) Don't use this to change a score of 2 to 0.

ITEM (CONT.) _____

_____
_____
_____
_____
_____

ITEM 7 SHALLOW AFFECT: Do you ever feel depressed? What does it feel like? *[distinguish between depression and emptiness/anger/frustration].* Have you lost anyone (death, divorce, etc.) whom you felt close to? What do you mean by close? How did it affect you? Go to the funeral? Currently close to anyone? Loner? Ever been in love? What did you love about them? (assess knowledge of person's interests, routines). Are you the kind of person that has strong feelings? What do you mean? Describe them?

_____
_____
_____
_____
_____
_____
_____
_____
_____
_____

ITEM 8 CALLOUS/LACK OF EMPATHY: Ever been cruel or abusive to animals? People? Break into houses and "trash" them for fun? Destroy things for fun? Ever been described as cold and callous? Gotten "carried away" in a fight? Do you enjoy hurting, mocking others? Victims? Provide specific examples where examinee was hurtful or neglectful (directly or by implication) *and see if he or she can appreciate his or her impact or how others might feel.*

_____
_____
_____
_____
_____
_____
_____
_____
_____

ITEM 16 FAILURE TO ACCEPT RESPONSIBILITY FOR OWN ACTIONS:
Do you think your sentences have generally been fair, lenient, or harsh?
What kind of job did your lawyers do? When you look back over your life,
who or what do you blame for the way it has turned out? Effects on victims? Others?

_____
_____
_____
_____
_____
_____
_____
_____
_____
_____

ITEM 10 POOR BEHAVIORAL CONTROLS: Has anyone ever described
you as short-tempered or hot-headed? Why? Get angry often? Describe it?
What makes you angry? What do you do when you get angry? Look for
a history of temper tantrums, assaults, etc.

_____
_____
_____
_____
_____
_____
_____
_____
_____

ITEM 4 PATHOLOGICAL LYING: Do people accuse you of not telling
the truth? Are you a good liar? How much has lying been a part of your
life? What age? Give me examples? Willing to lie to get what you want?
Lied to police? How much have you lied during this interview? *Look for a
history of aliases, discrepancies between record and interview data, inconsistencies during the interview.*

_____
_____
_____
_____
_____
_____
_____
_____

ITEM 5 CONNING/MANIPULATIVE: Has anyone described you as a con man or hustler? Why? Are you one? What do you mean? Is it easy for you to talk others into giving you what you want? How? By what means? Convince others of your point of view? Anything you wouldn't do for 5 million dollars? Loner? Look for a history of fraud, scams, etc.

_____

_____

_____

_____

_____

_____

_____

_____

_____

ITEM 9 PARASITIC LIFESTYLE: If able-bodied is an issue, assess onset of disability and consider entire life span (see *Rating Booklet*).

_____

_____

_____

_____

_____

_____

_____

_____

ITEM 13 LACK OF REALISTIC, LONG-TERM GOALS: What will you do when you get out? Live where? Work? How will you stay away from crime, alcohol, drugs? What do you see yourself doing in 5 to 10 years? Assess past history for lack of planning. *Assess whether current plans have been thought out and researched (i.e., phone calls, letters to places of residence, employment) or just fantasy based.* If incarcerated, consider release date.

_____

_____

_____

_____

_____

_____

_____

_____

_____

ITEM 1 GLIBNESS/SUPERFICIAL CHARM: Record *specific* statements as well as comments [with dates] from the record. Evasiveness or a tough guy, macho image are criteria that also contribute to scoring. *Not all subjects who receive a score of 1 on this item are subjectively charming to all examiners.*

_____
_____
_____
_____
_____
_____
_____
_____
_____

ITEM 2 GRANDIOSE SENSE OF SELF-WORTH: Do you have any special skills or talents? Is there anything you couldn't do if you put your mind to it? Do you see yourself as a follower or leader? Loner? Record *specific* statements made by the subject as well as comments [with dates] from the record.

_____
_____
_____
_____
_____
_____
_____
_____
_____

DIAGNOSIS/RECOMMENDATIONS: _____
_____
_____
_____
_____
_____
_____
_____
_____
_____

ENDNOTES

1. Refer to the *Rating Booklet* (not the *Manual*) during the interview. *Questions included in this section of the CIS are necessary but not sufficient for PCL-R administration and scoring.* Use the Rating Booklet and Interview and Information Schedule as guides for developing additional questions (Hare, 1991b, 1991c). Question as extensively as needed to assess the degree to which PCL-R items match lifelong patterns.

REFERENCES

Gacono, C., & Hutton, H. (1994). Suggestions for the clinical and forensic use of the Hare Psychopathy Checklist–Revised (PCL-R). *International Journal of Law & Psychiatry, 17*:(3), 303–317.

Gacono, C. B. (1998). The use of the Psychopathy Checklist–Revised (PCL-R) and Rorschach in treatment planning with antisocial personality disordered patients. *International Journal of Offender Therapy and Comparative Criminology, 42*:(1), 49–64.

Hare, R. (1991a). *The Hare Psychopathy Checklist–Revised (PCL-R)*. Toronto, ON: Multi-Health Systems.

Hare, R. (1991b). *The Hare PCL-R: Rating Booklet*. Toronto, ON: Multi-Health Systems.

Hare, R. (1991c). *The Hare PCL-R: Interview and Information Schedule*. Toronto, ON: Multi-Health Systems.

Appendix B: A Forensic Psychological Evaluation

J. Reid Meloy
University of California, San Diego

The Honorable Justice Forall
Los Angeles County Superior Court
1523 First Street
Los Angeles, CA 90000

> RE: Sampson, Samuel
> No: 56712
> DOB: March 5, 1953

Dear Judge Forall:

I am submitting this evaluation pursuant to your order dated October 24, 1997 concerning Mr. Samuel Sampson. The purpose of this evaluation is to determine whether the defendant would constitute a danger to the health and safety of others if he was supervised as an outpatient, and whether he would benefit from such status (Penal Code §1603 and §1604).

Database I reviewed approximately 800 pages of documents provided to me by the Los Angeles County District Attorney's Office. These documents included psychological and psychiatric evaluations before and after the violent offenses of 1989; summary reports and progress notes from Signet and Trenton State Hospitals from 1990 to the present; newspaper articles; letters from the defendant's sister and husband; criminal investigation reports of the May 27 and July 12, 1989 offenses; autopsy reports and photographs from the crime scene of July 12, 1989; psychiatric data from Thames General Hospital and Los Angeles County Medical Services; various civil and criminal transcripts concerning the defendant; and recent reports from both Los Angeles and Anaheim County Conditional Release Programs.

I also conducted personal and telephonic interviews with Susan Stewart, the defendant's sister (telephone interviews on November 4 and 22, 1997); Taylor Jones, the defendant's psychologist and psychotherapist (personal interview on October 31, 1997); and Judith Weiss, Community Program Director from Anaheim County (telephone interview on November 18, 1997).

I interviewed Mr. Sampson for three and one-half hours at Trenton State Hospital on November 12, 1997. I also interpreted the results of the following psychological tests in the preparation of this report: the Rorschach Test (administered by Dr. Pasquel on December 7, 1996); the Minnesota Multiphasic Personality Inventory–2 (completed at Trenton on October 24, 1996); the Millon Clinical Multiaxial Inventory III (completed on November 7, 1997); and the Hare Psychopathy Checklist–Revised, scored by me following the review of all other data.

Instant Offense Mr. Sampson killed his parents, Joseph and Lorraine Sampson, at 0400 on July 12, 1989 in their bedroom at 1234 Maple Street, Pasadena, California. He assaulted his father with a bat while he slept and then stabbed him multiple times with a 10½-inch carving knife. He then stabbed his mother while she was standing and accosting him. He was found Guilty, and Not Guilty by Reason of Insanity, and was admitted to Signet State Hospital on January 18, 1991 on a dual Penal Code §1026 commitment from both Los Angeles and Smith Counties.

On May 27, 1989, six weeks earlier, Mr. Sampson had attempted to murder two men in a restaurant in Dublin, California. He had entered the establishment with a companion, Kevin Wrich, to meet a third man. While they were ordering beers, the defendant drew a Harrington and Richardson .380 semi-automatic pistol from underneath his fatigue jacket and fired multiple times at both men. He then fled the restaurant and was arrested as he stood naked in the San Francisco Bay, yelling and covering himself with seaweed.

Mr. Sampson was admitted to Thames General Hospital in Smith County on May 30, 1989 on a 72-hour hold. He was then transferred to Los Angeles County Medical Services in Martinez on June 2. He remained there until June 21, when he was released to his parents. Family and individual outpatient treatment continued. On July 9, 1989, he confessed to his therapist and father that he had killed his cat, and then 3 days later he murdered his parents.

Following the murder of his parents, he waited for 4 hours and then contacted his attorney, Michael Stewart, now married to his sister. He requested that Mr. Stewart take him to see a psychiatrist, Joseph Browne, MD, which he did. He had seen Dr. Browne a week earlier. Mr. Sampson confessed to them that he had killed his parents, he was taken to Ryan Crisis Center, and subsequently arrested by the police.

Social and Developmental History Mr. Sampson was the second child born to Joseph and Lorraine Sampson on March 5, 1953. His sister, Susan, is 1 year older. He was raised in an intact, Roman Catholic, upper middle class family in which both parents were active in the community. His father owned a department store, Sampson Sales, in Pasadena, California. Mr. Sampson's history is consistent with that of a severe conduct disorder, childhood-onset type. This diagnosis predicts the development of antisocial personality disorder in adulthood. His history is positive for 7 of the 15 conduct disorder criteria (*DSM–IV*): stealing without confrontation of the victim (he would steal neighbor's mail); running away from home overnight at least twice (at age 10, he would sneak out, drink alcohol, and eventually come home intoxicated); lying (he would lie to his parents to cover his drinking); truancy (he was often truant from school); destroying other's property (his sister reported that he would destroy her toys, rip off the arms and legs of dolls, and would destroy building lights and windows); initiating physical fights (he would fight regularly from age 6 onward); and physical cruelty (he would beat his sister from age 11–16 years of age with his fists; he also attempted to drown her when she was 7 years old). There are also anecdotal observations ranging from this last cited incident until the attempted murders in Dublin, California, of Mr. Sampson displaying a smile when this violence was occurring. These continual observations strongly suggest the presence of expressed sadism in Mr. Sampson's personality: that is, the experience of pleasure when he is inflicting pain or suffering on others. This observation, however, has not been documented since the instant offense.

His relationship with his parents, which he characterizes as "poor to fair," could be described as intensely conflictual with father and intense and controlling with mother. This pattern is consistent over time, and ranges from mutually contemptuous anger felt by both father and son, to a symbiotically close relation to mother, in which the defendant felt "unconditional love." This pattern is consistent with narcissistic and antisocial character development. It is nicely captured in a note by Holly Payne, MA, a psychologist doing family therapy with the Sampsons 1 month *before* the killings: "Family dynamics appear to be a symbiotic tie between son and mother and a distant, but controlling father, creating double messages for patient regarding independence/dependence and possibly sexual identity problems."

There does not appear to be a history of physical or sexual abuse of Mr. Sampson. Data indicate that he was disciplined with a belt by his father and occasionally slapped on the face. He also did not witness his father assaulting his mother, nor any other physical violence in the family. Mr. Sampson describes his father's anger toward him as "a silent contempt. It was his job to figure out what was wrong with me and point it out, it was a negative relationship. I was afraid of him, I didn't like to see him." The parents were extremely well liked in the community. Father was gregarious; mother tended to be dutiful and kept her feelings contained.

Sexual History Mr. Sampson's sexual history is notable for its early experimentation and subsequent failures. He first had sexual intercourse with a babysitter at home when he was 10 or 12 years old. He reports that his parents caught them one evening "with her pants down" and that ended his sexual activity with her. He denied any sexual activity through high school. He is heterosexual in orientation, but did not have success as an adolescent nor as a young adult with women. He appears to have had two girlfriends prior to his incarceration; one with whom he lived in Tennessee for 1 year, a girl 5 years his senior, before returning to California; and one in California (a year before the violent offenses) who rejected him. He did have one girlfriend at Trenton, a patient, which also lasted for 1 year and was sexual. He denies any history of "one-night stands" and has never been married or fathered children.

Military History Mr. Sampson served in the Marine Corps for 1 year and then was discharged. His personal writings reveal constant battles with authority figures, and he states that he was discharged for a shoulder injury. There are other data that indicate he may have been generally discharged for drug and alcohol abuse, but this has not been confirmed.

Education History The defendant completed junior college after a protracted period of attending school following his military service. He reports, "I didn't enjoy school," but paradoxically did excel in the boy scouts and became an Eagle Scout when he was 16 years old — as reported by him.

Cruelty to Animals There does not appear to be a history of cruelty to animals other than the killing of the cat 3 days prior to the double homicide. "I liked cats, but they're not much use, disloyal shits. I killed the cat when I was psychotic." His articulated reasons for this incident varied among the people he told.

Work History Mr. Sampson's work history is transient and unstable, generally doing tasks below his estimated level of intelligence, which is in the above average to bright normal range. He reports brief stints with a paper route, as a janitor, in his father's furniture store, gas station work, tree trimming service, sugar refinery, work with a surveyor, work for the city of Martinez, and odd jobs for his father.

Weapons History Mr. Sampson has had an extensive weapons history. He denies any history of hunting, only target shooting. He has been trained by the Marines in the use of weapons. He has owned or possessed the following weapons: .22 automatic pistol in high school, a Winchester Model 73 30-.06 at age 24, a .357 magnum revolver in early adulthood, and a .22 target revolver. He also possessed the H&R .380 pistol that he borrowed from a friend for the May 27 shootings. There were also multiple weapons in the house where he lived before the offenses due to the drug dealings and robberies occurring there. These included 12-gauge and 18-gauge shotguns. He denies any interest in owning or possessing a weapon at present.

Prior Criminal History Mr. Sampson does not have a documented criminal history prior to the two 1989 offenses, although he does report petty criminal activity and drug offenses, including possession, use, and sales. He also reports an arrest at age 14 when he stole a pipe and two arrests for drunk in public. He also attempted an insurance fraud by staging a car accident in a sugar spill.

Medical History His medical history is unremarkable. There are no significant childhood illnesses or injuries reported. He had respiratory problems as an adolescent and does report current allergies. He also is a Hepatitis B carrier.

Family Criminal and Psychiatric History There is no history of family criminal activity. Alcohol abuse is present in the biological family. His maternal aunt is reportedly an alcoholic, and his sister is a self-reported alcoholic who is in recovery treatment. Mother and father drank daily, but no one reported its interference with their functioning.

Drug and Alcohol History Mr. Sampson has an extensive drug and alcohol history. Caffeine was used at 10 years old; alcohol was first ingested at 5 years of age; by 12, the defendant was drinking regularly, two to three times per week. It reportedly relieved his emotional pain. He was using alcohol when he returned to California and continued to abuse alcohol up to the time of the violent offenses; nicotine was used in the form of cigarettes, beginning at age 10 and continuing to age 30; cocaine has been used about 20 times in early adulthood; amphetamine was used in high school, approximately 10 times, and once at age 25; sedative-hypnotics were used in high school, and Mr. Sampson used Valium once with a needle; opiates were used once at age 22; cannabis was smoked daily from age 16 to 25; hallucinogens were used about 20 times (LSD) in high school, and mushrooms (peyote) 4 times; inhalants were sniffed briefly at age 12; phencyclidine has never been used. Mr. Sampson was a dependent polydrug and alcohol user throughout his entire adolescent and young adult life until the time of the offense.

Psychiatric History There is no documented psychiatric treatment history prior to the offenses in 1989. Although the cause of the psychosis in mid-1989 is arguable as either drug induced, and therefore organic, or functional, it is clear that he was psychotic at the time, manifested by grandiose and persecutory delusions and auditory hallucinations. The psychosis lasted for a period of more than 1 month and less than 6 months and does meet the criteria for schizophreniform disorder. Mr. Sampson was only treated with low doses of neuroleptics, initially with little success during the time he was hospitalized between the offenses, and subsequently the course of the psychotic disorder appears as if it would have remitted naturally. All his medications were discontinued at Signet State Hospital on October 29, 1991, and there has been no reoccurrence of psychotic symptoms since. He was considered a diagnostic mystery at Signet because he did not appear to meet the initially diagnosed criteria for paranoid schizophrenia. His psychopathic personality, however, did become more obvious to his treating psychiatrists once his psychosis remitted; it was mostly expressed in his detachment, lack of bonding, and lack of remorse and guilt concerning his crimes.

Clinical Interview I met Mr. Sampson at Trenton State Hospital on November 12, 1997 for our interview. He was cordial and anxious throughout the time I spent with him, and was articulate and thoughtful. At times his laughter was inappropriate, especially when he devalued himself and his history. There were also times when his narcissism was apparent through a rather contemptuous attitude toward others.

Mr. Sampson is a 38-year-old White male appearing neat and clean and wearing glasses and hospital clothing. I began by asking him about his stay at Trenton. "I've been here 4 years, the humane treatment is better here, it's less personal at Signet. I've worked on a deeper level. My underlying anger, I'm gaining insight into me as a personality, at Signet I was driven, determined. But not well rounded. I didn't used to bond, now I'm different. I have the Smith's in Anaheim, they adopted me and are like family. But I don't know what I want out there. I also have my AA sponsors, I believe I can bond to others, but physical separation makes it difficult. I'm reluctant to engage with patients, because there's always a sense of loss, it's painful to the ego, I don't know. . . ."

When asked to describe his deceased father, he said, "He was very conservative, family oriented, typical Italian type, social, community responsibility, not good with children, he had emotional faults which I picked up. He didn't spend time with the kids, not ideal for kids. He had a strong personality, good with friends and peers. I disappointed him, his anger was too great." He described his mother: "The martyr. She filled in for dad on all the activity, upbringing. Did very good. Warm and loving in a way, but didn't look out for herself very well, moralistic issues weren't dealt with. She loved me unconditionally."

When asked to describe his childhood, he said, "I was unmanageable before the age of 10. My grandfather died when I was 10, my dad and our relationship went down. I was stealing, throwing mud balls at cars, a bully in school, fighting all the time, to anybody. I was angry, no needs met at home, misery and shit I didn't want."

His earliest memory, often an important template for later behavior and perception: "I'd feel lonely at night, lay down behind the door to hear the TV set. One time they came out and thought I was asleep and said, 'oh, isn't he cute.' When I was asleep I was cute, when I was awake, totally different!" His earliest memory of father: "I was stuck in the woodbox while he worked. He put me back in, that was my world. I was OK if he left me alone." His earliest memory with mother: "I'm playing in the kitchen with my sister, playing astronauts, she would interact with us."

After the gathering of the historical data noted earlier in this report, I asked Mr. Sampson about the time prior to the offenses. "I'd felt alright in Tennessee (after military). I was progressing pretty well, had a girlfriend Rebecca. People living with us in Memphis. Then I returned to school and California. It felt suffocating. I moved back with my parents. It was a dumb shit thing to do, a rerun of a bad movie." When asked why he did this, he said, "My social skills were so poor, and I had such a negative view." He worked in a sugar factory, began junior college, and was self-medicating with alcohol and marijuana. This continued for several years and the defendant began socializing with drug dealers. He would work part-time jobs, but continued an unstable social and work history.

In mid-1988, he had a girlfriend and moved out of the home into a garage. This also appears to be the time when Mr. Sampson was told to leave his parents' home due to a money-making scheme in which he tricked a teller to release money to him ($3,000) against his father's wishes. He was told to get out of the home by his mother. He began selling marijuana at this time and also was surrounded by weapons in the home of his friend and was continuing to possess weapons himself. It is unclear what exactly precipitated his psychotic break, but it was probably a combination of the drug and alcohol ingestion, rejection by his family, rejection by his new girlfriend, and the climate of paranoia that is manifest in drug dealing surroundings.

He reports, "I began crying in May 1989. I was emotionally scaling unknown regions. It went on for a couple of days, auditory and visual hallucinations. I became an apparition in the mirror. I had done some methamphetamine a week before. I passed out on the floor with my pants down and they left me there. I was having command hallucinations saying, 'Go shoot someone.' I went and shot a coke dealer in a bar with my friend's .380 auto pistol (laughs). My friend pushed me to go pick up some coke in Oakland and then Dublin. The guy bought me a beer, I heard voices and shot him. Neither one died, but hurt bad. I jumped into the water of Dublin Bay, naked and putting seaweed on my head."

"I was in jail. I don't know if it was drugs and it doesn't make any difference. My parents bailed me out, stayed with my sister for a week, then my parents as an outpatient. No medications—I refused them. I was in and out of psychosis, bungling around the house. Worried about the drug dealer I shot, no one would talk to me. I met with a psychologist. I killed my cat. I thought it was a reincarnation of a former wife, I thought he was talking to me. I stomped on it. I was crying."

On July 12, 1989, Mr. Sampson committed the instant offense. "Voices were tormenting me. People talking on the astral plane, TV voices talking to me, dead people and witches. Circular thinking, the end of the world, retribution for my sins and crimes, guilt. I was a mass of jelly. I tried to call for help that evening. They came back at 10 or 11 p.m. and went to bed. I went to bed to go to sleep, and the auditory hallucinations continued. I was responsible for the ills of the world. Feeling awful. Interplanetary war. All I loved would die. It won't stop unless I kill my parents. I ran downstairs, grabbed a knife in the kitchen, baseball bat. I hit him in the head, he grabbed me, we pushed back and forth. I stabbed him once, but the autopsy said two or three times. He collapsed, she jumped out of bed and ran around to him. (How were you feeling?) Numb and terrified. (Thinking?) She grabbed me and pushed me back. I said I have to kill you. She let go and the knife went into her throat, the autopsy said three times. She fell down, a fountain of blood. (How did you feel?) Lost. I stood there and cried. I ran around the house then. In so much pain, but I couldn't cut myself. The auditory hallucinations stopped. Oh, no, this isn't real. I set dad next to mom, put a blanket over them, sat on the floor, for a couple of hours. Called my brother-in-law and asked him to drive me to the doctor. Told him what had happened. They took me to Thames Hospital. I thought no one really died. I then tried suicide in jail. I felt sorry for the two deputies cause my head was swinging from a rope."

When asked how he felt about the killings, he began to cry. "A loss for them and me, confused. I'm better at a great cost to someone else. If I hadn't killed, I would be dead, the way I was going. I feel whole, but I don't like me sometimes. I haven't spoken to any family members. My paternal grandmother died the next year."

He recounted his treatment in the hospitals as "emotional development. It stopped when I began using drugs. I learned how to grow up here with healthy models." When asked about his anger, he reported that he is angry daily, with a frequency of 2 to 20 times. "I like people, but I'm insecure. Anger was easy, the only emotion. I'm still angry, mostly at myself for not taking a positive view. I didn't get my wakeup till later."

When asked about his 5-year projection, he said, "employed, I'd form attachments easily, I want to continue artwork, sculpture, painting. I need to see about relations with women." When asked about conscience, he said, "I was raised Roman Catholic. Guilt was a panacea for moral behavior. I never hurt other people, but couldn't communicate. I pay attention to others now, but I don't like being scrutinized."

He was able to state that his first signs of decompensation would be unresolvable anger and deviation from his long-term goals of work and school.

He verbally agreed to all the terms and conditions of the Anaheim Conditional Release Program.

Mental Status Exam Oriented to person, place, and time. Alert, anxious, cooperative. Affect blunted and sometimes inappropriate to thought content. No formal thought disorder. Speech is normal in rate and volume. No evident delusions or hallucinations. No thought insertion, withdrawal, stealing, or broadcasting. Concentration and attention normal. Memory tested for short- and long-term retrieval, normal. Concept formation normal for average to above average IQ. No homicidal or suicidal ideation or intent. Appearance casual and neat. Personal hygiene is normal.

Review of Hospital Records I reviewed the summary notes from Signet and Trenton for the past 10 years and the clinical notes from December 4, 1996 to November 12, 1997. Initial notes from the past year indicate that Mr. Sampson is superficial, guarded, aloof, angry, passive–aggressive, capable of empathy, isolative, motivated for treatment, and works very hard at solitary tasks. His anger and bitterness have apparently decreased during the past year with a concomitant rise in depressive symptoms. He appears to let go of his anger more appropriately. His psychotherapist for the past 3 years, Taylor Jones, PhD, reports that he has seen him weekly for a total of 150 to 200 sessions. He stated that he is currently working on trust issues, and that most of the transference work concerning father is complete. He describes him as "obsessive compulsive. He knows he's angry, and sublimates through painting. He may be neurotically organized, and feels helpless because of the current situation. He is not sure about people. Mythical people are safer. He expects betrayal by others."

Suicide History Mr. Sampson has made two suicide attempts, the most serious on August 5, 1989, when he cut his throat and slashed his abdomen. He also made a suicide gesture between offenses at the Los Angeles County Medical Services with a piece of glass.

Psychological Testing Mr. Sampson was administered the MMPI–2, MCMI–III, and Rorschach as noted in the database section of this report. The test results are reviewed in turn.

MMPI–2 The Minnesota Multiphasic Personality Inventory–2 was completed at Trenton on October 24, 1996. The test was computer scored. I consulted with James Hess, PhD, a noted authority, while interpreting the results.

Mr. Sampson produced a valid profile with no indications of conscious or unconscious distortion or defensiveness. He produced a two-point clinically elevated 45 profile. It describes an individual who is educated, charming, and presents superficially quite well. This person, however, is generally out of touch with his feelings, quite angry, and sensitive to rejection. He wants to be liked and respected, but is rather immature and narcissistic. Good controls are present unless the person is rejected or using alcohol. This may create a flash point that could lead to an explosive event, followed by covering over and denial of its importance. On the surface, this individual is warm and caring, but has no loyal or enduring relations and does not tend to bond to others. Generally there is emotional passivity, and also the harboring of strong, unconscious dependency needs. Sexuality is most comfortable in situations where controls are greatest and distance can be maintained. This individual has found a mental health "persona," but he is still overcontrolled. Subtle signs of depression and anxiety do indicate positive features, but these feelings are still deeply buried. He is still quite angry at authority figures, sublimated through a more traditionally feminine behavior, such as artistic or cultural pursuits. He probably had parents where one was very authoritarian and he learned to be a survivor through any means necessary.

Treatment should involve individual and group psychotherapy where he is actively engaged and confronted by strong clinicians, and has an opportunity to bond to a group and recognize that others can care about him.

MCMI-III The Millon Clinical Multiaxial Inventory–III was completed by the patient on November 7, 1997, almost 1 year after the MMPI-2. It was scored and interpreted through National Computer Systems, and the report is reproduced here verbatim from the computer printout. Aspects of this report have been integrated into my findings:

"A distinct tendency toward avoiding self-disclosure is evident in this patient's response style . . . on the basis of the test data the patient is exhibiting psychological dysfunctions of mild severity. This man exhibits a veneer of friendliness and sociability, yet shows contempt for conventional morals. Although he is able to make a good impression on casual acquaintances, he frequently displays his characteristic impulsiveness, restlessness, and moodiness to family members and close associates. Rather untrustworthy and unreliable, he persistently seeks excitement and often engages in self-dramatizing behavior. His relationships are shallow and fleeting, and he often fails to meet routine responsibilities. His communications frequently are characterized by caustic comments and callous outbursts, and he often acts rashly, using insufficient deliberation and poor judgment. Seen often as irresponsible and undependable by others, he exhibits short-lived enthusiasms that are followed by disillusionment and resentment."

"Unlikely to admit responsibility for personal or family difficulties, he has an easily circumvented conscience, and he may be quite facile in denying the presence of psychological tension or conflict. Interpersonal problems are rationalized, especially those that he engenders, and blame is readily projected onto others. Self-indulgent and insistent on getting his way, he reciprocates the efforts of others with only minimal loyalty and consideration."

"When crossed, subjected to minor pressures, or faced with potential embarrassment, he often is provoked to abandon responsibilities with minimal guilt or remorse. Unfettered by the restrictions of social conventions or the restraints of personal loyalties, he is quick to free himself from encumbrances and obligations. His superficial affability collapses easily, and he quickly jettisons those who challenge his autonomy or beliefs. Although infrequent, his temper outbursts may turn into uncontrollable violence. More typically, he is impetuous and imprudent, throwing caution to the winds, driven by a need for excitement and an inability to delay gratification, with minimal regard for consequences. Adventure seeking, he restlessly chases one capricious whim after another, and is likely to travel an erratic course of irresponsibility, delighting in defying and challenging social conventions. He appears to have a poor prognosis for staying out of trouble."

Rorschach This test was administered to the patient on December 7, 1996 at Trenton State Hospital. I rescored the protocol and analyzed it using the RSP3 program produced by Rorschach Workshops.

Mr. Sampson scored positive for the Depression Index, which is a positive prognostic indicator given his antisocial history, and suggests frequent and intense feelings of depression that will be consciously denied.

His affects inconsistently influence his thinking and decision making. He is considered an ambitent, meaning he does not have a clear pattern of problem solving, a finding that is common among psychiatric patients. He tends to take a simplified, item-by-item approach to problems. His modulation of emotion is poor, and parallels that of a 7-year-old boy, a finding that is average for antisocial personality disordered males. He also tends to avoid emotionally provoking stimuli outside himself, and is highly defended against his own affect. At the time of testing, he was experiencing distress and discomfort, and finds his emotional states confusing. He shows high levels of felt anxiety or helplessness, which is not consistent with psychopathy.

His capacity for control and stress tolerance is normal, and generally will not falter unless stress is extreme or prolonged.

His self-perception is characterized by extreme self-absorption, but he shows no indications of pathological narcissism. He has a capacity for balanced introspection and insight, a positive prognostic indicator, and volitional psychological resources are in the average range. His self-image, however, is more imaginative than real, with a marked sexual preoccupation.

His interpersonal perceptions show a distinct interest in others as whole, real, and meaningful individuals. He also experiences needs for closeness to others that are normative. He is not characterologically angry, but is oppositional and will often be defensively authoritarian. He will often see others as potential adversaries, despite his wishes that they not be, and may self-aggrandize with them to shore up his self-esteem for the expected rejection.

His cognitive processes tend to be simple and less complicated than expected for his age. He is an underincorporator, meaning that he will scan the stimulus field and often miss important sources of data because of his haphazard approach to visual cues around him. His aspirations do not outstrip his abilities. He tends to view the world in rather unconventional and idiosyncratic ways, but his reality testing is unimpaired. There is no indication of borderline or psychotic impediments in his ability to distinguish between internal and external reality. Likewise, his ideation is generally normative, with slightly more faulty conceptualizing than one would like to see. He shows no clinical evidence of formal thought disorder, although he is prone to errors in judgment.

Hare Psychopathy Checklist–Revised Mr. Sampson scored 26 on the PCL-R, placing him in the moderate range of psychopathic disturbance. Among male prison inmates, he would score at the 59.3 percentile, meaning that he would be slightly above average for psychopathy in that setting. Among male forensic psychiatric patients, he would score at the 77.3 percentile, ranking him as more psychopathic than most patients in such a setting. This score suggests that Mr. Sampson is not a primary or severe psychopath, although he probably would have scored in the higher range 15 years ago. Part of this change is due to the aging process, and part of it may be due to treatment. Nevertheless, at present he shows some capacity to form emotional relationships and to accept prosocial values. He also shows indicators of both anxiety and depression, which are important predictors of successful treatment of psychopathically disturbed patients.

Psychodiagnosis (*DSM–IV*)

AXIS I:	303.90	Alcohol dependence, in hospital remission
	304.80	Polysubstance dependence, in remission
	295.40	Schizophreniform Disorder, in remission
AXIS II:	301.70	Antisocial Personality Disorder with additional histrionic, narcissistic, and passive–aggressive traits (moderate psychopathy)
AXIS III:		Hepatitis B carrier
AXIS IV:		Problems related to social and legal factors
AXIS V:		GAF 65 (current)

Findings and Opinions

1. The defendant shows no clinical signs or symptoms of an AXIS I mental disorder. There are psychological test indices that suggest masked depression, a good prognostic indicator.

2. The defendant has an extensive alcohol and drug abuse history, which is his greatest vulnerability as an outpatient. He will be at high risk to consume alcohol again, despite commitment and involvement in the AA programs at Trenton. He recognizes this vulnerability.

3. The defendant has a personality disorder that is presently described as a moderately psychopathic antisocial personality. He is not a primary psychopath, which would make him a significant risk for continued violence and criminality on release. His level of psychopathic disturbance predicts a decreased risk of criminality on release and some meaningful gains from treatment during the past 12 years. His moderately positive changes in demeanor and his increased willingness and ability to manage his anger appear genuine and should not be considered faked. Nevertheless, he will continue to evidence both histrionic and narcissistic character patterns, will anger easily, will resist authority at times, may be suggestible and confused about his feelings at times, will defend against strong dependency needs, and will be inclined to engage in mischievous behavior while in the community, including deception of his clinician.

4. His other major vulnerability besides alcohol abuse (and other stimulant drugs) will be rejection by women. He has some confusion around his own gender identity and sexual preferences. Although this is unconscious, his intensely dependent relationship on his mother, and her reinforcement of his grandiosity and antisociality, make him particularly vulnerable to narcissistic insults from women. His relations need to be carefully monitored so that he does not emotionally connect with a woman who is using drugs or is emotionally unstable. He will also tend to form hostile-oppositional relations with males, expecting the treatment of contempt he perceived from his father. Careful teaching of appropriate social skills with both men and women will be useful.

5. Although he does have a significant weapons history, I see no reason to predict a return to weapons possession unless he decompensates or begins to use illicit drugs.

6. Despite his propensity for anger, and its unmodulated expression, his controls are normal and he is not behaviorally impulsive. He also thinks about his anger now, and can have insight into it. He will continue to benefit from individual psychotherapy with an active, strong clinician.

7. The motivational dynamics for the killing of his parents need to be further explored. The overt precipitant—that is, his psychosis—is evident,

but it is not clear *why* his psychosis was expressed through parricide. I suspect that it was narcissistic rage toward a perceived father who rejected him and a perceived mother who controlled him, delusionally set forth at the time as a necessary act to redeem himself. These underlying dynamics need to be explicated and should not be avoided by paying attention only to the psychosis. After all, most people with psychosis do not murder.

8. He appears to have a support system in Anaheim County — namely, the Smith Family. I was unable to reach them by telephone. Although at one time he had a substantial amount of money from his parents' estate, his sister informed me that $110–$125,000 of it was negotiated back to her as part of a wrongful death settlement in 1993. My conversation with Dr. Weiss of the Anaheim program indicates that they are favorably impressed with Mr. Sampson, but are concerned that they "have been had." Her program has outlined a comprehensive plan for Mr. Sampson that I have reviewed and find satisfactory for this patient.

9. Mr. Sampson's potential victim pool consists of two groups: first, individuals that he targets for homicide when he is delusional to fulfill some grandiose purpose. His history indicates four such victims: a friend, a stranger, and his parents. Two of these victims were actually killed. This violence tends to be planned and purposeful, despite its delusional basis, and is carried out over the course of a few hours. The aftermath of this form of *predatory* violence in Mr. Sampson is increased psychotic agitation without guilt or remorse. It is my opinion that he is at virtually no risk for this form of violence in the future if he remains nonpsychotic. This can be easily monitored through the Conrep program and core standards of treatment. The second victim pool group consists of anyone who wounds, criticizes, or insults him. This group has included a variety of people throughout his life, such as his sister and other peers. The historical violence in these cases has been physical assault without a weapon. Mr. Sampson has not engaged in this form of violence during the past 12 years at the state hospitals, despite an available victim pool (other patients and staff) and certain narcissistically wounding events that are bound to occur in such a setting. The absence of such *affective*, impulsive violence bodes well for low risk in the future, and Mr. Sampson may simply have outgrown physical aggressiveness in response to interpersonal threat to his narcissistic equilibrium. It is likely that, instead, he responds through unmodulated, and often frequent, verbal anger, and may devalue these objects in fantasy. Nevertheless, these mechanisms, his age, and his general isolation substantially reduce the risk of this form of violence in the future.

I do have some concerns about his sadistic impulses because they were apparent to me during the interview in the form of sadomasochistic feelings directed toward himself. One would not expect these impulses to go away, and his treating clinician should watch carefully for pleasant affect expressed by Mr. Sampson when he expresses devaluation of himself or others. This needs to be carefully explored so that he can work on it therapeutically, but I do not see it increasing his risk of violence at present.

I also am not concerned about a threat to his sister, Susan. Although I understand her fear of him, I see no basis in present reality for her to be frightened. Mr. Sampson has no intent to reestablish his relationship with her, and it is a term and condition of his treatment that he will not contact her.

Opinion and Recommendation It is my opinion that Mr. Samuel Sampson would not constitute a danger to the health and safety of others if placed in the Anaheim Conditional Release Program at this time, and would benefit from such status. I would also make the following recommendations:

a. He initially be placed in Hope House, a 12-person, 24-hour supervised housing, for at least 6 months.

b. He be randomly tested for drug and alcohol abuse twice weekly, then decreased to once per week.

c. The Anaheim Conrep program personally interview the Smiths before the defendant is released, and set whatever visitation limits seem appropriate.

d. Structure the patient so that he can continue his artistic pursuits, and whatever educational goals he sets. He should also be required to earn some money through work so that he is self-supportive.

e. He should be assigned to an active and engaging psychotherapist who can both support and confront, and who is familiar with psychopathic disturbance, its underlying psychodynamics, and expected countertransference reactions.

f. Collateral contacts should be substantial so that any deception or manipulation can be identified quickly and easily.

Thank you so much for this interesting case. If you have any questions, please telephone me.

J. Reid Meloy, PhD, ABPP
Diplomate, Forensic Psychology
American Board of Professional Psychology
Fellow, American Academy of Forensic Sciences
Associate Clinical Professor of Psychiatry
University of California, San Diego

Appendix C: The Use of the Psychopathy Checklist–Revised (PCL–R) and Rorschach in Treatment Planning With Antisocial Personality Disordered Patients

Carl B. Gacono
Private Practice, Austin, Texas

Often ignored within correctional settings, the need for *thorough* screening, treatment planning (Maruish, 1994; Mortimer & Smith, 1983), and outcome assessment is no more conspicuous than among the heterogeneous group of individuals who compose a disproportionate percentage of the population, those diagnosed as Antisocial Personality Disorder (ASPD; American Psychiatric Association, 1994). Although ASPD patients constitute only a small proportion of adult community populations (females = 1%, males = 3%; American Psychiatric Association, 1994), their ubiquitous presence in a correctional environment (50%-75%; Hare, 1996) stimulates a clinical need for careful evaluation at all phases of treatment (screening, treatment planning, progress).

Although sharing similar behavioral features, ASPD patients vary greatly with respect to treatment amenability. Those elevated in psychopathy (psychopaths; PCL-R ≥ 30; Hare, 1991) evidence poor treatment response[1] (Ogloff, Wong, & Greenwood, 1990; Rice, Harris, & Quinsey, 1990). Not a surprising finding in that psychopaths participate in more institutional misbehavior (Gacono, Meloy, Sheppard, Speth, & Roske, 1995; Wong, 1988) and present a higher risk for both violent and nonviolent reoffense (Hare, McPherson, & Forth, 1988; Williamson,

International Journal of Offender Therapy and Comparative Criminology, 42(1), 1998   49-64
© 1998 Sage Publications, Inc.

Hare, & Wong, 1987) than nonpsychopaths (PCL-R ≤ 30). Psychopathic Rorschachs reveal corresponding personality deficits in all areas related to attachment (perceptual, affect, attachment desire, expectations of cooperative, mutual relationships; Gacono & Meloy, 1994, 1996) and subsequently the presence of most if not all variables associated with negative treatment response (Hilsenroth, Handler, Toman, & Padawer, 1995). Whereas to date there is no known, empirically validated treatment for psychopaths (PCL-R ≥ 30), the prognosis for nonpsychopathic ASPDs is considerably better.

Whereas the PCL-R total score identifies severe ASPD patients at greatest risk for treatment failure, item analysis provides a foundation for treatment planning in nonpsychopathic ASPDs, one of several clinical applications that have only been mentioned antidotally (Becker & Quinsey, 1993; Gacono, in press; Gacono & Hutton, 1994). Together, PCL-R and Rorschach data provide several levels of personality information and a method for monitoring treatment progress (Gacono, 1990; Gacono & Hutton, 1994; Meloy & Gacono, 1995).

THE PSYCHOPATHY CHECKLIST-REVISED

The Hare Psychopathy Checklist-Revised (PCL-R; Hare, 1991; Hare, Hart, & Harpur, 1991) provides a standardized method for assessing core psychopathic personality characteristics (Meloy, 1988) and behaviors. The PCL-R is a 20-item, 0- to 40-point scale consisting of two stable, oblique factors (Hare et al., 1991).

Factor 1 items contain core characteristics of glibness and superficial charm (1), grandiose sense of self-worth (2), pathological lying (4), conning/manipulative (5), lack of remorse (6), shallow affect (7), callous/lack of empathy (8), and failure to accept responsibility for own actions (16). Characterized by egocentricity, callousness, and remorselessness, Factor 1 correlates with *DSM-III-R*'s (*Diagnostic and Statistical Manual of Mental Disorders*, third edition, revised; American Psychiatric Association, 1987) narcissistic and histrionic personality disorders (Hare, 1991) and self-report measures of Machiavellianism and narcissism (Harpur, Hare, & Hakstian, 1989; Hart & Hare, 1989). Emotionally detached, ASPD patients elevated on Factor 1 lack emotional distress and attachment capacity necessary to initiate and sustain psychotherapy.

Factor 2 items contain proneness to boredom (3), parasitic lifestyle (9), poor behavioral controls (10), early behavioral problems (12), lack of realistic, long-term goals (13), impulsivity (14), irresponsibility (15), juvenile delinquency (18), and revocation of conditional release (19), and are characterized by an irresponsible, impulsive, thrill-seeking, unconventional, and antisocial lifestyle.[2] Factor 2 correlates with the ASPD diagnosis, criminal behaviors, lower socioeconomic background, lower IQ, and less education, and self-report measures of antisocial behavior (Hare, 1991; Harpur et al., 1989). Elevated Factor 2 scores alert the clinician to deficient ego functions, diminished controls, and consequently a need for therapeutic structure. When elevated, the PCL-R total score (combined factors) assures poor treatment outcome (Ogloff et al., 1990; Rice et al., 1990).

PCL-R administration requires *access* to collateral *historical/background* information and a semistructured interview (Hare, 1991). Interview alone is *never* sufficient for scoring. PCL-R scores range from 0 to 40 with a cutoff ≥ 30 designated as the threshold for primary psychopathy.[3] Psychopathic offenders are more prone to institutional violence, general and violent recidivism (Hare & McPherson, 1984; Harris, Rice, & Cormier, 1991; Hart, Kropp, & Hare, 1988; Rice et al., 1990; Serin, 1991, 1992; Serin, Peters, & Barbaree, 1990; Wong, 1988), and treatment failure (Ogloff et al., 1990; Rice et al., 1990) than those with low scores.

THE RORSCHACH TEST

Although some controversy lingers concerning the reliability and validity of the Rorschach Test, any empirical basis for general criticism is lacking (Weiner, 1996). Two recent meta-analytic studies of Rorschach validity (Atkinson, 1986; Parker, Hanson, & Hunsley, 1988) demonstrated that "conceptual, theory-based studies of the Rorschach indicate adequate validity values approximately equivalent to those found for the Minnesota Multiphasic Personality Inventory (MMPI)" (Weiner, 1996, p. 208). As Parker et al. (1988) point out:

> The MMPI and Rorschach are both valid, stable, and reliable under certain circumstances. When either test is used in the manner for which it was designed and validated, its psychometric properties are likely to be adequate for either clinical or research purpose. (p. 373)

The validity of the Rorschach depends on *what it is used for* rather than inherent weaknesses in its psychometric properties. The test was "designed and intended for use as a personality assessment instrument . . . scales or indexes that correlate consistently and significantly with observable aspects of personality functioning" (Weiner, 1996, p. 207). Several areas of demonstrated validity include differentiating trait and state personality variables, measuring developmental change in children and adolescents, identifying experienced distress in war veterans with posttraumatic stress disorder, treatment planning, and monitoring improvement in psychotherapy (Weiner, 1994, 1996; Weiner & Exner, 1991).

INTEGRATING THE PCL-R AND RORSCHACH

PCL-R administration provides a standardized method for quantifying and organizing *observable* attitudes and behaviors. Through the PCL-R record review and interview, the clinician formulates an Axis II diagnosis (*DSM-IV*; American

Psychiatric Association, 1994) and gains understanding of the ASPD individual's primary character style.[4]

Item analysis suggests specific areas that require intervention. For example, in a low scorer (PCL-R < 20), 0 points on Items 1 (*glibness/superficial charm*) and 2 (*grandiose sense of self worth*) coupled with a score of 2 on Items 3 (*proneness to boredom*), 14 (*impulsivity*), and 15 (*irresponsibility*) rules out a narcissistic or psychopathic disorder, suggests borderline features, and indicates the clinical need for structure and interventions designed to increase impulse control and problem-solving skills. One or 2 points on Item 10 (*poor behavioral controls*) signal the need for anger management training.

The Rorschach adds to and refines hypothesis generated by the PCL-R. It provides information concerning (see Tables 2 and 4) problem solving and response style (Lambda, introversive, extratensive), processing (Zd; overincorporation, underincorporation), reality testing (X–%), perceptual accuracy and conventionality (F+, X+, P; Does the individual see the world as most others?), controls and current stress levels (D/adjD; Does the current testing reflect a chronic or situational condition and which affective states are contributing to overload?), levels of emotionality and how the subject deals with them (FC:CF+C, Afr; i.e., avoidance), self-perception (W:M, Fr+rF, MOR; grandiose vs. inadequate), coping resources (EA, CDI), desire for affectional relatedness (T), and interpersonal interest, maturity, and expectations (H, (H), COP, AG; Does the person expect cooperation in human relations? Aggression? Are relationships based on imagination or reality?). PCL-R items *quantify* observable attitudes and documented behaviors, whereas Rorschach data *correlate* with them. The PCL-R and Rorschach assess different but complementary personality dimensions.

CASE EXAMPLES[5]

Steve and Dave were incarcerated, Caucasian males in their mid to late 20s carrying a diagnosis of Antisocial Personality Disorder (American Psychiatric Association, 1987). Consistent with treating severe character pathology, Steve and Dave began treatment within an institutional setting (Gacono, 1985; Kernberg, 1984). They were voluntary participants in a state offender treatment program. Group treatment was based on principles of Reality Therapy and included sections on Rational Behavior Training (RBT; Maultsby, 1979), criminal thinking (Walters, 1990; Yochelson & Samenow, 1977), anger management, and relapse prevention (Gorski & Miller, 1982; Marlatt & Gordon, 1985).

Concurrent to group participation, both subjects participated in one-to-one counseling. Steve completed 9 months of short-term psychodynamic therapy (Strupp & Binder, 1984). His treatment focused on grief work and identity issues related to a history of sexual abuse. Dave attended 16 months of supportive counseling, which included problem solving and assertiveness training. Both were rated as improved by their treating therapists.[6]

PCL-Rs and initial Rorschachs were administered prior to treatment as a routine part of admissions testing (see Tables 1-4). PCL-Rs were administered and independently scored by two experienced raters, with final item scores being determined by rater consensus. The second Rorschach was administered after 10 months of treatment. A third Rorschach was administered to Dave 16 months into treatment. These latter Rorschachs were administered by a clinical psychologist or advanced graduate psychology intern as a routine part of program evaluation. All five Rorschachs were rescored by CBG for reliability, with rater consensus between CBG and the test administrator determining final scores. All protocols were then rescored independently by LAB (an experienced, Ph.D.-level rater) and yielded the following reliabilities: location, 99%; space, 100%; developmental quality, 92%; determinants, 87%; a/p, 100%; form quality, 94%; pairs, 96%; content, 96%; populars, 100%; Z scores, 91%; and special scores, 67%.[7]

The Rorschach Comprehensive System (Exner, 1993) evaluates Rorschach data in several clusters and constellations (see Tables 2 and 4) useful for formulating treatment strategies. *Mediation variables* assess the extent to which an individual is oriented toward making conventional or acceptable responses. *Ideation variables* address how inputs become conceptualized and used. *Processing* reveals processing effort/motivation and processing efficiency. The *Affect cluster* examines the role of emotion in psychology and functioning. The *Self-perception cluster* provides a picture of self-image and self-esteem. *Interpersonal variables* reveal how an individual perceives and relates to others (Exner, 1993). Select variables and ratios (see Tables 2 and 4) will be used to illustrate *expected* treatment progress.

CASE 1: STEVE

Steve's initial PCL-R score is 23 (see Table 1), placing him in the low end of the moderate range (Gacono & Hutton, 1994). He is not a psychopath. None of his Factor 1 items are prototypic (scored 2). Despite narcissistic traits, he is not an *arrogant* narcissist; not a pathological liar; has some capacity for affective experience, attachment, empathy, and remorse; and accepts some responsibility for his antisocial behavior (Items 6, 7, 8, & 16). Despite attachment difficulties (Items 11 & 17), one T response and 2 COPs on the Rorschach (see Table 2) support attachment potential and "expectations of cooperative human interaction," even in the context of self-focus (Fr = 1).[8]

Given above-average intelligence (Zachary, 1986), high levels of treatment motivation,[9] and the absence of a sexual deviation, Steve's prognosis is favorable, despite his ASPD diagnosis. Had Items 1 and 2 (narcissism) and Items 6, 7, and 8 (shallow affect)[10] been prototypic (2s), concurrent to a T-less Rorschach protocol with Fr = 1, treatment prognosis would have been dismal.

Factor 2 items indicate a "later" rather than early onset for antisocial behavior (*early behavior problems* = 1, *juvenile delinquency* = 0), prognositically a positive

TABLE 1
STEVE'S PCL-R PROTOCOL

Item	Factor 1	Factor 2	Total Score
1. Glibness/superficial charm	1		1
2. Grandiose sense of self-worth	1		1
3. Need for stimulation/proneness to boredom		1	1
4. Pathological lying	1		1
5. Conning/manipulative	1		1
6. Lack of remorse or guilt	1		1
7. Shallow affect	1		1 (0-1)
8. Callous/lack of empathy	1		1
9. Parasitic lifestyle		1	1
10. Poor behavioral controls		2	2
11. Promiscuous sexual behavior			2
12. Early behavioral problems		1	1
13. Lack of realistic, long-term goals		1	1
14. Impulsivity		1	1
15. Irresponsibility		1	1
16. Failure to accept responsibility for own actions	1		1
17. Many short-term marital relationships			2
18. Juvenile delinquency		0	0
19. Revocation of conditional release		2	2
20. Criminal versatility			1
Total	8	10	23

sign. One-point scores on Items 3, 14, and 15 indicate some impulse control, coping resources, and capacity for delay ($M = 3$). However, as indicated by 1-point scores, instead of 0s, and supported by Rorschach data (EA, M), Steve is in need of comprehensive skills training (Ross, Fabiano, & Ewles, 1988), including anger management (PCL-R Item 10 = 2; S–% = .25). Concurrent to an ASPD diagnosis, a cluster B personality style containing narcissistic, histrionic, and borderline traits is suggested.

Steve's low Lambda is consistent with his elevated Zd, indicating an inefficient problem-solving style and a tendency to become overinvolved with stimuli (Exner, 1993). Low Lambda combined with a tendency toward introversion[11] (EB) suggest that overincorporation (Zd) may be in part due to self-criticalness associated with the need "to avoid error or failure" (Exner, 1993, p. 409). In ASPD patients, this pattern relates to suspiciousness and can correlate with an early history of abuse-induced vigilance. Other cognitive deficits include perceptual accuracy problems (X+%, F+%), unconventional thinking (Xu%, P), reality testing difficulties (X–%), and cognitive slippage (WSum6; SCZI). The pervasiveness of these thinking problems suggests the need for cognitive-behavioral

TABLE 2
SELECT RORSCHACH VARIABLES FOR STEVE

	Pre	Post
R	13	16
Lambda	.44	.33
EA	4.5	9.5
EB	3:1.5	6:3.5
D/adjD	0/0	0/1
Ideation		
Ma:Mp	3:0	6:0
M–	0	1
M	3	6
WSum6	30	30
Mediation		
P	4	7
X+%	.46	.63
F+%	.50	.50
X–%	.31	.13
Xu%	.23	.25
S–%	.25	.00
Affect		
FC:CF+C	1:1	1:3
PureC	0	0
Afr	.30	.45
T	1	1
Y	0	1
V	1	2
Processing		
Zd	4.5	–1.5
W:M	10:3	8:6
Self-perception		
3r+(2)/R	.46	.56
Fr+rF	1	1
FD	0	2
MOR	1	0
Interpersonal		
COP	2	2
AG	0	0
H	1	2
(H)	1	2
Hd:(Hd)	1:0	1:0
Constellations		
SCZI	4	1
DEPI	3	4
CDI	3	1
S-CON	7	6

group therapy augmented by psychodynamic therapy.[12] Due to Steve's history, range of affect, and testing data suggesting bonding potential (T = 1; PCL-R Item 7), introversion, and the capacity for empathy (M = 3; PCL-R Item 8) and remorse (V = 1; PCL-R Item 6), a short-term psychodynamic therapy was included in his treatment.

Treatment progress. Successful treatment should reveal increases in coping resources, reality testing, conventional thinking, emotional control, emotional tolerance, accurate perceptions of self and others, and interpersonal relatedness. Steve's Rorschach *supports* treatment gains. Organized resources (EA) increase (4.5 to 9.5) without subsequent decreases in controls (D/adjD = 0/1). Now within a normative range (Exner, 1993), coping resources have increased (CDI, 3 to 1). Capacity for delay and perhaps empathy increased (M doubles). A predominant introversive problem-solving style surfaces.

Lambda remains similar but now organizing is more efficient, less strained, and more accurate (X–%, .31 to .13). Perceptual accuracy without affect (F+%) remains constant; however, improvement in X+% (.46 to .63) may suggest less emotionally caused disruptions. Perhaps the disruptive effects of anger on thinking has lessened (S–% = .00). Although the level of cognitive slippage (WSum6) remains stable, Steve is better able to identify what is "popularly" seen by others (P = 4 to 7). Not unexpected for an ASPD individual, unusual perceptual accuracy remains pervasive (Xu%). Observable gains in Steve's judgment and problem-solving skills accompanied these Rorschach changes.

Despite continued difficulties with affect modulation (FC:CF+C), Steve is more tolerant of affect (FC:CF+C = 1:3, Afr) and now allowing "new" affective states, such as anxiety (Y). Greater tolerance for emotions is essential to relapse prevention in that negative emotions compose "high risk situations." Although self-focused (EgoC = .56), Steve's self-appraisal lacks grandiosity, is more realistic (W:M), and includes increased psychological mindedness/rumination, some painful (V = 2; perhaps guilt) and some with objectivity (FD = 2). His self-focus, absent the malignant narcissism, may even be a source of "ego strength." Interest in others has increased (M, H, (H)). Combined observable behaviors and Rorschach data suggest improvement to a *maintenance stage*[13] (Prochaska, DiClemente, & Norcross, 1992).

CASE 2: DAVE

Given above-average intelligence (Zachary, 1986), high levels of treatment motivation (*action stage*), and the absence of a sexual deviation, Dave's low PCL-R score (PCL-R = 15; see Table 3) is prognostically promising. Zero scores on glibness and grandiosity (Items 1 & 2), 1 point on failure to accept responsibility for own actions (Item 16), and low scores on lack of remorse (Item 6 = 1), shallow affect (Item 7 = 0), and callous lack of empathy (Item 8 = 1) rule out a narcissistic or psychopathic disorder and are consistent with his below-average Egocentricity Ratio (3r+(2)/R; as noted in Table 4). Dave's 3r+(2)/R, 4 morbid responses (MORs), and the absence of a reflection response suggest a damaged rather than grandiose sense of self.

Dave's T response, a prognostically positive sign, coupled with low scores on PCL-R Items 6, 7, and 8 indicate a desire and capacity for attachment. Like Steve and other nonpsychopathic ASPD patients (Afr < .50 = 49%; Gacono & Meloy, 1994), Dave is not *without* affect but *intolerant* of it (Afr = .38). The absence of points on Items 11 (*promiscuous sexual behavior*) and 17 (*short-term marital relationships*) also support bonding capacity. Dave has been exclusively involved with one sexual partner, who became his wife, for approximately a decade. The composite data suggest a cluster C, avoidant style concurrent to an ASPD diagnosis (additional data will also support a passive-aggressive personality; Mp>Ma+1, S = 3).

Factor 2 scores indicate behavioral problems originating in childhood (PCL-R Items 12 & 18). Early onset of antisocial behavior coupled with elevated Factor 1 scores are consistent with a psychopathy diagnosis (Smith, Gacono, & Kaufman, 1997), and fortunately this is not the case. Dave's impulse controls are deficient but not absent (PCL-R Items 3, 14, 15; D/adjD = 0/0). A source of strength, Item 9 (*parasitic lifestyle* = 0) indicates that Dave has held legal employment the majority of his adult life. Despite vacillation by CBG on scoring Item 10 (*poor behavioral controls*, anger problems) 1 or 2, any points for an incarcerated ASPD felon on this Item alerts the clinician to needed anger management skills.

Dave's low Lambda suggests difficulties identifying the most economical means for confronting a task and is consistent with him being easily overwhelmed by emotional laden stimuli. His Rorschach suggests moderate to severe problems with perceptual accuracy (Mediation, X+%, F+%), unusual thinking (Xu%), reality testing (X-%; M-), coping (CDI), affect modulation and tolerance (FC:CF+C; C = 2; Afr), hostility (S = 3), and depression (DEPI). A comprehensive life skills training program is recommended to (a) begin to address these deficits (Ross et al., 1988), (b) orient him to the treatment process, and (c) further assess his treatment amenability.

Dave's combination of hostility (S = 3), passivity (Mp>Ma+1), and damaged sense of self (MOR = 4) manifest in a diagnosable passive-aggressive disorder and identify another area for treatment intervention (i.e., assertiveness training). Although interested in others (M = 7, H = 3), past relationships, including his childhood, have been toxic and resulted in the lack of expectations for positive human interaction (COP = 0).

Dave's initial Rorschach is consistent with an avoidant, passive, inadequate individual who would "peddle his bicycle" in order to sell drugs. Unlike Steve who demonstrated high levels of self-focus and some "narcissism," Dave's inadequacy requires direct intervention, as a basic sense of being damaged underlies his avoidant, passive-aggressive style.

TABLE 3
DAVE'S PCL-R PROTOCOL

Item	Factor 1	Factor 2	Total Score
1. Glibness/superficial charm	0		0
2. Grandiose sense of self-worth	0		0
3. Need of stimulation/proneness to boredom		1	1
4. Pathological lying	1		1
5. Conning/manipulative	0		0
6. Lack of remorse of guilt	1		1
7. Shallow affect	0		0 (0-1)
8. Callous/lack of empathy	1		1
9. Parasitic lifestyle		0	0
10. Poor behavioral controls		1	1 (1-2)
11. Promiscuous sexual behavior			0
12. Early behavioral problems		2	2 (1-2)
13. Lack of realistic, long-term goals		1	1
14. Impulsivity		1	1
15. Irresponsibility		1	1
16. Failure to accept responsibility for own actions	1		1
17. Many short-term marital relationships			0
18. Juvenile delinquency		1	1
19. Revocation of conditional release		2	2
20. Criminal versatility			1
Total	4	10	15

Treatment progress. Successful treatment should result in improved perceptual accuracy and reality testing, better affect tolerance, less hostility, increased self-esteem, greater assertiveness, more interest in others, and better skills for assessing interpersonal relationships (judgment, self and other appraisal). Dave's Rorschach suggests treatment gains but also highlights areas for continued work.[14]

Still an unconventional thinker (Xu%), important gains are indicated in perceptual accuracy (X+%, F+%) and reality testing (X–%). Not perfect (M- = 1), Dave can now exercise "better judgment" in interpersonal relationships, one of several factors contributing to his avoidant/passive-aggressive style.

Growing confidence, both personally (handling emotions) and interpersonally, has contributed to increased self-esteem (3r+(2)/R, .36 to .50); however, his is still tarnished by a basic sense of damage (MOR = 3), residue from a neglectful and deprived childhood. Dave now associates positive attributes with interpersonal interactions (COP = 2), possibly a by-product of his therapeutic alliance and certainly an avenue through which his damaged self might, over time, be modified. Although test data and self-report confirm increased confidence in managing emotions, affect tolerance (FC:CF+C = 0:2; Afr = .41), depression (DEPI = 6),[15]

TABLE 4

TABLE 4
SELECT RORSCHACH VARIABLES FOR DAVE

	First	Second	Third
R	22	28	24
Lambda	.22	.56	.33
EA	12	8.5	10.0
EB	7:5	7:1.5	8:2
D/adjD	0/0	0/0	0/0
Ideation			
Ma:Mp	1:6	2:5	1:7
M–	1	1	1
M	7	6	8
WSum6	12	25	10
Mediation			
P	6	5	5
X+%	.41	.43	.46
F+%	.25	.50	.50
X–%	.14	.07	.04
Xu%	.45	.43	.50
S–%	.00	.00	.00
Affect			
FC:CF+C	0:4	1:2	0:2
PureC	2	0	0
Afr	.38	.47	.41
S	3	4	3
T	1	1	1
C'	3	1	1
Y	1	0	0
V	2	1	4
Processing			
Zd	+2.5	–1.5	–2.0
W:M	6:7	6:7	3:8
Self-Perception			
3r+(2)/R	.36	.43	.50
Fr+rF	0	0	0
FD	1	2	0
MOR	4	4	3
Interpersonal			
COP	0	2	2
AG	0	0	2
H	3	3	2
(H)	0	1	1
Hd:(Hd)	3:3	6:1	5:2
Constellations			
SCZI	1	2	1
DEPI	6	4	6
CDI	3	2	2
S-CON	5	5	5

and anger (S = 3) remain problematic. His passive-aggressiveness (Mp>Ma+1; S = 3) continues to be a treatment focus.

DISCUSSION

As previously indicated, both Steve and Dave were treatment successes. Although this case study format, absent any comparison patients, cannot be used to confirm *actual* treatment effects, Rorschach changes are consistent with *expected* treatment influences, and despite therapeutic impact, variables and ratios (see Tables 2 and 4) support the temporal stability of the test (Exner, 1993; Weiner & Exner, 1991).

Although Steve's PCL-R score (23) was greater than Dave's (15), both scores were relatively low, neither patient was psychopathic, and both were amenable to treatment. It's interesting that both were low Lambda introversives, who produced T = 1 protocols. This intriguing "finding" stimulates more questions than answers. Nonpsychopathic ASPDs exhibiting this Rorschach triad may be attractive treatment candidates due to their desire for interpersonal relatedness (T = 1), their vulnerability to emotional distress, and, perhaps, capacity to foresee the consequences of their behavior, all contributing to the increased likelihood of them requesting psychotherapy. Introversion might contribute to a form of psychological-mindedness (M & FD),[16] increasing the probability of treatment success. In contrast to high Lambda, often defensive, always coarthed forensic patients (Bannatyne, 1996; Bannatyne, Gacono, & Greene, 1999), low Lambda ASPD patients' openness, discomfort with self, and problem-solving style characterized by "difficulty identifying the most economical ways of handling task demand(s) . . . do not always use their resources effectively . . . preoccupations and/or apprehensions often interfere with concentration or logical reasoning, and thus they often fail to perceive easier or economical solutions, which leads to an overinvolvement with stimuli around them" (Exner, 1993, p. 409), make them apt candidates for a combined dynamic/life skills treatment approach. Any relationship between these variables and positive treatment response in ASPD patients, however, awaits future study.

Combined, the PCL-R and Rorschach form a useful method for treatment planning with ASPD patients. The Rorschach also aids in monitoring treatment progress. Limited institutional resources (time, staff, money) for correction's growing ASPD populations will continue to demand effective and comprehensive treatment planning to ensure their effective use. Financial losses and failed treatment can and do result from the shortsighted neglect of careful assessment and treatment matching (Gacono, 2000; Gacono et al., 1995). The challenge to correctional psychologists and message to administrators is straightforward, like the message of a popular oil filter commercial, "You can pay me now [careful psychological assessment] or pay me later [failed programming, wasted resources]."

ACKNOWLEDGMENTS

The author extends appreciation to Dr. John Rubel for comments and suggestions and to Dr. Lynne Bannatyne for rescoring Rorschachs. The views expressed in this article are solely the author's.

NOTES

1. ASPD base rates typically exceed 50% in correctional settings, whereas less than 25% of the population would be psychopathic (Hare, 1996).

2. Items promiscuous sexual behavior (11), many short-term marital relationships (17), and criminal versatility (20) are not included in the two-factor structure, yet when elevated, provide additional evidence of attachment difficulties.

3. Subjects receive a score of 0, 1, or 2 on each item depending on whether the trait is absent (0), some elements apply (1), or a reasonably good match occurs (2). Mean PCL-R scores (Hare, 1991) are somewhat higher in prison ($M = 23.37$, $SD = 7.96$) than forensic psychiatric populations ($M = 20.56$, $SD = 7.79$).

4. Because an ASPD diagnosis relies primarily on behavioral criteria, ASPD subjects frequently meet criteria for one of the other personality disorders or display traits of an additional disorder (i.e., histrionic, narcissistic, borderline, avoidant, passive-aggressive, etc.).

5. The records of two ASPD patients who staff believed had "benefitted" from a state prison treatment program are offered to highlight the use of PCL-R and Rorschach data in treatment planning. Historical information has been withheld or altered to ensure the anonymity of Steve and Dave.

6. Both cases were offered blind to PCL-R or Rorschach scores. Self-report and staff observation indicated that Steve and Dave displayed less impulsiveness, better affect tolerance, reduced anger, a complete elimination of violent acts, increased self-esteem, and assertiveness, and were less sensitive to criticism.

7. Reliability was determined by comparing *every* response from CBG's final sequence of scores with LAB's corresponding independently coded sequence response scores. To be counted as a "hit" (agreement), determinants had to have achieved the same level of form domination (FC, CF, C) while special scores needed the same level (1 or 2); any deviation was counted as a "miss" (nonagreement). Lowered percentage agreement for determinants and special scores reflect this stringent procedure. When agreement was adjusted for special scores without considering level, agreement rose to the acceptable 80% cutoff.

8. Texture (T) responses indicate desire for affectional relatedness; a prognostically positive but unusual finding in ASPDs (whereas 79% of adult ASPD males are T-less [Gacono & Meloy, 1994], only 11% of nonpatient adults are [Exner et al., 1995]) and a likely contributor to Steve's request for one-to-one counseling.

9. Steve was in an *action* stage of treatment (Prochaska, DiClemente, & Norcross, 1992). During this stage, "individuals modify their behavior, experiences, or environment in order to overcome their problems" (p. 1104).

10. Steve is affectively avoidant (Afr = .30) but not without affect.

11. Reduced R (R = 13) results in an ambitent style on Protocol 1. Steve's predominant introversive style surfaces on the second 16 response protocol.

12. The combination of cognitive-behavioral techniques within a psychodynamic framework (Gacono & Meloy, 1988) would be an example of prescribed or technical eclecticism (Lazarus, 1989; Stricker, 1994). Cognitive restructuring and life skills can increase the ASPD patient's ability to tolerate deeper therapeutic work.

13. The *maintenance stage* is designated by "the stage in which people work to prevent relapse and consolidate the gains attained during *action*" (Prochaska, DiClemente, & Norcross, 1992, p. 1104).
14. Only the first and third Rorschach will be discussed. The second "transitional" Rorschach is presented for the reader's review. Dave remains in the latter phases of the *action stage*.
15. Like many other ASPD patients who manifest borderline personality organization and elevate on DEPI, Dave described his "depression" as boredom or emptiness.
16. As noted in Tables 2 and 4, both patients produced FDs and Vs.

REFERENCES

American Psychiatric Association. (1987). *Diagnostic and statistical manual of mental disorders* (3rd ed.). Washington, DC: Author.
American Psychiatric Association. (1994). *Diagnostic and statistical manual of mental disorders* (4th ed.). Washington, DC: Author.
Atkinson, L. (1986). The comparative validities of the Rorschach and the MMPI: A meta-analysis. *Canadian Psychology, 27*, 238-247.
Bannatyne, L. (1996). *The effects of defensiveness on select MMPI2 and Rorschach variables for schizophrenic forensic outpatients.* Ph.D. dissertation presented to the faculty of Pacific Graduate School of Psychology, Palo Alto, CA.
Bannatyne, L., Gacono, C., & Greene, R. (1999). Differential patterns of responding among three groups of chronic psychotic forensic outpatients. *Journal of Clinical Psychology.*
Becker, J., & Quinsey, V. (1993). Assessing suspected child molesters. *Child abuse and Neglect, 17*, 169-174.
Exner, J. (1993). *The Rorschach a comprehensive system volume 1: Basic foundations* (3rd ed.). New York: John Wiley.
Exner, J., Colligan, S., Hillman, L, Ritzler, B., Sciara, A., & Viglione, D. (1995). *A Rorschach workbook for the comprehensive system 4th edition.* Asheville, NC: Rorschach Workshops.
Gacono, C. (1985). Mental health work in a county jail: A heuristic model. *Journal of Offender Counseling, 5*(1), 16-22.
Gacono, C. (1990). An empirical study of object relations and defensive operations in antisocial personality. *Journal of Personality Assessment, 54*, 589-600.
Gacono, C. (2000). Suggestions for the institutional implementation and use of the Psychopathy Checklists in forensic and clinical practice. In C. B. Gacono (Ed.), *The clinical and forensic assessment of psychopathy: A practitioner's guide.* Mahwah, NJ: Lawrence Erlbaum Associates.
Gacono, C., & Hutton, H. (1994). Suggestions for the clinical and forensic use of the Hare Psychopathy Checklist-Revised (PCL-R). *International Journal of Law and Psychiatry, 17*(3), 303-317.
Gacono, C., & Meloy, R. (1988). The relationship between cognitive style and defensive process in the psychopath. *Criminal Justice and Behavior, 15*(4), 472–483.
Gacono, C., & Meloy, R. (1994). *The Rorschach assessment of aggressive and psychopathic personalities.* Hillsdale, NJ: Lawrence Erlbaum Associates.
Gacono, C., & Meloy, R. (1996). Attachment deficits in antisocial and psychopathic personalities. In M. Hilsenroth (Chair), *Use of the Rorschach in the diagnosis of DSM-IV Cluster B Personality Disorders.* 1996 International Rorschach Congress, Boston, MA.
Gacono, C., Meloy, R., Sheppard, K., Speth, E., & Roske, A. (1995). A clinical investigation of malingering and psychopathy in hospitalized insanity acquittees. *Bulletin of the American Academy of Psychiatry and Law, 23*, 387-397.
Gorski, T., & Miller, M. (1982). *Counseling for relapse prevention.* Independence, MO: Herald House-Independence Press.
Hare, R. (1991). *The Hare Psychopathy Checklist-Revised.* Toronto, Canada: Multi-Health Systems.
Hare, R. (1996). Psychopathy: A clinical construct whose time has come. *Criminal Justice and Behavior, 23*(1), 25-54.

Hare, R., Hart, S., & Harpur, T. (1991). Psychopathy and the DSM-IV criteria for antisocial personality disorder. *Journal of Abnormal Psychology, 100*(3), 391-398.

Hare, R., & McPherson, L. (1984). Violent and aggressive behavior in criminal psychopaths. *International Journal of Law and Psychiatry, 7,* 35-50.

Hare, R., McPherson, L., & Forth, A. (1988). Male psychopaths and their criminal careers. *Journal of Consulting and Clinical Psychology, 56,* 710-714.

Harpur, T., Hare, R., & Hakstian, R. (1989). A two-factor conceptualization of psychopathy: Construct validity and implications for assessment. *Psychological Assessment, 1,* 6-17.

Harris, G., Rice, M., & Cormier, C. (1991). Psychopathy and violent recidivism. *Law and Human Behavior, 15,* 625-637.

Hart, S., & Hare, R. (1989). Discriminant validity of the Psychopathy Checklist in a forensic psychiatric population. *Psychological Assessment: A Journal of Consulting and Clinical Psychology, 1,* 211-218.

Hart, S., Kropp, P., & Hare, R. (1988). Performance of male psychopaths following conditional release from prison. *Journal of Consulting and Clinical Psychology, 56,* 227-232.

Hilsenroth, M., Handler, L., Toman, K., & Padawer, J. (1995). Rorschach and MMPI-2 indices of early psychotherapy termination. *Journal of Consulting and Clinical Psychology, 63*(6), 956-965.

Kernberg, O. (1984). *Severe personality disorders: Psychotherapeutic strategies.* London: Yale University Press.

Lazarus, A. (1989). *The practice of multimodal therapy.* Baltimore, MD: Johns Hopkins University Press.

Marlatt, G., & Gordon, J. (1985). *Relapse prevention: A self-control strategy for the maintenance of behavioral change.* New York: Guilford.

Maruish, M. (1994). *The use of psychological testing for treatment planning and outcome assessment.* Hillsdale, NJ: Lawrence Erlbaum.

Maultsby, M. (1979). *Freedom from alcohol and tranquilizers.* Lexington, KY: Rational Self-Help Books.

Meloy, R. (1988). *The psychopathic mind: Origins, dynamics, and treatment.* Northvale, NJ: Aronson.

Meloy, R., & Gacono, C. (1995). Assessing the psychopathic personality. In J. Butcher (Ed.), *Clinical personality assessment: Practical approaches* (pp. 410-422). New York: Oxford University Press.

Mortimer, R., & Smith, W. (1983). The use of the psychological test report in setting the focus of psychotherapy. *Journal of Personality Assessment, 47*(2), 134-138.

Ogloff, J., Wong, S., & Greenwood, A. (1990). Treating criminal psychopaths in a therapeutic community program. *Behavioral Sciences and the Law, 8,* 81-90.

Parker, K., Hanson, R., & Hunsley, J. (1988). MMPI, Rorschach, and WAIS: A meta-analytic comparison of reliability, stability, and validity. *Psychological Bulletin, 103,* 367-373.

Prochaska, J., DiClemente, C., & Norcross, J. (1992). In search of how people change: Application to addictive behaviors. *American Psychologist, 47*(9), 1102-1114.

Rice, M., Harris, G., & Quinsey, V. (1990). A follow-up of rapists assessed in a maximum security psychiatric facility. *Journal of Interpersonal Violence, 4,* 435-448.

Ross, R., Fabiano, E., & Ewles, C. (1988). Reasoning and Rehabilitation. *International Journal of Offender Therapy and Comparative Criminology, 32,* 29-35.

Serin, R. (1991). Psychopathy and violence in criminals. *Journal of Interpersonal Violence, 6,* 423-431.

Serin, R. (1992). The clinical application of the Psychopathy Checklist Revised (PCL-R) in a prison population. *Journal of Clinical Psychology, 48*(5), 637-642.

Serin, R., Peters, R., & Barbaree, H. (1990). Predictors of psychopathy and release outcome in a criminal population. *Psychological Assessment: A Journal of Consulting and Clinical Psychology, 2,* 419-422.

Smith, A., Gacono, C., & Kaufman, L. (1997). A Rorschach comparison of psychopathic and nonpsychopathic conduct-disordered adolescents. *Journal of Clinical Psychology, 53*(4), 289-300.

Stricker, G. (1994). Reflections on psychotherapy integration. *Clinical Psychology: Science and Practice, 1*(1), 3-12.

Strupp, H., & Binder, J. (1984). *Psychotherapy in a new key: A guide to time-limited dynamic psychotherapy.* New York: Basic Books.

Walters, G. (1990). *The criminal lifestyle: Patterns of serious criminal conduct.* Newbury Park, CA: Sage.

Weiner, I. (1994). Rorschach assessment. In M. Maruish (Ed.), *The use of psychological testing for treatment planning and outcome assessment.* Hillsdale, NJ: Lawrence Erlbaum.

Weiner, I. (1996). Some observations on the validity of the Rorschach Inkblot Method. *Psychological Assessment, 8*(2), 206-213.

Weiner, I., & Exner, J. (1991). Rorschach changes in long-term and short-term psychotherapy. *Journal of Personality Assessment, 56,* 453-465.

Williamson, S., Hare, R., & Wong, S. (1987). Violence: Criminal psychopaths and their victims. *Canadian Journal of Behavioral Science, 19,* 454-462.

Wong, S. (1988). Is Hare's Psychopathy Checklist reliable without the interview? *Psychological Reports, 62,* 931-934.

Yochelson, S., & Samenow, S. (1977). *The criminal personality: Volume 1. A profile for change.* New York: Aronson.

Zachary, R. (1986). *Shipley Institute of Living Scale: Revised manual.* Los Angles: Western Psychological Service.

Appendix D: Selected Psychopathy Bibliography by Subject

Barbara J. Sparrow
University of Texas, Austin

Carl B. Gacono
Private Practice, Austin, Texas

PSYCHOPATHY

Andersen, H. S., Sestoft, D., Lillebaek, T., & Gabrielsen, G. (1996). Prevalence of ICD-10 psychiatric morbidity in random samples of prisoners on remand. *International Journal of Law and Psychiatry, 19*, 61–74.

Belmore, M. F., & Quinsey, V. L. (1994). Correlates of psychopathy in a noninstitutional sample. *Journal of Interpersonal Violence, 9*, 339–349.

Blackburn, R. (1996). Psychopathy and personality disorder: Implications of interpersonal theory. In D. J. Cooke, A. E. Forth, J. P. Newman, & R. D. Hare (Eds.), *Issues in criminological and legal psychology: No. 24. International perspectives on psychopathy* (pp. 18–23). Leicester, UK: British Psychological Society.

Blackburn, R. (1998). Psychopathy and personality disorder: Implications of interpersonal theory. In D. J. Cooke, A. E. Forth, & R. D. Hare (Eds.), *Psychopathy: Theory, research, and implications for society* (pp. 269–301). Dordrecht, The Netherlands: Kluwer.

Blair, J., Sellars, C., Strickland, I., Clark, F., Williams, A., Smith, M., & Jones, L. (1996). Theory of mind in the psychopath. *Journal of Forensic Psychiatry, 7*, 15–25.

Blair, R. J. R. (1995). A cognitive developmental approach to morality: Investigating the psychopath. *Cognition, 57*, 1–29.

Blair, R. J. R., Jones, L., Clark, F., & Smith, M. (1995). Is the psychopath morally insane? *Personality and Individual Differences, 19*, 741–752.

Brown, S. L., Forth, A. E., Hart, S. D., & Hare, R. D. (1992). The assessment of psychopathy in a noncriminal population [Abstract]. *Canadian Psychology, 33*(2a), 405.

Chandler, M., & Moran, T. (1990). Psychopathy and moral development: A comparative study of delinquent and nondelinquent youth. *Development and Psychopathology, 2*, 227–246.

Cleckley, H. (1976). *The mask of sanity* (5th ed.). St. Louis, MO: Mosby.

Coid, J. W. (1992). DSM–III diagnosis in criminal psychopaths: A way forward. *Criminal Behavior and Mental Health, 2*, 78–94.

Cooke, D. J., & Michie, C. (1997). An Item Response Theory analysis of the Hare Psychopathy Checklist. *Psychological Assessment, 9*, 3–13.

Cooney, N. L., Kadden, R. M., & Litt, M. D. (1990). A comparison of methods for assessing sociopathy in male and female alcoholics. *Journal of Studies on Alcohol, 51*, 42–48.

Davies, W., & Feldman, P. (1981). The diagnosis of psychopathy by forensic specialists. *British Journal of Psychiatry, 138*, 329–331.

Devita, E., Forth, A. E., & Hare, R. D. (1990). Family background of male criminal psychopaths [Abstract]. *Canadian Psychology, 31*(2a), 346.

Dickie, I., Malcolm, P. B., & Forth, A. E. (1997). Correlates of the Psychopathy Checklist: Screening Version in incarcerated offenders [Abstract]. *Canadian Psychology, 38*(2a), 14.

Foreman, M. (1988). *Psychopathy and interpersonal behavior.* Unpublished doctoral dissertation, University of British Columbia, Vancouver, British Columbia.

Forth, A. E., Brown, S. L., Hart, S. D., & Hare, R. D. (1996). The assessment of psychopathy in male and female noncriminals: Reliability and validity. *Personality and Individual Differences, 20*, 531–543.

Forth, A. E., Kisslinger, T., Brown, S., & Harris, A. (1993). Precursors to psychopathic traits in a sample of male and female university students [Abstract]. *Canadian Psychology, 34*(2a), 380.

Fulero, S. M. (1995). Review of the Hare Psychopathy Checklist–Revised. In J. C. Conoley & J. C. Impara (Eds.), *Twelfth mental measurements yearbook* (pp. 453–454). Lincoln, NE: Buros Institute.

Gacono, C. B., & Hutton, H. E. (1994). Suggestions for clinical and forensic use of the Hare Psychopathy Checklist–Revised (PCL–R). *International Journal of Law and Psychiatry, 17*, 303–317.

Gacono, C. B., & Meloy, J. R. (1988). The relationship between cognitive style and defensive process in the psychopath. *Criminal Justice and Behavior, 15*(4), 472–83.

Gacono, C. B., & Meloy, J. R. (1994). *Rorschach assessment of aggressive and psychopathic personalities.* Hillsdale, NJ: Lawrence Erlbaum Associates.

Gonçalves, R. A. (1996). Psychopathy and adaptation to prison. In D. J. Cooke, A. E. Forth, J. P. Newman, & R. D. Hare (Eds.), *Issues in criminological and legal psychology: No. 24. International perspectives on psychopathy* (p. 60). Leicester, UK: British Psychological Society.

Grann, M., Tengström, A., Långström, N., & Stålenheim, E. G. (1998). Reliability of file-based retrospective ratings of psychopathy with the PCL-R. *Journal of Personality Assessment, 70,* 416–426.

Gray, K. C., & Hutchinson, H. C. (1964). The psychopathic personality: A survey of Canadian psychiatrists' opinions. *Canadian Psychiatric Association Journal, 9,* 452–461.

Green, C. J. (1988). The Psychopathy Checklist. *Journal of Personality Disorders, 2,* 185–187.

Haapasalo, J. (1994). Types of offense among the Cleckley psychopaths. *International Journal of Offender Therapy and Comparative Criminology, 38,* 59–67.

Haapasalo, J., & Pulkkinen, L. (1992). The Psychopathy Checklist and nonviolent offender groups. *Criminal Behavior and Mental Health, 2,* 315–328.

Hare, R. D. (1980). A research scale for the assessment of psychopathy in criminal populations. *Personality and Individual Differences, 1,* 111–119.

Hare, R. D. (1982). Psychopathy and the personality dimensions of Psychoticism, Extraversion, and Neuroticism. *Personality and Individual Differences, 3,* 35–42.

Hare, R. D. (1983). Diagnosis of antisocial personality disorder in two prison populations. *American Journal of Psychiatry, 140,* 887–890.

Hare, R. D. (1985). A comparison of procedures for the assessment of psychopathy. *Journal of Consulting and Clinical Psychology, 53,* 7–16.

Hare, R. D. (1991). *The Hare Psychopathy Checklist–Revised.* Toronto, Ontario: Multi–Health Systems.

Hare, R. D. (1993). *Without conscience: The disturbing world of the psychopaths among us.* New York: Simon & Schuster.

Hare, R. D. (1995). Psychopaths and their victims. *Harvard Mental Health Letter, 12,* 4–5.

Hare, R. D. (1996a). Psychopathy and antisocial personality disorder: A case of diagnostic confusion. *Psychiatric Times, 13,* 39–40.

Hare, R. D. (1996b). Psychopathy: A clinical construct whose time has come. *Criminal Justice and Behavior, 23,* 25–54.

Hare, R. D. (1997). The NATO Advanced Study Institute on psychopathy, Alvor, Portugal, 1995. *Journal of Personality Disorders, 11,* 301–303.

Hare, R. D. (1998a). The Hare PCL–R: Some issues concerning its use and misuse. *Legal and Criminological Psychology, 3,* 101–122.

Hare, R. D. (1998b). The NATO Advanced Study Institute. In D. J. Cooke, A. E. Forth, & R. D. Hare (Eds.), *Psychopathy: Theory, research, and implications for society* (pp. 1–11). Dordrecht, The Netherlands: Kluwer.

Hare, R. D., Forth, A. E., & Hart, S. D. (1989). The psychopath as prototype for pathological lying and deception. In J. C. Yuille (Ed.), *Credibility assessment* (pp. 24–49). Dordrecht, The Netherlands: Kluwer.

Hare, R. D., Forth, A. E., & Strachan, K. (1992). Psychopathy and crime across the lifespan. In R. DeV. Peters, R. J. McMahon, & V. L. Quinsey (Eds.), *Aggression and violence throughout the life span* (pp. 285–300). Newbury Park, CA: Sage.

Hare, R. D., Harpur, T. J., Hakstian, A. R., Forth, A. E., Hart, S. D., & Newman, J. P. (1990). The Revised Psychopathy Checklist: Reliability and factor structure. *Psychological Assessment: A Journal of Consulting and Clinical Psychology, 2,* 338–341.

Hare, R. D., & Hart, S. D. (1992). Psychopathy, mental disorder, and crime. In S. Hodgins (Ed.), *Mental disorder and crime* (pp. 104–115). Newbury Park, CA: Sage.

Hare, R. D., & Hart, S. D. (1995). Commentary on antisocial personality disorder: The DSM–IV field trial. In W. J. Livesley (Ed.), *The DSM–IV personality disorders* (pp. 127–134). New York: Guilford.

Hare, R. D., Hart, S. D., Forth, A. E., Harpur, T. J., & Williamson, S. E. (1993, January/February). Psychopathic personality characteristics: Development of a criteria set for use in the DSM–IV antisocial personality disorder field trial. *American Psychiatric Association DSM–IV Update,* pp. 6–7.

Hare, R. D., Hart, S. D., & Harpur, T. J. (1991). Psychopathy and the DSM–IV criteria for antisocial personality disorder. *Journal of Abnormal Psychology, 100,* 391–398.

Hare, R. D., McPherson, L. E., & Forth, A. E. (1988). Male psychopaths and their criminal careers. *Journal of Consulting and Clinical Psychology, 56,* 710–714.

Hare, R. D., Strachan, C., & Forth, A. E. (1993). Psychopathy and crime: An overview. In C. R. Hollin & K. Howells (Eds.), *Clinical approaches to the mentally disordered offender* (pp. 165–178). Chichester, England: Wiley.

Harpur, T. J., Hakstian, R., & Hare, R. D. (1988). Factor structure of the Psychopathy Checklist. *Journal of Consulting and Clinical Psychology, 56,* 741–747.

Harpur, T. J., & Hare, R. D. (1994). The assessment of psychopathy as a function of age. *Journal of Abnormal Psychology, 103,* 604–609.

Harpur, T. J., Hare, R. D., & Hakstian, R. (1989). A two–factor conceptualization of psychopathy: Construct validity and implications for assessment. *Psychological Assessment: A Journal of Consulting and Clinical Psychology, 1,* 6–17.

Harpur, T. J., Hare, R. D., Zimmerman, M., & Corryell, W. (1990, August). *Dimensions underlying DSM–III personality disorders: Cluster 2.* Paper presented at the annual meeting of the American Psychological Association, Boston, MA.

Harpur, T. J., Hart, S. D., & Hare, R. D. (1993). Personality of the psychopath. In P. T. Costa & T. A. Widiger (Eds.), *Personality disorders and the five-factor model of personality* (pp. 149–173). Washington, DC: American Psychological Association.

Harris, G. T., Rice, M. E., & Quinsey, V. L. (1994). Psychopathy as a taxon: Evidence that psychopaths are a discrete class. *Journal of Consulting and Clinical Psychology, 62,* 387–397.

Harry, B. (1992a). Criminals' explanations for their criminal behavior: Part I. The contribution of criminologic variables. *Journal of Forensic Sciences, 37,* 1327–1333.

Harry, B. (1992b). Criminals' explanations for their criminal behavior: Part II. A possible role for psychopathy. *Journal of Forensic Sciences, 37,* 1334–1340.

Hart, S. D. (1994). Development and validation of a new scale for the assessment of psychopathy. *Dissertation Abstracts International: Section B: The Sciences and Engineering, 54*(8-B), 4438.

Hart, S. D., Cox, D. N., & Hare, R. D. (1995). *Manual for the Psychopathy Checklist: Screening Version (PCL:SV).* Toronto: Multi–Health Systems.

Hart, S. D., & Dempster, R. J. (1997). Impulsivity and psychopathy. In C. D. Webster & M. A. Jackson (Eds.), *Impulsivity in principle and practice* (pp. 212–232). New York: Guilford.

Hart, S. D., Forth, A. E., & Hare, R. D. (1991). The MCMI–II as a measure of psychopathy. *Journal of Personality Disorders, 5,* 318–327.

Hart, S. D., & Hare, R. D. (1994). Psychopathy and the Big 5: Correlations between observers' ratings of normal and pathological personality. *Journal of Personality Disorders, 8,* 32–40.

Hart, S. D., & Hare, R. D. (1996). Psychopathy and antisocial personality disorder. *Current Opinion in Psychiatry, 9,* 129–132.

Hart, S. D., & Hare, R. D. (1997). Psychopathy: Assessment and association with criminal conduct. In D. M. Stoff, J. Brieling, & J. Maser (Eds.), *Handbook of antisocial behavior* (pp. 22–35). New York: Wiley.

Hart, S. D., & Hare, R. D. (1997). The association between psychopathy and narcissism: Theoretical views and empirical evidence. In E. Ronningstam (Ed.), *Disorders of narcissism – Theoretical, empirical, and clinical implications* (pp. 415–436). Washington, DC: American Psychiatric Press.

Hart, S. D., Hare, R. D., & Harpur, T. J. (1992). The Psychopathy Checklist: Overview for researchers and clinicians. In J. Rosen & P. McReynolds (Eds.), *Advances in psychological assessment* (Vol. 7, pp. 103–130). New York: Plenum.

Helfgott, J. B. (1997). The relationship between unconscious defensive process and conscious cognitive style in psychopaths. *Criminal Justice and Behavior, 24,* 278–293.

Hemphill, J. F., Hayes, P. J., & Hare, R. D. (1994). Gough's Socialization scale and psychopathy [Abstract]. *Canadian Psychology, 35*(2a), 48.

Hemphill, J. F., Hemphill, K. J., & Hare, R. D. (1992). Attributions for criminal events by criminal psychopaths and correctional staff [Abstract]. *Canadian Psychology, 33*(2a), 406.

Hobson, J., & Shine, J. (1998). Measurement of psychopathy in a UK prison population referred for long-term psychotherapy. *British Journal of Criminology, 38,* 504–515.

Holmes, C. A. (1991). Psychopathic disorder: A category mistake? *Journal of Medical Ethics, 17,* 77–85.

Hookham, R. E. (1994). The Cognitive Style Questionnaire: A cross-validation study, employing the MCMI-II and the Hare Psychopathy Checklist, revised with a population of incarcerated males. *Dissertation Abstracts International, 55*(3-B), 1185.

af Klinteberg, B. (1996). The psychopathic personality in a longitudinal perspective. *European Child & Adolescent Psychiatry, 5,* 57–63.

af Klinteberg, B., Humble, K., & Schalling, D. (1992). Personality and psychopathy of males with a history of early criminal behavior. *European Journal of Personality, 6,* 245–266.

Kosson, D. S., Steuerwald, B. L., Forth, A. E., & Kirkhart, K. J. (1997). A new method for assessing the interpersonal behavior of psychopathic individuals: Preliminary validation studies. *Psychological Assessment, 9,* 89–101.

Levenson, M. R. (1992). Rethinking psychopathy. *Theory and Psychology, 2,* 51–71.

Levenson, M. R. (1995). Physio-sociology or psychology of conscience? Reply to Smith. *Theory and Psychology, 5,* 139–144.

Levenson, M. R. (1996). Psychopathy and conscience. In D. J. Cooke, A. E. Forth, J. P. Newman, & R. D. Hare (Eds.), *Issues in criminological and legal psychology: No. 24. International perspectives on psychopathy* (pp. 94–99). Leicester, UK: British Psychological Society.

Levenson, M. R., Kiehl, K. A., & Fitzpatrick, C. M. (1995). Assessing psychopathic attributes in a noninstitutionalized population. *Journal of Personality and Social Psychology, 68,* 151–158.

Lilienfeld, S. O. (1994). Conceptual problems in the assessment of psychopathy. *Clinical Psychology Review, 14,* 17–38.

Lilienfeld, S. O. (1996). The MMPI-2 Antisocial Practices content scale: Construct validity and comparison with the Psychopathic Deviate scale. *Psychological Assessment, 8,* 281–293.

Lilienfeld, S. O. (1998). Methodological advances and developments in the assessment of psychopathy. *Behaviour Research and Therapy, 36,* 99–125.

Lilienfeld, S. O., & Andrews, B. P. (1996). Development and preliminary validation of a self-report measure of psychopathic personality traits in noncriminal populations. *Journal of Personality Assessment, 66,* 488–524.

Livesley, W. J. (1998). The phenotypic and genotypic structure of psychopathic traits. In D. J. Cooke, A. E. Forth, & R. D. Hare (Eds.), *Psychopathy: Theory, research, and implications for society* (pp. 69–79). Dordrecht, The Netherlands: Kluwer.

Livesley, W. J., Jackson, D. N., & Schroeder, M. (1989). A study of the factorial structure of personality pathology. *Journal of Personality Disorders, 3,* 292–306.

Livesley, W. J., Jackson, D. N., & Schroeder, M. (1992). Factorial structure of traits delineating personality disorders in clinical and general population samples. *Journal of Abnormal Psychology, 101,* 432–440.

Loza, W., & Simourd, D. (1994). Psychometric evaluation of the Level of Supervision Inventory among male Canadian federal offenders. *Criminal Justice and Behavior, 21,* 468–480.

Mackay, I. (1991). "Psychopathic disorder: A category mistake?" A legal response to Colin Holmes. *Journal of Medical Ethics, 17,* 86–88.

Marshall, L., & Cooke, D. J. (1996). The role of childhood experiences in the aetiology of psychopathy. In D. J. Cooke, A. E. Forth, J. P. Newman, & R. D. Hare (Eds.), *Issues in criminological and legal psychology: No. 24. International perspectives on psychopathy* (pp. 107–108). Leicester, UK: British Psychological Society.

McCord, W., & McCord, J. (1964). *The psychopath: An essay on the criminal mind.* Princeton, NJ: Van Nostrand.

Meloy, J. R. (1988). *The psychopathic mind: Origins, dynamics, and treatments.* Northvale, NJ: Jason Aronson.

Meloy, J. R., & Gacono, C. B. (1995). Assessing the psychopathic personality. In J. Butcher (Ed.), *Foundations of clinical personality assessment* (pp. 410–422). Oxford, England: Oxford University Press.

Meloy, J. R., & Gacono, C. B. (1998). The internal world of the psychopath: A Rorschach investigation. In T. Millon, E. Simonsen, & M. Birket–Smith (Eds.), *Psychopathy: Antisocial, criminal, and violent behaviors* (pp. 95–109). New York: Guilford.

Millon, T., & Simonsen, E., Birket-Smith, M., & Davis, R. D. (Eds.). (1998). *Psychopathy: Antisocial, criminal, and violent behavior.* New York: Guilford.

Morey, L. C. (1988). The categorical representation of personality disorder: A cluster analysis of DSM–III–R personality features. *Journal of Abnormal Psychology, 97,* 314–321.

O'Kane, A., & Fawcett, D. (1996). Psychopathy and moral reasoning: Comparison of two classifications. *EDRA: Environmental Design Research Association, 20,* 505–514. (Unconfirmed)

O'Kane, A., Fawcett, D., & Blackburn, R. (1996). Psychopathy and moral reasoning: A comparison of two classifications. *Personality and Individual Differences, 20,* 505–514.

Pescitelli, D., Dawda, D., & Hart, S. D. (1998). Reliability and validity of the Screening Version of the Psychopathy Checklist (PCL:SV) in university students [Abstract]. *Canadian Psychology, 39*(2a), 121–122.

Porter, S. (1996). Without conscience or without active conscience? The etiology of psychopathy revisited. *Aggression and Violent Behavior, 1,* 179–189.

Presse, L., Jordan, S., & Christopher, M. (1992). Moral reasoning and criminal psychopathy [Abstract]. *Canadian Psychology, 33*(2a), 406.

Prins, H. (1995). What price the concept of psychopathic disorder? *Medicine, Science, and Law, 35,* 307–315.

Raine, A. (1986). Psychopathy, schizoid personality, and borderline/schizotypal personality disorders. *Personality and Individual Differences, 7,* 493–501.

Raine, A. (1992). Schizotypal and borderline features in psychopathic criminals. *Personality and Individual Differences, 13*(6), 717–721.

Reed, J. (1996). Psychopathy: A clinical and legal dilemma. *British Journal of Psychiatry, 168,* 4–9.

Reise, S. P., & Oliver, C. J. (1994). Development of a California Q-set indicator of primary psychopathy. *Journal of Personality Assessment, 62,* 130–144.

Reise, S. P., & Wink, P. (1995). Psycholegal implications of the Psychopathy Q-Sort. *Journal of Personality Assessment, 65,* 300–312.

Rettinger, L. J., & Andrews, D. (1991). Assessment of the construct validity of the Psychopathy Checklist [Abstract]. *Canadian Psychology, 32*(2a), 205.

Rettinger, L. J., & Andrews, D. (1992). Personality and attitudes correlates of the Psychopathy Checklist [Abstract]. *Canadian Psychology, 33*(2a), 406.

Richards, H. J., & McCamant, K. (1996). Narcissism and psychopathy: Concurrent validity of the PCL–R, the Rorschach, and the MCMI. In D. J. Cooke, A. E. Forth, J. P. Newman, & R. D. Hare (Eds.), *Issues in criminological and legal psychology: No. 24. International perspectives on psychopathy* (pp. 131–135). Leicester, UK: British Psychological Society.

Rime, B., Bouvy, H., & Rouillon, F. (1978). Psychopathy and nonverbal behavior in an interpersonal situation. *Journal of Abnormal Psychology, 87*, 636–643.

Robins, L. N. (1978). Etiological implications in studies of childhood histories relating to antisocial personality. In R. D. Hare & D. Schalling (Eds.), *Psychopathic behavior: Approaches to research* (pp. 255–271). Chichester, England: Wiley.

Rogers, R. (1995). *Diagnostic and structured interviewing: A handbook for psychologists.* Odessa, FL: Psychological Assessment Resources.

Rogers, R., & Bagby, R. (1995). Dimensions of psychopathy: A factor analytic study of the MMPI Antisocial Personality Disorder scale. *International Journal of Offender Therapy and Comparative Criminology, 38*, 297–308.

Rogers, R., & Dion, K. (1991). Rethinking the DSM–III–R diagnosis of antisocial personality disorder. *Bulletin of the American Academy of Psychiatry and Law, 19*, 21–31.

Rogers, R., Dion, K. L., & Lynett, E. (1992). Diagnostic validity of antisocial personality disorder: A prototypical analysis. *Law and Human Behavior, 16*, 677–689.

Rogers, R., Duncan, J. C., Lynett, E., & Sewell, K. W. (1994). Prototypical analysis of antisocial personality disorder: DSM–IV and beyond. *Law and Human Behavior, 18*, 471–484.

Ruegg, R. G., Haynes, C., & Frances, A. (1997). Assessment and management of antisocial personality disorder. In M. Rosenbluth & I. D. Yalom (Eds.), *Treating difficult personality disorders* (pp. 123–172). San Francisco: Jossey-Bass.

Salekin, R., Rogers, R., & Sewell, K. (1996). A review and meta-analysis of the Psychopathy Checklist and Psychopathy Checklist–Revised: Predictive validity of dangerousness. *Clinical Psychology: Science and Practice, 3*, 203–215.

Schroeder, M., Schroeder, K., & Hare, R. D. (1983). Generalizability of a checklist for assessment of psychopathy. *Journal of Consulting and Clinical Psychology, 51*, 511–516.

Serin, R. C. (1992). The clinical application of the Psychopathy Checklist–Revised (PCL–R) in a prison population. *Journal of Clinical Psychology, 48*, 637–642.

Serin, R. C. (1993). Diagnosis of psychopathy with and without an interview. *Journal of Clinical Psychology, 49*, 367–372.

Simcox, A. M. (1992). A descriptive study of Iowa prisoners classified by the Psychopathy Checklist. *Dissertation Abstracts International, 53*(1-B), 574.

Simourd, D., Bonta, J., Andrews, D., & Hoge, R. D. (1990). Criminal behavior and psychopaths: A meta-analysis [Abstract]. *Canadian Psychology, 31*(2a), 347.

Simourd, D., Hoge, R. D., Loza, A., Rowe, R., & Simourd, L. (1998). A comprehensive assessment procedure for use with adult offenders [Abstract]. *Canadian Psychology, 39*(2a), 26.

Smith, R. J. (1995). Psychopathy one more time: Comment. *Theory and Psychology, 5*, 131–137.

Stevens, G. F. (1993). Applying the diagnosis of antisocial personality to imprisoned offenders: Looking for hay in a hay-stack. *Journal of Offender Rehabilitation, 19*, 1–26.

Stevens, G. F. (1994). Prison clinicians' perceptions of antisocial personality disorder as a formal diagnosis. *Journal of Offender Rehabilitation, 20*, 159–185.

Stone, G. L. (1995). Review of the Hare Psychopathy Checklist–Revised. In J. C. Conoley & J. C. Impara (Eds.), *Twelfth mental measurements yearbook* (pp. 454–455). Lincoln, NE: Buros Institute.

Templeman, R., & Wong, S. (1994). Determining the factor structure of the Psychopathy Checklist: A converging approach. *Multivariate Experimental Clinical Research, 10*, 157–166.

Tennent, G., Tennent, D., Prins, H., & Bedford, A. (1990). Psychopathic disorder: A useful clinical concept? *Medicine, Science, and the Law, 30,* 38–44.

Tennent, G., Tennent, D., Prins, H., & Bedford, A. (1993). Is psychopathic disorder a treatable condition? *Medicine, Science, and the Law, 33,* 63–66.

Thomas-Peter, B. A. (1988). Psychopathy and telic dominance. In M. J. Apter, J. H. Kerr, & M. P. Cowles (Eds.), *Progress in reversal theory* (pp. 235–244). Amsterdam: North-Holland.

Thomas-Peter, B. A. (1992). The classification of psychopathy: A review of the Hare vs. Blackburn debate. *Personality & Individual Differences, 13,* 337–342.

Thomas-Peter, B. A. (1996). The structure of emotion in personality disordered aggressors: A motivational analysis. *Journal of Forensic Psychiatry, 7,* 26–41.

Trevethan, S. D., & Walker, L. J. (1989). Hypothetical versus real-life moral reasoning among psychopathic and delinquent youth. *Development and Psychopathology, 1,* 91–103.

Vitelli, R. (1997). Validation of the LSI-R in a prison setting [Abstract]. *Canadian Psychology, 38*(2a), 17.

Widiger, T. A. (1998). Psychopathy and normal personality. In D. J. Cooke, A. E. Forth, & R. D. Hare (Eds.), *Psychopathy: Theory, research, and implications for society* (pp. 47–68). Dordrecht, The Netherlands: Kluwer.

Widiger, T. A., Cadoret, R., Hare, R. D., Robins, L., Rutherford, M., Zanarini, M., Alterman, A., Apple, M., Corbitt, E., Forth, A. E., Hart, S. D., Kultermann, J., Woody, G., & Frances, A. (1996). DSM-IV antisocial personality disorder field trial. *Journal of Abnormal Psychology, 105,* 3–16.

Widiger, T. A., & Corbitt, E. (1993). Antisocial personality disorder: Proposals for DSM-IV. *Journal of Personality Disorders, 7,* 63–77.

Widiger, T. A., & Corbitt, E. (1995). Antisocial personality disorder: Proposals for DSM-IV. In W. J. Livesley (Ed.), *The DSM-IV personality disorders* (pp. 127–134). New York: Guilford.

Widiger, T. A., Frances, A. J., Pincus, H. A., Davis, W. W., & First, M. (1991). Toward an empirical classification for DSM-IV. *Journal of Abnormal Psychology, 100,* 280–288.

Widiger, T. A., Frances, A., Spitzer, R. L., & Williams, J. B. W. (1988). The DSM-III-R personality disorders: An overview. *American Journal of Psychiatry, 145,* 786–795.

Widiger, T. A., & Lynam, D. R. (1998). Psychopathy and the five-factor model of personality. In T. Millon & E. Simonsen (Eds.), *Psychopathy: Antisocial, criminal, and violent behavior* (pp. 171–187). New York: Guilford.

Widom, C., & Newman, J. P. (1985). Characteristics of non-institutionalized psychopaths. In D. Farrington & J. Gunn (Eds.), *Aggression and dangerousness* (pp. 57–80). New York: Wiley.

Wong, S. (1985). *Criminal and institutional behaviors of psychopaths.* Ottawa, Ontario: Programs Branch Users Report, Ministry of the Solicitor General of Canada.

Wong, S. (1988). Is Hare's Psychopathy Checklist reliable without the interview? *Psychological Reports, 62,* 931–934.

Wong, S., & Templeman, R. (1988). High and low psychopathy groups derived by cluster analyzing Psychopathy Checklist data [Abstract]. *Canadian Psychology, 29*(2a), 854.

Zagon, I. (1995). Psychopathy: A viable alternative to antisocial personality disorder? *Australian Psychologist, 30,* 11–16.

Zagon, I., & Jackson, H. (1994). Construct validity of a psychopathy measure. *Personality and Individual Differences, 17,* 125–135.

Children and Adolescents

Blair, R. J. R. (1997). Moral reasoning and the child with psychopathic tendencies. *Personality and Individual Differences, 22,* 731–739.

Brandt, J. R. (1994). Assessment of psychopathy in a population of incarcerated adolescent offenders. *Dissertation Abstracts International, 54*(9-B), 4908.

Brandt, J. R., Kennedy, W. A., Patrick, C. J., & Curtin, J. (1997). Assessment of psychopathy in a population of incarcerated adolescent offenders. *Psychological Assessment, 9,* 429–435.

Christian, R. E., Frick, P. J., Hill, N. L., Tyler, L., & Frazer, D. R. (1997). Psychopathy and conduct problems in children: Implications for subtyping children with conduct problems. *Journal of the American Academy of Child and Adolescent Psychiatry, 36,* 233–241.

Forth, A. E. (1995). *Psychopathy and young offenders: Prevalence, family background, and violence.* Unpublished report, Carleton University, Ottawa, Ontario.

Forth, A. E. (1996). Psychopathy in adolescent offenders: Assessment, family background, and violence. In D. J. Cooke, A. E. Forth, J. P. Newman, & R. D. Hare (Eds.), *Issues in criminological and legal psychology: No. 24. International perspectives on psychopathy* (pp. 42–44). Leicester, UK: British Psychological Society.

Forth, A. E. (1997). Psychopathy and risk of recidivism and violence in male young offenders [Abstract]. *Canadian Psychology, 38*(2a), 88.

Forth, A. E., & Burke, H. C. (1998). Psychopathy in adolescence: Assessment, violence, and developmental precursors. In D. J. Cooke, A. E. Forth, & R. D. Hare (Eds.), *Psychopathy: Theory, research, and implications for society* (pp. 205–229). Dordrecht, The Netherlands: Kluwer.

Forth, A. E., & Tobin, F. (1996). Psychopathy and young offenders: Rates of childhood maltreatment. *Forum on Corrections Research, 7*(1), 20–24.

Frick, P. J. (1996). Callous-unemotional traits and conduct problems: A two-factor model of psychopathy in children. In D. J. Cooke, A. E. Forth, J. P. Newman, & R. D. Hare (Eds.), *Issues in criminological and legal psychology: No. 24. International perspectives on psychopathy* (pp. 47–51). Leicester, UK: British Psychological Society.

Frick, P. J. (1998). Callous-unemotional traits and conduct problems: Applying the two-factor model of psychopathy to children. In D. J. Cooke, A. E. Forth, & R. D. Hare (Eds.), *Psychopathy: Theory, research, and implications for society* (pp. 161–187). Dordrecht, The Netherlands: Kluwer.

Frick, P., O'Brien, B., Wootton, J., & McBurnett, K. (1994). Psychopathy and conduct problems in children. *Journal of Abnormal Psychology, 103,* 700–707.

Gretton, H., McBride, M., O'Shaughnessy, R., & Hare, R. D. (1994). Predicting patterns of criminal activity in adolescent sexual psychopaths [Abstract]. *Canadian Psychology, 35*(2a), 50.

Gretton, H., McBride, M., O'Shaughnessy, R., & Hare, R. D. (1997). Sex offender or generalized offender? Psychopathy as a risk marker for violence in adolescent offenders [Abstract]. *Canadian Psychology, 38*(2a), 15.

Hirst, D. J. (1993). Inpatient adolescent MMPIs: A look at the subtle/obvious subscales and the Psychopathy Checklist. *Dissertation Abstracts International, 53*(9-B), 4956.

Hume, M. P., Kennedy, W. A., Patrick, C. J., & Partyka, D. J. (1996). Examination of the MMPI-A for the assessment of psychopathy in incarcerated adolescent male offenders. *International Journal of Offender Therapy and Comparative Criminology, 40,* 224–233.

Lewis, K., & O'Shaughnessy, R. (1998). Predictors of violent recidivism in juvenile offenders [Abstract]. *Canadian Psychology, 39*(2a), 95.

Lynam, D. R. (1996a). Early identification of chronic offenders: Who is the fledgling psychopath? *Psychological Bulletin, 120,* 209–234.

Lynam, D. R. (1996b). Pursuing the psychopath: Capturing the fledgling psychopath in a nomological net. *Journal of Abnormal Psychology, 106,* 425–438.

Lynam, D. R. (1998). Early identification of the fledgling psychopath: Locating the psychopathic child in the current nomenclature. *Journal of Abnormal Psychology, 107,* 566–575.

Mailloux, D. L., Forth, A. E., & Kroner, D. G. (1997). Psychopathy and substance use in adolescent male offenders. *Psychological Reports, 81,* 529–530.

McBride, M. (1998). *Individual and familial risk factors for adolescent psychopathy.* Unpublished doctoral dissertation, University of British Columbia, Vancouver, British Columbia.

McBurnett, K., & Pfiffner, L. (1998). Comorbidities and biological correlates of conduct disorder. In D. J. Cooke, A. E. Forth, & R. D. Hare (Eds.), *Psychopathy: Theory, research, and implications for society* (pp. 189–203). Dordrecht, The Netherlands: Kluwer.

Myers, W. C., & Blashfield, R. (1997). Psychopathology and personality in juvenile sexual homicide offenders. *Journal of the American Academy of Psychiatry and the Law, 25,* 497–508.

Myers, W. C., Burket, R. C., & Harris, E. H. (1995). Adolescent psychopathy in relation to delinquent behaviors, conduct disorder, and personality disorders. *Journal of Forensic Sciences, 40,* 436–440.

O'Brien, B. S., & Frick, P. J. (1996). Reward dominance: Associations with anxiety, conduct problems, and psychopathy in children. *Journal of Abnormal Child Psychology, 24,* 223–240.

Ridenour, T. A. (1996). Utility analyses of the Psychopathy Checklist–Revised and Moffitt's taxonomy for a rehabilitation program for juvenile delinquents. *Dissertation Abstracts International: Section B: The Sciences and Engineering, 57*(6-B), 4086.

Rogers, R., Johansen, J., Chang, J. J., & Salekin, R. T. (1997). Predictors of adolescent psychopathy: Oppositional and conduct-disordered symptoms. *Journal of the American Academy of Psychiatry and the Law, 25,* 261–271.

Smith, A. M., Gacono, C. B., & Kaufman, L. (1997). A Rorschach comparison of psychopathic and nonpsychopathic conduct disordered adolescents. *Journal of Clinical Psychology, 53,* 289–300.

Sullivan, L. (1996). *Assessment of psychopathy using the MMPI-A: Validity in male adolescent forensic patients.* Unpublished master's thesis, Department of Psychology, Simon Fraser University, Burnaby, Canada.

Toupin, J., Mercier, H., Déry, M., Côté, G., & Hodgins, S. (1996). Validity of the PCL-R for adolescents. In D. J. Cooke, A. E. Forth, J. P. Newman, & R. D. Hare (Eds.), *Issues in criminological and legal psychology: No. 24. International perspectives on psychopathy* (pp. 143–145). Leicester, UK: British Psychological Society.

Trevethan, S. D., & Walker, L. J. (1989). Hypothetical versus real-life moral reasoning among psychopathic and delinquent youth. *Development and Psychopathology, 1,* 91–103.

Vitelli, R. (1998). Childhood disruptive behavior disorders and adult psychopathy. *American Journal of Forensic Psychology, 16*(4), 29–37.

Watt, K., Ma, S., Lewis, K., & O'Shaughnessy, R. (1997). The relationship between parental criminality and youth psychopathy [Abstract]. *Canadian Psychology, 38*(2a), 14.

Wootton, J. M., Frick, P. J., Shelton, K. K., & Silverthorn, P. (1997). Ineffective parenting and childhood conduct problems: The moderating role of callous unemotional traits. *Journal of Consulting and Clinical Psychology, 65,* 301–308.

Cross-Cultural Issues

Barrigher, P. L. (1997). Differences in the Hare Psychopathy Checklist–Revised scores among African American and White offenders. *Dissertation Abstracts International: Section B: The Sciences and Engineering, 57*(12-B), 7715.

Cooke, D. J. (1994). *Psychological disturbance in the Scottish prison system: Prevalence, precipitants, and policy.* Edinburgh: Scottish Home and Health Department.

Cooke, D. J. (1995). Psychopathic disturbance in the Scottish prison population: Cross-cultural generalizability of the Hare Psychopathy Checklist. *Psychology, Crime, and Law, 2,* 101–118.

Cooke, D. J. (1996a). Psychopathy across cultures. In D. J. Cooke, A. E. Forth, J. P. Newman, & R. D. Hare (Eds.), *Issues in criminological and legal psychology: No. 24. International perspectives on psychopathy* (pp. 24–29). Leicester, UK: British Psychological Society.

Cooke, D. J. (1996b). Psychopathic personality in different cultures: What do we know? What do we need to find out? *Journal of Personality Disorders, 10,* 23–40.

Cooke, D. J. (1998). Psychopathy across cultures. In D. J. Cooke, A. E. Forth, & R. D. Hare (Eds.), *Psychopathy: Theory, research, and implications for society* (pp. 13–45). Dordrecht, The Netherlands: Kluwer.

Côté, G. (1990). Interrater reliability and interrater agreement with the French version of the Hare's Psychopathy Checklist [Abstract]. *Canadian Psychology, 31*(2a), 391.

Côté, G., & Hodgins, S. (1991). L'échelle de psychopathie de Hare: Validation de la version français: I. *Bulletin de Psychologie, 45,* 14–20.

Côté, G., & Hodgins, S. (1996). *L'Échelle de psychopathie de Hare - Révisée: Éléments de la validation de la version française.* Toronto: Multi-Health Systems.

Côté, G., Hodgins, S., Ross, D., & Toupin, J. (1994). *L'échelle de psychopathie de Hare: Un instrument et la validation de sa version français.* Communication présenté au Congrès de Psychiatrie et de Neurologie de Langue Française, Masson, France.

Freese, R., Müller-Isberner, R., & Jöckel, D. (1996). Psychopathy and co-morbidity in a German hospital order population. In D. J. Cooke, A. E. Forth, J. P. Newman, & R. D. Hare (Eds.), *Issues in criminological and legal psychology: No. 24. International perspectives on psychopathy* (pp. 45–46). Leicester, UK: British Psychological Society.

Hodgins, S., Côté, G., & Ross, D. (1992). Predictive validity of the French version of Hare's Psychopathy Checklist [Abstract]. *Canadian Psychology, 33*(2a), 301.

Knect, T. (1996). Der neugefasste psychopathiebegriff. *Schweiz Rundsch Med Prax, 85*(1–2), 9–13.

Kosson, D. S., Smith, S. S., & Newman, J. P. (1990). Evaluation of the construct validity of psychopathy in Black and White male inmates: Three preliminary studies. *Journal of Abnormal Psychology, 99,* 250–259.

Molto, J., Carmona, E., Poy, R., Avila, C., & Torrubia, R. (1996). The Psychopathy Checklist–Revised in Spanish prison populations: Some data on reliability and validity. In D. J. Cooke, A. E. Forth, J. P. Newman, & R. D. Hare (Eds.), *Issues in criminological and legal psychology: No. 24. International perspectives on psychopathy* (pp. 109–114). Leicester, UK: British Psychological Society.

Neary, A. M. (1991). DSM-III and Psychopathy Checklist assessment of antisocial personality disorder in Black and White female felons. *Dissertation Abstracts International, 51*(7-B), 3605.

Raine, A. (1985). A psychometric assessment of Hare's checklist for psychopathy in an English prison population. *British Journal of Clinical Psychology, 24,* 247–258.

Shine, J. H. (1996). The use of the Psychopathy Checklist–Revised in the UK [Letter]. *Forensic Update, 47,* 33–34.

Shine, J. H., & Hobson, J. A. (1997). Construct validity of the Hare Psychopathy Checklist, Revised, on a UK prison population. *Journal of Forensic Psychiatry, 8,* 546–561.

Gender

Cooney, N. L., Kadden, R. M., & Litt, M. D. (1990). A comparison of methods for assessing sociopathy in male and female alcoholics. *Journal of Studies on Alcohol, 51,* 42–48.

Forth, A. E., Brown, S. L., Hart, S. D., & Hare, R. D. (1996). The assessment of psychopathy in male and female noncriminals: Reliability and validity. *Personality and Individual Differences, 20,* 531–543.

Forth, A. E., Kisslinger, T., Brown, S., & Harris, A. (1993). Precursors to psychopathic traits in a sample of male and female university students [Abstract]. *Canadian Psychology, 34*(2a), 380.

Hamburger, M. E., Lilienfeld, S. O., & Hogben, M. (1996). Psychopathy, gender, and gender roles: Implications for antisocial and histrionic personality disorders. *Journal of Personality Disorders, 10,* 41–55.

Loucks, A. D., & Zamble, E. (1994). Criminal and violent behavior in incarcerated female federal offenders [Abstract]. *Canadian Psychology, 35*(2a), 54.

Louth, S. M., Hare, R. D., & Linden, W. (1998). Psychopathy and alexithymia in female offenders. *Canadian Journal of Behavioural Science, 30*, 91–98.

Murphy-Peaslee, D. M. (1995). An investigation of incarcerated females: Rorschach indices and Psychopathy Checklist scores. *Dissertation Abstracts International: Section B: The Sciences and Engineering, 56*(1-B), 531.

Neary, A. M. (1991). DSM–III and Psychopathy Checklist assessment of antisocial personality disorder in Black and White female felons. *Dissertation Abstracts International, 51*(7-B), 3605.

Nicholls, T. L., Douglas, K., & Ogloff, J. R. P. (1997). Risk assessments with female psychiatric patients: Utility of the HCR-20 and PCL:SV [Abstract]. *Canadian Psychology, 38*(2a), 111–112.

Piotrowski, N., Tusel, D. J., Sees, K. L., Banys, P., & Hall, S. M. (1996). Psychopathy and antisocial personality disorder in men and women with primary opioid dependence. In D. J. Cooke, A. E. Forth, J. P. Newman, & R. D. Hare (Eds.), *Issues in criminological and legal psychology: No. 24. International perspectives on psychopathy* (pp. 123–126). Leicester, UK: British Psychological Society.

Rutherford, M. J., Alertman, A. I., & Cacciola, J. S. (1996). Reliability and validity of the Revised Psychopathy Checklist in opiate- and cocaine-addicted women. In D. J. Cooke, A. E. Forth, J. P. Newman, & R. D. Hare (Eds.), *Issues in criminological and legal psychology: No. 24. International perspectives on psychopathy* (pp. 136–141). Leicester, UK: British Psychological Society.

Rutherford, M. J., Alterman, A. I., Cacciola, J. S., & McKay, J. R. (1998). Gender differences in the relationship of antisocial personality disorder criteria to Psychopathy Checklist–Revised scores. *Journal of Personality Disorders, 12*, 69–76.

Rutherford, M. J., Alterman, A. I., Cacciola, J. S., & Snyder, E. C. (1996). Gender differences in diagnosing antisocial personality disorder in methadone patients. *American Journal of Psychiatry, 152*, 1309–1316.

Rutherford, M. J., Cacciola, J. S., & Alterman, A. I. (1992). The Psychopathy Checklist-Revised with women. In *Problems of Drug Dependence 1991* (Research Monograph Series #119, p. 2). Rockville, MD: NIDA.

Rutherford, M. J., Cacciola, J. S., Alterman, A. I., & McKay, J. R. (1996). Reliability and validity of the Revised Psychopathy Checklist in women methadone patients. *Assessment, 3*, 43–54.

Salekin, R., Rogers, R., & Sewell, K. (1997). Construct validity of psychopathy in a female offender sample: A multitrait-multimethod evaluation. *Journal of Abnormal Psychology, 106*, 576–585.

Salekin, R., Rogers, R., & Sewell, K. (1998). Psychopathy and recidivism among female inmates. *Law and Human Behavior, 22*, 109–128.

Silbaugh, D. L. (1993). The Cognitive Style Questionnaire: A cross-validation study, utilizing the MMPI and the Hare Psychopathy Checklist with a population of incarcerated females. *Dissertation Abstracts International, 53*(12 B), 6574.

Strachan, C. (1993). *Assessment of psychopathy in female offenders*. Unpublished doctoral dissertation, University of British Columbia, Vancouver, British Columbia.

Forensic Issues

Cunningham, M. D., & Reidy, T. J. (1998). Antisocial personality disorder and psychopathy: Diagnostic dilemmas in classifying patterns of antisocial behavior in sentencing evaluations. *Behavioral Sciences and the Law, 16*, 333–351.

Douglas, K. S., & Ogloff, J. R. P. (1998). Comparing the relationship of psychotic and psychopathic symptoms to violence in psychiatric patients [Abstract]. *Canadian Psychology, 39*(2a), 98.

Elliott, C. (1991). The rules of insanity: Commentary on "Psychopathic disorder: A category mistake?" *Journal of Medical Ethics, 17,* 89–90.

Elliott, C. (1992). Diagnosing blame: Responsibility and the psychopath. *Journal of Medicine & Philosophy, 17,* 199–214.

Freese, R., Müller-Isberner, R., & Jöckel, D. (1996). Psychopathy and co-morbidity in a German hospital order population. In D. J. Cooke, A. E. Forth, J. P. Newman, & R. D. Hare (Eds.), *Issues in criminological and legal psychology: No. 24. International perspectives on psychopathy* (pp. 45–46). Leicester, UK: British Psychological Society.

Gacono, C., Meloy, J. R., Sheppard, K., Speth, E., & Roske, A. (1995). A clinical investigation of malingering and psychopathy in hospitalized insanity acquittees. *Bulletin of the American Academy of Psychiatry and the Law, 23,* 387–397.

Gacono, C., Meloy, J. R., Speth, E., & Roske, A. (1997). Above the law: Escapees from a maximum security forensic hospital and psychopathy. *Journal of the American Academy of Psychiatry and the Law, 25,* 547–550.

Hare, R. D. (1998a). Psychopaths and their nature: Implications for the mental health and criminal justice systems. In T. Millon & E. Simonsen (Eds.), *Psychopathy: Antisocial, criminal, and violent behavior* (pp. 188–212). New York: Guilford.

Hare, R. D. (1998b). The Hare PCL-R: Some issues concerning its use and misuse. *Legal and Criminological Psychology, 3,* 101–122.

Harris, G. T., & Rice, M. E. (1994). Psychopaths: Is a therapeutic community therapeutic? *Therapeutic Communities: International Journal for Therapeutic & Supportive Organizations, 15,* 283–299.

Harris, G. T., Rice, M. E., & Cormier, C. A. (1994). "The effectiveness of therapeutic communities for psychopaths": Reply. *Therapeutic Communities: International Journal for Therapeutic & Supportive Organizations, 16,* 147–149.

Harris, G. T., Rice, M. E., & Quinsey, V. L. (1993). Violent recidivism of mentally disordered offenders: The development of a statistical prediction instrument. *Criminal Justice and Behavior, 20,* 315–335.

Hart, S. D., & Hare, R. D. (1989). Discriminant validity of the Psychopathy Checklist in a forensic psychiatric population. *Psychological Assessment: A Journal of Consulting and Clinical Psychology, 1,* 211–218.

Heilbrun, K., Hart, S. D., Hare, R. D., Gustafson, D., Nunez, C., & White, A. (1998). Inpatient and post–discharge aggression in mentally disordered offenders: The role of psychopathy. *Journal of Interpersonal Violence.*

Hill, C. D., Rogers, R., & Bickford, M. E. (1996). Predicting aggressive and socially disruptive behavior in a maximum security forensic psychiatric hospital. *Journal of Forensic Sciences, 41,* 56–59.

Howard, R. C. (1990). Psychopathy Checklist scores in mentally abnormal offenders: A re-examination. *Personality and Individual Differences, 11,* 1087–1091.

Howard, R. C., Bailey, R., & Newman, F. (1984). A preliminary study of Hare's Research Scale for the Assessment of Psychopathy in mentally abnormal offenders. *Personality and Individual Differences, 5,* 389–396.

Kropp, P. R. (1994). The relationship between psychopathy and malingering of mental illness. *Dissertation Abstracts International, 54*(11-B), 5945.

Kruh, I. P., & Brodsky, S. L. (1997). Clinical evaluations for transfer of juveniles to criminal court: Current practices and future research. *Behavioral Sciences and the Law, 15,* 151–165.

Meloy, J. R., & McEllistrem, J. E. (1998). Psychopathy and bombing: An integrative review. *Journal of Forensic Sciences, 43,* 556–562.

Nedopil, N., Hollweg, M., Hartmann, J., & Jaser, R. (1996a). Comorbidity of psychopathy with major mental disorders. In D. J. Cooke, A. E. Forth, J. P. Newman, & R. D. Hare (Eds.), *Issues in criminological and legal psychology: No. 24. International perspectives on psychopathy* (pp. 115–118). Leicester, UK: British Psychological Society.

Nedopil, N., Hollweg, M., Hartmann, J., & Jaser, R. (1996b). Comorbidity of psychopathy with major mental disorders. In D. J. Cooke, A. E. Forth, & R. D. Hare (Eds.), *Psychopathy: Theory, research, and implications for society* (pp. 257–268). Dordrecht, The Netherlands: Kluwer.

Nicholls, T. L., Douglas, K., & Ogloff, J. R. P. (1997). Risk assessments with female psychiatric patients: Utility of the HCR-20 and PCL:SV [Abstract]. *Canadian Psychology, 38*(2a), 111–112.

Ogloff, J. R. P. (1996). Legal issues associated with the concept of psychopathy. In D. J. Cooke, A. E. Forth, J. P. Newman, & R. D. Hare (Eds.), *Issues in criminological and legal psychology: No. 24. International perspectives on psychopathy* (pp. 119–122). Leicester, UK: British Psychological Society.

Ogloff, J. R. P., & Lyon, D. (1998). Legal issues associated with the concept of psychopathy. In D. J. Cooke, A. E. Forth, & R. D. Hare (Eds.), *Psychopathy: Theory, research, and implications for society* (pp. 401–422). Dordrecht, The Netherlands: Kluwer.

Patrick, C. J., & Iacono, W. G. (1989). Psychopathy, threat, and polygraph accuracy. *Journal of Applied Psychology, 74*, 347–355.

Rasmussen, K., & Levander, S. (1996a). Crime and violence among psychiatric patients in a maximum security psychiatric hospital. *Criminal Justice and Behavior, 23*, 455–471.

Rasmussen, K., & Levander, S. (1996b). Individual rather than situational characteristics predict violence in a maximum security hospital. *Journal of Interpersonal Violence, 11*, 376–390.

Rasmussen, K., & Levander, S. (1996c). Violence in the mentally disordered: A differential clinical perspective. In D. J. Cooke, A. E. Forth, J. P. Newman, & R. D. Hare (Eds.), *Issues in criminological and legal psychology: No. 24. International perspectives on psychopathy* (pp. 127–130). Leicester, UK: British Psychological Society.

Rasmussen, K., Levander, S., & Sletvold, H. (1995). Aggressive and non-aggressive schizophrenics: Symptom profile and neuropsychological differences. *Psychology, Crime & Law, 2*, 119–129.

Reed, J. (1996). Psychopathy: A clinical and legal dilemma. *British Journal of Psychiatry, 168*, 4–9.

Rice, M. E., & Harris, G. T. (1992). A comparison of criminal recidivism among schizophrenic and nonschizophrenic offenders. *International Journal of Law and Psychiatry, 15*, 397–408.

Rice, M. E., & Harris, G. T. (1995). Psychopathy, schizophrenia, alcohol abuse, and violent recidivism. *International Journal of Law and Psychiatry, 18*, 333–342.

Rice, M. E., Harris, G. T., & Cormier, C. A. (1992). An evaluation of a maximum security therapeutic community for psychopaths and other mentally disordered offenders. *Law and Human Behavior, 16*, 399–412.

Stålenheim, E. G. (1997). Psychopathy and biological markers in a forensic psychiatric population. *Acta Universitatis Uppsaliensis, Comprehensive Summaries of Uppsala Dissertations from the Faculty of Medicine, 701*.

Stålenheim, E. G., & von Knorring, L. (1996). Psychopathy and Axis I and Axis II psychiatric disorders in a forensic psychiatric population in Sweden. *Acta Psychiatrica Scandinavica, 94*, 217–223.

Stålenheim, E. G., & von Knorring, L. (1998). Personality traits and psychopathy in a forensic psychiatric population. *European Journal of Psychiatry, 12*, 83–94.

Stålenheim, E. G., von Knorring, L., & Oreland, L. (1997). Platelet monoamine oxidase activity as a biological marker in a Swedish forensic psychiatric population. *Psychiatry Research, 69*, 79–87.

Sullivan, L. (1996). *Assessment of psychopathy using the MMPI–A: Validity in male adolescent forensic patients.* Unpublished master's thesis, Department of Psychology, Simon Fraser University, Burnaby, Canada.

Wintrup, A., Coles, M., Hart, S., & Webster, C. D. (1994). The predictive validity of the PCL–R in high-risk mentally disordered offenders [Abstract]. *Canadian Psychology, 35*(2a), 47.

Zinger, I. (1996). The misuse of psychopathy in Canadian court proceedings. In D. J. Cooke, A. E. Forth, J. P. Newman, & R. D. Hare (Eds.), *Issues in criminological and legal psychology: No. 24. International perspectives on psychopathy* (pp. 157–159). Leicester, UK: British Psychological Society.

Zinger, I., & Forth, A. (1998). Psychopathy and Canadian criminal proceedings: The potential for human rights abuses. *Canadian Journal of Criminology, 40,* 237–276.

Industrial and Organizational Psychology

Babiak, P. (1995). When psychopaths go to work: A case study of an industrial psychopath. *Applied Psychology: An International Review, 44,* 171–178.

Babiak, P. (1996). Psychopathic manipulation in organizations: Pawns, patrons, and patsies. In D. J. Cooke, A. E. Forth, J. P. Newman, & R. D. Hare (Eds.), *Issues in criminological and legal psychology: No. 24. International perspectives on psychopathy* (pp. 12–17). Leicester, UK: British Psychological Society.

Gustafson, S. B. (1996). Aberrant self-promotion: The dark side of normal. In D. J. Cooke, A. E. Forth, J. P. Newman, & R. D. Hare (Eds.), *Issues in criminological and legal psychology: No. 24. International perspectives on psychopathy* (pp. 61–62). Leicester, UK: British Psychological Society.

Gustafson, S. B., & Ritzer, D. R. (1995). The dark side of normal: A psychopathy-linked pattern called Aberrant Self-Promotion. *European Journal of Personality, 9,* 147–183.

Psychophysiology, Emotion, and Learning

Alm, P. O., af Klinteberg, B., Humble, K., Leppert, J., Sorensen, S., Tegelman, R., Thorell, L. H., & Lidberg, L. (1996). Criminality and psychopathy as related to thyroid activity in former juvenile delinquents. *Acta Psychiatrica Scandinavica, 94,* 112–117.

Alm, P. O., af Klinteberg, B., Humble, K., Leppert, J., Sorensen, S., Thorell, L. H., Lidberg, L., & Oreland, L. (1996a). Psychopathy, platelet MAO activity and criminality among former juvenile delinquents. *Acta Psychiatrica Scandinavica, 94,* 105–111.

Alm, P. O., af Klinteberg, B., Humble, K., Leppert, J., Sorenson, S., Thorell, L., Lidberg, L., & Oreland, L. (1996b). Psychopathy, platelet MAO activity and criminality among juvenile delinquents grown up. In D. J. Cooke, A. E. Forth, J. P. Newman, & R. D. Hare (Eds.), *Issues in criminological and legal psychology: No. 24. International perspectives on psychopathy* (pp. 6–11). Leicester, UK: British Psychological Society.

Arnett, P. A. (1997). Autonomic responsivity in psychopaths: A critical review and theoretical proposal. *Clinical Psychology Review, 17,* 903–906.

Arnett, P. A., Howland, E. W., Smith, S. S., & Newman, J. P. (1993). Autonomic responsivity during passive avoidance in incarcerated psychopaths. *Personality and Individual Differences, 14,* 173–184.

Arnett, P. A., Smith, S. S., & Newman, J. P. (1997). Approach and avoidance motivation in incarcerated psychopaths during passive avoidance. *Journal of Personality and Social Psychology, 72,* 1413–1428.

Blair, R. J. R., Jones, L., Clark, F., & Smith, M. (1997). The psychopathic individual: A lack of responsiveness to distress cues? *Psychophysiology, 34,* 192–198.

Blair, R. J. R., Sellars, C., Strickland, I., Clark, F., Smith, M., & Jones, L. (1995). Emotional attributions in the psychopath. *Personality and Individual Differences, 19,* 431–437.

Christianson, S., Forth, A. E., Hare, R. D., Strachan, C., Lidberg, L., & Thorell, L. (1996). Emotion and memory in criminal psychopaths. *Personality and Individual Differences, 20,* 437–443.

Cornell, D. G., Roberts, M., & Oram, C. (1997). The Rey Osterrieth complex figure test as a neuropsychological measure in criminal offenders. *Archives of Clinical Neuropsychology, 12*, 47–56.

Cripps, J. E. (1997). *The association between the neutralization of self-punishment, guilt, and psychopathy among extrafamilial child molesters.* Unpublished master's thesis, Carleton University, Ottawa, Ontario.

Day, R., & Wong, S. (1990). Lateral processing of emotional stimuli [Abstract]. *Canadian Psychology, 31*(2a), 339.

Day, R., & Wong, S. (1996). Anomalous perceptual asymmetries for negative emotional stimuli in the psychopath. *Journal of Abnormal Psychology, 105*, 648–652.

Dolan, M. (1994). Psychopathy: A neurobiological perspective. *British Journal of Psychiatry, 165*, 151–159.

Fedora, O., & Reddon, J. R. (1993). Psychopathic and nonpsychopathic inmates differ from normal controls in tolerance to electrical stimulation. *Journal of Clinical Psychology, 49*, 326–331.

Folsom, J., Lawson, J. S., & Inglis, J. (1992). Learning disabilities and psychopathy in a male prison population [Abstract]. *Canadian Psychology, 33*(2a), 405.

Forth, A. E., & Hare, R. D. (1989). Slow cortical potentials in psychopaths. *Psychophysiology, 26*, 676–682.

Gacono, C. B., & Meloy, J. R. (1993). Some thoughts on Rorschach findings and psychophysiology in the psychopath. *British Journal of Projective Psychology, 38*, 42–52.

Gillstrom, B., & Hare, R. D. (1988). Language-related hand gestures in psychopaths. *Journal of Personality Disorders, 2*, 21–27.

Halle, P., & Hodgins, S. (1996). Perspectives actuelles sur la psychopathie: Données neuropsychologiques et hypotheses neurobiologiques. *Révue de Neuropsychologie, 6*, 471–504.

Hare, R. D. (1984). Performance of psychopaths on cognitive tasks related to frontal lobe functions. *Journal of Abnormal Psychology, 93*, 133–140.

Hare, R. D. (1988). Psychopathy, affect, and behavior. In D. J. Cooke, A. E. Forth, & R. D. Hare (Eds.), *Psychopathy: Theory, research, and implications for society* (pp. 105–137). Dordrecht, The Netherlands: Kluwer.

Hare, R. D., & Craigen, D. (1974). Psychopathy and physiological activity in a mixed-motive game situation. *Psychophysiology, 11*, 197–206.

Hare, R. D., & Forth, A. E. (1985). Psychopathy and lateral preference. *Journal of Abnormal Psychology, 94*, 541–546.

Hare, R. D., & McPherson, L. M. (1984). Psychopathy and perceptual asymmetry during verbal dichotic listening. *Journal of Abnormal Psychology, 93*, 140–149.

Hare, R. D., Williamson, S. E., & Harpur, T. J. (1988). Psychopathy and language. In T. E. Moffitt & S. A. Mednick (Eds.), *Biological contributions to crime causation* (pp. 68–92). Dordrecht, The Netherlands: Martinus Nijhoff.

Harpur, T. J., & Hare, R. D. (1990). Psychopathy and attention. In J. Enns (Ed.), *The development of attention: Recent research and theory* (pp. 501–516). Amsterdam: North-Holland.

Hart, S. D., Forth, A. E., & Hare, R. D. (1990). Performance of criminal psychopaths on selected neuropsychological tests. *Journal of Abnormal Psychology, 99*, 374–379.

Hayes, P. J., & Hare, R. D. (1994). Psychopathy, language, and violence [Abstract]. *Canadian Psychology, 35*(2a), 48.

Howard, R., Payamal, L. T., & Lee, H. N. (1997). Response modulation deficits in psychopaths: A failure to confirm and a reconsideration of the Patterson–Newman model. *Personality and Individual Differences, 22*, 707–717.

Howland, E. W., Kosson, D. S., Patterson, C. M., & Newman, J. P. (1993). Altering a dominant response: Performance of psychopaths and low-socialization college students on a cued reaction time task. *Journal of Abnormal Psychology, 102*, 379–387.

Intrator, J., Hare, R., Strizke, P., Brichtswein, K., Dorfman, D., Harpur, T., Bernstein, D., Handelsman, L., Schaefer, C., Keilp, J., Rosen, J., & Machac, J. (1997). Brain imaging (SPECT) study of semantic and affective processing in psychopaths. *Biological Psychiatry, 42,* 96–103.

Kandel, E. (1992). Biology, violence, and antisocial personality. *Journal of Forensic Sciences, 37,* 912–918.

Kiehl, K. A., Hare, R. D., & Brink, J. (in press). Semantic and affective processing in psychopaths: An event-related potential (ERP) study. *Psychophysiology.*

af Klinteberg, B. (1997). Hyperactive behaviour and aggressiveness as early risk indicators for violence: Variable and person approaches. *Studies on Crime and Crime Prevention, 6,* 21–34.

af Klinteberg, B. (1998). Biology and personality: Findings from a longitudinal project. In D. J. Cooke, A. E. Forth, & R. D. Hare (Eds.), *Psychopathy: Theory, research, and implications for society* (pp. 139–160). Dordrecht, The Netherlands: Kluwer.

af Klinteberg, B., Humble, K., & Schalling, D. (1992). Personality and psychopathy of males with a history of early criminal behavior. *European Journal of Personality, 6,* 245–266.

Kosson, D. S. (1996a). Psychopathic offenders display performance deficits but not overfocusing under dual-task conditions of equal priority. In D. J. Cooke, A. E. Forth, J. P. Newman, & R. D. Hare (Eds.), *Issues in criminological and legal psychology: No. 24. International perspectives on psychopathy* (pp. 82–89). Leicester, UK: British Psychological Society.

Kosson, D. S. (1996b). Psychopathy and dual-task performance under focusing conditions. *Journal of Abnormal Psychology, 105,* 391–400.

Kosson, D. S. (1998). Divided visual attention in psychopathic and nonpsychopathic offenders. *Personality and Individual Differences, 24,* 373–391.

Kosson, D. S., & Harpur, T. J. (1997). Attentional functioning of psychopathic individuals: Current evidence and developmental implications. In J. A. Burack & J. T. Enns (Eds.), *Attention, development, and psychopathology* (pp. 379–402). New York: Guilford.

Kosson, D. S., & Newman, J. P. (1986). Psychopathy and allocation of attentional capacity in a divided-attention situation. *Journal of Abnormal Psychology, 95,* 257–263.

Kroner, D. G., & Forth, A. E. (1995). The Toronto Alexithymia Scale with incarcerated offenders. *Personality and Individual Differences, 19,* 625–634.

Kroner, D. G., & Forth, A. E. (1996). Affective processing in psychopaths: A salient–content perspective. In D. J. Cooke, A. E. Forth, J. P. Newman, & R. D. Hare (Eds.), *Issues in criminological and legal psychology: No. 24. International perspectives on psychopathy* (pp. 90–93). Leicester, UK: British Psychological Society.

Kroner, D. G., & Forth, A. E. (1997). Affective and cognitive processing in violent psychopaths [Abstract]. *Canadian Psychology, 38*(2a), 11.

Kroner, D. G., & Forth, A. E. (1998). Negative and positive endorsement of affective information in violent psychopaths [Abstract]. *Canadian Psychology, 39*(2a), 132.

Kroner, D. G., & Weekes, J. R. (1996). Balanced Inventory of Desirable Responding: Factor structure, reliability, and validity with an offender sample. *Personality and Individual Differences, 21,* 323–333.

Lapierre, D., Braun, C. M. J., & Hodgins, S. (1995). Ventral frontal deficits in psychopathy: Neuropsychological test findings. *Neuropsychologia, 33,* 139–151.

Lewis, C. E. (1991). Neurochemical mechanisms of chronic antisocial behavior (psychopathy): A literature review. *Journal of Nervous & Mental Disease, 179,* 720–727.

Lilienfeld, S. O., Hess, T., & Rowland, C. (1996). Psychopathic personality traits and temporal perspective: A test of the short time horizon hypothesis. *Journal of Psychopathology and Behavioral Assessment, 18,* 285–314.

Louth, S. M., Hare, R. D., & Linden, W. (1998). Psychopathy and alexithymia in female offenders. *Canadian Journal of Behavioural Science, 30,* 91–98.

Louth, S. M., Williamson, S., Alpert, M., & Hare, R. D. (1994). Poverty of affect in the speech of psychopaths [Abstract]. *Canadian Psychology, 35*(2a), 48.

Louth, S. M., Williamson, S., Alpert, M., Pouget, E. R., & Hare, R. D. (1998). Acoustic distinctions in the speech of male psychopaths. *Journal of Psycholinguistic Research, 27*, 375–384.

Marshall, L. (1996). The processing of affective words by psychopaths. *Issues in Criminology and Legal Psychology, 26*, 18–22.

McBride, M., Boer, D., & Hare, R. D. (1997). Psychopathy and arousal in criminal and noncriminal populations [Abstract]. *Canadian Psychology, 38*(2a), 147.

Meyers, C. A., Berman, S. A., Scheibel, R. S., & Hayman, A. (1992). Case report: Acquired antisocial personality disorder associated with unilateral left orbital frontal lobe damage. *Journal of Psychiatry & Neuroscience, 17*, 121–125.

Miller, J. D., & Hill, J. K. (1997). Examining the relationship of anxiety and psychopathy in the Social Personality Inventory [Abstract]. *Canadian Psychology, 38*(2a), 13.

Newman, J. P. (1994). Psychopathy and anxiety as separate influences on response modulation [Abstract]. *Psychophysiology, 31*, S7.

Newman, J. P. (1997). Conceptual nervous system models of antisocial behavior. In D. Stoff, J. Brieling, & J. Maser (Eds.), *Handbook of antisocial behavior* (pp. 324–335). New York: Wiley.

Newman, J. P. (1998). Psychopathic behavior: An information processing perspective. In D. J. Cooke, A. E. Forth, & R. D. Hare (Eds.), *Psychopathy: Theory, research, and implications for society* (pp. 81–104). Dordrecht, The Netherlands: Kluwer.

Newman, J. P., & Brinkley, C. A. (in press). Reconsidering the low-fear explanation for primary psychopathy. *Psychological Inquiry.*

Newman, J. P., & Kosson, D. S. (1986). Passive avoidance learning in psychopathic and nonpsychopathic offenders. *Journal of Abnormal Psychology, 95*, 252–256.

Newman, J. P., Kosson, D. S., & Patterson, C. M. (1992). Delay of gratification in psychopathic and nonpsychopathic offenders. *Journal of Abnormal Psychology, 101*, 630–636.

Newman, J. P., Patterson, C. M., Howland, E. W., & Nichols, S. L. (1991). Passive avoidance learning in psychopaths: The effects of reward. *Personality and Individual Differences, 11*, 1101–1114.

Newman, J. P., Patterson, C. M., & Kosson, D. S. (1987). Response perseveration in psychopaths. *Journal of Abnormal Psychology, 96*, 145–148.

Newman, J. P., & Schmitt, W. (1998). Passive avoidance in psychopathic offenders: A replication and extension. *Journal of Abnormal Psychology, 107*, 527–532.

Newman, J. P., Schmitt, W., & Voss, W. (1997). The impact of motivationally neutral cues on psychopathic individuals: Assessing the generality of the response modulation hypothesis. *Journal of Abnormal Psychology, 106*, 563–575.

Newman, J. P., & Wallace, J. F. (1993a). Diverse pathways to deficient self-regulation: Implications for disinhibitory psychopathology in children. *Clinical Psychology Review, 13*, 699–720.

Newman, J. P., & Wallace, J. F, (1993b). Psychopathy and cognition. In P. Kendall & K. Dobson (Eds.), *Psychopathology and cognition* (pp. 293–349). New York: Academic Press.

Newman, J. P., Wallace, J. F., Schmitt, W. A., & Arnett, P. A. (1997). Behavioral inhibition system functioning in anxious, impulsive and psychopathic individuals. *Personality and Individual Differences, 23*, 583–592.

Newman, J. P., Widom, C. S., & Nathan, S. (1985). Passive-avoidance in syndromes of disinhibition: Psychopathy and extraversion. *Journal of Personality and Social Psychology, 48*, 1316–1327.

O'Brien, B. S., & Frick, P. J. (1996). Reward dominance: Associations with anxiety, conduct problems, and psychopathy in children. *Journal of Abnormal Child Psychology, 24*, 223–240.

Ogloff, J. R., & Wong, S. (1990). Electrodermal and cardiovascular evidence of a coping response in psychopaths. *Criminal Justice and Behavior, 17,* 231–245.

Palmer, W. R. T. (1997). Enhancing release prediction using current, potentially dynamic, predictors and survival analysis [Abstract]. *Canadian Psychology, 38*(2a), 87.

Paris, J. (1996). Antisocial personality disorder: A biopsychosocial model. *Canadian Journal of Psychiatry, 41,* 75–80.

Patrick, C. J. (1994). Emotion and psychopathy: Startling new insights. *Psychophysiology, 31,* 319–330.

Patrick, C. J. (1995, Fall). Emotion and temperament in psychopathy. *Clinical Science,* 5–8.

Patrick, C. J., Bradley, M. M., & Lang, P. J. (1993). Emotion in the criminal psychopath: Startle reflex modulation. *Journal of Abnormal Psychology, 102,* 82–92.

Patrick, C. J., Cuthbert, B. N., & Lang, P. J. (1994). Emotion in the criminal psychopath: Fear image processing. *Journal of Abnormal Psychology, 103,* 523–534.

Patrick, C. J., & Erickson, L. M. (1994). Emotional imagery and startle reflex modulation in psychopathic and nonpsychopathic criminals [Abstract]. *Psychophysiology, 31,* S75.

Patrick, C. J., & Miller, M. W. (1994). Psychopathy and startle potentiation during noxious stimulus anticipation [Abstract]. *Psychophysiology, 31,* S76.

Patrick, C. J., & Zempolich, K. A. (in press). Emotion and aggression in the psychopathic personality. *Aggression and Violent Behavior.*

Patrick, C. J., Zempolich, K. A., & Levenston, G. K. (1997). Emotionality and violent behavior in psychopaths: A biosocial analysis. In A. Raine & P. A. Brennan (Eds.), *Biosocial bases of violence* (pp. 145–161). New York: Plenum.

Patterson, C. M., & Newman, J. P. (1993). Reflectivity and learning from aversive events: Toward a psychological mechanism for the syndromes of disinhibition. *Psychological Review, 100,* 716–736.

Raine, A., O'Brien, M., Smiley, N., Scerbo, A., & Chan, C. J. (1990). Reduced lateralization in verbal dichotic listening in adolescent psychopaths. *Journal of Abnormal Psychology, 99,* 272–277.

Raine, A., & Venables, P. H. (1988a). Enhanced P3 evoked potentials and longer recovery times in psychopaths. *Psychophysiology, 25,* 30–38.

Raine, A., & Venables, P. H. (1988b). Skin conductance responsivity in psychopaths to orienting, defensive, and consonant-vowel stimuli. *Journal of Psychophysiology, 2,* 221–225.

Serin, R. C., & Kuriychuk, M. (1994). Social and cognitive processing deficits in violent offenders: Implications for treatment. *International Journal of Law and Psychiatry, 17,* 431–441.

Siever, L. J. (1998). Neurobiology in psychopathy. In T. Millon & E. Simonsen (Eds.), *Psychopathy: Antisocial, criminal, and violent behavior* (pp. 231–246). New York: Guilford.

Smith, S. S., Arnett, P. A., & Newman, J. P. (1992). Neuropsychological differentiation of psychopathic and nonpsychopathic criminal offenders. *Personality and Individual Differences, 13,* 1233–1243.

Smith, S. S., Newman, J. P., Evans, A. M., Pickens, R., Uhl, G. R., Wydevan, J., & Newlin, D. B. (1993). Psychopathy is not associated with increased D2 dopamine receptor Taql A or B gene marker frequencies in incarcerated substance abusers. *Biological Psychiatry, 33,* 845–848.

Stålenheim, E. G., Eriksson, E., von Knorring, L., & Wide, L. (1998). Testosterone as a biological marker in psychopathy and alcoholism. *Psychiatry Research, 77,* 79–88.

Stålenheim, E. G., von Knorring, L., & Oreland, L. (1997). Platelet monoamine oxidase activity as a biological marker in a Swedish forensic psychiatric population. *Psychiatry Research, 69,* 79–87.

Stålenheim, E. G., von Knorring, L., & Wide, L. (1998). Serum levels of thyroid hormones as biological markers in a Swedish forensic psychiatric population. *Biological Psychiatry, 43,* 755–761.

Thomas-Peter, B. (1996). The structure of emotion in personality disordered aggressors: A motivational analysis. *Journal of Forensic Psychiatry, 7,* 26–41.

Thornquist, M. H., & Zuckerman, M. (1995). Psychopathy, passive avoidance learning, and basic dimensions of personality. *Personality and Individual Differences, 19,* 525–534.

Williamson, S. E. (1991). *Cohesion and coherence in the speech of psychopathic criminals.* Unpublished doctoral dissertation, University of British Columbia, Vancouver, British Columbia.

Williamson, S. E., Harpur, T. J., & Hare, R. D. (1991). Abnormal processing of affective words by psychopaths. *Psychophysiology, 28,* 260–273.

The Rorschach Test

Gacono, C. B. (1988). *A Rorschach analysis of object relations and defensive structure and their relationship to narcissism and psychopathy in a group of antisocial offenders.* Dissertation, United States International University, San Diego, California.

Gacono, C. B. (1990). An empirical study of object relations and defensive operations in antisocial personality disorder. *Journal of Personality Assessment, 54,* 589–600.

Gacono, C. B. (1992). A Rorschach case study of sexual homicide. British *Journal of Projective Psychology, 37*(1), 1–21.

Gacono, C. B. (1996a). Human figure drawings of a serial, sexual murderer. *International Network for Projective Drawing and Pictorial Symbolism, 1*(2), 9–10.

Gacono, C. B. (1996b). The Rorschach and the diagnosis of antisocial and psychopathic personality. In D. J. Cooke, A. E. Forth, J. P. Newman, & R. D. Hare (Eds.), *Issues in criminological and legal psychology: No. 24. International perspectives on psychopathy* (pp. 52–56). Leicester, UK: British Psychological Society.

Gacono, C. B. (1997). Borderline personality organization, psychopathy, and sexual homicide: The case of Brinkley. In R. Meloy, M. Acklin, C. Gacono, J. Murray, & C. Peterson (Eds.), *Contemporary Rorschach interpretation* (pp. 217–238). Hillsdale, NJ: Lawrence Erlbaum Associates.

Gacono, C. B. (1998). The use of the Psychopathy Checklist–Revised (PCL–R) and Rorschach in treatment planning with antisocial personality disordered patients. *International Journal of Offender Therapy and Comparative Criminology, 42*(1), 49–64.

Gacono, C. B., & Meloy, J. R. (1991). A Rorschach investigation of attachment and anxiety in antisocial personality disorder. *Journal of Nervous and Mental Disease, 179*(9), 546–552.

Gacono, C. B., & Meloy, J. R. (1992). The Rorschach and the DSM–III–R antisocial personality: A tribute to Robert Lindner. *Journal of Clinical Psychology, 48*(3), 393–405.

Gacono, C. B., & Meloy, J. R. (1993). Some thoughts on Rorschach findings and psychophysiology in the psychopath. *British Journal of Projective Psychology, 38*(1), 42–52.

Gacono, C. B., & Meloy, J. R. (1994). *Rorschach assessment of aggressive and psychopathic personalities.* Hillsdale, NJ: Lawrence Erlbaum Associates.

Gacono, C. B., & Meloy, J. R. (1997). Rorschach research and the psychodiagnosis of antisocial and psychopathic personalities. *Rorschachiana, 22,* 130–145.

Gacono, C. B., & Meloy, J. R. (1997). Attachment deficits in antisocial and psychopathic personalities. *British Journal of Projective Psychology, 42*(2), 47–55.

Gacono, C. B., Meloy, J. R., & Berg, J. (1992). Object relations, defensive operations, and affective states in narcissistic, borderline, and antisocial personality disorder. *Journal of Personality Assessment, 59*(1), 32–49.

Gacono, C. B., Meloy, J. R, & Bridges, M. (2000). A Rorschach comparison of psychopaths, sexual homicide perpetrators, and nonviolent pedophiles: Where angels fear to tread. *Journal of Clinical Psychology.*

Gacono, C., Meloy, J. R., & Heaven, T. (1990). A Rorschach investigation of narcissism and hysteria in antisocial personality disorder. *Journal of Personality Assessment, 55*(1&2), 270–279.

Heaven, T. R. (1989). The relationship between Hare's Psychopathy Checklist scores and selected Exner Rorschach variables in an inmate population. *Dissertation Abstracts International, 49*(8-B), 3442.

Meloy, J. R., & Gacono, C. B. (1992a). A psychotic (sexual) psychopath: "I just had a violent thought." *Journal of Personality Assessment, 58*(3), 32–49.

Meloy, J. R., & Gacono, C. B. (1992b). The aggression response and the Rorschach. *Journal of Clinical Psychology, 48*, 104–114.

Meloy, J. R., & Gacono, C. B. (1993). A borderline psychopath: "I was basically maladjusted." *Journal of Personality Assessment, 61*(27), 358–373.

Meloy, J. R., & Gacono, C. B. (1995). Assessing the psychopathic personality. In J. Butcher (Ed.), *Foundations of clinical personality assessment* (pp. 410–422). Oxford, England: Oxford University Press.

Meloy, J. R., & Gacono, C. B. (1998). The internal world of the psychopath: A Rorschach investigation. In T. Millon, E. Simonsen, & M. Birket-Smith (Eds.), *Psychopathy: Antisocial, criminal, and violent behaviors* (95–109). New York: Guilford.

Meloy, J. R., Gacono, C. B., & Kenney, L. (1994). A Rorschach investigation of sexual homicide. *Journal of Personality Assessment, 62*(1), 58–67.

Murphy-Peaslee, D. M. (1995). An investigation of incarcerated females: Rorschach indices and Psychopathy Checklist scores. *Dissertation Abstracts International: Section B: The Sciences and Engineering, 56*(1-B), 531.

Richards, H. J., & McCamant, K. (1996). Narcissism and psychopathy: Concurrent validity of the PCL-R, the Rorschach, and the MCMI. In D. J. Cooke, A. E. Forth, J. P. Newman, & R. D. Hare (Eds.), *Issues in criminological and legal psychology: No. 24. International perspectives on psychopathy* (pp. 131–135). Leicester, UK: British Psychological Society.

Smith, A. M., Gacono, C. B., & Kaufman, L. (1997). A Rorschach comparison of psychopathic and nonpsychopathic conduct disordered adolescents. *Journal of Clinical Psychology, 53*, 289–300.

Substance Abuse

Alterman, A. I., & Cacciola, J. S. (1991). The antisocial personality disorder diagnosis in substance abusers. *Journal of Nervous and Mental Disease, 179*, 401–409.

Alterman, A. I., Cacciola, J. S., & Rutherford, M. J. (1993). Reliability of the Revised Psychopathy Checklist in substance abuse patients. *Psychological Assessment: A Journal of Consulting and Clinical Psychology, 5*, 442–448.

Alterman, A. I., McDermott, P. A., Cacciola, J. S., Rutherford, M. J., Boardman, C. R., McKay, J. R., & Cook, T. G. (1998). A typology of antisociality in methadone patients. *Journal of Abnormal Psychology, 107*, 412–422.

Alterman, A. I., Rutherford, M. J., Cacciola, J. S., McKay, J. R., & Boardman, C. R. (1998). Prediction of 7 months methadone maintenance treatment response by four measures of antisociality. *Drug and Alcohol Dependence, 49*, 217–223.

Darke, S., Kaye, S., & Finlay-Jones, R. (1998). Antisocial personality disorder, psychopathy and injecting heroin use. *Drug and Alcohol Dependence, 52*, 63–69.

Darke, S., Kaye, S., Finlay-Jones, R., & Hall, W. (1998). Factor structure of psychopathy among methadone maintenance patients. *Journal of Personality Disorders, 12*, 162–171.

Gerstley, L. J., Alterman, A. I., McLellan, A. T., & Woody, G. E. (1990). Antisocial personality disorder in substance abusers: A problematic diagnosis? *American Journal of Psychiatry, 147*, 173–178.

Hemphill, J., Hart, S. D., & Hare, R. D. (1994). Psychopathy and substance use. *Journal of Personality Disorders, 8*, 169–180.

Loza, W. (1993). Different substance abusing offenders require a unique program. *International Journal of Offender Therapy & Comparative Criminology, 37,* 351–358.

Mailloux, D. L., Forth, A. E., & Kroner, D. G. (1997). Psychopathy and substance use in adolescent male offenders. *Psychological Reports, 81,* 529–530.

Piotrowski, N., Tusel, D. J., Sees, K. L., Banys, P., & Hall, S. M. (1996). Psychopathy and antisocial personality disorder in men and women with primary opioid dependence. In D. J. Cooke, A. E. Forth, J. P. Newman, & R. D. Hare (Eds.), *Issues in criminological and legal psychology: No. 24. International perspectives on psychopathy* (pp. 123–126). Leicester, UK: British Psychological Society.

Piotrowski, N. A., Tusel, D. J., Sees, K. L., Banys, P., & Hall, S. M. (in press). Psychopathy, antisocial personality, and other personality disorders in opiate addicts: Assessment and treatment issues. In *Problems of Drug.*

Rutherford, M. J., Alertman, A. I., & Cacciola, J. S. (1996). Reliability and validity of the Revised Psychopathy Checklist in opiate- and cocaine-addicted women. In D. J. Cooke, A. E. Forth, J. P. Newman, & R. D. Hare (Eds.), *Issues in criminological and legal psychology: No. 24. International perspectives on psychopathy* (pp. 136–141). Leicester, UK: British Psychological Society.

Rutherford, M. J., Alterman, A. I., Cacciola, J. S., & McKay, J. R. (1997). Validity of the Psychopathy Checklist–Revised in male methadone patients. *Drug and Alcohol Dependence, 44,* 143–149.

Rutherford, M. J., Alterman, A. I., Cacciola, J. S., & McKay, J. R. (1998). Gender differences in the relationship of antisocial personality disorder criteria to Psychopathy Checklist–Revised scores. *Journal of Personality Disorders, 12,* 69–76.

Rutherford, M. J., Alterman, A. I., Cacciola, J. S., McKay, J. R., & Cook, T. G. (1996). Object relations and reality testing in psychopathic and antisocial methadone patients. *Journal of Personality Disorders, 10,* 312–320.

Rutherford, M. J., Alterman, A. I., Cacciola, J. S., & Snyder, E. C. (1996). Gender differences in diagnosing antisocial personality disorder in methadone patients. *American Journal of Psychiatry, 152,* 1309–1316.

Rutherford, M. J., Cacciola, J. S., & Alterman, A. I. (1993). The predictive validity of the Psychopathy Checklist–Revised in treated opiate addicts. In *Problems of Drug Dependence 1992* (Research Monograph Series #132, p. 156). Rockville, MD: NIDA.

Rutherford, M. J., Cacciola, J. S., Alterman, A. I., & McKay, J. R. (1996). Reliability and validity of the Revised Psychopathy Checklist in women methadone patients. *Assessment, 3,* 43–54.

Smith, S. S., & Newman, J. P. (1990). Alcohol and drug abuse/dependence disorders in psychopathic and nonpsychopathic criminal offenders. *Journal of Abnormal Psychology, 99,* 430–439.

Tourian, K., Alterman, A., Metzger, D., Rutherford, M., Cacciola, J. S., & McKay, J.R. (1997). Validity of three measures of antisociality in predicting HIV risk behaviors in methadone maintenance patients. *Drug and Alcohol Dependence, 47,* 99–107.

Treatment

Blackburn, R. (1990). Treatment of psychopathic offender. *Issues in Criminological and Legal Psychology, 16,* 54–66.

Dolan, B., & Coid, J. (1993). *Psychopathic and antisocial personality disorders: Treatment and research issues.* London: Gaskell.

Gacono, C. B. (1998). The use of the Psychopathy Checklist–Revised (PCL–R) and Rorschach in treatment planning with antisocial personality disordered patients. *International Journal of Offender Therapy and Comparative Criminology, 42,* 49–64.

Gacono, C. B., Nieberding, R., Owen, A., Rubel, J., & Bodholdt, R. (2001). Treating juvenile and adult offenders with conduct disorder, antisocial, and psychopathic personalities. In J. Ashford, B. Sales, & W. Reid (Eds.), *Treating clients with special needs* (pp. 99–129). Washington, DC: American Psychological Association.

Garrido, V., Esteban, C., & Molero, C. (1996). The effectiveness in the treatment of psychopathy: A meta-analysis. In D. J. Cooke, A. E. Forth, J. P. Newman, & R. D. Hare (Eds.), *Issues in criminological and legal psychology: No. 24. International perspectives on psychopathy* (pp. 57–59). Leicester, UK: British Psychological Society.

Harris, G. T., & Rice, M. E. (1994). Psychopaths: Is a therapeutic community therapeutic? *Therapeutic Communities: International Journal for Therapeutic & Supportive Organizations, 15,* 283–299.

Harris, G. T., Rice, M. E., & Cormier, C. A. (1994). "The effectiveness of therapeutic communities for psychopaths": Reply. *Therapeutic Communities: International Journal for Therapeutic & Supportive Organizations, 16,* 147–149.

Hemphill, J. (1992). *Psychopathy and recidivism following release from a therapeutic community treatment program.* Unpublished master's thesis, Department of Psychology, University of Saskatchewan, Saskatoon, Saskatchewan.

Hemphill, J. F., & Wong, S. (1991). Efficacy of the therapeutic community for treating criminal psychopaths [Abstract]. *Canadian Psychology, 32*(2a), 206.

Hughes, G., Hogue, T., Hollin, C., & Champion, H. (1997). First-stage evaluation of a treatment programme for personality disordered offenders. *Journal of Forensic Psychiatry, 8,* 515–527.

Kristiansson, M. (1995). Incurable psychopaths? *Bulletin of the American Academy of Psychiatry and the Law, 23,* 555–562.

Lösel, F. (1996). Management of psychopaths. In D. J. Cooke, A. E. Forth, J. P. Newman, & R. D. Hare (Eds.), *Issues in criminological and legal psychology: No. 24. International perspectives on psychopathy* (pp. 100–106). Leicester, UK: British Psychological Society.

Lösel, F. (1998). Treatment and management of psychopaths. In D. J. Cooke, A. E. Forth, & R. D. Hare (Eds.), *Psychopathy: Theory, research, and implications for society* (pp. 303–354). Dordrecht, The Netherlands: Kluwer.

Meloy, J. R. (1995). Antisocial personality disorder. In G. Gabbard (Ed.), *Treatment of psychiatric disorders* (2nd ed., pp. 2273–2290). Washington, DC: American Psychiatric Press.

Mulder, R. T. (1996). Antisocial personality disorder: Current drug treatment recommendations. *CNS Drugs, 5,* 257–263.

Ogloff, J., Wong, S., & Greenwood, A. (1990). Treating criminal psychopaths in a therapeutic community program. *Behavioral Sciences and the Law, 8,* 81–90.

Reid, W. H., & Burke, W. J. (1989). Antisocial personality disorder. In American Psychiatric Association (Ed.), *Treatments of psychiatric disorders* (Vol. 3, pp. 2742–2749). Washington, DC: Author.

Reiss, D., Grubin, D., & Muex, C. (1996). "Psychopaths" in special hospital: Treatment and outcome. *British Journal of Psychiatry, 168,* 99–104.

Rice, M. E., & Harris, G. T. (1992). A comparison of criminal recidivism among schizophrenic and nonschizophrenic offenders. *International Journal of Law and Psychiatry, 15,* 397–408.

Rice, M. E., Harris, G. T., & Cormier, C. A. (1992). An evaluation of a maximum security therapeutic community for psychopaths and other mentally disordered offenders. *Law and Human Behavior, 16,* 399–412.

Serin, R. C. (1995). Treatment responsivity in criminal psychopaths. *Forum on Corrections Research, 7*(3), 23–26.

Tennent, G., Tennent, D., Prins, H., & Bedford, A. (1993). Is psychopathic disorder a treatable condition? *Medicine, Science, and the Law, 33,* 63–66.

Whitely, S. (1994). The effectiveness of therapeutic communities for psychopaths. *Therapeutic Communities: International Journal for Therapeutic & Supportive Organizations, 16,* 146–147.

Wong, S., & Elek, D. (1989). Treatment of psychopaths: A review of the literature [Abstract]. *Canadian Psychology, 30*(2a), 292.

Yates, P., & Nicholaichuk, T. (1998). The relationship between criminal career profile, psychopathy, and treatment outcome in the Clearwater sexual offender program [Abstract]. *Canadian Psychology, 39*(2a), 97.

Violence, Sexual Violence, and Risk

Barbaree, H., Seto, M., Serin, R., Amos, N., & Preston, D. (1994). Comparisons between sexual and nonsexual rapist subtypes. *Criminal Justice and Behavior, 21,* 95–114.

Blackburn, R., & Coid, J. (1998). Psychopathy and the dimensions of personality disorder in violent offenders. *Personality and Individual Differences, 25,* 129–145.

Brown, S. L., & Forth, A. E. (1995). Psychopathy and sexual aggression against adult females: Static and dynamic precursors [Abstract]. *Canadian Psychology, 36*(2a), 19.

Brown, S. L., & Forth, A. E. (1997). Psychopathy and sexual assault: Static risk factors, dynamic precursors, and rapist subtypes. *Journal of Consulting and Clinical Psychology, 65,* 848–857.

Burke, H. (1997). *Offenders' perceptions of factors related to outcome (success or failure) upon release from prison.* Unpublished master's thesis, Carleton University, Ottawa, Ontario.

Conacher, G. N., & Quinsey, V. L. (1992). Predictably dangerous psychopaths. *The Lancet, 340,* 794.

Cooke, D. J. (1989). Containing violent prisoners: An analysis of Barlinnie special unit. *British Journal of Criminology, 129,* 129–143.

Cornell, D., Warren, J., Hawk, G., Stafford, E., Oram, G., & Pine, D. (1996). Psychopathy in instrumental and reactive violent offenders. *Journal of Consulting and Clinical Psychology, 64,* 783–790.

Douglas, K., Ogloff, J. R. P., & Nicholls, T. L. (1997). The assessment of risk for violence in psychiatric inpatients [Abstract]. *Canadian Psychology, 38*(2a), 111.

Firestone, P., Bradford, J. M., Greenberg, D. M., Larose, M. R., & Curry, S. (1998). Homicidal and nonhomicidal child molesters: Psychological, phallometric, and criminal features. *Sexual Abuse: Journal of Research and Treatment, 10*(4), 305–323.

Firestone, P., Bradford, J. M., Greenberg, D. M., McCoy, M., Larose, M. R., & Curry, S. (1998). Risk factors for recidivism in incest offenders [Abstract]. *Canadian Psychology, 39*(2a), 96.

Firestone, P., Bradford, J. M., McCoy, M., Greenberg, D. M., Curry, S., & Larose, M. R. (1998). Recidivism in convicted rapists. *Journal of the American Academy of Psychiatry and the Law, 26,* 185–200.

Forth, A. E. (1995). *Psychopathy and young offenders: Prevalence, family background, and violence.* Unpublished report, Carleton University, Ottawa, Ontario.

Forth, A. E. (1996). Psychopathy in adolescent offenders: Assessment, family background, and violence. In D. J. Cooke, A. E. Forth, J. P. Newman, & R. D. Hare (Eds.), *Issues in criminological and legal psychology: No. 24. International perspectives on psychopathy* (pp. 42–44). Leicester, UK: British Psychological Society.

Forth, A. E. (1997). Psychopathy and risk of recidivism and violence in male young offenders [Abstract]. *Canadian Psychology, 38*(2a), 88.

Forth, A. E., & Brown, S. L. (1997). Psychopathy and sexual assault: Static risk factors, emotional precursors, and rapist subtypes. *Journal of Consulting and Clinical Psychology, 65,* 848–857.

Forth, A. E., & Burke, H. C. (1998). Psychopathy in adolescence: Assessment, violence, and developmental precursors. In D. J. Cooke, A. E. Forth, & R. D. Hare (Eds.), *Psychopathy:*

Theory, research, and implications for society (pp. 205–229). Dordrecht, The Netherlands: Kluwer.

Furr, K. (1994). Prediction of sexual or violent recidivism among sexual offenders: A comparison of prediction instruments. *Annals of Sex Research, 6,* 271–286.

Furr, K. (1996). Characteristics of sexual assaults on female prison staff. *Forum on Corrections Research, 8*(2), 25–27.

Gacono, C. B. (1992). A Rorschach case study of sexual homicide. *British Journal of Projective Psychology, 37,* 1–21.

Gacono, C. B., Meloy, J. R., & Bridges, M. (2000). A Rorschach comparison of psychopaths, sexual homicide perpetrators, and nonviolent pedophiles: Where angels fear to tread. *Journal of Clinical Psychology, 56,* 757–777.

Gacono, C., Meloy, J. R., Sheppard, K., Speth, E., & Roske, A. (1995). A clinical investigation of malingering and psychopathy in hospitalized insanity acquittees. *Bulletin of the American Academy of Psychiatry and the Law, 23,* 387–397.

Gacono, C., Meloy, J. R., Speth, E., & Roske, A. (1997). Above the law: Escapees from a maximum security forensic hospital and psychopathy. *Journal of the American Academy of Psychiatry and the Law, 25,* 547–550.

Glover, A. J. J. (1993). Identification of violent incarcerates using the Test of Criminal Thinking and the revised Psychopathy Checklist. *Dissertation Abstracts International, 53*(12A), 4253.

Gordon, A., Wong, S., & Salofske, D. (1998). An evaluation of the construct validity of the Violence Risk Scale-Experimental Version (VRS-E1) [Abstract]. *Canadian Psychology, 39*(2a), 98.

Grann, M., Långström, N., Tengström, A., & Kullgren, G. (in press). Psychopathy (PCL–R) predicts violent recidivism among criminal offenders with personality disorders in Sweden. *Law and Human Behavior.*

Gretton, H., McBride, M., O'Shaughnessy, R., & Hare, R. D. (1994). Predicting patterns of criminal activity in adolescent sexual psychopaths [Abstract]. *Canadian Psychology, 35*(2a), 50.

Gretton, H., McBride, M., O'Shaughnessy, R., & Hare, R. D. (1997). Sex offender or generalized offender? Psychopathy as a risk marker for violence in adolescent offenders [Abstract]. *Canadian Psychology, 38*(2a), 15.

Hare, R. D. (1981). Psychopathy and violence. In J. R. Hays, T. K. Roberts, & K. S. Soloway (Eds.), *Violence and the violent individual* (pp. 53–74). Jamaica, NY: Spectrum.

Hare, R. D., Forth, A. E., & Strachan, K. (1992). Psychopathy and crime across the lifespan. In R. DeV. Peters, R. J. McMahon, & V. L. Quinsey (Eds.), *Aggression and violence throughout the life span* (pp. 285–300). Newbury Park, CA: Sage.

Hare, R. D., & McPherson, L. M. (1984). Violent and aggressive behavior by criminal psychopaths. *International Journal of Law and Psychiatry, 7,* 35–50.

Harris, A. J. R., & Forth, A. E. (1998). Psychopathic sexual deviants: The intersection of Hare's conception of psychopathy and measures of sexual deviance [Abstract]. *Canadian Psychology, 39*(2a), 132.

Harris, A. J. R., & Hanson, R. K. (1997). The Psychopathy Checklist (Screening Version): Utility in the community supervision of sex offenders [Abstract]. *Canadian Psychology, 38*(2a), 2.

Harris, G. T., & Rice, M. E. (1994). The violent patient. In M. Hersen & R. Ammerman (Eds.), *Handbook of prescriptive treatments for adults* (pp. 463–486.) New York: Plenum.

Harris, G. T., Rice, M. E., & Cormier, C. A. (1991). Psychopathy and violent recidivism. *Law and Human Behavior, 15,* 625–637.

Harris, G. T., Rice, M. E., & Quinsey, V. L. (1993). Violent recidivism of mentally disordered offenders: The development of a statistical prediction instrument. *Criminal Justice and Behavior, 20,* 315–335.

Harris, G. T., Rice, M. E., & Quinsey, V. L. (in press). Appraisal and management of risk in sexual aggressors: Implications for criminal justice policy. *Psychology, Public Policy, and Law.*

Hart, S. D. (1996). Psychopathy and risk assessment. In D. J. Cooke, A. E. Forth, J. P. Newman, & R. D. Hare (Eds.), *Issues in criminological and legal psychology: No. 24. International perspectives on psychopathy* (pp. 63–67). Leicester, UK: British Psychological Society.

Hart, S. D. (1998a). Psychopathy and risk for violence. In D. J. Cooke, A. E. Forth, & R. D. Hare (Eds.), *Psychopathy: Theory, research, and implications for society* (pp. 355–373). Dordrecht, The Netherlands: Kluwer.

Hart, S. D. (1998b). The role of psychopathy in assessing risk for violence: Conceptual and methodological issues. *Legal and Criminological Psychology, 3,* 123–140.

Hart, S. D., & Hare, R. D. (1996). Psychopathy and risk assessment. *Current Opinion in Psychiatry, 9,* 380–383.

Hart, S. D., Hare, R. D., & Forth, A. E. (1994). Psychopathy as a risk marker for violence: Development and validation of a screening version of the Revised Psychopathy Checklist. In J. Monahan & H. Steadman (Eds.), *Violence and mental disorder: Developments in risk assessment* (pp. 81–98). Chicago: University of Chicago Press.

Hart, S. D., Kropp, P. R., & Hare, R. D. (1988). Performance of psychopaths following conditional release from prison. *Journal of Consulting and Clinical Psychology, 56,* 227–232.

Hayes, P. J., & Hare, R. D. (1994). Psychopathy, language, and violence [Abstract]. *Canadian Psychology, 35*(2a), 48.

Heilbrun, K., Hart, S. D., Hare, R. D., Gustafson, D., Nunez, C., & White, A. (in press). Inpatient and post-discharge aggression in mentally disordered offenders: The role of psychopathy. *Journal of Interpersonal Violence.*

Hemphill, J. F., & Hare, R. D. (1996). Psychopathy Checklist factor scores and recidivism. In D. J. Cooke, A. E. Forth, J. P. Newman, & R. D. Hare (Eds.), *Issues in criminological and legal psychology: No. 24. International perspectives on psychopathy* (pp. 68–73). Leicester, UK: British Psychological Society.

Hemphill, J. F., Hare, R. D., & Wong, S. (1998). Psychopathy and recidivism: A review. *Legal and Criminological Psychology, 3,* 141–172.

Hemphill, J. F., Templeman, R., Wong, S., & Hare, R. D. (1998). Psychopathy and crime: Recidivism and criminal careers. In D. J. Cooke, A. E. Forth, & R. D. Hare (Eds.), *Psychopathy: Theory, research, and implications for society* (pp. 375–399). Dordrecht, The Netherlands: Kluwer.

Hersh, K., & Gray-Little, B. (1998). Psychopathic traits and attitudes associated with self-resorted sexual aggression in college men. *Journal of Interpersonal Violence, 13,* 456–471. (Unconfirmed)

Hodgins, S. (1997). An overview of research on the prediction of dangerousness. *Nordic Journal of Psychiatry, 51*(Suppl. 39), 33–38.

Kandel, E. (1992). Biology, violence, and antisocial personality. *Journal of Forensic Sciences, 37,* 912–918.

Kosson, D. S., Kelly, J. C., & White, J. W. (1997). Psychopathy-related traits predict self-reported sexual aggression among college men. *Journal of Interpersonal Violence, 12,* 241–254.

Kroner, D. G., & Forth, A. E. (1997). Affective and cognitive processing in violent psychopaths [Abstract]. *Canadian Psychology, 38*(2a), 11.

Lalumière, M. L., & Quinsey, V. L. (1996). Sexual deviance, antisociality, mating effort, and the use of sexually coercive behaviors. *Personality and Individual Differences, 21,* 33–48.

Lewis, K., & O'Shaughnessy, R. (1997). Psychopathy in instrumental and reactive violent offenders [Abstract]. *Canadian Psychology, 38*(2a), 14.

Lewis, K., & O'Shaughnessy, R. (1998). Predictors of violent recidivism in juvenile offenders [Abstract]. *Canadian Psychology, 39*(2a), 95.

Looman, J., Abracen, J., Maillet, G., & DiFazio, R. (1998). Phallometric nonresponding in sexual offenders. *Sexual Abuse: Journal of Research and Treatment, 10*(4), 325–336.

Loucks, A. D., & Zamble, E. (1994). Criminal and violent behavior in incarcerated female federal offenders [Abstract]. *Canadian Psychology, 35*(2a), 54.

Loza, W., & Dhaliwal, G. K. (1997). Psychometric evaluation of the Risk Appraisal Guide (RAG): A tool for assessing violent recidivism. *Journal of Interpersonal Violence, 12,* 779-793.

Malcolm, P. B. (1996). Millhaven's sex offender intake assessment: A preliminary evaluation. *Forum on Corrections Research, 8*(2), 18-21.

Meloy, J. R., Gacono, C. B., & Kenney, L. (1994). A Rorschach investigation of sexual homicide. *Journal of Personality Assessment, 62*(1), 58-64.

Myers, W. C., & Blashfield, R. (1997). Psychopathology and personality in juvenile sexual homicide offenders. *Journal of the American Academy of Psychiatry and the Law, 25,* 497-508.

Nadeau, B., McHattie, L., Mulloy, R., & Smiley, W. C. (1998). Psychopathy and phallometric assessments of sex offenders [Abstract]. *Canadian Psychology, 39*(2a), 95.

Newlove, T., Hart, S. D., Dutton, D. G., & Hare, R. D. (1992). Psychopathy and family violence [Abstract]. *Canadian Psychology, 33*(2a), 405.

Patrick, C. J., Zempolich, K. A., & Levenston, G. K. (1997). Emotionality and violent behavior in psychopaths: A biosocial analysis. In A. Raine & P. A. Brennan (Eds.), *Biosocial bases of violence* (pp. 145-161). New York: Plenum.

Pham, H. T., Remy, S., Dailliet, A., & Lienard, L. (1998). Psychopathy and evaluation of violent behavior in a psychiatric security milieu. *Encephale, 24*(3), 173-179.

Polaschek, D. L. L. (1997). New Zealand rapists: An examination of subtypes. In G. M. Habermann (Ed.), *Looking back and moving forward: 50 years of New Zealand psychology* (pp. 224-231). Wellington, New Zealand: New Zealand Psychological Society.

Prentky, R., & Knight, R. (1988). *Antisocial personality disorder and Hare assessments of psychopathy among sexual offenders.* Unpublished manuscript, Massachusetts Treatment Center, Bridgewater, MA.

Quinsey, V. L., Rice, M. E., & Harris, G. T. (1995). Actuarial prediction of sexual recidivism. *Journal of Interpersonal Violence, 10,* 85-105.

Rasmussen, K., & Levander, S. (1996a). Crime and violence among psychiatric patients in a maximum security psychiatric hospital. *Criminal Justice and Behavior, 23,* 455-471.

Rasmussen, K., & Levander, S. (1996b). Individual rather than situational characteristics predict violence in a maximum security hospital. *Journal of Interpersonal Violence, 11,* 376-390.

Rasmussen, K., & Levander, S. (1996c). Violence in the mentally disordered: A differential clinical perspective. In D. J. Cooke, A. E. Forth, J. P. Newman, & R. D. Hare (Eds.), *Issues in criminological and legal psychology: No. 24. International perspectives on psychopathy* (pp. 127-130). Leicester, UK: British Psychological Society.

Rasmussen, K., Levander, S., & Sletvold, H. (1995). Aggressive and nonaggressive schizophrenics: Symptom profile and neuropsychological differences. *Psychology, Crime & Law, 2,* 119-129.

Rice, M. E., & Harris, G. T. (1992). A comparison of criminal recidivism among schizophrenic and nonschizophrenic offenders. *International Journal of Law and Psychiatry, 15,* 397-408.

Rice, M. E., & Harris, G. T. (1995a). Psychopathy, schizophrenia, alcohol abuse, and violent recidivism. *International Journal of Law and Psychiatry, 18,* 333-342.

Rice, M. E., & Harris, G. T. (1995b). Violent recidivism: Assessing predictive validity. *Journal of Consulting and Clinical Psychology, 63,* 737-748.

Rice, M. E., & Harris, G. T. (1997). Cross-validation and extension of the Violence Risk Appraisal Guide for child molesters and rapists. *Law and Human Behavior, 21,* 231-241.

Rice, M. E., Harris, G. T., & Quinsey, V. L. (1990). A follow-up of rapists assessed in a maximum security psychiatric facility. *Journal of Interpersonal Violence, 4,* 435-448.

Salekin, R., Rogers, R., & Sewell, K. (1996). A review and meta-analysis of the Psychopathy Checklist and Psychopathy Checklist-Revised: Predictive validity of dangerousness. *Clinical Psychology: Science and Practice, 3,* 203-215.

Salekin, R., Rogers, R., & Sewell, K. (1998). Psychopathy and recidivism among female inmates. *Law and Human Behavior, 22,* 109-128.

Serin, R. C. (1991). Psychopathy and violence in criminals. *Journal of Interpersonal Violence, 6,* 423–431.

Serin, R. C. (1996). Violent recidivism in criminal psychopaths. *Law and Human Behavior, 20,* 207–217.

Serin, R. C., & Amos, N. L. (1995). The role of psychopathy in the assessment of dangerousness. *International Journal of Law and Psychiatry, 18,* 231–238.

Serin, R. C., & Kuriychuk, M. (1994). Social and cognitive processing deficits in violent offenders: Implications for treatment. *International Journal of Law and Psychiatry, 17,* 431–441.

Serin, R. C., Malcolm, P. B., Khanna, A., & Barbaree, H. E. (1994). Psychopathy and deviant sexual arousal in incarcerated sexual offenders. *Journal of Interpersonal Violence, 9,* 3–11.

Serin, R. C., Peters, R. D., & Barbaree, H. E. (1990). Predictors of psychopathy and release outcome in a criminal population. *Psychological Assessment: A Journal of Consulting and Clinical Psychology, 2,* 419–422.

Seto, M. C., Barbaree, H. E., & Serin, R. C. (1994). Comparison of low-fixated and high-fixated child molesters [Abstract]. *Canadian Psychology, 35*(2a), 51.

Seto, M. C., Khattar, N. A., Lalumiere, M. L., & Quinsey, V. L. (1997). Deception and sexual strategy in psychopathy. *Personality and Individual Differences, 22,* 301–307.

Stone, M. H. (1998). The personalities of murderers: The importance of psychopathy and sadism. In A. E. Skodol (Ed.), *Psychopathology and violent crime* (pp. 29–52). Washington, DC: American Psychiatric Press.

Webster, C. D., Harris, G. T., Rice, M. E., Cormier, C. A., & Quinsey, V. A. (1994). *The Violence Prediction Scheme: Assessing dangerousness in high risk men.* Toronto: Centre for Criminology, University of Toronto.

Weiler, B. L., & Widom, C. S. (1996). Psychopathy and violent behaviour in abused and neglected young adults. *Criminal Behaviour and Mental Health, 6,* 253–271.

Widiger, T. A., & Trull, T. J. (1994). Personality disorders and violence. In J. Monahan & H. Steadman (Eds.), *Violence and mental disorder: Developments in risk assessment* (pp. 203–226). Chicago: University of Chicago Press.

Williamson, S. E., Hare, R. D., & Wong, S. (1987). Violence: Criminal psychopaths and their victims. *Canadian Journal of Behavioral Science, 19,* 454–462.

Wintrup, A. (1996). *Assessing risk of violence in mentally disordered offenders with the HCR-20.* Unpublished master's thesis, Simon Fraser University, Burnaby, British Columbia.

Wintrup, A., Coles, M., Hart, S., & Webster, C. D. (1994). The predictive validity of the PCL-R in high-risk mentally disordered offenders [Abstract]. *Canadian Psychology, 35*(2a), 47.

Wong, S. (1985). *Criminal and institutional behaviors of psychopaths.* Ottawa, Ontario: Programs Branch Users Report, Ministry of the Solicitor General of Canada.

Wong, S. (1996). Recidivism and the criminal career of psychopaths: A longitudinal study. In D. J. Cooke, A. E. Forth, J. P. Newman, & R. D. Hare (Eds.), *Issues in criminological and legal psychology: No. 24. International perspectives on psychopathy* (pp. 147–152). Leicester, UK: British Psychological Society.

Yates, P., & Nicholaichuk, T. (1998). The relationship between criminal career profile, psychopathy, and treatment outcome in the Clearwater sexual offender program [Abstract]. *Canadian Psychology, 39*(2a), 97.

Zamble, E., & Palmer, W. (1996). Prediction of recidivism using psychopathy and other psychologically meaningful variables. In D. J. Cooke, A. E. Forth, J. P. Newman, & R. D. Hare (Eds.), *Issues in criminological and legal psychology: No. 24. International perspectives on psychopathy* (pp. 153–156). Leicester, UK: British Psychological Society.

Zanatta, R. (1996). *Risk of violent recidivism: A comparison of dangerous and non-dangerous offenders.* Unpublished master's thesis, Simon Fraser University, Burnaby, British Columbia.

Author Index

Subject Index